Commendations for *Alternative Futures: India Unshackled*

Can a radically different and progressive future India emerge, overcoming the systemic injustices – economic, ecological, political, social, cultural – of today? Any such seemingly utopian vision to become feasible must show that it is workable and reachable. The great strength of this book, making it a must read, is that it does both. It points to different experiences in India that already embody the values and actual practices that are needed for such functionality. And it looks at the struggles of various social actors whose coming together could forge the collective agency that makes this project achievable.

Achin Vanaik
Retired Professor of International Relations and Global Politics, University of Delhi

This is an important book. Today, when stable social structures as we knew them are engulfed in change and decay, there is sometimes an attempt to seek isolated explanations for the chaos in economic, ecological and cultural causation. This book makes a refreshing attempt to focus on intersectionalities of many paradigms to both understand the dysfunction of our present lives, as well as engage with a possible convivial future. Several of the writers have demonstrated alternatives that are eminently doable, and these will be major sources of strength and positive energy as we move into the future.

Ilina Sen
Feminist activist and scholar, Mumbai

Envisioning the future of a rapidly changing world needs a global understanding. This is a difficult task. As humanity enters the era of Econocene in which the market has become the changemaker, local understandings based on close links with both past and present can help shape human futures along alternative avenues. This book is a bold attempt towards such a task, across an impressive array of subjects and themes that have the much needed explicit and implicit interconnections. This makes the book globally significant.

Jayanta Bandyopadhyay
Former Professor, Indian Institute of Management Calcutta

Humans are integral to nature. What distinguishes them is the capacity to introspect and an awareness of being the symbol of a larger truth in nature. When nature's elements are in harmony, the world is a better place. Our aim is to raise our consciousness to this fact – which is what the contributors to this book have attempted to do. I cannot wait to read it in full.

Leela Samson
Dancer, choreographer, teacher

Alternative Futures is about the future of humankind and I am a woman of the present, forged by the past and wary of the future. How can I blurb/blurt about this book. There is a word in English: 'pipe dream'. It ostensibly means delusions borne of smoking opium. But there is something more to it. A pipe which is a kind of a tunnel that always opens towards the light.

This real light at the end of the tunnel makes all the contributors to this volume write not in vague general terms but in concrete specific terms. It's interesting to read authors who are otherwise steeped in the murky present talking longingly about the future. I congratulate both the editors for coming up with this book. It's obvious that their activist-theorist background has immensely contributed to making of the *Alternative Futures*.

Pradnya Pawar
Marathi poet & writer, Mumbai

Perhaps for the first time, it is possible for human beings to reach far beyond their basic needs and build a decent society – not just for a few but for everyone. The day has come to dream big and work hard: to sweep away poverty, injustice, caste, patriarchy, violence, exploitation, and also to build the institutions of liberty, equality, solidarity and sustainability. This enlightening collection, written by some of India's finest thinkers and activists, opens our eyes to these new horizons. It also tells us about the sterling efforts that are already being made, away from the glaze of the mainstream media, to build an alternative future. Essential reading for all those who believe that another world is possible.

Jean Drèze
Honorary Professor, Delhi School of Economics

Being caught up in everyday crises that demand urgent attention, compelled to work in fields of power with alien rules and tools, can we imagine other, better worlds? In this salutary set of essays, some of India's leading activists and scholars look past our preoccupation with the present towards visions of ecologically and socially just futures. Like all dreams that have inspired concerted action, they deserve our keenest consideration.

Amita Baviskar
Professor of Sociology, Institute of Economic Growth, Delhi

This book is timely when India is facing an economic, political and social crisis and its people seem to despair and ask "where do we go from here?" The authors, well known in their own fields, try to answer these questions that may not solve all the problems but give a sense of direction to the journey ahead. This book should thus become a text book for ongoing reflection on the future of India.

Walter Fernandes
Writer & researcher, North Eastern Social Research Centre, Guwahati

A fantastic group of authors and editors delineate an optimistic future for India, a practical utopia which is also an inspiration for the rest of the world. Drawing on ancient wisdom and institutions, progressive ideologies, years of activism, and latest contributions from diverse sciences, this book analyzes what could be done across the full range of human endeavour, from basic needs to governance to justice and sustainability.

Joan Martinez Alier
Ecological economist, Autonomous University of Barcelona

At time of rapid economic change with far reaching, often irreversible consequences, it is refreshing to find two seasoned practitioners and thinkers on alternative modes of development join forces and suggest ways ahead for a society as complex as India's. Even those who differ with specifics of the cases examined and the arguments advanced will not be able to ignore this work. It is especially welcome as it straddles many divisions, between human and natural sciences, advocacy and constructive action and between local and national arenas. The issues of the environment could not be de-linked from the wider quest for social justice and an inclusive societal order but here they are seen as integral in a host of ways. Reading and engaging with this book will be a richly rewarding experience.

Mahesh Rangarajan
Professor of History and Environmental Studies, Ashoka University, Sonepat

To enact radical socio-ecological transformations, we first need to imagine them. This is what this book brilliantly does, it decolonizes our imaginary! These are the futures I wanna live, what about you?

Federico Demaria
Editor of "Degrowth: A Vocabulary for a New Era"

Young people of India, please read this book. Please have a dialogue about the ideas in this book. Don't pre-judge them. Some may seem old fashioned, some utopian, some too new or radical. But these ideas come from men and women who have spent decades trying to build your country and your future. In some cases, they have been tested on the ground directly; in others, they have been recovered from the past or borrowed from times to come. Use the multicoloured strands in this volume, for tomorrow is yours to weave.

Rohini Nilekani
Chair, Arghyam, Bengaluru

This is a timely publication, capturing collective wisdom of varied social movements over the last 40 years. Veteran activist researchers from environment, political, progressive cultural, women's rights and human rights movements have critically reflected on the dynamics of their struggles and provided future vision. Their analysis is informed by right based perspective and commitment for striving for entitlements of the marginalized sections of society. This insightful work will help all those who want to build a society based on foundations of social justice, gender justice, environmental justice and distributive justice. This reader will provide food for thought, debate, discussion for study circles to strengthen social sector, civil society initiatives and development studies.

Vibhuti Patel
Chair, Advanced Centre for Women's Studies, Tata Institute of Social Sciences, Mumbai

Alternative Futures: India Unshackled aims to instill the notion that futures are always open and multiple. Faced with the closure of a future with futures by the present ideologies of growth, modernization and development – as the only possible or credible paths to an allegedly single future of wealth and material abundance for all – the authors of this courageous and farsighted volume enlighten those of us searching for alternative ways of living worldwide on many aspects of the cultural and ecological transitions our societies need to undergo in order to preserve and enhance the pluriverse. From environmental governance to radical democracy, from craft to agroecology, from water to education and much more this volume provides concrete tools and ideas for moving effectively toward post-patriarchal, post-capitalist and pluriversal worlds. *India Unshackled* is the product of the South Asian dissenting imagination at its best; it shows why the task of liberating the future from its modernist shackles is one of the most radical goals and acts of imagination critical theory and activism can pursue at present.

Arturo Escobar
Professor of Anthropology, University of North Carolina, Chapel Hill

This is an indispensable collection in which eminent practitioner-intellectuals distill the debates on a range of new issues – socio-cultural justice, political practice, ecological and economic priorities – that demand engagement in the anthropocence. I would use this as a first go-to collection for an accessible, open-minded and informed discussion of the many issues that impinge on public life today.

Susie Tharu
Retired professor, Department of Cultural Studies, English and Foreign Languages University, Hyderabad

This book is very important as it is aimed at producing an alternative framework of development. In the absence of such an alternative, we remain just slogan shouters. Though, because of the attack of fascism we all are busy giving priority to save and protect whatever little democracy we are left with, it is very important to talk about radical alternatives, which this book does. I would love to take its message all over the country.

Jignesh Mevani
Rashtriya Dalit Adhikar Manch

We are mired today in the age of precarity, of loss, of profound injustice and unimaginable violence. And we are trapped in the debilitating fictions of post-truth rule; in tweets that supplant rich traditions of argumentation, dissent and disagreement; and in the utter disregard for life, liberties, dignity, equality, diversity, self-respect, fraternity and pluralism – indeed privacy and constitutional morality – guaranteed under our Constitution. *Alternative Futures: India Unshackled* restores our faith in the power of dreams: daring us to dream of insurgent constitutionalism, and resurrecting memories of other worlds, other times, that we must reclaim for our present and our futures.

Kalpana Kannabiran
Feminist sociologist & writer

With over 600 vibrant pages, from Shiv Vishwanathan's future dreaming to Manisha Gupte's revisionings of sex-gender – via water and energy abundance, food sovereignty, craft economies, language and learning, dissent and self-governance – the intellectuals and activists in this book not only model Indian futures, they will lead readers in the West to new imaginaries.

Ariel Salleh
Political Economy, University of Sydney & Author of "Ecofeminism as Politics"

Many Indians nowadays prefer to locate their utopias in the past. This is an old tradition and is often used very creatively, as Gandhi did. But the past that is being invoked in India now neither has any critique of the present nor does it supply any vision of the future; it is a past packaged in self-righteousness, hiding deep feelings of inferiority and an inability to face the future. It is, therefore, a pleasure to welcome this lively collection of papers, some of them open challenges to conventional models of development, progress and statecraft. Future studies are the markers of a self-confident intellectual community, unafraid to face dark times. For they still have a future to think of. We should be beholden to the editors and the authors for the ambitious intellectual challenge they have posed for us and our rulers.

Ashis Nandy
Senior Fellow and Former Director, Centre for the Study of Developing Societies

ALTERNATIVE FUTURES
INDIA UNSHACKLED

EDITED BY

Ashish Kothari and K. J. Joy

authors
UPFRONT

First published in India in 2017 by:
Paranjoy Guha Thakurta for AuthorsUpFront Publishing Services Private Limited
Copyright © 2017 Ashish Kothari and K. J. Joy
The copyright of the individual essays is vested with the respective author of the essay.

Cover design: Neena Gupta
Cover illustration: Ashish Kothari
Inside illustrations: Bindia Thapar, originally prepared for National Biodiversity Strategy and Action Plan process coordinated by Kalpavriksh.

eBook available on Amazon Kindle

Foreword

One of the most delightful possibilities of a book like this, a mark of its hospitality, is its invitation to an errant writer to write the Foreword. So an absentee essay[1] transforms itself in its second incarnation into a Foreword, describing not the book which is formidable in its competence, but the future as a possibility. I admit my generation dreamt of the future at a different level from the participants of the book. Here one senses a politics of anxiety, of responsibility, where ecology and justice in particular become all encompassing words for a world of possibilities. For my generation, the future was the domain of dissent, of the possibility of eccentricity. As a student, I was proud that it was Ananda Coomaraswamy and not Daniel Bell who coined the word 'the post-industrial society'. I loved pointing out that Jules Verne's Captain Nemo was actually an Indian prince displaced by the mutiny. To make assurance double sure, I would add that ET as an extra-terrestrial was an idea invented by Satyajit Ray and pursued by Steven Spielberg. It was not just the Science Fiction (SF) part of the future that fascinated me. In fact, SF hardly found a hold in India and the fascination Indians had for the detective novel hardly extended to SF. Partly our mythology was so rich, so replete with aliens, monsters, witches that one did not need SF as a genre. But SF or not, the Indian national movement was definitely futuristic. Whether one considers Coomaraswamy, Geddes, Saha or Gandhi, one realises the national movement was futuristic in myriads of ways. First, one must emphasise that Gandhi was no luddite. His *ashrams* were futuristic, ethical and scientific experiments, laboratories of disciplined minds thinking of the future while the rest of the world slumbered. Patrick Geddes who was first professor of sociology dreamt of futuristic cities and a futuristic science. In fact, he wanted India to embody the idea of a post-Germanic science, a science that went beyond the extractive competence of the mine and the dreams of a steam engine. Tagore's Santiniketan was partly a shared dream between Geddes and the poet dreaming of a futuristic university. Meghnad Saha and the *Science and culture* group realised the danger of synthetic chemistry for products like lac, indigo, madder and hoped that a science as a rishi-hood of the future would protect our primary products. The future, they warned, could raise prospects of obsolescence, erasure, triage, that if progress was one side of the coin, obsolescence was the other. A.K. Coomaraswamy in fact wrote that the Indian national movement had to fight a guerrilla war against the museum as it smelt of death and formaldehyde. In fact, futurism was the constant refrain of the national movement, a dream that fades out in the first decades of independence. In that sense, Gandhi's sense of Swadesi and Swaraj were a heuristics for the future, an idea which some of the essays take up as eco-swaraj.

There is a second point, a composite of style and content, that one must emphasise. Our futurism was playful, dissenting and epistemic for India; the future was a compost heap of dissenting and defeated imaginations. The future was an anthology of differences, a thesaurus of diversity which democracy hoped to keep alive. Part of it arose from the ethical contract, the responsibility our activists at Chipko, Lokayan, Kalpavriksh felt that India could not develop linearly like the West, that the tribal, the nomad could not disappear but had to be part of the possibilities of the future. Secondly, that India would always have to be a society that existed in multiple time because only a society with multiple time *made* democracy a set of pluralistic possibilities. As a result, the future in India had to be a social contract between the oral, the textual and the digital. The world of the Brundtland Report is too narrow, too provincial a language to build the idea of sustainability. Sustainable futures in India meant alternative futures. Individual choice alone was inadequate. What one needed was the copious availability of alternative epistemologies and technologies. The future would never be singular or hegemonic because then the future becomes a warrant for genocide or extinction.

One word will occur again and again throughout these set of essays: sustainability. Sustainability should not be thought of an English term, a prim word invented by a governess, but a polysemic world, dreaming diversity and inventing an array of vernacular ideas, reinventing word and world. Dissenting epistemologies become critical for this world, but the word epistemology itself needs to be redefined. It is not just a laboratory system of legitimating or validating a scientific fact, an excuse for political correctness in science. One has to move beyond the official world and think of epistemology as related to life, lifeworld, lifestyle, livelihood, lifecycle. Epistemologies have to be plural so one senses the power of coping, and *jugaad* as we appreciate the potency of the scientific method. Dissenting epistemologies are critical to open up the world of the future. Think of the world of energy and as we move beyond electricity, nuclear, solar, wind, waste, we are moving to different epistemological worlds, where efficiency needs plurality to remain meaningful. Alternative energy systems and alternative epistemologies go together. This is what Gandhi tried to articulate with his two words Swadesi and Swaraj. Swadesi refers to the local, to the neighbourhood, to the vernacular, the parochial. Swaraj is cosmic, oceanic, planetary. It demands an ethic of responsibility where the neighbourhood reaches out to the cosmos, where a dewdrop resonates with the ocean. It is an ethics of scale, of panarchy, where the future is a pretext for constantly reinventing democracy beyond the electoral and majoritarian imaginations. The future thus becomes an attempt to rethink the frames of imagination, between the body, the sensorium, nature, language and technology. One has to speak of the future at least in an introduction, in holistic terms. One often gets caught in silos of the mind where the future gets so obsessively specialised that the whole is less than the sum of the parts and that is one tragedy the future cannot survive. In this context, one must add that one group hardly cited in future studies today is the Theosophists. The movement is dismissed as a cranky set of frauds despite being the mainstay of the original Congress party. Few remember that Allan Octavian Hume was not just President of Congress but a great ornithologist, who wrote a text on agricultural policy looking at local proverbs, and a person who wished to lead the Theosophist movement. Theosophy provided a literal circus of epistemologies which created new futures for childhood (Montessori), new notions of art and colour (Kandinsky and Roerich), new articulations of diversity (Alfred Wallace). The celebration of past and futures they delved in has still to be matched. The future in that sense is rarely a celebration, a festival of possibilities. It becomes more a domesticated list of the possible imposing of restraint on wild thought or dreams of action.

To the playfulness that Theosophy created, one must add a sense of ethics. Play is required to guarantee that the future does not become a dismal science, an obsession with methodologies and techniques. At the least, one must add the clown, the trickster, the Shaman to the social scientist as high priest and expert. One must summon the storyteller so that the language of social science and technology does not become arid. We need to remember that social scientists make poor storytellers. We tend to leave out the unexpected from the future, by becoming too extrapolative, by consolidating on current imaginations without allowing for surprise and emergence. One has to go beyond current categories, particularly in economics, where the current ideas of efficiency, rationality and cost-benefit might be adequate. Futures have to have a sense of surprise, of ambush, of tentativeness, and basing them on current syllabi and ideology dooms them to a procrustean past. Questioning categories and epistemologies becomes part of the everydayness of the future. The legislator with his/her wish list is obvious in each of these essays. Their competence is obvious but what the future needs is a dream, a creativity of a different kind. The Franco-Greek philosopher, Cornelius Castoriadis put it pithily. He said one must distinguish between the imagination and the imaginary. The imagination springs from an extrapolation of current categories and concepts. If we say nation state, we have already created a cartography around boundary, state, citizen, sovereignty, security. The imaginary is a horizon, it dreams of worlds which have yet to appear, of possibilities still to be thought through, even of worlds still to be constructed. I am wagering this book has more of the imaginary as possibilities because Swaraj in that heuristic sense has to go beyond the current syllabus of thought. The realism of the future needs a touch of the surreal to be acceptable. The danger here is the current logic of development Jesuitically positing sequences and predictable scenarios. The current human development indicators, the millennial indices lack both a sense of dream and nightmare, partly because of the poverty of dissent, partly because too many of our futurists belong to the think tanks of today. Luckily this anthology, rooted in ecological and social activism and a critique of economic categories, might guarantee that the emancipations of the future do not break down into dull scenarios. This is critical because one finds it difficult to accept today that both liberal and left imaginations have little to offer the future except the chains of current thought. If the content is a wish list if not a dream, one senses interesting efforts to go beyond current diktats. The quirky and the eccentric are struggling past the dismally technocratic. The high priests survive but the Shaman delivers the punchlines.

Books on the future in India tend to be of two kinds. The first, deeply embedded in social science and ecology tend to be professional, almost as if the future is a behavioural science. The second tends to be literary, open to SF scenarios, have a touch of the utopian and the impossible. This book is more of the first kind and a consolidation of some of the best essays in that genre. But any book on the future to me is a project in process and I always insist on more. I want the literary to combine with the scientific to create a wider world of conjectures. I wish they had more SF scenarios, and even invited a prophet and an astrologer not just as a sign of grace and humour but as an acknowledgement that insights today come from manifold directions.

Secondly, I wish there was more on war and violence, on genocides, because many of the alternative realities that we are dreaming of need to go beyond the logic of genocide, apocalypse and extinction. Extrapolations are important but we need new creation myths of the future, a summons to a storytelling of a different kind.

Thirdly, one wishes that there was a sense of evil. A positivistic, well behaved future does not appeal to me. The future could be a necropolis. Violence and its future need a longer discourse. But maybe one is listing all this because one is looking through the window at the richness of the effort. Yet *as* the window creates both the power of desire and the objectivity of distance, one must greet this book both as good news and as the beginnings of a project. The future has become a tenuous project in recent times where the past becomes an obsession. The varieties of the future might provide the therapy for a society obsessed with rewriting the past. In that sense, the future and the ethics of the future might be a liberating possibility in more ways than one. It might teach our current regime that the future can be a creative possibility, a way of escaping the current mediocrity of options. In fact, J. P. Donleavy, the author, once said "the future is a different country where we will behave differently". If the book just does that, it might open a new generation to the possibilities of a playful democracy. One can hardly ask for more in a Foreword.

Shiv Visvanathan

Endnotes

1. 'Editors' note: Shiv was requested to contribute an essay for the book, and the 'errantness' he mentions is about the essay never arriving! But we are delighted to have his foreword instead.

Preface

Journeys to this Book ... and Beyond

We present this book with a personal note from each of us, a brief collective note on the journey of the book. Our more substantive views on the issues this book deals with are laid out in the introductory and concluding essays.

(Ashish's journey)

Since 1978, just into high school, I've been protesting and resisting. Critiquing government policies that prioritise business and growth over ecological and human rights, supporting peoples' movements against displacement and dispossession, challenging conservation programmes that exclude people and development policies that exclude other species. There are plenty of fires around, so fire-fighting is a more than full-time job.

It is not, however, satisfactory. Not so much because the victories seem to be less than the defeats (this is to be expected given the force of the capitalist, statist, casteist and patriarchal juggernaut we are up against). More because all too often, I found myself in an overwhelmingly negative atmosphere, saying the 'no' word way more than I'd like to. 'No' to this, 'no' to that.... But yes to what, I asked myself? Yes to what, asked an increasingly impatient number of people who, even if sympathetic to our protests, wanted to know what were our answers to meeting human needs and aspirations.

It's not that I was not aware of solutions. In our travels my companions in Kalpavriksh and I frequently came across initiatives on the ground that appeared to be answering the question 'yes to what?' This was particularly true of the domain of biodiversity conservation, where we documented and promoted the concept and practice of Community Conserved Areas (CCAs), later to become an internationally recognized phenomenon, or of co-management by various actors, as alternatives to exclusionary, western wildlife protection policies adopted in India and elsewhere. Or of organic farming as a solution to food needs that did not poison the earth as did the Green Revolution approach. Or of decentralized water harvesting vs. mega-dams.

These explorations and realisations were however sporadic and in a few specific sectors. They did not amount to a comprehensive answer to the question 'yes to what?' Some of us began to explore the key principles and lessons emerging from these grassroots initiatives, to see if there were common threads emerging. Around 2011-12 I wrote a couple of exploratory pieces on 'radical ecological democracy' (RED), proposing a preliminary synthesis of these principles. Then Aseem Shrivastava and I consolidated this in our 2012 book *Churning the Earth: The Making of Global India,* in which we critiqued economic globalization as also laid out a skeleton of radical alternatives to such globalization. But the critique was 300 pages, the alternatives 100, still an imbalance I was not satisfied with.

Soon after the book Kalpavriksh initiated the Vikalp Sangam process, attempting to document and network movements, groups and individuals working on alternatives in the entire range of human endeavour. From 2014 till now, this has yielded several hundred stories and over a dozen detailed case studies, ten confluences of people in various parts of India, and outreach materials like articles, booklets, and films. Most important, it has increased our understanding of the common threads, encapsulated in an evolving document 'In Search of Alternatives' which is a sort of collective visioning of the future that we want (see http://www.kalpavriksh.org/images/alternatives/Alternativesframework4thdraftMarch2016.pdf).

Around the time the Vikalp Sangam process was started, I also wondered what it would be like to ask some prominent thinkers, activists, and activist-thinkers what their vision of the future was. What could India in 2047, a century after Independence, or even 2100, look like, if one were to let one's imagination and hopes run free? How could we get there, were there already some signs that indicated possibilities and probabilities? And so this book.

This journey of discovery within India has been made even more exciting by the fortune of visiting and getting connected to alternative initiatives in some other parts of the world. Many collectives and individuals are envisioning more just, equitable, wiser futures, many of them based on actual experience that shows the feasibility of such visions. This volume from India is a humble contribution to this most important of human tasks: the quest for a healthy planet for ourselves and for all of life that we are part of.

(Joy's journey)

When Ashish invited me to be part of this book project as a co-editor with him I very happily accepted it without even thinking about the extent of work involved and whether I would be able to do justice to it, given my numerous other commitments. The main reason for my getting involved in this is that the theme of the book, *Alternative Futures,* appealed to me greatly and I also saw it as a natural progression to what I have been doing over the last 30-35 years. I have been part of collectives and organisations that have, in a way, shaped my journey as an activist and as a researcher. The slogan 'sangharsh-aur-nirmaan' (struggle/resistance and reconstruction) popularised by Shahid Shankar Guha Niyogi also had a great influence on me, like many others, who got into socio-political movements in the 1980s'.

I got my grounding in 'politics based on alternatives' while I was a full time activist with Mukti Sangharsh Movement (MSM), an anti-drought mass movement of the toiling people in Sangli district (Maharashtra, India). MSM taught me that along with resistance or saying 'no' to destructive projects it is also important that toilers articulate what they want and mobilise themselves around a positive agenda. Though MSM started with mobilising the Employment Guarantee Scheme (EGS) workers, it soon became a collective space for participatory studies, experimentation and developing peoples' alternatives to government's plans, programmes and projects. MSM organised struggles to implement these alternatives that helped to change the character of EGS work in the region and also pressurized the government to restructure public irrigation schemes on more equitable, sustainable lines. Baliraja dam, born out of the struggle against indiscriminate sand excavation from the river Yerala, a tributary of Krishna River, soon became the mascot of equitable water distribution. The struggle against Uchangi dam in Kolhapur district (Maharashtra) was also fought on the basis of an alternative plan and forced the government to accept it. There are many such examples.

MSM also brought together political activists, people's science movement activists and pro-people scientists and technologists to conceptually engage with developmental issues, experiment and develop alternatives. The vision of a 'biomass based decentralized, sustainable and equitable agro-industrial society' emerged from this collective search.

My journey into the arena of alternatives got politically sharpened because of my association with Shramik Mukti Dal (SMD), a New Left political trend in Maharashtra. For SMD, creation of an exploitation free society (in terms of class, caste, patriarchy, ethnicity, etc.), that is materially and spiritually enriched and in harmony with nature is the goal of radical social transformation. According to SMD revolution is not merely taking control of the means and methods of production developed by modern capitalism (which are detrimental to both nature and humans) but also developing them in a sustainable manner without compromising on the primary productivity of the ecosystem, and also increasingly shifting the base of development to renewable resources. SMD also believes that it is important to involve toiling masses in developing alternatives in all sectors that affect their lives. In fact fighting the state on the basis of people's alternatives can further expand the frontiers of peoples' power (*samantar sattha* or parallel power).

Since 1990-91 Society for Participative Ecosystem Management (SOPPECOM) provided the institutional space for me in this journey. SOPPECOM was set up primarily to pursue the different elements of the alternative vision (of a biomass based, decentralised, sustainable and equitable agro-industrial society) in a more systematic and grounded manner. SOPPECOM could come up with an alternative paradigm in the water sector characterized by integration of sources, sustainable water and land use, equitable access and participatory management. The alternative proposal to restructure the destructive Sardar Sarovar Project (SSP) by my friend Suhas Paranjape and I under the guidance of K. R. Datye in the 1990s', was another important contribution that we could make in the water-environment-development sector, towards reconciling the polarised discourse in the water sector around large versus small.

In 2014 Kalpavriksh initiated the Vikalp Sangam process and I have been fortunate to get associated with it. The Sangams that I could attend were eye openers to me through new exposures to a wide variety of alternatives in various sectors under different bio-physical, socio-economic and cultural contexts.

This book is thus a very significant milestone in my journey so far, and has been a tremendous learning experience. The diverse sectors and authors the book could string together and the alternative ideas, concepts, experiences they have brought forth have been mindboggling. Collectively they can help us to get out of the shackles of the ever-growing cynicism of 'there is no alternative' (TINA) syndrome and provide the contours for a better tomorrow.

(our collective journey towards this book)

After joining hands for this book, our first tasks were to conceive the broad framework or brief that we would send the authors, to list the topics we wanted covered, and identify possible authors for each. All of these were continuously adapted and modified over the first few months, as we got comments on the themes from prospective authors, some authors did not work out and we had to look for others, and the list of themes too kept growing as we realised more and more gaps in our first list. From the initial idea of perhaps 15 essays or so, it grew to over 30 (and yet gaps have remained, as we explain in the introductory essay)! Given our restless minds, we not only kept adding topics and authors, but also activities, such as the dialogue of authors that we organised in February 2016 (see essay by Bajpai and Bhagat). As the saying goes in Hindi, we are good at *apne pair pe kulhadi marna* ('dropping the axe on our own foot'). And why not, as long as the end result is worth it?

All this started in October 2014, and we are now sending the book to press in mid-2017. Nearly three years of an exciting, sometimes frustrating or banal, often surprising, and always educational journey – a journey with many co-travellers.

Acknowledgments

We would like to profusely thank the following, without whom the future of this book would have been considerably imperilled!

All the authors, for readily agreeing to write an essay that must have taken them out of their comfort zones, for bearing with our repeated and annoying queries and multiple edits, for participating in the authors' dialogue, and for some welcome advise on various aspects of the process of putting this book together.

Nagmani Rao for some (or rather, lots of!) sharp copyediting, and much else besides.

The Centre for the Study of Developing Society (CSDS), Kalpavriksh and SOPPECOM for organizing the authors' dialogue in partnership with Oxfam India in February 2016. In CSDS, particular thanks to Aditya Nigam and Jayasree Jayanthan; in Kalpavriksh, Shrishtee Bajpai and Sujatha Padmanabhan; and in SOPPECOM, Sarita Bhagat.

Paranjoy Guha Thakurta for readily agreeing to publish this book, and Manish Purohit for patiently seeing it through.

Sanjeev Kumar Aggarwal of Utsav Films for filming the authors' dialogue, and John D'Souza for transforming the footage into short clips covering author presentations and discussions, for public viewing (available at https://www.youtube.com/playlist?list=PL0MSps3jx9ML8OKnIHN7Q7waqSN1jP_8Y).

Oxfam India for unconditional support to the whole process of putting together the book, including sponsorship of the authors' dialogue.

Jayanta Bandopadhyay for being part of the first few steps of this journey.

None of the above, of course, are to be thanked for any errors and weaknesses that remain in the book, for which we accept complete responsibility.

Ashish Kothari and K. J. Joy

Contents

Economic Futures

Socio-cultural Futures

INTRODUCTION

Envisioning India's Future: an introduction[1]

Ashish Kothari and K. J. Joy

A Bit about the Book

Envisioning the future is a perilous task. However good one's understanding of history, and strong one's faith in the lessons it teaches us, however robust our systems of modelling using the best methodologies and technologies available to us, we could still be horribly, embarrassingly wrong. But then, the vision could also turn out to be correct; more important, it could actually even influence the course of current events such that at least elements of it come true. Look at science fiction: how often has it turned out to be science fact!

Our brief to the exciting galaxy of authors in this volume was to indulge in some such vision-setting, for a moment letting the imagination run riot, not get caught in the shackles of what is 'realistic' and 'feasible'. But since we did not want this to be an exercise *only* in imagination, we also requested authors to build on the current context, and to provide actual examples and instances from the past or present that point to the real possibility of such visions coming true. The essays in this collection range from the somewhat cautious to the adventurously imaginative, and we believe they all have value in providing us direction, hope, and an inkling of what may yet be.

In this opening essay we mainly provide an overview of the collection, clubbing the essays into four key spheres of human existence: political, socio-cultural, economic, and ecological. In the concluding essay we elaborate more on these arenas, sketching a futuristic vision of justice, equity, and ecological wisdom. We acknowledge here that the framework of four spheres we are using for both the opening and the concluding essays, is based on an ongoing process of dialogue and sharing of experiences that we are involved with, the Vikalp Sangam or Alternatives Confluence,[2] as also on some of our previous work on an alternative paradigm called radical ecological democracy or '*ecoswaraj*' (see, for instance, Kothari, 2014).

The division of the 32 thematic essays in this volume into the four spheres is necessarily imperfect, for the essays and the topics they cover do not neatly fit into any one arena, and the spheres themselves overlap with each other (a bit like the Olympics symbol!). We would like to avoid the academic trap of neat categorization. Nevertheless, we believe this framework provides us a basis for analysis, as also for envisioning of the future.

Key Elements of the Future
Ecological futures

India's imperilled environment has been the subject of much research, activism, and action. The staggering loss of ecosystems and biodiversity, the toxification of our water, air, and soil, the erosion of productive soils, and a host of other problems are evidence of the unsustainability of human activity in India (as indeed in the world as a whole, as shown by recent studies on how we have crossed several planetary boundaries, notably Rockstrom *et al.,* 2009). In such a situation, what futures can be envisioned that rescue us from the steep decline into ecological collapse?

Safeguarding the ecosystems and biodiversity that sustain us is clearly a crucial part of what needs to be done. Over the last few decades there have been many initiatives, both within and outside government, towards this. These include protected areas and legal protection to particular species, 'reserving' forests for restricted use, and other governmental measures; they also include widespread community initiatives that sustain either ancient practices like sacred ecosystems or enable new ones as a response to scarcity, wildlife decline, or other situations. Unfortunately, the former in particular, have mostly been within an exclusionary conservation paradigm that attempts to separate people from nature; and simultaneously the state has been rather generous in giving over critical ecosystems to 'development' projects such as mining and dams.

In this volume, Kartik Shanker, Meera Anna Oommen and Nitin Rai point to the problems of such paradigms and to how neo-liberalism has promoted commodification in several forms. They argue for a holistic approach that integrates conservation ideals with social and environmental justice. They propose a reconciliation ecology that aims for greater conservation values for the countryside and recognizes that ethnic and linguistic influences have resulted in heterogeneous, multi-use landscapes with an amazing array of bio-cultural diversity. Any conservation approach has to embrace community and traditional knowledge as an ethical and moral imperative to distributive justice so that it can address a variety of issues ranging from inequalities to oppression.

Clearly such an approach calls into question also the overall model of environmental governance in India. Sharachchandra Lele and Geetanjoy Sahu point out that though the country has very many laws for protecting the environment, aided by a pro-active judiciary (which has even interpreted the Constitutional right to life as including the right to a clean environment), the current state of the environment is deplorable. Presently, environmental governance has four major issues: regulatory failure, limits to judicial activism, domination of neo-liberal growth ideas and the assumption that conservatism is environmentalism. They argue that the future of environmental governance has to start with embracing environmentalism as a way of life, that is, quality of life, sustainability, and environmental justice. Second, institutional design has to be re-worked, such that it can encompass biophysical and social justice goals. Better environmental governance requires a change in value systems, concern for social justice and a belief in the democratic process.

One specific aspect of India's natural resources that is under severe and increasing crisis is water. We have this strangely contradictory situation in which all cultures in the country have revered water as sacred, have considered rivers or the sea as the birthplace of life, and yet everywhere we have allowed their degradation into polluted, encroached, overexploited or drained out ecosystems. There is also significant inequality in access to water for various purposes. With water crises looming large across many parts of India, paradigm shifts are needed in how we manage this crucial element of nature. This is what Shripad Dharmadhikary and Himanshu Thakkar write about, pointing to the need to move away from the extreme anthropocentrism and inequity of current water use to one where water is seen as an integral part of ecosystems, and its multifaceted values (cultural, sustenance, and economic) are considered. A fundamental shift towards the core values of sustainability, equity, efficiency, and democratization is needed. The authors provide some examples of seeds of hope, both from official sources as well non-governmental actors, and suggest elements of a future vision as also its achievement through institutional changes, creating successful examples, and replicating them at a larger level.

Basic to an ecologically just and sustainable future, and to social and economic equity that we deal with below, is the issue of energy. Access to sufficient quantities of energy is an important determinant of human well-being. With climate change, the sources of energy and mode of generation have become very critical. Harish Hande, Vivek Shastry, and Rachita Misra argue for the availability of affordable clean energy technology that can meet both development goals and environment quality. Central to this is the promotion of Decentralized Renewable Energy (DRE), which provides an opportunity to improve access to modern energy services for the poorest members in society. This essay lays out possibilities for the future by engaging with various policy levels, and the financial and technological changes that are required to promote sustainable development and equitable distribution of resources. To ensure energy access for differentiated populations of rural and urban centres, the authors highlight initiatives such as DRE extension and integration, policy convergence for low carbon village development, energy entrepreneurship as a livelihood, and community resource centres. India's energy future lies in creating a collaborative economy where changes in consumption patterns are promoted, and access to energy services is deemed higher than ownership.

Political futures

Relations of power are integral to all interactions in society, from interpersonal and family life to global governance. These relations are contained within a complex web of hierarchies, inequities, and complementarities. For this volume we use the term 'political' to include collective processes and institutions of decision-making at various levels from village and city (or collectives within these) to state, nation, and the globe.

In many ways India is an intensely hierarchical society, with inequities in power manifested in all spheres of life from the family to the nation. Traditional inequities based on caste, ethnicities, gender, wealth, and status in the ruling hierarchy have been added to in recent times by one's position in the state's hierarchy and the increasing dominance of capitalism in the market. The interplay amongst all these is complex and at times contradictory, but the predominant reality is one of a society with intense inequities in power. The representative form of democracy India has adopted has not managed to achieve a fundamental change in this situation, despite the potential advantage that marginalized communities with large populations have in an electoral set-up where majority votes can be made to count. In such a situation, what changes are needed to achieve a society with greater political equity and access?

M. P. Parameswaran envisions a rural unit that is politically, economically and in other ways self-governing; we describe this in greater detail in the 'Economic Futures' section below.

Pallav Das, in his essay on power, lays out the contours of inequities, traditional and new, and notes that in response to attempts to change the status quo, the state or entrenched forces are responding increasingly with violence. He then investigates the organic attempts at resistance rooted in the traditions of communities, and asks whether these show us the way to an egalitarian power structure based on the 'commons'? He proposes that peoples' movements and progressive forces forge a 'New Power Alliance' that has the experience and the motivation to challenge the existing power structure and its economically exploitative and environmentally ruinous agenda.

Aruna Roy, Nikhil Dey and Praavita Kashyap, using their vast grassroots experience in making governance more accountable, examine what changes are needed in India's democratic framework. The emergence and spread of mass movements demanding transparency, accountability, wages, and community rights, have pressed the nerve centres of the entire neoliberal structure. Campaigns such as those for Right to Information, and Guaranteed Employment have increased our understanding of the nature and challenges of participatory democracy. They have shown that despite a neoliberal economy and polity, what seems impossible can be achieved. They propose the idea of direct democracy, through a 'rainbow coalition of grassroots social movements', somewhat akin to what Das has proposed. Such a coalition would allow cross-fertilization of ideas and bring out intricate connections between economic, social, and political rights with ecological rights.

One specific aspect of political structure is law. India has a complex Constitution, one of the world's largest bodies of law, and a large repertoire of judicial interpretations of law, in themselves path-breaking. In this context Arpitha Kodiveri examines the opportunities and limitations of law, describes the range of factors (social, political, economic, and cultural) that influences it, and lists three major daunting challenges: access to justice, social acceptance of law, and multiple forms of injustice. She then argues for a legal future that strives for a social democracy, by engaging with the principles of decentralization, equality and innovation in justice delivery. She proposes opening up of the legislature and the judiciary to the participation of citizens in making law as well as resolving legal disputes. Central to this, is the creation of mediation centres that can play a crucial role in establishing a constant connection between law and society, to bring out layers and complex notions of identity.

A recurrent theme in India, especially in the debates that take place within civil society regarding various aspects of society, is the relationship between different political ideologies, or different ideological and philosophical traditions that have political ramifications. The debate is often divisive, as orthodox and rigid positions are taken leading to a Gandhi vs. Ambedkar vs. Marx vs. whomever else or a religion and spirituality vs. rationalist, or a traditional vs. modern schism. Are there ways to overcome these divides, can something be found in all or many of these ideologies to arrive at either a grand synthesis, or some sort of unity in diversity that assists in realizing an equitable, just, and sustainable society?

Aditya Nigam and Bharat Patankar address this challenge in different ways. The former draws on some important early to mid-twentieth century Indian thinkers to propose the concept of radical social democracy, an idea for the future that appeals for a change in what Ambedkar called the social conscience of the people. In its practice, it would institutionalize the ethics of sharing, so that resources become part of the commons. Radical social democracy will strive for systems that do not fall prey to powerful oligarchies, and instead enable institutional forms that can provide space for the plurality of visions for the imagined future. It will, at the very least, give people the opportunity to make informed choices when problematic questions arise that may not lend themselves to easy resolutions. It will be a socialism freed of the state, 'deeply connected to actual lived practices on the ground and drawing its principles and norms from them'. In this, and other ways, such a system, liberated from historical contestations, could integrate many ideals of Gandhi, Ambedkar, M.N. Roy, Iqbal, Tagore, and other critical thinkers who may otherwise be seen as contradicting each other.

Patankar approaches the issue from the standpoint of theory. He argues for a multilinear critical theory, one that recognizes human existence as the combination of various social, political, economic and cultural relations, and emerges from the multilinearity[3] of exploitation, the evolution of struggles and the evolution of dreams of a future society. In his effort in developing this multilinear critical theory, Patankar draws insights from writings of Ambedkar, Phule, Marx and Kosambi. A society of liberated humanity is a dream that can come true, says the author, if the approach for total transformation has the base of such a theory.

Finally, relevant to political futures is a crucial question: what is India's role in the global order? Muchkund Dubey deals with this question through a focus on the United Nations (UN), which has a crucial role in creating a peaceful world in which people of all nations could prosper. He points out that the 1960s' and 70s' were a golden era of international cooperation; however, by the 1990s', the major powers succeeded in weakening this by dismantling the UN's capacity to deliver public goods to the international community. Dubey argues for a new, dynamic and democratic multilateral governance of the future world order. Central to this will be to restore and revamp the essential functions and enhance the capacity of the UN. It should become a voice for people through effective participation of all countries and civil society organizations. This would also require democratization of the decision making process in the IMF and the World Bank, and bringing WTO under the UN framework, ensuring accountability of multinational corporations, global surveillance, and regulation of international financial markets. India's role should be an initiative for restructuring the world order, by building a global coalition for a new dynamic and democratic multilateralism, including trying to bring on board countries like China (and other BRICs nations).

Economic futures

While the origin of the word 'economy' refers to the management of *oikos* (our home/family in Greek), here we are referring to it mostly as the management of materials and finances. India's economy, building on a long history of primary production (farming, pastoralism, fisheries, forestry) as also secondary (textiles, crafts, metalwork, and much else), has shifted after Independence from a predominantly state-led ('socialist', at least in part) to a predominantly corporate or corporate state-led (increasingly 'capitalist') character. Using conventional parameters it is today one of the world's largest economies. But it is also clear that this model of economic development that India has adopted has not led to well-being and prosperity for all and also appears to be unsustainable, given the natural and human resources we have. This is all the more so with the globalized economy that we have gone in for, especially after 1991 (Shrivastava and Kothari, 2012). Can a different economic future be envisioned in which the problems of gross inequality, marginalization of hundreds of millions, and ecological unsustainability are tackled and there is sustainable well-being for all?

Under this theme we have essays covering pastoralism, agriculture and food, biomass based agro-industrial development, crafts, industry, energy, localization, transportation and markets. Together they unfold crucial aspects of a future that can be economically and ecologically regenerative and democratic.

Pastoralism, as a way of life and livelihood activity, predates settled agriculture. Ilse Köhler-Rollefson and Hanwant Singh Rathore, the latter himself a pastoralist, bring out the contribution it makes to both the economy and ecological systems in India, though very often it goes unnoticed. It is an insightful food production system developed by livestock keepers through observation and knowledge, over many generations. Despite a natural nexus with the green economy, these people are not strongly organized and superseded by industrial production. The authors argue for an enabling environment that can integrate pastoral production with nature conservation, ensure space for pastoralists in the landscape, and develop combined livestock production and environmental protection as an attractive 'career' option for young people. According to them the future of pastoralist production will be a decentralized form of livestock keeping and optimal use of local biomass. They also propose pathways – such as documentation of indigenous livestock production, alternate livestock development framework and development of value chains – to promote and support pastoralism.

Agriculture (cultivation), another primary sector of production, is intimately connected to nutritional security, livelihoods and ecology, though since the introduction of green revolution agriculture this relationship is increasingly under threat because of commercialization and high external input based agriculture. Bharat Mansata, Kavitha Kuruganti, Vijay Jardhari and Vasant Futane, (three of them part or full-time farmers) briefly outline the history of ancient forests' roots of food and farming and its nutritional security to forest dependent communities. Government policy paradigms have ignored the traditional knowledge systems and skill sets of farmers, especially women, and *adivasis*. These authors argue for a future which assures Anna Swaraj (food sovereignty) and food security to all, dignified livelihoods to farmers, ecological sustainability, and co-evolution. Central to this is biodiverse, ecological farming – a path of agro-ecology, based on careful management of natural resources by small-scale farmers – several examples of this are presented. Such a path will reduce vulnerability to fluctuations and extremes of climate and weather conditions, and increase self-reliance towards food sovereignty.

Crafts offer us a transition from the primary sectors to the secondary sectors of the economy. There are two essays on secondary sectors – crafts and industries. According to Uzramma, craft industries in India have retained their relevance throughout the Industrial Age, in spite of the domination of high-energy industrial production. This provides an opportunity for India to by-pass the option of high-energy industrialization which benefits only a few, in favour of low-energy, dispersed craft industries, which could usher in democracy in production, a basic building block for true social equity. Craft industries use low-cost infrastructure and need small capital investment, which make it possible for ownership of production to be widely held. With the looming threat of climate change, India's low-energy craft industries will gain in viability. Traditional Indian craft products, like the heritage craft practices of other civilizations, embody specific cultural traits that give them a distinctive identity, highly valued in contemporary markets. In recognition of all these aspects, democratic rights of producers to raw material, institutional finance, and the legal ownership of their specific product identities must be guaranteed by the State.

Dunu Roy begins his essay on industry and industrial workers with a brief history of industrialization in the world and the parallel patterns in India. In the organized, formal sector of Indian industry, labour laws are somewhat functional, primarily because of the organised strength of the work-force. Workers in the informal sector are self-employed – there is the absence of an employer to negotiate with, lack of access to credit, transportation, markets, skills, and space to carry on livelihoods. Then there is the 'illegal' sector, in which working people do not have even the minimum protection of the law as they are deemed illegal. Workers in all these sectors have been creatively registering their opposition to disinvestment and restructuring, privatization and foreign investment, denial of organizing rights and fair wages, contractual labour and labour law reforms, demolitions and evictions. This has fuelled resistance to the state-corporate strategy of division and consolidation. However, according to Roy, the future of industrial work lies in a radical change of two crucial determinants of capitalist society,that is, competition and profit. The essay provides a few examples of movements that have been trying to challenge these determinants, but the real problem lies in the absence of a politics and theorization that can go beyond these attempts by workers, and challenge and change all structures of exploitation, inequality, and injustice.

The discourse around economic reforms – liberalisation, privatization and globalization – in the country has moved beyond mere critique to articulation as well as grounding of alternative ideas and approaches. There are several essays that deal with this important issue, discussing possibilities for regional and local economies, and conceptualising *bazaars* for local exchanges.

According to Aseem Shrivastava and Elango Rangasamy, the corporate market economy has equated development with economic growth and that has led to huge ecological damage and destruction of human communities. Globalisation has resulted in the centralisation of power with a few nations and companies, who regulate the tightly networked business economy. The essay argues for localisation and regionalisation of economies that are ecologically stable and renewable. It would mean clusters of 20-30 villages, with a town as a hub, which are collectively self-sufficient; and a panchayat academy as a crucial institution of learning. Such an economy will be a 'Network Growth Economy'. The essay lists out strategies to achieve a new, decentralised, economic architecture, which will challenge the industrial and globalised economy. An example is given of Kuthambakkam village in Tamil Nadu, which anchored itself in the vision of Gram Swaraj when Elango, one of the authors of this essay, was *sarpanch* (village head). The village now enjoys good concrete roads, an effective drainage system, safe drinking water, manufacture-based livelihoods, and energy-efficient street lighting, in addition to having *pucca* houses. This village is an example of decentralized, ecologically more sensitive and renewable economy.

Related to this is the essay by K. J. Joy, on how the biomass based strategy can revitalize or regenerate the rural economy and ecology, opening up a sustainable and equitable developmental pathway. If a typical family of five persons can either produce or get access to about 18 tons of biomass then it can meet all needs like food, fodder and fuel, and still have enough left for a decentralised, energy efficient agro-industrial development in rural areas. The essay details how bulk biomass can be used in infrastructure sectors like water, buildings, roads, etc., with already available technologies that have significant cost,

11

energy saving, employment, and participatory advantages over conventional technologies. If renewable energy sources can also be brought in then the energy required for processing biomass also becomes available in a dispersed manner. The author proposes a concept of integrated production-cum-energy generation units (IPEUs) for all this.

M. P. Parameswaran takes the above possibilities further with a far-reaching vision of a vibrant, self-reliant village in the Kerala of 2047. Based on peoples' movements and the combined inspiration of Gandhi, Jaiprakash Narayan, and Marx, the village has aimed at increasing longevity free of morbidity till a balance is reached between birth rate and death rate and the population stabilizes, increasing freedom from dependence on alienated work, and increasing equality, diversity and tolerance. This was achieved by enhancing the decentralized planning process already experimented with in Kerala, people choosing their own candidates rather than allowing political parties to do so. This process was supported by significant stress on alternative education through a set of dedicated teachers, social security for children and the elderly, a cyclical agricultural system enabling food security, local manufacturing of a range of products (exchanged with other products in neighbouring panchayats), and redistribution of unoccupied homes to those with inadequate housing, and decentralized water and energy self-sufficiency. The combination of a rural base with some urban amenities converted the area into a rurban one. Various hurdles along the way were resolved through strong democratic dialogue and knowledge generation.

Rajni Bakshi briefly traces 2500 years of history to map the characteristics of the Indian market culture. According to her, contemporary notions of growth and technological advancement have changed both modes and relations of production. In a market culture of limitless accumulation, there is need to explore the possibility of a culture based on the notion of sufficiency and common good. The essay visualizes a village level economy, which will be self-sustaining for essentials and capable of expanding space for a non-monetised exchange. Such an economy will have community-based systems of protection and revitalisation of natural resources. The starting point of such a bazaar is to change the aspiration of accumulation into the ethics of commons and public goods.

The Indian city is facing multiple crises, including the abysmal living conditions of most of its residents, especially the poor. It also causes multiple crises outside of its limits, in its parasitic relationship with the village. How can these be changed?

Rakesh Kapoor looks at the major challenges that urban India faces in the next three decades and beyond, including poor infrastructure, highly inadequate water and electricity supply, slums, waste disposal, and poor public transport. Amongst the underlying causes of these is poor governance, financial weakness, the lack of innovation and populist schemes. Arguing that a better quality of life for Indians – urban and rural – requires fundamental departures from current approaches, mindsets and institutions, Kapoor suggests a radically different vision for urban *plus* rural India 2047, built around the ideas of dispersed urbanization with small towns as development and skilling hubs, innovative mechanisms for financing, public authorities at multiple levels to regulate the uses of land and water, empowering urban local bodies (ULBs) or urban local governments (ULGs) for decentralized governance, innovation in sustainable resource use and solutions for urban areas to create 'regenerative' and 'smart' cities, and low carbon pathways. This suggested future will be based on extensive use of renewable energy sources, minimal waste generation, minimum ecological footprint, provision of decent housing to all citizens and resilience to disasters. Kapoor notes that the ultimate challenge for Indians, including political leaders, is to first of all *envision* another future for urban *plus* rural India, and then to take along all constituents of our population to achieve that vision.

One of the crucial sectors of urban India is transportation. Although most cities have extensive urban planning, despite all flyovers, road widening, and other road infrastructure projects, the problem of traffic is intensifying with each passing year. Sujit Patwardhan explores the contemporary scene, and details out the vision for the future of transport in urban India. According to him, transport planning in India has been predominantly car centred, resulting in edging out of the bicycle, carriages, and other modes of public transport. It has also resulted in greater rate of increase in levels of pollution. The essay proposes people-centric sustainable transport that can make a city pleasant and safe, where people can walk, cycle and reach destinations without dependence on automobiles. Central to this is the environment-centric city planning that will promote compact forms of residential development, reduced dependence on automobile transport, mixed land use planning, protection of natural assets of the city and effective waste management.

Sustainable and equitable futures are closely linked to technology choices that society makes, amongst other things. Dinesh Abrol engages with the question of technology within a broader frame of political economy. The contemporary technological systems are guided by the dominant neo-liberal knowledge production, which is extremely extractive in nature and results in increasing inequality. The research and development institutions are centralized and have closed their doors to alternate forms of science and technology. For example, the agro-ecosystems and landscapes have drastically degraded due to current models of monoculture and chemical-intensive agriculture. Today, India is facing a growing reliance on the capitalist mode of production and consumption. The essay explores technological alternatives in agriculture and rural industrialization programmes, sustainable transportation, energy sector and housing or habitat development. It urges strategies that prioritize the process of development of changes in the dominant structures and the existing cultural norms of consumption, by protagonists committed to pursuing peoples' democracies and socialist democracies. The basic needs of peasantry and working class are their priority. The essay argues for technological alternatives that can play a significant role in the above, and that can trigger a radical transformation in socio-technical systems, guided by social equity driven ecological transformation with alternate social carriers of innovation and development.

Socio-cultural futures

India's ancient civilizational features are rapidly changing under the influence of modernization, but they nevertheless provide a foundation and continue to be a factor in social and cultural life. Contradictions and complementarities abound in the relations of caste, class, gender, age, ethnicity, ability, geography, kinship, demographics, sexuality, and in the interplay of tradition and modernity. Profound inequities and exploitation are found alongside with equally strong solidarity and harmony. In what may appear to be an increasingly confusing complexity, what futures can be envisioned that minimize the conflicts and maximize the complementarity, in which diversity is more a source of strength than of divisiveness?

The section on socio-cultural futures has essays dealing with language, art, media, knowledge, health, sexuality, dalits and caste, gender, adivasis, and minorities. Most of these also straddle the economic, political and socio-cultural spheres.

One crucial aspect of culture is language. India is a land of at least 780 living languages – one out of every eight languages in the world. According to Ganesh Devy, languages are worldviews rather than just modes of communication and lack of this recognition along with stress on economic viability, have resulted in the disappearance of many indigenous languages. The technological revolution in terms of communication has profoundly affected the way the modern world communicates and several ethnic and cultural groups are facing the threat of elimination. The essay argues that we need to support languages that are not popular or in the mainstream or have not reached the cities. This would mean harnessing initiatives to protect languages to a much greater extent, such as maintaining e-libraries, literary societies and initiating magazines of and for indigenous languages. India will be able to face the challenge of securing its great language diversity only by embracing its multi-linguistic and multi-cultural identity.

Learning and education opportunities are at the heart of culture (and much else of what is contained in this book). Tultul Biswas and Rajesh Khindri point out education plays a crucial role in the transmission of ideas, life experiences, culture, knowledge, language, and so on, from one generation to the other. The school, as an agency of imparting education, becomes a vital site of these transmissions. However, school systems are also responsible for reinforcing inequalities and prejudices that are already prevalent in the society. The dysfunctional government school system in India is populated by students from the most marginalised sections of the society. On the other hand, private schools reflect the highly class stratified Indian society, and do not even engage with the students from the marginalized sections. Such stratification is further amplified with caste, religion, and gender inequalities that are deeply embedded in the Indian society. Education has been reduced to business and there is no space for the creative and holistic development of a child. Inspired by the ideas of Avijit Pathak, this essay argues for the vision of future education that can open up opportunities and unleash the potential towards the development of a balanced, just, and responsive students and teachers. Examples of a few initiatives that have moved away from the conventional school structure and opened new ways of creating interactive, inclusive, open-ended learning environment show that such a future, even though challenging, is possible.

Sudha Gopalakrishnan explores the inheritance and contemporary representation of art (limited to the performing arts) in India. India has been a land of various traditional art forms like arts, theatre, dance, and music; these have also been sites of resistance to and ridicule of the dominant establishment. However, market-oriented approach to performing arts has degraded the legacy of art forms, and reduced them to mere economic ends. The essay argues that the future of art has to balance the context-specific significance with relevance to the larger world. This type of a 'balance' can be struck by creating public spaces, collectives, and organisations that work on exploring and preserving local cultures. Art also has to transgress beyond established/conventional boundaries to enable the cultural flow. It can also be systematically archived and preserved. A new possibility of art would entail recognising its renewable potential or something that creates value.

Paranjoy Guha Thakurta looks for what alternative media should strive to bring to the public sphere, as also how to make it more responsive to the segments of the population and issues often shut out by the profit-driven corporate media. The emergence of oligopoly in the Indian media has resulted in the loss of heterogeneity and plurality. It has become unresponsive and has squeezed its coverage of issues like agriculture, Dalits, marginalized farmers, and environment. The digitisation of media has resulted in a transformed flow of information in spite of the access divide around the world, and gives hope for a democratic future. An ideal scenario would be that aggregation and dissemination of the information in the digital world is not controlled by a powerful few; rather ordinary concerned citizens of the country collect and disseminate information regulated by an independent body, which can deter errant journalists. The essay suggests the need for people of different backgrounds, yet of the same persuasion, to come together. Media practitioners should collaborate with whistle blowers, representatives of civil society and political activists to bring out unpleasant truths and deliver greater transparency.

According to Rajeshwari Raina, in the era of neo-liberalism, knowledge has been reduced to mere achievement of economic ends. A highly centralised science and technology establishment serves only the state and the private sector corporations. Policymaking, higher education, scientific research, production of commodities, all the knowledge enterprises, accept knowledge's monetised version. The essay envisions the future of knowledge in India based on democratic values and community-based knowledge systems. Such a system will integrate and decentralise the inter-linkages between diverse natural, social, physical, and financial assets. Central to this is the creation of institutional arrangements that integrate diverse knowledge systems and abide by the principles of equality and justice. The scientific community has to mobilise itself to do the right kind of science in democratised, decentralised ways with the capacity of inclusion and deliberation. This relates closely to Abrol's essay on technology.

Abhay Shukla and Rakhal Gaitonde say that the history of the development of the health system in India is marked by consistent gaps between the rhetoric expressed in policy documents, and the actual resources allocated for the realization of these policies. India has a policy like National Rural Health Mission (NRHM), based on a model of participatory planning and community-based governance, but the implementation is swayed by the logic of commodification of the health sector under the neo-liberal framework. The essay argues for a Health Systems Approach, to move towards the democratization of the public health system and socialization of the private health care system. Central to this approach is a Universal Health Care (UHC) System that will bring in the vast majority of public and private health care providers under a single integrated system, including multiple systems of health. This system will be publicly managed and funded. UHC will require radical changes in provisioning, governance and financing, such that it can ensure free access to quality health care for the entire population, along with ensuring a decent and secure income and professional satisfaction for health care professionals.

One of the questions philosophy has always wrestled with is: what is it that makes our lives meaningful? Arvind Narrain looks at this from the perspective of multiple sexualities, noting that the answer provided by late capitalism is consumption, which claims to satisfy various (created) human needs. The deeply unsatisfactory nature of this claim is best gestured to by the anti-hero in Brett Easton Ellis's 'American Psycho', who finds out that an existence in which 'to consume' is the very definition of what it is to be human, kills the human within you. This essay is written in the spirit of trying to decipher how one derives meaning in life in the contemporary era. While there are many possible answers, this essay argues that at least two concepts are deeply meaningful to human existence. The first is the notion of love for one person and the second is the notion of love in a wider sense, which can be characterized as the love of justice or empathy for the suffering other. These two concepts are explored biographically by going to three queer lives lived on the margins of the societal consensus, namely, the lives of Swapna and Sucheta as well as Chelsea Manning.

Dalits have lived in the most inhuman conditions through history. According to Anand Teltumbde, the Dalit movement has failed to recognise class consciousness, such that, even policies like reservations, has only benefitted better off sections of the Dalits. The majority of Dalits still do not have access to elementary education, health, employment, democratic rights and modern values, as caste identities continue to dominate the Indian public sphere. Central to his vision is the abolishment of caste and communal consciousness from the public spaces so that humanity can march towards a society based on the principles of liberty, equality and fraternity. He also offers a ten-point agenda for this transformation, including outlawing castes, abolition of political reservations, separation of politics and religion, freezing reservation to the present population and revamping it, keeping distributive justice as its core, and adoption of proportional representation system.

If we can envision a caste-free India, can we also envision a future without gender inequities and patriarchy? Yes, it is possible, says Manisha Gupte. The notions of patriarchy that legitimise the control of men over women's production, reproduction, and sexuality dominate the present world. The author brings out glimpses of India without gender binaries and patriarchy. A society without gender binaries will refute sexual interactions as power-laden transactions; people will have reproductive and sexual rights; women will have open and safe access to private and public spaces and inequalities related to caste, class and religion would be abolished. The essay argues for intersectional approach (of class, caste, patriarchy, ethnicity,) and re-visioning of politics through lived realities of the subordinated, to fight the issues of inequality and injustice. This will force the removal of any kind of hierarchies related to caste, gender, class, ethnicity, and sexuality and will strengthen the values of equality, democratic participation by centre-staging the knowledge and the wisdom of people who witness and experience discrimination.

Another marginalized group in India are ethnic (including religious) minorities. Irfan Engineer looks at the evolution of religious identities in colonial and post-colonial India and the consequent dilution of community living. Due to the deepening of communal consciousness by cultural entrepreneurs, stronger prejudices and contests have emerged. The Constitution of India has granted stronger privileges to minorities without recognizing the differentiated intensity with which they experience discrimination and marginalisation. On the other hand, 'fundamentalists' have used these loopholes to create communal ripples. Taking the example of a *Mohalla* (neighbourhood) committee in Bhiwandi, the essay proposes the building of local social networks and groups of diverse communities to tackle communal tensions. According to him, it is rather difficult to envisage the future of minorities under the present political regime and a society dominated by the capitalist notions of development. However, alongside the struggle for social justice, inclusion, and livelihoods, the essay envisions a struggle for democratization of culture. This would mean an intra-inter struggle of communities and deconstruction of identities by the marginalized, such that the differentiation of the majority and minority becomes irrelevant.

Adivasis have been amongst the most marginalized in India, variously persecuted, dispossessed, neglected, vilified, and looked down upon. Gladson Dungdung brings out this reality in his essay, showing the multiple ways in which adivasis have never been treated as equal citizens, and their history has rarely been part of the dominant narrative of what India is. In recent times the alienation of adivasis from their lands by the globalized development process has become even more acute. It is not surprising that many of them wonder if they ever gained independence. Even the welfare approach of the state towards adivasis has been inappropriate and violative of their culture (including their languages), ecological connections, governance systems, and autonomy. In such a context, Dungdung paints an alternative future that would consist of territorial autonomy, well-being or development paths built on their own worldviews and aspirations, action on urgent problems of health and education, communities regaining their lost lands, territories and resources, and full rights to self-determination, self-reliance and self-rule. Through this, Dungdung says that perhaps adivasis 'can also help the rest of Indian society to become more equitable, just, and ecologically sustainable.'

Is a Coherent Vision Emerging?

Given the very wide range of themes being dealt with, and the diverse backgrounds of the authors, it is not expected that there will be a single common vision emerging in this volume. Indeed this may not even be desirable, for there is no reason to prioritise a single vision over a plurality. Nevertheless, we do think that some broad common trends, such as the quest for ecological sustainability and socio-economic justice and equity, the exploration of a more accountable and deep democracy, and the celebration of diversity of various kinds (without allowing this to degrade into divisiveness), do show themselves as threads through the volume. Admittedly, this is partly due to the choice of authors that we as editors made, but only partly, for in many cases we were not fully aware of the kinds of positions they would take. The complex and complicating factors are, however, in the detail of what people have said about sustainability and equity and justice, not only the broad strokes.

We deal with this finer grained analysis, including in it our own perspectives, in the concluding essay. We elaborate there what India in 2100 could be,[4] as told by a woman addressing a large gathering taking place simultaneously in many sites. She tells of a civilization based on five crucial intersecting spheres: direct political democracy in which all people have the right, capacity, and forums to take part in decision-making; economic democracy in which the means of production and the forms of consumption are publicly controlled ('public' here meaning collectivities of people, not the state), local self-reliance takes precedence over larger scale economic relations, and relations of caring and sharing are brought back centre-stage in place of monetary or commodified ones; social justice which strives towards equity and mutual respect amongst various sections of people as also the abolition of divisive categories like caste; cultural and knowledge diversity in which all forms of knowing and being are respected; and all these built on a base of ecological sustainability, resilience and wisdom that includes rebuilding a relationship of respect and oneness with the rest of nature. She provides a number of examples from the early 21st century that already provided an inkling of what transformations were possible. It is not a picture of everything being rosy and positive, but of one where the processes of equity, justice, and ecological wisdom have been firmly set into place, and much transformation already achieved.

Impossible Utopias?

Some readers of this volume are likely to be critical of the often 'utopian' nature of the visions expressed by authors. Those who posit such futures are charged of being dreamy-eyed, unrealistic, living in their own worlds. This is understandable, for we are constantly made aware of how serious a situation we are in, how difficult it is to make even small changes and then to sustain them… and for those with historical knowledge, how many revolutions have started with similar visions but failed to achieve them.

Understandable, yes, but not, we contend, justified. Movements based on ideals of equity, justice, ecological sustainability, fairness, peace, and so on, may have failed to achieve ideal states, but they have pushed open spaces for significant transformations. One has to only look at the women's movements, or the struggles of indigenous peoples or of those labelled as 'disabled', or of those fighting for democratic reforms, or those shaking off colonial shackles, to realize how much they have achieved. If the pioneers of these movements had given up on their dreams as soon as they hit the first hurdle, or even before that, by heeding the sceptics around them, we would have seen no such transformations.

Several international agreements, and the Constitutions of many countries, contain utopian elements in them. Yet we do not dismiss them outright. On the contrary, they become guiding documents for action and policy to move towards, or to hold up when human rights and ecological violations take place. Vision documents can be like beacon lights we can see in the distance when struggling through a fog or a dark night, since at least they provide us some hope and a direction to head towards. We have, for too long, been suppressed by notions of what is 'practical' and 'realistic', stripping us of the power to dream. We contend that this act of dreaming, of envisioning, is an entirely legitimate and necessary exercise particularly in the current context of despair and cynicism stuck in the quagmire of material reality.

As stated by Argentinian movie director Fernando Birri, cited by Eduardo Galeano:

'Utopia is on the horizon. I move two steps closer; it moves two steps further away.
I walk another ten steps, and utopia runs ten steps further away.
As much as I may walk, I never reach it.
So what's the point of utopia? The point is this: it makes us continually advance.'[5]

In any case, those who are selling us the quintessential American dream, where each of us will have immense economic wealth and the latest cars and automated house and so on, are proving to be selling us not only impossibilities but also insane greediness for material acquisitions as providing the 'good life'. It is a nightmare, not a dream: the planet can simply not sustain such promises, and the gross inequities being created in trying to achieve them are leading us to perilous social conflicts. And so, as one of us has written previously in association with another colleague: 'Between the seemingly 'impossible' path (of a radical ecological democracy) and the manifestly insane one, we prefer the former' (Shrivastava and Kothari, 2012).

What the Book Does Not Cover

Diverse and wide-ranging as the essays in this volume are, there are still major gaps and limitations in coverage. We were aware of some even as we were requesting this set of essays, and identified some more along the way. Subjects like spirituality, religion, and other aspects of culture (other than language), are either missing or dealt with indirectly. Of the primary occupations, fisheries are absent altogether. Human rights,[6] and within that the specific element of child rights or of 'differently abled' people, is another thematic gap, as is the issue of rights to land and the commons. Minorities in areas other than religion have not been dealt with. There is no specific focus on youth. An essay on macro-economics would have been a useful addition, as would have been one on the future of work. And sports and recreation remains neglected – somehow it was never part of our field of vision till too late! Finally, several essays cover a part of the themes they take up, not necessarily comprehensively, partly due to restrictions of space, partly depending on the expertise of the author(s).

Though the essays are not focused on particular regions, it is apparent that in their collective geographical coverage there are gaps, such as north-eastern India, and the island communities.

Readers will undoubtedly find other such gaps, which the editors take sole responsibility for. We realise also that covering the entire range of themes and sectors would need several volumes. Hopefully this volume can stimulate more such writing and dialogue, covering missing themes and regions, in an ongoing process of visioning India's future.

Finally, it should be clear but nonetheless worth stating, that neither this volume nor any of the authors in it are claiming to be *the* definitive vision or voice on the subjects dealt with. On each of these subjects, there can be diverse perspectives, even more so when we are talking about *possible* visions of the future, not only analysis of what has gone past and what is present. Also, there is no claim that all the perspectives and visions presented here are consistent with each other. However, our hope is that this set of 30-odd essays provides some elements of a coherent collective vision based on the common elements of justice, equity, and sustainability, and stimulates more such reflection and thinking and dialogue, to make such a vision more robust, inspiring, and ultimately, actionable.

Endnotes

1. We acknowledge the contribution of Shrishtee Bajpai of Kalpavriksh, who drafted the summaries of essays that we have used as a base for describing the key points of each author.
2. See http://kalpavriksh.org/index.php/alternatives/alternatives-knowledge-center/353-vikalp-sangam-coverage; see especially 'The Search for Alternatives: Key Aspects and Principles', http://kalpavriksh.org/images/alternatives/Articles/Alternativesframework3rddraftVSprocess20mar2015Eng.pdf. In this note the arenas are referred to as pillars, and the social and cultural are dealt with separately, which we have merged in this essay.
3. The author has adapted this algebraic concept to engage with social theory from a multipronged and eclectic perspective.
4. It is worth pointing out here that there is an inconsistency in the time frame that different authors have taken; many have spoken about India in 2100, but a couple have considered scenarios for 2047 (100 years after India's independence). This is partly due to unclear communication by the editors to the authors, and partly due to the authors wanting to provide either an extended (2100) or a shortened (2047) scenario.
5. https://creatologue.com/2011/09/01/what-purpose-does-utopia-serve/.
6. A promised essay on this did not come in on time.

References

Kothari, A., 2014, 'Radical Ecological Democracy: Way forward for India and beyond', *Development,* 57(1), pp. 36–45.

Rockstrom, Johan, Will Steffen, Kevin Noone, Åsa Persson, F. Stuart Chapin, Eric Lambin, Timothy M. Lenton, Marten Scheffer, Carl Folke, Hans Joachim Schellnhuber, Björn Nykvist, Cynthia A. de Wit, Terry Hughes, Sander van der Leeuw, Henning Rodhe, Sverker Sörlin, Peter K. Snyder, Robert Costanza, Uno Svedin, Malin Falkenmark, Louise Karlberg, Robert W. Corell, Victoria J. Fabry, James Hansen, Brian Walker, Diana Liverman, Katherine Richardson, Paul Crutzen and Jonathan Foley, 2009, 'Planetary Boundaries: Exploring the safe operating space for humanity', *Ecology and Society* 14(2): Art. 32, Available at http://www.ecologyandsociety.org/vol14/iss2/art32/ (accessed on 15 January, 2017).

Shrivastava, A. and A. Kothari, 2012, *Churning the Earth: The Making of Global India,* New Delhi: Viking and Penguin Books India.

ECOLOGICAL FUTURES

Changing Natures: a democratic and dynamic approach to biodiversity conservation

Kartik Shanker, Meera Anna Oommen and Nitin Rai

Summary

This essay provides a brief historical background of the dominant conservation paradigm and its social-political context before calling for a holistic approach. It stresses that both exclusionary conservation and development in the last century share a common past in the legacies of large-scale socio-political processes such as colonialism, post-colonial agendas and neoliberalism. While this approach has had some positive outcomes for the conservation of endangered species and habitats, it has also resulted in the creation of conservation silos and disenfranchised communities. The recent turn to commodification of conservation areas through tourism and carbon sequestration interventions has accentuated material and discursive conflicts.

This essay argues for reconciliation ecology that aims for greater emphasis on heterogeneous, multi-use landscapes which can create a greater engagement with conservation for civil society in general, and result in better outcomes for biodiversity. This holistic approach is a departure from an exclusionary paradigm, replacing it with a vision for the future that conforms to the ideals of social and environmental justice while striving towards achieving conservation targets.

Introduction

India encompasses an enviable diversity of flora and fauna within its territorial boundaries. Despite being one of the 17 mega-diversity countries in the world, and host to four global biodiversity hotspots, India has perhaps lost fewer of its large vertebrates to complete extinction than many others. This outcome is the result of a range of factors including (but not restricted to) a long history of conservation and tolerance to species accorded by human communities throughout the length and breadth of the country, and the numerous

25

historical and political contingencies and biophysical features that together sustain this impressive diversity. On the flip side of this optimistic outlook can be found issues such as local extinctions of species, habitat loss and the overwhelming negative impacts of development and of conservation itself: of dispossession, loss of livelihoods and the loss of cultural diversity and dignity. The conservation scenario in India therefore remains a paradox with elements of hope entwined with loss.

Protected areas have now become a global model for the conservation of biological diversity with some scholars even demanding that half the land area of the earth be enclosed as a formally protected network in order to stem the decline in biological diversity (Wilson, 2016). Modern day conservation in India, comprising largely of protected area (PA) establishment and legal protection of threatened species outside PAs, has its roots in British colonial era initiatives premised on the demarcation and notification of areas initially for timber management and later as wildlife reserves (Saberwal & Rangarajan, 2003; Rangarajan, 1996a). American discourses on sustainability and dessication such as those of Marsh (1864) and romanticist contributions such as Muir, Thoreau and Leopold were also influential in determining forestry and conservation trajectories (Guha, 1989; Saberwal, 1997). A focus on colonial era practices and extra-local influences, however, hides the longer history of forest protection that India has experienced for many centuries. Forests have always been an important resource for kings, colonial rulers and now the independent state, and therefore been protected and controlled in a variety of ways (Trautmann, 2015). It is safe to assume that such control by the state will continue into the future. The social and ecological costs of such top down conservation and control approaches have, however, been high.

As researchers and practitioners working in this field, we attempt a critical appraisal of key aspects of conservation in India with a view to suggesting approaches that are already pertinent and likely to become even more so in the next few decades. More specifically, we argue that the continuing emphasis on inviolate conservation and 'pristine' landscapes has had adverse social and ecological consequences. Though the numbers of certain species may have increased, this, by itself, need not mean that there have been positive impacts at a broader level, and in some cases, the increase itself has had some social and economic costs such as herbivores raiding agricultural crops. The shortcomings of the protected area model call for the adoption of a holistic approach that not only interrogates the different elements within the conventional conservation framework, but also incorporates concerns related to uneven development, socio-economic inequalities, and ethical and cultural specificities, all of which lead to multi-scale and multi-actor power differentials. In our opinion, such an approach could provide a viable alternative to the exclusionary

26

paradigm and hopefully usher in a vision for the future that conforms to the ideals of social and environmental justice while striving towards achieving conservation targets. Further, we submit that a broader environmental and social agenda is of paramount importance in an era of unprecedented global transformations ranging from climate change to the local and regional impacts wrought by globalisation and industrialisation.

We begin this essay with a brief historical sketch of the development of the dominant conservation paradigm in India, and the socio-political context that generated it. In this section, we stress that as the comparative histories of tropical developing countries affirm, both exclusionary conservation and development in the last century share a common history in the legacies of large-scale socio-political processes such as colonialism, post-colonial agendas and neoliberalism. Hence, there is a need to view conservation and development as linked agendas. In the sections following this, we use a simple thematic interrogation (of what? where? who? and how?) to offer suggestions for a broadening of the conservation agenda from a protection-centric model to a more spatially as well as socially heterogeneous framework that could adequately address India's long-term ecological and social goals.

Conservation and Development: two sides of the same coin

Across most of the world, modern conservation has been largely driven by notions of wilderness as 'pristine' nature and the need to protect such landscapes from a variety of human-induced impacts. While the assumption of pristineness itself has been called to question both in terms of its authenticity and of its questionable creation as a political project across colonial landscapes, it should suffice to say that conservation in India too has followed a similar trajectory. A focus on protected areas (especially officially created, exclusionary ones) remains the hallmark of the conservation movement globally, as well as in India. Although there were also pre-colonial forms of this conservation approach (e.g. protection of individual species such as elephants, establishment of hunting preserves and forest patches along the boundaries of kingdoms), the colonial period consolidated the idea of exclusionary conservation (Trautmann, 2015). During British rule in India, the control of forests was taken over by the state to fuel various colonial enterprises such as plantation development, ship-building and the construction of railways. Forests were put under a system of intense management for production of timber (scientific forestry) while at the same time placing restrictions on traditional practices such as shifting cultivation and hunting by forest communities (Guha, 1983; Pouchepadass, 1995). Although wildlife, especially species involved in crop-raiding and direct attacks, were systematically eradicated during the earlier colonial period, concerns about scarcity of animals for hunting prompted the establishment of reserves for the purpose of managing wildlife populations (Rangarajan, 1996a; 1996b; 1998). Many of these reserves were demarcated as the continuations or extensions of already existing royal hunting preserves. By the end of the colonial period, forests in India were thus simultaneously under intense production for timber and intense 'protection' for hunting.

Independent India continued with the management of forests for timber and the hunting of wildlife in reserves until 1972 when a global movement in conservation and a growing awareness of environmental degradation resulted in the enactment of the Wild Life Protection Act by the Government of India. The Act banned hunting of listed species and protected areas were notified mostly as wildlife sanctuaries and national parks across the country. Additional forest, grassland, marine, and mountain areas came under these conservation categories even as India continued to lose forests outside these islands of protection, to meet its development goals. The intensification of conservation within protected areas and the conversion of forests outside for developmental purposes has not only continued, but in recent years accelerated to worrying levels.

At the core of the conservation discourse leading up to this period was the reliance on presumably inviolate, wild and pristine landscapes for the singular purpose of conserving biological diversity. That such pristine areas do not exist outside of a political construct is often ignored with the result that landscapes that have had long histories of people's use and residence are targeted for conservation and eventual displacement of the people who historically managed and produced these landscapes. The notification of these landscapes as PAs has resulted in adverse social and ecological outcomes such as the displacement of people and the curbing of local management and traditional use systems (Wani and Kothari, 2007). As a consequence of the negative implications of protected areas, the decades leading up to the new millennium saw the initiation of a number of inclusive approaches to conservation. These include the Integrated Conservation Development Projects (ICDPs) of the 1980s' to more recent community-based conservation (CBC) with a focus on poverty alleviation models and their variants. ICDPs were top-down strategies that were aimed at reducing the resistance to exclusionary approaches while not changing the essence of the fortress approach (Hughes and Flintan, 2001). In India, a number of initiatives such as Joint Forest Management (JFM) and the 'India Ecodevelopment' projects were initiated around some protected areas to reduce pressure on forests and garner community support (Sundar, 2005; Shahabuddin, 2010).

Following on the heels of the global turn towards neo-liberalisation, India too liberalised its economy in 1991. The slow but sure integration of the Indian economic system with global markets resulted in the increasing commodification of nature. Over the years, commodification has taken several forms, such as the valuation of forests for its subsequent conversion to non-forest purposes on payment for each hectare of forest diverted; or the conversion of protected areas into tourism destinations through the construction of these areas as pristine and wild. Neoliberal policies have also been instrumental in catalysing large-scale changes in modified landscapes through their impact on land use, agricultural practices, and food security and sovereignty (Shrivastava and Kothari, 2012). In addition, neoliberal commodification has also been the key driver of payments for ecosystem services (PES) strategies such as REDD and REDD+ (Dressler and Roth, 2011; Büscher *et al.*, 2012) which are now also being employed in India with unclear benefits for conservation or communities (Jha, 2012; Lele, 2012; Ghosh, 2015).

To summarise, a broader look at large-scale land-use and conservation trajectories in tropical developing countries (including India) over the past century or so reveals that there are common overarching processes such as colonialism and neo-liberalism. Though not without their own regional and place-based specificities, colonial practices were instrumental in the transformation of the tropics along several fronts such as deforestation and plantation agriculture. At the same time, to overcome the scarcities induced by excessive extraction, colonial policies eventually prompted the establishment of exclusionary protected areas, which resulted in adverse impacts such as exclusion of people from native lands, the creation of inequalities, and the erosion of cultural connections with land (Grove, 1995).

Recently, economic neo-liberalisation has brought about shifts in agricultural commodity production and increase in demand for land resulting in the separation and intensification of agricultural production and state led conservation within their respective 'zones'. The establishment of protected areas for conservation lends itself to its eventual commodification for tourism and more recently as repositories of carbon. Thus, neoliberal policies have been increasingly integrated into the conservation agenda under which capitalist expansion and conservation are not only deemed compatible, but also desirable (Igoe & Brockington, 2007; Castree, 2010). The socially problematic outcomes of conservation interventions mandates a more inclusive and ethical strategy with a strong foundation in the principles of social and environmental justice. In the sections below, we critique the contemporary approach to conservation and present approaches that we believe offer a more sustainable and holistic alternative.

What: re-imagining diversity

Conservation in India has historically revolved around charismatic large mammals and the protection of their populations and habitats. Terrestrial mammals like elephants, rhinos, tigers, lions and primates still command a significant proportion of time, effort and financial resources in the country's conservation efforts. Even on the marine side, large iconic vertebrates such as sea turtles garner both headlines and money (Shanker, 2015). While this focus on flagships has been valuable for raising the profile of conservation in the public eye, and may have been relevant during the early part of the conservation phase, it is necessary to revisit the contemporary relevance of this approach. Single species efforts need to be evaluated not only on their positive outcomes, but also for their counter-productive impacts and inadequacies that affect India's conservation context as a whole. For example, there are pockets of extensive conflict between elephants and humans in north eastern and southern India when populations have spilled over from nearby sanctuaries, resulting in numerous problematic impacts (Münster & Münster, 2012; Barua *et al.*, 2013). Similarly, conservation of green turtles both locally and in nearby Sri Lanka may have led to increases in foraging populations in the Lakshadweep Islands, which has led to both direct and indirect (through decimation of sea grass patches) conflict with fishers (Arthur *et al.*, 2013). Many large herbivores such as elephants and sea turtles are charismatic icons for conservation, but are also known to be ecosystem modifiers, with transformative effects on tree and sea grass communities respectively (Lal *et al.*, 2010; Christianen *et al.*, 2014). In Bharatpur National Park for instance, grazing by domestic water buffaloes created the wetland habitat that was essential for birds. When grazing was banned by the Forest Department, the vegetation grew so rapidly that the habitat transformed and bird densities dropped to alarming levels, provoking the department to allow grass cutting by people to mimic grazing (Lewis, 2003). These cases demonstrate that a single species focus can impede or even act counter to the larger goals of biodiversity conservation.

Another frequently raised caveat is that a focus on an iconic species or small group of species can divert attention away from a variety of others, perhaps equally deserving in attention but lacking in charisma. The Indian wild pig is a case in point. Despite being one of the most problematic species of crop-raiding animals in the country, very little research attention has been focused on this important species. The case often made for the reliance on large mammals and other iconic species (as flagships, umbrellas and indicators) is also that they serve as surrogates for other diversity and can be effective tools to spatially prioritise areas for conservation. In general, it has been found that many such 'indicator' species do not serve as particularly good surrogates for biodiversity in general (Andelman and Fagan, 2000; Das *et al.*, 2006). The extensive diversity of plants, as well as terrestrial and marine invertebrates which dominate some of these ecosystems both in terms of abundance and diversity, and which have the potential for a variety of human benefits (many still undocumented) do not get adequately represented in these species-centric studies/strategies. By ignoring this diversity, we also ignore important ecosystem processes and functions.

In other cases, successful species conservation has resulted in increases in populations of large vertebrates that have historically been involved in conflicts with people (elephants, wild pig, macaques). Many local communities who are involved in long-term antagonistic relationships with such species, or find themselves engaged in new conflict where there may have been none earlier, blame either the State (as custodians of these species) or conservationists (as guardians) for these conflicts. Forest margins, especially the peripheries of parks with large vertebrates, are likely to continue as zones of escalated conflict under better protection regimes that result in the spillover of species.

Moving on from flagships, one of the primary imperatives of conservation efforts in India should be to broaden the notion of biodiversity, that is, to understand diversity at different scales, to appreciate the value of biodiversity in terms of its utilitarian, aesthetic, symbolic and intrinsic benefits, and for the preservation of long-term ecosystem function and services. However, as much as conservation needs to conceptually broaden its canvas to include lesser known species, given the scale of diversity, more single species studies and interventions will be neither easy, nor efficient or desirable. Moreover, research on tropical systems has drawn explicit attention to the importance of maintaining and facilitating ecological and evolutionary processes (Gardner *et al.*, 2009). Planning for long-term persistence of biological diversity and ecosystem services requires a shift from species-based to process-based thinking, and perhaps by complementing long-term in-depth studies with 'satisficing' strategies – approaches that can provide good enough solutions (Simon, 1956) to a greater number of species and habitats. This also requires a concomitant shift in perspective from a protected-areas-as-islands mentality to a more holistic conservation framework that addresses landscape mosaics which comprise land uses that range from high to low diversity, as well as an openness towards embracing more efficient research methodologies.

In this vision, conservation would privilege processes which enable the long-term maintenance of biological diversity and ecosystem services such as the maintenance of meta-populations, pollination and climate regulation. Prioritisation exercises would accommodate a much broader range of taxa and use modern conservation planning methods that include principles of complementarity (Margules and Pressey, 2000) wherein areas are selected, not individually, but to maximize their benefit as a whole, or even better, as a network. Conservation would also then mandate the exploration of fundamental socio-economic trade-offs and networks and large-scale influences on an equal footing with ecological processes. Closer examinations of neoliberal and globalising agendas that bring about large-scale changes in land use, agrarian practices and urbanising processes that affect the mobility of populations, and trade policies that impact food security would need to be a part of this shift to a broader conservation agenda. Understanding these changes is essential to tackling conservation challenges due to the interlinked and considerable outcomes of these processes on biodiversity and landscapes.

Where: from exclusionary enclaves to reconciled landscapes

Broadening the notion of biodiversity begs for a larger spatial spread of conservation initiatives beyond these exclusionary spaces (Chazdon *et al.*, 2009; Shankar Raman, 2015). In the past century, protected areas have no doubt played an important role in saving endangered species and habitats in India. However, their creation and spatial configuration have been the consequence of historical contingency. The existence of royal hunting grounds and preserves and the exclusionary practices of Indian forestry transitioned easily into a formal network that has little to do with the principles mandated by formal conservation planning exercises. Significant biophysical spaces such as the marine realm have hardly any representation in the conservation network. Moreover, the restriction of wildlife to protected areas has resulted in reduction in connectivity, alteration of genetic flows, reduction of home ranges, increase in local abundances of wildlife causing conflict with humans and erosion of local peoples' ability to live with wildlife. In the current conservation scenario, areas outside the formal PA network are accorded little value by conservationists themselves, and are perceived by local people as spaces where wildlife should not be occurring. Often, local people consider wildlife spilling over into the countryside as government property, a widespread perception with antecedents in colonial and recent conservation practices which enclosed wildlife in exclusionary reserves and removed them from outside parks (see Treves, 1999, for a similar pattern in Africa). Frequently, the fallout of such a perception is escalated conflict, especially retaliatory attacks on endangered species of conservation significance. A range of hidden dimensions from uncompensated psychosocial impacts to opportunity and transaction costs have increasingly been shown to be contributing to the problem (Barua *et al.*, 2013).

The critical question for future conservation is whether the current PA network would be capable of serving the greater goal of conservation that not only protects select species, but also achieves its long-term ecological processes-based goals. By setting a strict protectionist agenda of securing a certain percentage of the country's area with too extreme a focus on the preservation of wilderness, we need to question whether we are ignoring or exacerbating issues in areas outside reserves which could nevertheless be of critical importance in the long-term maintenance of biological diversity and ecosystem services. In addition, unfettered development in these areas is likely to impact not just the biodiversity in these locations. Through a variety of ecological, geographic, and social processes, the biodiversity in adjacent (or even distant) locations, which may include high priority areas for conservation, would also be impacted.

The outcomes of this narrow focus are not only ecological, but also social such as retaliatory attacks on species, organised protests against conservation practices and acts of every day resistance. Examples of increasing human-wildlife conflict include leopard attacks on humans, elephant raids on agriculture and the constant but not very visible impacts of primate and herbivore related crop losses (Karanth *et al.*, 2013). These wildlife induced impacts combine with the livelihood implications of protected area establishment such as curtailment of access and displacement to give rise to vocal campaigns by human rights groups against the establishment of protected areas (Bijoy, 2011).

In any case, 'pristine' protected areas with no human activity are conceptually a paradox. On the one hand, the enforcing authority (say government) will need to be present to ensure that there is no unauthorized presence in the area. Second, those in favour of such pristine areas (typically conservation biologists and urban conservationists) will argue that their presence is required for research and monitoring. In effect then, like colonial preserves for hunting, this then becomes little more than a land grab for yet another elite section of society.

Considering these problematic impacts, a revised framework for conservation is in order.

For many years, Michael Rosenzweig has championed the idea that species richness patterns across the globe are largely driven by the species-area relationship, that is, the larger the area, the more the species. The corollary, of course, is that when the available area for species disappears due to one reason or another, in the long run, the total number of species that can be supported will also decline (Rosenzweig, 2001). Hence, the preservation of enclaves that form a tiny fraction of the Earth's area will never be sufficient either for the long-term maintenance of species and even less so for that of critical ecological services. In his proposal for 'reconciliation ecology', Rosenzweig argues that human landscapes must therefore be managed to be friendlier to biodiversity, creating a win-win system for both humans and non-human species (Rosenzweig, 2003a, b). While the idea is not new and has been subjected to scrutiny, controversy and support, it is appealing at more levels than just its biological implications of greater areas for species survival.

The biological consequences of such a project lie in transforming or maintaining human dominated or influenced landscapes in different ways. For a range of smaller and motile taxa, it may be possible to make the matrix itself less hostile. This may come about by marginally altering land use policies to promote diverse vegetation types. For other taxa, it may be necessary to create corridors and refuges that allow them to use larger landscapes that are currently inaccessible to them. In the Indian context, which is dominated by less intensive agricultural practices and a diversity of traditional use systems, a reconciliatory approach might be a more feasible solution than a strict PA vs. non-PA division. Moreover, in many parts of India, management regimes such as common property land use have traditionally incorporated at lease some features of reconciled landscapes. Low intensity agriculture and pastoral landscapes in the country often serve as biodiversity friendly matrices.[1] Hence, 'reconciliation' landscapes that have benefits for both people, biodiversity and ecosystem services are not hard to imagine in India.

However, the cultural implications of this project may be even more profound. A combination of traditional property and resource management systems, production and extraction practices, locally-suited agricultural varieties and livestock breeds, religious factors, ethnic and linguistic influences have resulted in heterogeneous, multi-use landscapes with an amazing array of bio-cultural diversity. When viewed from this perspective, there is a wide constituency of people who, by living on the land and working it, already fall within the ambit of conservation, though not explicitly categorised or articulated as such; globally there is recognition of such practices as Indigenous Peoples and Community Conserved Territories and Areas, or ICCAs (www.iccaconsortium.org). Current development and agricultural (including pastoral and fisheries) practices are rapidly transforming landscapes from diverse multi-cropped areas to single cropped and high yielding areas. For reconciliation approaches to work in such changing contexts there needs to be better integration of conservation and agricultural policy.

Reconciliation ecology therefore envisages greater conservation values for the countryside and hinges on the re-conceptualization of landscapes and seascapes as connected, historical and dynamic. Recognizing that these landscapes were historically used and managed by local residents and that landscapes are connected to each other and therefore allow the movement of many species will not only extend the area under a new conservation paradigm but also reduce the conflicts that form part of the current conservation practice. This is likely to be not only more effective, but more socially just (and therefore viable in the long term) than Wilson's 'half-earth' alternative (2016) which would also create more area for biodiversity and wildlife but at the considerable cost of further marginalising communities and alienating people from nature.

In practical terms, this would involve the move to a more dynamic categorisation of conservation areas where the focus is not on conservation alone but a multiple set of ecological and livelihood priorities that are negotiated amongst local and regional stakeholders. This will mean, however, that practices that are seen to fundamentally alter the landscapes such as intensive agriculture, mining and large infrastructural projects will have to be regulated and are likely to affect the industrialisation goals of the state. We therefore believe that any discussion of conservation needs to necessarily include a reconsideration of the economic growth models which currently assume that conservation can happen in biodiversity islands while the rest of the land and sea is put under some form of intense production.[2] The future of conservation in India is therefore intrinsically linked to the developmental approach that the government and local stakeholders can negotiate amongst themselves.

Who: saviours, scoundrels and scapegoats

The issue of conservation governance dealing with *who* takes conservation decisions, has become quite well-established in the last few years, at least at global levels, as recognised by both the Convention on Biological Diversity (CBD) and by the International Union for Conservation of Nature (IUCN) (Borrini-Feyerabend *et al.*, 2013). In conceptual terms, modern Indian conservation is a mix of several ideologies ranging from utilitarian colonial and post-colonial extraction to Western romanticist notions among elite intellectuals and conservationists who were influential in the creation of exclusionary spaces that today constitute India's parks. As Cronon (1995) explains in the case of North America, this cultural tradition of 'undisturbed wilderness' is also characterised by misperceptions about historical use of land and by an erasure of history (e.g., colonial land grabs). Together this has resulted in a modern tendency to view any kind of use of natural spaces, species or resources as abuse. The exclusion of people from their land went hand in hand with both systems. In the colonial period, extractive practices for imperial expansion were justified in the form of the White Man's burden which mandated the colonist to manage the native and his land as the latter was considered to be incapable of taking care of his own legacy. A similar throwback from colonial times is visible in the treatment of local communities and tribal populations by conservationists. Although this has been pointed out several times, a point worth reiterating is a tendency to treat people living inside or close to protected areas as the primary threats to species and ecosystems without adequately problematising the milieu that brings about local extractive practices.

In India, these values can be traced to a spectrum of ethical standpoints adopted by conservationists and other stakeholder groups over the years. Reflecting a wider conservation agenda that includes diverse stakeholder groups and multiple use landscapes, as suggested by Norton (2000), we urge for the adoption of a more pluralistic and inclusive ethic. This calls for the contextual adoption of a continuum of human values related to biological diversity that are not only held by conservationists but also by tribal communities, agriculturalists, pastoralists, urban folk and numerous other stakeholder groups.

While there have been sporadic efforts to involve people in conservation in India, little has changed about the underlying approach. The much touted eco-development initiatives of the government were aimed at reducing dependence on the forest through the provision of alternative livelihoods. The goal of increasing incomes from non-forest based livelihoods was met through the establishment of eco-development committees (EDCs) consisting of local peasants and forest dwellers but under the control of the forest department. The forest department pushed the formation of these EDCs and undermined the role of constitutional local bodies (Sundar, 2000). At the same time, civil society advocacy of and guidance on more inclusionary, participatory conservation pathways such as joint protected area management based on co-governance, diversification of governance types and co-existence have been ignored by official agencies; even formal commitments under legally binding instruments like the Convention on Biological Diversity's Programme of Work on Protected Areas which enjoin India to move towards rights-based, participatory conservation, have not been implemented (Kothari *et al.*, 1996; ATREE *et al.*, 2007a, b). Even the few measures for participation that were officially mandated in the Wild Life Protection Act (WLPA) and the National Wildlife Action Plan, such as Sanctuary Advisory Committees, have not been implemented for any protected area. On the contrary, conservation has become more centralized and exclusive. Even as legislation for granting of forest rights, the Forest Rights Act (FRA), was being notified, the WLPA was being strengthened and inviolate areas for tiger conservation were being legislated (Bijoy, 2011).

Local participation in conservation and forest management received a boost in 2006 with the notification of the Forest Rights Act. This unprecedented legislation gives adivasis and traditional forest dwellers rights, not just to livelihoods such as cultivation and forest produce harvest, but also, and more relevant to our account, the right to manage and conserve areas according to their customary practice. This is an empowering legislation under which many communities have in the last few years begun to claim rights. It is worth noting that while state governments have been willing to grant rights to individual households for cultivation of forest land, there has been resistance by the state, and especially the forest administration, to granting rights to the community for use and management of forests. The reason for the reticence is that community forest rights (CFR) threaten state control over forests and landscapes. Even in cases where CFRs have been granted, communities have found it difficult to exercise their conservation rights due to the conflict between the FRA and the WLPA in determining who controls conservation areas (Rai, 2014). Neither of these legislations has a process laid out for post rights situations. In the decade since the FRA has been notified, there have been a few examples of local conservation efforts within protected areas. After years of struggle, communities in 3 protected areas have received CFR rights: Biligiri Rangaswamy Temple Tiger Reserve (BRT, Karnataka), Shoolpaneshwar Wildlife Sanctuary (Gujarat) and Simlipal Tiger Reserve (Odisha). In BRT, although rights were granted in 2011, *gram sabhas* have not been allowed to exercise their rights due to the singular implementation of the WLPA over the FRA (Madegowda *et al.*, 2013).

Much of the recent scholarship on conservation endorses the 'principle of local support', which proposes that conservation cannot succeed without local communities. This often serves as the *raison d'etre* for involving local people, but as Brockington (2004) points out, this premise is often overrated, as the realities of power have shown that conservation alliances have routinely marginalised the poor, displaced people from their native lands or excluded them in different ways. In other words, the idea of local support is a myth given that the communities are powerless to defend their rights or interests in the face of more powerful interests who determine conservation goals. Following Brockington's argument, we would like to emphasise that community involvement should not be contingent on whether a project will succeed or fail (without community support) but rather, on the ethical and moral imperatives relating to justice and democratic principles.

How: dynamic systems, plural solutions

In our essay, we have argued that there need to be changes in three dimensions: what, where and who. First, we need to re-imagine diversity so that it accommodates a broader array of life forms, what Charles Darwin (1859) might have referred to as 'grandeur in this view of life'. This re-imagination needs to occur not merely in the corridors of science, but in society. This vision of biodiversity then accords value for a variety of landscapes, not just the select preserves that house a few iconic species. Hence, we propose that conservation is best served by landscapes that reconcile a range of human use and biodiversity values, emphasizing ecosystem function and process as well as justice and equity. We suggest going beyond the current categories of protected areas to acknowledge a range of community-based and customary areas such as the indigenous peoples' and community conserved territories and areas or ICCAs (Pathak, 2001). Finally, we need to abandon any approaches that lead to further alienation between people and environment, such as exclusionary areas would do. Broadly, a proportion may very well need to be designated as free of extractive use or destructive activities, but such designations need not exclude people from those areas. In fact, we endorse the notion that communities that are connected with the land and the sea are the best stewards of the environment and resources. We emphasise that the biggest driver of ecosystem and biodiversity decline today are current economic growth models based on accumulation at any cost which has resulted in not only enormous social and economic inequality but also ecological degradation at unprecedented scales.

In summary, our vision is for a landscape that contains many constantly changing ecological and social elements which acknowledges that these systems are governed by non-equilibrial processes and cannot therefore be managed as static systems. We envision connected landscapes that are open for access by all citizens. This will mean putting more land under common property regimes managed by nested democratic institutions.[3] We need to move to a more dynamic categorisation of conservation areas to facilitate the inclusion of more land into a new conservation rationale where the focus is not on conservation alone but a multiple set of priorities that are negotiated amongst local and regional stakeholders. This will result in making more areas biodiversity friendly and accommodate species in landscapes that are currently seen to be unfriendly to biodiversity such as agricultural and urban landscapes. For example, cities may have relatively little biodiversity and certainly few endangered or iconic species (though there are some), but they have a disproportionate effect on the environment, as well as policy relating to it. It therefore becomes imperative to re-imagine conservation in these spaces. While there is a recent focus on urban biodiversity and conservation, and there have been some successes at city-wide scales, we suggest that small communities work best together. We envision a neighbourhood scale greening of cities with a city scale focus on certain icons that can promote and sustain interest in conservation.

The proposal for such a democratic and dynamic approach to conservation has been made for India in the past, and most comprehensively in the National Biodiversity Strategy and Action Plan (Kalpavriksh and TPCG, 2005). Amongst the major actions listed in the NBSAP were a landscape approach for conservation; a move to a public trust doctrine for land and water management; a decentralized nature governance structure; and recognition of local knowledge and management systems. The NBSAP, which was prepared by a coalition of civil society groups, was rejected by the Ministry of Environment and Forests, which had commissioned the plan in the first place. The rejection of the plan indicates the challenges that face efforts to change the nature of biodiversity conservation governance in India. We imagine a future in which both state and society are open to questioning and revising established conservation practice and welcome new and hybrid ways of governing nature based on customary and scientific knowledge through democratic processes.

In order to achieve these goals, we need to engage constantly both with nature as well as with society to find equitable and appropriate paths to environmental conservation and sustainability. Both knowledge and action need to be democratised in order to adopt an equitable ethic and approach to addressing. Although inputs from the natural sciences have dominated conservation frameworks, an increasing acceptance of the need for ecology and society to be managed as an interlinked system has led to an increased analytical focus on conservation social science in the past few decades. Political ecological and historical explorations that deal with asymmetric power relations, the analysis of fortress conservation, and neoliberal approaches have been important axes of political enquiry. Of particular relevance in this context would be the acceptance of topics that dare not be broached, which upset the long-held tenets of the 'Edenic sciences' (Robbins and Moore, 2013) such as hunting and sustainable use that often provoke the ire of animal rights activists and radical conservationists.

Conservation in socially heterogeneous systems also brings into context the different constituencies of knowledge that could inform future directions. While the dichotomy between scientific and traditional knowledge has been explored at a theoretical level, (Agrawal, 1995) two practical cautions are significant. Firstly, there is a privileging of scientific knowledge, despite the fact that this form of science is often normative, reflecting the biases and preferences of its providers (Lackey, 2007). An examination of this politics of science at the science-policy interface is especially pertinent because conservation biology is a 'mission-driven discipline' which often requires its practitioners to take a stand, and advocacy for a particular cause should be scientifically and ethically justified (Chan, 2008). Similarly, there is also a need to examine the 'new traditionalist discourse' (which valorises traditional systems as benign, sustainable and exclusively indigenous) not only in terms of the claims of sustainability of different traditional practices, but also its embedding in social domination and subordination (Sinha *et al.*, 1997). The power to produce certain forms of knowledge gives selected actors the power to govern in specific ways. We hope to see in future a democratic production of knowledge in which more forms of knowledge are included enabling what Visvanathan (2005) has called 'cognitive justice'.[4] This will ensure more equitable conservation governance than is currently the case.

Finally, we would like to emphasise a critical concept that is inherent in the idea of this collection of essays – that futures are intertwined. Environment issues are connected to development, health, education, poverty, dignity, democracy and justice. We believe that the path to a better environmental future lies in being able to understand and act on these connections. This calls for the breaking down of boundaries that separate areas of enquiry and of action.

In closing, we would like to emphasise a brave new hopeful vision for environmental conservation that requires us to think beyond the boundaries of ecology. Our social, psychological and physical well-being is closely linked to the health of the planet, but we can only achieve those goals by adopting a pluralistic philosophy to human-environment relations and by instituting processes which promote connections, at every level, with nature, in all its forms.

Endnotes

1. Pl. also see Food and Agriculture Futures essay in this volume.
2. Pl. also see Localisation Futures, Dare to Dream, and Concluding essay of this volume.
3. Pl. also see Democracy, and Power futures essays in this volume.
4. Pl. also see Knowledge Futures essay in this volume.

References

Agrawal, A., 1995, 'Dismantling the Divide between Indigenous and Scientific Knowledge', *Development and Change*, (26), pp. 413-39.

Andelman, S.J. and W.F. Fagan, 2000, 'Umbrellas and Flagships: Efficient conservation surrogates or expensive mistakes?' *PNAS* (97), pp. 5954 – 59.

Arthur, R., N. Kelkar, T. Alcoverro and M. D. Madhusudan, 2013, 'Complex Ecological Pathways underlie Perceptions of Conflict between Green Turtles and Fishers in the Lakshadweep Islands', *Biological Conservation,* (167), pp. 25–34.

ATREE, Council for Social Development, Himal Prakriti, Kalpavriksh, Samrakshan, SHODH, Vasundhara, Wildlife Conservation Trust, and WWF-India, 2007, *Proposed Guidelines on Identification of Critical Wildlife Habitats, Co-existence and Relocation related to Tiger Reserves: Suggestions to the*

National Tiger Conservation Authority, Future of Conservation Network, http://kalpavriksh.org/images/CLN/FOC/foc20073.pdf (accessed 1 Feb, 2017).

ATREE, Foundation for Ecological Security, Himal Prakriti, Kalpavriksh, Samrakshan Trust, SHODH, Vasundhara, Wildlife Conservation Trust, and WWF-India, 2007, *Proposed Guidelines for Identification of Critical Wildlife Habitats in National Parks and Wildlife Sanctuaries under Scheduled Tribes and Other Traditional Forest Dwellers (Recognition of Forest Rights) Act 2006,* Future of Conservation Network, India.

Barua, M., S. A. Bhagwat and S. Jadhav, 2013, 'The Hidden Dimensions of Human-Wildlife Conflict: health impacts, opportunity and transaction costs', *Biological Conservation* (157), pp. 309-16.

Berry, W., 1981, 'Solving for Pattern', in, The Gift of Good Land: Further Essays Cultural and Agricultural, Originally published in the Rodale Press periodical, *The New Farm,* (Volume/Number unavailable).

Bijoy, C. R., 2011, 'The Great Indian Tiger Show', *Economic & Political Weekly,* XlVI (4), pp. 36–41.

Borrini-Feyerabend, G., N. Dudley, T. Jaeger, B. Lassen, N. Pathak Broome, A. Phillips and T. Sandwith, 2013, *Governance of Protected Areas: From understanding to action,* Best Practice Protected Area Guidelines Series No. 20, Gland, Switzerland: IUCN.

Brockington, D., 2004, 'Community Conservation, Inequality and Injustice: myths of power in protected area management', *Conservation and Society* 2(2), pp. 411-32.

Bryant, R.L., 1998, 'Power, Knowledge and Political Ecology in the Third World: A review', *Progress in Physical Geography* (22), pp. 79-94.

Büscher, B., S. Sullivan, K. Neves, J. Igoe & D. Brockington, 2012, 'Towards a Synthesized Critique of Neoliberal Biodiversity Conservation', *Capitalism, Nature, Socialism* (23)**,** pp. 4-30.

Cafaro, P., and R. B. Primack, 2014, 'Species Extinction is a Great Moral Wrong: sharing the earth with other species is an important human responsibility', *Biological Conservation* (170)**,** pp. 1-2.

Carruthers J., 1989, 'Creating a National Park: 1910-1926', *Journal of Southern African Studies,* (15), pp. 188-216.

Castree, N. M., 2010, 'Neo-liberalism and the Biophysical Environment 1: What neo-liberalism is, and what difference nature makes to it', *Geography Compass* (4), pp. 1725-33.

Castree, N. and B. Braun, (eds.), 2001, *Social Nature: Theory, Practice and Politics,* Massachusetts, USA: Blackwell Publishers.

Chan, K. M. A., 2008, 'Value and Advocacy in Conservation Biology: Crisis Discipline or Discipline in Crisis?', *Conservation Biology* 22(1), pp. 1-3.

Chazdon R. L., C. A. Harvey, O. Komar, D.M. Griffith, B.G. Ferguson, M. Martínez Ramos, H. Morales, R. Nigh, L. Soto Pinto, M. Van Breugel and S. M. Philpott, 2009, 'Beyond Reserves: A Research Agenda for Conserving Biodiversity in Human-modified Tropical Landscapes', *Biotropica* 41(2) pp. 142-53.

Christianen, M. J., P. M. Herman, , T. J. Bouma, L. P. Lamers, M. M.van Katwijk, T.van der Heide, P. J. Mumby, B. R. Silliman, S. L. Engelhard, M. van de Kerk, and W. Kiswara, 2014, 'Habitat collapse due to overgrazing threatens turtle conservation in marine protected areas', *Proceedings of the Royal Society of London B, Biological Sciences* 281(1777), pp. 2013-2890.

Cronon, W. A., 1995, 'The Trouble with Wilderness, or, Getting Back to the Wrong Nature', in, *Uncommon Ground: Rethinking the Human Place in Nature*, New York: W.W. Norton & Company Inc.

Darwin, C., 1859, *On the Origin of Species by Means of Natural Selection, or the Preservation of Favoured Races in the Struggle for Life*, London: John Murray.

Das, A., J. Krishnaswamy, K. S. Bawa, M. C. Kiran, V. Srinivas, N. S. Kumar and K.U. Karanth, 2006, 'Prioritisation of Conservation areas in the Western Ghats, India', *Biological Conservation* (133), pp. 16-31.

Demerit, D., 2001, 'Being Constructive about Nature', in *Social Nature: Theory, Practice and Politics*, N. Castree and B. Braun (eds.), Massachusetts, USA: Blackwell Publishers.

Dressler, W. and R. Roth, 2011, 'The Good, the Bad, and the Contradictory: Neoliberal Conservation Governance in Rural Southeast Asia', *World Development* (39), pp. 851-852.

Escobar, A., 1995, *Encountering Development: The Making and Unmaking of the Third World*, Princeton, USA: Princeton University Press.

Gardner, T. A., J. Barlow, R. Chazdon, R. M. Ewers, C. A. Harvey, C. A. Peres and N. S. Sodhi, 2009, Prospects for tropical diversity in a human-modified world, *Ecology Letters* 12: pp. 561-82.

Ghosh, Soumitra, 2015, 'Capitalisation of Nature: Political Economy of Forest/Biodiversity Offsets', *Economic & Political Weekly*, 50(16):pp. 53-60.

Grove, R. H., 1995, *Green Imperialism: Colonial Expansion, Tropical Island Edens, and the Origins of Environmentalism*, Cambridge and New York: Cambridge University Press.

Guha, R, 1983, 'Forestry in British and post-British India: a historical analysis', *Economic & Political Weekly* 18(44), pp. 1882-96.

Guha, R., 1989, 'Radical American Environmentalism and Wilderness Preservation: A Third World Critique', *Environmental Ethics*, (11), pp.71-83.

Herrnstein, R. J., and C. Murray, 1994, *The Bell Curve: Intelligence and Class Structure in American Life*, New York, USA: The Free Press.

Hughes, R. and F. Flintan, 2001, *Integrating Conservation and Development Experience: A Review and Bibliography of the ICDP Literature*, London: IIED.

Igoe, J. and D. Brockington, 2007, 'Neoliberal Conservation: A Brief Introduction', *Conservation and Society* 5(4), pp. 432-49.

Jha, S., 2012, 'Does REDD+ induce inclusive exploitation of forest people?' *Current Conservation* 6 (1), pp. 14-19.

Kalpavriksh and TPCG, 2005, *Securing India's Future: Final Technical Report of the National Biodiversity Strategy and Action Plan*, Pune/Delhi: Kalpavriksh.

Karanth, K.U., and K. K. Karanth, 2012, 'A Tiger in the Drawing Room: Can Luxury Tourism Benefit Wildlife?', *Economic & Political Weekly* XLVII (38) pp. 38-43.

Karanth, K. K., A. M. Gopalaswamy, P. K. Prasad, and S. Dasgupta, 2013, 'Patterns of Human-Wildlife Conflicts and Compensation: Insights from Western Ghats Protected Areas', *Biological Conservation* (166), pp.175–85.

Kothari, A., N. Singh, and S. Suri, (eds.), 1996, *People and Protected Areas in India: Towards Participatory Conservation*, New Delhi: Sage Publications.

Lackey, R.T., 2007, 'Science, Scientists and Policy Advocacy', *Conservation Biology* 21(1), pp. 1-17.

Lal, A., R. Arthur, N. Marbà, A.W. Lill, and T. Alcoverro, 2010, 'Implications of conserving an ecosystem modifier: Increasing green turtle (*Chelonia mydas*) densities substantially alters seagrass meadows', *Biological Conservation* (143), pp. 2730-738.

Lele, S., 2012, 'Buying our way out of environmental problems,' *Current Conservation* 6 (1), pp. 11-13.

Lewis, M., 2003, 'Cattle and Conservation at Bharatpur: A Case Study in Science and Advocacy', *Conservation and Society* 1(1), pp. 1-21.

Madegowda, C., N. D. Rai, and S. Desor, 2013, 'BRT Wildlife Sanctuary (Karnataka): A case study' in Desor, S. (ed), *Community Forest Rights under Forest Rights Act: Citizens' Report 2013*, Pune: Kalpavriksh, Bhubaneshwar: Vasundhara, and Delhi: Oxfam India, pp. 50 – 57.

Margules, C. R. and R. L. Pressey, 2000, 'Systematic conservation planning' *Nature*, (405), pp. 242 – 53.

Marsh, G. P., 1864, *Man and Nature, or Physical Geography as Modified by Human Action*, New York: C. Scribner.

Münster, D. and U. Münster, 2012, 'Human-Animal Conflicts in Kerala: Elephants and Ecological Modernity on the Agrarian Frontier in South India', in Münster, U. D. Münster and S. Dorondel (eds.), *Fields and Forests: Ethnographic Perspectives on Environmental Globalisation*, Munich, Germany: Rachel Carson Centre Perspectives, pp. 41-50.

Naughton-Treves, L., 1999, 'Whose animals? A history of property rights to wildlife in Toro, Western Uganda', *Land Degradation and Development* (10), pp. 311-28.

Neumann, R.P., 1992, 'Political ecology of wildlife conservation in the Mt. Meru area of northeast Tanzania', *Land Degradation and Rehabilitation* 3(2), pp. 85-98.

Norton, B.G., 2000, 'Biodiversity and environmental values: in search of a universal earth ethic', *Biodiversity and Conservation* 9(8), pp.1029-44.

Pathak, N., 2001, *Community Conserved Areas in India: A Directory*, Pune/Delhi: Kalpavriksh.

Pouchepadass, J., 1995, 'Colonialism and Environment in India: comparative perspective', *Economic and Political Weekly* 30(33), pp. 2059-67.

Rai, N. D., 2014, 'View from the podu: Approaches for a Democratic Ecology of India's Forests', in *Democratising Forest Governance*, Lele, S. and A. Menon, (eds.), New Delhi: Oxford University Press, pp. 25-62.

Rangan, H., 2000, *Of Myths and Movements: Rewriting Chipko into Himalayan History*, London, UK: Verso.

Rangarajan, M., 1996a, *Fencing the Forest: Conservation and Ecological Change in India's Central Provinces, 1860-1914*, New Delhi: Oxford University Press.

Rangarajan, M., 1996b, 'Environmental Histories of South Asia: A Review Essay', *Environment and History* 2(2): pp.129-43.

Rangarajan, M., 1998, 'The Raj and the Natural World: the war against 'dangerous beasts' in colonial India', *Studies in History* 14(2), pp. 265-99.

Robbins, Paul and Sarah A. Moore, 2013, "Ecological anxiety disorder: diagnosing the politics of the Anthropocene", *Cultural Geographies*, 20(1): 3-9.

Rodney, W., 1973, *How Europe Underdeveloped Africa*, London: Bogle-L'Ouverture Publications & Dar-Es-Salam: Tanzanian Publishing House.

Rosenzweig, M. L., 2001, 'Loss of speciation rate will impoverish future diversity', *PNAS* 98(10), pp. 5404-410.

Rosenzweig, M. L., 2003a, 'Reconciliation ecology and the future of species diversity', *Oryx* 37(2), pp. 194-205.

Rosenzweig, M.L., 2003b, *Win-Win Ecology: How the Earth's Species can Survive in the Midst of Human Enterprise*, London, UK: Oxford University Press.

Saberwal, V. K., 1997, 'Science and the dessicationist discourse of the 20th century' *Environment and History* 4(3), pp. 309-43.

Saberwal, V. and M. Rangarajan, 2003, *Battles over Nature: Science and the Politics of Conservation*, New Delhi: Permanent Black.

Shahabuddin, G., 2010, *Conservation at a Crossroads*, New Delhi: Permanent Black.

Shankar Raman, T. R., 2015, 'Expanding the conservation landscape', *Seminar* (673), http://www.india-seminar.com/2015/673/673_shankar_raman.htm (accessed 1 Feb, 2017).

Shanker, K., 2015, *From soup to superstar: the story of sea turtle conservation along the Indian coast*, New Delhi: Harper Collins.

Sharma, M., 2011, *Green and Saffron: Indian Environmentalism and Hindu Nationalist Politics*, New Delhi: Permanent Black.

Shrivastava, A. and A. Kothari, 2012, *Churning the Earth: The Making of Global India*, New Delhi: Penguin, India.

Simon, H. A., 1956, 'Rational choice and the structure of the environment', *Psychological Review* 63(2), pp. 129-38.

Sinha, S., S. Gururani and B. Greenberg, 1997, 'The 'new traditionalist' discourse of Indian environmentalism', *The Journal of Peasant Studies* 24(3), pp. 65-99.

Sundar, N., 2000, 'Unpacking the 'Joint' in Joint Forest Management', *Development and Change*, 31(1), pp. 255-79.

Sundar, N., 2003, 'The construction and deconstruction of 'indigenous' knowledge in India's Joint Forest Management Programme,' in *Indigenous Environmental Knowledge and its Transformations: Critical Anthropological Perspectives*, A. Bicker, R. Ellen and P. Parkes (eds.), UK: Routledge, pp. 79-100.

Trautmann, Thomas, 2015, Elephants and Kings: *An Environmental History*, Chicago: University of Chicago Press.

Visvanathan, S, 2005, 'Knowledge, Justice and Democracy', in Leach, M., I. Scoones, and B. Wynne (eds), Science and Citizens, New Delhi: Orient Longman, pp. 83–94.

Wani, M. and Kothari, A., 2007, 'Protected areas and human rights in India: the impact of the official conservation model on local communities', *Policy Matters* (15), pp.100-114.

Wilson, Edward O, 2016, *Half Earth: Our Planet's Fight for Life*, New York: Liveright.

Zackey, J., 2007, 'Peasant Perspectives on Deforestation in Southwest China –Social Discontent and Environmental Mismanagement', *Mountain Research and Development* 27(2), pp.153-161.

Environmental Governance in Future India: Principles, Structures and Pathways

Sharachchandra Lele and Geetanjoy Sahu

Summary

The current state of environmental governance in India is suffering from multiple contradictions. On one hand, the country has series of rules and regulations for the protection and safeguarding of biodiversity, water, air, and so on. Moreover, Indian judiciary has been proactive in support of environmental concerns and has even declared the right to clean environment to be a fundamental right to life. On the other hand, the current state of the environment in India is deplorable, major rivers in India are highly polluted, forests are diverted for dams, mining, etc. and India is among the 20 most polluted countries in the world.

This essay explores the reasons for the complex nature of environmental governance and suggests that the future of environmental governance should envisage a transformed value system and framework of environment and development. Presently, environmental governance has four major issues: regulatory failure, limits to judicial activism, domination of neo-liberal growth ideas and the assumption that conservatism is environmentalism.

The essay argues that the future of environmental governance has to start with embracing environmentalism as a way of life, that is, quality of life, sustainability, and environmental justice. Second, institutional design has to be re-worked, such that it can encompass biophysical and social justice goals. Better environmental governance requires a change in value systems, concern for social justice and a belief in the democratic process.

Introduction

The environment is implicated in all human activities, spheres, locations and scales: production and consumption, domestic and commercial, urban and rural, local and global. Consequently, the governance of the environment is also a vast topic, covering the use of natural resources such as forests, water and minerals as well as the disposal of waste products and other impacts that emerge, such as air and water pollution, and questions of biodiversity loss and climate change.

In this essay on re-imagining the future of environmental governance in India, we cover some of the overarching issues, but focus particularly on issues related to pollution regulation at multiple levels—the day-to-day monitoring and enforcement by pollution control boards, the setting of standards, and the regulation of potentially polluting industrial projects through the environmental clearance process—leaving other dimensions such as governance of forest and water resources to other essays.[1] Given, however, the strong connection between 'local' pollution (air, water, soil or solid waste) and the 'global' pollutant that is causing climate change (CO_2),[2] we include a discussion on the governance of carbon emissions in this essay. We use the term environmental governance rather than environmental management or pollution regulation because we include not just polluters and regulators, but also the pollutees, that is, those experiencing the pollution, wider civil society groups, the judiciary, and the state that sets up and influences many of these processes and institutions, including the legal framework governing pollution.

After a brief overview of the current state of affairs and its likely causes, we present an alternative vision that involves shifts in normative ideas, ideologies, institutions and cultures, and the bounding assumptions we make in developing this vision. We then offer a few thoughts on how a transition towards this vision might begin.

Current Context: progress or regression?

In assessing the current state of environmental governance in India, one faces the classic dilemma of whether the glass is half-empty or half-full. On the one hand, following the 1972 Stockholm Conference, a constitutional amendment in 1976 made it incumbent upon the state to 'to protect and improve the environment and to safeguard forests and wildlife of the country' (article 48A). A Department of Environment was then formed (which later became a Ministry) and a series of laws were enacted, relating to air, water, wildlife, forests, and then later biodiversity, genetic material, hazardous chemicals, and more specific aspects. Currently, between the centre and the states, there are over 200 statutes that relate directly or indirectly to environmental protection. Perhaps no other country in the world has as many environmental rules and regulations as we have in India! Pollution Control Boards (PCBs) have been set up in all states to enforce pollution related laws, and special agencies and structures have been created for conserving biodiversity and for saving tigers. Industries are being required to install pollution control technologies and green ratings initiating by civil society organizations do seem to exert pressure on industries to reduce pollution (Powers *et al.*, 2011). Moreover, in the past three decades, the judiciary has become quite supportive of environmental protection, declaring the right to a clean environment as being part of the fundamental right to life, enlarging the scope for public interest litigation (PIL), and taking a very active role in cases of Delhi air pollution, Palar river clean-up and India-wide forest management, among others (for more details, see Sahu, 2014). The National Green Tribunal was set up to reduce the burden of litigation on the Supreme Court and is currently playing a valuable role.

At the same time, the state of India's environment continues to deteriorate. A WHO report in December 2014 stated that of the 20 most air-polluted cities in the world, 13 were in India. Most Indian rivers are polluted by sewage, and an increasing number are now getting affected by industrial pollution—the number of polluted rivers rising from 121 to 275 in five years (CPCB, 2015). Solid waste disposal is presenting major problems and affecting villages around all major cities. Forests are being diverted to non-forest activities such as mining, dams and roads at an unprecedented rate (CSE, 2012). The list seems to go on and on. And environmental conflicts have increased dramatically—around mining, dams, pollution, water scarcity, forest rights and several other issues. While some of this increase may be due to increased awareness amongst communities about their rights, there is no doubt that the frequency of violation of environmental rights[3] has increased as the pressure on the environment escalated. This is particularly true in the post-1991 period, when the liberalization of the Indian economy for the sake of economic growth translated into rapid industrialization, as described vividly by Shrivastava and Kothari (2012). Not surprisingly, environmental historian Ramachandra Guha (2013) has described recent India as 'an environmental basket-case'.

Multiple Causes of the Predicament

The reasons for this state of affairs are complex. First and foremost, there are regulatory failures at multiple levels. In the case of day-to-day monitoring and enforcement of pollution, the PCBs do a very poor job of enforcing the plethora of laws. Processing paperwork for 'consent to establish' and 'consent to operate' takes the place of actual environmental monitoring, corruption is rampant, and transparency and accountability are very limited. The major reason for this is the manner in which the PCBs have been structured. While statutorily set up as independent regulatory bodies, they retain the worst of both worlds—the rules and regulations of government departments but the uncertainty in funding of an autonomous body. Moreover, the governing bodies of the PCBs are filled with bureaucrats and industry representatives, and the CEOs of the PCBs are also bureaucrats on temporary postings, rather than professionals (Lele *et al.*, 2015). At another level, the process of anticipatory regulation of environmental impacts of large projects through the 'environmental clearance' process set up under the Environment Protection Act is also significantly flawed (Menon & Kohli, 2009). Environmental impact assessments (EIAs) that feed into this process are sloppy or bogus, public hearings are often a sham, land acquisition is permitted to be carried out even before projects receive environmental clearances, and the conditions imposed at the time of giving clearances are rarely complied with post-facto.[4] Here, the flaw is both in the poorly designed process as in the absence of agencies with the ability and authority to monitor compliance with the law. Moreover, the EIA notification of 1994 has been amended more than twenty times over the last two decades in ways that accommodate the interests of the project proponents. Finally, there are areas where standards are inadequately framed, such as heavy metal pollution in water (Jamwal *et al.*, 2016), or regulations do not exist at all, such as groundwater exploitation.

Second, while an activist judiciary might compensate for the state's abdication of its responsibility to implement the law, the limits and indeed the dangers of such judicial activism are becoming apparent now. To begin with, the activism has always been limited to the upper echelons (some High Courts and the Supreme Court); the lower courts in particular and the excessively complicated judicial system in general continue to prevent swift action against environmental polluters, who can get stay orders at will and escape with light fines if they ever get convicted (Lele *et al.*, 2015). Moreover, the implementation of pro-environment judgements through monitoring committees (in the absence of a responsive state) has been found to have serious limitations (Sahu 2010). Equally important, when 'activism' leads to consistent crossover into the domain of the executive, the results can be positively harmful, as in the case of the amazing 'continuing writ of mandamus' in the Godavarman case (Rosencranz & Lele, 2008),[5] or the Supreme Court and later the NGT trying to dictate the choice of technology or the date of vehicle obsolescence in the case of urban air pollution. Finally, the 'environmentalism' of the Indian judiciary has serious limits: it focuses on 'green' issues but not on their social justice dimensions (as when it sought the removal of all forest 'encroachments' without understanding the complex history of the problem (Sarin, 2014), and it eventually bows to the rhetoric of development and 'eminent domain' for state-led projects such as the Sardar Sarovar project on the Narmada river (Sahu, 2014).

Third, the larger socio-political context is not favourable to strong environmental regulation. Successive governments have been obsessed with industrialization and economic growth, and have not only refused to fix the holes in the process and institutional arrangements, but have gnawed away at existing regulations in various ways: appointing weak ministers, who in turn appoint compromised clearance and appraisal committees, cut funds, and more recently, openly advocate the gutting of environmental laws in the name of rationalisation.[6] Whatever little attempts have been made, such as trying to limit the forested areas in which coal mining could be permitted, have been actively and concertedly watered down in inter-ministerial battles, with pressure from the highest level, no matter which party has been in power.[7] The shift in the nature of the discourse can be gauged from the fact that the Ministry of Environment has in recent times focused more on proving how it is business-friendly than on how it is a strong defender of the public's right to a clean environment. This speaks volumes of the influence that the corporate sector has had on environmental policy.

Moreover, it is not only governments and industry working in cahoots: the public constituency for a clean environment continues to be limited or even shrinking as the consumerist boom enthrals the common man. As the gains from a post-liberalisation economic boom have accrued to the middle and upper classes, the only environmentalism that has flourished is a 'conservationism' focused on saving tigers without questioning the ecological footprint of the saviours' lifestyles. What little opposition may exist to the impacts unleashed by industrialisation on communities in the hinterland is being squelched by the state: witness the systematic decimation of the anti-nuclear protests at Kudankulam (Anonymous, 2012; Sudhakar & Vijaykumar, 2012), or of Greenpeace India for mobilizing opposition to coal mining in tribal India (Kothari, 2015; Subramanian, 2015). And while those whose livelihoods are immediately threatened by dams, nuclear plants or mines may oppose such projects in the short run, it would be fair to say that most of them do not see an alternative developmental pathway. Not surprisingly then, *Adivasi* youth in central India continue to migrate to towns even in areas where dispossession-related displacement is not visible and where their parents lay claim to community forests under the Forest Rights Act.[8] In the case of over-exploitation of groundwater, the virtual absence of any regulation is mirrored in the absence of any serious social movements against such depletion, because in most locations virtually everybody—rural or urban, rich or poor, peasant or capitalist—is complicit in this particular form of environmental depletion. In other words, while the political economy of capitalism plays a very significant role, significant cultural changes involving changing attitudes towards the environment and towards consumption are taking place (Wilhite, 2008), possibly triggered by technological change that paints a vision of a limitless future.

Thus, the current state of environmental governance in India is the product of a complex interplay between citizens-as-consumers, citizens-as-producers and citizens-as-rights-holders, and their organized manifestations in the state, the corporate sector, the judiciary and civil society. The solutions recommended have often been partial at best. The corporate sector and upper and middles classes of course tend to see development as the solution to everything—basically using an Environmental Kuznets Curve argument, backed up by a belief in technology and the market.[9] The judiciary takes a top-down command-and-control approach, stepping into the breach left by a retreating state, even if the band-aid nature of such interventions is sometimes obvious and even if these interventions repeatedly cross the line between the judiciary and the executive and involve micro-managing selected cases. The same environmentalist judiciary continues to permit state projects that displace rural communities (as in the case of the Sardar Sarovar project) or that expose rural citizens to unacceptable levels of risk (as in the case of the Kudankulam nuclear power plant) by accepting the state's claims of due diligence and eminent domain. And activists, swimming against the tide of consumerism and pressing against the heavy hand of the state,[10] continue to speak in multiple tongues:[11] conservationists focus on top-down enforcement, social activists focus on transparency and decentralization, while a newer generation of sustainability enthusiasts pins its hopes on technological fixes. A holistic approach to environment and development, and therefore to environmental governance, is yet to be shaped.

What Should Future Environmental Governance Look Like?

A progressive vision for environmental governance in future India would be founded upon new value frameworks and ideas of environment and of development, institutional arrangements based on new design principles, and vibrant processes that bring about positive synergy between individuals and institutions.

Outlining Our Environmentalist Principles

To begin with, environmentalism would be understood not as something apart from development (Narain, 2015), but in fact a multi-dimensional philosophy about a way of life. It would include a close relationship with Nature as a goal in itself while recognizing that meeting even basic human needs involves modifying Nature. It would include an ethical position about respecting the rights of future generations as well as of intra-generational justice in the use of Nature's resources and disposal of waste generated by this use. In other words, environmentalism would not be just about sustaining a certain lifestyle into the future, but also about rethinking the content of that lifestyle itself, as well as its repercussions on others (human and non-human) in the present, that is, quality of life, sustainability as well as environmental justice (Lele, 2013). Closely coupled to these values would be concern for social justice (concern for the marginalised). Conversely, economic growth as a social goal would be replaced by a focus on meeting basic needs and the quality of life for all within environmental limits (Joy *et al.*, 2004)—with the understanding that these limits may be flexed through technological innovation but may not be broken, and, in tinkering with them, one must observe the 'precautionary principle'.[12] Finally, there would be a deep commitment to democratic governance, for its own sake, as the process to be adopted in taking decisions about balancing between material needs, non-material quality of life, long-term sustainability, equity and justice.[13]

The second feature of a progressive environmental governance framework would be an institutional design that is adapted to the biophysical and the social context as well as to the goals outlined above. Here, the eight design principles outlined by Ostrom (1990) have been found to be valuable for the context of local-level common pool resources with no wider externalities. But this framework has some limitations, which become apparent even in the context of forests and water resource governance, and which become particularly severe in the context of pollution problems. To begin with, even if one assumes that resources such as pastures have only local biophysical linkages, the Ostrom design principles primarily speak to the goal of 'efficient' use, not necessarily sustainable use — communities may collectively decide that wiping out the resource is the optimal thing to do. Secondly, as is often noted in the case of forests, heterogeneity of local interests (e.g., between fuel-wood collectors, timber growers, and graziers) and wider linkages (e.g., between local actions in the forest and their downstream hydrological impacts or impacts on rare wildlife that may be seen as a global heritage) are ubiquitous and cannot be addressed through the Ostrom framework (Lele, 2004). The case of pollution is extreme: pollution is usually a unidirectional externality from an 'upstream/upwind' polluter to a 'downstream/downwind' pollutee (or group of pollutees): e.g., upstream tanneries and downstream farmers in Vellore (Sahu, 2010), or upstream textile industry and downstream farmers in Tiruppur (Srinivasan *et al.*, 2014). Thus, if environmental governance is to meet both environmental justice and sustainability goals, institutional design will have to use a combination of two principles: decentralization of operational authority to improve efficiency and to address local common-pool problems where they exist, and overarching regulation that balances the rights of the producers to livelihoods and those of others to a clean environment (Farrell & Keating, 2000). Furthermore, the goal of democratic process requires a variety of attributes: legitimacy, transparency, accountability, and inclusiveness. For actual effectiveness, the organizations would need strong 'capability', that is, technical and administrative skills, leadership, and resources. Equally, conflict resolution and adjudication support is essential. Finally, a more systemic approach would mean looking at prevention as much as cure.

Translating these Principles into a Vision

To translate these broad principles into a description of an environmentally sound future for India, we must first clarify what 'boundary assumptions' we make. We assume that India's population will have stabilized at around 1.5 billion, that more than half of this population will be in urban locations or non-farm occupations, and that the economy will be a mix of small and large private players, with the state (at multiple levels) playing a robust regulatory role. Technology will continue to play a very important role, but social control over technologies will be much more democratic than it is today.

In this context, what shape will environmental governance take? Let us focus on pollution control, an activity currently carried out by state-level PCBs. In a future India, the PCBs may remain at the state level, but they would have several other features that draw upon the principles outlined above within the boundary conditions indicated:

- *For jurisdictional parsimony and environmental linkages*: Subdivisions of the PCBs would follow administrative jurisdictions (city boundaries, district boundaries) but their planning and standard-setting would be done using biophysical units such as watersheds and air-sheds[14] and with district-level consultative committees. Environmental clearances for new industries would rest with the PCBs (not with state or central committees) and would be given, based on cumulative impact assessment at these biophysical scales. At the same time, PCBs would have the authority to make multiple bodies (municipalities, utilities, planning authorities) work in tandem to ensure consistent approaches.[15]

- *For administrative skill and leadership*: The Chair of the Governing Board of the PCB would be chosen through an open application/nomination process by an independent multi-disciplinary selection committee, and the Chief Executive of the PCB (currently called Member-Secretary) would be a professional hired by the PCB through a similar open process and a renewable contract (not an IFS officer coming on deputation as is currently the case).

- *For downward accountability and inclusiveness*: A third of the members of the Governing Board of the PCB would be explicitly representing potential pollutees, through a combination of elected officials from different municipal and district-level panchayati raj institutions and eminent public individuals and activists. A third would be technical experts, selected by the same multi-disciplinary selection committee mentioned above. Bureaucrats heading other government departments or agencies or local bodies would not be present on the Governing Board. Potential polluters (industries, commercial groups) would not be represented on the Board, but would be part of consultative processes in setting of standards. Potential pollutees would be part of public hearings on environmental clearances for large projects, of social audits of the performance of the PCBs, and would have standard forums for interaction with their representatives on the Governing Board.

- *For transparency*: Deliberations of the Governing Board would be telecast/webcast publicly, as would be all hearings involving appeals against punitive orders/show-cause notices. All environmental data would be collected and analysed 'double-blind' (the PCB itself and an educational/research organization) and made publicly available via the internet in local languages within hours of sampling. All environmental clearance data would be mandatorily shared through similar media.

- *For legitimacy*: Being a statutory body confers some legitimacy, but PCBs will also *earn* legitimacy by publicly presenting, adopting and implementing 5-year pollution reduction goals and demonstrating effectiveness, fairness and transparency.

- *For financial resources*: Pollution cesses – on vehicles proportional to distance travelled (with a rising slab rate) but inversely proportional to passengers carried, on industries in proportion to production capacity, and on municipalities proportional to sewage production – would fund the activities of the PCB. Rebates for reductions in pollution intensities and surcharges for increases in these intensities would apply.

- *For standard setting*: States would compete with each other in setting higher (not lower) standards. The process of standard setting itself would be continuous and demystified. A large budget for medical research on human epidemiology of pollutants and ecological research on ecosystem impacts would be complemented by support to engineering institutions for research on monitoring and pollution abatement technologies. At all stages of standard-setting, independent expert and wider public input will be mandatorily sought.

- *For prevention at source*: A holistic approach would be adopted, wherein prevention or reduction at source would be given greater attention than simply end-of-pipe solutions. This would be in the form of shifts in industrial processes, brought about not by just making technologies available for such shifts but by changing taxation policies drastically, so as to shift feedstock from petroleum to biomass.[16] Again, holism would mean that 'solutions' that breed their own problems, such as the use of biotechnology (Richardson, 2012), would be eschewed in favour of more 'nature-based' processes. The same approach would apply to other sectors, such as agriculture, where shifting to low-input or organic agriculture would obviate the need for heavy investment in remediation of fertilizer runoff into streams and pesticide residues in food.

- *For anticipatory regulation*: To encourage reduction at source and prevent irreversible damage, the idea of anticipatory regulation would shift from its current weak and complex form of consent-processing and limited project-wise environmental impact assessments (EIAs) to more comprehensive cumulative impact assessments, and ex-ante identification of acceptable and unacceptable activities in different areas. Similarly, for water pollution, regulation would start by identifying (through a participatory process) the use for which a water body is meant, and then implement catchment-level limits on the pollutant load that can keep the water body fit for that use.

- *For technically sound and transparent monitoring*: The PCB would focus on meeting environmental standards through monitoring and enforcement, not focusing as they do now on issuing permits and licenses. Water quality in streams, lakes, various effluent discharge points and ground water would be monitored through large numbers of low-cost sensors that continuously upload data to publicly visible websites and display boards. Air quality sensors and emission sensors would also be set up in large numbers across urban areas and at industrial point sources; vehicular emissions would also be monitored real time and shared publicly along with enforcement data, so that it would be clear whether the heaviest polluters got penalised or not. PCB's monitoring would be supported (and verified) by citizen-level monitoring programmes. Simultaneously, PCBs would have major outreach programmes to help polluting industries achieve better compliance at lower cost.

- *For enforcement*: PCBs would have powers of seizure and arrest for major violations. But this would be complemented by social sanctions—naming and shaming of the heaviest polluters. A strong effort at recruiting staff with strong environmental commitment into the PCBs would be complemented by culture building and internal and external vigilance to minimize corruption.

- *For conflict resolution*: Third parties would have explicit *locus standi* to file cases where enforcement is weak.[17] The Courts would have dedicated green benches at all levels starting from the lowest Courts. Expert testimony would be a standard procedure in court cases. Pollution affected persons would have *locus standi* in courts. Court procedures would be simple and time bound, with disposal of pollution cases within months. At the same time, the courts themselves would refrain from over-use of the *suo moto* route for creating litigation and from getting involved in enforcing environmental laws or micro-managing environmental solutions. They would focus instead on ensuring ease of access to judicial remedy to the layperson and speedy disposal of environmental cases.

- *For building public awareness and support*: The government would provide substantial support for pollution literacy campaigns, as well as other complementary activities to build awareness but also a culture of support for environmental enforcement. This would include working with consumer groups (to build consumer awareness about products consumed), trade unions and other labour groups (to link pollution and occupational health concerns) and with industry groups (to convince them of fairness of standard-setting and enforcement and the need for them to reduce profit expectations). A substantial part of environmental awareness building would be bottom-up, with civil society groups leading the effort.

Integrating Carbon and Pollution Governance

CO_2 emissions will be a major concern in all environmental governance in future India and it will be fully integrated into the governance of pollution. A multi-level institutional framework will translate national commitments into state and district-level carbon budgets that allow for regional variation in needs and abilities. The carbon-emission content of all consumption will be communicated to consumers through sophisticated messaging techniques. More importantly, technologies of energy generation and of industrial production will have shifted to a 'maximise-renewables minimise carbon' mode. The connection between carbon-friendly and local environment-friendly production and consumption technologies will be exploited to the hilt. Carbon taxes will be used to subsidise technological and institutional innovation, including mass transport and transition to carbon-friendly urbanisation patterns and lifestyles. Dispersed urbanisation, each in close contact with its rural periphery and drawing preferentially upon local rather than global resources, will be the norm.

How Does One Get There?

Outlining a vision is far easier than figuring out pathways for reaching it. With the ongoing attempts to dilute environmental laws, one wonders whether the state-led gains of the 1970s' and 1980s' and the judiciary-led gains of the 1990s' and 2000s'—all driven by strong civil society movements—will in fact be lost in the pursuit of economic growth that has become the focal point of state policy over the past decade or more.[18] This focus has bred more confrontation (*sangharsh*) and left little space for creative movement (*nirmaan*) towards the wider environmentally sound development paradigm mooted earlier in this essay.

Nevertheless, one sees sparks in various places. Judicial activism and innovation has led to the creation of several long-term participatory environmental governance mechanisms—environmental monitoring and clearance committees headed by retired judges and involving experts, civil society groups and state agencies. The Dahanu Taluka Environment Protection Authority is one example—an authority that has attempted to ensure that industrialisation of the Dahanu region at the border of Maharashtra and Gujarat was guided and regulated more meaningfully than would have been the case under normal operation of environmental laws and enforcement (Sahu & Chawla, 2011). A similar authority was created in the Palar basin to address the problem of tannery-induced water pollution. Both institutions suffered from limitations, but the possibility they opened up for more participatory environmental governance, rather than a purely technocratic one, remains noteworthy (Sahu, 2010).

A more recent example is the ongoing mobilization around lakes in Bengaluru city. These human-made irrigation tanks that provided water for cultivation in a rural landscape got converted to recipients of sewage when the surroundings urbanized. A significant movement has, however, emerged over the past 5 years to clean up these lakes (Baradwaj, 2014). From being a purely middle-class campaign to have a nice location for a morning walk, the movement has diversified into a broader water management campaign. Sewage treatment plants (STPs) are being set up on lakeshores to treat incoming sewage before letting it out into the lake. Citizen groups are monitoring the functioning of these STPs, and guarding against inflow of any other sewage. Neighbouring apartments that have their own STPs are now applying for permission to discharge treated wastewater into the lakes (Express News Service, 2016). Research groups are continuously sampling lake quality, studying the additional role of reed beds in purifying the water, and trying to set up open 'dashboards' on the internet that will display quantity and quality of lake water continuously.[19] These diverse groups are putting pressure on the PCB and on the municipal body to deliver on the possibility of a multi-functional lake system. In parallel, a few citizen groups are working on reducing their own water consumption.[20] The long-term changes in jurisdiction and planning are yet to take place, but the scarcity of water in the region is generating a lot of concern and interest in alternative solutions, that we believe might eventually force such changes.

The challenge of environmental governance is in some ways a subset of the larger challenge of democratic governance that our country has been facing since post-independence. Some of the core issues are common, viz., how does one create institutions to deliver on certain normative criteria if the criteria are not shared by the population that the institutions serve? Indian society has inherited value systems and structures that are not often conducive to democratic governance – including patriarchy, caste and xenophobia or parochialism. These have been reinforced by processes of colonialism, post-colonial centralization of authority and corporate capitalism. The same forces are partly responsible for the environmental predicament. But environmental issues are also somewhat different because of the complexities introduced by biophysical processes and technological changes, particularly the multi-scalar nature of these processes and the linkages they introduce across administrative and political boundaries. Bringing about better environmental governance will require a change in values away from consumerism and anti-democratic functioning and also the unleashing of the positive potential in technology and institutions.

Endnotes

1. Pl. see essays on Conservation, Energy, and Biomass futures in this volume.
2. Much of modern industrial growth, the consequent pollution created by the production process, and the waste it generates at the consumer end are all rooted in a carbon-based economy (CGCSCI, 2006, Chpt. 5).
3. These include both statutory rights, such as rights under various environmental laws, and constitutional rights, such as the right to life, right to a healthy environment and right to livelihood.
4. For more details, see Kohli & Menon, 2005, and Kohli and Menon, 2009.
5. This Supreme Court case began in 1995 and continues till today, with more than 2000 orders issued, covering all states and all kinds of forestry matters. The Court, in 2002, constituted a Central Empowered Committee accountable only to itself, and through it, not only took over the role of the Forest Advisory Committee (FAC) that normally made recommendations on forest diversions, but went into many other domains such as clearance of working plans and investigation of forest clearance violations by mining companies, to name a few. There was at one point open confrontation between the Court and the Ministry as to the powers of the two committees and the composition of the FAC.
6. 'T S R Subramanian panel proposes new law, institutions to fast track green clearances', *Down to*

Earth, 20 Nov 2014, available at http://www.downtoearth.org.in/news/t-s-r-subramanian-panel-proposes-new-law-institutions-to-fast-track-green-clearances-47482.

7. For instance, see Chakraborty and Sethi, 2015.

8. Based on field observations in Dindori district, Madhya Pradesh by Venkat Ramanujam, PhD scholar, ATREE, and discussions with Dilip Gode, activist, Gondia district, Maharashtra. See also Shah, 2010.

9. The Environmental Kuznets Curve is a purportedly inverted-U shaped curve describing the relationship between economic growth and environmental quality. The underlying argument is that 'although economic growth usually leads to environmental deterioration in the early stages of the process, in the end the best – and probably the only – way to attain a decent environment in most countries is to become rich' (Beckerman, 1992), because wealth enables societies to eventually tackle environmental problems. This is akin to Simon Kuznets' argument that economic growth initially results in an increase in economic inequality but eventually inequality reduces.

10. See Guha, 2008.

11. Akin to, but updated forms, of the six varieties of Indian environmentalism identified by Gadgil and Guha, 1995, pp.111.

12. The concept that if the environmental impacts of a product or action are unknown or uncertain, then the product should not be used or the action should not be taken.

13. Such a multi-dimensional vision has been articulated by several scholars at various times in specific contexts. For instance Joy *et al,*. (2004) in the context of watershed development or Lele *et al.,* (2013) in the context of water management. A comprehensive set of principles is now emerging through the Vikalp Sangam process: see http://kalpavriksh.org/index.php/alternatives/alternatives-knowledge-center/353-vikalp-sangam-coverage.

14. Just as a watershed refers to an area drained by a particular stream, an air-shed refers to a region where topography and wind patterns result in much of the air pollution remaining confined to that particular region.

15. As against the current picture of urban authorities permitting high rise buildings without ensuring that sewerage or water supply arrangements exist, or without factoring in the transport needs it would generate and the air pollution consequences of the same.

16. This is intimately linked to the reduction of fossil fuel consumption: not only does the modern method of processing chemicals depend heavily on fossil fuel use, but also the feedstock of modern chemical industries is petroleum (CGCSCI, 2006, Ch. 3). It is these petrochemicals that constitute the biggest source of local pollution. Major taxes on petroleum products will then serve to curb their use in feedstock and the consequent pollution that they generate.

17. Currently, their ability to file cases depends entirely on the judiciary's openness to PILs.

18. One area in which there continues to be some space for forward movement is forest rights. The passing of the landmark Forest Rights Act 2006 gave rights to hundreds of village communities in eastern Maharashtra (especially Gadchiroli and Gondia districts) and thousands of such communities in Odisha state is an obvious example of a governance shift in the forest sector (see

Shrivastava & Mahapatra 2013). We have not discussed it here for reasons of scope, as outlined at the beginning of this essay.

19. See www.atree.org/research/ced/lwl/BangaloreWater.
20. See http://biometrust.blogspot.ca.

References

Anonymous, 2012, *Eminent Indians Speak Out Against Harassment of Anti-Nuclear Activists in Koodankulam*, available at http://www.dianuke.org/eminent-indians-speak-out-against-harassment-of-anti-nuclear-activists-in-koodankulam/ (Last accessed 12 Feb 2017).

Baradwaj, A., 2014, *Awareness and participation towards encouraging sustainable urban water management: A case study of the Jakkur Lake, Bangalore*, M.A. (Creative Sustainability) Thesis, Department of Design, Aalto University.

Beckerman, W., 1992, 'Economic growth and the environment: Whose growth? Whose environment?' *World Development*, 20(4): pp. 481-96.

CGCSCI, 2006, *Sustainability in the Chemical Industry: Grand Challenges and Research Needs, Report of Committee on Grand Challenges for Sustainability in the Chemical Industry*, National Research Council, Washington D.C.:National Academies Press.

Chakraborty, S. and N. Sethi, 2015, 'Final number of inviolate coal blocks down from 206 to less than 35', *Business Standard*, 2 September 2015, http://www.business-standard.com/article/economy-policy/final-number-of-inviolate-coal-blocks-down-from-206-to-less-than-35-115090200004_1.html (Last accessed 12 Feb 2017).

CPCB, 2015, *River Stretches for Restoration of Water Quality*,MINARS/37/2014-15, New Delhi: Central Pollution Control Board.

CSE, 2012, *Public Watch Report*, New Delhi: Centre for Science and Environment.

Express News Service, 2016, 'Treated Water From Apartment Complex to Fill up Puttenahalli Lake', *The New Indian Express*, 26 January, http://www.newindianexpress.com/cities/bengaluru/Treated-Water-From-Apartment-Complex-to-Fill-up-Puttenahalli-Lake/2015/05/18/article2820404.ece (Last accessed 12 Feb 2017).

Farrell, A. and T. J. Keating, 2000, 'The globalization of smoke: Co-evolution in science and governance of a commons problem', paper presented at *Constituting the Commons: Crafting Sustainable Commons in the Millennium*, organized by International Association for the Study of Common Property (IASCP), at Bloomington, Indiana, 31 May – 4 June.

Gadgil, M. and R. Guha, 1995, *Ecology and Equity: The Use and Abuse of Nature in Contemporary India*, New York and London:Routledge.

Guha, R., 2008, The rise and fall of Indian environmentalism, http://ramachandraguha.in/archives/the-rise-and-fall-of-indian-environmentalism.html (Last accessed 12 Feb 2017).

Guha, R., 2013, 'The past & present of Indian environmentalism', *The Hindu*, 27 March, http://www.thehindu.com/opinion/lead/the-past-present-of-indian-environmentalism/article4551665.ece (Last accessed 12 Feb 2017).

Jamwal, P., S. Lele and M. Menon, 2016, 'Rethinking water quality standards in the context of urban rivers', paper presented at *Urbanization and the Environment*, Eighth Biennial Conference of the Indian Society for Ecological Economics, organized by INSEE, IISc, ATREE, and NIAS, Bangalore, 4-6 January.

Joy, K. J., S. Paranjape, A. K. Kiran Kumar, R. Lele and R. Adagale, 2004, '*Watershed Development Review: Issues and Prospects*, CISED Technical Report, Bangalore: Centre for Interdisciplinary Studies in Environment and Development.

Kohli, K. and M. Menon, 1994, *Eleven Years of the Environment Impact Assessment Notification, 1994; How Effective Has It Been?*, Pune: Kalpavriksh, Just Environment Trust and Environment Justice Initiative (Human Rights Law Network).

Kohli, K. and M. Menon, 2009, *Calling the Bluff: Revealing the State of Monitoring and Compliance of Environmental Clearance Conditions*, Pune: Kalpavriksh.

Kothari, A., 2015, 'MHA: A Ministry for Hounding Activists?', *India Together*, available at *http://indiatogether.org/government-crackdown-on-the-activism-sector-reeks-of-arbitrariness-and-illegitimacy-op-ed* (Last accessed 12 Feb 2017).

Lélé, S., 2004, 'Beyond State-Community Polarisations and Bogus "Joint"ness: Crafting Institutional Solutions for Resource Management', in *Globalisation, Poverty and Conflict: A Critical "Development" Reader*, M. Spoor (ed.), Dordrecht, Boston & London: Kluwer Academic Publishers, pp. 283-303.

Lele, S., 2013, 'Environmentalisms, Justices, and the Limits of Ecosystems Services Frameworks', in *The Justices and Injustices of Ecosystems Services*, T. Sikor (ed.), Oxon, U.K.: Earthscan/Routledge, pp.119-39.

Lele, S., N. Heble, B. K. Thomas and P. Jamwal, 2015, *Regulation and Compliance in Industrial Water Pollution: The Case of the Vrishabhavathy River, Bangalore*, (unpublished manuscript), Bangalore: Ashoka Trust for Research in Ecology and the Environment.

Lele, S., V. Srinivasan, P. Jamwal, B. K. Thomas, M. Eswar and T. M. Zuhail, 2013, *Water Management in Arkavathy Basin: A Situation Analysis*, Environment & Development Discussion Paper No. 1, Bangalore: Ashoka Trust for Research in Ecology and the Environment.

Menon, M. and K. Kohli, 2009, 'From impact assessment to clearance manufacture', *Economic & Political Weekly* 44(28), pp. 20-23.

Narain, S., 2015, 'India's environment: a review of four decades', in *State of India's Environment 2015*, S. Narain (ed.), New Delhi: Centre for Science and Environment, pp.11-20.

Ostrom, E., 1990, *Governing the Commons: The Evolution of Institutions for Collective Action*, New York: Cambridge University Press.

Powers, N., A. Blackman, T. P. Lyon and U. Narain, 2011, 'Does disclosure reduce pollution? Evidence from India's green rating project', *Environmental and Resource Economics*, 50(1); pp. 131-55.

Richardson, B., 2012, 'From a fossil-fuel to a biobased economy: The politics of industrial biotechnology', *Environment and Planning C: Government and Policy*, 30(2): pp. 282-96.

Rosencranz, A. and S. Lélé, 2008, 'Supreme Court and India's Forests', *Economic & Political Weekly*, 43(5), pp. 11-14.

Sahu, G., 2010,'Implementation of Environmental Judgments in Context: A Comparative Analysis of Dahanu Thermal Power Plant Pollution Case in Maharashtra and Vellore Leather Industrial Pollution Case in Tamil Nadu', *LEAD: Law, Environment and Development Journal*, 6(3): 335-53.

Sahu, G., 2014, *Environmental Jurisprudence and the Supreme Court*, New Delhi: Orient Blackswan.

Sahu, G. and M. Chawla, 2011, 'Environmental Movement in Dahanu: Competing Pulls', *Economic & Political Weekly*, 46(49): 10-14.

Sarin, M., 2014, 'Undoing Historical Injustice: Reclaiming citizenship rights and democratic forest governance through the Forest Rights Act', in *Democratizing Forest Governance in India*, S. Lele and A. Menon (eds.), New Delhi: Oxford University Press, pp. 100-48.

Shah, A., 2010, *In the Shadows of the State: Indigenous politics, environmentalism, and insurgency in Jharkhand, India*, Durham: Duke University Press.

Shrivastava, A. and A. Kothari, 2012, *Churning the Earth: The Making of Global India*, New Delhi: Penguin India.

Shrivastava, K. S. and R. Mahapatra, 2013, 'Bamboo rising', *Down To Earth*, 31 March. http://www.downtoearth.org.in/coverage/bamboo-rising-40053 (Last accessed on 12 Feb 2017).

Srinivasan, V., D. S. Kumar, P. Chinnasamy, S. Sulagna, D. Sakthivel, P. Paramasivam and S. Lele, 2014, *Water Management in the Noyyal River Basin: A Situation Analysis*, Environment & Development Discussion Paper No. 2, Bangalore: Ashoka Trust for Research in Ecology and the Environment.

Subramanian, S., 2015, 'India's war on Greenpeace', *The Guardian*, 11 August, http://www.theguardian.com/world/2015/aug/11/indias-war-on-greenpeace (Last accessed on 12 Feb 2017).

Sudhakar, P. and S. Vijaykumar, 2012, 'Kudankulam: 11 protesters held on sedition charges', *The Hindu*, 20 March, http://www.thehindu.com/news/national/tamil-nadu/kudankulam-11-protesters-held-on-sedition-charges/article3013635.ece (Last accessed on 12 Feb 2017).

Wilhite, H., 2008, *Consumption and the Transformation of Everyday Life: a view from South India*, London: Palgrave Macmillan.

The Future of Water in India

Shripad Dharmadhikary and Himanshu Thakkar

Summary

Water planning around the world is extremely anthropocentric and it is assumed that water is only for human use. Within the human community also, this usage is prioritized to benefit the rich. The essay stresses the need of radical change in the decision-making process, mindset, and framework that go behind these decisions.

India is blessed with reasonably regular monsoon, a large number of perennial and seasonal rivers, the Himalayas percieved as an inexhaustible source of water, availability of groundwater as a decentralised source and traditional water management systems. However, water resources development authorities have shown blatant disregard to these blessings and have focussed on extractive policies of building big dams, big hydropower projects, large-scale irrigation and river interlinking projects and also unsustainable use of groundwater.

The essay lists out the key elements of the future of the water sector in India and argues for a vision based on core values of sustainability, equity, efficiency, and democratization. Water should be seen as an integral part of ecosystems rather than a resource only for human use. Even looking at human use, it is required that multifaceted factors are taken into cognizance such as cultural value, sustenance value, and economic value. Access to the poor is particularly important to focus on.

The paper shows how groundwater is India's water lifeline and need to move towards its sustainable use, making rainwater, local water systems, rivers, wetlands, forests and community driven regulation as key components of the future and not large dams or inter linking of rivers, which seem like mainstay of current estabishment paradigm. The paper provides some examples of seeds of hope, both from official sources as well non governmental actors. There are suggestions for what all will constitute future vision, but key issue is not what but how to achieve the vision.

The strategy to achieve this vision will be to keep fighting for institutional level changes, challenge wrong and destructive efforts, create successful examples, and replicate them at a larger level. The paper concludes that we have long way to go before we can achieve desirable state of water resources governance.

Introduction

Someone has correctly said that the future is not what happens but what we create. When we think of the future of water, it is clear that there can be multiple futures. Each future scenario is a trajectory taking off from today in a direction that is determined by the choices we are making, the decisions we have taken. In today's planning lies tomorrow's future.

This is obvious from the current state of water resources. Each of the serious issues in the sector can be traced back to the choices we have made in the past. These choices relate to how water is to be stored and used, how much water is to be stored and used, when, how and where it is to be used, how we govern (including who decides) and manage our water resources, rivers, their catchments, wetlands, forests, mountains, groundwater and other water bodies, and indeed, even in choices about what the water is to be used for. The sum total of these choices can be said to define our framework towards water and water resources.

One of the central and defining features of our prevailing mindset has been the notion that any drop of water that is not extracted out for human use is a "waste". This has been stated in so many words in umpteen policy and planning documents. Consider this statement from the 1st Five Year Plan (GoI, 1950):[1]

> 'A more recent appraisal of the water resources of the country, based on an empirical formula co-relating the river flow in each basin with its rainfall and temperature, gives the total annual flow as equivalent to 1356 million acre-feet for the Indian Union. Of this only 76 million acre-feet or 5.6 per cent are at present being used for purposes of irrigation; the rest flow waste to the sea.'

Sixty six years later, little has changed in this approach, or in the other elements of the current mindset. Some of the other elements include total anthropocentric planning – water seems to be on earth only for use of humans, and even within the human community, it seems to be prioritized for the benefit of the rich and the powerful – a belief that we can extract water to a limitless extent, from rivers, lakes, and the ground; manipulate prevailing ecosystems without bothering about the consequences; a faith that we can meet ever-increasing demands of water without any bounds, and that we need not question whether all expressed desire or demand for consumption of water needs to be met, especially if it is the consumption of the elite and the powerful with significant consequences for the system in which water exists; a naïve conviction that we can pour all sorts of toxic and other effluents into water without creating any problems or that we can take care of such problems in future, need not bother now; and an attitude that we can take and turn around any element of the water cycle, twist and change its pathways, re-shape waterways, rivers, drainage patterns to suit our desires, take water wherever we want, and justify, and even glorify it as a 'conquest of nature', establishing humankind's superiority over the entire natural world.

So when we think of the future of water in India, we need to first understand the decisions we are making, the decision making processes and systems and the mindset and framework which defines these decisions. If these elements remain as they now are, we are likely to see a future that is more or less an extrapolation of what has come to pass over the last few decades. And it is not going to be a pleasant one. It is a future where we are likely to see most of our rivers having dried up, or reduced to a seasonal trickle. Often, even this trickle is likely to mostly contain sewage and toxic effluents. Groundwater would have been exhausted or plummeted to unsustainable depths or be of unusable quality in most areas of the country. Most water resources would be heavily polluted leading to sickness and ill-health of large sections of the population. The rich, however, would be protected by provision of bottled water, water purification devices and exclusive access to cleaner water sources. While rivers would be linked to each other and all water extracted and transported to farms mostly growing commercial crops, we would also find many areas where even drinking water is scarce and poor people would be suffering from regular crop losses. Since most surface water sources would have turned toxic, it will lead to disease and social strife among the poor, but the rich classes will also not be able to escape these consequences, since the whole ecology would be affected. Sounds familiar? Well, familiar policies and practises will lead to a familiar future. Examples of water conflict are now common across India: between people and state (Narmada dams,[2] hydropower projects in North East India), people and corporations (e.g., Coca Cola and its extraction of groundwater),[3] state and state (e.g., Cauvery), and so on.[4]

A different water future however is also possible. For that to happen, we need to choose the appropriate path.

A starting point for this is the recognition of the realities as well as the blessings of water in India.

Ignoring the Blessings

While studying the water sector in India the traditional official view that comes up is that India has only about 2.4 per cent of earth's land, 4 per cent of earth's renewable water and yet 18 per cent of global human population (GoI, 2012b).[5] Then the UN norms of per capita water availability are paraded to say that India is water stressed or will soon become a water scarce area. In reality these macro figures hide more than they reveal.

India is in fact fortunate to have a number of blessings in the water sector. The first blessing is the large number of rivers that we have, many of them perennial, and others seasonal. The rainfall that we get with regularity of a calendar is the second major blessing. The third major blessing we have is the Himalayas in the north, which are considered the third pole of the world. It is considered an almost inexhaustible source of water (water tower). The fourth major blessing of India is the groundwater sources available in a decentralized way, which can also be used as a bank and insurance in addition to being a lifeline, when other sources fail, provided they are used in a sustainable way. Another major blessing that we would like to include in this list is India's rich traditional knowledge of water harvesting and water conservation technology and management systems.

However, the way we have gone about water resources development in India in the last hundred odd years, it seems we do not value any of these blessings. Our emphasis and priority has been building big hydropower and irrigation projects (mostly big dams), and the latest in this list is the river linking project. Secondly, our consumption patterns, both of water and everything else in which water is embedded (what many like to call virtual water) is not sustainable or wise. This is reflected in many different ways, but to illustrate, the North-West-India areas of Punjab and Haryana have predominantly water intensive paddy-wheat cropping cycle, which is not sustainable considering the water availability, with average annual rainfall in two states being 636 mm and 555 mm respectively (IMD, 2015). Similarly, large parts of Maharashtra and Karnataka that are growing sugarcane and have a huge number of sugar factories are low rainfall drought prone areas where these activities are totally inappropriate. The Krishna river basin that spans across Maharashtra, Karnataka, Telangana and Andhra Pradesh is declared a closed basin and large parts of the basin are drought prone and perennially facing water scarcity. Yet from these very basins, over three billion cubic meters of water are getting diverted on an annual basis, to high rainfall Konkan area, only for hydropower generation and then mostly flowing down to sea.[6] To give an idea of how big this quantity of water is, it is equal to 1.2 million Olympic size swimming pools or almost twice the live capacity of the massive Ujani Dam in Maharashtra.

The Vision

If we want a different future, we have to put in place an entirely different vision for the water sector, a vision with the core values of sustainability, equity, efficiency and democratization. Such a vision would start with how we look at water. We need to understand, appreciate and respect water as both, an integral part of, as well as sustainer of the ecosystem. Our vision needs to be based on the fact that water on this planet is not meant only for human use but for all living (and non-life) forms. By definition, what we do is mostly anthropocentric (in addition to anthropogenic and based on human values), yet, we would need to take care that we are not trampling on and encroaching on the right to water of others on Earth. Even looking at human 'use' of water, we would need to take cognisance that water plays a multifaceted role in human life and economy. It has cultural, aesthetic, sustenance, economic, and commercial values. Our vision and approach to water would need to ensure balance amongst all these values.

Such a vision would ensure that even as the needs of human society are met, our rivers and streams would be as close to free-flowing as possible and not bound by large structures and impoundments. Our vision would look at wetlands not as wastelands, to be encroached upon, but as important parts of the water system in their own right. Water – in rivers, streams, lakes, ponds – would be clean and unpolluted, with the quality so good that people could just walk to the water and drink it, at most places. And that water bodies would remain public commons so that people could actually have the right to walk up to them. Control of water would remain in public hands, and not be privatized. Access to water would be a right of everyone, and would not be denied to anyone because of any reasons like a person's caste, economic status and so on. In such a vision, there would be harmony between human society and water systems.

What could be some of the key elements of such a vision?

* Respect water as an ecosystem and as a sustainer of ecosystems;
* Understand that water is not meant only for human use, but also for other life (and non-life) forms;
* Harvest water where it falls, protect local water systems, wetlands and create more of them;
* Achieve sustained existence of rivers[7] including environment flows from all existing dams;
* Recognise that groundwater is our water lifeline and will remain so for a long time to come; and if we want to sustain that water lifeline, we need to ensure that we

harvest water where it falls and make groundwater recharge a focus area of our water policy and programs;

- Recognise the groundwater recharge systems, protect them and create more such systems;
- Recognise wetlands as an integral and significant part of water systems in their own right and stop treating them as 'wastelands';
- Restore and maintain the quality of water in rivers, streams and all water bodies;
- Community driven regulation of groundwater use, indeed of all water use;
- Democratic decision making starting with prioritization of needs, options assessment, selection of right option, implementation and management;
- Participation based on awareness, information and understanding;
- Sensible, judicious, wise and responsible consumption of water as per democratically accepted priorities;
- Adopt smart urban water management options: priority for not long distance but local water sources, total recycling of waste water, protection of urban water bodies, maximizing rainwater harvesting, groundwater recharge;
- Sustainable industrial water use – based on appropriate citing policy and also complete water reuse and recycle;
- Learning to understand and value aquifers, rivers, wetlands, local water bodies, rainwater;
- Achieving cropping patterns that are appropriate to the local agro-climatic characteristics;
- Adopt and encourage water saving cropping methods (e.g., System of Rice Intensification, also applicable for other crops besides rice);
- Organic and locally appropriate agriculture to eliminate harmful chemicals and minimize use of water (with particular attention to encouraging dry-land farming);
- Energy systems based on renewable sources (excluding large hydro), decentralized generation, local grids;[8]
- Sustainable mountain environment;
- Creating reliable and transparent information systems regarding water, including embedded/virtual water use;[9]
- Democratic institutions, decision making, monitoring, compliance, regulation;
- Achieving optimum benefits from existing infrastructure;
- Understanding the special place, role, and concerns of North East, Tribal areas, Himalayas, Western Ghats, Coastal areas, Deltas, dry-land areas;

- Demand Side Management[10] ensuring that use of water is within sustainable limits and that it is done in the most efficient way possible;
- Ensuring fulfilment of basic needs of all through rights based approach that prioritizes equity. One of the important aspects would be to ensure that access to water is tied to basic /livelihood needs and not land ownership;
- Learning to say NO to unsustainable demands on water;
- Understanding the unique role of water in nature as an embedded element;
- Democratic governance of each resource, area and project, including decision making processes;
- Informed decision making process with all necessary studies done before the decision, both at project level and at basin level;
- Free, prior and informed consent of all concerned for all major interventions;
- A siting policy for water use activities in line with the ecological situation and water availability;
- Water resources development and management decisions taking changing climate into account, the effects already visible in terms of changing monsoon, increased droughts, floods and hailstorms, melting glaciers, increasing sea level rise;
- Understanding and ensuring the key role rivers play in taking the sediment right up to the deltas and the coastal areas, and in sustaining the freshwater-saltwater mix in such areas on which ecosystems and fisheries are dependent, not allowing dams to hamper this role;
- Prior, credible Environment and Social Impact Assessment, Cumulative Impact Assessment; achieving compliance through participatory environmental governance;
- Managing water as commons, ensuring that everyone has access to it for meeting basic needs, and that control on water is not privatised.

This is certainly not an exhaustive or a comprehensive list, but only presents some key elements. What is important is that there are many robust examples of implementation of these elements in the country, even as the dominant practices go largely in the opposite direction.

Some Illustrative Examples

In this section we are providing brief descriptions of some examples where some of these strategic steps have been implemented.

One of the most interesting admissions, confirming that the current paradigm of large-dams driven irrigation has failed not only the environment but also the farmers has come from the Chief Minister of Maharashtra, Devendra Fadnavis. On 21 July 2015, in his statement to the Maharashtra Assembly, he said:

'Maharashtra has the country's 40 per cent large dams, but 82 per cent area of the state is rain fed. We have moved away from our vision of watershed and conservation…We did not think about hydrology, geology and topography of a region before pushing large dams everywhere. But this has to change'.

Coming from the Chief Minister of a state that has the highest number of large dams in the country (See GoI, 2012a), and twice that of the state with the second highest number, that is, Madhya Pradesh, and yet has been facing terrible droughts and farmers' suicides on a large scale on a regular basis, this is an admission that the future of water needs to go on a different trajectory. The trajectory has also been indicated clearly by the Chief Minister – decentralized rainwater harvesting through peoples' participation is one of its main pillars. While this initiative is reportedly showing good results even in the short time since it has been taken up, there is concern that such thinking does not seem to extend to a more comprehensive vision of water resources. This is evident from the fact that the same Government has annulled the river zone regulation norms.

Of course, the idea is not new. Like most of the elements of a different trajectory that we are proposing, this too has been around for many years. Struggles against large dams, like the *Narmada Bachao Andolan*, have strongly advocated such an approach as the real solution[11] to problems of droughts, water supply, agricultural water needs, etc. There are a number of people who have done experiments with such work, obtained great results, demonstrating that decentralized water harvesting is a far more effective solution to water problems than large dams can provide. Several of these examples are mentioned in the paragraphs that follow.

Local Water System: traditional wisdom

The traditional water harvesting technology and management systems can certainly be counted as one of India's blessings in water sector. This has been most brilliantly described by well known Gandhian, Anupam Mishra, in his now famous books like *Aaj bhi khare hai talab*, ('the ponds are still standing', published in 1993) and *Rajasthan ki Rajat Bunde* ('the golden drops of Rajasthan', 1995). There is a lot we can learn from this wisdom even today, while being mindful of the caste systems and its inherent injustices. In many parts of India these systems and knowledge are still in use, or being revived, to meet water needs in judicious ways.

Watershed Development: Maharashtra

There are many examples of successful watershed development works—Maharashtra possibly has one of the largest number. Maharashtra has been one of the progressive states in the country when it comes to watershed development, participatory water management and a pioneering discourse surrounding equitable sharing of available water sources. The state has had a number of remarkable stories like Ralegan Siddhi and Hivare Bazaar, the work of Samaj Parivarthan Kendra (SPK) and Society for Promoting Participative Ecosystem Management (SOPPECOM) on water users associations in Waghad and Palkhed, work of Paani Panchayat on equitable sharing of irrigation water particularly arguing for allocation of water even to the landless, work of AFARM, *Pani Sangarsh Chalwal* (Water Struggle Movement) of South Maharashtra, and others, in addition to a number of centrally funded and state funded watershed programs like Drought Prone Area Program (DPAP), Integrated Wasteland Development Program (IWDP), Adarsh Gaon Yojana, etc. The state has had its share of stalwarts like Late Vilasrao Salunkhe, Anna Hazare, Popatrao Pawar, Late Dr. Mukundrao Ghare, Smt. Kalpanatai Salunkhe, to name just a few. They talked about not only increasing water availability, but also allocating and managing the available water resources equitably and sustainably and many other facets of participatory watershed management which were strongly rooted in equity, gender sensitivity, social realities and ecological sustainability.[12]

Well Recharging and Check-dams: Gujarat

While Gujarat is known for the massive Sardar Sarovar Dam and the movement against the dam, namely the Narmada Bachao Andolan, students of water resources development also know it for widespread well recharging and check-dam construction through social movements. The significance of this work can be gauged from a paper by researchers of International Water Management Institute and others (Shah *et al.,* 2009), where, after assessing the relative impacts of large dams, groundwater recharge and decentralised water harvesting structures, the authors conclude that per Billion Cubic Meter (BCM) of water, large dams served 17,150 ha, groundwater storage served 237,910 ha and decentralised water harvesting structures served 2,532,000 ha. So for the same volume of water, groundwater storage served about 14 times more land that the land served by large dams and decentralised water harvesting methods served 148 times more land. Though the value per hectare of crops and milk was higher for land served by large dams, the aggregate value of crops and milk from the lands served by groundwater and decentralised water harvesting was each double the value of output from land served by dams for the state as a whole during the period under review. The water productivity (Rs./BCM) from groundwater and decentralised water harvesting was thus 6.14 and 30 times higher, respectively, than that from large dams. These figures not only destroy the myth that large dams are more productive, they establish clearly that large dams should be at best the option of last resort after decentralised water harvesting and groundwater recharge systems.

Rivers: Arvari river parliament in Alwar

It is well known that the work of repair, maintenance of *johads* (traditional tank systems of Rajasthan) and creation of more such structures with involvement of communities, led by the Tarun Bharat Sangh in Rajasthan[13] led to rejuvenation of some of the local streams that used to be dry soon after monsoon. In fact the then President of India went in March 2000 to the communities to honour them for their achievement, possibly the first time this ever happened. But less well known is the effort of the communities who came together in the form of a river parliament to manage the river Arvari once it was rejuvenated. There is a lot that the official water management can learn from this effort, even though the Arvari river Parliament may not be as active now as in the past.

While these ideas have been around for decades, there are also many new and innovative ideas that have come. One example of such innovations is System of Rice Intensification.

System of Rice Intensification

The system of rice intensification (SRI) is a new and evolving alternative to conventional methods of rice cultivation[14]. In this method, rice seedlings are transplanted early (eight to 12 days old compared to 21 days in the conventional method). They are transplanted in un-puddled condition; the seedlings are widely spaced. The fields are alternately kept wet and dry; they are not flooded until the panicle initiation stage (1-3 cm. of water in the field during the reproductive phase). The field is drained twenty five days before harvest and organic manure is used as much as possible. Mechanical weeding should start around ten days after transplantation; at least two weedings are necessary, more are recommended. It is supposed to provide better growing conditions in the root zone, save inputs, improve soil health and optimise water use efficiency. The rice plants grown with this method are more drought and flood tolerant and hence cope much better in changing climate.

India has over 24 million hectares under irrigated paddy. If SRI were to be applied on all this land we would be able to increase our irrigated area by at least 50 per cent, using the water now being used for paddy irrigation. It would also lead to a 50 per cent increase in rice production. Both these factors would have huge implications for water resource management in India in the years to come. SRI kind of methods have also been found to be effective in a number of crops including wheat, sugarcane, pulses, among others. The question that immediately springs to mind is: With such far-reaching implications why is the government not actively pushing the adoption of SRI with necessary priority?[15] There is now state support for SRI in at least a few states (for example, Tripura, Tamil Nadu, Andhra Pradesh, Bihar, Odisha, among others) and many states do so wholeheartedly, but the support is not there from the Centre, nor is it integrated into the whole set of agricultural policies and programs.

There are many other examples, including some from the urban areas (such as Bhuj water harvesting work for slums, Chennai rooftop harvesting, Bengaluru water harvesting and recycling in Rainbow Drive and other colonies, revival of lakes with benefit of groundwater recharge, Hivare Bazar in Maharashtra as an example of groundwater regulation by the community, etc.,[16] but we are not going into details of these here.

World Commission on Dams: A new framework for decision making

Undoubtedly, the biggest and strongest social campaigns and movements on water issues have happened around the issues of large dams, which is truer for India than possibly most other countries. Here it is not possible to go into the details of these campaigns. However, since India continues to be one of the biggest dam builders in the world, it needs to be highlighted that large dams, including large hydro and even small hydro projects remain highly contested projects in India. Many projects have been stopped because of such protests, including Bhopalpatnam-Ichampalli in Maharashtra/AP, Koel Karo in Jharkhand-Bihar, and Silent Valley in Kerala. One prominent case in point is the stoppage of the highest capacity hydropower project of India, the 2000 MW Subansiri Lower Hydropower project on Assam-Arunachal Pradesh border in Brahmaputra basin in North East India, since December 2011. The work had to be stopped following long mass based campaign in Assam, when over Rs. 5000 crores (50 billion) were already spent on the project. The events[17] that followed around the project have vindicated every issue that the movement has raised since the work was stopped.

In this context, to indicate the road ahead, we must mention the report of the World Commission on Dams (WCD, 2000), made public in November 2000 by Nelson Mandela. This 12 member Commission was set up through a collective effort in which the World Bank, the governments, the industry, the campaigns and the anti dam movements were involved. The report did not say that large dams are all bad or that large dams should not be built, but it did say that in too many cases disproportionate costs have been paid, the benefits have been lower than projections and better alternatives were ignored. The report provided a framework for arriving at better decisions in future. In India, where dams have increasingly become an end in itself rather than the means to an end, the WCD guidelines can indeed be very useful. Any project that follows the WCD guidelines is likely to have much better public acceptance. We would strongly urge that the framework provided by the WCD be made the basic framework for decisions around not just dams but all major water sector interventions. While the Government of India has been reluctant to accept this framework when the WCD had released its report, many of the key principles were already present in India's policy and legal regime and subsequent to the report launch several other principles from the WCD have also been included. Thus, there is already a basis on which to build, and take up the WCD framework, as a holistic framework. This would play a big role in shifting the future of water in India to a more sustainable and equitable direction.

The Strategy

How to achieve the vision is certainly a far more difficult exercise than putting it together. Even preparing a credible road map for achieving the vision is not an easy task. Here indeed, past experience could be in many ways useful though not always a full guide. It is going to be tough to achieve the vision if we look at our current trajectory. The strategy should be to keep fighting for institutional changes that will help tweak the trajectory towards achieving such a vision, and create successful examples and learn right lessons from such experiences for replication at the larger level, bringing necessary policy, legal and institutional changes. At the same time, there is also a need to have strategies that would enhance resistance to unsustainable and inequitable water projects and processes.

Signs of Hope

One encouraging sign is that several official documents and processes have had to take cognizance of some of the elements of a new vision.

The admission by Maharashtra CM in his speech before the state legislature on 21 July 2015 that large dams seem to have failed the state is a part of several instances where the official machinery and establishment have started acknowledging – often grudgingly – the failure of the past and current paradigm, and have started accepting the validity and need for many of the elements of the framework that is being proposed in this paper.

For example, the National Water Policy (NWP) adopted in 2012, has a clear priority for the use of water, one that reflects the need for equity, the need to provide first for basic needs, and for the needs of the environment (GoI, 2012b).

> 'Safe Water for drinking and sanitation should be considered as pre-emptive needs, followed by high priority allocation for other basic domestic needs (including needs of animals), achieving food security, supporting sustenance agriculture and minimum eco-system needs. Available water, after meeting the above needs, should be allocated in a manner to promote its conservation and efficient use'.

Unfortunately, the policy and the Union Water Resources Ministry (now renamed as Union Ministry of Water Resources, Ganga Rejuvenation and River Development) are totally silent on how to achieve this objective.

The National Water Policy (GoI, 2012b) also calls for environmental flows in all rivers, saying (Sec. 3.3):

> 'Ecological needs of the river should be determined, through scientific study, recognizing that the natural river flows are characterized by low or no flows, small floods (freshets), large floods, etc., and should accommodate developmental needs. A portion of river flows should be kept aside to meet ecological needs ensuring that the low and high flow releases are proportional to the natural flow regime, including base flow contribution in the low flow season through regulated ground water use' (pp. 4).

However, there is no real implementation of this stipulation.

There is also a recommendation (Sec 2.2) to have a National Water Framework Law, about which, the NWP says:

> 'Such a framework law must recognize water not only as a scarce resource but also as a sustainer of life and ecology. Therefore, water, particularly groundwater, needs to be managed as a community resource held, by the state, under public trust doctrine to achieve food security, livelihood, and equitable and sustainable development for all. Existing Acts may have to be modified accordingly' (pp. 4).

Indeed there is urgent need to ensure community driven regulation of groundwater management, but there is absolutely no credible movement in that direction or for such a framework law.

In recent years, the new Central Government, in May 2014, has initiated a major program for Ganga Rejuvenation, with the aim to restore the wholeness of the river. It has asserted that the principles on which the Ganga Rejuvenation will be based (and, hopefully, the same principles will apply to other rivers in the country too) are that of *aviraldhara* (uninterrupted, continuous and connected flow), *nirmaldhara* (unpolluted flow) and geological and ecological integrity.'

The first ever joint report between Union Water Resources Ministry and Union Ministry of Environment and Forests (March 2015) on assessment of environment flows in rivers in India[18] showed another hopeful sign for the future of Indian rivers. However, that report is still under elaboration and development, and so we need to wait to see its implementation.

In Uttarakhand, a number of significant developments before and after June 2013 flood disaster have seen cancellation and stoppage of work on a number of disastrous projects and declaration of a stretch of Bhagirathi river as Eco Sensitive Zone. In these developments, the civil society, some regulatory agency persons, judiciary and media have played important roles. In this still unfolding saga,[19] there is not only hope for some tributaries of Ganga, but there are also seeds for learning for states and nations across the Himalayas. But it remains to be seen what lessons we learn from possibly the worst ever flood disasters of India.

In the context of heavily dammed rivers, one could mention the example of the Chalakudy Puzha Samrakshan Samithi's efforts (Latha *et al.*, 2012)[20] at developing a different reservoir operation scheme to ensure better downstream flows as an intermediate strategy.

Lest one gets too optimistic, it is important to note that while many of these developments are as yet mere expressions of intentions, actions taken by the Government are still following largely the earlier approaches. For example, the Maharashtra Government does not seem to have any intention of breaking free of the stranglehold of water guzzling crops like sugarcane which take up disproportionately high share of water in the state or abandon many of the dam projects that came through corrupt decisions and without credible processes. At the national level, the Government is aggressively pushing programs like the Interlinking of Rivers and even on the Ganga, the approach on ground shows no break from the failed experience of the past thirty to forty years of dealing with its pollution. So one must exercise caution in assessing whether the Government is serious about incorporating new approaches and breaking away from the past practices that have caused such grave problems.

In Conclusion

Practices are still dominated by the old thoughts, and even as some of the newer ideas are given a place, one cannot help feeling that this is just lip-service. The key is to push for the establishment to put their money where their mouth is, and ensure that once some of these aspects find a place in the official documents, they are also implemented in practice, and properly. This will require continuous vigilance and push by all sections of the society, including media, judiciary, academics and civil society among other actors. Meanwhile, citizens can also continue to spread decentralized water harvesting and use/management initiatives.

With such efforts, a different future for water in India is possible, a future where rivers flow, where waters are largely unpolluted, the basic needs of all people are met, water is also available for non-humans, and continues to play its role in ecology and nature.

Endnotes

1. Chapter 26, Irrigation and Power.
2. See www.narmada.org for more details.
3. See, for example, http://www.righttowater.info/rights-in-practice/legal-approach-case-studies/case-against-coca-cola-kerala-state-india/ (Last accessed 5 June 2016).
4. Joy *et al.*, 2008, is a good reference for more details and cases.
5. Para 1.1, Preamble, National Water Policy 2012, New Delhi: Ministry of Water Resources, Government of India.
6. This is not to suggest that all water flowing to sea is a waste, but to say that the water artificially transferred from a deficit basin to high rainfall area is not even serving much useful purpose.
7. For more details on the principles of managing our rivers, see Delhi Declaration on Rivers adopted at the first India Rivers Week during November 2014, at: https://sandrp.wordpress.com/2015/01/17/let-our-rivers-live-delhi-declaration/ (Last accessed 5 June 2016).
8. See also essay on Energy Futures in this volume.
9. Embedded or virtual water is the water consumed in the process of manufacturing or producing a good. For example, production of milk would need water for drinking by the milch animal, as well as for processing, packaging etc. All this water, divided by the quantity of milk produced, would give the water "embedded" in a litre of milk. This is also sometimes referred as "virtual water" which the milk contains or represents.
10. Demand Side Management basically means adjusting water use demands to meet objectives of efficiency, conservation, equity, sustainability, etc. This could include a slew of measures including proper cropping patterns, water saving cropping methods, financial incentives and disincentives, reducing losses, reuse and recycle, among others. See SANDRP blog for a detailed analysis of this statement, at https://sandrp.wordpress.com/2015/07/26/we-pushed-large-dams-not-irrigation-cm-fadnavis-assembly-speech/ (Last accessed 5 June 2016).

11. Sometimes this is phrased as 'alternatives to large dams'. However, something is an alternative if it does things similar to the original. In case of large dams, however, the benefits that can be delivered by them are much lesser than what a decentralised system can, and come at much higher costs. Thus, it's not correct to call the latter as 'alternatives'. Rather, they should be described as the 'real solutions'.

12. For details of some recent cases, see: https://sandrp.wordpress.com/2014/07/22/local-initiatives-for-drought-proofing-maharashtra/ and https://sandrp.wordpress.com/2015/05/19/digging-deeper-into-water-scarcity-after-watershed-development/ (Last accessed 5 June 2016).

13. There are many other noteworthy efforts in Rajasthan, including the one called *chauka* system practised in grazing lands, an innovation led by Laxmansingh in Laporia (Dudu Tehsil in Jaipur district), see for some details: http://www.downtoearth.org.in/news/the – chauka-magic-20492 and https://sandrp.wordpress.com/2013/11/18/dharati-ratan-annual-festival/ (Last accessed 5 June 2016).

14. See also essay on Food and Agriculture Futures in this volume.

15. For more details, see: http://sandrp.in/sri/sriintro (Last accessed 5 June 2016).

16. There are a number of publications and resources on such examples, including, say: *Aaj bhi Khare hai talaab* (Hindi, 1993) & *Rajasthan ki Rajat Bunde* (Hindi, 1995), both by Shri Anupam Mishra (Gandhi Peace Foundation), see for details: http://www.indiawaterportal.org/articles/aaj-bhi-khare-hain-talaab-book-anupam-mishra and http://scroll.in/article/677189/for-more-than-20-years-a-slim-book-has-helped-indian-farmers-become-self-reliant-in-water, (both last accessed on 5 June, 2016); SANDRP blogs (e.g. https://sandrp.wordpress.com/2014/06/13/gawadewadi-a-success-story-of-participatory-small-scale-water-conservation/ (Last accessed 5 June 2016) and CSE, 1999.

17. For example, NHPC agreed to make huge changes in the structural and operational parameters of the project following multiple official committee reports.

18. For details, see: https://sandrp.wordpress.com/2015/04/15/mowr-report-on-assessment-of-e-flows-is-welcome-needs-urgent-implementation/ (Last accessed 5 June 2016). The actual report is an unpublished document.

19. For details, see: https://sandrp.wordpress.com/2015/06/18/two-years-of-uttarakhand-flood-disaster-of-june-2013-why-is-state-centre-gambling-with-the-himalayas-the-ganga-lives-of-millions/ (Last accessed 5 June 2016).

20. See also: https://sandrp.wordpress.com/2013/09/28/public-pressure-leads-to-changes-in-kerala-dam-operation/ (Last accessed 5 June 2016).

References

CSE, 1999, *Dying Wisdom – Rise, Fall and Potential of India's Traditional Water Harvesting Systems*, New Delhi: Centre for Science and Environment.

GoI, 1950, *First Five Year Plan,* New Delhi: Planning Commission, Government of India. Available at http://planningcommission.nic.in/plans/planrel/fiveyr/1st/1planch26.html (Last accessed on 4 Sept. 2004).

GoI, 2012a, *National Register of Dams*, New Delhi: Central Water Commission, Ministry of Water Resources, Government of India.

GoI, 2012b, *National Water Policy*, New Delhi: Ministry of Water Resources, Government of India.

IMD, 2015, *Rainfall Statistics of India – 2015*, Report no. ESSO/IMD/HS R. F. REPORT/04(2016)/22, New Delhi: Indian Meteorological Department.

Joy, K. J., Biksham Gujja, Suhas Paranjape, Vinod Goud, Shruti Vispute (eds.), 2008, *Water Conflicts in India – A Million Revolts in the Making*, New Delhi: Routledge.

A. Latha, Ravi S.P., and Rajneesh P., 2012, *Linking Rivers – Reviving Flows, Towards Resolving Upstream-Downstream Conflicts in Chalakudy River Basin*, Pune: Chalakudy Puzha Samrakshana Samithi and Kerala State Resource Centre of the Forum with Forum for Policy Dialogue on Water Conflicts in India.

Mishra, Anupam, 1993, *Aaj Bhi Khare Hain Talab*, Gandhi Peace Foundation, Delhi. Available at http://www.indiawaterportal.org/sites/indiawaterportal.org/files/aaj_bhi_khare_hain_talaab_anupam_mishra.pdf.

Mishra, Anupam, 1995, Rajasthan ki Rajat Boondein, Gandhi Peace Foundation, Delhi. Available at http://www.indiawaterportal.org/sites/indiawaterportal.org/files/rajasthan_ki_rajat_boondein_anupam_mishra_lowresolutionversion_0.pdf.

Shah, Tushaar, Ashok Gulati, Hemant P, Ganga Shreedhar, and R. C. Jain, 2009, 'Secret of Gujarat's Agrarian Miracle after 2000', *Economic & Political Weekly*, XLIV (52), Dec 26, pp. 45-55.

WCD, 2000, *Dams and Development – A New Framework for Decision Making, the Report of the World Commission on Dams*, London: Earthscan.

Energy Futures in India

Harish Hande, Vivek Shastry, Rachita Misra[1]

Summary

A prerequisite for ensuring any basic services, such as housing, health, education, entrepreneurship opportunities, access to finance, etc., is the availability of energy. This essay argues for the availability of affordable clean energy technology that can meet both development goals and environment quality. Central to this is the promotion of Decentralized Renewable Energy (DRE), which provides an opportunity to improve access to modern energy services for the poorest members in society. This essay lays out possibilities for the future by engaging with various policy level, financial, and technological changes that are required to promote sustainable development and equitable distribution of resources.

To ensure the energy access for differentiated populations of rural and urban centres, this essay highlights initiatives such as DRE extension and integration, policy convergence for low carbon village development, energy entrepreneurship as a livelihood, and community resource centres. India's energy future lies in creating a collaborative economy where changes in consumption patterns are promoted and access to energy services is deemed higher than ownership.

Introduction

Energy poverty is a major barrier to rural, economic and social development. According to National Sample Survey Organisation (PIB, 2011) data, fuel and light constitute the second highest expenditure after food in rural areas. Improving access to modern energy sources is an important means of realizing rural development, and a catalyst for other spheres of human development. A prerequisite for ensuring guaranteed provision of any basic amenities and productive utilizations is the availability of reliable power supply. It is imperative that affordable clean energy technologies are promoted to meet both developmental goals and environmental quality.

In India, the electricity sector contributes to about 47 per cent of all the CO_2 emissions, with high possibility of these figures increasing in the coming decade (Planning Commission, 2014). The big challenge India faces today is to provide electricity and modern energy access to an additional 240 million people and sustainable cooking for 840 million (WEO, 2015) mainly located in rural areas. Recent policy efforts to switch existing commercial and urban users to clean energy sources have also picked up pace. There is a large scope for clean energy interventions including Decentralized Renewable Energy (DRE), energy efficiency and improved cooking solutions in these areas. DRE offers the opportunity to improve access to modern energy services for the poorest members of society, which is crucial for achieving many of the seventeen Sustainable Development Goals, beyond the Affordable and Clean Energy goal (UN, 2015).

Energy is often a prerequisite and sometimes a catalyst for provision of other related amenities such as housing, health, education, entrepreneurship opportunities, skills training, access to finance, etc. As rightly pointed out by the UK Department for International Development (DFID), demand for energy is a 'derived demand', especially for the urban and rural poor, wherein no one wants energy in itself but rather the allied services it can provide including cooking, water heating, lighting, refrigeration, water pumping, transport and communications, etc, which are necessary preconditions for poverty alleviation of masses (DFID, 2002). This energy requirement also has environmental implications.

Environment & Development: opposing paradigms?

'... (Malthus) said that we would raise population enough to lower our living standards again. Well, we have raised the population, we did have this massive gain in productivity, rise in living standards, we've had huge progress and now we have to ask can we sustainably live with the planet and keep the gains to productions' (Jeffrey Sachs)?[2]

There are varied perceptions and opinions about the relationship between economic growth and preservation of environmental quality. It is believed that increased extraction of natural resources will ultimately lead to augmented accrual of waste and concentrated pollution, causing the rate of extraction becoming greater than the rate of regeneration of the resource base. The widely acclaimed Environmental Kuznets Curve (EKC) hypothesis, postulated by Kuznets propounds this 'trade-off between environment and development', implying that developing nations and economies in transition will have to forego environmental quality for the sake of attaining higher echelons of socio-economic development (Panayotou, 2003).

However, the EKC hypothesis is based on the preconceived notion that economies in transition will follow the carbon exhaustive developmental trajectories that was followed earlier by the developing nations. Currently, developing nations do not have the luxury to duplicate the emission trajectories and energy consumption pathways that had been adopted by the developed nations during their phases of industrialization due to the imminent danger of climate change lurking ahead. Developing nations will feel these impacts most severely, although they have the least responsibility towards being the causal agents of climate change. Developing nations are therefore faced with a dual undertaking – alleviating poverty levels of the population and maintaining environmental quality and natural resource base for our future generations, without increasing the threat of climate change.

These two paradigms of economic growth and environmental preservation may not be contradictory in nature after all. To achieve this equilibrium, a sustainable development framework needs to be structured which relies on leapfrogging into a Renewable Energy regime to provide clean, appropriate and efficient energy to the underserved segment of the society. However, as critics like Mansoor Khan (2013) have pointed out, growth cannot be an infinite, exponential curve that is typically imagined by the proponents of development. Further, development trajectories need to consider a sustainable co-benefits approach which propagates adoption of several mitigation options which also have other 'co-benefits' for sustainable development attached (CSTEP, 2015). The co-benefits of DRE interventions in livelihoods, housing, education, etc., are explored in more detail in the later sections.

Energy Projections: current models and shortcomings

In 2006, the Planning Commission, Government of India, presented a report on Integrated Energy Policy (IEP). The primary guiding factor for energy demand projections in the IEP report was the need to increase economic growth and GDP. It stated,

'India needs to sustain an 8% to 10% economic growth rate, over the next 25 years, if it is to eradicate poverty and meet its human development goals. To deliver a sustained growth rate of 8% through 2031-32 and to meet the lifeline energy needs of all citizens, India needs, at the very least, to increase its primary energy supply by 3 to 4 times and, its electricity generation capacity/supply by 5 to 6 times of their 2003-04 levels' (Planning Commission, 2006, pp. xiii).

Prayas (2015) reviewed three broad approaches to energy demand estimation:

- Energy needed for achieving certain GDP growth. This approach might not look at socio-economic conditions, equality of access and equitable developmental goals.
- Energy needed for achieving developmental objectives or desirable outcomes, represented by some proxies, which could be indices like the Human Development Index (HDI).
- Disaggregated, bottom-up assessment of energy needs where specific developmental goals form a detailed normative framework.

The Central Electricity Authority (CEA) carries out an elaborate exercise every five years, called the Electric Power Survey (EPS) for forecasting the future electricity requirements of the country. The main aim of the EPS is to assess electricity demand—thus it is not a normative framework. For example, the 17th EPS report states that, 'The electricity consumption by the end consumer is the guiding factor for evaluating the electricity demand for the future' (CEA, 2007, pp. 45). In other words, it looks at what the consumption by end consumer would be, but not how much should be needed, and for which purpose.

Several analysts have shown a strong association between HDI of various countries and their per capita electricity consumption (Pasternak, 2000). A corollary is that this HDI-electricity use co-relation can be used to work out the required per capita electricity consumption for a desired HDI (say 0.7). When the data is plotted, the per capita electricity consumption needed to ensure an HDI of 0.7 comes to about 2300 kWh per year, and at the generation end this is equivalent to 2895 kWh.

It should be noted that there are several outliers that may be of interest. For example, there are countries like Ecuador (1055 kWh, HDI 0.695) and Peru (1106 kWh, HDI 0.723) that have achieved HDI of 0.7 and above with relatively smaller per capita electricity consumption per year. On the other hand, there is South Africa with HDI of only 0.597 but a consumption of 4803 kWh per capita per year.

While the HDI-electricity consumption correlation is robust, it hides great differences between the structures of the economies across various countries and their health and education services. It could also mask the inequitable distribution of services within the countries, with the poorer sections consuming much less electricity than the average population. Hence, the outliers may be of more interest than those that lie on the best fit line. These outliers can show how the same HDI can be achieved with less per capita electricity use, by ensuring equitable access to services, and reducing wasteful consumption at the top of the pyramid.

According to a 2008 report by a global consortium, the Ecological Footprint (EF) of the planet was 1.78 global hectares (gha) per capita (WWF *et al.*, 2012, pp. 140-44). It can also be inferred from the report that at a sustainable level of footprint, the HDI possible is around 0.55. To achieve an HDI of 0.7 countries would require an EF of 3.14 gha, much higher than the current (2008) global sustainable bio-capacity. This indicates that the conventional approach to achieving a high HDI is unsustainable and there is a need to re-examine these approaches.

Also needing re-examination is India's Intended Nationally Determined Contribution (INDC) submitted to the United Nations Framework Convention on Climate Change (UNFCCC) in October 2015. While the proclamation of reducing the emissions intensity by 33 – 35 per cent of 2005 levels by 2030 looks ambitious on the face of it, the resulting trebling of emission intensity 'shamefully hides behind the poor' (Kothari & Adve, 2015). The ecological footprint of the richest 1 per cent of Indians is over 17 times that of the poorest 40 per cent (Shrivastava & Kothari, 2012).

Prayas (2015), reviewed several studies that indicated that an energy supply of 1200 to 1800 kgoe (kilogram(s) of oil equivalent) per capita per year would be needed to provide energy for a dignified living. Further, the International Energy Agency (IEA) calculated per capita total primary energy supply in 2011 to be 1884 kgoe (IEA, 2013, pp. 48). Thus, it is safe to say that the current global energy supply can meet the energy needs of everyone on this planet, provided it is distributed equitably.

To deliver complete energy access and meet the growing aspirations, it is essential for the ambitious plan to produce 40 per cent of electricity by non-fossil sources to have a massive thrust on Decentralized Renewable Energy (DRE), towards a worthy vision of democratic, equitable development.

DRE for Equitable Growth: visions and pathways

Envisioning equitable access to energy services requires a radical change in our approach to consumption as well as generation. On the consumption end, a number of supply side energy efficiency measures have been taken up, such as replacing bulbs with LEDs and labelling efficient appliances; and better demand side management is possible through demand response, time-of-day pricing, etc. These measures still do not go far enough to fundamentally address the nature of wasteful consumption discussed earlier. That would call for a systemic behavioural change that makes the end-users aware of their consumption patterns and create compassion to save electricity for those at the bottom of the energy ladder.

On the generation end, provision of reliable power supply for all would create enormous pressure on the already strained centralized grid. This would translate to the construction of more coal fired power plants, large hydro projects, etc., that will need huge investments and requirement for land resources to build infrastructure, having adverse impacts on our environment and disruptive consequences for communities. Conventional power plants also have longer gestation periods, and in remote areas and hilly terrains, the cost of grid extension is substantially high (Nouni *et al.,* 2007). In addition, the business and development opportunity cost of waiting for grid connection is often unaccounted for. Under such circumstances, DRE solutions (stand-alone home energy systems, decentralized micro-grids, grid-connected mini-grids, etc.,) play a crucial role in offsetting some of the required demand for electricity generation without causing environmental degradation.

While the case for DRE in remote rural areas is sufficiently clear, less discussed is its role in grid connected regions. The visions for the future need not erase the existing grid. However, there needs to be a strong focus on drastically reducing fossil fuel based electricity production and nuclear and large hydro sources that has been a subject of human safety and social unrest issues. Unreliable day time electricity disproportionately impacts small businesses in rural as well as urban areas (Akshatha, 2015), which can be addressed by decentralized generation like micro-grids and rooftop systems. Scaling up RE and DRE, its planned integration with the grid, together with penetration of energy efficient appliances would lay the foundation for a future with responsible consumption at the point of generation, reducing losses and the need for large unclean power sources.

So, what does that future look like?

The future would be for all citizens – rural, migrant and urban – to be energy self-sufficient, for each citizen or community to own, produce, and use energy responsibly (under democratic, community based control and management, sourcing locally available resources, with full knowledge of the impacts of their consumption on society and environment) and productively (using efficient, decentralized means to generate and sustain employment). The future would be for the sun, wind, water and waste to power our houses, our work and our communities.

And how do we get there?

Rural: Complete Productive Decentralization

Urban migration in India continues to increase because of decreasing employment opportunities in rural India, increasing distress from the effects of environmental degradation including climate change, and a continuing absence of basic amenities in infrastructure, healthcare, finance and education. Large scale displacements as a result of infrastructure projects are also sometimes a reason. On one level, migration indicates the growing regional imbalance and the urban-rural gap in the development story. Taking this migration as a natural phenomenon, the government's plan is to build 100 smart cities to absorb this burgeoning migrant population, albeit an absence of serious discussion on affordability and social equity. At the end of the day, cities are more energy intensive, and the decisions we make today will commit the remaining carbon emission capacity into our infrastructure.[3]

The vision for rural India should be to leverage DRE to create long-term sustainable livelihoods, and enable access to basic amenities.

DRE can enable electricity access in regions where grid extension is more expensive, and also increase reliability in regions where the grid already exists. Powering rural India completely with DRE can succeed as a vision only when DRE also succeeds in increasing productive livelihood opportunities towards meeting rural needs and aspirations. Further, with appropriate financing and operational models, end-users and communities can take ownership of these DRE systems. There is also a possibility of creating entrepreneurs to provide these services on a need basis. Designing DRE as bankable assets for the rural users makes them credit worthy and facilitate access to mainstream financing for other developmental needs. The question is therefore not whether these aspirations have to be sacrificed for environmental goals, but whether DRE can be massively scaled up to focus more on productive, decentralized rural development, where the environmental benefits are merely a useful by-product.

Technology and Policy Pathways

- *Integrated district level planning:* Integrated energy planning at a district level would broadly involve three related activities – energy mapping, ecosystem analysis and needs assessment. Energy mapping involves grassroots assessments of low access regions where electricity is unavailable, unreliable and inadequate. To facilitate energy access, it would be prudent to not only consider technological factors, but also criteria such as a supportive policy environment, innovative and affordable financing solutions, and institutions for skill development and so on. Needs assessment would also bring out the energy challenges in other sectors such as agriculture, health, education, etc., making it possible to incorporate clean energy interventions in these sectors.

- *Low carbon village development:* Developing low carbon plans for villages would require a cross sectoral approach that focuses on fostering the entire ecosystem necessary for creating sustainable livelihood opportunities and services that will uplift the standard of living in the long term. This requires looking beyond infrastructure development, and moving towards a convergence of schemes that integrate DRE and create a conducive policy environment for financial inclusion, sustainable livelihoods, health and education. For example, the central government's Saansad Adarsh Gram Yojana (SAGY) leverages the capacity of the MPs to transform villages into Adarsh Grams (model villages) of holistic development in social, human, economic and personal fronts.

- *Clarity on grid extension and DRE integration:* Lack of sufficient information about future grid extension plans and grid complementarity would disincentivize investors and possible players from entering the DRE space. Grid extension plans should be made publicly available so that off grid energy companies can plan accordingly and customers can know their communities' situation when deciding on buying solar products. Energy mapping and techno-economic studies have to be enforced while evaluating the current and future electrification strategy for states.

- *Energy in livelihood missions:* The National and State Rural Livelihood Missions in India work with a goal of poverty alleviation, but start with the assumption of access to reliable electricity. In reality, rural and remote areas across the country still reel under heavy power failures that worsen in the summer. When such an energy scenario is tied to livelihood promotion, it results in a heavy reliance on fossil fuels such as diesel and kerosene, which also eat into the earned income of the households and enterprises. Making a clear link between energy access through DRE and livelihood improvement can help change the way programs are planned.

- *Energy Efficiency in Rural Livelihoods:* To address industrial energy consumption, the Bureau of Energy Efficiency (BEE) has initiated a number of energy efficiency measures to reduce consumption in medium to large industries and clusters. Further, attractive rooftop-solar net metering schemes are now available to encourage industries and commercial establishments to produce and consume their own electricity. However, the role of energy efficiency in livelihood appliances for the rural market has rarely been discussed. Power unavailability or severe scarcity makes the use of electric livelihood appliances like sewing machines, *roti* rolling machines, photocopiers, printers, flour mills, etc., unviable for rural households. While it is possible to solar power these appliances to open up new livelihood opportunities, currently inefficient motors and other components result in prohibitive costs for backing these appliances with DRE. Adaptive innovation of technologies has to be supported to increase the efficiency of small livelihood appliances, and incentives have to be provided to back these livelihoods with DRE. This can lead to true decentralization of services, and therefore better quality of life.

Capacity Building and Financing Pathways

- **Small, low cost loans:** Innovative mechanisms could include bank guarantee for loans to energy entrepreneurs and end users (to reduce risk of bankers), interest subsidy and margin money subsidy (to reduce on-going or one-time cost of end users). These should be promoted as part of Priority Sector Lending. Creation of targets and monitoring of these targets through the State Level Bankers' committee (SLBC) could be an important way of ensuring compliance. Increased access to seed-financing and low cost debt financing for small and medium sized energy entrepreneurs is necessary to facilitate the growth of clean energy enterprises in the region.

- **Banker awareness creation:** Banks should be encouraged to engage in decentralized energy financing, with appropriate targets and monitoring. This can be undertaken through training and capacity building workshops at various banking levels, particularly in North-eastern and East Indian states where financing is yet to pick up. These workshops must encompass practical demonstrations and discussions with financiers who have engaged in energy lending.

- **Skill development:** To reduce the cost of training and skill development incurred by individual entrepreneurs, there must be a thrust on creating curriculum and teaching modules for training of RE technicians (as part of electricians' and fitters' programs), operators and micro-entrepreneurs. The existing Industrial Training Institutes (ITIs) and Rural Development and Self Employment Training Institutes (RSETIs) can then be utilized to disseminate these courses at the local level and build manpower on the ground. This can be combined with the work of the Skill Development Mission and Rural Livelihood Mission at the state level.

Case Study: Energizing Livelihoods, *ONergy Solar*[4]

In Raidighi (West Bengal), Arun the owner of a paper mill factory is able to work for longer hours and with more precision because of the installment of solar powered lights and fans. Arun is able to create party strings, which he sells in Kolkata because of the reliable source of light and electricity. Like the above paper mill factory, several other small businesses, self-help groups and other groups have been supported in providing reliable source of electricity and lighting and increasing their monthly income and livelihoods.

Case Study: Low Carbon Rural Development, *EDF and FCN*[5]

Environmental Defence Fund and Fair Climate Network's pilot low-carbon rural development project began in five states: Karnataka, Tamil Nadu, Andhra Pradesh, Telengana and Odisha, and extending to Bihar, Maharashtra and Uttarakhand. In Chittor, Andhra Pradesh,with the introduction of the CROSS FCS Biogas Unit, B. Devi's kitchen environment has drastically improved. The biogas unit was constructed near her house in November 2014. Now, she and her husband have time to spend with their children, that was previously spent gathering firewood and preparing meals. The overall objective of this work is to help farmer households improve their livelihoods and adaptation capacity, while adopting a low-carbon development pathway.

Case Study: Pico-Hydro Power for Households, *Small-Scale Sustainable Infrastructure Development Fund (S3IDF)*[6]

In Karnataka, in many rural areas, especially in the hilly regions and coastal districts, the terrain conditions make grid electricity supply either inaccessible or unreliable. However, these areas provide ideal sites for small pico-hydro systems. Pico-hydro (or small hydro-power) systems can generate sufficient power for household usage. In 2010, S3IDF provided 20 families, living in locations that are conducive to pico-hydro systems, with gap-filling finance and bridge support with the help of Prakruti Hydro Labs (PHL), a technology supply company that installs pico-hydro systems. These pico-hydro systems have improved the economic and living conditions of these 20 poor families by providing them with access to a perennial and renewable energy source.

Case Study: Energy Efficient Rural Livelihoods, *SELCO Foundation*[7]

In Bondeli village deep in the forested region along Goa-Karnataka border, 50 households are powered by an oversized 10kW micro-grid installed by MG Solar

Powertronics. Families here grow rice, and women spend a couple of hours each day to mill this rice to make flour. The alternative is to spend on transporting bags of rice to the nearest town 40 km away, and the village is completely cut off during monsoon. While the village would've benefited from a small 2HP flour mill, the ones available in the market are inefficient, and the existing inverter in this village would not have been able to handle the starting current from these appliances. SELCO Foundation identified this gap and retrofitted the flourmill with a higher efficiency motor along with a Variable Frequency Drive (VFD) to reduce the starting current. This intervention made the flourmill compatible to run on the existing micro-grid. It is now owned by the village committee, and a member is designated to operate it as a local business.

Urban Poor: DRE solutions for an inclusive informal city

As discussed above, development and urbanization in India has been largely supplemented by a surge of rural-urban migration. While this rate of migration and population growth has been high, the cities have been unable to keep up with it in terms of infrastructure as well as basic service delivery. This, furthers the economic divide, deepens urban poverty and increases the growth of slums and informal settlements. According to the 2011 census, 17 per cent of urban population lived in slums, while 1 out of every 5 was a migrant construction worker. In addition, according to the International Energy Agency (IEA), around the world, a total of 208 million people living in urban areas do not have access to electricity. In India itself, this number is as high as 5.7 million (Shrinivasan, 2013). These communities end up using unsustainable fuels, such as kerosene or biomass, which are not only harmful for the environment, but also impact their health and are not economically sustainable.

But when looking at urban poor specifically, it is important to note that this group is not as homogenous as it may seem. On a closer look, we realize that because the marginal utility is very high amongst this group, the way the urban poor are able to access resources also differs significantly. And this is directly related to their nature of tenure and livelihood security in the city. While some live in notified slums and have metered electricity, others have a very transitional role, living on daily wages and moving in and out of the city, or encroach public or private land around the city depending on their livelihood and economic needs (eg., informal migrant labour colonies, street vendors, nomadic craft communities).

a. Notified slums: The recognized and notified slums by the government have access to a metered electricity connection. However, because of the way these slums are planned and constructed (not incorporating aspects of natural light and ventilation), they are energy intensive and also result in high electricity bills, and lower savings per month. In addition, because these households also serve as workshops or spaces of small household industries, lack of lighting and poor working conditions also result in lower productivity.

Capacity Building, Technology and Design Pathways

- *Energy auditing:* Energy auditors need to be trained locally, who can provide door to door services in the communities. Conducting the assessment, performing the calculations and monetizing the assessment in terms of savings, can make the solution to communicate with the households easy. The saving is the difference between the current usages patterns and the suggested efficient technology.
- *Financial services:* Energy efficiency packages can be added to the portfolio of banks. These would promote the use of CFLs, star rated products, efficient cook stoves etc.

Policy Pathways

Slum Redevelopment Schemes and Policies should look at energy efficiency. By incorporating simple passive architecture and construction technologies, efficiency in material usage and construction technology can be enforced by the government.

b. *Informal communities and livelihoods* – The flexibility of solutions that can be offered by DRE can help result in energy solutions that look at formalizing the informality in our cities. In this section we would look at developing an energy pathway for communities that are transitional in nature. These may include:

- *Informal migrant construction labourers:* They look for seasonal employment opportunities in the city and work as unskilled daily wage labourers. They move between their native village and the city, or within the city from one encroached land to another, depending on the proximity to their work site.
- *Nomadic craft communities:* They travel from one city to another, depending on the market and festivals. They live along the main streets, where they work and live in the same space.
- *Street vendors:* They move around neighbourhoods selling their goods or services, and do not have a fixed location or infrastructure.

Technology and Design Pathways

Shared resources and community centres: While, on one hand, migration needs to be tackled at the source itself, by looking at appropriate sustainable development of rural areas, we also need to look at policy responses in destination sites as well, i.e., the urban areas. Keeping in mind the flexible energy needs and temporary nature of the communities, decentralized renewable energy solutions can be deployed to serve the communities with clean energy solutions. The case study below talks about a model that can be used to make technology more affordable by either looking at community ownership of the system, or creating a livelihood opportunity out of it for a particular entrepreneur. By creating an entrepreneur that owns the technology and rents it to the migrant communities on a daily basis, the model would look at minimizing the capital cost on installation and serving the flexible needs of the community.

The model can also be seen as an example of a collaborative economy, where it promotes a sustainable way of development by bringing about a change in the consumption pattern, where access is deemed higher to ownership. Especially valuable for the interim needs of the informal communities in the city, the solution can be scaled up to serve a 'kinetic city'[8] allowing for flexibility in usage, while facilitating more equitable distribution of resources. Leveraging on existing public infrastructure, solar powered community centres can be created to serve the energy and livelihood needs of the migrant communities. Other examples are the models of bike sharing, Laundromats, sharing work spaces, rental tools, etc.

Case Study: Integrated Energy Centers, *SELCO Foundation*[9]

Integrated Energy Centres (IECs) are solar powered community centres that can host a range of basic services and activities lacking in communities. Energy centres are essentially solar powered independent service centres for rural/urban/peri-urban spaces where a combination of energy services (such as lighting, mobile charging, charged batteries, and others) can be provided on a daily/monthly rental basis. The IEC can also serve as a health unit, education centre, livelihood centre or a community space. Each IEC is custom designed to cater to the need in a community and to best suit local environments and situations. Income generated by the IEC through the various services goes towards recovering costs including running, maintenance and capital costs of the centres. Such a shared system reduces the burden on customers of owning the systems and can be run by an entrepreneur who can be financed using external funding. These centres become a hub for the underprivileged to access services that are either difficult to obtain or unreliable. Examples of IECs facilitated by SELCO Foundation can be seen in Kariammana Agrahara slum in Bangalore, and Kanbargi slum in Belgaum, Karnataka.

Cities: Energy Self Sufficiency

The energy and water demands of cities are likely to be key determinants, playing an important role in the future and sustainability of city infrastructure. Buildings account for 40 per cent of total electricity consumption (lighting, air conditioning and plug loads), and are projected to increase to 76 per cent by 2040 (CSE, 2014).

For cities to address their energy demand, the vision has to be for every house and commercial establishment to be self-sufficient in energy (rooftop PV + efficient appliances + solar water heaters) and water (rain water harvesting + grey water recycling). There could also be self-sufficient communities and co-ops, where energy produced in one part of the community can be shared by the other residents. In the United States, for example, the conversation is already shifting from green buildings and net-zero buildings to 'Living Buildings' that produce/collect more water, energy and food than they consume. With almost 60 – 70 per cent of our building stock yet to be built by 2030, this will have huge ramifications.

With the right set of incentives, both residential and commercial sectors are poised to be ideal markets for rooftop solar systems. In order to facilitate the most effective utilization of rooftop solarsystem, energy efficient appliances would have to become prevalent in the market. Market potential already exists with people using inverters and batteries which produce power that is more expensive (Rs 20/kWh) power than solar (Rs 7/kWh). Utility business models have to evolve, to enable a competitive environment for entrepreneurs/ businesses to offer attractive services.

Policy Pathways

Changes would be required in the incentives and mandates for households, commercial establishments as well as state distribution companies.

- *Building codes and city development plans*: Building codes and urban development plans determine land usage (residential versus commercial areas), including the number of floors that can be constructed in specific areas. In the current system, residential areas suddenly turn into high-rises and commercial areas, allowing the number of built floors to increase, and increasing the risk of shading solar panels of the neighboring house. Therefore, creating building codes and plans, laying them down for a 20-year period is critical in protecting the interests of home owners who invest in rooftop PV systems or solar water heating systems.

- *Mandated inclusion of solar systems in new construction*: With codes and plans in place, it would be possible for governments to create mandates for new houses, apartment complexes and technology parks/special economic zones larger than specific square feet areas, to have rooftop PV systems and solar water heating systems. Today's cities are often being built by a handful of real estate developers. This warrants that developers be brought under the ambit of these mandates after due consultation on the best solutions. Leading the way, Uttar Pradesh government has made installation of rooftop solar panels mandatory for residences and offices constructed on an area of more than 5000 sq. feet. A building owner will have to reserve 25 per cent of the area for the purpose.

- *Meeting RPOs through rooftop and off grid*: Strict enforcement of Renewable Purchase Obligations (RPOs)[10] and nurturing the Renewable Energy Certificate (REC) market will enhance investors' confidence in DRE technologies. Currently, most State utilities are unable to meet their RPOs, and this is not strictly enforced by the regulators. Provisions could be introduced whereby the utilities could use distributed generation assets such as decentralized micro grids and rooftop PV systems within their jurisdiction to meet their obligations.

- *Generation for self-sufficiency under CSR:* With regard to large commercial establishments and companies, there could be provisions within India's CSR law to include "Generation of Power using renewable energy sources for self-sufficiency" as a recognized intervention for social responsibility towards which company profits could be utilized. If all of the industrial and commercial establishments move to captive RE generation, the cross subsidy that currently exists between these sectors and the residential segment would have to be re-structured to only support the most vulnerable sections of the society, with other users paying the true price.

Financing Pathways

- *Incentives for households*: Across the state of Karnataka, the requirement to have solar water heating systems in all new buildings that first came into effect in 2007 has considerably improved the uptake. However, in addition to this mandate, it was the rebate being provided for every house with a solar water heating system and an indication of a 2-4 year payback that piqued the interest of new home owners. Similar to the case of Solar water heaters, low interest loans at 2-4 per cent per annum, routed through nationalized banks can provide households with the required credit to purchase capital intensive rooftop systems. Since RE is already under the priority sector lending category, reducing interest rates and using funds such as National Clean Energy Fund (NCEF) to bridge the gap could be feasible and easy to implement.

- *Third party leasing models*: Another way of reducing the upfront capital costs for households and commercial establishments is through Third party solar leasing models. A commercial company owns and operates the SPV system on the building owner's rooftop. The building owner does not pay the upfront cost of the SPV system but instead leases the system by paying fixed monthly installments over a specified period of time and consumes the electricity generated by the leased system at a price that is sometimes cheaper than that charged by utilities (TERI, 2014).

While such models have been accepted in the western countries, India faces unique challenges to its implementation. Residential rooftops are generally considered private, usable spaces where third party intrusion may not be acceptable. However, providing the right incentive for both home owners as well as generators through effective implementation of feed-in tariff mechanisms and creating a portfolio of low interest loans for rooftop systems can go a long way in increasing adoption for households, small businesses and small institutions in the urban space.

Technology Pathways

- *Efficient appliances*: Energy efficient appliances – TVs, mixer grinders, washing machines – must become widely available and backed by reliable manufacturers and suppliers. This would require both consumer awareness as well as government policies, including incentives that increase demand and propel manufacturing.
- *Retrofitting batteries and new storage*: Due to poor electricity reliability in cities, inverters and Diesel Generators with batteries are already being used on a large scale. If technology innovations can support retrofitting of these batteries enabling them to also charge from solar, it could reduce the financial outflow required of households and commercial establishments. Improvements in storage technology could also bring significant changes.

Vision for the energy ecosystem

The realization is finally dawning that there cannot be one silver bullet solution; no one size fits all for DRE solutions. Customization is a critical part of realizing the vision. Though the solutions have to be deployed very rapidly to achieve complete energy access, the implementation will require multiple approaches, all of which have to be supported in parallel. Each of the solution deployment visions mentioned above will be supported by strong networks in design, manufacturing, service, awareness and governance.

- *Design and manufacturing*: A more people-focused and human-centric approach to design for energy products and solutions (for both rich and poor) will bolster stronger, more field-ready and feasible technology applications. Manufacturing would, therefore, be driven by the learnings of such iterative design combined with energy efficiency and field performance of products (across diverse community segments). Supporting frugal innovations, local manufacturing and fabrication using local materials can strengthen the decentralized technology ecosystem for clean energy, while also creating more enterprises and livelihoods.

- *Service networks*: Service and installation networks for renewable energy would be widespread with RE service centers within every 20-30 km radius, managed and operated locally. Such service centers could be co-located with existing appliance servicing shops, and also with training institutes like ITIs and polytechnics. Trained individuals in rural and urban areas – technicians and operators – will be equipped to manage the centers and address doorstep servicing needs of households and institutions. In areas with strong Self Help Group (SHG) networks, specific SHGs could themselves own and operate the RE service center as an energy cooperative. Local entrepreneurship including mechanics, electricians, mobile repair shops, SHGs with RE as their core livelihood and relatively larger implementers to support with technology supply, spare parts and know-how (as required), could together form a strong service network system that can be replicated across the country – in rural, urban and tribal contexts.

- *Conservation awareness:* Indian cities are driven by economics – while a certain percentage of the population engages voluntarily in austerity measures and conservation of energy and water, the larger percentage is more likely to respond to economic indicators and incentives to change consumption patterns. While it is important to not over-estimate the potential of energy efficiency measures, appropriate incentives (and disincentives) and awareness programs have to be designed to avoid unwanted and wasteful consumption of energy by both rural and urban households. Information about alternative practices has to be disseminated widely to effect behavioral impacts on energy intensive power users. Transparent billing mechanisms that clearly show the amount of subsidy given to each user would be helpful in phasing out these subsidies to reveal the true cost of power supply in the future.

- *A more accepting government and banking structure*: The practitioner perspectives in India are growing, with diverse examples of technological and financial innovations that have succeeded in different contexts. Despite these advances, the voices of these practitioners are feeble, as a result of which millions of people that can be served every day still remain in the dark. While successive governments have set ambitious policies, and renewable energy has finally been categorized under priority sector lending, India needs a governance structure that is receptive to the voices of practitioners, social enterprises and entrepreneurs, especially empowering small community collectives and cooperatives. Similarly, bankers must become more open to lending credit to proven DRE technologies, especially to rural customers at the bottom of the pyramid. This is paramount for DRE to be scaled up meaningfully.

Endnotes

1. The authors would like to acknowledge the contributions of Surabhi Rajagopal and Juhi Chatterjee at SELCO Foundation.
2. Quoted from a lecture at London School of Economics, 2015.
3. http://www.washingtonpost.com/news/energy-environment/wp/2015/10/09/why-earths-future-will-depend-on-how-we-build-our-cities/?wpmm=1&wpisrc=nl_green.
4. More brief case studies available on their website: http://onergy.in/case-study.php.
5. Details of the case study can be accessed at https://www.edf.org/sites/default/files/india_low_carbon_rural_development_fact_sheet.pdf.
6. Details of the case study can be accessed at http://s3idf.org/assets/2012/03/Pico-Hydro%20Power%20for%20Households.pdf.
7. More brief case studies available on their website: http://onergy.in/case-study.php.
8. Rahul Mehrotra defines Kinetic City as 'a city in motion – a three-dimensional construct of incremental development. The Kinetic City is temporary in nature and often built with recycled material…It constantly modifies and reinvents itself…The processions, weddings, festivals, hawkers, street vendors, and slum dwellers all create an ever-transforming streetscape- a city in constant motion, where the very physical fabric is characterized by the kinetic' (Huyssen, 2008, pp. 207).
9. More about IECs on the SELCO Foundation website: http://www.selcofoundation.org/wp-content/uploads/2014/05/IEC_updateMarch2013.pdf.

10. 'Renewable Purchase Obligation refers to the obligation imposed by law on some entities to either buy electricity generated by specified 'green' sources, or buy, in lieu of that, 'renewable energy certificates (RECs)' from the market. The 'obligated entities' are mostly electricity distribution companies and large consumers of power. RECs are issued to companies that produce green power, who opt not to sell it at a preferable tariff to distribution companies' (Ramesh, 2013).

References

Akshatha, M., 2015, 'Power holidays for industries under BESCOM limits: Good or bad?' *Citizen Matter. in,* November, Bangalore. Available athttp://bangalore.citizenmatters.in/articles/power-holidays-for-industries-under-bescom-limit-analysis (Accessed on 17 May, 2016).

CEA, 2007, *Report on the Seventeenth Electric Power Survey of India,* New Delhi: Central Electricity Authority, Government of India.

CSE, 2014, *Energy and Buildings,* New Delhi. Available at http://www.cseindia.org/userfiles/Energy-and-%20buildings.pdf (Accessed on 17 May, 2016).

CSTEP, 2015, *A Sustainable Development Framework for India's Climate Policy: Interim Report,* Bangalore: Center for Study of Science Technology and Policy. Availableat http://www.cstep.in/uploads/default/files/publications/stuff/30683f0adbd6f81820ab9a37eb55c7b0.pdf (Accessed on 13 March, 2016).

DFID, 2002, *Energy for the Poor: Underpinning the Millennium Development Goals,* United Kingdom: Department for International Development.

Huyssen, A., 2008, *Other Cities, Other Worlds: Urban Imaginaries in a Globalizing Age,* Durham: Duke University Press.

IEA, 2013, *Key World Energy Statistics,* Paris: International Energy Agency.

IEA, 2015, *India Energy Outlook,* Paris: International Energy Agency.

Khan, M., 2013, *The Third Curve – The End of Growth as we know it* (1st edition), Mumbai: Mansoor Khan Productions Private Limited.

Kothari, A., & N. Adve, 2015, 'A Flawed Climate Road Map', *Economic & Political Weekly,* 50(42), pp.14-17.

Nouni, M.R., S.C. Mullick, and T.C. Kandpal, 2008, 'Providing electricity access to remote areas in India: An approach towards identifying potential areas for decentralized electricity supply', *Renewable and Sustainable Energy Reviews,* 12(5), pp.1187–220. http://doi.org/10.1016/j.rser.2007.01.008 (Accessed on 1 May, 2017).

ONergy, 2015, ONergizing Livelihoods, http://onergy.in/case-study.php (Accessed January 16, 2016).

Panayotou, T., 2003, *Economic Growth And The Environment,* Presented at the United Nations Economic Commission for Europe, Geneva.

Pasternak, A.D., 2000, *Global Energy Futures and Human Development: A Framework for Analysis.* Oak Ridge: US Department of Energy. Available at http://newmaeweb.ucsd.edu/courses/ MAE119/WI_2015/PDF-PublishedDocuments/GlobalEnergyFutures_and_HumanDevelopment_ Pasternack-2000.pdf (Accessed on 13 March, 2016).

Planning Commission, 2006, *Integrated Energy Policy: Report of the Expert Committee*, New Delhi: Govt. of India.

Planning Commission, 2014, *The Final Report of the Expert Group on Low Carbon Strategies for Inclusive Growth,* New Delhi: Government of India. Available at http://planningcommission.gov.in/reports/ genrep/rep_carbon2005.pdf (Accessed on 24 Jan, 2016).

Prayas, 2015, *How Much Energy Do We Need Towards End-Use Based Estimation For Decent Living*, Pune: Prayas (Energy Group).

Ramesh M., 2013, 'Renewable purchase obligations enforcement is not our remit: Power regulator' *The Hindu Business Line*, February. http://www.thehindubusinessline.com/economy/renewable-purchase-obligations-enforcement-is-not-our-remit-power-regulator/article4428240.ece (Accessed on January 16, 2016).

Shrivastava, A. and A. Kothari, 2012, *Churning the Earth: The Making of Global India.* Delhi: Viking Books / Penguin India.

Shrinivasan, R., 2013 (March 22), '17% of urban India lives in slums: Census', http://timesofindia. indiatimes.com/india/17-of-urban-India-lives-in-slums-Census/articleshow/19118219.cms (Accessed on 27 August, 2017).

TERI, 2014, *Reaching the Sun with Rooftop Solar,* New Delhi: The Energy and Resources Institute.

United Nations, 2015, Sustainable development goals. Available at http://www.un.org/ sustainabledevelopment/sustainable-development-goals/ (Accessed on 18 Feb, 2016).

WWF, ZSL, GFN, & ESA,2012, *Living Planet Report 2012: Biodiversity, Biocapacity and Better Choices.* Available at http://www.footprintnetwork.org/images/uploads/LPR_2012.pdf (Accessed on 19 January, 2016).

POLITICAL FUTURES

The Power Equation and India's Future

Pallav Das

Summary

The power equation in India is marked by a high degree of inequality. The essay probes its evolution in the country – from caste to the consolidation of capitalism in the contemporary society, and their insidious nexus with politics. It explores why women, backward castes and dalits, and various religious and ethnic minorities have been traditionally accorded an inferior socio-economic position in society, and how the forces of modernization, in their attempt to nudge this imbalance in power to a more just place, have been met with a new and more pernicious development, that of physical violence, which has become increasingly frequent, intense and brazen. The essay then investigates the organic attempts at resistance rooted in the traditions of indigenous communities taking shape in the Indian hinterland. Could these decentralized and community based traditional structures show us the way to an egalitarian power structure based on the 'commons'? The essay concludes with the idea of forging a 'New Power Alliance' that has the experience and the motivation to challenge the existing power structure and its economically exploitative and environmentally ruinous agenda.

Introduction

What should the power equation look like in the future in India? That, obviously, depends on how the people of this country view their current relationship with its existing construct. Is there general satisfaction among them about how power, particularly political and socio-economic power, is distributed and shared in the various societal structures that impact their lives? Conversely, if there is discontent regarding how people interact with power then what are the available avenues for addressing that dissatisfaction? How accessible are those avenues to the people in general, and in fact, how meaningfully successful have attempts at the redress of grievances (and attempts at change) been, historically? Is the existing power equation in India working to everyone's satisfaction? And, why is there a need to change it in the future?

This essay attempts to explore the nature of power in India, its historical roots and evolution, and its impact on the current socio-economic conditions in the country. Based on this discussion, it will further examine the need for change in how the power equation operates within the Indian society. Finally, it will inquire into the ways in which the path to the new future could unfold, the impediments and possible circumventing routes, and what the new power dynamic could look like in an economically egalitarian, politically radical and environmentally sane society.

The Layers of Power

Robert Dahl, the political theorist closely associated with the pluralist conception of power and its rather unconvincing attempt at empiricism, formulated a somewhat austere but tenable definition of the notion of power. 'My intuitive idea of power', Dahl said, 'is something like this: *A* has power over *B* to the extent that he can get *B* to do something that *B* would not otherwise do' (Dahl, 1957, pp. 202-03). Defining an abstruse term like power in simple words is not easy, yet Dahl's definition does manage to signify the cold logic of power – the compulsion of an individual or a collective *B* to comply with the will of an *A,* acutely aware of the negative consequences of non-compliance. Power, then, as traditionally understood, is a relational concept operating within a certain societal structure, and the location of individuals or groups within that structure defines their access to power with an unequivocal expression of inequality. Who has control over material resources in a society and how it is maintained, and how social institutions are configured and to whose advantage, are also factors to the access to power. Wealth, status, education, influence, knowledge, and even raw muscle, are some of the ways in which power is expressed in a society. Needless to say, the inequality inherent in power relations is sustained through all possible means – manipulation of thought, coercion, cooption, deception, inducements, fear, threat of violence and of course the use of an existing advantageous position to ensure continued dominance.

Power and Structural Violence

In any society, the relationships of power get fused into its structure over time. One of the more astute examinations of that very link between power and the structure of society is by Johan Galtung, a Norwegian mathematician and sociologist, specifically in the context of conflict within and between societies. Galtung identifies three ways in which power is exercised in a society – through ideas, inducements and punitive action. The disempowered are expected to follow and contribute to the functioning of the operative ideology, which is determined for them by those who wield power and have control over material resources. They do so in exchange for remuneration set for them, but any refusal on their part to participate in that process could lead to a commensurate amount of punishment, which again is a part of the dynamic of power. For Galtung, the inequality inherent in this power relationship leads to systemic oppression of one group by the other. It is a situation where a section of society is marginalized, exploited, degraded and debased without actually experiencing physical violence. Galtung calls this the condition of 'structural violence', as it closes all avenues for the disempowered to exercise any agency in their own lives, ultimately being forced to accept the control of others over their lives and their prospects, reflecting a classic case of complete socio-psychological impairment. Structural violence, in fact, is not imposed upon the disempowered using a formal or a legal code. Instead, it becomes a part of the dominant culture, which mutually reinforces its ideological imperative. Media, popular culture and religion help shape society's attitudes and beliefs towards structural violence and consolidate its position as the dominant narrative of power in society.

A significant determinant of the stability and efficacy of any kind of power relationship is the internalization of its logic as well as the operating process by actors on both sides of the equation. The Indian caste system is probably the most successful illustration of that societal order. While power is expressed, implied and accepted in India in many universally recognizable and known forms, both modern and pre-modern, the caste system is unique to the country because it is rooted in an intangible yet powerful notion of 'purity' of a person and even a group. In fact, a person derives his or her relative purity from that which is ascribed to a caste to which he or she belongs. The explanation of relative purity of a particular caste group is defined on the basis of their occupation (the purity of priesthood versus the impurity of scavenging) or if one was to give credence to the mythical origins disclosed in the Rig Vedic *Purusha Sukta* (the Hymn of Man), to which part of the human form of Lord Brahma was it constituted from (the head or the foot, etc.). These would essentially remain implausible and dubious until and unless there was a uniform agreement among all actors to accept that explanation as an axiom.

While the caste system has had a pernicious influence traditionally on the power dynamics in India, the basic coordinates of the current power structure in the country have become clearly evident over the last quarter century of neo-liberal fundamentalism – an exceedingly centralized pretend democracy which is run by an entrenched political class spread across a perfunctory and convenient ideological divide. It operates in close association with corporate elite pursuing an economic agenda of ceaseless growth, running overwhelmingly on fossil fuels, and blind to its ecological consequences. To make sure that this pact between the economic and political elite continues uninterruptedly, there is a tacit understanding of minimal or no intervention in the social structure and its power dynamic. It ensures that the boat never rocks.

If the current power dynamic in India causes inequality, discrimination and ecological stress, what, then, should it look like in the India of the future, where these problems have been successfully addressed? To change the existing equation of power completely, one would have to create another dynamic, which is based on the equality of status between various actors, where power is redistributed and shared equally and decisions are designed to promote the good of everyone. At a societal level, then, the traditionally disempowered groups would have to intervene at the place where power is located, the state being one of the easily identifiable ones. In India, however, given how tradition and history have situated power in various places in the society, the task has always been more complex. But, at the same time, the opportunities for challenging and changing entrenched power are also more numerous.

Power and the State

In his book, 'Change the World Without Taking Power', the Irish Marxist sociologist, John Holloway ponders over the relevance of the state in effecting radical socio-political change. Taking inspiration from the Zapatista movement in the Chiapas province of Mexico, he contrasts the two distinct interpretations of the term, power, in the Spanish language, to explain his distrust of the conventional revolutionary trajectory towards change – '*poder hacer*' or the power to create, to do, as opposed to '*poder sobre*', or power over, 'the power of domination and subjugation which stifles the power of the people to create' (Ross, 2005). Holloway makes this important distinction to explain his disenchantment with the revolutionary angst and preoccupation with capturing state power. 'If we focus our struggles on the state, we have to understand that the state pulls us in a certain direction. It seeks to impose upon us a separation of our struggles from the society; it separates leaders from the masses. It draws us into a different way of thinking and it pulls us into a process of reconciliation with reality, and that reality is the reality of capitalism' (ibid.).

The explicit pursuit of state power compromises our ability to look for creative answers to the class centric and elite focused notion of power, and we end up in the same maze of command and subordination. In our desire for change in the societal power structure we should be looking to channel people's own frustration and outrage about the oppression and discrimination in their lives into creative action. Consequently, we can neither wait for the next election nor for the next revolution, because as Holloway states, 'substituting one state power for another just repeats the same problem over and over again and eventually exhausts the revolution. This is the old way of thinking about the revolution and it doesn't work anymore' (ibid.).

Holloway believes that localized attempts at creating alternatives would lead to organized political assertiveness at the grassroots level and create autonomous spaces within and outside the capitalist system as well as the power structure. He refers to this process as the creation of 'cracks' in the system. It is immaterial as to what the size of that crack is; it could be an organized strike in a major industry or the establishment of a small farmers' cooperative or the students' refusal to attend classes to protest the high cost of education. As the incidence, intensity, amplitude and the reach of these events increases, the actors involved would become alive to their individual and collective power, and gain further experience at how to express it through more concerted action. Like small cracks in a wall, which deepen and converge with pressure, these spaces within society come together to allow the possibility of the collapse of the edifice.

The Search for Alternatives

What do these cracks look like in the current scenario in India? Some very interesting experiments are emerging from deep in the hinterland. In 2013, for instance, the residents of the village of Mendha Lekha in Maharashtra's Gadchiroli district decided to transfer the ownership of their farmlands to the Gram Sabha, or the Village Assembly – a total of 200 ha belonging to 52 families (Pallavi, 2013). The village is in the *adivasi* (indigenous communities) belt of the state and the Gond tribal community of this area considers land as a community resource and not as individual property. This has resonance in the revolutionary concept of the 'commons' (air, water, forests, etc.) but goes a step further because it organizes cultivable land into collective ownership. Even though the erstwhile owners cultivate most of the land in Mendha Lekha, decisions about its use are taken collectively. This ensures that the land stays in the ownership of the village and individual owners are not tempted to sell to land sharks operating in the adivasi region. As Devaji Tofa, a community leader said, 'With private ownership, people tend to get selfish and isolated' (ibid.).

The poverty rate for rural adivasi areas in Maharashtra is an astounding 56%, and 54% tribal children in India are chronically undernourished.[1] As their forests get destroyed, land gets cleaved and gouged for mining, and water sources become foul, the tribal communities are looking for alternatives. Mendha Lekha created the first crack in the local power structure in 2009, when it became one of the first two villages in India to win community rights over forests under the Forests Rights Act. Following this the village was able to take over the management of forest produce (particularly bamboo), water harvesting in the forests, as well as organizing income generating projects, there. The gram sabha ensures hundred per cent employment in the village, and every working adult gets work according to their capability. Women have an equal stake in the new power dynamic and form fifty percent of all management committees. Also, there are strict term limitations for serving on committees and people are selected instead of being elected to them.

The decentralized and community oriented power structure in Mendha Lekha shares many of its progressive attributes with the Zapatista communes in Chiapas, Mexico and the Kurdish communitarian organizations in the Rojava region of Northern Syria. Direct democracy, bottom up model of development, cooperative rather than market fundamentalist economy, gender egalitarianism, consultative, non-hierarchical decision making – it is a concerted attempt at framing a new power dynamic in Chiapas and Rojava. The Zapatistas have withdrawn from the state apparatus of Mexico and the Kurds aspire to a stateless society, both quite certain of their ideological moorings. The Gond adivasi communities of Mendha Lekha, grounded in the earth and modest by culture would never lay claim to such lofty ambitions: yet, they have taken the first necessary steps towards recalibrating the power dynamic in their immediate surroundings. 'Our government is in Mumbai and Delhi, but we are the government in our village' (*Mumbai Dilli mein hamaari sarkar, hamaare gaon mein hum hi sarkar*) is the slogan that reflects this philosophy. The experiment is a reminder of Holloway's conception of 'the power to create' and is a bold challenge to the state's 'power over' that they have lived under for all these years (Pathak, 2001; Pathak, *et al.*, 2008). Is it possible to replicate this experiment elsewhere in India? How can this crack in the power structure become deeper and wider? The most significant aspect of Gadchiroli's demographics is that its population is nearly 40 per cent tribal and overwhelmingly so in the rural areas. The district abuts other adivasi majority areas in Maharashtra and in the adjoining states, Chhattisgarh and Andhra Pradesh as well. With similar attributes of access to natural resources and sharing the progressive adivasi traditions, communities in these areas should have been expected to adopt the Mendha Lekha model of decentralized power and decision making quite readily. Yet, the reality is somewhat different.

The most important factor behind the replication of successful socio-political experiments is the proof of their sustainability, ease and regularity of communicating that success to a larger audience and, most importantly, the absence of any kind of wanton and gratuitous pressure, which would prevent the possibility of the first two conditions. There have been substantial hitches in this regard in Gadchiroli. The adivasi hinterland of central India is witnessing a power struggle focused on its rich natural resources. The extractive pressures of neo-liberalism reached these parts soon after the opening of the Indian economy. Concomitant with that, the ultra-left Naxalite rebellion against the state also gained ground owing to the disaffection and alienation of the local communities from the developmental process. As would be expected, this conflict for power has severely destabilized the lives of the people in this region, including in Gadchiroli district.

The Mendha Lekha experiment came into the crosshair of, both, the Naxalites and the state. The forces of the armed rebellion have been furious at the success of the initiative because it emerges out of a convergence of the adivasi community's traditional ability to manage its affairs, particularly the commons, and a state sponsored policy like the Forests Rights Act (FRA). Espousing a militant strategy for the capture of the state and a top down model of decision making, the ultra-left, it seems, is anxious to confront any initiatives which seek to transfer power at the local level, however limited it may be. Consequently, to discourage any possibility of its replication, the Naxalites came down hard on the Mendha Lekha initiative, and community leaders and local officials were threatened, publicly humiliated in 'people's courts' and even kidnapped for the crime of being 'the agents of the state'. On the other hand, the state tried to back track on its promise of granting 'community forest rights' under FRA. Last year, the Forest Department, in a typical case of bureaucratic artifice, asked the gram sabhas in Maharashtra to pass a resolution to reinstate the Joint Forest Management Committees, which in fact had been made redundant by FRA (Pallavi, 2014). This move would have prevented the villages from taking independent decisions regarding the management of their forests, a right, which they had struggled long and hard to get. Given the immense pressures from all sides, it is not surprising that building on the Mendha Lekha model of decentralization of power in India has been somewhat sporadic and minimal. Of late, though, several other communities in this part of Maharashtra have gained community forest rights and are asserting some form of autonomy.

Power and the Commons

The experiment at Mendha Lekha has opened up a distinct new possibility for mounting a challenge to the existing power dynamic in India, despite running into setbacks and strife after a promising beginning. Most importantly, it has allowed the possibility of the idea of the 'commons' to gain new recognition in the country due to the strategic and well-organized manner in which the village community was able to use the Forests Rights Act to manage its immediate natural resource of the bamboo forests. The community, however, went beyond the limited scope of a state sponsored policy initiative and decided to transfer the ownership of their farmlands to the gram sabha, thus underscoring the power imperative of its own intentions. In a rudimentary sense the idea of the 'commons' refers to the resource people have in common, what they share and don't have to pay for. But, recent scholarly work on the subject has further flushed out its context and meaning. Massimo De Angelis, a professor of Political Economy at the University of East London and the author of 'The Beginning of History: Value Struggles and Global Capital' (De Angelis, 2010) has highlighted three identifying elements of the commons. 'First, all commons involve some sort of common pool of resources, understood as non-commodified means of fulfilling peoples' needs. Second, the commons are necessarily created and sustained by *communities* – communities are sets of commoners who share these resources and who define for themselves the rules according to which they are accessed and used. The third and most important element in terms of conceptualizing the commons is the verb 'to common' – the social process that creates and reproduces the commons' (ibid.). De Angelis explains the notion of 'to common' or 'commoning' with reference to the medieval customs of collecting wood in the forests or setting up villages on the king's land, which were recognized as rights by the sovereign. The important point here, and of relevance to the present context of the commons, is that these rights were not granted by the king, but it was the existing customs which were 'acknowledged as de facto rights' (ibid.).

People's own agency in expressing and acquiring collective ownership over their immediate resources is the operative aspect of power that emerges out of the idea of the commons. Recently, another path breaking experiment was undertaken in Telengana, this time concerning groundwater in the drought prone district of Mahbubnagar (Bhaduri *et al.*, 2015). To address the issue of a continually plunging water table, the borewell owners of Chellapur village decided to pool their groundwater to create a water grid. The results were quite impressive – the irrigated area doubled and the grain production increased by a massive 240 per cent. What was most remarkable, however, was that a village community came together with an NGO to implement a strategy, which stepped away from the conventional notion of groundwater as private property and adopted a 'commons' approach of collective ownership. Even those who didn't have their own borewells were allowed to share groundwater at a price. The collective approach was environmentally sound too, as it helped in controlling competitive digging of wells, ultimately reducing the pressure on the level of groundwater. These experiments at sharing local resources demonstrate a significant 'crack' in the power structure and will be replicated in areas with similar predicaments.

The idea of the 'commons' has not only provided proactive radical alternatives for development policies, it has also inspired democratic resistance towards destructive initiatives taken up by the state in the name of economic growth. The hard battle the local communities in Niyamgiri in Orissa fought and won against the Vedanta mining company (*The Hindu,* 2010)[2] and the continuing tenacious struggle in opposition to the POSCO Steel project (DTE staff, 2015) also in Odisha, are prime examples of the ideological tussle currently in progress in the country. There are a number of similar struggles taking place all over India where the communities are resisting takeover of their natural resources. These contests are all the more relevant in the adivasi heartland of the country. Capitalism depends for its survival on endless growth, for which it needs to extend its reach to the farthest corners for natural resources, to enclose new 'commons' for exploitation and extraction. The central Indian peninsula is one of those last remaining areas of abundance. But, along with that need for resources, the global capital also requires to commodify spheres of life and social processes, which have been hitherto untouched by the market and its pernicious logic of profit, such as the adivasi areas. These socio-economic transformations act as potent displays of the power of capitalism. And by extension of that logic, accomplishing these transformations makes it even more powerful. Yet, the peaceful resistance efforts such as the one mounted in Niyamgiri, help in the creation of an alternative. The resolve of the adivasi communities in central India to neither open up their commons for extraction nor get co-opted into the operative logic of the market is an expression of their own sense of power, which they derive from their egalitarian socio-economic beliefs rooted in their customs. This compelling blend of democratic resistance and traditional practices centred on the commons is necessary for challenging corporate hegemony over the developmental model in India and is going to be a significant determinant of the future of the power equation in the country.

Power and the Solidarity of the Excluded

The commons model is relevant beyond the adivasi area of India. There are a large number of ecosystem and agriculture dependent communities in the country, including substantial populations of pastoralists and fishers, which can benefit from that approach. In these areas it is important to seek to regain power in the manufacture of traditional crafts, production from basic agricultural commodities, and aquatic and other kinds of nature-based produce by linking them through a localized system of exchange.[3] The commons model, in fact, is the only one able to ensure the sustenance of the cultural and ecological context of the people's lives. The traditional village republic in India was built upon the exchange of goods and services, which were locally sourced. While it was rife with social inequalities, it was nonetheless an efficient model based on economic self-sufficiency. But it was unglued by colonialism and mercantilism and then destroyed by industrial and finance capital when India opened itself up to globalization.

A small beginning could be made in the shape of a network of a farmers' cooperative providing local produce; an alternative energy grouping offering access to solar and other clean sources of power; and ancillary services groups – a crafts guild manufacturing basic tools for daily life as well as traditional handicrafts and a group of lawyers and scribes for providing legal advice in cases of conflict or for dealing with extra local administrative authorities. The farmers' cooperative would also have experts in traditional medicine for guiding people towards a healthy lifestyle. Additionally, the alternative energy grouping would include in its purview the technical aspects of digital connectivity, and the crafts guild would encompass the larger ambit of education inspired by Mahatma Gandhi's idea of 'Nai Taleem'.[4]

These groups would be formed on the basis of equal status for all adult men and women within the organization, and as equal investors sharing in surplus. This would ensure that profit motive does not become an overriding factor as it has in capitalist exchange. The Dharani Farmer's Cooperative in Andhra Pradesh and the Khamir Textile Cooperative in Kutch in Gujarat are recent examples of successful initiatives propelled by similar ideas.[5] These groups would also trade with others in the network on the basis of equality, by assigning mutually acceptable value for all goods and services. A network would have a representative committee based on equal participation of both genders to solve intra network issues and also represent it outside. The members would nominate the representatives for a fixed duration and their work would not be remunerative. Ideally, such a network would not be spread over more than a typical block in an Indian district, for it to be self-sufficient and self-operative.

The most important problem for crafting such a network would be how to deal with the residual feelings of caste and community solidarity and related notions of superiority and subordination, which people would probably carry into such networks from their earlier lives. Given that these groupings and networks would be made out of choice and with the sound intent of an egalitarian existence, they would self-select people with respect for those attributes. Those who feel uncomfortable with the idea of equality would either not join or leave in some time. If such a network were able to display success and longevity as a 'crack' within the existing system, then it would become a power structure worthy of replication. Conversely, however, if the experiment becomes replicable it would come under immense pressure from the existing power dynamic, which would either try to co-opt it with major changes or choke it through pressure on its material independence. It could also face physical violence and efforts at elimination if it becomes a major threat to the existence of the current system of power.

Recalibrating Power, Challenging Violence

Violence and poverty are two overlapping categories of socio-economic abuse in India and dalits, tribals, Muslims, ethnic minorities and women continually suffer their consequences – more than other sections of the Indian population. Furthermore, in the last few decades a large part of this cross-section has also faced the impact of environmental degradation the most – particularly loss of traditional nature based livelihoods, dislocation due to developmental projects, loss of agricultural land due to desertification, water shortages or deluges caused by climate change, and leading an environmentally deleterious life in urban ghettoes (Shrivastava and Kothari, 2012). They also face regular human rights violations for any signs of dissent, and even active state repression in case their dissent is perceived as anti-national rebellion.

While Johan Galtung's analysis of power examines the violence and discrimination present in the structure of power that defines human interactions, the threat of apparent violence has always existed behind the expression of power. Hannah Arendt, the German-American political theorist, whose work preceded that of Galtung by a few decades, examined the nature of the relationship between the two concepts and found that they were distinct from each other and blatant violence, at most, is a perversion of power. Power, according to Arendt is, 'the human ability not just to act but to act in concert. When we say of somebody that he is "in power" we actually refer to his being empowered by a certain number of people to act in their name' (Arendt, 1970, pp. 143). The Brahmin, thus, represents the collective power of Sanatan Dharma of Brahminical Hinduism, by becoming the 'true' repository of ritual purity around which the caste system is organized. And, then, as if talking about repression against the 'untouchables', Arendt states, 'Even the most despotic domination we know of, the rule of master over slaves, who always outnumbered him, did not rest on superior means of coercion as such, but on the organized solidarity of the masters' (ibid., pp.149). In the Indian context, the anxiety for compliance that the Brahminical order had created among the lower castes through the socially organized instruments of pollution and exclusion, seldom forced the need for threat of violence to be activated. According to Arendt, power is not created through violence; in fact, when power devolves to violence it is eventually destroyed. In words, which turned out to be quite prophetic in her analysis of totalitarian states, Arendt affirmed that, 'Power and violence are opposites; where the one rules absolutely, the other is absent. Violence appears where power is in jeopardy, but left to its own course it ends in power's disappearance' (ibid., pp. 155).

In contemporary India there is a continuum, which operates from the aggregated constitutional promise of equality for all, to the personalized space where the possibility as well the eventuality of discrimination and sometimes, physical violence, is habitual, and ingrained. The distance between the poles is so enormous that often the legal and moral limits imposed by the constitution are insolently breached without much of a consequence on the other end. Violence against dalits and lower castes, women, and religious and ethnic minorities represents the power of the ritually sanctified personalized space which expands and contracts at will and melds when needed with similar organic spaces, confident of its safe distance from constitutional probity. Is the rise in class, caste, communal, gender, ethnic and environmental violence in India a pointer towards the beginning of the unravelling of its power structure? Is violence the betraying sign of a change, albeit quite slow and messy? It feels as if the notion of power known to this country, however pernicious it was, is stretched at its seams and collapsing routinely. Violence fills the vacuum sporadically but without really being able to provide long-term stability to the structure. The present moment, consumed as it is by corporate and financial greed is truly a moment of oppressive indifference for anyone who doesn't share its logic of immediate gratification and sustained profit. What it shares, however, with the predicament of a substantial subset of the population of the country is the violence it has committed to the ecology and the climate in the country and worldwide. As D. R. Nagaraj, the Kannadiga literary critic said in his prescient comment about the rapid changes taking place post liberalization, 'In this modern nation, Muslims, Harijans, tribals and the poor will all be decimated. They will be crushed to pulp under the weight of desire and machines' (cited in Vajpayi, 2011 pp. 115). But, is that their declared destiny? There has to be an alternative to decimation.

The New Power Alliance

It is true that in a literal Marxist sense the oppressed groups in India don't form an economic class but as Nicos Poulantzas, the Greek Marxist theorist envisaged, they do share a similar 'class position', as survivors of economic and ecological oppression as well as physical violence originating from an unequal access to power. Called the New Power Alliance (NPA), this group – women, tribals, dalits, Muslims and lower castes – stands at the cusp of an alliance forming moment to challenge their subjugation by entrenched power elite.[6] In the process can they effect a revolutionary political and ecological transformation that India desperately needs, now? The 'common' here is the threat of destruction, which leads to the 'common' of the promise of struggle. As survivors of violence these groups cannot afford to use violent means of resistance themselves because, that would amount to a cooption into the methods of the oppressor, and thus prevent them from making the stark contrast needed to project their unique identity. Moreover, unlike the ultra-left rebellion in the forests of central India, these groups are diffused all through rural and urban India and could be crushed by the state machinery if given the perception of being armed. As a medium term strategy, these groups, in fact, need to persuade the ultra-left group to give up arms and join a peaceful resistance movement towards change in the power structure.

All revolutionary discourse, in some form or the other, has affirmed and encouraged the course of action, which moves towards the establishment of people's power. The idea of change, when it is detached from the pursuit of state power, frees people from the anxiety of large-scale mobilization to challenge the established nexus between corporations and the political and bureaucratic elite in India. The socio-psychological space which is essential for creative alternatives to the current power dynamic is often clouded by uncertainty and the threat of failure, because the task is so huge and the adversary so intimidating and 'powerful'. The power dynamic has to be challenged at strategic levels without getting too overwrought about its size and scope, as well as its desired impact on the ultimate goal of changing the power equation. That wisdom is becoming apparent in more and more meaningful ways all over India, as modest and yet very effective grassroots challenges emerge on the horizon without the need for loud proclamations. That's what has begun changing the power dynamic in India.

The Future of Power

So, finally, to come back to the initial question, based on the above discussion – what could the power equation look like in the future in India, say fifty years from now? Could the Indian society evolve into a stateless dispensation free of stratification, self-regulated and self-organized, where the traditional notion of power itself becomes completely redundant? What would the society look like if wealth, status, education, influence, networks – all the necessary attributes of power under free market fundamentalism – become irrelevant to human engagements in India? To paraphrase Robert Dahl, '*A* would exercise no power over *B* in pursuit of any task and vice versa, yet the two would form a relationship of equality, reciprocity and sharing where all the necessary tasks of their lives get done under the rubric of mutual care'. If this ideal (some would even call it utopian) future was attained then what would the transformed shape of the power dynamic look like in India? Let us explore that future:

Power and the political economy

- The essential logic of economic activity would be the fulfilment of livelihood needs and not the logic of accumulation.
- Cooperative forms of production would be the basis of industry. All decisions regarding the raising of capital, setting up of infrastructure and machinery, production targets, etc., and other day-to-day activities would be taken through an informed consultative and democratic process. All personnel would have an equal say in the decision making process, whatever be the nature of their specialization.
- Banks and financial institutions would also be cooperatively owned and would work on behalf of the people. The chief aim of the banks would be to facilitate and sustain economic activity in its area of operation and not to make profit.
- The chief economic unit would be an eco-region, roughly similar to a current state in India. It would be created on the basis of its common ecological and geographical features – it could for instance be a coastal mangrove area or a mountainous region or a flat arid area. All economic activity in an eco-region would be designed around its ecology, and would maintain its integrity.
- All eco-regions would be small units comprising not more than ten current districts. Large contiguous tracts of similar ecological and geographical features would be divided into smaller units.
- All economic activity would be guided by the larger goal of maintaining environmental equilibrium and all industrial and production activity would have to submit itself to periodic public audits.
- All surpluses would be shared equally among the members of a particular production unit.
- Economic activity would not be guided by the notion of endless growth. In fact, whenever a situation warrants it, de-growth would be introduced to bring an industry or a production unit back to equilibrium.

Power and political structures

- In a politically egalitarian India all formal structures of decision-making (as far as possible) would be formed on the basis of direct democracy (Kothari and Das, 2016).

- Institutions formed by representational elections would be downwardly accountable, i.e. to those groups and people they are representing.
- All elected bodies would be completely transparent and would work under the oversight of watchdog committees at that level.
- All elected offices (at national, state and other levels) would be restricted to two terms but they would not be successive. You would have to give yourself a break of at least one term before trying for another one. No elected or representational office would be for more than two years.
- The expenditure for elections would be done through a collective fund and every candidate would have access to an equal amount. The time allotted for canvassing would be sufficient to make an outreach but not unnecessarily lengthy. All elections would be conducted, as far as possible, at the same time, so as to optimize election expenditure.
- All offices would submit to a right to recall halfway through a term, if a minimum agreed upon number of people were to ask for that option to be explored.
- All elected chambers would have equal representation for women and men.

Power and the social structure

- All citizens of the country would be considered equal in their legal, economic and social status.
- All communities would be considered equal. No traditional notions of ritual superiority of communities or religious groups would be accepted in the social or legal spheres. There would be legal sanctions and penalties for any expression or practice of discrimination based on community association.
- Both sexes would have equal social and legal status. They would have access to equal opportunities for education and employment.
- Religious beliefs would be strictly personal and would not be allowed to influence public decision making process.
- The family unit would be encouraged not to be guided by any residual patriarchal influence. Female as well as male role models would be encouraged to be followed and emulated by the youth and the kids.

Conclusion

While it's tempting to imagine a scenario where the state has withered away to usher in an egalitarian dynamic of power in society, and those who've been traditionally and historically deprived of any say over their own current circumstances as well as future prospects are in a position to exercise their will, it is also quite sobering to look at the realistic picture. The task of reaching that desired goal is challenging to say the least. Yet, the journey to that imagined future is the most exciting that one could take, and also the most essential to propel the human evolution to the next desired level of equality.

Endnotes

1. Poverty data 2004-05, www.tribal.nic.in (Last accessed 26 June 2016).
2. http://www.thehindu.com/news/national/it-is-no-to-vedantas-mine-project-in-orissa/article591546.ece (Last accessed 26 June 2016).
3. See essays on Craft, Localisation, and Market Future essays in this volume.
4. Nai Taleem or 'New Education' was symbolic of the holistic manner in which Mahatma Gandhi approached India's struggle against British colonialism – not just as a political battle but also as an initiative towards socio-economic resurgence. He imagined education to be the fundamental element towards the creation of a new society, where the Indian youth were not just learning to be the most efficient little clerks for the colonial government. Gandhi emphasized the importance of learning traditional crafts as the method for getting an insight into history, geography, science and mathematics. This unique restructuring of pedagogy towards the skills of the backward castes in the Indian social system was a clever way in which he wanted to move away from the upper caste stranglehold on knowledge through its emphasis on reading, writing and abstract conceptualization. Unfortunately, however, Nehru and the rest of the elite in post-independence India ignored Gandhi's revolutionary ideas about education and gradually laid them to rest after his assassination.
5. www.timbaktu-organic.org (last accessed 26 June 2016); www.khamir.org (last accessed 26 June 2016).
6. See also Democracy Futures essay in this volume.

References

Arendt, H., 1970, *Crisis of Republic*, New York: Harcourt Brace.

Bhaduri, A, Bakka Reddy, 2015, *Groundwater as commons demonstrated in Mahbubnagar*, Telengana, http://www.indiawaterportal.org/articles/groundwater-commons-demonstrated-mahbubnagar-telangana (Last accessed 26 June 2016).

Dahl, R., 1957, *The Concept of Power*, www.unc.edu/~fbaum/teaching/articles/Dahl_Power_1957.pdf pp-202-03) (Last accessed 26 June 2016).

De Angelis, M., 2010, *An Architektur interview with Massimo De Anglis*, http://www.e-flux.com/journal/on-the-commons-a-public-interview-with-massimo-de-angelis-and-stavros-stavrides/ (Last accessed 26 June 2016).

DTE staff, 2015, Posco To Withdraw Investment From Odisha, *Down To Earth*, 3 April, http://www.downtoearth.org.in/news/posco-to-withdraw-investment-from-odisha – 49272 (Last accessed 26 June 2016).

Kothari, A. and P. Das, 2016, 'Power in India: Radical Pathways', in *State of Power 2016*, Amsterdam: Transnational Institute, https://www.tni.org/en/publication/power-in-india-radical-pathways (Last accessed 26 June 2016).

Pallavi, A., 2013, 'Mendha Lekha residents gift all their farms to gram sabha', *Down to Earth*, http://www.downtoearth.org.in/news/mendha-lekha-residents-gift-all-their-farms-to-gram-sabha-42127 (Last accessed June 26 2016).

Pallavi, A., 2014, 'Maharashtra forest department gets flak for its August 15 diktat', *Down to Earth*,http://www.downtoearth.org.in/news/maharashtra-forest-department-gets-flak-for-its-august-15-diktat-45634 (Last accessed June 26 2016).

Pathak, N., 2001, *Tribal Self-Rule and Natural Resource Management: Community Based Conservation at Mendha-Lekha*, Maharashtra, India, Pune/Delhi: Kalpavriksh and London: IIED.

Pathak, Neema, Erica Taraporewala, Milind Wani, Arshiya Bose and Ashish Kothari, 2008, *Towards Self-Rule and Forest Conservation in Mendha Lekha Village*, Gadhchiroli,http://www.iccaconsortium.org/wp-content/uploads/images/media/grd/mendha_india_report_icca_grassroots_discussions.pdf (Last Accessed 26 June 2016).

Ross, J., 2005, *How To Change The World Without Taking Power*, http://www.counterpunch.org/2005/04/02/how-to-change-the-world-without-taking-power/ (Last accessed 26 June 2016).

Shrivastava, A. and A. Kothari, 2012, *Churning the Earth: The Making of Global India*, Delhi: Viking/Penguin India Books.

Vajpeyi, A., 2011, *'Let Poetry Be a Sword!': How D.R. Nagaraj changed the way we read Gandhi and Ambedkar*, History Faculty Publication Series, Paper 2, http://scholarworks.umb.edu/cgi/viewcontent.cgi?article=1001&context=history_faculty_pubs (Last accessed 26 June, 2016).

Allowing People to Shape Our Democratic Future

Aruna Roy, Nikhil Dey, Praavita Kashyap, with the MKSS

'Time present and time past
Are both perhaps present in time future
And time future contained in time past.
If all time is eternally present
All time is unredeemable.
What might have been is an abstraction
Remaining a perpetual possibility
Only in a world of speculation.
What might have been and what has been
Point to one end, which is always present....'
(Eliot, 1936)

Summary

The essay explores social movements that have challenged the elite and have creatively used the non-electoral democratic space to have their voices heard, such as, MKSS, RTI and rights-based legislations. The coming up of mass movements, led by the people demanding transparency, accountability, wages, community rights, have pressed the nerve centres of the entire neoliberal structure. The rights-based campaigns led a discourse that went beyond counter-rhetoric and initiated much better understanding of the nature and challenges of participatory democracy.

The essay proposes the idea of direct democracy through a 'Rainbow coalition of grassroots social movements'. Such a coalition would facilitate cross-fertilization of ideas and bring out the intricate connections between economic, social, political rights with ecological rights. The essay raises a vexing question of finding space for the above vision in the midst of global power and financial capital, suggesting that the movements should strive for utopia by constantly bringing in the logical causality of democratic practice.

Introduction

Given the fact that democracy reflects complexity, dreams of the future are bound to be hazy, untidy and unfinished; the wonder lies in its ability to serve as a platform of our collective conscience. Unlike other utopian concepts, it does not allow space for the luxury of self-deception. Expectations rise and fall with its successes and failures, but hope stays to push the process on. We often overlook the etymology of the word – an acknowledgement that this system places ordinary people at the centre of its theory and practice. History has vindicated this hypothesis in keeping collective conscience and wisdom alive. Collective interest defines a more equitable, inclusive, and sustainable world.

The current evaluative discourse is coloured by the perceptions of the privileged. Despite misgivings Indian democracy has kept the electoral machine working. We might acknowledge collective action, but we rarely acknowledge the power and presence of collective thought. The challenging task of preparing a democratic vision for the future will have to give space and acknowledge the deliberate subaltern efforts of the past and the present. Since ordinary citizens do not have easy access to the visible and formal mainstream platforms of public debate, their opinion, aspirations and expectations can often be drawn from popular public action. As persons located in what is sometimes called 'peoples' or social movements' in India, this document will reflect and share, the hope that kindles and helps articulate our vision of the future.

With Independence in India, came democracy, and in theory at least, a government by the people. At the same time, those who were forced to share power and discard privilege found it extremely difficult to deal with the notion of peoples' participation. They worked to quickly adjust to the new Constitutional and legal framework, and used their existing power and influence to focus on areas where the electoral system could be manipulated and captured. The ruling classes with the underpinning of the feudal and colonial past continue to haunt us. They have succeeded in elite capture, and use every trick possible in the electoral system to regain and retain power. The displaced feudal chief has often come back as the elected leader. The dilemma is that though identity politics has been effective in a limited sense to overcome marginalization, it has also strengthened the basic caste structure in India; and given birth to a non-accountable elite that has captured leadership based on the idea of caste loyalties. The market has also created new elite. Contemporary democratic practice faces huge challenges and yet it is one of our only areas of hope.

India's future will last only as long as our commitment to democracy lasts. The elite critique of democracy is dismissive of its basic principles. During the independence movement, there was an understanding amongst elite groups of the need for freedom of expression and fundamental rights born from personal experience. Many of the leaders had spent years in jail, and had been part of a very sustained and celebrated national movement. This peoples' movement for freedom was enriched by the Gandhian principles of *satyagraha*, as well as vigorous debates between different ideological strains that were simultaneously working on a blueprint for the independent nation state. Democracy was the lowest common denominator, as all groups realized that the multiple identities, along with the intrinsic plurality and diversity across the subcontinent required space for expression and participation.

The elites within each group have continued to reap the benefits of an iniquitous economic and social milieu. A sophisticated exercise comprising extreme use of force against sub-national movements, and co-option of their leadership, has helped integrate the elites of those communities into the 'national mainstream'. An imperfect democracy has given marginalized people some space and voice, but their leadership has disproportionately benefited from the 'representative' character of the democratic framework. In fact, dissent voiced by large numbers of marginalized people has given their leadership an opportunity to join the mainstream elite – although they remain at the margins of that elite club. Neoliberal globalization and the market economy have given these elites an opportunity to better themselves – often at the cost of the economy, and by using their power and 'leadership' to squeeze their communities. A section of the poor – particularly tribal communities under siege for their mineral resources, land, water, and forests – has turned towards an armed counterforce for help and support. Many other small and decentralized efforts have attempted to assert their democratic right to participation. As community based struggles multiply, and dissent is manifested against the economic model using democratic modes of struggle, the elite leadership has begun to express impatience with democracy itself. For the poor and marginalized, democracy is a lifeline for expression and dissent.

As these social and economic struggles for equality and expression continue, democracy becomes a ground for contestation, at a level of concept and practice. Participation, decentralization, and self-rule are ideas that do not essentially question the nation state, but do help give space to more voices of dissent. Decentralization and self-rule also raise issues of internal democracy, especially in the entrenched hierarchies of caste Indian society. Democracy remains an imperfect place essential for the survival of these adversarial groups. For the poor and marginalized, perhaps the real challenge is to use democratic space to return to its conceptual roots and establish participatory modes which give each citizen a voice at all points and at all times. That is why the nature of democratic assertion has turned revolutionary slogans on their head: from an idea of overthrowing the state to laying ownership over the state – *'Yeh sarkar hamari aapki, Nahin kisi ke baap ki'* (this state is ours, it does not belong to anyone's father). It is this assertion that gave birth to the idea that people in a democracy can, and will, themselves ask questions and demand answers at all times. It also leads us down the path of a more institutionalized idea of a participatory democracy. For them, then, the nation state is themselves.

Social Movements and Participatory Politics

Peoples' movements (like the Narmada Bachao Andolan, Chipko Movement, Chhattisgarh Mukti Morcha) have tried to address issues related to power structures, but not been completely successful in preventing or overcoming the capture of electoral politics by the elite. At the same time, they have very effectively and creatively used the non-electoral democratic space to have their voices heard. Independent India has witnessed progressive social movements emerge from amongst India's most marginalized communities. The Narmada Bachao movement for example was one of the first anti-dam struggles in India that brought together people from across the country in support of the residents of the dam-affected area. The movement changed India's understanding of dams and fundamentally questioned the mainstream narrative of development. These movements have influenced Indian democracy, politics and development, in profound ways. It is a continuing irony that despite these efforts, the largest numbers became the fringe, and the minority elite continues to classify itself as the mainstream. Despite this classification, as exceptions on the fringes of the 'mainstream', the assertions of peoples' movements for equal participation and voice, marks the intersection of an uneasy engagement – between representative democracy and participatory democracy, between complementary and adversarial politics.

Those at the lower ends of the socio-economic hierarchy realized soon enough, that the struggle for freedom had to continue even after Independence. The structure of non-violent civil disobedience, a legacy of the national movement, shaped the struggle for justice and equality and influenced public action. The leadership of the freedom struggles pre-occupied with removing an external adversary faced the challenge of running the government, and its identification with the concerns of the poor, marginalized, and exploited took a subordinate place.

Ambedkar, who had struggled to find equal space for dalit and marginalized communities within the national movement, was far more sceptical and perhaps more realistic than Gandhi about what self-rule would mean. He quite rightly concentrated on a strong Constitutional framework, while realizing the limitations of law and governance in a democracy that inherited a feudal society and a market economy. Ambedkar's insightful apprehensions expressed just before the adoption of the Constitution continue to be relevant today:

> 'On the 26th of January 1950, we are going to enter into a life of contradictions. In politics we will have equality and in social and economic life we will have inequality. In politics we will be recognizing the principle of one man one vote and one vote one value. In our social and economic life, we shall, by reason of our social and economic structure, continue to deny the principle of one man one value.
>
> How long shall we continue to live this life of contradictions? How long shall we continue to deny equality in our social and economic life? If we continue to deny it for long, we will do so only by putting our political democracy in peril. We must remove this contradiction at the earliest possible moment or else those who suffer from inequality will blow up the structure of political democracy which this Assembly has so laboriously built up.'
>
> – *B.R. Ambekar's speech to the Constituent Assembly on November 25, 1949*[1]

Democratic Governance – claiming a share of power

The capture of representative democracy by elite structures shifted the focus of subaltern social movements to an ever-growing demand for participation and equality. In the complex and fractured divisions of class, caste, religion and gender, language and regional diversities, it has suited the ruling elite to dismiss peoples' participation in governance as disarray and chaos, accusing such efforts as contributing to inefficiency and 'misgovernance'. There is a litany of clever, misinformed myths created to reduce democracy to just the casting of the vote. The failure of performance because of corruption and arbitrary use of power became pinned to the rhetoric of socialism, equality, and *garibi hatao* (poverty alleviation). The proponents of inequality used the frustration with failure to discredit and dump ideas themselves; the market was offered as the panacea to all ills. The State seemed to respond to the demand for decentralization with the 73rd and 74th amendments to the Constitution (respectively providing greater powers to elected rural and urban bodies, at local levels), that did bring a vast number of elected representatives into the political sphere. However their real power was in question as the liberalization of India's economy in 1991 took away economic decision-making from local communities (Shrivastava and Kothari, 2012).

Markets and the Politics of Profit

In this market driven scenario it was argued that only purchasing power could meet basic needs. However, for the huge numbers without privileges of birth and money, the State cannot become irrelevant. While the State ironically reduced its own role, the most disadvantaged were struggling to ensure that the State did not abdicate its basic responsibility. The campaigns and struggles sought to re-establish the argument that the State had an obligation to protect the interests of the people against the unaccountable power of money.

Economic liberalization brought affluence to some and growth rates began to rise. The disadvantaged remained fighting for survival as before, as they continued to look for work and the basic necessities of health and food, to survive. The 'market' quite clearly failed to meet their basic minimum needs. They had no money to use the private hospitals, schools that mushroomed even in relatively small villages. Latest figures from India's Socio Economic Caste Census of 2014 show how far we have to go, particularly in rural India, even after almost 70 years of independence. 'Of the 300 million households surveyed, an overwhelming majority (73 per cent) live in villages. Of this rural population, less than 5 per cent earn enough to pay taxes, only 2.5 per cent own a 4-wheeler vehicle and less than 10 per cent have salaried jobs. Rural India has depressing statistics in education where access to education remains skewed with only 3.5 per cent of students graduating and around 35.7 per cent of residents who can't read or write'.[2]

Reforming the reforms

With the persistence of extreme poverty came the reinvention of basic concepts of reform. 'Land reform' meant facilitation of transfer of land to the rich, and land developers, symbolized by the passage of the SEZ Act. 'Labour reform', meant the dismantling of labour protection laws. Large numbers of people at the base of the economic pyramid felt the shrinking of responsibility and accountability of agencies of the State.

The corporate sector began to dabble in development efforts, and corporate social responsibility (CSR) was presented as the more efficient form of 'charity' to the 'destitute'. In one sense this took the discourse back to an earlier generation when development was considered assistance to the poor or marginalised in the form of welfare rather than empowerment. What is worse, today CSR appears to be a way for companies to enhance their social image; it can also be used to fund government programmes in partnership with companies, making dangerous incursions into the arena of government. Model villages, projects, schools, and a 'reformed' and liberalised media began to look for 'happy stories' to promote the new design. Electronic and print media were 'liberated' from the burden of being the 'fourth estate'. The reality reflected in human development indicators have continued to aggregate stories of malnutrition, starvation, illiteracy, and poor health. A new interpretation of civil society intervention called public private partnerships (PPP) emerged. The private sector was enabled to play the development role for government, for a price. Independent or more politically conscious 'civil society' was not a part of this framework.

Through the Looking Glass – the MKSS, the RTI, and democratic explorations

A group of activists moved to a tiny village, Devdungri in central Rajasthan in mid 1987 at the cusp of market globalization. Living and working through the late 80s' and early 90s', they watched from the 'grassroots' an India being overtaken by events across the world. A little over 1000 people came together on the 1st of May 1990 in a small town called Bhim to form the Mazdoor Kisan Shakti Sangathan (MKSS). The ruling elite saw it as a quixotic effort, out of sync with the times. For them, a workers and peasants organization was seen as aligned to Moscow and Beijing, born irrelevant. The MKSS and its constituents were deeply uncomfortable with the so-called market paradigm. It continued to swim against the tide – albeit in a limited area in Rajasthan. The early and mid 90s', saw the beginnings of the campaign for Right to Information (RTI) and the battle for guaranteed wage employment. The people of the area demanded work, minimum wages, and copies of the accounts and documents of development expenditure. This pressed on the nerve centres of corruption and exploitation in the administrative system. The demand for transparency and access to official records had begun. It was initially met with incredulity and denial by the system – that the provision of records was an 'impossible' demand to meet.

Hum Janenge, Hum Jiyenge (We will Know, We will Live)

At the time, some social movements supportive of the MKSS' land and minimum wage struggles were deeply sceptical about the RTI campaign, perceived as a dilution of its core concerns. Ordinary people thought differently, they saw the direct link between basic needs juxtaposed with exploitation and manipulation of records with impunity. The stealing and deprivation was experienced everyday when development funds were stolen, false entries made in the records. Mohan*ji*,[3] a member of the MKSS, a *dalit* activist, singer, composer and lyricist, composed a song in 1990 where he sang:

'pehle waale chor bhaiya bandookon se maarte thhe,
abhi waale chor to kalmon se maare re – Raj choron ka!'

(The earlier thieves used to kill with guns, the thieves of today kill with pens – The state is made of thieves!)

Disclosure of papers exposed real thieves. This time the arbitrary use of caste and class power did not work in the face of irrefutable 'evidence'. The innovative platform of the '*jan sunwai*' (public hearing) evolved as a mode to audit official accounts and implementation in the public domain, worked to establish the truth. A new dynamic was born, almost like a chemical reaction. The dissemination of information and ensuing debates brought a dramatic change in power relationships. The hearings brought the poor and the middle class together in a new alliance. The focus was State irresponsibility, lack of financial transparency and a need for accountable governance.

India not Shining – pressure for new enactments

When the India Shining campaign failed to give the Bharatiya Janta Party (BJP) a second term, it was seen as an acknowledgement and as an assertion of popular will against the neo-liberal reform driven model of development. The MKSS witnessed the organic growth of a powerful movement emerging for transparency, the Right to Information, and a democratic demand for a share in governance. The marginalized wanted a more responsive, accountable government in which they could participate. 'Peoples' movements' reflected the political aspirations of people within a democratic framework of rights.

In 2004, the newly elected United Progressive Alliance (UPA) Government (anchored by the Congress party but with several other parties including the Left parties), acknowledged the nature of the mandate by issuing a set of promises, through the National Common Minimum Programme (NCMP). At least three landmark legislations articulated by social movements were passed: The Right to Information Act, the National Rural Employment Guarantee Act, and the Scheduled Tribes and Other Traditional Forest Dwellers (Recognition of Forest Rights) Act (in short, the Forest Rights Act). The basic structure of these legislations were drafted with inputs from peoples' movements, that included a broad cross section, including people living at the grassroots, academics, journalists, even retired judges. These legislations provided a new set of significant entitlements to the people, and recognized the democratic need to empower ordinary citizens and fix responsibility on the State to deliver. These promised legislations would not have been passed without sustained campaigning and pressure on the UPA Government.

The persistent pressure on government, political parties, and a public debate, clause by clause, even as the legislations were being forwarded to parliament later, marked a new period in the engagement of peoples' organizations and movements with the mainstream policy making process. A broad coalition in support of these legislations emerged in and out of parliament, as social movements, one section of the Congress, and the Left parties worked together to make the promises in the NCMP a reality. These legislations began to be used from the date of their passage. The laws such as the RTI sustained and strengthened the movements. Despite repeated attempts to amend and dilute the law, including by the Courts, the use of the RTI has grown. It has changed power relationships, starting from the poor in the village who had to beg the powerful even to access basic entitlements like food and employment, to the ordinary person who could now ask questions of the Supreme Court and the Prime Minister's office and demand accountability. In addition, people have been able to play a role in exposing major scams relating to coal block and spectrum allotment, land deals, and development policy and allocation, in every aspect of governance and power. It is manifest in the movement's expanding impact, with a growing capacity to protect the legislation.

The election result of 2004 was a clear rejection of the 'India Shining' Campaign of the National Democratic Alliance (NDA) and therefore presented a unique moment in the political discourse. The UPA, in its first term (2004-2009) had two contradictory streams – one which recognised the strong reaction of the unorganised sector and agricultural communities to a growth trajectory that had often come at their cost, the other celebrated the growth rate, and insisted on a corporate driven growth agenda. Thanks to this stream in the UPA, foreign domestic investment and stock market indices continued to be a more important indication of success than increased spending and utilization of rural development funds. Reform led to a series of international treaties and trade agreements determining the economic policies with a deep impact on peoples' lives. On the other hand the National Common Minimum Program (NCMP) of the UPA's first term was a set of promises to the people of India. The rights-based legislations promised in the NCMP became a part of an accountable set of measures and legislations. They were backed by the Left parties who played an important role in counter-veiling corporate interests and supporting the rights-based legislations. In UPA's second term (2009-14), in the absence of a clear set of promises, and with the Left parties having left the coalition, the new rights-based legislations under consideration including the Land Acquisition Act and the Food Security Act, were severely diluted before being passed by Parliament. The nature of Indian democracy was changing once again.

How Democratic is 'Civil Society'?

'Civil society' grew but its extremely diverse character was still to be acknowledged and understood. In contemporary political phraseology, the conglomerate of non-party political formations is sometimes referred to as a part of 'civil society'. Civil society is made up of a range of organizations; including many that specifically identify themselves as non-political. While civil society is a more recent term, the earlier phraseology like NGOs, and voluntary organizations failed to distinguish between the objective and working process of different organizations. Even where terms like 'community-based organizations' (CBOs) were used it did not identify what the particular purpose of the organization would be. Therefore one of the most important ways to define any organization is to identify its purpose and connect it with its politics. In an India divided by class, caste, gender and religion, the crisscross of feudal, modern, bigoted and the rational, no one definition could cover all. The label civil society was and is a misnomer that tries to standardize a very plural people. Different formations might sometimes agree on the importance of an issue, but expectations and ideas are varied and often contradictory. Therefore it is important for all organizations to make clear their purpose, alliances and broad political ideology. Even for those who choose not to call themselves political, the rest of us need to understand their politics within the democratic framework – whom they prioritize, why, what their positions are on equality in access to resources and decision making. The new emphasis on equality and access to decision-making is what has led to the varied movements for a participatory democracy.

Civil society organizations need to be classified in a manner similar to the way political parties are, by their ideologies and their constituencies. At a time when political mobilizations are taking place around popular issues, there are claims and counter claims from different sides of the ideological spectrum, on representing 'the people'. It is therefore extremely important to understand who 'the people' are, and what conception there is of the future. For the MKSS, State, people, and civil society have been and will remain a deeply interlinked complex web that needs to be better understood for the greater common good.

From Rhetoric to Practice

Although the MKSS was never aligned to a political party it accepted that democratic processes are deeply political. To that extent the MKSS has been and remains a political organization, aligned to the rights of the poor and marginalized.

The MKSS began to shape the tools and means with people who stood to gain the most through participatory democracy – to analyze the cause and the effect of law and policy, to trace the benefits. The popularly accepted rhetoric of transparency and accountability had to be used, to transform and truly democratize the structures of government and governance. Governance in independent India had to be made far more inclusive and participatory, and all the processes of governance needed to be made transparent along with all the manifestations. It became clear, that forcing the structures of power to take note, change their relationship with the citizen, and incorporate such changes in law and practice, was imperative for the struggle towards any form of equality.

The campaigns for the right to work, right to information, right to food, all addressed basic questions of entrenched inequality and injustice. The discourse matured and went beyond mere counter-rhetoric and demands. The indifference to government and governance changed to a demand for participation, and an assertion that the functioning of democracy must be bottom up. In this paradigm, 'good governance' as defined by international agencies like the World Bank was challenged and juxtaposed with the real demands and architecture of 'democratic governance' as defined by people's movements. Participation of ordinary people and social movements in the pre-legislative, legislative, implementation, and auditing process, was an essential cornerstone of the definition of democratic governance. Therefore the top-down approach of thrusting policies formulated by corporates and technocrats on the people and defining their implementation as 'good governance' was being continually questioned. Instead people insisted that democratic participation extended beyond the vote to ensure people and their voices were incorporated within every act of governance. The importance of using statistics, building theoretical frameworks, drafting policies, and legislations, answering the critiques, had become clear to such campaigns and movements when they began to stake a claim in the decision-making process. This also initiated a much better understanding of the challenges of the nature of participatory democracy. The transformation of a common sense idiom into the language of governance was a singular contribution of all the peoples' campaigns of the last two decades; examples include the movement towards 'tribal self-rule' in many *adivasi* regions of central and eastern India, or the work of Urban Setu in Bhuj at empowering urban citizens with information, enabling them to be part of the town's governance.[4]

Attack on Rights Based Legislations and Freedom of Expression

The last decade of both the UPA II government and the new Modi-led BJP government have seen determined attempts from the ruling elite to undermine and dilute the rights-based legislations. The rights-based legislations and the right to participate are under threat. In 2014, a new government came to power where the political dispensation has fashioned a critique of the last government, with a spurious argument that India's economic decline was because of rights based laws – even legislations unanimously supported in parliament. It seems like the frontal attacks have now been replaced by attempts to surreptitiously undermine the laws and even the basic framework of the Constitution. Dissent from the mainstream, accepted paradigm of development is seen as a threat. The right to freedom of expression is not an esoteric right confined to intellectual debates and rights – it is fundamental to a healthy democracy. People who have the courage and the commitment to face the ire of the state, and who question the arbitrary use of power are targeted. Yet they continue to try and use the space created by constitutional guarantees to restrict their rights by the government and its agents.

The unease of the government, past or present, demonstrates how these rights based participatory laws are actually changing basic relationships between the voter and the representative. The design of the RTI enabled citizens to realize their sovereignty, changing the unequal relationship between citizens and government. It has challenged concentrations of power, and made the state accountable and responsive to the common citizen. The RTI has grown into an immensely popular movement with approximately 5-8 million RTI applications a year. While the RTI has had huge successes, the act of filing an RTI and even getting part of an answer triggers off a process of challenging the arbitrary use of power. Users have threatened entrenched power with focused questions. Even though more than 46 of them have been murdered because they dared to challenge the impunity of the powerful, the number of applications continues to increase. The RTI has evolved into a decentralized, self-generated process, enabling ordinary people to participate in governance to the best of their ability, using constitutional legitimacy and asserting the right to sovereignty. The legal imagination of the RTI Act can be seen in the proviso to its exemption clause (section 8) for instance: 'Provided that the information which cannot be denied to the Parliament or a State Legislature shall not be denied to any person.' It is the first law that puts the elected representative at par with the voter and penalises the officer personally for not providing information.

From Transparency to Accountability

India has survived an onslaught on the rights-based legislations by a hostile political regime. Questions have advanced from transparency towards accountability. The conception of the RTI came from ordinary people, and they faced the problems of lack of accountability. In Bhilwara, celebrating Ambedkar Jayanti (Babasaheb Ambedkar's birth anniversary), a group of dalits defined their concept of journeying towards a more accountable and equal society.

They said they needed: '*Jankari, Sunwayi, Karvayi, Bhaghidari, Surakshsa*' (information, hearing, time bound action, participation, and protection). The MKSS added the sixth – an open democratic platform like the Jan Sunwai. Popularly known as the 'Bhilwara Principles', they have become part of the political lexicon of the MKSS.

The last decade has seen rights-based movements make extraordinary gains with a slew of legislations, while the larger framework and direction of development and politics marched on in the opposite direction. We are faced with a question of whether these embryonic movements of widespread decentralization, participatory and incremental political change, eventually produce an alternate vision to address some of the fundamental crises of our time – the human and ecological condition.

Social movements in India have provided some signs of hope and credible alternative paradigms. With the RTI for instance, there are a million mutinies (between 8 to 10 million annual applications) against corruption and arbitrary action. The RTI Act is an example of a huge, deliberate, and popular search for alternatives. If one were to zoom in to examine the details of the applications, we would see that the RTI Act is strongly based on the principles and the human urge for equality and participation defining the natural trajectory of a popular movement. There is a desire for transparency and to transmute the obvious logic of democratic rights into accountability. The RTI has created and crafted a practical tool that every ordinary citizen can use. This expression of a right does not reject the necessity of representative democracy, but underscores the need for accountability.

Workers and peasants in central Rajasthan had a daily struggle to access everyday necessities. They were sharp enough to realize that their battle for copies of the muster rolls, bills and vouchers, contained very broad principles of transparency, the right to information, the right to expression, the right to life and indeed the right to demand equality.

It is perhaps the same common sense assertion of what is needed, that led to a simple and straightforward demand for the Employment Guarantee Act. '*Har haath ko kaam do, kaam ka poora daam do!*' (Let every labouring hand get work and give full (just) wages for every work) was the slogan that actually put forth a most obvious universal desire to be gainfully employed and receive a fair and just remuneration for work done. Ask any worker or citizen anywhere in India whether they subscribe to these basic principles of work and there will be universal affirmation. Work is essential to life, livelihood, and the joy of human existence. With that there must be dignity, equality, and the ability to make life choices. The demand for a stipulated number of days of work at minimum wages cannot be seen as a fulfilment of that human urge. It is the beginnings of establishing every individual's right to work, employment, and livelihood. In neo-liberal times, this very small demand seemed an impossible dream. There was a universal discussion of a shrinking state in a time when the state took on the responsibility for policing dissent and enforcing free trade. It was acknowledged that huge numbers of people would suffer the ill effects of this global market economy. Safety nets were to be designed to keep a drowning population's nose just above the water level. If the RTI was frowned upon as giving too many political rights to the citizen, the idea of enshrining any economic or development rights in law should have been rejected outright. And yet the NREGA was legislated at the time when neo-liberal globalization was in its full stretch.

The potential in Indian democracy reached a kind of fruition when the RTI and NREGA together pushed a spate of rights-based legislations that put the citizen at the centre of economic, social, and political entitlements. When the time came for implementation, information had to be extracted from bureaucrats who had every reason to hide their deeds and misdeeds. Guaranteed employment had to be provided by functionaries who were most threatened by it. That is why these movements have forced a discourse on a vision of democracy that would challenge the concentration of power and vested interests of the ruling elite. This manifested itself in not only proposing, but also attempting to institutionalize within the laws, the modes of participation and accountability to the people.

The Challenge of Institutionalizing Direct Democracy

For the citizen, the RTI represents a huge breakthrough from the limitations of the once in five-year vote syndrome of representative democracy where they are trapped without practical avenues of participation. The RTI allowed the citizen to make links to transparency, accountability and participation as initiated and controlled by citizens. This is a fundamental first step in moving toward direct democracy. In the lexicon of peoples' movements, this is also a different paradigm from one that assumes that change will only come after the overthrow of the state and its replacement by another, better (read, us) set of rulers. Through the provision of slogans that move from *humara paisa, humara hisab* (our money, our accounts) to *paise humare aap ke, nahin kisi ke baap ke* (money is ours not yours or your dynasty's) and then to *sarkar humare aap ki, nahin kisi ke baap ki* (government is ours not yours or your dynasty's), the RTI movement laid its claim to governance itself, at all times and on all matters. This enables and empowers all citizens at all times to question any decision-makers and legitimizes the value of their opinion.

The institutionalizing of direct democracy also requires us to go beyond slogans and rhetoric and work out the nuts bolts and procedures of the direct democracy paradigm. In social audits therefore, it is not just a group of people coming together to express an opinion on a matter and calling it a *jan sunwai* or a social audit. Like any audit procedure it requires a set of necessary conditions, a certain amount of facilitation, ensuring access to understandable information, a platform that records peoples' comments and necessary outcomes. All this needs to be done on a regular basis whether or not there are groups in that area. Similarly a participatory pre-legislative consultative process requires a set of procedures before it can really be considered a credible paradigm of decision-making. The RTI has enabled the practical institutionalization of peoples' participation and direct democracy.

Transparency was obviously only a first step. But knowing was not enough, there had to be the capacity to enforce accountability: to ask questions and secure answers, to examine, to analyze, to suggest, monitor, and audit whatever was being done in the name of the people. The popular slogan *humara paisa, humara hisab* (our money, our accounts) began to be incorporated in the concept of public audits and statutory social audits. While the constitutional right to freedom of speech and expression had given democratic space to people to express themselves, it was the vote that gave them the power to seat and unseat rulers. Bringing rulers to account in a day-to-day fashion has only happened through these institutionalized forms of participatory governance. The RTI gave the right to demand answers, and social audit empowered every citizen to ensure compliance. These are small persistent modes for a continual attempt to break concentrations of power that exist even in an elected government. It answers the often heard supercilious remark from the system, 'you voted them in, now suffer them!'

The RTI and social audit are generic modes that can be used by all movements fighting for justice on the basis of truth. They can only function in a synergetic relationship with democratic space and practice. In fact they string together a rainbow coalition of the marginalized. The RTI has shown it has a transformative potential for any individual or movement facing unaccountable power. The idea of public audit moves beyond information towards institutionalized accountability. These are cultural movements, changing relationships, and bringing about change even in those who use it to question.

The RTI is not a magic wand capable of creating utopia but it is an expression of how common sense, collective action, and democratic practice can come together to change things on an ongoing basis. We can confidently say that the RTI has already strengthened our democracy in important ways, and posterity will still see it as landmark legislation and as seminal to fostering direct democracy. Most importantly, the human rights, ecological and social movements for justice, equality and freedom intertwine to represent human aspirations for a sustainable future.

Vision for the future

We stand at a point in history when apparently rulers of countries around the world have accepted capitalism, the market, and economic growth as a dominant development paradigm. The capitalist framework not only accepts inequality but also encourages it. It is a system that has not managed to provide the majority (i.e., particularly in the global south) access to basic human needs. It has corroded justice and dignity. Wealth is concentrated in smaller and smaller groups of affluent people and corporations, encouraging phenomenal and irrational greed. It asserts without a qualm that the continued deprivation of a majority of people is an inevitable but manageable corollary. The most blatant and unsustainable consequence of this paradigm is the threat to ecological balances and the future of the Earth. It is not just climate change but also the plunder of finite resources at an alarming and unrelenting pace. At this pace evidence tells us the Earth will collapse. And yet, the dominant paradigm hurtles on.

Independent grassroots peoples' movements are perhaps an organic attempt to address the tension between political equality of the vote and continued social and economic inequality of social identities and capitalism. These democratic movements have asserted rights to fundamentally question inequality of all kinds. They have used the political equality of the vote, to show its limitations, and used participation so gained, to fight economic and social inequality. Social movements have begun to construct, brick by brick, the architecture of participatory democracy, a vision which details the possibility of incremental but fundamental change. The growing synergy between peoples' movements has also allowed an organic cross-fertilization of ideas, to enable people to see the intrinsic connections between economic, social and political rights, with ecology and the control over natural resources. Control over natural resources is vital to the existence of communities. It is understood too, that only the equal rights of community-owned natural resources will ensure their organic and sustained regeneration.

The Rainbow Coalition of Peoples' Movements

The whole range of movements, organizations and persons engaged in participatory democracy for control over natural resources and in participatory decision-making is a rainbow coalition. One of the safeguards is that everyone has equal access to power based on citizenship. The RTI movement has been the empowering of people within that political equality. The coalition between those saying local decision-making and those saying that the basis of decision-making must be equal access to information and common property resources, that whole range comes together to deepen the understanding of how decisions can be taken at the local level. Everyone has great expertise and experience in each area and the coming together gives us a composite understanding. So the coming together helps us construct a social economic political framework based on participatory decision-making.

It is clear that the growth obsession is a spiral to self-destruction. Will 'participatory' decision-making, local markets, grassroots movements, and social constructs based on equality be able to counter the myths of consumer satisfaction sold by global power of finance and capital? Can an alternate vision of a more just, equitable, and sustainable future find space to communicate and spread globally? Can we have a democratic polity that respects plurality and the sanctity of basic equality, and human rights for all?

As Ambedkar pointed out, social hierarchies and unbridled capitalism are inimical to democracy. There are enough popular voices that seek to weave together, pluralism, justice, and equality in democratic practice. How can rationality win the battle against the arguments for instant gratification? In fact, the strength of popular movements is their tenacity to state the rational, and to never let these questions be passed by. They understood, as Eliot did, that logical causality binds the present irrevocably to the past and the future. It is a vision that accepts the rights of all, while diligently and persistently exploring the possibilities of democratic practice. It is imperative to protect the fundamental right to express with freedom in a democracy. The voices, which speak truth to power, persist and continue to articulate, keeping democracy's legacy alive.

Eduardo Galeano, quoting Fernando Birri said, 'Utopia is on the horizon. As I move two steps closer; it moves two steps further away. I walk another ten steps and the horizon is ten steps further away. ... I'll never reach it. So what's the point of a utopia? The point is: to keep us walking' (Manrique et al., 2001).

When we move beyond the radical revolutionary idea of overthrow of the state – the problem is, what will the new state look like and how to ensure that the new set of rulers will not fall prey to the same power problems? So with the RTI the government is answerable to each individual at all times, laying claim to the state. The continual process of breaking concentrations of power is strengthened by the RTI. It will always seem like there is a further horizon. The point is to keep going, to keep learning and to collectively participate in building better futures.

Acknowledgement

As we all know, thinking is not dependent on literacy, and our mental vocabulary is not restricted by the ability to read or write. Collective thinking and writing gives us the space to acknowledge the wisdom of the people. All writings, including articles, memorial lectures, convocation addresses and speeches accredited to individuals working in the MKSS, owe their ideas, ideology and theoretical assumptions to the MKSS collective.

Endnotes

1. See details in http://parliamentofindia.nic.in/ls/debates/vol11p11.htm (Accessed in March 2017).
2. For details refer to http://edition.cnn.com/2015/08/02/asia/india-poor-census-secc/ (Accessed in March 2017).
3. In India the word '*ji*' suffixed to a name is used to accord respect.
4. See http://bhujbolechhe.org/en/partners/urban-setu-initiative-kutch-nav-nirmav-abhiyan and https://www.academia.edu/5875292/Setu_Bhuj_Bridging_governance_gap (Accessed in March 2017).

References

Eliot, T.S., 1936, 'Burnt Norton', in *Collected Poems: 1909–1962*, London: Faber and Faber.

Manrique, J., Eva Golinger and Eduardo Galeano, 2001, 'Galeano' (an interview), BOMB, No. 75 (Spring), pp. 54-59, http://www.jstor.org/stable/40426766 (accessed 18 April 2017).

Shrivastava, A. & A. Kothari, 2012, *Churning the Earth: The Making of Global India,* Delhi: Viking/ Penguin India Books.

Legal Futures for India

Arpitha Kodiveri

Summary

The essay examines the opportunities and limitations of law in India and gives the examples that illustrate its dynamic nature and the range of factors (social, political, economic, and cultural) that influence it. The essay argues for a legal future that strives for a social democracy, by engaging with the principles of decentralisation, equality and innovation in justice delivery.

The Indian legal system has three major daunting challenges: access to justice, social acceptance of law, and multiple forms of injustice. To combat these challenges, the essay proposes opening up of the legislature and the judiciary to common citizens as a method of actively engaging citizens impacted by legal issues to participate in the process of making law as well as resolving legal disputes. Central to this, is the creation of mediation centres that can play a crucial role in establishing a constant connection between law and society to bring out layers and complex notions of identity.

Introduction

W. H. Auden (1940) in his poem 'Law, like Love' writes:
Law is neither wrong nor right,
Law is only crimes
Punished by places and by times,
Law is the clothes men wear
anytime, anywhere,
Law is Good morning and Good night.

Others say, Law is our Fate;
Others say, Law is our State;

138

Others say, others say
Law is no more,
Law has gone away.

(Auden, 1940, pp. 113)

Law as Auden describes it determines the everyday and is omnipresent in our lives. More so he describes the law as a site of struggle where its source, implementation and interests are contested and like love these struggles bring with them possibilities as well as a constant churn of transformation. India's legal history stands testament to such struggle where multiple interests are debated whilst embedded in a complex societal fabric. This social fabric is contextualized by issues of caste, class, poverty and gender. There have been several critical junctures in India's legal travails but a few key moments have been – the making of India's Constitution in 1950 which serves as the supreme legal framework; the political emergency in 1975 which in some ways paved the beginning of human rights; women's rights and environmental movements; and the economic reforms of 1991, to name a few. These critical junctures have seen the passing of some progressive legal opinions and legislations and some that are regressive and violate the ethos of the Constitution. Yet this fragmented nature of law is what allows it to act as an enabler as well as a constraint in our path to seek social, economic, political and ecological justice. The law is subject to a myriad of influences from social movements to mere expression of economic intent, it is the negotiation of these influences that the law to an extent facilitates or defines.

Extending from this abstract understanding of the legal realm in India as one where influences, powers and interest are negotiated, I would like to elicit this dynamic nature of law in recent examples where these interests have been negotiated through street protests, parliamentary processes, and the enforcement and implementation of law. It is through these examples that I would like to chronicle the opportunities and limitations that the use of law has as an instrument in achieving sustainability, equity and justice before venturing into the possible legal futures.

On 16 December 2012 'Nirbhaya' a 23 year old physiotherapy intern was brutally gang raped in Delhi. This act of violence triggered country wide protests demanding safety for women and justice for the victim. This demand for justice increased the pressure on the judiciary to react appropriately to the crime. What often goes unnoticed is how this country-wide unrest and street protests created an avenue for direct engagement with the judiciary and legislature. The demand for safety of women was couched with an urgent need for legal reforms that could address these demands. These protests, along with the pressure from other sources like the international media, resulted in the formation of a judicial committee headed by Justice Verma which suggested reforms to the existing criminal law framework (Narang, 2014). These reforms were then adopted in the form of the Criminal Law (Amendment) Ordinance, 2013, which altered the legal landscape while dealing with crimes against women. The challenge still remains that despite this legal framework the amount of time taken to address rape cases continues to be slow despite the setting up of six fast track courts (Shakil, 2014). The case has however increased the amount of public discussion on violence against women and the number of cases reported has increased since the Nirbhaya incident (Narang, 2014). It is here that the challenge emerges where progressive legal reforms that cross the institutional barriers of the judiciary and the legislative through a judicial committee set the foundation for legal redress for victims of violence. Yet, for the reforms to be implemented, it requires a drastic shift in the functioning of the judiciary whose institutional memory needs to dramatically absorb these reforms. This, in many ways, is a key challenge that the use of legal reforms puts forth which requires a paradigm shift in its functioning. The use of street protests provided for increased public discussion and created an enabling environment for more women to come out and report their cases but the institutional response to these reports remain weak. This was a unique instance where the law responded to the nationwide protests. There was a sense of unison in the legal and public imagination. This however does not occur often.

Let us now take the case of Section 377 of the Indian Penal Code which states:

> 'Unnatural offences—whoever voluntarily has carnal intercourse against the order of nature with any man, woman or animal—shall be punished with imprisonment for life, or with imprisonment of either description for a term which may extend to ten years, and shall also be liable to fine.'

This section criminalizes sexual activities which are 'against the order of nature'. This is a case where the Lesbian, Gay, Bisexual and Transgender (LGBT) community were criminalized within the existing legal framework. Its constitutionality came to be challenged in the High Court of Delhi by the Naz Foundation and it went on to be decriminalized where adult consensual sexual activities in private were permitted. When this decision came to be challenged in the Supreme Court, Section 377 was upheld. This exposes one of the core challenges that are embedded in the use of law and the courts in particular, for justice. The hierarchical structure, which allows for appeals to higher courts which at times can allow for better redress, can also result in a change from a progressive to a regressive decision. This occurred in the present case. What is more important to note is that in the case of Nirbhaya there was a semblance of alliances across different segments of society in relation to its demand for justice while in the present case this alliance building is still taking place. The degree of social acceptance towards the LGBT community is quite low and this brings us to the other challenge and opportunity that the law presents. The challenge is whether striking down Section 377 would create more social acceptance towards the community or if an evolved societal imagination that allows for acceptance would result in the same being reflected in law. This inter-relationship is present in most cases concerning marginalized communities and the law becomes the site for contestation.

In the case where the Narmada Bachao Andolan tried to challenge the construction of the Sardar Sarovar Dam on the grounds that it would cause large scale displacement of *adivasis* and other local communities in the area, the Supreme Court dismissed the petition on the basis that the larger purpose of the dam was to provide water for irrigation and drinking purposes especially to non-riparian states like Rajasthan. This hierarchy of the rights of water of certain communities at the cost of compromising the right of adivasis to their land and waters is another instance where judicial discretion in interpreting a legal dispute reinforces power structures. Such preference of the rights of one community at the cost of the other is a complex balancing act but the scales often weigh heavier to the side of those communities that are more powerful by virtue of aligning with the development agenda of the state and correspond to state interests. The language of rights is thus fraught with the question where legitimate rights holders are denied rights by giving preference to claims emerging from communities more powerful.

The legislature as a site for struggle or the push for drafting new legislations to address injustice have been successful, yet like the other approaches of using the law, they come with their specific set of challenges. The Forest Rights Act is an example where historical injustice committed to forest dwelling communities by denying them their rights in forest areas through colonial forest laws was challenged and their rights were recognized. This is an example where the political struggle found its expression in a new legislation, and it was possible because these efforts were complemented by political will in the then United Progressive Alliance government to pass such a law. The legislature also acts as what John Austin (1980), a noted legal philosopher called a space where law becomes the command of the sovereign, and this can be seen in the proposed amendments to India's environmental laws[1] and the passing of a new land ordinance[2] that shrinks the democratic space available for communities impacted by it to articulate their interests[3]. In this case the political will is moving towards growth centric legal amendments. The challenge then of achieving the goals of social, economic and political justice through shaping legislative discourse in India is that it is subject to the changing priorities of the government in power.

These instances illustrate the challenges associated with using the law and the ability of law to address injustice. These challenges can be located more broadly in problems of access to justice, social acceptance of law and law's ability to address the multifaceted nature of injustice.

Future of Law

In 2047 I would envision that the law has been able to break down existing power structures that maintain social, economic and political inequality in India. The law achieves this ideal of justice by opening up the legislature and judiciary to greater citizen participation where citizens have internalized the virtues of rights and rule of law. There are three components to this vision of law.

Firstly, ensuring access to justice by changing the current form of the legislature and the judiciary to be more localized and citizen driven.

Second, enabling the making of a society where values of justice, equality and sustainability are virtues that are prioritized and expressed through law.

Third, ensuring access to justice by expanding the existing notion of procedure accepted by law, particularly in relation to evidence. By expanding the notion of procedure what I am aiming at is the loosening of procedural barriers particularly criteria of what amounts to evidence. I propose a radical shift where criteria for evidence under the Indian Evidence Act, 1972 are softened to accommodate communities or citizens who have been marginalized from gaining access to such evidence, particularly when it is being produced to access rights. An example of this is in the Forest Rights Act, 2006 where communities who are unable to provide evidence such as land records for claiming their rights within forest areas can produce a statement by an elder reduced to writing[4]. This softening of criteria will enable access to justice by overcoming the evidentiary barrier. Evidence as understood legally usually involves state-legitimized facts, or scientific information whose authenticity is usually ensured by the recommendation of certain labs by state actors. This monopolization of evidence in the hands of the state, particularly in access to rights, acts as a barrier for communities unable to afford the costs of sourcing such evidence. The Right to Information Act, 2005 acts as a critical link in breaking this monopolization of legal evidence by the state, but this continues to involve a process of engaging with the state in request for information. It is the lack of this complete disengagement with the state which frames the evidentiary barrier to rights. In light of the procedural innovation as put forth in the FRA, I propose that community generated legal evidence like oral histories should be considered authentic and accepted by law. Testimonies of events already enter the realm of legally accepted form of evidence to validate the happenings of an incident. I propose the expansion of this notion of evidence to apply to rights claims. For instance in the case of a claimed right to cultural heritage for a community, oral histories and songs that allude to such cultural links should be considered as authentic evidence. These three arms will have to feed into each other to allow law to break the existing power structures by creating enough room for them to be challenged by citizens. It would also impact these power centres which may take the form of large corporations or the state.

Opening up the Legislature and Judiciary

Presently the functions of the legislature and judiciary are controlled by the state, with limited scope for citizen participation. Citizen participation is curtailed to electing a representative government and contributing to functioning of local authorities which were a product of decentralization. To enable more citizen engagement I propose the complete restructuring of the current form of the legislature and the judiciary. This restructuring is grounded in the values of access to justice and citizen controlled process of formulation of law and dispute resolution.

The legislature is presently composed of two houses of parliament the Lok Sabha (House of the People) and Rajya Sabha (Council of States) which act as two avenues to balance the interests of the centre and the state. It is my contention that within this structure the process of law making becomes an act of power struggle between elected political parties in the different houses while the citizens impacted by the bill are sometimes invited to provide comments on the proposed legislation.

What if we open up the legislature to a third house at the lowest unit level of governance where bills can be proposed, debated and discussed? The 73rd and 74th amendment to the Indian Constitution[5] devolved executive and administrative powers to rural and urban areas but did not devolve legislative powers. The relevance of laws is specific to the realities in different geographies and this subjectivity is not adequately captured in the Rajya Sabha. This decentralization of legislative powers will prevent the law becoming the command of the sovereign and engender accountability to citizens in the legislative process. This process will allow for the making of more nuanced legislation as the impact of the proposed legislation on different communities will be negotiated. For direct democracy to be realized there is a need for legislative intent to be subject to debate and critical analysis which has the power to reshape and change it.

To illustrate how this would function we can take the example of the proposed land ordinance. The ordinance proposed to do away with the consent clause for the acquisition of land either for public purpose[6] or public-private partnership projects. If this third house of parliament were alive this amendment to the existing land acquisition act would require the approval with two-thirds majority of the different *grams* (village units) and municipality units (assuming here that this will function as the lowest unit of governance) to this bill. The resistance to the introduction of this clause by Adivasi's, Dalits and farmers can be legitimately expressed in the third house and the upper houses will be legally bound to consider this resistance and alter the bill. This may seem like a herculean task to involve the different grams and municipality units. Yet this will ensure that the consent and considerations of the impacted population are adequately taken into account in the legislative decision making process.

This structure will also give the grams and municipality units' agency in introducing laws applicable to their area making legislative response more specific to the issues experienced in the area, and provide an avenue for customary laws to find its way into the formal legal process. The challenges with this approach are many as it may result in multiplicity of laws and create more conflict, yet it can act as a potential medium to strengthen the relationship between the citizen and the state structures in the legislative process.

The judiciary in India is a multi-layered and complex structure which is suffering from issues of inefficiency and access to justice. The present judicial structure consists of the courts, namely, the district courts, High courts and the Supreme Court as well as specialized courts and tribunals like the administrative tribunals and the Lok Adalats[7] which form a part of the alternative dispute resolution mechanisms available. The present structure has tried to address the question of access to justice by diversion of disputes to specialized legal avenues like the National Green Tribunal, reducing the burden on courts; expanding the notion of *locus standi*[8] through the public interest litigation system thereby increasing access to courts (Bhagwati & Dias, 2012). Present attempts have been the establishment of *Gram Nyayalayas*[9] (village courts) in different panchayats. Though the state has attempted through these different methods to increase access to justice, whether these approaches actually increases access is yet to be studied. I speculate that though the present structure attempts to address the question of access to justice it falls short, as it does not place sufficient emphasis on methods of mediation and negotiation.[10] The adversarial method of conflict resolution can cost the parties to the dispute as the goal is to win and the decision is in the hands of a judge, whereas in a mediation proceeding the parties to the dispute work together to resolve the dispute giving them more agency in deciding the outcome.

The setting up of localized mediation centres which can be formally recognized can prove to be an interesting alternative. Though Lok Adalats tried to establish localized access to the judiciary they continued to rely on the discretion of judges which can alienate solutions which the parties to the dispute may arrive at. Mediation centres controlled by the citizens and assisted by the legal aid centre can pave the way for a new model to create an active judicial presence in different areas and reduce the burden on courts.

An ideal for law to be able to break the existing power structures is that it has to be supported by a society where justice, equality and sustainability are paramount. To realize this ideal state it would require a constant connection between law and society which would entail an interaction with social norms, customary laws with the formal legal system. Customary laws provide a historical basis for understanding norms and conflict resolution methods within particular communities and its interaction with the formal legal system has been ridden with conflict. In 2047 customary laws enjoy an interesting equation with the formal legal system where they gain the acceptance of the latter, but in areas of conflict, the customary law will prevail unless it is contrary to the virtues of justice, equity and sustainability as internalized by society. The reason customary law would prevail is to enable cultural and societal norms particular to that community to exist and avoid being eroded by new legal structures that come with statutory law. This hierarchy of customary law to statutory law can be broken in instances where it violates the ideal of justice, equity and sustainability. An example that can be seen in present times, where a Khap panchayat[11] in Uttar Pradesh ordered women to be raped as punishment for their brother marrying outside his caste (Bhatia, 2015). With the opening up of the judiciary and the legislature this interaction and negotiation would be more possible.

In 2047 every process of law making and implementation will involve the rights holders in its negotiation. The law will be more layered with laws ranging from the national, state to the local level with the Constitution continuing to be the supreme law of the land. In an event of conflict between different laws priority would be given to the local laws, followed by state laws and then central laws, which will make judicial interpretation more locally relevant. However, if any of these layers of law conflict with the Constitution, the constitutional position on the issue would prevail. With mediation being a dominant method of dispute resolution it will allow for more organic settlement of disputes where the settlement being an agreement between the two parties can move beyond the frame of the local, state and national laws. Another change that would occur in 2047 is that when India is a signatory to any international treaties, in order to realize her obligations under these, she would mandatorily incorporate the ethos of the international treaty into domestic legislation. This incorporation will be subject to the three tiered legislative process described earlier.

Pathways

As I laid down my vision, I was keen to study other interventions which were already moving towards this ideal to arrive at the suggested pathways. My search for these interventions led me to interview three innovators in the space of law and justice—Deepta Sateesh, Director of the Law + Environment + Design Laboratory, Danish Shiekh, a human rights lawyer at the Alternative Law Forum and Gulika Reddy, who is the founder of Schools of Equality. These three new interventions are moving towards the two aspects of my vision. The first being access to justice and the other being the creation of an enabling environment for a society to prioritize justice, equality and sustainability. It is tough to place these initiatives into either of these aspects but I have chosen to do so, based on the greater emphasis on one of these aspects.

Access to Justice by Designing New Possibilities

Access to justice is traditionally viewed as the lack of the ability of law to respond to injustices due to lack of legal protection or judicial and institutional access. In my vision I propose to address this by opening up the legislature and judiciary for more citizen engagements. The Law + Environment + Design Laboratory adds another dimension to this question of access to justice by stating that the language of the law itself is a barrier in its use and suggests the need to move beyond its text heavy nature to something more accessible which is visual. This democratizes the knowledge of law, enabling a participatory process either in the making of law or its implementation, and of developing legal strategies. Deepta Sateesh suggests that at times it might also be excessive reliance on the legal framework in addressing injustice that creates a perception of the lack of legal redress or lack of access to justice. She articulates that the legal struggles need to be complemented with spiritual, social and cultural resources and creative intervention. This showcases that opening up of the judiciary and legislature needs to be accompanied with creative intervention that makes the language of law accessible and even look beyond the law to resolve or address conflict.

The Law + Environment + Design Laboratory was set up in 2011 as a collaborative effort between environmental lawyers from Natural Justice and Designers from the Srishti School of Art, Design and Technology. It was created with the vision to challenge existing legal, environmental, social, cultural and economic frameworks with interdisciplinarity. The experiments at the lab reveal the potential for design and design methodology to navigate some of the challenges that the use of law entails.

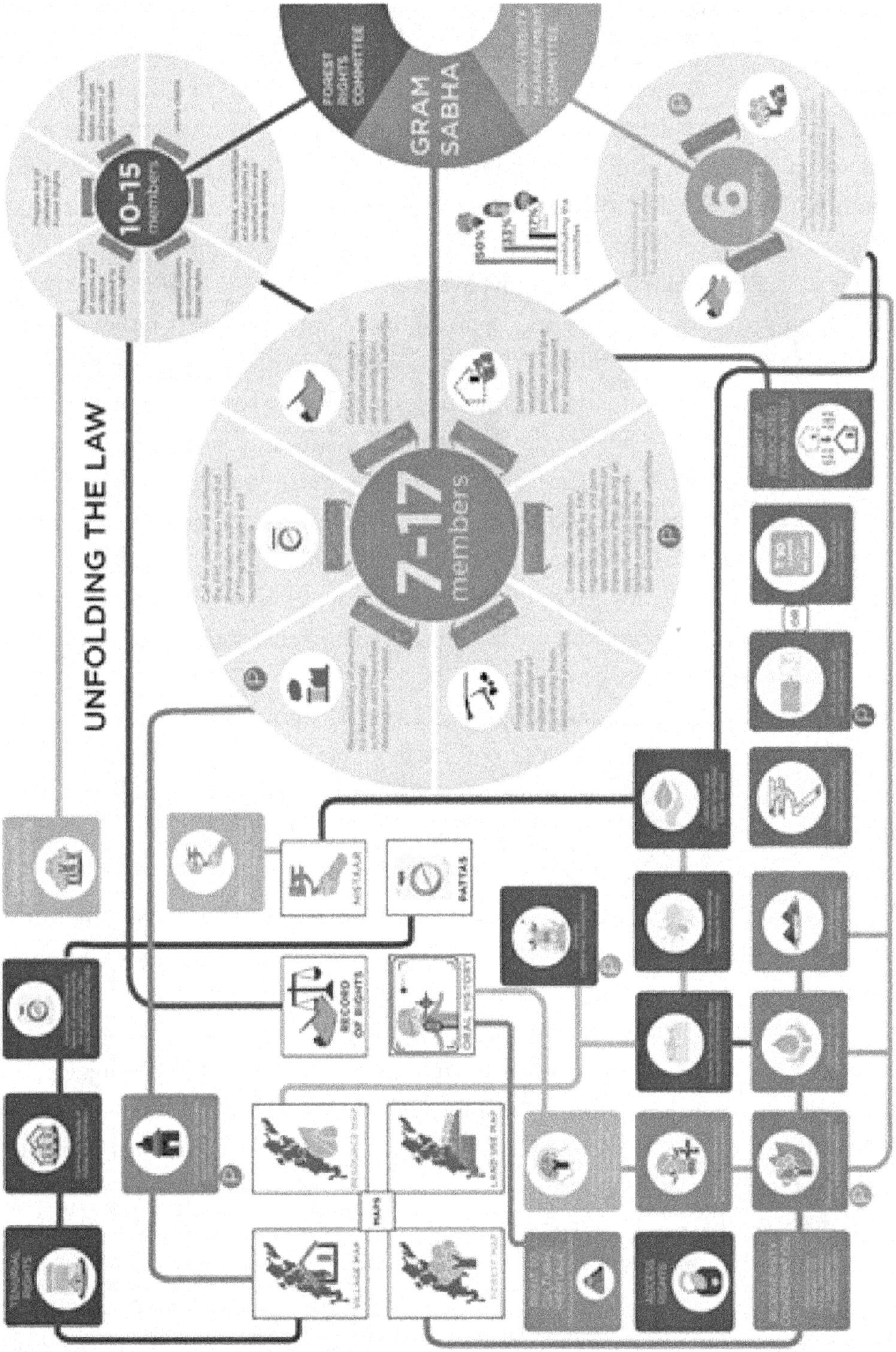

Figure 1: The use of the visual medium in an infograph to navigate the Forest Rights Act, 2006 sourced from the Law+Environment+Design Laboratory website available at http://srishti.ac.in/ledlab/

'The ground is complex and the law tends to simplify or generalize and the language of the law can distance or alienate people from using it', says Deepta Sateesh, as she begins to reveal her journey of working with the law in assisting communities in their struggle to assert their rights over resources. The first experiment of bringing these two disciplines together was when designers worked on communicating the Forest Rights Act, 2006 to pastoral communities in Kutch and Sariska who were engaged in a struggle to assert their rights under the Act. The problem with the implementation of such a progressive Act is a matter of communicating the nature of rights available within it and how to access them. The visual medium provides an interesting opportunity to dilute the text heavy nature of law making. The use of the visual medium acts as a way of democratizing the knowledge of law, enabling a richer engagement of communities which this law impacts and citizens in the future. It fundamentally challenges the approaches towards lawyering where legal strategies are constructed by lawyers. Instead, through the visual medium, it opens up the conversation with other stakeholders who are likely to be impacted by such legal action. The first experiment resulted in the creation of a board game on the Forest Rights Act, 2006 and a paralegal toolkit. This experiment further provides a new lens to look at the problem of access to justice as not one of lack of access to redress or other institutional aspects but locates it in the language of the law.

'Law can only act as one outlet and design provides an opportunity to explore others', is what Deepta Sateesh says to describe the point where legal intervention cannot address all aspects or impacts that a community may face from a particular injustice.

The next experiment with law and design was to revive the myths and narratives of the Khoi-San community in South Africa to provide an alternative way to address the collective trauma that they had experienced from a historical process of marginalization. The legal struggle could not address this collective trauma and there was a need for a design intervention to complement the legal efforts. This came in the form of a graphic novel that built on the power of narratives that rebuild the myths of the Khoi-San people and the story of their ancestors to provide spiritual and cultural relief in their struggles. This showcases that the experience of injustice cannot always be resolved or addressed by law alone and there is a need to complement legal efforts with the use of narratives or other creative methods that can engage communities.

'There is a dissatisfaction or dissonance with the way policies are being implemented on the ground; this, to an extent, is because the law generalizes the particularity of places and relationships', states Deepta Sateesh, as she highlights the possibilities that design holds for law. She states that the distance between the law or legal framework and its context of implementation is a product of the colonial frame that we continue to sit within. It is her vision to use design as a way of understanding the frame that is particular to India and to then begin to propose different ways to navigating conflict from there.

Society that Prioritises Equality and Justice

The two interventions featured here are moving towards this ideal by expanding the scope of existing legal structures to understand the complexity of identity based discrimination through a comprehensive anti-discrimination law and the other by incorporating human rights education in the school curriculum through Schools of Equality.

Towards a comprehensive anti-discrimination law

'One example I often refer to is what my colleague Sumathy describes – where in a Kolkata village a Dalit female to male (Trans-man) was in a relationship with an upper caste woman. The upper caste family wanted the relationship to come to an end. In their efforts to do so, they inflicted violence, the Dalit Trans-man was stripped and paraded nude. In such an instance will one look at it as a question of caste atrocity, gender identity or a question of sexual orientation. How can a legal framework that's insular grapple with something like this?', says Danish, as he begins to lay out the framework for a comprehensive anti-discrimination law. The underlying principles that fuel this effort is the idea of intersectionality and the need for law to embrace the complex notion of identity as well as acknowledging the multiple strands of discrimination that take place with a single individual or instance of injustice.

The landscape of discrimination law in India is variegated, dispersed and lacks insight into the intersecting and unifying nature of discrimination across recognized identity markers. The Indian Constitution provides a guarantee against discrimination on a number of prohibited grounds including race, caste, place of birth and sex, but the manner in which these have been operationalized through legislation and policy measures leaves a lot to be desired. It is here that the efforts of Danish and the Alternative Law Forum lie in enabling the articulation for such a comprehensive framework. Danish recounts that the first time this conversation took place was in 2012 where the LGBT movement was discussing the path ahead and an element that emerged was non-discrimination. This piqued his interest and he began to research on the need for a new discrimination framework. More so now, he emphasizes, given the regime change due to which religious minorities are particularly vulnerable. It is this unique ability of the project to understand questions of intersectionality and indirect discrimination that allow for it to pave the way for a new legal future for India.

The idea of intersectionality was first developed by Kimberle Crenshaw, an American scholar in the field of critical race theory, when she was speaking about black women (Crenshaw, 1991). So if you are a Dalit and a woman, you aren't facing two distinct discriminations, but rather a particular experience of discrimination as a Dalit woman. We haven't had much discussion on intersections yet. In terms of legislations, the Persons with Disabilities Act and the Prevention of Atrocities Act deal with discrimination against certain categories. But how does one go about dealing with discrimination on multiple grounds was a question posed by Jayna Kothari, an advocate in the Bangalore High Court, in the consultation held by the Alternative Law Forum in 2012, for understanding the need for a comprehensive anti-discrimination law (Sheikh, 2014). It is this intersectionality that this project aims to address. The other aspect is the lack of an expansive interpretation of Article 15 of the Constitution where only five grounds of discrimination are protected. Danish states that,

'There is little or no recognition of the concepts of indirect discrimination and reasonable accommodation in India law, whether constitutional or statutory. Both Articles 15 and 16 have specific affirmative action provisions for women, children, 'scheduled castes and tribes' and 'other backward classes'. On the whole, attention has been spent instead on the limits of affirmative action. In practice, however, reservations have come to be regarded as the most important, if not the only, means of taking affirmative action. The problem then is that we haven't focused on how to make reservations more effective, how to ensure that once you get individuals into institutions how do you deal with more systemic effects of discrimination and exclusion against them.'

These aspects then lay the foundation for the need for an anti-discrimination legislation to address what Danish refers to as 'analogous experiences of different communities who are discriminated against'.

The efforts are presently underway in working towards a draft document that will showcase the legal framework for a potential legislation. Presently they are occurring at two levels. One, the doctrinal, where there is an extensive mapping of existing laws and its protection of discrimination on certain grounds and then the aspect of narratives or lived experience of discrimination. The team has been interviewing activists, civil society lawyers and individuals on how they experience discrimination on the basis of their identity. They then intend to bring both these aspects together which Danish recounts is a messier process than he describes it to be. 'The challenges with this project are many' says Danish, the first being to make the case on the ground for the viability of such an initiative.

Despite this challenge he states that the only way to build political consensus around issues of discrimination is to forge alliances across different groups, given that experiences of discrimination can overlap. He concludes that there is a need for building alliances between vulnerable communities by recognizing the larger notion of discrimination as opposed to an isolated experience of injustice.

This effort of developing a comprehensive anti-discrimination framework will provide a legislative base for society to prioritize the need for equality and justice. It will do so by enabling victims of multiple strands of discrimination to seek the shelter of law. As Danish Sheikh says, 'Prejudice is not going to end soon so we need a system that is accessible and a system where if something happens to me I can seek remedy; when I face indirect discrimination, to be able to give it a name, which I have not been able to do yet'.

Schools of equality

'Growing up in India, I felt anger at the normalization of social injustice. My belief that the law was a powerful instrument for social change motivated me to go to law school,' says Gulika Reddy, as she describes her path towards this initiative. Upon graduating from law school she worked as a human rights lawyer in the Madras High Court. It was here that she realized that good legislation is only part of the solution. Several other challenges exist which lie outside the ambit of litigation. These related to lack of rights awareness, access to counsel and ineffective implementation of the law. To address these issues she set up a new collaborative program that brought together non-governmental organizations (NGOs) and National Law Schools to organize periodic rights awareness programs and dispense free legal aid for indigent and marginalized women. Despite receiving free legal assistance she notices that women at the awareness workshops expressed reluctance to approach the legal system, as they felt further victimized by the judicial process and functionaries under the law. It became apparent to her that insensitivity present within the Court system was symptomatic of widely held beliefs about women and gender roles in society.

Recognizing that gender socialization begins early and is reinforced by societal institutions, culture and media, she started Schools of Equality, an activity-based program that runs alongside the mainstream curriculum in high schools and encourages students to examine issues relating to equality and shift social attitudes that perpetuate gender-based violence and other forms of social injustice. As a part of the programme, they will interact with leaders from social justice movements, lawyers, artists, writers, photographers, musicians, performance artists, and therapists to articulate their views on equality and social justice. The programme enables students to understand diversity and equality, preparing them to address issues that they are faced with as members of society. What Schools of Equality attempts to do is address the challenge of social acceptance of a legal framework. The program allows students to interrogate and engage with the idea of equality and challenge the perception of identity and its impact on the way discrimination is experienced. Gulika recounts an interesting experiment where students were asked to pen down an entire constitution. In their experience of doing so they have been able to address questions of discrimination at the basic level of a 'joke' and reflect on their own practices of discrimination (Shenoy, 2015). This also provides them with the opportunity to engage with the law and understand its spirit which will cultivate a culture of social acceptance of progressive legislations and criticism of regressive ones based on the standards of equality.

They are presently working with schools for underprivileged youth in Kadapa, a rural district in Andhra Pradesh. Her efforts through the Schools for Equality do provide a pathway for establishing a critical link between law and society in the case of discrimination. Though the program in many ways centres on the question of human rights and discrimination, it holds a key in bridging the link between an active citizen engagement in making laws and resolving disputes to a society where such values of equality are understood.

Conclusion

These legal visions provide an insight into the potential legal futures and pathways for India to allow for the law to contribute more effectively to the pillars of Vikalp Sangam.[12] I would like to conclude with the view that law as a site of struggle will continue to act as a space where these pillars are realized or challenged but law as Auden says, is like love which is flippant, confusing yet eternally fulfilling.

'Like love we don't know where or why,
Like love we can't compel or fly,
Like love we often weep,
Like love we seldom keep.'

(Auden, 1940, pp.113)

Endnotes

1. In 2014 the present government formed a High Level Committee chaired by T.S.R. Subramanian to review four key environmental legislations. The recommendations of this Committee sought

to dilute present environmental clearance processes with a single-window clearance by suggesting amendments to the four key legislations. Details of the recommendation are available at http://www. accessinitiative.org/blog/2014/11/recommendations-high-level-committee-review-environmental-laws-india (Last visited 24 November, 2015). These recommendations went on to be rejected by a parliamentary standing committee set up on the issue.

2. In 2014 the Modi led government introduced amendments to the present Right to Fair Compensation and Transparency in Land Acquisition, Rehabilitation and Resettlement Act, 2013 through an ordinance. The most concerning of the proposed amendments was to do away with provisions which required consent of the gram sabha in the case of projects being undertaken for public purpose and those undertaken under a public-private partnership. Though the land ordinance lapsed, the state governments have been empowered to make amendments in the state laws in accordance to the ordinance.

3. The democratic space for communities is shrinking because of the reducing spaces for community engagement in the process of gaining environmental clearance and land acquisition based on the proposed amendments.

4. Rule 13 (i) of the Rules as amended in 2012 of the Scheduled Tribes and Other Traditional Forest Dwellers (Recognition of Forest Rights) Act, 2006.

5. 73rd and 74th amendment to the Constitution were brought about in 1992 for the establishment of the Panchayat Raj system in rural areas and Municipalities in urban areas to realize the objective of localized governance.

6. Public purpose has been defined in Sec 2 (1) of the Right to Fair Compensation and Transparency in Land Acquisition, Rehabilitation and Resettlement Act, 2013.

7. Lok Adalat or people's court was an initiative by Justice P.N. Bhagwati to introduce a non-adversarial system of dispute resolution in villages.

8. The rule of *locus standi* refers to the requirement that a person who brings a case before the court should have suffered a legal injury. This rule has been altered in the case of Public Interest Litigation where any person can institute a case before the court, if there is a question of public interest.

9. Gram Nyayalayas are village courts established by the Gram Nyayalayas Act, 2008 to ensure speedy justice.

10. Mediation here is being referred to as a formal process where parties to the dispute, guided by a mediator, arrive at workable solution to the dispute derived by the parties.

11. Khap panchayats are panchayats in rural areas composed primarily of male village elders.

12. The pillars specifically are ecological sustainability, social well-being and justice, direct and delegated responsibility, economic diversity and cultural and knowledge democracy; see 'The Search for Alternatives: Key Aspects and Principles', at http://www.vikalpsangam.org/about/the-search-for-alternatives-key-aspects-and-principles/#_ftn1.

References

Alternative Law Forum, 2012, *Report on the Consultation of Antidiscrimination Laws*, available at https://www.scribd.com/doc/255882558/Consultation-on-Anti-Discrimination-Law (Last accessed 21 April, 2015).

Auden, W.H, 1940, *Another Time*, New York: Random House.

Austin, G., 2003, *Working a Democratic Constitution: A History of the Indian Experience*, New Delhi: Oxford University Press.

Austin, J., 1980, *Lectures on Jurisprudence or Philosophy of Positive Law*, London: Spottiswoode and Company.

Bhagwati, P.N. and C.J. Dias, 2012, 'The Judiciary in India: A Hunger and Thirst for Justice', *NUJS Law Review*, 5 NUJS L. Rev. pp. 171-88.

Bhatia, Gautam, 2015, *Horizontal Discrimination, Article 15 (2) and the possibility of a Constitutional Civil Rights Act*, available at https://www.academia.edu/9736139/Article_15_2_and_a_Constitutional_Civil_Rights_Act (Last accessed 10 September, 2017).

Crenshaw, Kimberley, 1991, 'Mapping the Margins: Intersectionality, identity politics and violence against women of color', *Stanford Law Review*, Vol. 43, July, pp. 1241-299.

Law+Environment+Design Laboratory website available at http://srishti.ac.in/ledlab/ (Last accessed 21 April, 2015).

Law+Environment+Design Laboratory, 2013, Viewbook available at http://srishti.ac.in/ledlab/wp-content/uploads/2014/04/LED_Viewbook_finalx.pdf (Last accessed 14 April, 2015).

Narang, Monika, 2014, 'Understanding Social and Legal Impacts of the Nirbhaya Movement, India', *International Journal of Development Research*, Vol. 4(6), pp. 1212-219, June.

Narmada Bachao Andolan V Union of India and others, Writ Petition (civil) 328 of 2002 available at http://indiankanoon.org/doc/1642722/ (Last accessed 24 November, 2015).

Sheikh, D, 2015, 'Notes from a presentation on a comprehensive antidiscrimination framework' at a workshop on antidiscrimination in NLSIU, Bangalore, Alternative Law Forum (December, 2014).

Shenoy, Sonali, 2015, On Schools of Equality, *Indian Express*, available at http://www.newindianexpress.com/cities/chennai/School-Students-Pen-their-Own-Constitution/2015/04/16/article2765897.ece (Last accessed 21 April, 2015).

Shakil, Sana, 2014, Slow trials at fast track courts, *Times of India* on http://timesofindia.indiatimes.com/city/delhi/Slow-trials-at-fast-track-courts-raise eyebrows/articleshow/45529797.cms (Last accessed on 21 April, 2015).

Suresh Kumar Koushal and another V NAZ Foundation and others, Civil Appeal No. 10972 of 2013 (http://judis.nic.in/supremecourt/imgs1.aspx?filename=41070).

For a Radical Social Democracy: Imagining Possible Indian Future/s

Aditya Nigam

'Pure time, then, is not a string of separate, reversible instants; it is an organic whole in which the past is not left behind, but is moving along with, and operating in, the present. And the future is given to it not as lying before, yet to be traversed; it is given only in the sense that it is present in its nature as an open possibility.'

– Muhammad Iqbal (2011, pp. 50)[1]

Summary

Drawing on the writings of some important early to mid twentieth century Indian thinkers, the essay proposes the concept of radical social democracy, an idea for the future that appeals for a change in what Ambedkar called the social conscience of the people. In its practice, it will institutionalize the ethics of sharing, so that the resources become part of the commons. The radical social democracy will relentlessly strive for the systems that do not fall prey to powerful oligarchies and enable institutional forms that can provide space for the plurality of visions for the imagined future.

Since the future is not a moment in time that is yet to arrive, rather it is shaped through every moment of our present, hence, it has to be imagined, taking into account the fact, that there are far more groups that have a stake in how it shapes up than ever before. The present form of parliamentary democracy, dominated by the party-form, reduces all politics and contestation to mass manipulation, where effectively oligarchies rule in the name of the masses, without allowing for complexities of any sort to be debated. Radical social democracy, at the very least, would give people the opportunity to make informed choices when problematic questions arise, that may not lend themselves to easy resolutions.

The Future, Here and Now

The future, goes an apocryphal saying, is not what it used to be.[2] It is difficult from our notions of linear time to imagine how something that has not yet come, could have already changed beyond recognition. The future is, after all, always something that is yet to come, a 'not-yet', to borrow Ernst Bloch's expression. And yet, it is interesting to think of the possibility of a time that never was, having so irretrievably changed that we might perhaps need to revisit all our temporal concepts—modernity, progress, history, future, development—so that we may understand the meaning of this enigmatic statement.

Once upon a time, our future used to be one of abundance, of 'man's' complete mastery over nature. It used to be a future that was driven by technology and large scale industry, where technology, it was believed, would liberate us from the everyday drudgery of work and we would be left free to enjoy the beauties of life, have time for aesthetic pursuits and write poetry. Human emancipation was imagined to be predicated upon the domination and control of Nature. All of Nature's bounties were for us to consume and enjoy. This was pretty much the global hegemonic vision that also ruled the imagination of the makers of modern India. Critics like Gandhi and Tagore were soon consigned to the safety of school textbooks, while *adivasi* cosmologies and their notions of their future were seen as signs of backwardness to be eradicated at all costs. Indeed, the power of this vision was most dramatically evident in the life and works of B. R. Ambedkar whose rejection of village autonomy and of traditional occupations and livelihoods was decisive, as was his embrace of modernity and technology. An important aspect of this global dream of a utopian future was the idea that certain modes of being belonged to an unviable past that had to be obliterated. Their backwardness was a drag that held back the rest of humanity from reaching the Promised Land. Thus was Time mapped on to Space in a way that made large parts of the non-Western world and its modes of being to be an embodiment of the past. Conversely, the present was also relocated elsewhere – in Europe – where History was apparently happening. It mattered little what your or my present actually was, for it was always only the past of an abstraction called World-History or World-System. That was where the future was arriving at any given moment. That present-becoming-future was the future for the rest of the world.[3]

We can resist such a construction by making a radical claim to the effect that we no longer recognize any such thing as a singular World which has only one present. We could join Tagore in wanting to 'kill the giant abstraction which is claiming the sacrifice of individuals all over the world under highly painted masks of delusion' (Bhattacharya, 1997, pp. 58).[4] And this would not be a very outlandish claim. After all, there are modes of being, once thought to be relics of the past, which have refused to oblige the moderns by disappearing into the pages of history. They will pretty much be part of our future which now has begun to already look different from what it used to only a few decades ago.

Nature too, has not been gracious enough to oblige us. It is already talking back, indeed striking back in anger. Climate change is an affliction of the condition called the *homo sapiens*, but it is not a condition that nature passively bears; on the contrary, it is like that sleeping snake at the bottom of the earth, which has been roused to fury.[5] The future now is no longer one where a part of humanity basks in aesthetic pleasures, having dispensed with another part of humanity and brought nature itself under its complete domination. It is a future, already arriving – a future where the moderns will have to make peace on equal terms with both the 'wretched of the earth' and an angry and uncompromising nature.

It is a future, in other words, that is already here. Everything that we do today—from building high energy consuming cities with flyovers and malls, to destruction of agricultural land for luxury living—will remain with us for decades to come, maybe even centuries; and in the case of plastics and nuclear waste, even millennia! It will affect everything, bringing in its train changes ranging from erratic and devastating climatic changes to destruction of our food security. As Iqbal's statement cited in the epigraph to this paper suggests, the future must be seen not as something that is 'yet to be traversed' but as a set of open possibilities connected deeply with the present, which is in turn structured by the past which continues to operate within it. A crucial point in Iqbal's assertion is that the future represents a set of open possibilities. In our times, I understand this to be a consequence of the fact that there are today far more people and social groups who have a stake in how the future shapes up, than there used to be some decades ago. No longer is it a matter for state and political elites, policy-makers, economists and corporations to decide. Whether there will be a nuclear power plant in Koodankulan or Jaitapur is a decision that can longer be left to this nexus of the political elite, experts and corporations – let us call it the power bloc. Nor can the decision to simply hand over the natural commons to corporations be left to them. There were movements and struggles against such moves earlier too; but what has changed significantly is that at a global level, the presence and legitimacy of other stakeholders has now become impossible to ignore.

Take for instance the idea of 'inter-generational equity', first mooted in the Stockholm Conference on Human Environment in 1972, which has become one of the key nodes around which revolve not only our critiques of what we do to our 'natural resources' but also the way in which we think of the future. In demanding that the present generation leave behind an earth for coming generations, in a condition at least as good as it was received in, the idea of inter-generational equity places upon the present the responsibility of shaping the future by exercising discretion and restraint. It forces us to acknowledge that the future is being shaped at every moment of our present, here and now. In other words, it is not a moment in time that is yet to arrive – a time that will begin when this burdensome prehistory of oppression ends. There is no apocalypse that will mark the end of the drudgery of historical time and lead us into the realm of Eternity. There is also no 'revolutionary moment' which will put an end, once and for all, to all exploitation and lead to a new beginning like a classless society without exploitation. It is no longer possible to assume that we can let capital wreak havoc now, in the hope that we will set it right once the revolution takes place, for there will be nothing left to set right at this rate.

The recognition that there are many more players in the field than the power bloc, leads to the enunciation of a fundamentally different set of normative principles.

One example from our recent history will suffice to explain this better. In the wake of the popular struggles against land acquisition, especially after the Singur and Nandigram (West Bengal) struggles, the debate on land acquisition acquired new urgency. Struggles against Special Economic Zones and mining through mass dispossession of tribal communities drew attention to larger questions of justice that had so far been ignored in the name of an inescapable economic logic. In that context, the Minister for Mines in the second term of the United Progressive Alliance (UPA) government (2009-14), B. K. Handique, made a proposal in parliament, giving the tribal communities 26 percent stake in the proceeds from mining. The proposal came from the group of ministers in the course of drawing up the Mines and Minerals (Development and Regulation) Bill and was vehemently opposed by industry bodies like the Federation of Indian Chambers of Commerce and Industry. Even though that proposal apparently went into cold storage, more recently the anti-mining struggle in Goa managed to get the Supreme Court to direct, in April 2014, the formation of a Permanent Fund by putting back 10 percent of the profits from iron ore mining in the state. The Supreme Court basically accepted the principle that a percentage of the mining should go back to the community and subsequent generations, acknowledging them too as stakeholders, even though the proportion of profits earmarked for it leave much to be desired. It is of course possible to see this move as an attempt at incorporation of dissent and a way of buying out resistance but it is equally important to recognize that this move too is being fiercely resisted by the mining corporations. In other words, it is a matter of profound conflict and contestation in which, often, such small changes can become the thin edge of the wedge for mass struggles and dissenting voices to transform the terms of policy and judicial discourse. Needless to say, this in no way represents an alternative vision of the world – a vision with which many movements on the ground operate.[6]

In another striking move, dubbed populist by the power bloc and intellectuals associated with it, the Aam Aadmi Party (AAP) government in Delhi has decided in principle to provide consumers 20 kilolitres of water a month (700 litres a day) free of cost. The argument for this measure advanced by the AAP is that water is the lifeline and cannot be treated as an economic good – at least up to a certain minimum level. Beyond that level, whoever wants to consume excess water must pay higher tariffs. This position runs fundamentally against any argument for the privatization of water. This argument clearly draws on the experience of numerous struggles and movements across the world and points towards a different ethic of living.

The future is now practically indistinguishable from our living present. That is why many contemporary movements are so deeply invested in the 'here and now'. For feminism it was always so – the struggle against patriarchy was never a deferred struggle. I have argued, elsewhere, that this concern with the 'here and now' marks our post-utopian moment more generally, and movements like the Dalit movement or the ecological struggles in particular too, are no longer prepared to wait for an indefinite future.

Technology and Indian Thought Traditions

If the future, for our nineteenth century forbears like Marx, was one of super-abundance and freedom from the drudgery of work through the sheer revolutionary power/s of technology and the productive forces, at the beginning of the twenty-first century that option no longer seems viable. In productivism lay the hope of the future, not only for Marxism but in fact, for all other modern ideologies, for much of the last three centuries. Today we seem to have arrived at the limit point of that imagination.

Already, by the middle of the twentieth century, Marxists like Herbert Marcuse were writing of the technological dystopia that the modern world was beginning to be (Marcuse, 1964). In his justifiably famous book *One-Dimensional Man*, he had spoken of the technological rationality of modern industrial society as something that increasingly tends towards totalitarianism of some form or the other. Technological optimism had already been severely dented with the rise of fascism and Nazism and reached its mid-century climax with the dropping of the atomic bomb by the so-called 'free world' over a hapless civilian population. That was where Marcuse had begun his story of the technological dystopia of the modern world.

India has had a robust tradition of the critique of technology and what Tagore termed 'machinicdemon' – *jantradaanav* (See Bhattacharya, 1997, p. 32). If there were those like Jawaharlal Nehru, B. R. Ambedkar and M. N. Roy, who shared the technological optimism of their times, there were figures like Gandhi and Tagore who struck a different note on this issue.

A relentless critique of modern technology is pervasive in Tagore's writings – both fiction and non-fiction. Gandhi's *Hind Swaraj*, of course, was an early and prescient text in this regard and his rejection of machine-based modern civilization was uncompromising. But there are interesting dissonances between the positions of these two giant figures of twentieth century India. Gandhi's early attack on machinery drew on his reading of Romesh Chandra Dutt's *Economic History of India*, which, according to his own account, made him weep when he first read it. His conclusion: 'It is machinery that has impoverished India. It is difficult to measure the harm that Manchester has done to us. It is due to Manchester that Indian handicraft has all but disappeared' (Parel, 1997, pp.107). Elsewhere, many years later, he underlined this basic point once again, when he said that what he objected to was, 'the craze for machinery, not machinery as such'. He explicated this further: 'The craze is for what they call labour-saving machinery. Men go on "saving labour" till thousands are without work and thrown on the open streets to die of starvation' (ibid., pp.166). It is clear from these statements that Gandhi's primary concern was with the labour displacing power of technology. But even more importantly, in this later statement, Gandhi tied up this opposition to machinery to the concentration of economic and political power: 'I want the concentration of wealth, not in the hands of the few, but in the hands of all. '*Today machinery merely helps a few to ride on the backs of millions*' (ibid., pp.166, emphasis added). This connection between machinery, industrialization and centralization was seen by many Indian thinkers through the nineteenth and twentieth centuries, but there were also some who believed that it was possible to have a modern industrialized economy without centralization and destruction of the rural economy.

While it is true that most thinkers of modern India had already accepted the superiority of modern science and technology, as persuasively argued by Partha Chatterjee (1994), it is interesting that even many of those who accepted the West's superiority in this regard, had deep reservations with regard to industrialism of the kind that the West embodied.[7] Right from the nineteenth century onwards, this attitude resulted from a commitment of the colonized intelligentsia to the rural population and concern for the appalling conditions of its existence. Thus an early modernist figure like Rammohun Roy too 'realized the strategic significance of the renovated and modernized village *panchayats*' (Ganguli, 1977, pp. 87). He maintained that these panchayats could be the building blocks of an economy 'reconstructed from the bottom upwards'. The future Indian economy, he believed, could not be a centralized structure (ibid., pp. 87).

Tagore was entirely in agreement with Gandhi as far as his critique of technology went but he discerned among the participants of Gandhi's Non-cooperation movement, the powerful presence of what he called the 'slave mentality'. And he could not quite absolve Gandhi himself of some responsibility in encouraging it: 'Where Mahatma Gandhi has declared war against the tyranny of the machine which is oppressing the whole world, we are all enrolled under his banner. But we must refuse to accept as our ally the illusion-haunted magic-ridden slave mentality that is at the root of all the poverty and insult under which the country groans' (Bhattacharya, 1997, pp. 84). For one thing, Tagore was deeply suspicious of Gandhi's presentation of the *charkha* as the alternative mantra to the domination of the machine. 'To one and all he simply says: Spin and weave, spin and weave...Is this the call of the New Age to new creation?' (ibid., pp. 81). Tagore saw in this cult of the charkha the potential to numb the mind, to reduce the human personality to banal levels: 'But if man be stunted by big machines, the danger of his being stunted by small machines must not be lost sight of' (ibid., pp. 82). Tagore revolted against the peculiar kind of 'political asceticism' that he had begun to identify with the Gandhian project. For, in the end, Tagore's was a call for the joyful celebration of life that was predicated upon the exaltation of the individual's capacity for reason and creativity: 'We have enough of magic in this country – magical revelation, magical healing, and all kinds of divine intervention in mundane affairs. That is exactly why I am so anxious to instate reason on its throne' (ibid., pp. 82).

On this point, Tagore seems to be considerably closer to Amebdkar, even though the latter differs with both Gandhi and Tagore on the general issue of machinery. Ambedkar experienced the advent of the machine and technology in general as immensely liberating, which is clearly linked to the fact that unlike Gandhi and Tagore, his reference point is the community of labour of the most degrading kinds – the labour that untouchable castes had been traditionally made to perform in Hindu society. Such labour obviously held little romantic appeal for him. But Ambedkar's response to 'Gandhism' on the question of machinery is not merely experiential. He underlines that what separates humans from animals is culture, which he sees as 'essential for man'. He underlines that a life of culture is made possible only when there is sufficient leisure (Rodrigues, 2002). Leisure means the lessening of the toil necessary for satisfying the physical wants of life. This toil, he argues, can only be lessened when machine takes the place of man. Machinery and modern civilization are thus indispensable for emancipating man from leading the life of a brute' (ibid., pp.159).

Both Gandhi and Ambedkar, it seems to me, were basing themselves on very real experiences of the impact of machinery on different sections of the population of India – even though neither of them actually experienced its impact directly at a personal level, though Ambedkar certainly had a closer acquaintance with it, via members of his family. It is difficult to deny the deeply unsettling impact of machinery and industrialization on large sections of the Indian population, leading to large-scale destitution, that so moved Gandhi.[8] It is equally difficult to deny the liberatory potential of machinery where it came to populations forced into the most degrading and humiliating forms of work, the Dalits. Nor is it possible, at a more general level, to deny Ambedkar's point about the availability of leisure through technology – something that more recent technologies do in terms of liberating women to some extent from the drudgery of household work.[9] It is interesting here to note that Rokeya Sakhawat Hossain's story 'Sultana's Dream',[10] published a few years before Gandhi's *Hind Swaraj*, actually visualized a women's utopia that was based on both a reversal of the division of labour and a vision of technology as liberating.[11] It is also not without significance that it is the imagination of control over solar power that forms an important ingredient of the technological basis of Rokeya's utopia.

Most discussions of the Gandhi-Ambedkar debate end up affirming one or the other of the positions, replaying old animosities and stances taken in relation to tradition and modernity. It is far more important, however, to recognize that both Gandhi and Ambedkar, and in a different sense, Tagore and Rokeya Sakhawat Hossain, articulate different responses to the question of technology that give voice to different aspects of an existential reality in a society like India's. Any contemporary discussion of their positions must take this point into account as an index of the complex terrain of India's encounter with modernity. Only then can we possibly begin to appreciate the fact that even when the imperative of ecology and global climate change force us to re-appraise our attitude to technology-fetishism, we cannot at the same time afford to ignore the fact that even today, there are domains of life where its impact is liberatory.

Radical Social Democracy – Ambedkar and M.N. Roy

'Democracy is another name for equality. Parliamentary democracy developed a passion for liberty. It never made even a nodding acquaintance with equality. It failed to realize the significance of equality and did not even endeavour to strike a balance between liberty and equality, with the result that liberty swallowed equality and made democracy a game and a farce.'

– B.R. Ambedkar[12]

In the above quote, Ambedkar makes a distinction between democracy, which he sees as synonymous with equality and *parliamentary democracy* – its actually existing, liberal form – that, in its passion for liberty, has ignored equality. The implication of his critique of parliamentary democracy is, obviously, that one needs to find other forms that will rectify the situation and bring democracy closer to its central concern, namely, equality.

Equality, however, must be understood in its broadest sense as equality along many different axes – class, caste, gender, community and so on. It is not possible to have equality in one arena alone. At one level, Ambedkar's efforts to institute 'safeguards' in the form of reservations in both employment and political representation, can be read as attempts to make democracy more egalitarian. However, these efforts could not go beyond safeguards for specific communities or social groups like the Dalits and Adivasis and even in those contexts, amounted to making the best of a bad deal. The larger question of what he called social democracy, however, remained quite unexplored.

It may be interesting at this point to bring M.N. Roy, another outspoken modern Indian critic of parliamentary democracy, into the discussion. For Roy too, one of the key elements responsible for the degeneration of democracy was 'parliamentarism' – the other being laissez faire. Between the two, they gave unbridled power to a small minority to exploit the majority. Roy actually zeroes in on the very idea of representation and delegation, integral to parliamentary democracy, as the villain of the piece. 'Constitutional pundits declare that this [representation] is democracy itself; but in reality it is a negation of democracy, based on the contempt for the demos' (Roy, 1981, pp.77). Roy's was a critique articulated in the context of the global experience of the rise of fascism and totalitarianism and he held the 'eclipse of the individual', in the service of the state in modern polities responsible for the malaise of parliamentary democracy. His critique of representation leads him to a rejection of the party-form as such, which he began to see as instrumental in the dissolution of the individual into an altogether threatening entity called the 'masses'. 'The purpose of election propaganda is to create a state of mass hysteria' (ibid., pp. 53).

In a very different way, Ambedkar's deepest suspicions too related to the question of the 'masses' – for he saw them all through the nationalist movement as entirely upper

Nigam

caste in character. In a context where the untouchables were a small minority, any mass mobilization was bound to be threatening to the interests of the minorities, in this case, the Dalits. Ambedkar's strategy was therefore to reject the very idea of the local – his critique of the villages being that they were 'sinks of localism' – and displace the entire question of Dalit emancipation to the terrain of the state. In contrast, Roy's critique led him towards what he called 'radical democracy', which he visualized as a network of local republics with people directly electing their representatives without the mediation of parties.

At a superficial level, these two might seem to be very contradictory visions – one which placed exclusive reliance on the state and the other that moved towards a network of local republics that sound suspiciously close to the Gandhian notion of *Gram Swaraj* or even Tagore's idea of *swadeshi samaj* (See Bhattacharya 1997, pp. 25).[13] However, I will argue that there is a link that connects the Ambedkarite search for social democracy to Roy's radical democracy. This link lies in the value Ambedkar places on the issue of social reform while arguing that in the final analysis, no law or state can ensure the protection of democratic values; it has to come from the '...social and moral conscience of society...' (Rodrigues, 2002, pp.122). In fact, he goes on to quote Edmund Burke to say that 'there is no method found of punishing the multitude' and that while law can punish a solitary offender, '...it can never operate against a whole body of people who are determined to defy it.' With such an understanding, it was hardly possible for Amebdkar to support a strong state-centric vision of social democracy. His argument, therefore, turned to the idea of a 'social conscience' of the people at large, which alone could '...safeguard all rights, fundamental and non-fundamental'. That is why, in this well known essay on 'Ranade, Gandhi and Jinnah', Ambedkar makes a case against the arguments of those he calls the 'political school of the intelligentsia' and accords priority to the issue of social reform over the political goal of self-government. 'The politicals never realized that democracy was not a form of government: *it was essentially a form of society*', he therefore asserts (ibid., pp.123). Elsewhere, in *What Congress and Gandhi Have Done to the Untouchables*, he goes one step further in arguing that 'self-government and democracy become real not when a Constitution based on adult suffrage comes into existence, but when the governing class loses its power to govern' (ibid., pp. 134). What precisely does this mean? Given that Ambedkar never supported the idea of the oppressed class(es) overthrowing the powerful 'governing class' by a revolution, I read this statement to mean that he visualized a possible scenario where the power of the governing class would be hemmed in by other countervailing powers that would represent, in some sense, the social conscience. Since Ambedkar was hugely sceptical of the majority community, this appeal to the social conscience could only make sense if the social itself was reconfigured. This reconfiguration does not make sense if one believes that the majority community can never change, for in that case, the Dalits would have to remain a permanent minority. Such a reconfiguration, it is evident, calls for a powerful social reform movement, one which cannot but be based on a serious intellectual challenge to the old order. Something of this kind is suggested by Ambedkar towards the end of his *Annihilation of Caste*:

> '...(T)he Hindus must consider whether the time has not come for them to recognize that there is nothing fixed, nothing eternal, nothing *sanatan*; that everything is changing, that change is the law of life for individuals as well as for society. *In a changing society, there must be a constant revolution of old values* and the Hindus must realize that if there must be standards to measure the acts of men, there must also be a readiness to revise those standards' (ibid., pp. 304, emphasis added).

It should be clear then that the idea of social democracy only becomes meaningful in the context of a society reconstituted through a radical change in ways of thinking. In Roy too, the idea of radical democracy is predicated on the idea of an intellectual revolution that had to precede any social revolution. In his later years, Roy was to elaborate the idea of an intellectual revolution into a full-fledged programme for an Indian Renaissance that would accomplish something of a modern transformation of our ways of life, not very different from the kind Ambedkar had in mind. One can wager that in a society thus transformed, Ambedkar too would have been willing to rethink his ideas on decentralization and local democracy. In a different way, then, this could tie up with the more general inclination among many early twentieth century Indian thinkers towards some combination of a modernized panchayat system blended with a cooperative economy.

Possible Indian Future/s

The futures that we imagine today, I have suggested earlier, will be crucially framed by what we do today. Our collective future/s can no longer be imagined in terms of transcendent ideals that must be realized by making the world conform to those ideals. Such transcendent utopianism has been at the root of our modern miseries, writ large across the global history of the twentieth century. Modernist utopias, irrespective of whether they were Marxist or liberal free market type (a code word for capitalist utopias), eventually became massive projects of social engineering that relied crucially on the state to enforce them. These projects were inherently violent, based as they were on the cognitive arrogance of the modern mind that sought to eliminate all signs of 'backwardness' and 'irrationality' by

165

bringing them in tandem with what it saw as the only way to be rational. Economically, such a vision was predicated upon the violent destruction of all 'pre-capitalist' forms of 'ownership' – non-individual, not codified in legal instruments, often based on use and access by communities. This was particularly true of adivasi or indigenous people's relation to their land and habitat, to the resources they accessed from them. The transformation of such pre-capitalist property into bourgeois private property was co-terminus with two things: the uprooting of traditional communities and the production of the individual property owner on the one hand, and the concentration of the new individualized property in a few hands on the other. In other words, it instituted mass dispossession and concentration of property in a few hands as part of the same mechanism, just as we see happening before our very eyes today. The political form so far called 'democracy' was, in effect, one of electoral oligarchies – call it 'party-cracy', if you will. The institutions called political parties became the instruments of keeping the new economic dispensation in place, thanks to their state-centric nature. Representation through parties was a way of containing egalitarian democratic urges, not a way of expanding them, as the philosopher Jacques Ranciere has recently reminded us.[14]

Our imagination of our collective future/s must therefore look beyond these, drawing appropriate lessons from the disastrous experiences of modernity. We must understand that capitalism was not an aberration in the modernist project but was integral to it – which is why socialism, even while it thought it was presenting an alternative to capitalism, in fact only mimicked it.

And yet, there was something in that socialist idea – an egalitarian ethos tied to an ethic of sharing – that was liquidated thanks to its dream of replicating capitalism's 'achievements' through an excessive reliance on the state. The idea was not transcendent, but rather, immanent in the lived practices of many indigenous/ adivasi communities. That is why the new movement of indigenous people in Bolivia led by Evo Morales, calls itself the Movement for Socialism. The difference between the modernist socialism of the twentieth century and the new twenty-first century socialisms will be that while the former believed that the whole world had to first undergo capitalist transformation before socialism could be realized, the latter believes that the natural commons cannot be privatized, that the earth cannot be reduced to land and a provider of 'natural resources'– a mere commodity or a 'factor of production'. Nor can water or air be transformed into economic goods or commodities for private corporations to profit from. The battle today, in other words, is for the commons. The battle is for reclaiming popular control over the commons not via the alienating and dubious agency of the state, but directly. In the world of nation-states and powerful global economic and financial institutions, however, much of this remains within the realm of utopia, since states remain even now the structural limit and the ultimate horizon of intelligibility, of relative autonomy vis-à-vis global powers. That is perhaps why even the Evo Morales story ultimately remains tragic because state-domination still remains a reality in Bolivia, as does extractivism, even if in somewhat modified form.

Nonetheless, a struggle is on, at this very moment, for reclaiming a part of the legacy of the socialist idea. The socialism of the future, it is clear, cannot be a state-directed enterprise. It has to be immanent; it has to be molecular. That is to say, it must be deeply connected to actual lived practices on the ground and drawing its principles and norms from them. There are many instances in India today where local communities have taken charge of their lives and worked wonders by relying on such lived practices. On the other hand, the logic of private property has transformed ordinary life practices of sharing into something called 'piracy', against which states and private corporations act in tandem, criminalizing them. That itself shows how powerful their presumed impact on corporate profits is understood to be. The socialism of the future will have to be relentlessly egalitarian in its practice and will have to institutionalize the ethic of sharing as one that undercuts the logic of private property. This socialism, if one wishes to call it that, it should by now be evident, will prioritize ecological concerns and those of well-being over abstract ones of development. The political form of that socialism can only be something like a radical social democracy that continuously strives to find institutional forms beyond those of direct participation and those of the political party – forms that are not susceptible to appropriation by powerful oligarchies.[15]

Perhaps the most daunting challenge today is to spell out a specifically Indian vision of possible futures. The difficulty lies in the virtual impossibility of reconciling various different imperatives that govern the way different futures are imagined. To take one very evident example, we could see how problematic the demand for the preservation of traditional livelihoods raised by various ecological struggles can be for Dalits.

Today, when predatory corporate capital is rapidly taking over all the natural commons and even privately owned agricultural land, the importance of the issue of preservation of traditional and not-so-traditional livelihoods of adivasi and peasant communities can hardly be overstated. At any rate, it has become necessary to oppose their forcible dispossession in the name of some large design or logic of History. At the very least, the imperative of justice demands that people be given the opportunity of making informed choices. However, for Dalits employed in some of the most degrading occupations like manual scavenging, the only possible release lies in leaving those occupations.[16] But, in the perverse world of Brahmanical Hinduism, the release was never easy. In the first place, there were little options for alternative employment available for people belonging to these social groups, since they had been aggressively denied all possibility of educating themselves and accumulating wealth. Badri Narayan's study of the *nara-maveshi* movement that continued for decades in the state of Uttar Pradesh, for instance shows how difficult it was for the scavenging *chamars* to refuse to carry the carcasses of dead animals, for they had to face violent reprisals for their refusal[17] (Narayan, 2011). It was not even possible for individual members of these castes, even till about a couple of decades ago, to escape to the city – so powerful was the control of the upper castes. It was not for nothing that Ambedkar saw the liberation of Dalits as linked to a dual flight – a flight from Hindu religion and a flight from the village to the city. This speaks of quite a different relation to the lived world from that of the adivasi or the peasant whose struggle revolves around the refusal to leave the land and livelihood.

Similarly, with the rise of Hindutva, the issue of minorities, especially Muslims, in India has become highly contentious in Indian politics once more.[18] A daily war of attrition is carried on by Hindutva forces that often use the Muslim/minority question as a proxy for settling issues of caste division in Hinduism. Untouchable castes can neither leave the fold and adopt another religion, as can be seen from the frantic campaigns around so-called *gharvapasi*, nor can they find an honourable place in Hindu society as is evident from the continuing daily instances of humiliation that occur across the length and breadth of the country. The communal question in that sense is, and has always been, a displaced caste question.[19]

But at another level, the communal issue goes much deeper, tied as it is to the question of nation and nationalism as such. Right from the days of the anti-colonial struggle, dominant Indian nationalism of all hues – secular and Hindu – designated the 'communal Muslim' as the antithesis of 'national/nationalist Hindu'. Much of this politics was closely tied to the imagination of the Indian nation as going back three thousand years to a hoary Hindu past. In order to justify their exclusiveness nations always inhabit such mythical times that apparently bestow them with a sense of eternity.

It is interesting that Gandhi refused such an exclusivist idea of nationhood. Indeed, as has been argued by scholars like Ashis Nandy, Gandhi's refusal of nation is tied to his repudiation of history. Actual empirical history to him was always a domain of conflicts and violence and proved nothing about the universal idea of love that marked all religions. It may not be altogether without significance that he chose to call his famous tract, his manifesto, *Hind Swaraj*. By designating the subject-object of his Swaraj as *Hind*,

Gandhi had made an important statement. India, to him, was not a pristine Bharat (or *Bharatvarsha*) whose roots lay far back in mythical time, an unadulterated entity whose purity the nationalists wanted to resurrect. It was rather the geographical entity called Hind – the India of *his time* – that encompassed within its flow, the different currents and tributaries that had joined it over centuries. It was therefore neither possible nor desirable to separate its different components from one another. Gandhi's Hind and Iqbal's Hindi (not the language but the inhabitants of Hind) resonate with the same sense of celebration of a vibrant world in motion – not one that is fixated on an imaginary mythical past.[20]

The past moves along with the present, says Iqbal, and operates within it. But the problem, as we know, is that there is not one past. The challenge of thinking of a common future is, therefore, a challenge of reconstituting our pasts as well, of rendering them legible in ways that are radically different from the ways in which nations and nationalisms constitute a singular past – that is to say by referring back to some pristine time which inevitably makes it exclusivist. Indeed, even for those who apparently live or lived in the same time, the pasts may not be the same. We know after all that the great battles that were fought by the Sramanic traditions like Buddhism, Jainism or the Ajivikas against the dominant Brahmanical one, have a different story to tell about what we assume to be the same past.[21] Many of lower caste revolts in the early twentieth century after all, drew precisely upon those traditions, especially Buddhism, in order to articulate their vision of an emancipated future.

The only way of imagining a common future, it seems then, is to liberate ourselves from actual, empirical history, somewhat in the manner of Gandhi, thereby sidestepping the actual history of conflicts. Historically situated contentions and conflicts that often determine the conduct of figures like Gandhi, Iqbal, Ambedkar or Tagore can actually become an impediment in appreciating what might be truly valuable in their thought. Their encounter, I suggest, needs to be restaged by liberating them from the limits set by their historical contexts. This is not to suggest that their differences can be ironed out. Rather, it is to suggest that we contemporize them, make them speak to us today rather than enchain ourselves in historical conflicts they were forced into.

The problem of imagining an exploitation-free future for India, it should be clear by now, is not really one that can be resolved by thinking of it only along one axis. If we think of the future only in terms of its being free of class exploitation, for example, we lose out on other important forms of oppression and exploitation that continue in our society like those linked to caste and patriarchy, which are part and parcel of our traditional

169

society. Over and above these, there are modern forms of exploitation and violence that mark our society which have to do with modern modes of being – the mass displacement of communities and populations from their traditional habitat and forms of livelihood. Thinking of the future in terms of a specific content therefore limits our understanding. We need to think in fact of political forms that will enable different struggles to impact upon the ways in which the society of the future shapes up. The idea of a radical social democracy that draws on both Ambedkar and Roy and indeed takes what is positive in the ideas of Gandhi and Tagore, opens up precisely such possibilities for us.

Endnotes

1. Some of Iqbal's ruminations on Time are, to some extent, influenced by early twentieth century French philosopher, Henri Bergson but that should not concern us here, just as it has never really mattered that Spinoza's fundamental move of making God immanent to the universe, in all probability drew from Eastern pantheistic ideas. Iqbal's explicit purpose in these lectures was the reconstruction of Islamic thought in the face of challenges of the modern age for which he drew liberally from different sources.

2. There are various possible authors of this statement, in its many variations and it is difficult to trace its origin. Some of the earliest seem to be poet and philosopher Paul Valery and litterateurs Laura Riding and Robert Graves – both in 1937. For a useful list of references and possible origins of the statement, see http://quoteinvestigator.com/2012/12/06/future-not-used/ (last accessed on 20 May 2015).

3. Those interested further can see an elaboration of this argument in the context of Indian nationalism in Nigam, 2006.

4. In a letter addressed to Gandhi, in response to the latter's request that Tagore give a statement in support of the Non-cooperation movement, Tagore actually sent out an angst-ridden critique of the abstraction called nationalism.

5. This expression has been used by the adivasi inhabitants of Jadugoda (Jharkhand) where uranium mining by the Department of Atomic Energy has unleashed radioactivity leading to high incidence of cancer among the local inhabitants. In the film *Buddha Weeps in Jadugoda*, by Jharkhand-based film-maker Shri Prakash, Ghanshyam Beruli of the Jharkhandi Organization Against Radiation, invokes this powerful image of a snake being roused to anger.

6. Borrowing from an expression used by Lester Brown, I have argued in another article, that a new Copernican revolution is already underway, which radically reverses the relationship between the economy and ecology and which must increasingly determine our understanding of 'economic development' in the twenty-first century. Interested readers may see Nigam 2010 for an elaboration of this argument. In that larger scheme of things, I suggest, it will be through small, imperceptible

changes that bigger changes will make their presence felt, whatever the intentions of the powers that be.

7. For a reading that complicates, in another way, the straightforward modern versus anti-modern or pro-development versus anti-development view of these divergent tendencies in Indian thought, see Srinivasan (2014).

8. Pl. see Craft Futures essay in this volume.

9. Interestingly, in the 1924 statement cited earlier, Gandhi himself lauds the Singer Sewing Machine as having saved the woman from the tedious process of sewing and seaming with her own hands (Parel, 1997, pp. 166). A caveat is necessary here though: while technology can in some respects be liberating from certain kinds of degrading work, one needs to recognize the prior existence of sexual and caste-based division of labour and that technology does nothing towards transformation of those relations and prejudices that go with them.

10. The story is available in digital form at http://digital.library.upenn.edu/women/sultana/dream/dream.html (last accessed on 23 September 2015).

11. This comparison has recently been made by Rajeswari Sunder Rajan in a lecture, 'Feminism's Futures: The Limits and Ambitions of Sultana's Dream'. The lecture was delivered as the first Begum Rokeya Sakhawat Hossain Memorial Lecture at the Centre for Women's Studies, and is now published (Sunder Rajan, 2015).

12. B.R. Ambedkar, Speech delivered at the All-India Trade Union Workers Study Camp, Delhi, September 1943 (Das, 2010, pp. 48).

13. Tagore wrote an important essay entitled 'Swadeshi Samaj' in 1905 which is available in virtually all Tagore collections. Its idea of a decentralized society was essentially anti-statist and was something Tagore held on to all through his life. Both Tagore's *swadeshi samaj* and Gandhi's *gram swaraj* are ubiquitous ideas scattered throughout their writings. Gandhi's pronouncements on gram swaraj are available in the collection, *Village Swaraj*, compiled by H. M. Vyas (1962) and published by Navajivan Publishing House, Ahmedabad. It is available online in pdf format at http://gandhiashramsevagram.org/pdf-books/village-swaraj.pdf (last accessed on 23 September 2015).

14. See Ranciere (2007).

15. At one level, then, such a vision of radical social democracy is not very different from that of 'radical ecological democracy' that some scholar-activists have been talking and writing about. See, for instance, Kothari (2014). Important in this vision of a radical ecological democracy, is the bottom-up imagination of a future society, that is to say, an imagination that starts from the everyday practices of ordinary people rather than from macro structures and concepts.

16. See essay on Dalit Futures in this volume.

17. Things have started and changing slowly over the years and lately some very vocal protests have emerged, witnessed for instance, in the struggle after the Una incident in Gujarat. The refusal to carry carcasses by Dalits in Gujarat, following the flogging of four dalit youth by cow vigilantes, received massive support not just within Gujarat, but elsewhere in the country as well.

18. See essay on Religious Minority Futures in this volume.

19. For an elaboration of this argument see Nigam, 2006 and Menon, 2006.
20. The reference here is of course, to Iqbal's famous lines 'Hindi hain hum, vatan hai Hindostan hamara.
21. Sramanic traditions were essentially counter traditions to the Vedic/Brahmanic one, which was largely a householder's or lay person's religion, heavily based on rituals that gave the Brahmans, as custodians of Vedic knowledge, a position of exclusive power. As against this, the sramanic traditions became associated with wandering ascetic renunciates who rejected Vedic ritualism as also the dominance of the Brahmans. Buddhism, in particular, also became associated with an egalitarian ethos that rejected caste distinctions.

References

Bhattacharya, Sabyasachi, (ed.), 1997, *The Mahatma and the Poet: Letters and Debates Between Gandhi and Tagore*, Delhi: National Book Trust.

Chatterjee, Partha, 1994, *The Nation and Its Fragments: Colonial and Postcolonial Histories*, Delhi: Oxford University Press.

Das, Bhagwan, (ed.), 2010, *Thus Spoke Ambedkar: A Stake in the Nation*, Vol. I, New Delhi: Navayana.

Ganguli, B.N., 1977, *Indian Economic Thought: Nineteenth Century Perspectives*, New Delhi: Tata Mc-Graw Hill Publishing Co. Ltd.

Iqbal, Muhammad, 2011, *Reconstruction of Religious Thought in Islam*, Delhi: Shivalik Prakashan.

Kothari, Ashish, 2014, 'Radical Ecological Democracy: A Path Forward for India and Beyond', *Development*, Vol. 57, (1), pp. 36-45.

Marcuse, Herbert, 1964, *One-Dimensional Man: Studies in the Ideology of Advanced Industrial Society*, Boston: Beacon.

Menon, Dilip M., 2006, *Blindness of Insight: Essays on Caste in Modern India*, Delhi: Navayana Publishers.

Narayan, Badri, 2011, *The Making of the Dalit Public in North India: Uttar Pradesh, 1950 – Present*, New Delhi: Oxford University Press.

Nigam, Aditya, 2006, *The Insurrection of Little Selves: The Crisis of Secular-Nationalism in India*, New Delhi: Oxford University Press.

Nigam, Aditya, 2010, 'Capital Myths and the 'New Copernican Revolution', *Economic & Political Weekly*, 2010, Vol. 45(38), 18 September, pp. 13-17.

Parel, Anthony J., (ed.), 1977, *Gandhi – Hind Swaraj and Other Writings*, New Delhi: Cambridge University Press/ Foundation Books.

Rancière, Jacques, 2007, *Hatred of Democracy*, London: Verso.

Rodrigues, Valerian, (ed.), 2002, *The Essential Writings of BR Ambedkar*, New Delhi: Oxford University Press.

Roy, M. N., 1981, *Power, Politics and Parties,* Delhi: Ajanta Publications.

Srinivasan, Janaki, 2014, 'The Path Not Taken? Contesting Development in Newly Independent India', in *Critical Studies in Politics – Exploring Sites, Selves, Power*, Nivedita Menon, Aditya Nigam and Sanjay Palshikar (eds.), Delhi: Orient Blackswan.

Sunder Rajan, Rajeswari, 2015, 'Feminism's Futures: The Limits and Ambitions of Rokeya's Dream', *Economic & Political Weekly*, Vol. 50(41), 10 October, pp. 39-45.

Multilinear Critical Theory:
For a Society of Liberated Humanity

Bharat Patankar

Summary

The essay argues for a multilinear critical theory, by probing the need and aspects of a theory that recognizes human existence as the combination of various social, political, economic and cultural relations. Aspects of a multilinear critical theory come from the multilinearity of exploitation, the evolution of struggles and the nature of the evolution of dreams of a future society.

A society of liberated humanity is a dream that can come true if the approach for total transformation has its base on a multilinear critical theory. Central to this theory is the synthesis of multiple theories, into a theory that cognizes the multiplicity and contradictory nature of human existence and can come up with an alternate transformatory process of exploitation-free society, through the socio-economic analysis of the world order.

The Context

In the era of imperialist globalization, to talk about multilinear critical theoretical approach is a challenging task. It is challenging, first, because it has to confront and come to grips with multidimensional reality. Second, it has to unfold or unravel the various social, economic and cultural existences of the same individual in the form of persons belonging to a particular class, caste, community, nationality, gender, race and cultural group. Thirdly, the relation between humans and nature, which is translated through the medium of social, economic and cultural existences and has a bearing on the very existence of humanity as a whole, has become more complex, because more and more aspects of nature are becoming new productive forces of today's social-economic system.

The Base for Multilinear Theory in India

With reference to India, and also the world, we should discuss the various points raised by Babasaheb Ambedkar, Mahatma Phule, Karl Marx and D. D. Kosambi in relation to the inevitability of the multilinear approach.[1] Ambedkar, in his 'What Survives of the Marxian Creed,' says,

'Apart from the general falsification of the Marxian thesis that socialism is inevitable, many of the other propositions stated in the lists have also been demolished both by logic as well as by experience ... What remains of Marx is a residue of fire. This residue in my view consists of four items: (i) The function of philosophy is to reconstruct the world and not to waste its time in explaining the origin of the world; (ii) There is a conflict of interest between class and class; (iii) That private ownership of property brings power to one class and sorrow to another through exploitation; (iv) That it is necessary for the good of society that the sorrow be removed by the abolition of private property.

(Ambedkar, 1987, pp. 444)

Along with this, in his book *Annihilation of Caste* (Writings and Speeches, Vol. I), he raises another question for socialists.

'That the social order prevalent in India is a matter which a socialist must deal with...is a proposition which in my opinion is incontrovertible. He will be compelled to take account of caste after the revolution, if he does not take account of it before the revolution. This is only another way of saying that, turn in any direction you like, caste is the monster that crosses your path. You cannot have political reform, you cannot have economic reform, unless you kill this monster.'

(1979, pp. 47)

He further says,

'There can be only one answer to this question, and it is that inter-dining and intermarriage are repugnant to the beliefs and dogmas which the Hindus regard as sacred. Caste is not a physical object like a wall of bricks or a line of barbed wire... Caste is a notion; it is a state of the mind. The destruction of caste does not therefore mean the destruction of a physical barrier. It means a notional change.'

(ibid., pp. 68)

At the same time, he points out,

> 'Now the first thing that is to be argued against this view is that the caste system is not merely a division of labour. It is also a division of labourers. Civilized society undoubtedly needs a division of labour. But in no civilized society is division of labour accompanied by this unnatural division of labourers into watertight compartments. The caste system is not merely a division of labourers – it is a hierarchy in which the divisions of labourers are graded one above the other. In no other country is the division of labour accompanied by the division of labourers.'

(ibid., pp. 47)

The quotes above raise some important points that Ambedkar wants to put forth. First, that any theory claiming to be a transformative theory has some things which are universal and some aspects which remain applicable to the particular era and also to the specific social formations. At the crux of the theory should be the theoretical aspects which are applicable over many historical eras. Gautam Buddha talked about his own thoughts in the same way. That is why he gave the message of *attadeepabhav* ('Be your own light'), and suggested that his followers should keep whatever is universal in his teaching and discard what has become obsolete. Second, he wants to point out that though the objective existence of certain phenomenon (in this case caste) is important for understanding the laws of motion of that phenomenon, for the purpose of abolishing exploitation and transcending towards the formation of a new society, the subjective aspect also is very important, sometimes more important. Thirdly, he wants to point out that binary exploitation (class) is not the only form of exploitation but graded inequality also is a very important basic form of exploitation which brings about division of labourers, which is more difficult to overcome. This therefore brings forth the suggestion towards adoption of a multilinear approach as the basis on which one could go towards critical theory.

D. D. Kosambi, in his *Introduction to the Study of Indian History*, says, 'For the purpose of this work, history is defined as the presentation, in chronological order, of successive developments in the means and relations of production' (Kosambi, 1975, pp. 1). Quoting Marx further, from his *Critique of Political Economy*:

> '...The totality of these relations of production constitutes the economic structure of society, the real foundation, on which arises a legal and political superstructure and to which correspond definite forms of social consciousness. The mode of production of material life conditions the general process of social, political and intellectual life. It is not

the consciousness of men that determines their existence, but their social existence that determines their consciousness' (Marx, 1859, as cited in Kosambi, 1975, pp. 425).

Kosambi further quotes:

'In studying such transformations it is always necessary to distinguish between the material transformation of the economic conditions of production, which can be determined with a precision of natural science, and the legal, political, religious, artistic or philosophic – in short, ideological forms in which men become conscious of this conflict and fight it out. As one does not judge an individual by what he thinks about himself, so one cannot judge such a period of transformation by its consciousness, but, on the contrary, this consciousness must be explained from the contradictions of material life, from the conflict existing between the social process of production and the relations of production. No social order is ever destroyed before all the productive forces for which it is sufficient having developed, and new, superior relations of production never replace older ones before the material conditions for their existence have matured within the framework of the old society'.

(ibid., pp. 426)

Here Marx is contradictory in his propositions. This contradictoriness could also be called as dialectical method. But there is a problem with these propositions in any case. Marx definitely gives secondary importance to the ideological forms wherein people become conscious of their condition. In his early writings, he says, 'But theory also becomes a material force once it has gripped the masses. Theory is capable of gripping the masses when it demonstrates *ad hominem*, and it demonstrates *ad hominem* as soon as it becomes radical. To be radical is to grasp things by the root. But for man the root is man himself' (ibid., pp. 251). Here Marx gives the solution to the contradiction in which he brings himself in the Critique of Political Economy. Thus, as Kosambi says, history cannot be a chronological order of successive development in the means and relations of production but also, very basically, changes in juridical, political, religious, aesthetic and philosophical forms of consciousness. When Marx says that existence determines consciousness, it cannot by any means be taken as the ensemble of forces and relations of production. Existence also includes cultural, ethical, ideological, religious dimensions. So these two aspects of existence always are in humanity as a single whole and not as eclectic summation of these aspects. In *Capital* (1972) Marx says,

'Capitalist production, by collecting the population in great centres, and causing an ever-increasing preponderance of town population, on the one hand concentrates the historical and motive power of society; on the other hand, it disturbs the circulation of matter between man and the soil, i.e., prevents the return to the soil of its elements consumed by man in the form of food and clothing; it therefore violates the conditions necessary to the lasting fertility of the soil. By this action it destroys at the same time the health of the town laborer and the intellectual life of the rural laborer. But while upsetting the naturally grown condition for maintenance of that circulation of matter, it imperiously calls for its restoration as a system, as a regulating law of social production, and under a form appropriate to the full development of the human race' (pp. 505).

Through this analysis Marx goes much beyond the narrow concept of revolution, which he himself proposes almost at the end of *Capital*, Volume I.

'The monopoly of capital becomes a fetter upon the mode of production, which has sprung up and flourished along with, and under it. Centralization of the means of production and socialization at last reach a point where they become incompatible with their capitalist integument. This integument is burst asunder. The knell of capitalist private property sounds. The expropriators are expropriated.'

(ibid., pp. 763)

From his early writings onwards, up until his 'Letter to Vera Zasulich' (1965), he has not given a straitjacketed stages theory through which history will go. But responding to Vera Zasulich, for example, he says that if the organized strength of the working class and the peasantry is sufficient to carry the *mirs* (traditional collective farms in Russia) to modern collective farms in a socialistic way, then it is not necessary for Russian social-economic situation to first go through bourgeois transformation and then to socialism (Marx and Engels, 1848, pp. 142). After the Paris Commune he corrects the mistake in the Communist Manifesto and writes in the Preface that Communards were showing sufficiently that the proletarian revolution cannot use the same state given by the bourgeois mode of production, but has to create its own proletarian state with proletarian democracy. Lastly it could be pointed out that though he says at the end of *Capital* that the 'expropriators are expropriated' – meaning thereby that the means of production created by the proletariat are made private property of the bourgeoisie and bourgeoisie then is expropriated from those means of production and collectively taken over by the proletariat – he has nevertheless held that the mode of production of the future liberated society has to emerge within the womb of capitalist society itself. This means the totality of the aspects of future society should keep getting shaped inside the womb of existing capitalist society. This necessitates developing various insights and theoretical propositions of Marx in a multilinear way and synthesizing these with the propositions of Ambedkar, Phule, etc. His farsighted theoretical proposition talks of exchange of matter between soil and humans. This carries the insight which could be thoroughly developed in the 21st century for dealing with the question of the relation between ecology and abolition of exploitation, with the creation of the new society of a healthy nature. This insight couldn't be used unless and until one adopts multilinear critical theoretical approach to understand Marx and others.

Phule had adopted multilinear critical theoretical approach towards understanding the causes of exploitation in India. An excellent example of this could be seen in his book *Shetkaryaca Asud* ('Whipcord of the Peasant', 1882). He tries to grasp the totality from multiple aspects – the materialist view of history should be taken to understand the evolution of the exploitation he confronted, in which he includes the aspects of evolution of the state, caste, class, and gender exploitation, and also the role of the ecological paradigm in this evolution. Surprisingly, even though he takes his own materialist standpoint of history and dialectical approach in this book, he starts the book with the semi-poetical lines, 'without knowledge wisdom was lost; without wisdom values are lost; without values progress is lost; without progress wealth is lost; without wealth Shudras are ruined; and all this happens because of one thing, the lack of knowledge' (Phule, 1969, pp. 189). Here apparently one would say how is knowledge given such a central role in the shaping of the future of humanity, in this case the toiling masses? If there is forceful separation of the mass of people from acquiring, developing and exchanging knowledge and, on the other side, if it is wielded by a minority of the people as an instrument of domination and exploitation, then of course it becomes a great material force. Women, *Shudras* and *Atishudras*[2] were supposed to have only experiential knowledge and were banned from developing this experiential knowledge into a scientific abstract knowledge, which creates a wall of separation between manual labour and mental labour. This separation, along with the ban on having control over natural resources by any means, cannot bring about anything but slavery to these excluded caste sections. This slavery is maintained on the basis of religio-cultural rules by punishing those who break the rules. So women's slavery as women and graded inequality with division of labourers into watertight compartments creates a situation which needs an alternative. This is not only in terms of new productive forces and relations of production but also in abolition of separation between manual and mental labour. It means creation of new ideological cultural consciousness on the basis of which a revolutionary praxis could become successful.

On this basis Phule uses a combined method:

- Understanding the nature of industry and imperialism with its effects on Indian social relations and economy;
- Effects on forest, agriculture, and water resources;
- Effects on caste relations;
- Effects on cultural values;
- Ideology and religion.

He gives alternative practices for going towards a new exploitation free society, a new dream. On this basis he proposes an alliance which he calls 'Stri-Shudra-Atishudra' alliance. In caste terms it meant, in those days, an alliance of all women and all non-brahman, non-trader and non kshatriya castes. Phule also had his perspective about toiling people. That is why he said, 'all men and women should become toiling people' (ibid., pp. 441). This proposition of Jotiba Phule can form the primary basis on which we can do a synthesis of critical theoretical propositions of Marx, Babasaheb Ambedkar, Phule himself, Kosambi, Gramsci, etc. Interestingly, this proposition not only contains the method of critical analysis of society, it also finds the roots of multifaceted exploitation and proposing concrete alternatives for changing the world. As Marx, in the spring of 1845, says in *Thesis on Feuerbach,* 'the philosophers have only interpreted the world, in various ways; the point is to change it' (Marx, 1975, pp. 423).

Ambedkar also tries to use a combined method. That is why he talks about:

- Annihilation of caste system;
- End of Brahmanism;
- Abolition of capitalism;
- Acceptance of a quasi-religion which doesn't contradict the scientific attitude towards social transformation;
- Abolition of gender exploitation.

So he talks about two enemies, capitalism and Brahmanism, embraces Buddhism with hundreds of thousands of his followers, resigns from the ministership in protest for reforms in the Hindu Code Bill as one of the instruments for going towards women's liberation and, the only comparison he does between philosophies is between Buddha and Marx.

From a comparative analysis of the approaches of Marx, Phule and Ambedkar, we come to the understanding that the first aspect of multilinearity flows from inevitable multilinearity of the aspects of exploitation and necessity of relatively autonomous and combined struggles for the end of this exploitation, along with the dream of a new society which has an ecologically sustainable character towards prosperity. The second aspect of multilinearity comes from the qualitatively different nature of historical evolution of various societies in the world and its effects on the existing social-economic structure. The third comes from the nature of evolution of the dream of future society, which compels taking into account the evolution of liberated humanity coming from people who are exploited on the basis of class, caste, gender, race, community, nationality etc., and at the same time to take note of geo-ecological and geographical differences between the various areas, nations and nationalities. Kosambi (1975), in certain ways, has taken note of some of these aspects.

Aspects of Multilinear Critical Theory

Based on the discussion above, we can come to the conclusion about some important aspects to be noted for the creation of the multilinear critical theory and synthesis of various critical theories for creation of exploitation-free society.

1. Exploitation is multifaceted and every factor has independent existence though intertwined with the other facets of exploitation. No facet of exploitation could be abolished without abolishing all the other facets. The struggles for the abolition of caste, class, gender, racial, etc., exploitations are then also going to be autonomous and yet intertwined.

2. No section of exploited people could be called as playing the role of vanguard in the creation of the new exploitation-free society. If at all we go by the logic of Marxist theory then, according to Jotiba Phule, women should become the vanguard for the creation of liberated humanity. Like in theory, where we are talking about multi-linearity about the transformatory movement we also have to talk about multilinear combined leadership of the social sections.

3. Dialectical shaping of each other by subjective critical consciousness of society and objective processes in the field of culture, mode of production, nature, should be the basis for understanding history, contemporary society, as well as the future march towards creation of liberated humanity. One-sided deterministic approach would lead to a mechanical conclusion and wrong propositions for the transformatory processes.

4. The world created by humans for themselves through their actions, and the remaining world of nature, should also be considered as being in a dialectical relationship. The changing role of any natural resource in its mode of use by humans would bring a change in all aspects of human society. At the same time, it would change the way the rest of nature affects the world created by humans.

5. Humans don't and cannot live on basic necessities like food and shelter, but they

also live on the basis of fulfilment of cultural, ideological, emotional, sexual, etc., requirements. They are the beings who want to rejoice when they are happy, to express their sorrows when they are sad, and anger in various forms. They want to express their love for nature also in various forms, and so on. Multilinear critical theory should take note of this nature of humans unified in the form of human existence.

6. On the background of the nature of human existence comes the question of religion. Though religion as such has a recent entry into human history, it has become a very important factor which should be dealt with if all sections of humanity, specifically exploited humans, have to be brought into, in Phule's words, 'ekmeylok' (unified humanity). Unless and until this happens total transformation of society and creation of a new society is impossible. From the standpoint of rationalism and scientific attitude it is understood today that religion is an irrational thing. Belief in heaven and gods is irrational and false. But there is a flaw in this kind of theory, because religion is a truth of human society created by society itself for some kind of necessity of life. In the introduction to his Critique of Hegel's Philosophy of Right, Marx says: 'Religious suffering is at one and the same time the expression of real suffering and a protest against real suffering. Religion is the sigh of the oppressed creature, the heart of a heartless world and the soul of soulless conditions. It is the opium of the people. The abolition of religion as the illusory happiness of the people is the demand for their real happiness. To call on them to give up their illusions about their condition is to *call on them to give up a condition that requires illusion*. The criticism of religion is, therefore, in *embryo the criticism of that vale of tears* of which religion is the *halo*' (pp. 244).

So the transformatory movement cannot take a position of opposing religion as an institution in terms of enmity. Any critical theory should address this question in terms of understanding the emergence of a particular religion and acceptance of it by millions of people. Only if one tries to understand this process, does the requirement of something like religion (which is not contradictory to the scientific or rational understanding) become obvious. Ambedkar and Phule tried to understand religion in the same way. This brings forth the question of whether human existence requires the aspect of what could be called as quasi-religion, or faith, which is not based on blind belief and mysticism. Religions like Buddhism or Phule's *Sarvajanik Satyadharma* (roughly translated, 'people's religion of truth') are to be considered to evolve the theory. Even after the 'soulless' conditions get transformed into conditions with soul, and the heartless world gets transformed into a world with heart, whether there is going to remain the necessity of religion is the problematic to be solved.

7. When natural resources like wind, solar energy, energy of the waves of the ocean, sound waves, light waves, etc., go on becoming part of the capital market and part of the production process as means of production or condition of production, then relations between nature and human creation becomes qualitatively different. Because these are the resources which are not palpable resources like ores or stones or natural gas. These are renewable resources which are not consumed in the production process, and which are part of the very basic ecological processes of nature. Today's stage of imperialist globalization is rapidly bringing these kind of resources into the capitalist realm but understanding about their relation to property ownership, to being a commodity, is not thought about at all. For example, if wind is used for electricity generation, it is the density and speed of the wind which is used and the issue doesn't remain only in the limits of relation of the wind to the production process but the relation of speed and density to it. This shows that basically capitalism has started going much beyond the framework of hitherto used means, conditions and instruments of production and this is only superficially understood or tried to be understood by a handful of attempts. This necessitates the multilinear theory which includes understanding of natural resources by using the method of natural sciences on the one hand and understanding of the new relations of human world with these resources and their functions by using the method of social sciences. It seems one has to go beyond this eclectic combination of the two sciences and go towards evolution of a unified theory dealing with both these aspects.

8. Emergence of cyberspace and 'virtual reality' has also created a new powerful and determining factor in the process of transformation of society. It exists in both subjective and objective worlds of human existence. Rather, it could be said where subjectivity ends and where objectivity starts is very difficult to decide in this space of human life. This also goes beyond the traditional understanding of the social relations of production, mode of production, instruments of production, means of production, etc. Despite this the sector occupies a very crucial role in today's world capitalist economy, and has to be thought about in terms of its role in the dream of an alternative society. This also requires a unified theory drawing from the fields of natural and social sciences.

9. The question of freedom and necessity, or freedom versus necessity, becomes very relevant and crucial in the period of imperialist globalization and ensemble of the

social formations in the world. This needs an understanding that the collective interest should be more important than individual freedom if one has to choose in terms of the end of exploitation and prosperity of all human beings. The multilinear critical theory has to deal with this question in such a way that these two things should not be counterposed as they have traditionally been. Ambedkar and Marx deal with this question in almost the same way though it is more correctly expressed by Marx: 'In place of the old bourgeois society, with its classes and class antagonisms, we shall have an association, in which the free development of each is the condition for the free development of all' (Marx & Engels, 1848, pp. 27). Here there is no contradiction between individual freedom and well-being of the collective.

Experiencing Necessity of Multilinear Critical Theory in Practice

This necessity was experienced during the people's movement even before the emergence of imperialist globalization. In the late 60s' and early 70s' world capitalism and the dominant mode of production, that is the capitalist mode of production in India was also in crisis. This crisis was felt by people because of rapidly increasing unemployment among the first young generation after independence, shortage of food-grains, because of the generalized droughts in many states, and obstacles felt by oppressed caste and class youth in getting educated at higher levels. This was also the period when the young generation of intellectuals threw themselves into the struggles of toiling farmers, agricultural labourers, adivasis, dalits, and women in emerging social movements. They started facing the problem of multiple identities, exploitations and cultural specificities in the same groups of people they were working with. I was working with my comrades in movements of three oppressed social sections – adivasis, agricultural labourers and working class. While we were trying to organize in an adivasi majority area, sometimes, because of the daily life circumstances, adivasis used to identify themselves only as adivasis and secondarily as agricultural labourers or toiling farmers. Adivasi women were getting oppressed and sexually exploited by the landholding caste people who of course belonged to the landowner class also. Women, while fighting against this oppression, *as women* found their identities as 'adivasi women' overshadowing their identity as women – a dilemma of gender oppression and class oppression as labourers.

This experience gave rise to the necessity of analysis of caste, gender, nationality and community independently as well as in relation to class. While conscious critical social practice emerged with these, integrated theoretical approach did not, and theory as well as practice have remained eclectic till now. Some fresh attempts for caste annihilation movement have recently emerged in Maharashtra. But because of the eclectic sectional movements of various classes and gender, it is becoming very difficult for organizations that had traditionally organised around class, mainly of the trade union kind, to lead and mobilize masses for caste annihilation movement, which these masses do not understand because of long-drawn ideological presentations and sectional movement practices. In fact, there should be a program based on a dream of an alternative society which is prosperous, ecologically balanced and based on decentralized production along with annihilation of caste, class, gender, race, and so on, in an integrated manner, with alternative cultural practices and values.[3] Such a program could only emerge out of multilinear critical theoretical approach which is capable of analyzing existing social-economic formations in India and the world. In other words, this program should have a potential such that every exploited section should feel compelled to go beyond their sectional interests and still feel that this would liberate them from all kinds of exploitation to give them a society of liberated humanity. This is not an easy task either theoretically or practically. However, until this happens the existing social order would remain intact and continue giving some concessions to the struggling people or suppress their struggles for some period.

It may be noted that in the academic field as well as theoretical work being done by those active in mass transformation movements, intellectuals are writing about caste and gender and even class in terms of the old realities which are not coinciding with the existing realities of caste, class, gender relations. For example, the percentage of people living off the caste jobs assigned by the traditional caste system has reduced to a great extent in India. Still, the theoretical discourse goes on as if that reality still existed. People doing research are not going to the roots of the caste system, as Babasaheb Ambedkar and Jotirao Phule did, for finding out the laws of motion of the caste system as a system. If this is not the basis of one's analysis, then only the superficial reality could be analyzed and that too in a schematic and descriptive way. But if one bases oneself on the laws of motion for analysis of today's caste system, then one would find that though the superficial and statistical reality has indeed changed, the laws of motion of the caste system have not changed. They are still in existence. We can only find certain glimpses or beginnings of analysis from the standpoint of laws of motion with regard to caste system and, we are still far away from the real understanding. This is also true about the radically changed nature of gender and class relations. Because of this, there is an absence of an alternative direction to these struggles. On top of this, understanding both of the intertwining of all these relations in the social formation and the effects of imperialist globalization has on this intertwining is totally lacking.

The realization through experience of the inevitability of multilinear critical theory also came about in the movements of rural toiling people in relation to Reliance Corporation's coal-based energy generation plant (it tried to start the plant in Raigad district of Maharashtra to produce 3000 megawatts electricity). The government and the company itself defended the project on the basis of shortfall of electricity generation for Maharashtra and the capability of the project to generate employment. Usually these projects are opposed on the basis of negative approach by saying that farmers should not be dispossessed of their land, and employment generated will not absorb the unemployment created by the dispossession. This is a defensive argument to maintain a status quo which does not give an answer to the illusionary developmental model imposed on the minds of the young generation of the affected families. At the same time looking at such struggles across India, they generally become losing struggles. There was an attempt in this particular movement in the Konkan region of Maharashtra to give an alternative, in a book published by the movement, *Towards a Prosperous and Beautiful Konkan: An Alternative Energy Plan*. A long-drawn struggle of five years, with mass participation of men and women, forced the state to revert acquired land. Along with this, the government had to agree to explore this alternative plan. This kind of approach has to get generalized, without remaining project-specific. It should be part of decentralized agro-industrial sustainable development which encompasses the alternative in the fields of ecological balance, land and water use, integrated water use, and development of the use of renewable resources.[4]

The movement could base its struggle on multilinear theoretical perspective against freely using wind as private property by the multinational and other kind of windmill companies. Here the movement achieved a victory to keep wind as a public resource and forced the government to make companies to pay for the use of this public resource.

A struggle for equitable water use based on minimum basic livelihood requirements in addition to drinking and domestic water use also threw up theoretical problems. Delinking right to this water use from the ownership of the land or house and assuring this amount of water before giving it to commercial use violates today's basis of giving right over water in proportion to ownership of land or other productive resource. In other words it challenges the practice of treating water as private property. This raises a theoretical question about the process of challenging private property in land and the industrial sector. The conventional concept of common property in land in an exploitation free society is to have big collective farms worked with big machinery like harvesters, etc. It also has no aspect of increased productivity from land by the use of organic farming and modern methods of water and land relationship based on root zone volumetric supply of water. It also has not got any aspect which deals with the kind of renewable energy based decentralized industries which would be related to specific products in agriculture, replacing fossil fuel raw materials. In short, renewable energy based decentralized agro-industrial complexes which could be easily collectively controlled by people themselves were not imagined in the older perspective. The old perspective accepted the capitalist model of industry and agriculture which makes centralization inevitable, which pollutes, saps the soil and labourers for enriching the centralized structure and endangers the sustainability and ecological balance and health of nature and humans. The means of production, forces of production and instruments of production, conditions of production and relation of the overall production processes to nature unquestioningly took the same form and content as the capitalist mode of production. The movement for equitable water distribution created these problematics, to be solved theoretically and to bring them into a practical program.

The creative practical movement which deals with gradually going towards establishing alternatives related to the future society requires a theory for going from subconscious to conscious to critical conscious thinking in activists working for change. This cannot come about merely through study circles. It requires a dialectical relationship between multinear critical theory and conscious practice of the movement which never loses the link with the final aim of exploitation-free society. To the extent these two aspects go on enriching each other, to that extent the process of social transformation doesn't take place suddenly at a particular point of time, but happens as an everyday process, unfolding towards the realization of the dream. The theory about this relation is also not developed to the extent which would fulfil the needs of the era of imperialist globalization.

Finally, one should be cautious about the multinear critical approach being endangered in falling into an eclectic approach. The need of the hour is that the multilinear approach should be a synthesis of various theoretical approaches into a single theoretical approach which cognizes the multiplicity and contradictions in actual life and emerges as a theory which gives analysis of the world social order and socio-economic formation in India. At the same time it comes up with alternative unified processes through which the established socio-economic formation in India could be transformed.

Unfolding Multilinear Critical Theory: a practical program towards total transformation

The following points emerge when considering how multilinear critical theory could unfold:
1. The vision of future society gives you the alternative in all fields of society to be brought into this world. These final alternatives should be translated into the kind of

immediate demands of the people which are not moving in circles in the established system but go on unfolding towards ultimate alternatives. At various stages these could be called as pre-figurative forms which would be developing through a series of movements into final unfolding. Such movements (unlike the circular movements within the established system) would encourage people to contribute creatively into a forward direction towards total transformation. This should be the major correction to be brought about urgently in the life of the circular movements which have become estranged from the ideology of transformation and their concrete processes of the same.

2. Any new society cannot emerge out of the old without having its own cultural ethos and value system. The totality of this could be called as Renaissance which unfolds the culture and values of the society of liberated humanity. But Renaissance is a thing which cannot be a movement based on a planned program and organized in a very systematic manner like the movements in other fields of life. This movement should come from the peoples' hearts in a spontaneous conscious manner. Thus the function of multilinear critical theory would be to point towards creation of inspiring points which would trigger the imagination of the people at large and then, they themselves, like wildfire, start unfolding a total process in this field.

3. It is also necessary for the movement based on multilinear critical theory to intervene in education in general and the field of science and technology in particular, because these fields are crucial for development of alternative productive forces based on renewables and the natural resources which are not exhaustible. This is a very laborious and tenuous task and needs patience and work with the scientists and technologists who are ready to participate in this process. Otherwise wind energy comes in as a part of renewable based productive force but the body of the tower used for harvesting wind comes from fossil raw materials creating pollution and using resource like water in large amounts and pollutes it too. One can say this becomes one of the major tasks to be undertaken for unfolding of social movement towards a society of liberated humanity.

4. A society of liberated humanity presupposes the process of withering away of the state.[5] Hence finding out the processes through which the very necessity of the state for any society could be abolished is essential. This involves incorporating a process of collective decision-making, decentralization, abolishing hierarchical structures of any kind, building the capacity of the population through mass education for enabling them to implement decentralized, collectively controlled processes of production.

At the same time simple methods of coordination rather than the current forms of democratic centralization should be evolved in all the organizations which are involved in transformatory process including political organizations.

5. It is very clear that organized violence is the main precursor for the beginning of exploitation and creation of state ruling over society, and threatening violent suppression of people. We have to think about the forms of movement which are non-violent but still determined. It is clear that this is a highly contentious point if we look at the historical process which the society has gone through till now. But we cannot ignore the truth that organized violence is always a precursor for creation not only of the state but also most prominently of all women's exploitation. The states in the world have acquired the instruments of violence of such a quality and quantity that they can demolish this world many times! Against this background, peoples' movements see participation by hundreds of thousands of people there by compelling violent forces of the state to withdraw, and the dream of going towards creating a society of liberated humanity cannot but adopt non-violent forms of the movement.

6. The main strength of any state was never its oppressive or violent power of killing thousands of people with the help of its armed machinery. Sanction given by the people at large for existence of the state as an institution is the major factor for its continued existence and that of its machinery. The process of searching how and through what processes this sanction is renewed by the state as an institution through the fields of culture, law, education, value systems, developmental patterns, etc., should go on and also unfold into a continual finding out of the non-violent forms. Experiences of various movements world over show that this process is possible on a wider scale and in a more consistent way.

7. Autonomy of the various aspects of the movement consistent with autonomy of the sectors in concretely existing society is the major precondition for development of the creative unfolding of these aspects and their merging into one process. Consideration of primacy of one aspect over another is proved wrong because even the established exploitative society has these varied aspects functioning in autonomous spontaneous ways, though connected with each other. So the movements in the fields of the economy, liberation from gender oppression, caste annihilation, creation of new culture, generation of new scientific and technological knowledge and programs, creative arts, should have their autonomy along with inter-wovenness, synthesizing into peoples' movement as a whole. This would require the formulations about

movements under the leadership of the proletariat or this or that section to be left aside and adopting democratic balance and coordination of the various movements as an alternative.

8. The various examples of actual movements and their contributions and drawbacks will help us in this unfolding as a multifaceted process. It is not necessary that these movements should be led by 'revolutionary' ideology. People can contribute in various movements without this kind of leadership. There are many examples of such kind, right from Paris Commune till now, including the movements the world over during the late 60s' and early 70s'.

9. It is also important to understand that there could be perspectives, experimentations, pre-figurative forms, which are leading towards society of liberated humanity, but there cannot be a blueprint of such a society. People would go on developing it through this process towards a reality in the future. Multilinear critical theory emerging out of dialectical dialogue between activists, thinkers and people can only become one of the mainstreams of this process. Without well-founded dreams no transformation can take place. But such dreams should have their feet firmly on the ground of the practical movement and actually existing situation of the period. Even where the dreams are not seen explicitly by the leading people in the movement, the masses themselves do so, such that new dreams become possible on the basis of the outcome of their struggle. The function of multilinear critical theory to bring about a society of liberated humanity is to come up with the dream that it is going to be possible and is also necessary.

Endnotes

1. This essay does not include M.K. Gandhi's thoughts and practice; there is need to understand and build these also into the multilinear critical theory, in particular the philosophy and practice of non-violence, the ability to mobilise millions of 'ordinary' people including women, and other such aspects.

2. These are expressions used for the castes who are not supposed to belong to the three higher *varnas*, that is, brahman, kshatriya and vaishya. In today's legal terminology all OBCs could be termed as shudras and BCs could be termed as atishudras.

3. Pl. see several other relevant essays in this volume, including those on Localisation, Dare to Dream, and the Concluding essay.

4. Pl. see essays on Biomass, Localisation, Energy and Water Futures in this volume.
5. Pl. see essay on Power Futures in this volume.

References

Ambedkar, B.R., 1987, *Writings and Speeches*, (Vol. 3), Mumbai: Education Department, Government of Maharashtra.

Ambedkar, B.R., 1979, 'Annihilation of Caste', in *Writings and Speeches*, (Vol. I), Mumbai: Education Department, Government of Maharashtra,

Kosambi, D.D., 1975, *An Introduction to the Study of Indian History*, Mumbai: Popular Prakashan.

Marx, K., 1972, *Capital* (Vol. 1), New York: International Publishers.

Marx, K. 1975, *Early Writings*, New York: Vintage Books.

Marx, K. 1965, *Letter to Vera Zasulich*, New York: International Publishers.

Marx, Karl and Frederick Engels, 1848, Manifesto of the Communist Party (Translated into English by Samuel Moore in cooperation with Frederick Engels in 1888); available in Karl Marx and Frederick Engels, 1969, *Selected Works*, Vol. One, Moscow: Progress Publishers. The Manifesto of the Communist Party is available at https://www.marxists.org/archive/marx/works/download/pdf/Manifesto.pdf (last visited 8 May 2017).

Phule, Jyotirao, 1969, *Shetkaryaca Asud ('Whipcord of the Peasant')*, *Samagra Wangmay* (Collected Works). Mumbai: Maharashtra Rajya Sahitya ani Sanskriti Mandal, Government of Maharashtra.

The Future World Order and India's Role in Shaping It[1]

Muchkund Dubey

Summary

The United Nations (U.N.) was created not only to prevent future wars, but also to seek out and address the root causes of war through its activities in social, economic, political and human rights fields. The vision was to create a peaceful world in which people of all nations could prosper. The 60s' and 70s' can be regarded as the golden era of international cooperation in the economic field. However, by the beginning of the 1990s', the major powers succeeded in weakening the organisation significantly by dismantling its capacity to deliver public goods to the international community. We are living in an unstable, disorderly world, where international norms of governance are enfeebled, particularly by the actions of a few powerful nations.

This essay argues for a new, dynamic and democratic multilateral governance of the future world order. Central to this will be to restore and revamp the essential functions and enhance the capacity (financially and for peacemaking) of the U.N. It should become a voice for people around the world through effective participation of all countries and civil society organisations. It should also be the arena for the global accountability of multinational corporations, global surveillance, and regulation of international financial markets. India should take the initiative for restructuring the world order by building a global coalition for a new dynamic and democratic multilateralism under the U.N.

The Post Second World War World Order

The post Second World War world order has been dominated by the hegemony of the major powers that emerged victorious from the War. At the institutional level, it has been underpinned by the United Nations and its family of organizations. It is basically a multilateral world order with a residue of hegemonism reflected in the veto power of the Permanent Members of the Security Council.

With all its deficiencies, the United Nations, in its objectives, original functions and structure, represented the highest level of excellence in the evolution of multilateralism. It was based on the twin pillars of a body of commonly shared human values and of basic principles of international law. The values represented by the United Nations consist of those which have been cherished by humankind through time immemorial. Some of these are peace, cooperation, harmony and solidarity derived from the awareness of common humanity. The others like fundamental freedoms, basic human rights, equality and justice, have evolved through the more recent strivings of humankind.

The United Nations was created not only to prevent another World War akin to WW II, nor even a possible Third world war, but (as per the Charter of the UN, 1945), 'to save the succeeding generations from the scourge of war'. One of the means by which the U.N. was meant to set about accomplishing this task was to seek to root out causes of war through its activities in the economic, social, cultural and human rights fields. The Charter contains extensive provisions in this regard. Besides, a whole network of institutions, including in particular the U.N. specialized agencies, have either been brought in association with or established by the United Nations to serve this purpose. The UNESCO Constitution describes this overall purpose of the Charter in a succinct manner: 'Since wars begin in the minds of men, it is in the minds of men that the defence of peace must be constructed'.

Throughout history, great thinkers and visionaries have aspired to 'one world'. Mahatma Gandhi had said: 'I would not want to live in a world that was not one world' (Asian Relations Organization, 1948). Jawaharlal Nehru had seen U.N. as the harbinger of such a world. At the Asian Relations Conference held in New Delhi in March-April 1947 he said: 'We have arrived at a stage in human affairs when the ideal of that "One World" and some kind of a world federation seems to be essential though there are many dangers and obstacles in the way.... We, therefore, support the United Nations structure which is painfully emerging from its infancy' (Asian Relations Organization, 1948).

Though the United Nations was by no means conceived as a world government, it was envisaged and structured as a central over-arching authority both in the military and non-military fields of security. The Charter left no scope for the functioning of a rival instrumentality for the prevention of 'threats to the peace, breaches of the peace, and acts of aggression'. The Charter envisaged no non-Charter response to threats to international security. The use of force without the Security Council's authorization was permitted only in an exercise of 'the inherent right of individual or collective self-defence' and that too only in the event of an 'armed attack'.

In the social, economic, cultural and human rights fields, the U.N., according to the Charter, represented the planetary system or the authoritative central piece of the international system. According to Article 1 of the Charter, the U.N. is 'to be a centre for harmonizing the actions of nations in the attainment of these common ends'. Article 57 provides that 'the various specialized agencies ... shall be brought into relationship with the United Nations'. Here please mark the use of the word 'shall'. This means that none of the agencies, including the World Bank, the IMF and the WTO has the choice of opting out of association with U.N. Article 59 which empowers the U.N. 'to initiate negotiations ... for the creation of any new specialized agencies required for the accomplishment of the purposes set forth in Article 55'. The hegemonist element in the Charter in the form of the veto was sought to be mitigated by such measures as 'Unite For Peace' adopted by the General Assembly, its direct role in the realm of disarmament and the initiatives taken by it for convening global conferences, including those on the issue of security and disarmament. However, the veto remained a ground reality by which the Permanent Members immunized themselves from any action to be taken against them under the enforcement provisions of the Security Council and made such action against other powers conditional upon unanimity among them.

In spite of numerous failures of the U.N., the period between the mid-60s' and the mid-70s' can legitimately be regarded as the golden era of international economic cooperation. That was the period when new organizations like UNDP, UNCTAD, UNIDO and UNEP were established. Schemes like the General System of Preferences (GSP), Integrated Programme of Commodity Market Organization, Compensatory Financing, Supplementary Financing, Special Drawing Rights and Debt Amelioration and Forgiveness were advanced and agreed upon. In the early 70s', two Declarations and Programmes of Action for the Establishment of a New International Economic Order were adopted. A Charter of Economic Rights and Duties was also promulgated. In the late 70s', the first International Development Strategy representing the closest approximation to development planning at the global level was adopted by the General Assembly.

But from the end of the 70s', major powers mounted a deliberate, well planned and concerted attack on the United Nations. By the beginning of the 1990s', they succeeded in weakening the Organization substantially, changing its agenda in the economic field beyond recognition and drastically whittling down its core competence. They also succeeded in putting their own economic policies beyond the pale of U.N. scrutiny and surveillance. The

U.N. was declared by these countries as incompetent to deal with its Charter functions in the realms of money, finance, trade, external indebtedness and development strategy. These functions were transferred to the IMF, World Bank and the WTO, the organizations which the major economic powers, by virtue of their voting strength or power to retaliation in the case of WTO, dominate and use as instruments for advancing their interest. The U.N. is now considered to be competent to deal only with disaster relief, post-war rehabilitation and construction, and humanitarian issues. Instead of being a negotiating forum for undertaking legally or morally binding commitments, the U.N. has become a debating society.

The major powers adopted a series of devices to bring the U.N. to its present state. They launched a false, misguided and misinformed campaign against the efficiency and the integrity of the United Nations. They derided and went back on the whole body of consensus that was achieved in the development field during the 60s' and the early 70s'. The other device they adopted for weakening the U.N. was to keep it's organizations on the brink of financial bankruptcy by withholding dues and applying budgetary squeeze in the form of 'zero nominal growth' in budget. A major factor accounting for the loss of autonomy of the United Nations and the distortion of its priorities has been its growing 'voluntarization', that is, the growing practice of putting the funding of its activities on a voluntary basis.

Even during the golden era, developed countries succeeded in maintaining their stranglehold over the world economy, using the rules and regimes governing the international economic order as an instrument for exploitation. Commodity prices continued to register a secular decline. Domestic agriculture of the major developed countries was kept outside the rules of GATT. Textile products were taken out of the purview of GATT rules from the early 70s' and developing countries were obliged to apply voluntary restrictions on their other competitive exports to developed countries. No dent was allowed to be made on the restrictive business practices of their transnational corporations and the effort made in the U.N. to keep an international surveillance over their activities and develop a code of conduct for their operation was abruptly brought to an end by the beginning of the 80s'. Even in its operational activities, the U.N. was not allowed to undertake programmes or projects which were likely to adversely affect the business of the companies of developed countries in the developing countries.

In the area of peacekeeping, the U.N. remained paralyzed during the Cold War for want of unanimity among the Permanent Members of the Security Council. This role was revived from 1989 to 1992 when the number of peacekeeping operations undertaken by the U.N.

was several times more than those during the entire Cold War period of over forty years. But just when the United Nations seemed to be doing justice to its Charter function relating to the maintenance of peace and security, the major powers stepped in to marginalize it once again in this sphere. For example, they did not authorize it to get involved in conflict situations in Iraq, Afghanistan and Syria. The outcome was the continuation of these conflicts involving massive scale killings, displacement and destruction.

The major powers and scholars of these countries have often claimed that the hegemony of these countries in the world order has been mainly responsible for maintaining peace during the post-war period. They have argued that their policy of deterrence based on the doctrine of mutual assured destruction prevented wars and maintained peace. But that was true only of inter-state wars among major powers; wars and conflicts remained endemic in Third World countries. Moreover, the policy of deterrence resulted in a nuclear arms race of unprecedented dimension. In the early 70s', it reached a stage where the world lived under the spectre of a 'nuclear winter'. This doctrine also resulted in the widespread adoption of a cult of militarism, not only by the two rival powers and their allies but also other countries of the world.

Even the reforms in the U.N. have been invariably driven by major developed countries, aimed at maintaining status quo in the international order, eliminate pluralism, stem dissent inconvenient to major powers and tighten their grip over the U.N. institutions. The overall effect has been general enfeebling of the U.N. brought about mainly by dismantling its capacity to deliver public goods to the international community and transferring its roles and functions to institutions which major powers control.

After the end of the Cold War, the United States emerged as the only superpower in the world, facilitated by the disintegration of the Communist system led by the Soviet Union. Other major military and economic powers joined it for maintaining the status quo in the world order. This was because they saw the main threat to their security coming from the rise of new powers, particularly in the Third World. Thus, instead of two rival power blocs contending for hegemony, there emerged a new alliance striving to establish its supremacy vis-à-vis the rest of the world. This alliance consisted of both, the East, the West, and Japan. China too was a member, albeit an informal one, of the new alliance. This alliance put in place a number of exclusive discriminatory regimes which had the purpose of freezing the level and structure of the development of developing countries. These included the Australia Group (for chemical weapons), the Missile Technology Control Regime (for missiles) and the London Club, later renamed as Nuclear Suppliers Group (for nuclear weapons). Some of the environmental regimes established at that time, like the Montreal Protocol, were also designed for the same purpose. The Agreement on Trade-Related Aspects of Intellectual Property Rights (TRIPS), the Agreement on Trade-Related Investment Measures (TRIMs), and the Agreement on Agriculture under the WTO had the effect of limiting the space for macro-economic policy making by developing countries and freezing their technological development at the current level.

Largely as a result of this consensus on the strategic objectives of major powers, the two years before the end of the Cold War and a decade after it, turned out to be very fruitful for progress in arms control and the strengthening of the non-proliferation regime. The United States and Soviet Union/Russia took parallel unilateral initiatives to eliminate tactical nuclear weapons. In the non-nuclear field, two major agreements were concluded: the treaty among the NATO and the now defunct Warsaw Pact countries to slash their conventional arms by almost half, and an unprecedented convention to ban the development, production, stockpiling, deployment and use of chemical weapons. The non-proliferation regime was strengthened as 40 states joined the NPT during this period including two major nuclear weapon powers (China and France), seven countries abandoned their nuclear weapon programmes voluntarily, and the NPT was extended indefinitely in 1995.

The second half of the 1990s' saw the consolidation of the superpower status of the United States. The U.S. Administration also arrogated to itself the discretion to act outside the U.N. either unilaterally or through 'coalitions of the willing', to intervene in troubled spots in the world in pursuance of its national interest. It waged wars in Kosovo, Iraq and Afghanistan and heavily bombarded the then Yugoslavia. Thankfully, the unilateral moment in world history did not last very long. The year 2001 marked the beginning of its end and by 2005, it was all but over. After that, there was a precipitate decline in the prestige and power of the United States.

A major factor bringing about this change was the shift of economic power balance from Europe and the United States to Asia. Major emerging Asian economies, particularly China and India, have grown up to three times faster than the United States and Europe, continuously for a period of nearly three decades. From the mid-1990s', China, Russia, India and other like-minded powers have been giving frequent calls for a multi-polar world order and taking action like the formation of groups such as BRICS (Brazil, Russia, India, China, South Africa) and SCO (Shanghai Cooperation Organisation), to bring this about.

Globalization has also brought about major differences in world power balance. Because of globalization, a major power, howsoever mighty, cannot work in isolation from other emerging powers. Moreover, globalization has facilitated the proliferation and strengthening of transnational actors, particularly national and international civil society organizations.

No power can now afford to ignore this phenomenon. The liberal world order led by the United States has also been challenged on normative grounds, which has given rise to a tide of anti-Americanism in a large swath of the Third World, particularly West Asia and Pakistan. Another major reason for the decline of the American order has been domestic – the rising income inequality, declining infrastructure and massive burden of debts. These burdens on the U.S. economy have been imposed in no small measures due to its involvement in the Iraq and Afghan wars which, according to one estimate, has a price tag of six trillion U.S. dollars (Acharya, 2015).

Future of the World

We are living in an unstable, disorderly, fractured, unequal and unjust world. The institutional mechanism for global governance is enfeebled and remains generally ineffective. International law is being flagrantly flouted by major powers and dictatorial regimes. This situation is unlikely to change and, most probably, would deteriorate in the coming decades.

We envisage the continuation of the current trend of recession, slow growth or stagnation in the economies of major developed countries. In emerging economies, particularly China, India, Russia, Brazil, South Africa and Turkey, the high rates of growth witnessed during the last 15 years have started slowing down. However, the potentiality for growth in most of these countries is still high. They have still a long way to go for catching up with developed countries in the areas of education, health and infrastructure. They are still far from being able to meet the minimum needs, particularly in the services sector, of their people.

Most of the other developing countries, particularly in Africa and South Asia, are likely to maintain the current momentum in their growth and may perhaps grow faster. They have even greater leeway to make in different sectors. Foreign aid is going to remain concentrated in these countries. To fuel the relatively high rates of growth in the emerging economies, their natural resources are likely to remain keenly coveted. Consequently, there is likely to be an increase in foreign investments in these countries in the coming years, particularly by India and China.

If the growth in the emerging economies and other developing countries is inclusive and equitable, it will not only have greater chance for being sustainable but will also have a positive impact on the world economy. This will very much depend upon drastic improvement in governance in these countries, their adoption of the right kind of development strategy and the space permitted to them by major economic powers for planning and carrying out their development activities.

But the world is likely to remain sharply divided between the rich and the poor and economically strong and weak nations. For, countries growing faster have still a long way to go before catching up the developed countries. Moreover, beyond a point, it is technology which keeps the growth momentum going. The vast numbers of these countries are likely to remain technologically backward in the next 3-4 decades. Moreover, the catch up is likely to be faster so far as the size of the economies is concerned, but when it comes to the standard of living measured in terms of per capita incomes, the distance separating the currently developed countries and the developing countries will continue to remain vast.

Military interventions by major powers in the name of the international community's right to protect but in reality designed to get rid of inconvenient rulers and governments, will continue to take place. So will be the brutal suppression of ethnic aspirations and democratic rights in pursuit of sectarian interests. Minorities will remain under threat in most dictatorial regimes and in those democracies which have adopted ethnicity or religion as the guiding principle of the state. Even in countries like India where democracy has taken firmer roots, minority communities will come under threat because of the recrudescence from time to time of majoritarian oppression and aggressiveness. It is very unlikely that stability will return in the near future to countries and regions which have gone through the process of regime change by armed intervention and those where war is being waged and sophisticated arms inducted on a large scale, for serving sectarian purposes or preventing a transition to some form of democratic governance.

At the institutional level, U.N. is likely to be further weakened and marginalized in the coming years. Its activities are likely to remain confined to technical assistance and relief operations financed through voluntary contributions and trust funds that give the contributors a firm control over the institution. Developed countries will continue to use the United Nations only as and when it suits their interest. The preference of the United States will remain to be for, to use the words of Joseph Nye, the eminent expert in security matters, 'multilateralism *a la carte*', in which U.N. is just one option. In the process, the current trend of building and strengthening structures outside the United Nations, which these countries control, will continue. These include NATO, G-7 and G-20. The proliferation of mega size regional arrangements like the Trans-Pacific Partnership, Trans-Atlantic Trade and Investment Partnership and new generation regimes for trade in services, environmental goods, etc., being negotiated outside the WTO, will lead to the marginalization of even WTO which has been a favourite institution of the developed countries. In this overall scenario, the U.N. Regional Economic Commissions that, till the mid-1970s', used to provide leadership in the realm of ideas and action at the international level, are likely to fade into a mere formal existence.

Several domains which have a crucial bearing on the future of the world, like the international financial system, information technology, activities in cyber space and outer space and those of the transnational corporations will continue to remain outside the U.N. Hence they would be subjected to minimal surveillance and control, under a very thin cover of international law. Finally, the United Nations will continue to remain a marginal player in conflict zones like Iraq, Afghanistan and Syria where ironically the only prospect for restoring peace lies in U.N. playing a central role. But the U.N. is being deliberately kept out by both the countries involved in the conflict as well as outside intervening powers.

Civil society organizations (CSOs) have now emerged as a major force influencing policies both at the national and international levels. In many countries including India, CSOs are both the repository and generator of knowledge in their respective domains and important vehicles for advocacy for bringing about changes in policies in the desired direction. At the national level, they are playing an extremely important role in making development inclusive, equitable and ecologically sustainable. At the international level, they have been making significant contributions to building a just and equitable world order.

In the coming decades, these organizations are expected to play a much greater role in carrying out their missions. However, they suffer from certain inherent limitations. For example, they function under severe resources constraint and on account of the miserly local philanthropy in developing countries, a large number of them rely on outside sources, to meet their funding requirements. Host governments often regard them as an instrument for advancing foreign countries' agenda, and their positions and activities on human rights and development issues are regarded as anti-development, anti-government and even anti-national. They are, therefore, kept under constant surveillance and their activities are clamped down from time to time. This happens even in countries having a democratic form of government, like India. The dictatorial regimes in any case leave them very narrow spaces for operation. In their functioning at the international level, there is often a lack of unity of purpose among them.

Democracy has gained ground globally mainly after the onset of the present phase of globalization, and particularly after the liquidation of the Soviet Union. Since then, country after country has overthrown dictatorial regimes and ushered in democracy in some form or the other. The more recent phenomenon in this regard has been the Arab

Spring. However, in most cases, countries aspiring to democracy have reached its doorstep without being able to enter into it. In many cases, the old order has reasserted itself either by directly suppressing the rising tide of democracy, or in the garb of a mere semblance of democracy. The situation has been made much more complicated, leading to strife, violence and endemic political instability, because of the intervention of Western powers to bring about regime change to suit their interest, in the name of promoting or ushering in democracy.

Movements for democracy will continue during the coming years. Many more democratic springs will arise in the process of which a few more countries may make a transition to democracy. But, by and large, the vast majority of the countries in the Third World will remain under authoritarian regimes or democracy will remain formalized in the form of domination by a single party.

In a paper published by the Carnegie Endowment for International Peace in 2015, the author, Alexei Arbatov, an eminent expert in security and disarmament issues, has concluded:

> 'It is obvious that the world is presently facing the most serious and most comprehensive crisis in the 50 years history of nuclear arms control. This crisis may quite possibly result in the total disintegration of the existing framework of treaties and regimes. In this event, the arms race will probably resume – with the direst military, political and economic consequences for mankind.'

> (Arbatov, 2015)[2]

In 2002, the United States withdrew from the Anti-Ballistic Missile Treaty. The Strategic Offensive Reductions Treaty (SORT) signed in 2002 was never fully functional. With the Strategic Arms Reduction Treaty (START-1) about to expire in 2009, the parties suddenly realized that there was nothing to replace it. The only positive measure was the agreement on the New START between President Barrack Obama and the then Russian President Dmitry Medvedev which effectively cut the deployed warheads by around 3000. An attempt to continue the process was made by President Obama in 2013 in a speech in Berlin in which he called for a further 30 per cent reduction in nuclear warheads down to about 1000 for each side. However, this proposal was not accepted by Moscow.

Lack of progress in arms control and in fact setbacks in it during the second decade of the new century was mainly because of the renewal of cold war between the U.S. and Russia. Russia is concerned about the U.S.'s global Ballistic Missiles Defence (BMD) programme, a sub-system of which has now been deployed in the Euro-Atlantic and the Asia-Pacific regions; and deployment by the U.S. of high-precision long-range conventional missiles. There is a real problem today of preserving the Intermediate-range Nuclear Forces (INF) Treaty and the New START Treaty.

Today development of missile defence system is no longer confined to the United States and Russia. National or multi-national defence missile programme are being pursued by China, India, Israel, Japan, NATO and South Korea.

A Vision for the Future World Order

The vision projected in the following paragraphs is that of the governance of the future world order underpinned by a new, dynamic and democratic multilateralism. The institutional form that it will take will be a revamped United Nations. An essential object of revamping will be the restoration to the United Nations of the functions in the economic and social fields provided in the Charter, but snatched away from it in the last few decades, and bringing under the U.N's purview the issues of global significance which have emerged recently. A key element of the renewal of the U.N. will be enhancing its capacity both financially and for peacekeeping. In this redesigned institutional structure of the world order, critical negotiations on disarmament will be multi-lateralized and a process of active and intensive law-making and norm-setting will be set in motion and completed within a specified time frame to serve as a basis for multilateral action and surveillance in areas which are yet to be brought on the U.N. agenda. The new multilateralism will be democratic in the sense that all those structures and processes within the United Nations that are still hegemonic will be democratized. This will include the expansion of the membership of the Security Council, democratization of the decision making process in the IMF and the World Bank, bringing WTO under the U.N. framework, and giving the people of the world a voice in the United Nations through an effective participation of civil society organizations in deliberations and decision making. A truly democratic United Nations is not possible without its constituent units, that is, the member states embracing democracy. Since a single form of democracy cannot be imposed as a pre-condition for the membership of the United Nations, negotiations will be undertaken for the member states to reach broad agreement on and generally follow such essential values of democracy as fundamental freedoms, human rights, respect for pluralism and diversity.

The future world order has to be in the nature and form of a new, dynamic and democratic multilateralism. This is not an option but a necessity, indeed an inevitability. It represents progress from a lower order of organizing human society to a higher order.

A retreat from it, as is becoming increasingly evident in the world today, cannot but end up in utter chaos in international life.

The new multilateralism will have to be underpinned by the United Nations. For, the U.N. is the only universal organization in the world. It is embedded in international law and mandated by all the nations of the world to deal with problems of a universal nature. Its Charter, even as it is, in large measure empowers it to discharge this crucial role. What is at stake today is the very character and features of the evolving world society. This cannot be left to be decided by a group of countries, howsoever powerful they may be, in their exclusive groupings. This has to be decided by an open discussion in the universal forum of the United Nations.

To discharge its role in the future world order, multilateralism under the United Nations will have to be put on the basis of a new paradigm. For this purpose, the United Nations will have to be revamped, strengthened and empowered in a radical manner. This will undoubtedly call for Charter amendment. This should not prove to be an insuperable task. The Charter has been amended in the past. Giving effect to an agreement on the expansion of the membership of the Security Council will in any case involve Charter amendment. For adequately empowering the U.N. financially and otherwise in order to enable it to mediate in the complex problems of the evolving world order, a thorough updating of the Charter is called for.

Restoring the Central Overarching Role of the U.N.

For putting in place a new multilateralism, it will be essential to reinstate the central overarching status of the U.N, in the international system. For this purpose it will be necessary to restore to the U.N. the jurisdiction it originally had in the Charter, in the hard core economic domains like money, finance, trade, and development strategy.

Second, new issues which have come to the forefront of global concern and solutions for which can be found only on a multilateral basis, should be squarely brought on the agenda of the United Nations. These include food security, energy security, water resources, equitable sharing of natural resources, cyber space and information technology. The U.N. should also be the arena for the global accountability of multinational corporations, global surveillance and regulation of international financial markets, channelling of surplus resources of the world for global development, particularly of the developing countries and for ensuring human security in a comprehensive sense of the term.

There is also an urgent need for extensive and active law-making and norm-setting in most of these areas. For all these areas we need framework agreements of the kind that prevails in the realm of climate change. These framework agreements should provide the basis for continuing intensive work in the nature of harmonization of policies, standard setting, commitments for action and their implementation.

Third, the association agreements with the IMF and the World Bank should be revised to bring them in line with those concluded by the Economic and Social Council with other specialized agencies and WTO should be brought into association with the United Nations under Article 57 of the Charter.

Fourth, the functions and the activities of the U.N. Regional Economic Commissions should be revived and strengthened in order to enable them to provide leadership at the regional level in pursuing the objectives of the United Nations. Regional integration and economic partnership agreements should be brought under their overall surveillance and should function in conformity with guidelines formulated by the Regional Economic Commission and endorsed by the General Assembly.

Fifth, the disarmament agenda of the United Nations should be expanded and strengthened. The U.N. should become the principal global forum for negotiations on arms control and disarmament. It is becoming increasingly evident that further progress in this area will be possible only if the current bilateral process is multi-lateralized. Moreover, the problem of instability and threat to international security posed by the recent developments in the areas of defensive weapon system, militarization of outer space and the development of a new generation of high precision long-range conventional missiles can be best resolved through discussion in the multilateral forum of the United Nations. In this connection, there is an urgent need for convening another Special Session of the U.N. General Assembly on Disarmament, i.e., SSOD-4, in order to reach a broad agreement on the agenda and objectives to be pursued.

Enhancing the Capacity of the United Nations

Enhancing the capacity of the United Nations is of crucial importance to enable it to discharge adequately and effectively its fully restored Charter functions as well as the new functions suggested in this paper. Among these, by far the most important are those related to the financial resources at the disposal of the United Nations. For this, the following actions are essential:

- U.N. must be given access to new and predictably recurring sources for financing its activities.
- Any deliberate denial of payment of dues to the Organization should not be permitted.

The Charter provision in this regard, including the denial of voting right, should be strictly applied.

- The prolonged financial blackmail against the U.N. by such devices as zero nominal rate of growth in the budget should be brought to an end.
- The process of the voluntarization of the funding of U.N. organizations should be halted and the earlier practice of the bulk of the finances of these organizations coming from accessed contributions should be restored.

In the peacekeeping arena, the recommendations made in the Agenda for Peace should be considered with a view to reaching agreement on them. These include establishment of a Peace Endowment Fund for financing peacekeeping operations and the creation of a Rapid Deployment Force of the U.N.

Democratization of Global Governance

This will call for the transformation of those structures of the U.N. system which are not sufficiently democratized. The first priority in this regard should be the expansion of both the permanent and regular membership of the Security Council and the phasing out of the veto right in the decision making process of the Council.

The decision making process in the IMF and the World Bank should be democratized by changing the composition of the quotas in these institutions so as to bring about a greater quota dispersal among member states.

Ensuring a more effective participation of the CSOs in U.N. deliberation and decision making is an essential and long-pending measure for democratizing global governance. As a first step, a global forum of the CSOs should be created which could be convened for a day or two prior to the annual session of the General Assembly. Conclusions and suggestions resulting from the deliberation in this forum could be fed into the decision making process of the Assembly. The next stage could be the creation of a Peoples' Assembly as a deliberative body complementing the General Assembly.

The global forum of the CSOs and its subsequent replacement, the Peoples' Assembly, will become an integral part of the U.N. system. The Charter amendments which are indispensable in any case will include a clause designating this body as a Permanent Organ of the United Nations. This Organ will report to the General Assembly and will be accountable to it in its conduct of business. During its session it will adopt resolutions on the basis of the same procedures as prescribed for the adoption of resolutions by the General Assembly. Each of these resolutions will be considered by the General Assembly under the respective agenda item with a view to taking decisions, as appropriate. The resolutions will be simultaneously addressed to the international community. They will form a part of U.N. documentation. It is expected that at least some of these resolutions will be pursued over a period of time and, by virtue of remaining a part of U.N. legislation, acquire a force of law.

It is not possible to go very far in democratizing an inter-governmental system like the U.N. without the democratization of its constituent units, that is, the member states. It is not practicable, as suggested in some quarters, to make the practice of a democratic form of government a condition for the membership of the United Nations. An enforcement of this condition will be suicidal for the multilateral system as most of the existing member states will be disqualified under this criterion. Another problem is that there is unlikely to be an agreement on the form of democracy that can be prescribed for being embraced universally. An attempt could, however, be made to reach a broad agreement on the essential values of democracy like fundamental freedoms, human rights, government by representatives elected by the people in a free and fair election, and respect for and celebration of cultural and ethnic diversity. The U.N. should consciously promote these values generally as well as in individual countries with the cooperation of the governments of the countries concerned. The promotion of such democratic values should be mainstreamed into U.N. activities through the provision of adequate finances and establishment of a separate institution for this purpose.

India's Role

India started with an idealistic and pro-active approach towards the United Nations. It viewed the U.N. as the world community's chosen instrument for preserving and advancing peace, fostering cooperation, promoting economic and social progress and establishing a just and equitable world order. Jawaharlal Nehru who shaped and piloted India's foreign policy during its formative years, believed in building a world government on the foundations of the United Nations. In the economic field, India continued to persist with its idealistic approach to the U.N. for several years after Jawaharlal Nehru's departure from the scene. India played a leading role in the negotiations on some of the seminal agreements and frameworks for international cooperation finalized during the golden era of U.N.'s activities in the field of development cooperation.

After the mid-1970s' when this era came to an end, India, like other developing countries, got reconciled to the process of the decline of multilateralism under the U.N. and did not take any major initiative to reverse it. When reforms came on top of the U.N. agenda after the cold war, India's sole objective seemed to be to pursue its candidature for being a Permanent Member of the Security Council. There is no doubt that reform of the Security Council is of crucial importance and India has a very strong case for becoming one of its Permanent Members. However, for want of agreement on several related issues, the prospects for expansion taking place in the near future do not seem to be particularly bright. There is, therefore, no reason for India to remain a prisoner of the pursuit of this objective and, in the process, not to discharge its historical role of contributing to the substantive restructuring of the United Nations.

It is in India's self-interest as well as its moral obligation to actively work for changing the world order. In the long run, it is also in the interest of all other countries of the world. India should not be diverted from this task by the temptation of sitting at the high table or regarding itself as a major status quo power. For, India is still at the receiving end of the present world order and is likely to remain so in the foreseeable future.

Any initiative that India takes in this regard will be in keeping with the ideals and values it has inherited from its past and which inspired its freedom movement. They also constitute the basic tenets of our foreign policy. India is obliged under Article 51 of its Constitution to 'promote international peace and security, maintain just and equitable relations between nations, and foster respect for international law and treaty obligations in the dealings of organized peoples with one another'.

Moreover, India is now widely recognized as a significant global military and economic power. It has thereby acquired greater capacity to influence world events. If it can manage to bring China, among others, on board, this influence would multiply manifold.

Building on the vision outlined in this paper, India should take the initiative for building a global coalition for a new dynamic and democratic multilateralism under the United Nations. The task of mobilizing worldwide support for this is going to be difficult and time-consuming. But this effort is worth undertaking. For, even if, in the ultimate analysis, a consensus is built on a scaled down version of the vision outlined in this paper, it will have the advantage of getting the major nations of the world engaged in a dialogue which is long overdue.

As regards the procedure, even though it will be essential to evolve a global consensus, tactically the blueprint for new dynamic and democratic multilateralism should be discussed first in a smaller group of like-minded countries, preferably IBSA (India, Brazil and South Africa). It should be discussed simultaneously in the regional groupings of developing countries. The discussion then could move up to the Group of 77 and the forum of the Non Aligned Movement. Side by side, it will be of critical importance to engage and seek the support of other BRICS member countries, that is, China and Russia.

Using China's clout is absolutely essential for making a move forward. Its support, among others, will be a major factor in mobilizing the support of developing countries as a whole and influencing the attitude of major powers. When China joined the United Nations in 1971, it functioned there basically as a status quo power. From the early 1990s', there was a convergence in the attitude of India which had until then been working for changing the status quo, with that of China, in that both of them started functioning as status quo powers. But recently there is evidence of both of them, particularly China, pushing for significant changes in the roles and institutions of the present world order, without necessarily causing an upheaval in it. China has recently taken unilateral initiatives for building infrastructure for global trade and development and reducing dependence on dollar as the international reserve currency.

Russia may also be persuaded to support an initiative for bringing about significant changes in the present world order because of the insecurity it perceives in the status quo, particularly after the recent revival of the cold war. The United States and its allies can be expected to resist any initiative for major changes, but in view of the changed global economic power balance and the security scenario, even they can be expected to realize that it will be both untenable and unrealistic to keep the present world order intact.

India's ability to gather support for the proposed initiative will depend critically on domestic developments in the country, particularly its capacity to sustain and enhance its economic strength, and its success in achieving an inclusive, equitable and ecologically sustainable development. It will also be essential for it to scrupulously adhere to international law and the values underlying the U.N., in its conduct of international relations, particularly in its dealings with its weaker and smaller neighbours.

Endnotes

1. A number of documents have been used as background material for this essay, without citing them for specific parts of the text; these are given in the References.
2. Page numbers not available.

References

Acharya, Amitav, 2015, *The End of American World Order,* New Delhi: Oxford University Press.

Arbatov, Alexei, 2015, *An Unnoticed Crisis: The End of History for Nuclear Arms Control?* Moscow:

Carnegie Endowment for International Peace, Carnegie Moscow Centre.

Asian Relations Organisation, 1948, *Asian Relations* (Report of the Proceedings and Documentation of the First Asian Relations Conference, (March-April, 1947), New Delhi: Asian Relations Organization.

Childers, Erskine and Brian Urquhart, 1994, *Renewing the United Nations System*, Uppsala, Sweden: Dag Hammarskjold Foundation.

Commission on Global Governance, 1995, *Our Global Neighbourhood*, The Report of the Commission on Global Governance, Commission on Global Governance, New York: Oxford University Press.

Dubey, Muchkund, 2005a, 'Multilateralism Besieged', *Indian Journal of International Law*, Vol. 45(2), April-June.

Dubey, Muchkund, 2005b, 'Comments' on the Report of the High-Level Panel on Threats, Challenges and Change, in *Reforming the United Nations for Peace and Security*, Yale: Yale Centre for the Study of Globalization.

Dubey, Muchkund, 2007, 'Reform of the UN System and India', in *Indian Foreign Policy: Challenges and Opportunities*, Atish Sinha and Madhup Mohta (eds.), New Delhi: Academic Foundation.

Dubey, Muchkund, 2013, 'India's Foreign Policy: Underlying Principles, Strategies and Challenges Ahead', in *India's Foreign Policy: Coping with the Changing World*, Dubey, M., Delhi: Pearson.

Qureshi, Moeen and Richard von Weizsacker, 1995, *The United Nations in its Second Half Century*, The Report of the Independent Working Group on the Future of the United Nations, Yale: Yale University Press.

United Nations, 1992, *An Agenda for Peace: Preventive Diplomacy, Peacemaking and Peacekeeping*: Report of the Secretary-General, United Nations Document A/47/277, New York: United Nations.

United Nations, 2004, *A More Secure World: Our Shared Responsibility*, Report of the Secretary-General's High-level Panel on Threats, Challenges and Change, New York: United Nations.

United Nations 2005, *In Larger Freedom: Towards Development, Security and Human Rights for All*, Report by Secretary-General of the United Nations, New York: United Nations.

ECONOMIC FUTURES

Pastoral Futures

Ilse Köhler-Rollefson and Hanwant Singh Rathore[1]

Summary

Pastoralists keep herds of animals to convert naturally available vegetation and crop aftermath into food, fertilizer, fibre, fuel and other products, and provide valuable agro-ecosystem services while doing so. Pastoral systems are ubiquitous in India, especially in the marginal rain-fed areas, and are based on elaborate traditional knowledge as well as complex social institutions. Unfortunately, they have received only scant attention from policy makers despite their enormous contribution to the livestock economy as well as the conservation of biodiversity. They have often remained invisible and continue to be regarded as backward, despite their natural nexus with the green economy. This is due, in part, to their poor organisation at national level, and has led to their exclusion from customary grazing areas and obstructions of their migratory paths.

This essay argues for an enabling environment that integrates pastoral production with nature conservation, ensures space for pastoralists in the landscape, and develops combined livestock production and environmental protection as an attractive 'career' option for young people. For ecological and public health reasons, the future of livestock production should be decentralised and tailored to make optimal use of local biomass. The essay proposes some of the pathways, such as documentation of indigenous livestock production systems, an alternative livestock development framework, capacity-building and support for young pastoralists, as well as development of value chains that promote and support pastoralism.

Current Context

Pastoralism is a 'social and economic system based on the raising and herding of livestock'[2] and India is blessed with a huge number and diversity of pastoral communities. India's pastoralists husband cattle, buffalos, sheep, goats, yaks, camels, pigs, and even ducks in systems that range from sedentary to nomadic (Köhler-Rollefson, 2013; Rao and Casimir,

2003). The degree of nomadism is not fixed, but often varies from year to year, depending on the amount of rainfall (Sharma *et al.*, 2003). Pastoralists often embrace nomadism, not out of an inherent urge to wander, but because their animals are more productive under this kind of management, as it increases their access to the essential resources of forage and water. In some places, such as Kutch and the Thar Desert, pastoralists themselves may be sedentary, but their animals are nomadic, going out to graze on their own. The important criterion setting pastoralism apart from other types of animal husbandry is that the animals forage by themselves either on natural vegetation or on harvested fields, instead of being stall-fed, that is, the animals go to the feed, instead of the feed being brought to them.

By means of their animals, pastoralists can 'harvest' biomass in the remotest and most unlikely corners of the country, from the high altitude alpine meadows in the Himalayas to the most inhospitable and driest nooks of the Thar Desert, from the mangroves in the Gulf of Kutch to the tiny islands in the Chilika lake and the swamps in the Bay of Bengal. Their herds utilize the crop aftermath of the Deccan Plateau and, throughout the country, the grass growing on roadsides. Resembling a combined harvester, except that they don't require fuel, pastoralist animals convert almost any type of biomass – excepting a few poisonous species – into organic fertilizer, meat, milk and work animals (probably in that order of predominance of use). Pastoralism is an ingenious food production system developed by livestock keepers through observation and knowledge gathered over many generations. Having its roots in the Near East some 9,000 years ago, pastoralism makes a large contribution to food security (Krätli *et al.*, 2013).

Pastoralists are ubiquitous in India although the more specialized groups among them have evolved in rain-fed, remote and difficult areas where crop cultivation is risky or impossible. Yet they are rarely seen by mainstream India. City people sometimes can catch a glimpse of an endless single file of gray cattle with long horns walks eastwards on the Jaipur-Delhi National Highway towards greener pastures in Haryana. After Diwali, one can see collectives of Raika shepherds – men, women and children – leading batches of adult sheep and lambs, troops of donkeys and strings of camels on the Udaipur-Chittor Highway to the lusher climes of Madhya Pradesh. In early summer, Gaddi shepherds thread their flocks and ponies through the traffic jam between Manali and the Rohtang Pass in Himachal Pradesh.

Despite their omnipresence, we know very little about pastoralists and what they contribute to India's economy and ecological systems. There are two reasons for this. Firstly, because of their itinerant way of life, they are difficult to 'grasp' and document. Secondly, although some of them have been studied by anthropologists, they have generally not been under the purview of livestock professionals and policy makers. The starting point of India's livestock scientists has been that pastoral nomads are backward and a nuisance, a notion inculcated in colonial times. As late as 1999, a social scientist of the Central Arid Zone Research Institute stated that 'The nomads in present times...are a menace to the whole society and their sedentarization is imperative...' (Bharara,1999).

This is unfortunate, for pastoralism is not only the foundation of the nation's livestock wealth and a crucial supplier of organic manure, upholding soil fertility in many parts of the country. It also plays a huge role in India's status as the world's largest exporter of sheep and goat meat, the largest dairy producer and the largest exporter of beef. Almost 100 per cent of the small ruminant meat, more than 50 per cent of the milk and the bulk of the large ruminant meat produced in India derive from pastoralist systems.

There are no reliable figures about the number of pastoralists in India, and in some cases we are not even aware of their existence. In 1993, it was estimated that India has 34 million pastoralists managing a livestock population of more than 50 million (Cincotta et al., 1993). In 2003, pastoralists were assessed to represent 6 per cent of the Indian population (Sharma et al., 2003).

Pastoralists have been the subject of enquiry of the National Commission on Denotified, Nomadic and Semi-nomadic tribes, together with other categories and types of nomads, hunter gatherers, shifting cultivators and service providers. The latest report of this Commission, published in 2008, makes frequent references to animal herding nomads, including the Gaddi of Himachal and the Rebari of Rajasthan to illustrate the difficulties of the nomadic way of life and underline its backwardness. It describes nomads as being marginalised from the social and economic mainstream, having a low human development index and a high deprivation index, being deprived from the gains of planned development, of not being empowered and of being carriers of social stigma (NCDNST, 2016).

This assessment is, on some level, very much at variance with the actual situation. For one, pastoral nomadic communities often had, and continue to have, a high reputation for honesty and for achieving sometimes impossible tasks. In Rajasthan it is said that every Rajput hero in the past had a Raika confidante, one example being Harmal Raika who is credited with tracking down the female camels that became the founding stock of Rajasthan's camel population (Srivastava, 1999). Furthermore, many ruling dynasties are of pastoral origin, for instance the Holkars of Indore descended from the Dhangar community in Maharashtra. The Yadavs, said to compose 20 per cent of India's population, are historically and mythologically associated with cattle-herding and continue pastoralist activities until today (Mahendrakumar, 2006).

Secondly, while pastoralists are indeed excluded from the mainstream and disregarded by government and decision makers, they make a major contribution to the Indian economy and to its GDP. In general they are not destitute, since their herds provide good income and represent a self-regenerating asset. A pastoralist owning 50 sheep has liquid assets of 2.5 lakh (250,000) and sells around 1.4 lakh (140,000) worth of livestock in addition to earning another Rs. 75,000 from manure (Kamal Kishore, personal communication).

On the other hand, it is certainly true that pastoralists face a huge number of problems and threats making it impossible or even dangerous for them to continue making a living from grazing animals. The pastoralists pointed out their dependence on communally and state owned grazing lands and how these were declining both in quantity and in quality. They feel threatened by the continuous decrease in grazing resources, and cited examples such as their exclusion from participation in the Village Forest Protection Committees that were promoted under the Joint Forest Management Programme, the allotment of *gochar* (grazing) land for private use at the discretion of District Collectors that is undercutting the resource base of pastoralists, and many cases of pastoralists being banned from their traditional grazing areas because these have come under various 'forest protection' or management schemes. Examples include: Malaimadu breeders in Tamil Nadu and the Grizzled Squirrel sanctuary, Toda buffalo breeders, camel breeders and the Kumbhalgarh Reserve in Rajasthan, the elimination of fallow areas, due to conversion of agricultural land, including barren and uncultivable land as well as cultural waste and permanent fallow to non-agricultural uses. In addition, irrigated agriculture has increased. Pastoralists regard several policy changes as absolutely essential, including the revival of traditional norms for use of grazing lands, land use policies that protect grazing areas and ensure sufficient space for their livelihoods, collaboration between the government departments responsible for the two components of their livelihoods, that is, animal husbandry and forest /environment. They also expect that educational facilities integrate and reinforce important elements of their culture and indigenous knowledge; that there is acknowledgement and support for their essential role in conserving India's farm animal genetic resources and valuable genetic traits; and that animal health and livestock extension services are suited to their particular situation and integrate/utilize the considerable indigenous (ethno-veterinary) knowledge of pastoralists.

Providing a more supportive and enabling policy environment would go a long way towards serving the needs of both, the nation in terms of food security, and themselves in terms of livelihoods. In development parlance, it would provide a 'win-win situation'. But for this to happen, some deeply ingrained attitudes and concepts about livestock production need to be overcome.

Critique

The principles underlying pastoral livestock production are different from those of scientific animal husbandry as it is taught at colleges and universities. Pastoralists keep herds of animals to convert naturally available, biodiverse vegetation and crop aftermath into food and fertilizer. Successful pastoralism is based on moving animals to access and metabolize all available biomass. For this reason, pastoral livestock has been selected for mobility, hardiness and the ability to cope with droughts and seasonal fluctuations in the availability of forage. The inputs to the system are labour, traditional knowledge and social institutions that ensure access to the biomass. The constraining factor to the system is availability and accessibility of vegetation. If this reduces, herd size adapts accordingly. This adaptability is incorporated into the system through a higher rate of losses, lower birth rates, and distress sales. The intrinsic ability to adjust herd/flock size ensures that long-term overgrazing is not really a problem, making these inherently self-regulating and sustainable systems. Diversity is another principle underlying pastoralism: keeping a herd with diverse animals, so as to optimize survival during droughts and other challenging conditions, but also being able to capitalize on 'good times' when biomass is aplenty.

In contrast, animal science and most western production systems focus on the animal and its output, regardless of overall system sustainability. By means of scientific animal breeding, types and strains of livestock have been created that are enormously productive, but require equally enormous inputs with respect to feed, medicines and housing. If feed is not available locally, it is brought in from the outside, often from other continents. For instance, in Europe, 70-80 per cent of the protein fed to livestock is imported from North or South America. Likewise, China became totally dependent on soybean imports after it replaced its local pig breeds with high performance imported breeds that can no longer be sustained on locally available household waste and biodiverse vegetation.

There are other major differences between pastoral and 'scientific' production. Pastoralists produce food in a decentralized way, providing valuable agro-ecosystem services while producing food – they fertilize harvested fields, and disperse and aid the germination of seeds. In contrast, 'modern' production is based on the confinement of large numbers of animals in one place to maximize 'efficiency'. This entails a huge accumulation of manure which, in the process, is transformed from an asset to a menace, ultimately leading to the pollution of groundwater and water bodies. Secondly, the disease pressure is high and animals often need routine application of veterinary drugs (antibiotics) to stay healthy, causing drug resistance in both livestock and people. Thirdly, there are major impacts on biodiversity, due to the association of industrial livestock production with the erosion of genetic (breed) diversity, spread of monoculture feed crops like soybean, and the use of veterinary medicines like Diclofenac that is responsible for the decimation of vulture populations. Fourthly, labour is minimized and rural income opportunities are eliminated. Finally, there are huge animal welfare concerns in these systems (PCIFAP, 2008).

The enormous social and environmental costs of these so-called 'efficient livestock production systems' are currently externalised to the public at large. Because of their huge political clout and influence on academic research, they have spread around the world, in a process referred to as 'Livestock Revolution', basically the equivalent to the Green Revolution, with a heavy focus on maximizing single outputs like milk and meat.

Pastoral production represents the other end of the spectrum: it is at the intersection between food production, agricultural biodiversity and ecosystem. Hence, in a recent publication by FAO, livestock keepers were hailed as 'guardians of biodiversity' (FAO, 2009), and pastoralism is said to be a natural nexus for the green economy (McGahey *et al.*, 2014). Despite having some advocates, especially in Africa, pastoralists are so far too poorly organized and not in a position to take on the scientific and political establishments that benefit from and promote industrial production.

Indian animal scientists, having been trained in the dominant Western mould of animal science, generally have not engaged with the plethora of locally grown livestock systems and tend to either ignore them or view them as an outdated and quaint cultural occupation, with the exception of institutions such as the National Bureau of Animal Genetic Resources. However, the western paradigm has already begun to crumble, as concerns about its collateral damage are rising among environmental groups, civil society and animal welfare people. The Food and Agriculture Organisation (FAO) of the United Nations is ringing alarm bells and has initiated a Global Agenda for Sustainable Livestock (GASL) to put livestock development on a more sustainable track.[3]

India is in an excellent position to provide an alternative and sustainable model for livestock production because of its pastoralist heritage, and its large number of locally adapted breeds. It is the country with the largest number of small-scale livestock keepers in the world and vegetarianism is culturally important, so excess consumption of meat may be less of a problem than in other countries where meat eating is part of the culture and even source of identity.

What India has to do is to provide an enabling environment to its pastoralists, integrate pastoral production with nature conservation, ensure space for pastoralists in the landscape and develop combined livestock production and environmental protection as an attractive 'career' option for young people. It can be done, but it requires inter-sectoral collaboration between bureaucrats and scientists that are currently divided and polarized into livestock people on one hand and forest/wildlife people on the other.

In May 2016, experts working with pastoralists throughout India issued the 'Kullu Call for the Recognition of the Importance of Common Pool Resources and Pastoralism for India's Livestock Sector'. They recommended recognition of the contribution of extensive livestock systems and pastoralism to the national GDP and to livelihoods; field research and national census/surveys to determine numbers and economic contributions of extensive livestock keepers; development of livestock policies that support extensive livestock keepers and are sensitive to their specific needs, including mobile services; securing tenure, access and rights to common pool resources for these livestock keepers; and recognition of the role of pastoralism in adaptation to climate change and in biodiversity conservation.

Vision of the Future in 2047

By 2047, India will have become the global leader in implementing and promoting a vision of livestock development that is now, at the time of writing, regarded as alternative and far-fetched, but that thirty years from now will have become validated as the only long-term and globally sustainable approach to raising livestock in tune with the availability of the world's natural resources.

This vision builds on India's pastoralist heritage and its range of locally adapted livestock breeds and promotes decentralized livestock keeping that is oriented towards making optimal use of local biomass. India will have deviated from the current global trend of establishing increasingly larger livestock units or factory farms and purposefully support pastoralism. There will have been recognition of the positive aspects of pastoralism as a means of production that is in tune with available resources, and that places emphasis on the well-being of animals. Pastoralism will be appreciated and supported as an important part of India's bio-cultural heritage.

Instead of undergoing a Livestock Revolution, India will have experienced a 'Livestock Keepers' Revolution' in which livestock keepers have become empowered – through education and organizational strengthening – to manage the country's livestock wealth in tune with the availability of natural resources. The controversy about grazing rights has been resolved. Livestock are no longer seen as antagonistic to forests and conservation, but have become integrated into an overall management plan for India's natural resources.

Livestock keeping has turned into a highly respected profession because it demands skills and dedication; its practitioners are recognized as agro-ecosystem providers who also monitor the local biodiversity and are rewarded for these services through a number of privileges. These broadly correspond to the concept of Livestock Keepers' Rights. This change in status, combined with secure income, will have motivated not only people whose forefathers were pastoralists, but also those from other social backgrounds to enter these jobs. While the work is physically demanding it also has many rewards, including being close to nature, dealing with animals, having access to healthy food and a good salary. For this reason it attracts a good number of mid career drop-outs from the corporate sector and computer based livelihoods.

Because Indian farm animals are not amassed and confined in large numbers, but are kept in mobile systems and in reasonably sized herds, the outbreak of diseases is minimized and application of antibiotics is reduced to urgent cases. Herbal medicines, based on traditional ethno-veterinary knowledge and validated by scientists, have replaced many industrially produced medicines (for example, ANTHRA, 2005). Livestock products from India are establishing an international reputation for being low in drug residues and for their high nutritional content and exquisite taste, due to biodiverse feeding patterns rather than reliance on genetically modified feed crops. Therefore there is significant export demand for them; however the Indian government has instituted a policy that puts the demands of its own population over export considerations.

Many rural jobs have been created through the development of local value addition activities, such as cheese and sausages which were set up twenty years earlier through an Indo-European and other programmes that supported gourmet cheese makers and sausage makers from Europe and other countries. Raw materials sourced from pastoralist livestock form the basis of a thriving cottage industry, making paper from dung and processing wool into felt, insulation materials, apparel, and home ware, etc. Defined local ecosystems are managed by collectives who have the mandate to ensure agro-ecosystem health with the help of livestock, and which process and market their own products.

One example is the Kumbhalgarh Agro-Ecological Collective (KAEC), which is tasked to manage the area that was once known as Kumbhalgarh Wildlife Sanctuary, in a sustainable way. This is an interdisciplinary team that includes specialists in livestock, forest, and biodiversity management and has the task of sustainable use of this ecosystem monitored by means of indicators that have been determined in a participatory manner. Sheep, goats, camels, and cattle are grazed in the Kumbhalgarh Sanctuary in a way that supports the conservation of wild mega-fauna, including leopards and wolves. The wool of Boti sheep, the milk and cheese of camels, the cheese and meat of goats, and the milk of Nari cattle are the basis of a range of branded products protected by a geographical indication that are available locally and in selected urban outlets. Local hotels and restaurants feature these products on their menus and have developed a number of dishes that are specific to the region. This draws significant numbers of visitors from urban areas who also have the opportunity to accompany the agro-ecosystem providers on their daily rounds. This way they learn about nature and the local environment.

Pathways

There are both international and national pathways that can be leveraged to support pastoralism and nurture its potential for food production, according to the vision outlined above.

International pathways

At the international level, there are two frameworks that support the sustainable management of biodiversity. These are the legally binding United Nations Convention on Biological Diversity (CBD) and the platform provided by Commission on Genetic Resources for Food and Agriculture (CGRFA) hosted by the FAO.

Since 2002, pastoralists, indigenous livestock keepers and their support organizations worldwide have advocated for 'Livestock Keepers' Rights' in these two fora. Livestock Keepers' Rights are a concept that encapsulates the policy support that pastoralists and other ecological livestock keepers require for their professional survival and for their continued engagement in livestock production (Köhler-Rollefson *et al.*, 2010; Köhler-Rollefson, 2013). Much of the momentum of this movement has come from India.[4]

One of the founding moments of this process was a meeting held in March 2002 in Rajasthan in which representatives of Changpa, Raika/Rebari, Gujjar, Toda, Dhangar, Malaimadu cattle breeders, Kurma sheep breeders, Vembur sheep breeders, Andhra Pradesh Sheep and Goat Rearers' Association participated, discussed their mutual problems and exchanged experiences. In an ensuing statement[5] they emphasized their role in the ecology of India, particularly their contribution of organic fertilizer, and their significant but largely unacknowledged contribution to India's economy in terms of food security, provision of draft animal power, as well as foreign exchange earnings (meat, fibre, for example, Pashmina wool). The role of pastoralists in the conservation of indigenous livestock breeds such as one humped camel, Toda buffalo, Nari and Malaimadu cattle, Deccani sheep was highlighted. These breeds harbour a wide variety of adaptive traits, being able to cope with harsh climates and landscapes and resisting diseases that affect crossbred animals. Without pastoralists they cannot be conserved.

The term Livestock Keepers' Rights (LKR) was coined by civil society during the World

Food Summit in Rome in June 2002. It was initially modelled on the 'Farmers' Rights' enshrined in the recently completed International Treaty of Plant Genetic Resources for Food and Agriculture (ITPGRFA). At this point in time, international attention to animal genetic resources began to pick up, but livestock keepers were not even regarded as stakeholders in their management. Arguing that livestock keepers are indispensable to the management of animal genetic resources, civil society suggested that Livestock Keepers' Rights and an equivalent to the ITPGRFA were needed to ensure the sustainable management of these resources at the global level. Over the next couple of years, the concept of Livestock Keepers' Rights was gradually fleshed out in a series of grassroots level consultations that took place in Kenya, India, Italy, Ethiopia, and South Africa. The Raika of Rajasthan were one of the groups that provided inputs at all stages of the discussion, together with hundreds of livestock keepers representing more than twenty countries. The process identified eight key elements or cornerstones of LKRs that would support small scale livestock producers to continue conserving their breeds. These were divided into three principles and five specific rights that build on existing international instruments and are articulated in the *Declaration on Livestock Keepers' Rights*[6] that has been signed by a large number of civil society organizations worldwide (Köhler-Rollefson *et al.*, 2010).

However, at the UN level, the policy process for an International Treaty on Animal Genetic Resources was stalled. While there was sympathy for Livestock Keepers' Rights during the First International Technical Conference on Animal Genetic Resources in Interlaken (Switzerland) in September 2007 and in which a delegation of Indian pastoralists participated, no substantial progress towards any legally binding framework was made. Then, in 2010, the adoption of the Nagoya Protocol on Access and Benefit Sharing under the Convention on Biological Diversity opened up new perspectives. In Article 12, it states,

'Parties shall endeavour to support, as appropriate, the development by indigenous and local communities, including women within these communities, of:

(a) Community protocols in relation to access to traditional knowledge associated with genetic resources and the fair and equitable sharing of benefits arising out of the utilization of such knowledge'

(CBD Secretariat, 2011, pp. 9)

One of the aims of the Nagoya Protocol is to ensure that indigenous and local communities receive benefits from their traditional knowledge related to genetic resources. As pastoralists are holders of such knowledge, they should be entitled to such benefits. A case can thus be made that in return for their knowledge about biodiversity conservation, pastoralists should receive the benefit of secure access to land as well as technical and organisational support to develop and market products from their unique genetic resources (Köhler-Rollefson and Meyer, 2014). The community protocols mandated by the Nagoya Protocol would be a first step in that direction, by putting the priorities, knowledge and genetic resources of pastoralist communities on record and proving their eligibility for such benefits.

National pathways

Unfortunately, the development of international legal frameworks is time consuming and cumbersome and, even if adopted and ratified, their implementation requires constant pressure and monitoring by civil society. It is therefore better not to wait for any major developments at that level, and instead promote and push the following agenda in India to support pastoralism and gradually inch the country towards the vision outlined above:

1. *Document India's indigenous livestock systems to better know what we have*

   One of the hurdles faced in gaining greater support for pastoralists is the lack of information about existing pastoral systems, their outputs and economic and other contributions. This absence of data currently makes it easy to brand them as unproductive and backward. A recent study of migratory shepherds from two *tehsils* (blocks) in Rajasthan provided evidence about the enormous amounts of meat generated in the system (Köhler-Rollefson *et al.*, 2015). We need such data for many other pastoralist systems as well, combined with more general information about the linkages between distinct communities, their breeds/animal genetic resources, and their resource base and customary rights.

   The tool of choice for establishing such a data-base is Biocultural Community Protocols (BCPs) as spearheaded by the LIFE Network in India and some other countries (Köhler-Rollefson *et al.*, 2012). As mentioned above, Community Protocols are mandated by the Nagoya Protocol on Access and Benefit-Sharing, to which India is a signatory. BCPs comply with the notion of community protocols and they also help to identify and build the capacity of community leaders and young people with a real interest in livestock and a passion for breeding that can serve as entry points for further activities. The Raika of Rajasthan, the Banni buffalo breeders and the Kutchi camel breeders of Gujarat as well as the Bargur Hill cattle breeders in Tamil Nadu have already established BCPs. Additional ones by the Kuruba shepherds, the Golla pastoralists of Odisha, the Bakkarwal and Kangayam cattle breeders are in process. This effort needs to be expanded across India to cover all major and minor pastoralist groups.

BCPs will benefit, and achieve greater impact and credibility, if scientists and academics contribute to them by establishing numbers, estimates of output, nutritional analyses of products, etc. So it would be desirable to involve them in the process and raise their awareness as well.

2. *Organisational strengthening of pastoralist groups*

Pastoralists are very weak in advocacy, largely because they are totally absorbed by their jobs. Traditionally Indian pastoralists have been organized on a caste (*samaj*) level and community decisions, especially about social issues were – and continue to be made – in caste panchayats. These are usually composed of very conservative male elders who try to keep traditional gender and social relations in place and are not necessarily forward looking. Hence the shift must be made to cross-caste professional associations. An example of this is the Jaisalmer Camel Breeders' Association which encompasses members of many different castes. These professional organizations would focus on the development of breeds, advocacy for rights and development of product and marketing opportunities.

3. *Recognition of Grazing Rights*

The recognition of grazing rights and the implementation of community forest rights as provisioned for by the Forest Rights Act are essential prerequisites for maintaining pastoralism. Pastoralists have been advocating for this consistently and at the national level since 2006 when the Forest Rights Act came into force. Local activities to this effect are in place at many locations in India, including by the Maldharis of Kutch, by the Raika, by various groups in Tamil Nadu.

4. *Development of an alternative livestock development framework*

An Indian alternative to the western livestock development paradigm has urgently to be developed. As mentioned above, the current western framework revolves around a narrowly defined concept of efficiency as amount of feed versus unit of product and does not consider social and ecological dimensions. Such an alternative framework is currently being developed with inputs from scientists around the world. Hopefully it will be introduced and presented for discussion at an international conference to be held in India soon. Once this is launched, there would be need for including and promoting it in veterinary and animal husbandry curricula to get away from the western bias.

5. *Development of value chains*

Pastoralists should be provided with support to develop value chains around their products – including meat and milk – to obtain premium prices. The control over the production process should remain in their hands. Capacity-building and training by experts in cheese-making, sausage-making, etc., would be important, as would be the inputs by designers to packaging and branding. There must be support for marketing infrastructure. For instance, there is a demand in India for camel milk to treat autism. In order to ship the camel milk from remote desert areas to the large cities, technologies are required to keep the milk frozen.

6. *Motivation of young people – incentives*

The most important point is to motivate young people and remove the stigma of backwardness that currently surrounds livestock herding. This can be done by establishing formal training and capacity building that values and builds on traditional knowledge but also incorporates new and innovative ideas and concepts at the junction between food security and biodiversity conservation.

Endnotes

1. We would like to thank Kamal Kishore for his reading and detailed comments on the manuscript.
2. http://www.thefreedictionary.com (Last accessed in March 2017).
3. See www.livestockdialogue.org (Last accessed in March 2017).
4. India plays a key role in international pastoral politics on another level as well. It currently hosts the Secretariat of WAMIP, the World Association of Mobile Indigenous People and, in 2010, an Indian NGO, MARAG, organised the Global Gathering of Women pastoralists from 36 countries which resulted in the Mera Declaration of the Global Gathering of Women Pastoralists. See http://www.iucn.org/wisp/resources/publications/good_practice_studies_/gender/?10816/MERA-Declaration (Last accessed in March 2017).
5. http://www.pastoralpeoples.org/docs/Alsipura_statement.pdf.
6. http://www.pastoralpeoples.org/docs/LKRdeclaration.pdf (Last accessed in March 2017).

References

ANTHRA, 2005, *Bank on Hooves: Your Companion To Holistic Animal Health,* Pune: Anthra.

Bharara, L.P., 1999, *Man in the Desert: Drought, Desertification and Indigenous Knowledge for Sustainable Development,* Jodhpur: Scientific Publications.

CBD Secretariat, 2011, *Nagoya Protocol on Access to Genetic Resources and the Fair and Equitable Sharing of Benefits Arising from their Utilization to the Convention on Biological Diversity : text and annex*, Montreal: Secretariat of the Convention on Biological Diversity.

Cincotta, R.P. and G. Pangare, 2003, 'Evidence of Transhumance in "Sedentary" Bharwad, Small Ruminant Pastoralists in Saurashtra' in *Pastoralists and Pastoral Migration in Gujarat*, R.P. Cincotta and G. Pangare, (eds.), pp. 39-43.

FAO, 2009, *Livestock Keepers: guardians of biological diversity*, FAO Animal Production and Health, Paper 167, Rome: FAO.

GOI, 2008, *Report Volume – I*, (June 30), National Commission for Denotified, Nomadic and Semi-Nomadic Tribes, New Delhi: Ministry of Social Justice and Empowerment. http://socialjustice.nic.in/pdf/NCDNT2008-v1.pdf (last accessed 28 March, 2015).

Köhler-Rollefson, Ilse, 2013, 'Livestock Keepers' Rights in South Asia', in *The Right to Responsibility: Resisting and Engaging Development, Conservation, and the Law in Asia*, Holly Jonas, Harry Jonas, and Suneetha M. Subramanian (eds.), Malaysia: Natural Justice and United Nations University – Institute of Advanced Studies, pp. 136-49. http://naturaljustice.org/wp-content/uploads/pdf/Part%20II,%20Chapter%207.pdf (last accessed 24 March, 2015).

Köhler-Rollefson, I., E. Mathias, H. Singh, P. Vivekanandan, J. Wanyama, 2010, 'Livestock Keepers' Rights: The State of Discussion', *Animal Genetic Resources*, 47, pp. 1–5.

Köhler-Rollefson, I., A. R. Kakar, E. Mathias, H. S. Rathore, J. Wanyama, 2012, 'Biocultural Community Protocols: tools for securing the assets of livestock keepers', in *Biodiversity and Culture: exploring community protocols, rights and consent*, PLA 65, London: IIED, pp. 109-18.

Köhler-Rollefson, I. and LIFE Network, 2007, *Keepers of Genes: The interdependence between pastoralists, breeds, access to commons and livelihoods*, Sadri: LIFE Network (India), www.pastoralpeoples.org/docs/keepersofgenes_web.pdf (last accessed 1 April, 2017).

Köhler-Rollefson, I. and H. Meyer, 2014, *Access and Benefit-Sharing of Animal Genetic Resources: using the Nagoya Protocol as a Framework for the Conservation and Sustainable use of Animal Genetic Resources*, Eschborn and Ober-Ramstadt, Germany: ABS Initiative and LPP. http://www.pastoralpeoples.org/wp-content/uploads/2014/12/ABS-for-AnGr-Final-201412041.pdf (last accessed 1 April, 2017).

Köhler-Rollefson, I., H. S. Rathore, D. Raika and J. Paliwal, 2015, *Documentation and Quantification of a Long Distance Migratory Sheep Husbandry System in Southern Rajasthan (Pali District), India*, Sadri: Lokhit Pashu-Palak Sansthan.

Krätli, Saverio, C. Huelsebusch, S. Brooks, B. Kaufmann, 2013, 'Pastoralism: A Critical Asset for Food Security under Global Climate Change', *Animal Frontiers* 3, pp. 42–50.

Mahendrakumar, M., 2006, 'Yadava, a Pastoral Caste of Kerala', *Anthropologist* 8(2), pp. 83-87.

McGahey, D., J. Davies, N. Hagelberg, and R. Ouedraogo, 2014, *Pastoralism and the Green Economy – a natural nexus?*, Nairobi: IUCN and UNEP.

PCIFAP, 2008, *Putting Meat on the Table: Industrial Farm Animal Production in America*, Executive

Summary, Pew Commission on Industrial Farm Animal Production. http://www.ncifap.org/_images/pcifapsmry.pdf (last accessed 28 March, 2016).

Rao, Aparna and M. Casimir, 2003, 'Nomadism in South Asia. An introduction', in *Nomadism in South Asia,* A. Rao and M. Casimir (eds.), New-Delhi: Oxford University Press, pp. 11-38.

Sharma, Vijay, I. Kohler-Rollefson and J. Morton, 2003, *Pastoralism in India: A Scoping Study.* Ahmedabad: IIM and Germany: League for Pastoral Peoples. http://r4d.dfid.gov.uk/PDF/outputs/ZC0181b.pdf (last accessed 24 March, 2015).

Srivastava, Vinay K., 1997, *Religious Renunciation of a Pastoral People,* New Delhi: Oxford University Press.

Anna Swaraj:
A Vision for Food Sovereignty and Agro-Ecological Resurgence

Bharat Mansata, Kavitha Kuruganti, Vijay Jardhari, Vasant Futane

'European travellers to India from the 16ᵗʰ to the 18ᵗʰ centuries were dazzled by the food abundance they witnessed.'

(George and Paige, 1988)[1]

Summary

The essay briefly outlines the roots of food and farming in India, noting its high diversity and dependence on natural ecosystems like forests. However, rapid urbanization has severely impacted the fertility and water cycles of nature, which are integral to ecological sustainability. Government policy paradigms have ignored the traditional knowledge systems and skill sets of farmers, especially women, and Adivasis, and the Green Revolution model has pushed farming and farmers towards a crisis of unsustainability, pollution, and impoverishment.

This essay argues for a future which assures Anna Swaraj, or food sovereignty and security to all, dignified livelihoods of farmers, ecological sustainability, and co-evolution. Central to this is biodiverse, ecological farming – a path of agro-ecology, based on careful management of natural resources by small-scale farmers. It will reduce vulnerability to erratic fluctuations and extremes of climate and weather conditions and will increase self-reliance for regaining food sovereignty. The essay lists out various examples that signify the future possibility and pathways to self-reliant farming systems.

A Historical Overview

Looking ahead, 30-50 years from now, any grounded vision of the future of food and

228

farming in India needs to first examine our roots. What are real historically demonstrated possibilities? How did our human ancestors in this ancient 'cradle of civilization' meet their food needs before the dawn of agriculture, 10,000 years back? Or in the 9,950 years that followed until the so-called 'Green Revolution', five decades ago? What agro-ecological conditions enabled India's richly evolved heritage of food and bio-cultural diversity to flourish? How much of these conditions and diversity still survive; and what significance do they have for a healthy, sustainable and inclusive vision of the future?

Though better endowed by Nature than most places on earth, we need to recognize our present grim farm crisis; and the severe food and livelihood insecurity of many millions of people marginalized by the modern path of 'economic development' – reckless urban-industrial-consumerist-militarist expansion – a monstrous infant in historical time. We also need to understand how, in the face of such onslaught, our traditional biodiverse, self-sufficient, regenerative farming transformed into an extractive, externally dependent, mono-cropping agriculture – devastating our rich bio-cultural and agro-ecological heritage.

It is helpful to trace our entropic path downhill – to guide us up again to higher recognizable levels of synergistic evolutionary possibility. This, the present essay tries to do. It then takes a hard look at the current state of affairs, the pits we are in, and the imperative of a fundamental change of direction, very soon.

The core of the essay suggests a broad integrated outline of a hopeful but achievable vision of food and farming – deeply related to our forests, soils, water, energy, biodiversity and culture as well – a future which assures *anna swaraj,* or food sovereignty and security to all, dignified livelihoods to farmers, ecological sustainability, health, and co-evolution. Finally, this essay looks at some existing initiatives and the pathways they point at for progressively realizing such a vision.

While food is also linked to pastoralism (fisheries too), this is covered elsewhere in this book.[2] We have thus restricted our focus to plant foods, cultivated and uncultivated, while recognizing that evolved integrated farming systems include animals, birds, fish, in symbiotic, multi-functional relationships, alongside crops, trees and water bodies, where feasible.

Ancient Forest Roots of Food and Farming

Food vastly preceded farming. For several million years since its earliest evolution, our human species, like all others, did not need to grow its food. Nature provided in abundance and rich, mind-boggling diversity. There are an estimated 80,000 plant species that provide humanly edible yield (Myers, 1985, pp. 156). Most of these are uncultivated plants – growing wild, requiring only labour for harvesting or gathering.

Much of our land in this Indian sub-continent was blessed by Nature with fertile soils teeming with life, abundant sunshine and water, thick forests, and wondrous biodiversity. India, at its roots, is an *aranya* (forest) civilization. Agriculture is barely 10,000 years old. It too was nourished by our rich forests that replenished farm fertility, recharged groundwater, and fed streams, rivers, lakes. Our enormous crop diversity originated in the diversity of uncultivated wilderness, before evolving over many generations of selection and farm-tending in diverse agro-ecological conditions.

In biodiverse natural forests, there is year-long supply of several hundred varieties of foods, ensuring diversity and wholesome nutritional balance in the local diets, minimizing the possibility of any 'hidden hunger' – micro-nutrient or other deficiency in food – leading to ill health.

Uncultivated forest food plants provide edible yield – leaf, fruit, berry, flower, seed, stem, tuber/root, or mushroom – usually at a certain time of the year, depending on the species. They are a life saver for the *adivasis*, including the landless, orphaned, aged and infirm, all integral and cared for in the adivasi *kutumba* or community-family, which includes Nature.

Summarising the merits of uncultivated forest foods in providing nutritional security to forest dependent communities, a recent study pointed out:

'They are (i) available round the year; (ii) easily and equitably accessible to forest dwellers; (iii) varied, enabling balanced nutrition; (iv) free or low-cost; (v) safe from contamination/ adulteration; (vi) packed with micro-nutrients, and rich in antioxidants; (vii) a vital safety net against increasing crop failures caused by climate change, erratic rainfall, and mounting ecological degradation, including water scarcity, and dead/depleted soils' (Deb *et al.,* 2014).

While there is voluminous published information on India's rich biodiversity and traditional knowledge of edible/useful species,[3] we sadly forget that there are very few people left – the last living bridges – that can pass on such knowledge to future generations.

Forests also provide vital ecosystem services, efficiently harvesting and storing the sun's energy, sequestering carbon, producing biomass, creating fertile topsoil and guarding against its erosion. They moderate the climate, mitigate global warming, provide oxygen, bring rain, recharge groundwater, replenish and cleanse our rivers and water bodies, buffer against floods, and provide habitats for rich biodiversity. They also provide the forest dwelling people a huge variety of useful produce – all free gifts of Mother Nature.

Traditional Poly-cultural Farming

The collection of forest produce by adivasi communities – where forests survive and are not enclosed – is supplemented with poly-cultural (mixed) farming of 40-50 different food crops in clearances. In the plains too, farming communities traditionally grew many varied crops to meet all their basic needs. Some still do. Such small scale, biodiverse farming – organic 'by default', and entirely self-sufficient with locally sourced inputs – minimizes the risk of extensive loss under adverse climatic conditions, besides providing more wholesome, balanced and fresh nourishment. For the past ten millennia, it has fed the inhabitants of this populous land, and proved its sustainability, especially if integrated with at least 30 per cent tree or forest cover.

In 'Tending the Earth', Winin Pereira elaborates on how traditional Indian agriculture 'rated high in all aspects of total productivity, sustainability, self-reliance, diversity, and the depth of its indigenous knowledge' (1993, back cover).

A century earlier, J. A. Voelcker, a reputed European agricultural expert of his time, wrote in his 'Report on Indian Agriculture':

'Certain it is that I at least have never seen a more perfect picture of careful cultivation ... Nowhere would one find better instances of ingenuity in device of water raising appliances, of knowledge of soils and their capabilities, and the exact time to sow and reap, as one would in Indian agriculture; and this is not at its best alone, but at its ordinary level. It is wonderful too how much is known of rotation, the system of mixed crops....'

(1891, reprint 1986, pp. 11)

Sir Albert Howard, considered the 'father of sustainable agriculture' in the west, worked for many years as 'the Imperial Economic Botanist' to the colonial government in India. He confessed that he regarded the peasants as his professors, and learnt from them how to grow healthy crops, practically free from disease, without the slightest help from artificial manures or insecticides (cited in Pereira, 1993, reprint 2009, pp 22).

As one of us, active with the Beej Bachao Andolan, has said:

'The traditional *barah-naja* system of mixed cropping, prevailing in Uttarakhand, is a good example of rich agriculture – combining *madua* and other millets with various pulses, beans, oilseeds, vegetables – that keeps farmers and Mother Earth healthy and happy!

'The so-called coarse grains and millets ... jowar, bajra, ragi/madua/nachhni, saanwa/ jhangora, kangni, cheena, kodo, kutki, ... are highly nutritious. They are greatly important for the farming of the future because they don't need irrigation; and they can withstand drought, flood and other climatic or environmental vagaries. They are also great in poly-cultural farming with numerous other food crops!'

(Jardhari, 2015)

Wealth of Crop Diversity

The late Dr. Richharia, perhaps the world's foremost rice scientist, estimated that India had 200,000 'ecotypes' or varieties of rice that evolved through growing over many generations in diverse agro-ecological conditions. Over 60,000 distinct varieties were collected by Indian agricultural research centres. Dr. Richharia personally supervised the collection of 19,000 rice varieties from just the state of Madhya Pradesh, which then included Chhattisgarh as well. Of these, 1,600 were high-yielding, comparable or superior in productivity to any modern 'High Response Varieties', grown with agro-chemicals. Many of the indigenous varieties Richharia collected were hijacked to the International Rice Research Institute (IRRI) in the Philippines (Alvares, 1986).

Similarly, India has mind-boggling diversity of numerous other crops adapted to local conditions. Each variety has unique features which may include nutritional/medicinal qualities, tolerance to drought/cold/flood/salinity, resistance to pests and diseases, etc.

Colonial Rule and Early Agricultural Recovery post Independence

Even before chemicals appeared, the exploitation of Indian farmers had begun during colonial rule. Many were forced to grow monocultures of opium, tobacco, cotton, indigo, tea, coffee, etc., year after year – for export – instead of diverse food crops for their own needs. The *Zamindari* (landlord) system and the high revenue extracted by the British rulers added to the farmers' woes. It is well documented that the 'Great Bengal Famine' too was essentially a creation of the colonial government (Mukerjee, 2011). But by and large, the soils of this land remained free of serious harm in the absence of chemical inputs, and heavy earth moving machinery.

After the British quit this country, Indian farming had a 15 year respite. The first Union Agriculture Minister, K. M. Munshi, inspired by Gandhi's vision of *gram swaraj*, or village self-governance and self-reliance, emphasized the paramount importance of restoring Nature's nutrient/fertility cycle and hydrological/water cycle in each village and bio-region – the core challenge of agro-ecological regeneration.

The *Handbook of Agriculture* of ICAR (1987) reveals that India's food yield steadily increased between 1951 and 1961. Both agricultural growth of total output of all crops, and increase in productivity, or yield per unit area, were higher all through the 1950s' compared to the Green Revolution years. But much of such increased farm yield was consumed in the countryside, re-emerging from impoverishment under alien oppression.

Notwithstanding the creditable recovery of Indian agriculture, Nehru's dream of urban-industrial expansion could only be pursued if agricultural surplus – particularly less perishable staples like rice and wheat – came to the cities.

1966: The Turn Downhill

Since our tall native grain varieties tended to 'lodge' (bend over) with the use of chemicals, 18,000 tonnes of Mexican seed of two dwarf wheat varieties were imported in 1966 by the Government of India – the highest movement of seeds in history – all the way across the world (Randhawa, 1986). The use of chemical fertilizers that year also saw a tremendous growth, about 60 per cent over the previous year. The floodgates to an ecologically devastating way of farming dependent on external, non-renewable inputs, opened wide that year.

Four decades later, India faced an epidemic of farmer suicides. Bhaskar Save addressed an Open Letter to M. S. Swaminathan, then Chairperson of the National Commission on Farmers:

'This country boasted an immense diversity of crops, adapted over millennia to local conditions and needs. Our numerous tall, indigenous varieties of grain provided more biomass, shaded the soil from the sun, and protected against its erosion under heavy monsoon rains. The introduced exotic dwarf varieties led to vigorous growth of weeds, which could now compete successfully with the new stunted crops for sunlight.

'The straw growth with the dwarf crops fell drastically... much less organic matter was available to recycle the fertility of the soil, leading to an artificial need for external inputs. Inevitably, farmers resorted to more chemicals; relentlessly, soil degradation and erosion set in.

'The exotic varieties, grown with chemical 'fertiliser', were more susceptible to 'pests and diseases', leading to more poison being poured. But the attacked insect species developed resistance and reproduced prolifically. Their predators – spiders, frogs, etc. – that biologically controlled their population, were exterminated. So were many beneficial species like the earthworms and bees. ...The spiral of ecological, financial and human costs mounted!'

(Save, 2008, 4th reprint 2016, pp. 10)

Current Crisis of Food and Farming

In March 2015, one of us wrote an Open Letter to the Prime Minister, expressing the agony of impoverished cultivators:

'... The farmer is reduced to an (absurd) economic situation of *aamdani athani kharcha rupaiya!* – only half a rupee recovered against every rupee spent. ... Over 300,000 Indian farmers have taken their lives in sheer distress of deepening indebtedness.

'...Thousands of years ago, our ancestors collected seeds from the forest by picking and choosing. Using such traditionally inherited seeds, scientists 'created' new seeds for industry to sell to hapless farmers. ... Today, neither our diversity of food crops remains, nor our farm saved seeds; neither cattle, nor manure. Instead of bullocks that feed on grass, plough the fields, and provide (free) organic fertilizer, we now have tractors, fed on oil, that spew pollution; ... and there are government subsidies for power tillers, but none for oxen, buffaloes or cows! ... At one time, rivers of milk and ghee were said to flow in this country! But now, where are our famed indigenous breeds of the *sindhi, gir, tharparkar, sahiwal* and the dark *pahadi* cow?

' ... We need to stop aping the American model, which is less than a hundred years old, while our traditional way of farming has evolved and proved its sustainability over thousands of years! ... Diversion of fertile farmland for huge malls, high-tech cities, and SEZs is a grave blunder and injustice. Some argue that farmers will get good compensation. But this exchange of land for money is like 'selling one's nose to buy a nose-ring'! Fertile land is irreplaceable. How many days will the money last?'

(Jardhari, 2015)

At least 150 million hectares of land is bleeding its fertility each year, seriously afflicted with soil erosion. We are annually losing 12,000 million tonnes of topsoil (or significantly more), washed away from largely bare lands. Even at a nominal value of Re 1 for each kg of eroded topsoil, the recurrent economic loss is a *staggering Rs 12 lakh crore (1.2 trillion) every year* (Vohra, 1985, pp. 4-6)!

With the upper absorbent layer of our soils increasingly eroded each monsoon from denuded lands, there is marked decline in groundwater recharge by rain soaked into the earth, while withdrawal has increased over twenty times since 1950. As a result, aquifer levels have fallen precipitously all over the country, resulting in serious water scarcity, threatening an even drier future. Barely 60 years ago, most regions had an abundance of groundwater within easy reach.

In 2006/7, India's National Commission on Farmers reported that the Green Revolution was experiencing 'technological fatigue'! It added that 40 per cent of the farming population would like to leave farming if provided an opportunity. This portends a quarter billion potential ecological and economic refugees streaming into urban slums and ghettos!

Increased urbanization has been uncritically promoted by governments of almost every political hue. Some economists believe that even distress urban migration is good for the economy, offering cheap labour. But where are the industrial/urban jobs for rural labour, with essentially farming skills? Housing, feeding and supporting a quarter billion people with new stable jobs is thus an absurd 'pie in the sky' proposition!

In 2011, there were 9 million less 'cultivators' than in 2001. While farmers are pushed out this way, the other sectors cannot create sufficient additional jobs for them. They thus end up joining the ranks of informal/unorganized agricultural labourers, getting just occasional or seasonal employment on daily wages. There were 36.8 million more such workers in 2011, compared to 2001 (Office of the Registrar General & Census Commissioner, India undated).

A December 2014 report of the NSSO 70th round survey found that the monthly average income of an agricultural household was around 6000 rupees. The daily average earnings per adult were around Rs. 107, below the minimum wages prescribed for unskilled workers. It also found that 6.26 crore (60.26 million) agricultural households in India (nearly 70 per cent of all agricultural households) run on a 'debt economy'. On an average, there is a deficit of Rs. 856 per month per household, with expenses exceeding receipts. This leads to deepening debt, and mounting distress.

If we accept the controversial 2011-12 poverty head count ratio, 81 per cent are from rural India. Simply stated, 81 per cent of all under-nourished and hungry people are in rural India. And there lies the biggest unconscionable irony of the situation created by our policy makers. India impoverished and made hungry the very people who work to feed others!

The 70th Round NSSO survey also revealed that between 2003 and 2013, rural land ownership declined by 14.86 million hectares. At 0.6 hectares of land owned on an average per household, that is an estimated 'dispossession' of 24.77 million households in one decade, whether for 'push' reasons or 'pull' reasons.

The belief that 'development' necessitates shifting people out of primary occupations, is questionable. Such uprooting is neither inevitable, nor without trauma and grave injustice. It is clear that solutions have to come from within agriculture, given that other sectors have no opportunities for the displaced, even as emphasis on those sectors at the expense of agriculture has significantly contributed to the problem.

Unregulated changes in land use and ownership – including changes in cropping patterns and the use of resources like groundwater – are driving the crisis. Large shifts of land away from agriculture as well as commons, and away from food production for local needs, contribute to greater risk in farming, employment-related stresses, and environmental degradation, given that such shifts are towards mono-cropping, intensive use of water and chemicals, and deteriorating household food security. In some areas, what passes off as 'food-grain production' largely goes into non-food uses, as with maize.

Paradoxically, in the midst of hunger-starvation, the overflowing storehouses with rotting food stocks bear stark testimony to how real food security is far removed from the edifice we built over the decades.

Most food consumers in India are actually food producers. In the lopsided approach India followed, prices were artificially kept suppressed through regulations and marketing restrictions for the food producers. This was ostensibly to provide cheap food for some imagined poor consumers elsewhere. Ironically, over a period of time, the food producers themselves are impoverished.

Poverty, malnutrition and ill health are particularly high in states like Odisha and Jharkhand which have seen high levels of industrialization and resource-grabbing from village communities to fuel the industries. The rupture created in the 'Nature-Agriculture-Culture-Community' continuum that long existed in India has been a cause *and* consequence of the mounting farm crisis.

Modern, chemical-intensive, mechanized farming commonly consumes 10 times as many calories in producing one calorie of food! Chemical fertilizers require huge amounts of fossil fuels in their production. So does the manufacture and operation of tractors, harvesters, irrigation pumps, etc. If we add the huge amount of energy consumed in transporting fertilizers and food over hundreds or thousands of miles, the 'energy inefficiency' of the modern, industrial system of agriculture is even starker. Its share in the world's carbon dioxide, methane and nitrous oxide emissions is very significant. The latter is 200 times more potent than CO_2 as a greenhouse gas!

We import 21 per cent of our nitrogenous chemical fertilizer, 40 per cent of phosphorus and 57 per cent of potash (Department of Fertilizers, undated) at increasing costs and these figures do not include the raw materials imported for manufacturing these fertilizers in India. India is increasingly dependent on imported fossil fuels to meet our energy needs.

Added to all of this is the crisis of climate change. Further enhancing the vulnerability of farmers are Free Trade Agreements in Agriculture. Such agreements, signed without deliberative democratic processes with citizens and elected bodies, have led to 'dumping' of heavily-subsidised produce from elsewhere; and the enclosure/appropriation of bio-cultural heritage and the commons by dubious Intellectual Property Rights (IPRs) on life forms.

Vision for Agro-Ecological Regeneration and Food Sovereignty

The vision is to provide local, adequate, nutritious, diverse and affordable food for all – respecting bio-cultural plurality – through protecting and promoting economically viable, ecologically regenerative, and socially just livelihoods, centred around farming, and the processing and distribution of food.

In the international discourse on poverty and hunger, it is recognized now that the most direct way of tackling poverty is to address issues in agriculture, particularly through empowering women farmers. Empowerment includes control over resources, acknowledged as of critical importance at the Rome Food Summit.

Similarly, agro-diversity and indigenous knowledge hold the key. Resource conservation is more crucial now than ever before, in this era of climate change. All of this requires a re-orientation towards food sovereignty, and a pragmatic, livelihoods-centred strategy, with an emphasis on agro-ecology and social justice.

An agro-ecological approach reaps multiple benefits:

* conservation and regeneration of soil fertility
* carbon sequestration
* water conservation and recharge
* greater energy efficiency
* greater diversity of crop produce for more balanced, poison-free nutrition
* reduced vulnerability to erratic fluctuations and extremes of climate and weather
* reduced vulnerability to rising prices and supply disruptions of imported agricultural inputs and fossil fuels
* increased self-reliance for regaining food sovereignty

There is growing realization that change – towards more biodiverse ecological farming – will be driven by compulsion, if not by choice. 'Business as usual is not an option', concludes the beacon International Assessment of Agricultural Knowledge, Science and Technology for Development (IAASTD), also known as the 'World Agriculture Report', endorsed by 60 nations, including India. Prepared by 400 agricultural experts and 1,000 multi-disciplinary reviewers – including national representatives and those of FAO, WHO, UNDP, UNEP and the World Bank – the Report recommends a path of agro-ecology, based on careful management of natural resources by small-scale farmers. It notes that GM crops are **not** the answer to hunger, poverty or climate change (IEG, 2010).

Towards Soil Conservation and Regeneration

All sloping land with a 30 degree gradient or more must be brought under 80 per cent cover of trees and perennials to check soil erosion under increasingly frequent torrential downpours/'cloudbursts'. In the plains too, at least 30 per cent tree-cover is needed on land that is not flooded in the monsoon.

Besides arresting erosion is the challenge of conserving and regenerating soil fertility. As K.M. Munshi repeatedly exhorted, healing the nutrient cycle of nature is vital. What comes from the soil must go back to the soil, either as mulch, manure or compost. A ground cover of dry leaves and/or green foliage, shielding the soil from the sun, also helps maintain its microclimate, essential for regenerating the organic life of the soil. If these 2 principles – returning organic waste/residue to the land, and keeping the soil well covered – are religiously followed (and no chemicals added), soil fertility will not decline. Indeed, where poly-cultural planting or crop rotation is followed, and perennials/tree crops are integrated on at least 30 per cent of the land, soil fertility will steadily improve, even without *any* external inputs.

Groundwater Recharge and Regaining Water Abundance

A far more holistic, economical and ecological option than big dams is to restore at least 30 per cent ground cover of mixed, indigenous trees and forests, with multiple benefits. This is the essential task of ecological water harvesting – the key to restoring an abundance of groundwater – as Bhaskar Save points out,

> 'The porous soil under thick vegetation and mulch is like a sponge that soaks and percolates to the aquifer an enormous amount of rain each monsoon. … The potential for natural water storage in the ground is many times greater than the combined capacity of all the major and medium irrigation projects/dams in India! Such decentralized storage – entailing no construction cost – is far more efficient too, as it is protected from the high evaporation losses of surface storage.'

(Mansata, 2015b, pp. 11)

Tank irrigation covered half the cropped area of the country a century ago. Now it covers less than 10 per cent. About 500,000 of the old tanks still survive, but too many lie badly neglected in the absence of de-silting and maintenance. Some experts suggest that well-constructed and maintained tanks at suitable sites, covering only 3 per cent of India's land, can store a quarter of its rainfall at just the cost of human labour, providing local employment as well, and significantly boosting agricultural productivity.

Each crore (10 million) spent on 'minor irrigation' supplies water to a five times larger area of land than spent on 'major' or 'medium' irrigation projects (Vohra, 1985). Yet the government has been spending five times more on major and medium irrigation schemes than on 'minor' irrigation. It is high time we rectify our ways. An important step would be to allocate future financial resources for water conservation through *gram sabhas* and *panchayats*. Fair allocation for irrigation and other needs too should be decided through local consensus.

Certainly, water wastage and diversion for non-priority uses must be curbed. Maharashtra, for example, has the maximum number of large and medium-sized dams in India, over 40 per cent of the country's total. But an estimated 70 per cent of their irrigation waters are channelled for growing water-guzzling sugarcane on less than 7 per cent of Maharashtra's cultivable land, progressively causing soil salinity and consequent barrenness within just a few decades. One acre of chemically grown sugarcane requires more water than 25 acres of organic jowar, bajra or maize. Much water is diverted too for hundreds of big sugar factories.

On the bright side, Maharashtra also has several outstanding examples of successful community watershed management schemes with equal entitlements to every local resident, irrespective of land-holding. So long as water remains scarce, natural justice demands this; for water is a common resource, and a birthright of all. Collective decision making and implementation as a community, respecting the rights of each overcomes the conflicts of a fragmented society, enabling 'win-win' benefits for all.

From Energy Mining to Energy Harvesting

With steadily depleting reserves of fossil fuels, the world is facing the critical challenge of transitioning from an age of fossil wealth to an age of biological wealth. Indeed, we need to remember it was biological wealth in the first place that created fossil wealth!

Photosynthesis is by far the most efficient way of harvesting renewable/solar energy for decentralized, equitable use with multiple benefits, including soil regeneration, carbon sequestration, groundwater recharge, and provision of diverse valuable products. Leading in efficient harvesting/storage of solar energy are our dense natural forests. Biodiverse 'food forests' and horticultural gardens of perennials come second, followed by organically cultivated poly-cultures of annual/seasonal field crops with minimal/zero external inputs. Amelioration of, and adaptation to, climate change are also best achieved by this low-cost path, which sequesters far more carbon for every rupee/dollar spent, compared to high-tech 'solutions'.

Agrochemicals must be progressively phased out. A realistic target of 10 per cent annual reduction should be announced as government policy. The money saved should be used to support ecological, safe food growing practices, and suitable budgetary allocations made for mainstreaming agro-ecology within the next ten years.

Regenerating Bio-Cultural Diversity

While India's rich biodiversity historically catered to almost every conceivable human need, scientists confess that they have taken only a preliminary look at some 10 per cent of many thousands of species. Our Western Ghats and North-Eastern states are among the world's 'hotspots' of such exceptionally rich – and still barely discovered – but increasingly threatened biodiversity.

The large number of crop varieties in centralized collections serve little purpose in enhancing India's food security and sovereignty unless they are widely regenerated on farms. One way is to mobilize farmers to each adopt one crop variety as custodian – for sharing its seeds with others. Of course, the varieties also need to be reintegrated in our diets and bio-culture.

We must be vigilant against GM crops too. One of us, Vasant Futane, a seasoned Vidarbha farmer, has stated: 'Our healthy indigenous seeds – the lifeblood of Indian agriculture, and many millions of self-reliant livelihoods – are inevitably contaminated by GM crops.'

The potential hazards of GM crops to human, animal and eco-system health have been testified by increasing numbers of independent scientific studies that have strongly cautioned against their commercial release or even open field trials (Antoniou *et al.,* 2012; Kuruganti, 2013). There is urgent need for a Biosafety Act to guard against GM crops, prohibited in organic farming.

Suitable government measures are also urgently needed to protect our collective heritage of traditional crop/plant varieties from privatization under restrictive IPRs, patents and licenses.

Prioritizing Land Use for Food Security and Equity

Land use must be prioritized for sustainably meeting India's nutritional and ecological security. Land under forests or farming must not be diverted for different purposes through forced land acquisition or other means. Rather, the millions of acres of barren/fallow/ degraded land – still capable of supporting plant growth – offer enormous potential for combining ecological regeneration with progressive local self reliance in meeting food needs. Such land, along with government support, should be made available to those with little or no land of their own, assuring secure rights to their families and descendants.

Equitable access to land for small family farms enhances food production and nutritional security. A study done by Genetic Resources Action International (GRAIN) found that small farms are much more productive, and far more efficient in optimally (and sustainably) utilizing resources. According to one UN study, policies supporting small producers and agro-ecological farming methods could double global food production in a decade (GRAIN, 2014). Agrarian reforms can and should be the springboard to moving in this direction.

Food for Health

Balanced, poison-free nutrition is vital for health. Some years ago, the Food Safety and Standards Authority of India reported that the toxic pesticides and chemicals contained in commonly purchased foods is enormously in excess of permissible limits, exposing consumers to unacceptable risk of myriad diseases.

Clearly, there is a health imperative for growing food organically without chemicals. This awareness is growing rapidly, creating a huge potential demand for such poison-free food, especially if it is also affordable and conveniently accessible.

Significant too is the diversion and degradation of industrially processed food for mass marketing, promoted with misinformation. Eating white 'polished' rice was portrayed as socially superior to consuming brown rice. But by removing rice bran, vital proteins, nutrients and vitamins (e.g., B-complex group) are also lost. With more industrial processing and additives in packaged foods, there is greater degradation of nutritive value, and increase of harmful substances.

The 'Green Revolution', emphasizing wheat and rice, contributed to imbalanced nourishment. We have neglected our many nutritionally superior types of millet. India's current production of cereals, if equitably distributed, can already meet the needs of every person. However, with pulses, fruits, and especially vegetables, India's per capita production is less than half of what is needed. These are the food categories where India particularly needs to boost production and more equitable consumption – for balanced nutrition and good health. Providing even a quarter acre to each rural family – for growing fruits, vegetables, edible legumes, herbs, etc. – would greatly enhance the health of the people. Urban food gardening too needs to be similarly promoted and supported.

Women and Agriculture

Women farmers are traditional custodians of seeds; and the backbone of a biodiverse agriculture for food self-sufficiency. They have more firmly resisted the industrial way of mono-cropping, preferring poly-cultural, traditional farming for local/family self-consumption.

Empowering women farmers – which includes control over resources – is critical. They must have equal rights as men in deciding land use, what crops to grow, and how. To strengthen such rights, their names should be included in ownership titles and land records. State support must go equally to them.

Government policies, projects, and bank loans – for agro-ecological regeneration and local self-reliance – need to prioritize women farmers. Small self-help groups or cooperatives of women farmers have a better record of sustainable use and management of resources.

Remunerative Returns and Bringing Youth Back to Farming

A primary cause of youth disenchantment with farming is the raw deal to agriculture in the modern economy, with net returns – deducting costs from income – witnessing a relentless decline, commonly dipping into the red.

With 70 per cent of people dependent on the land for their livelihood needs, it was a grave blunder to keep food prices artificially depressed, even as the costs of everything else, including agricultural inputs, increased. Worse, middlemen/traders in farm produce were allowed to earn more at the cost of farmers. By making farmers subsidize urban folk – rich and poor – they were plunged deeper into debt each year. Ensuring remunerative returns for agriculture is vital to bring youth back into farming.

The government must institute a high-powered 'Farm Income Commission' to remedy the unjust neglect of farmers. Sustainable organic farming particularly needs to be incentivized with far-sighted policies and measures, recognizing its vital environmental services, superior health benefits, and huge savings in the import of progressively scarce and expensive fossil fuels and chemicals.

Farmers must again feel valued and respected, not treated as a dispensable burden. They should be free to set the prices of their produce, and farmers' markets supported for selling directly to consumers, without restrictions.

The growing awareness among consumers – sensitive to health, ecology, and social justice issues – has spurred a new movement of 'Community Supported Agriculture'. Banding together with local organic farmers, consumers provide themselves with fresh, wholesome foods, while ensuring remunerative returns for cultivators. Young consumers volunteer their services to help farmers. Some farms have birthed a new 'agro-ecological tourism' with opportunities for learning and meaningful participation, quite different from consumer tourism.

India needs to reintegrate agro-ecology at all levels of education – for the young and old, rural and urban alike. At the start of each monsoon, rural schools should take a month long break from academics to engage in planting on farms and forest regeneration projects. In urban schools too, at least one or two weeks of early monsoon engagement in planting would sensitize the young to nature and the lives of farmers.

The conveniences of urban centres and the possibilities for greater socio-cultural interaction have been a major attraction drawing people to cities. 'Rurbanization' of the countryside for meeting important non-food needs in the larger villages, and in and around small towns, can check such urban migration, even reverse it.

Organic SRI with Traditional Crops

SRI (System of Rice Intensification) is being practiced in many parts of the world, including India. In suitable conditions, farmers have doubled their productivity while reducing seed and water inputs.[4]

With innovative use of the SRI approach to grow other crops, the acronym now stands for 'System of Root Intensification'. It is being successfully adopted to organically cultivate diverse traditional crops, including millets. It can significantly increase food production, compensating for any decline feared through discontinuing chemicals. As agro-chemicals are phased out, organic SRI of traditional crops can be progressively adopted to grow the surplus of cereals/pulses required to feed urban areas. Smaller farmers, who follow mixed cropping of various millets, legumes, etc., for local self-provisioning, may also pursue SRI if it is successfully adapted to poly-cultures.

Urban and Peri-Urban Agriculture

In the historical evolution of cities, many continued to self-provision much of their food needs by growing in and around the urban areas until the density of population and constructed structures greatly increased. Such urban and peri-urban agriculture needs to be widely adopted again, even as the decongestion of parasitical cities progressively continues with rural and 'rurban' areas steadily becoming more attractive.

Urban agriculture in Cuba made huge strides in the past quarter century under compelling circumstances (Mansata, 2008). Within India, there is a significant urban food gardening movement shaping in Mumbai, Pune and Bangalore.

Initiatives and Pathways Pointing to the Future

There are already numerous initiatives/experiments on the ground, pointing towards future possibilities for our food and farming systems. While many individual farmers have successfully adopted the agro-ecological path, some have looked to community collaboration for collective benefit. Yet others have explored approaches that create new local rural-urban linkages, benefiting both farmers and consumers. Some examples are given below.

1) **Bhaskar Save, the 'Gandhi of Natural Farming' (1922-2015)**

   Save's farm in southernmost coastal Gujarat – low intervention and zero external input – is a veritable food forest; *and* a net supplier of water, energy and fertility to the local ecosystem, rather than a net consumer. It has inspired 3 generations of organic farmers.

   About 10 acres are under a natural orchard of coconut and *chikoo/sapota*, with fewer trees of various other species. Two acres are under seasonal field crops grown in traditional rotation. A nursery area raises coconut saplings that are in great demand. The farm yield – in all aspects of total output, nutritional quality, taste, diversity, water conservation, energy efficiency, and economic profitability – is superior to any farm using chemicals. The costs (mainly labour for harvesting) are minimal.

   Save's success in decreasing and eliminating external inputs, while achieving high productivity, is a model for promoting food security; and his method of tree-cropping – integrating short lifespan, medium lifespan and long lifespan species – has been hailed as potentially revolutionary for wasteland regeneration, while also offering sustainable and rewarding livelihoods to large numbers of people (Mansata, 2010). A residential learning centre at Save's farm (www.bhaskarsavenftc.in), offers a 5-day residential introductory workshops on natural farming in Hindi, Marathi, Gujarati and English. More such agro-ecological demonstration and learning centres are needed in every bioregion.

2) **Women's Sangams in 85 villages of Medak District, Telangana**

   The work of Deccan Development Society (DDS) with women's *sangams* (collectives) in semi-arid Medak district (Telangana) is an outstanding example of a cooperative community-centred, community-governed initiative. Here, Dalit women – including landless, exploited women – transformed their lives to secure greater autonomy by collectivizing themselves, taking control over their local natural resources and optimizing their sustainable use.

   The leadership abilities of the illiterate but extremely knowledgeable Dalit women – encouraged and groomed by the organization – made the Sangams vibrant platforms for local planning and execution of livelihood improvement programmes based on natural resources. Interventions included developing micro-watersheds, and regenerating 'ceiling surplus' plots of land (usually degraded/fallow/distant) assigned to landless households by the government. DDS supported collective land leases (and purchases) by the women's *sangams* for joint cultivation, re-popularizing diversity-based traditional ecological agriculture in the region. It also pursued social forestry. Re-establishing seed sovereignty by reviving local seed diversity and associated knowledge was a major thrust.

The sangams pioneered a unique food security programme in 32 villages. Centred on local production, storage and distribution of millets, this was supported initially by Government of India under an employment generation programme. It entailed only one-fifth the cost normally incurred by the government for collecting, storing and provisioning grain under its centralised PDS model. This too was just a one-time investment for the Government, into a village level Community Grain Fund. It was utilized for regenerating fallow lands and provided much employment to villagers, especially women.

For those who own land, the investment (received over three years) is advanced by the sangam as an interest-free loan to be repaid over six years in the form of millets. Such grain repayment to the sangam is stored within the village in low cost, traditional ways.

With transparent, participatory wealth ranking processes, poorest households are identified for food subsidy – millets collected as repayment from landowners are distributed to them at very low rates over six 'hungry months' of the year. The sale proceeds are ploughed back into the Community Grain Fund, for investing in more land development the next season, consciously enhancing social equity.

The sangam women have been pioneers in re-imagining and creating new favourable markets for themselves. They realized they have many products which they both produce and consume. But as producers, when they sell, they get very low prices; while as consumers, they buy small quantities at significantly higher prices.

Putting in their own equity, the women created a 'Market of the Walk-Outs' that buys and sells within the women's groups across 80 villages. As producers, they pay themselves better than what local traders offer. As consumers, they gain by getting 10 per cent member-discount on bulk orders. Led by a committee of eleven women, this is a unique 'rural to rural' cooperative marketing effort amongst the poorest sections – worth understanding and replicating.

3) Belgaum Organic Food Club

This is a rural to urban direct marketing effort without middlemen in a 'Consumer Supported Agriculture' model, in Belgaum, Karnataka. Led by farmers like Abhay Mutalik Desai, it was founded by 8 farmers, with a 'second line' of around twenty more farmers. They began weekly supplies of 'food baskets' of various organic vegetables, cereals and pulses to 400 urban middle-class consumer households in Belgaum, from whom they collected 8 weeks' advance as working capital for the producer collective. The price band was fixed uniformly for various vegetables for easier transactions, and to protect producers and consumers from market volatility. Organic food baskets were packed to customized orders of consumers, delivered to their doorstep – a win-win situation for both farmers and consumers.

However, the experiment, started in 2000, was halted after prolonged rains in 2004 that severely disrupted the supply chain. By then, the collective was also tired of spending energy in packing and delivering baskets to suit specific requests of consumers, who were getting too choosy about what they want. The farmers wanted to focus on farming. Looking back, the OFC pioneers believe that their venture can benefit by investing in consumer education, and assigning marketing to employed staff – two big problems they faced. They find greater demand now for organic food than ever before. Keen to restart, they say: 'As genuine organic producers, our greatest need is to find genuine and committed organic buyers!'

Several groups of farmers in different parts of the country have also successfully collectivized their marketing – earning a better return – through newly created institutions of 'Farmer Producer Organizations', in different forms, owned and controlled equally by the farmers themselves, through equal share-holdings and equal votes. Professional employees handle marketing, accounting, and general administration. A good example is Dharani Cooperative, AP, supported by Timbaktu Collective; also Sahaja Samrudha, Karnataka.

4) Adivasi Poly-cultural Farming in South Odisha

The Kondh adivasis inhabiting the Niyamgiri foothills in Bissam, Cuttack, and Muniguda blocks of Rayagada District, southern Odisha, have traditionally been self-reliant in meeting all their food needs. They collect many varieties of uncultivated foods from nearby forests, and also practice dryland (rainfed) farming of 40-50 traditional crop varieties, grown in surrounding clearances. The food harvested is largely for self-consumption, with excess shared within the community, or sold in local markets.

In recent years, this traditional self-reliant culture faced external threats, including mining. 'Living Farms' has been working locally to help strengthen the traditional methods and system of adivasi *Kutumba* or community self-governance; and to deepen the leadership of women in protecting and regenerating their forest and agro-biodiversity.

Local food and seed festivals are organized to share knowledge and seeds; also to celebrate, worship, and thank the land, forest, water, and village deities. Community dialogues are held between elders and the youth, vulnerable to external, disruptive influences.

5) **Grassroot Seed Initiatives and Movements**

A several-decades old pioneering community initiative in seed conservation and sharing is the Beej Bachao Andolan (BBA) of Uttarakhand. Following several Beej Yatras across the state, it revitalized the traditional ecologically sustainable Barahnaja system of mixed cropping of millets/cereals, pulses, oilseeds (mandua, ramdana, maize, kutu, jowar, rajma, gahath, bhat, naurangi, urad, moong, ragadwans, bhangjiri, til, san, bhang, etc.) for providing diverse, balanced and wholesome nutrition.

The BBA network of farmer-members possesses/grows between them about 200 bean varieties, 100 rice varieties, 8 wheat varieties, 27 varieties of 5 millets, 10 maize varieties, 3 amaranth varieties, several varieties of pulses, oilseeds, and so on.

Elsewhere in India, numerous *Beej Melas* (Seed Festivals) have been collaboratively organized in Nagpur, Mumbai, Pune, Bangalore, Hyderabad, Kolkata, Delhi, Bhubaneswar, Chandigarh, Kerala, etc. Local, regional and pan-India seed networks have emerged. The MINI network collaborates for the revival of indigenous millets. In 2014, many seed savers, including those from the national Alliance for Sustainable and Holistic Agriculture (ASHA), united to form the *Bharat Beej Swaraj Manch* or India Seed Sovereignty Alliance. Without Beej Swaraj or Seed Sovereignty, Anna Swaraj or Food Sovereignty is not possible.

Endnotes

1. The quote is drawn from the Indian edition of the book, published in 2007. Page number unavailable.
2. See also essay on Pastoral Futures in this volume.
3. For details see: i) National Institute of Science Communication and Information Resources [CSIR], Undated (a multi-volume encyclopedia on India's biological wealth); ii) Publications

and Information Directorate [CSIR], Undated (provides summary information on over 5,000 useful plant species, including their local names in various vernacular languages for easy cross-identification); iii) Indian Council of Forestry Research and Education (ICFRE), Undated (provides an account of almost 600 uncultivated food yielding species from various forested regions of India); iv) Watt, Sir George, 1889-90.

4. For details: http://sri.ciifad.cornell.edu; http://www.sri-india.net/.

References

Alvares, Claude, 1986, 'The Great Gene Robbery', *The Illustrated Weekly of India*, March 23.

Antoniou, Michael, Claire Robinson and John Fagan, 2012, *GMO Myths and Truths*, Bombay: Earthcare Books.

Deb, Debal, Kavitha Kuruganti, V. Rukmini Rao and Salome Yesudas, 2014, *Forests as Food Producing Habitats*, Bhubaneshwar: Living Farms.

Department of Fertilizers, Undated, *Indian Fertilizer Scenario 2013*, New Delhi: Ministry of Chemicals and Fertilizers, Government of India. http://fert.nic.in/sites/default/files/Indian%20Fertilizer%20 SCENARIO-2014_0.pdf (last accessed 30 March, 2017).

George, Susan and Nigel Paige, 1988, *Food for Beginners*, New York: Writers and Readers Publishing. Indian Edition, 2007, New Delhi: Orient Longman.

GRAIN, 2014, *Hungry for Land: small farmers feed the world with less than a quarter of all farmland*, 28 May. https://www.grain.org/article/entries/4929-hungry-for-land-small-farmers-feed-the-world-with-less-than-a-quarter-of-all-farmland (last accessed 30 March, 2017).

IEG (Independent Evaluation Group: World Bank, IFC and MIGA), 2010, *International Assessment of Agricultural Knowledge, Science and Technology for Development (IAASTD)*, Washington: Independent Evaluation Group, Working Paper, Report No. 57645, The World Bank Group; available at http://documents.worldbank.org/curated/en/636821468316165959/ pdf/576450NWP0Box31am0review0v40issue02.pdf (last accessed 16 May, 2017).

Indian Council of Forestry Research and Education, Undated, *Food from Forests*, Dehradun: (ICFRE).

Jardhari, Vijay, 2015, '*Open Letter to the Prime Minister of India*', https://foodwebsandus.wordpress. com/2015/09/24/a-farmers-plea/ (last accessed 16 May, 2017).

Kuruganti, Kavitha, 2013, *Adverse Impacts of Transgenic Crops*, New Delhi: compiled for Coalition for a GM-Free India.

Mansata, Bharat, 2015a (3rd Reprint), *Organic Revolution: The Agricultural Transformation of Cuba since 1990*, Kolkata: Earthcare Books.

Mansata, Bharat, 2015b (3rd Reprint), *The Vision of Natural Farming*, Kolkata: Earthcare Books.

Mukerjee, Madhusree, 1911, *Churchill's Secret War: The British Empire and the Ravaging of India during World War II*, New York: Basic Books.

Myers, Ed Norman, 1985, *The Gaia Atlas of Planet Management*, London & Sydney: Pan Books.

National Institute of Science Communication and Information Resources [CSIR], Undated, *The Wealth of India*, available at http://www.niscair.res.in/activitiesandservices/products/wealth-of-indiaFolder2010.pdf (last accessed 16 May, 2017).

Office of the Registrar General & Census Commissioner, India, Undated, *2011 Census of India*, Ministry of Home Affairs, Government of India; http://censusindia.gov.in/ (last accessed 16 May, 2017).

Pereira, Winin 1993 (Reprints, 2007, 2009), *Tending the Earth*, Kolkata: Earthcare Books.

Publications and Information Directorate [CSIR], Undated, 'The Useful Plants of India'.

Randhawa, M.S., 1986, *A History of Agriculture in India*, Volume 4, New Delhi: Indian Council of Agricultural Research.

Save, Bhaskar, 2008 (4th Reprint, 2016), *The Great Agricultural Challenge*, (transcribed by Bharat Mansata), Bombay: Earthcare Books.

Voelcker, John Augustus, 1891, *Report on the Improvement of Indian Agriculture*, London: Eyre and Spottiswoode, reprinted in1986, London: Agricole Reprints Corporation.

Vohra, B.B., 1985, *Land and Water*, New Delhi: Indian National Trust for Art and Cultural Heritage (INTACH).

Watt, Sir George, 1889-90 (digitized, 2006), *A Dictionary of the Economic Products of India'* (10 volumes), Oxford: Oxford University.

Crafts Show the Way for Indian Industrialization

Uzramma

Summary

In India craft industries have retained their relevance throughout the Industrial Age, in spite of the domination of high-energy production since the Industrial Revolution. Commercial mass production in the Western world was founded on exploitation, an example of which is the early factory production of cotton textiles in the nineteenth century, which used slaves to grow and pick cotton and young children to spin yarn.

The survival of craft industries in India into the twenty-first century opens an opportunity for us to by-pass the option of high-energy industrialization which benefits the few, in favour of low-energy, dispersed craft industries, which could usher in democracy in production, a basic building block for true social equity. Craft industries use low-cost infrastructure and need small capital investment, which make it possible for ownership of production to be widely held. With the looming threat of climate change, India's low-energy craft industries will gain in viability.

Traditional Indian craft products, like the heritage craft practices of other civilizations, embody specific cultural traits, which give them a distinctive identity, highly valued in contemporary markets.

This essay argues that in recognition of the vast potential of these industries, democratic rights of producers to raw material, institutional finance, and the legal ownership of its specific product identities must be guaranteed by the State.

The Current Potential for Crafts in India

Surely India in the early twenty-first century is in an enviable position to build up a vibrant industrial future. Today India, on the linear scale of industrialization, is considered 'less developed'. From this linear perspective there is only one way forward, but is it really so? Does the path to corporate industrialization taken by the 'developed' world have to be the path blindly followed in India? In my opinion India's living craft practices in the early twenty-first century put it in an enviable position to fashion an industrial future specific to India's own particular circumstances.

Since we are not part of the over-industrialized 'developed' countries, we can leapfrog the era of energy intensive industrial revolution technology with its dependence on dwindling fossil fuels, its pollution and social disruption, its entropic threats to life on earth. Our living artisanal industries, unique in the world for their size and vitality, allied to the new post-industrial technologies of ecological energy generation and communications, can direct an industrialization suited to our particular circumstances, built on our historical strengths, for the benefit of our people. The features of craft production – its use of renewable energy, minimal dependence on fossil fuels, inexpensive infrastructure, informal skill transfer mechanisms, its small scale of individual units dispersed throughout the country – together provide a rational blueprint for future industrial viability. A substantial part of industrial production through craft can disperse the gains of production throughout the rural countryside and can provide the basis for a democratic production regime.

Craft can challenge the claim to universality of Western industrialization and its appropriation of modernity. The all-enveloping nature of that model in which technology serves the needs of capital leaves no room within it for a search for alternative paths, though it has always been accompanied by protest and dissent. In its very early days the Luddites protested in England by famously breaking machines that replaced skilled labour with unskilled. The most profound critique of industrial technology directed by capital came from Karl Marx: 'We have seen how machinery does away with co-operation based on handicrafts, and with manufacture based on the division of handicraft labour' (Marx, 1965, pp. 300).

The genie of energy-intensive technology that was released from the bottle of the Industrial Revolution brought with it increased productivity, but at what cost? Environmental degradation, pollution, global warming, industrial ghettos and the disruption of society have been the outcomes of such technology. Since the development of industrial technology since its early days has been in the hands of the owners of capital, it has served the interests of capital at the cost of society. Again as Marx pointed out, 'Machines were, it may be said, the weapon employed by the capitalists to quell the revolt of specialized labour' (McLellan, 2000, pp. 321).

And let us not forget: the technological leap that such a process took was fuelled by extraction of natural resources from colonized lands, by forcible suppression of the industries of colonized peoples, and by their physical exploitation. One of the best known theatres of the violence of the industrial revolution was the cotton textile industry of India.

'Various and innumerable are the methods of oppressing the poor weavers…such as by fines, imprisonments, floggings, forcing bonds from them, etc.,' wrote William Bolts in 1772 (Chomsky, 1993, pp. 12). Through a series of savage measures the Indian cotton textile industry which had dominated world cotton textile trade for centuries became in twenty-one years – between 1814 and 1835 – a net importer in relation to Britain, and the dominance over world cotton textile trade, which India had held for centuries, passed into the hands of the colonial power. The table below brings out this changed equation in imports and exports.

Table 1: British cotton goods exported to India and Indian cotton goods imported into England

Year	British Cotton Manufacture Exported to India (In Yards)	Indian Cotton Piece Goods imported into Great Britain (In Yards)
1814	818,208	1,266,608
1821	19,138,726	534,495
1828	42,822,077	422,504
1835	51,777,277	306,608

Source: Beauchamp, 1935, pp. 29

In the literature of economic history the replacement of artisan manufacture by machine is described in triumphalist terms. The narrative of social history, however, details the vast costs to people and societies that underpinned the change – industrial production was built on human exploitation. Take the making of cotton cloth, which was the cradle of Industrial Revolution in Britain three hundred years ago, when the first machines driven by the steam engine were invented to replace Indian hand-made cotton yarn. For the new industry cotton was shipped to Lancashire from America, where it was grown and picked by slave labour.

'Slavery and cotton marched together', as Eric Hobsbawm (2010) says. Without slave labour in the growing and picking of cotton, and children and women to work the machines in the early factories, industrial production of cotton textiles in England and America could not have been established.

Lancashire set about decimating the millennia-old Indian industry, beginning with importing cotton yarn into India. This of course destroyed the household yarn spinning of the country, impoverishing millions of women. An individual spinner tells her story in a letter to the Bengali newspaper *Samachar Darpan* in the 1820s', quoted by Gandhi in *Young India* in 1931 (*Appendix A*). Force and violence was used in India by the East India Company and later continued by the British Crown, to ensure that cotton was denied to local industry (Satya, 1997). besides swinging taxation on every stage of cloth making in India (see testimony of F. C. Brown, *Appendix B*), punitive import duties in England and nominal duties on English cloth brought into India.

The great tragedy of the industrial revolution is that over the last two centuries it has so firmly established the domination of society by the market economy, that all other economic systems, however more humane, more attuned to the natural world they may be, now appear as utopian and impractical. The lessons of history are unlearned – how civilizations perished because they were unable to change course and abandon destructive practices. The lessons of nature are being ignored, of the cataclysms that are in store for the human race if it persists in following the currently dominant economic system.

Dissent has been a continuing counterpoint to industrialization in the West. Henry David Thoreau in the nineteenth century 'saw the potential for the destruction of nature for the ends of commerce'; Rachel Carson's book *Silent Spring* published in1962 sounded the alarm about pesticide use. Both these passionate indictments have shaped modern environmentalist concerns against the violation of nature by technology, concerns that are intensifying today when the disastrous effects of over-industrialization by mass production are ever more evident. Greater dissent is being voiced at an increasing volume.

From this critique a real change of direction towards sane, sustainable, democratic economic practice may yet emerge. Wendell Berry's retreat into 'simple living', Naomi Klein's battle against the corporate world, the Occupy movement, the growing organic product movement, and a revival of socialist ideals may yet make a strong coalition against the multinational industrial confederacy.

But contemporary dissent towards industrialization within industrialized countries seems at present to limit itself to rejecting the outcomes of excessive industrialization, and it may be difficult from that perspective to move beyond dissent into a creative alternative. That creative alternative is visible only where non-capitalist production exists on a large scale, which is nowhere more than in India. While in industrialized countries craft has become a hobby or has been relegated to a niche, India, unlike the hyper-industrialized countries, retains its large scale of craft production. Today when the climate crisis threatens life on earth, when it is clear that industries dependent on 'dirty energy' will not score high on the viability scale for long, India's living craft industries give the country a huge advantage in planning its industrial future.

Ivan Illich, the Austrian philosopher suggested that,

'Two-thirds of mankind still can avoid passing through the industrial age, by choosing right now a post-industrial balance in their mode of production which the hyper-industrial nations will be forced to adopt as an alternative to chaos' (Illich, 1973).

It is unfortunate that policy makers in India seem blind to the fact that high-energy industrialization is not sustainable and will not lead us to the promised land of a good life of all and to the advantage that the massive scale of contemporary craft production in this country allows us. We seem to have accepted the maxim that 'There is No Alternative'; that India and other 'developing' countries can modernize only by following the well-trodden path of energy-and-capital intensive industrialization. Will this path bring prosperity? Yes, to a few – India now has a hundred dollar billionaires, with a combined wealth at present of $346 billion (Forbes India Magazine, 2014). At the same time India also has a quarter of the world's malnourished people. The point is, as the World Food Programme points out, the gap between the rich and the poor has increased during the high economic growth phase. This is because the profits of high-capital industry go into only a few pockets. If we continue in this direction the gap will continue to widen, with immiseration for the many and increasing wealth for the few. Industrialization in India has not been able to provide livelihoods to people. As many reports point out only a small percentage of the working age population is employed in the organized sector. That is the present situation; the future, if we continue on this path, could be even bleaker. Technology research firm Gartner predicts software, robots and smart machines will take over one out of three jobs in another 10 years (Srinivasan, 2015).

Should we not take a different kind of path to economic growth, pursue a different kind of industrialization that would narrow that gap that would bring a good life to millions? Is such a course of action possible? In my view it is not only possible but in fact vital, for Indian policy makers to see the crafts sector as a viable, sustainable, large-scale production system that bypasses high-energy industrialization that would ensure an equitable distribution of wealth and therefore a good life for a substantial part of India's people.

Policy makers neglect the potential of craft as viable modern industry in terms of both rural employment and low-energy production, ignoring the fact that the vast majority of manufacture in India is outside organized industry, and a large part of that 'unorganized' segment consists of craft industries. Much of these are still linked to their local markets, cutting out the need for transport, another critical factor in saving energy.

India today retains its thriving artisan practices where the ownership of the means of production is well within the reach of most craftspeople; a weaver setting up his own loom can be sure of repaying its cost within a year. Imagine how that would disperse the profits of industry throughout society! India has close to the largest number of people in the world engaged in craft activities – some estimates put that number at 200 million persons. Ninety percent of the world's handlooms are in India. With its vast numbers of craft practitioners, its thriving artisan practices using renewable energies, its plentiful natural resources, its variety of micro-climates and its diverse cultures, it is well placed to achieve a 'post-industrial balance'. That balance, I suggest, is available to India thanks to a sturdy backbone of skill-based craft industries scattered throughout the remotest villages, which often have close relations with nearby small factory production. For instance, artisan brass work throughout the country gets its raw material of brass sheet made in small local brass mills, while artisanal practices of lost wax casting use scrap metal from the same small factories. Small glass factories supply the artisanal small-bead industry of Papanaidupeta in Andhra Pradesh. This kind of productive interdependence between craft production and large corporate industry located in industrial ghettos is impossible; now that the small glass factories of Firozabad are being pushed out of the market by bigger fish the Papanaidupeta bead makers are struggling.

There is no dispute that we have inherited a great craft tradition. It was craft production that gave India the largest share (24.4 per cent) of world trade in the year 1700,[1] not to speak of meeting its own needs in entirety, whether in villages, towns or palaces. India dressed its large and varied population (about twenty seven per cent of the world population in 1700)[2] in cotton cloth, built houses, modest and grand, from mud, brick and lime mortar, built bridges that survive to this day, made the finest steel in the world, learnt non-ferrous metal work from the Middle East and silk weaving from China. Indians early on mastered industrial chemistry and the skills of dyeing and tanning. The many indigenous Indian industries of earlier days – iron and steel, paper, building and masonry, sugar, distillation of various kinds, textiles of silk and cotton, leather, wood, metal, bamboo, stone, glass, ceramics, ship and boat-building, musical instruments, wooden carts, gold and silver jewellery, varnishes and gums, adhesives and paints, food preservation, dyeing, printing, painting, tool-making and many others were viewed with awe and wonder by early Europeans.

Civilizations developed industries based on their particular circumstances. Several ancient civilizations developed specific techniques of production that reflected their particular genius, or served their particular needs, and which they supplied to the rest of the world. Paper and printing were invented in China to carry the printed word over the vast range of the Chinese empire. Exports of silk made China rich and the Chinese managed to keep silk a secret for over 1000 years. However, in CE 550 the secret of silk became known to other countries when two monks managed to smuggle some silkworm eggs out of the country. Porcelain in China was perfected to a high art, its secrets revealed to Europe by a French Jesuit, Father Francois Xavier d'Entrecolles in 1712,[3] reckoned to be the first recorded instance of industrial espionage.

Indian mastery of dyeing and printing of cotton was legendary.

'The quality of Indian dyeing too was proverbial in the Roman world, as we know from a reference in St Jerome's 4th century Latin translation of the Bible, Job being made to say that wisdom is even more enduring than the 'dyed colours of India' (Irwin, 1962, as cited by Bean, 1989, pp. 360).

Such admiring comments are found throughout recorded history, and museums are full of cotton textiles dyed and printed in India, still bright after centuries. In the Ashmolean Museum of Oxford you will find pieces of printed Indian cloth found in Egypt, known to scholars as the 'Fustat textiles', which have been carbon dated from the 13th to the 17th centuries.

Indian natural dyeing, with a history stretching back millennia, was the first casualty of the early chemical industry of Europe. English and German chemists set about to replicate it artificially.

Indigo is not just a dye, in both Indian and Chinese medicinal traditions, it is commonly known as a cure for skin diseases. In the days when indigo was grown in Kadapa district of Andhra Pradesh people with skin troubles used to offer to step into the indigo vats to do the beating of the indigo solution. Synthetic indigo has never been able to reproduce either the distinctive carmine undertones, or the medicinal qualities of the real thing.

Indians were masters of steel making in early times: they were the first to produce high quality steel, called *wootz* by the Europeans who first encountered these. 'Though an ancient material, *wootz* steel also fulfills the description of an advanced material, since it is an ultra-high carbon steel exhibiting properties such as super-plasticity and high impact hardness … a feat unlikely to be surpassed by advanced materials of the current era' (Srinivasan & Ranganathan, 1997).

Demonstrations of their iron making techniques were given by the Agaria community, traditional iron-smelters, at Gandhi Ashram in Varanasi in 1990, and in 1993 during the 1st Congress of Traditional Sciences at the Indian Institute of Technology, Mumbai – places new to them.

'You may change the charcoal, the source of the ore, the place or climate and the Agaria engineer takes one or two experiments to settle on the new combination of different factors to deliver the sponge again', says Sahasrabudhey (undated, pp. 2). Continuing, he says, 'It is fascinating to note, how it is done with no gadgets to measure parameters or even time.' He describes how the master sits apart and watches, from time to time instructing his sons and nephews who work the bellows, charge the furnace, and remove the slag. Sahasrabudhey elaborates:

> '...deep into the forest and mountain ranges... there are villages where in a number of houses one can find the red glow in the small furnaces; iron smelting goes on here.... There must be Agaria workmen even now who know how to make wootz, who may even be doing it' (Sahasrabudhey, undated, pp. 1).

Not only are ancient skills remarkable in themselves, but also the objects, materials and processes that were produced by these ancient skills embodied characteristics specific to their cultures, characteristics which can give our modern industries their defining identities. A particular example of a cultural trait invested in modern industry is the Japanese skill of miniaturization, in bonsai, *netsuke, inro* (miniature sculptures), recognized as a major influence on contemporary design particularly of electronic devices, emerged from their particular circumstances:

> 'Japanese product is highly characterized by its miniaturization, due to the economic profit, resources limitation, traditional aesthetic and space limitation. Small object designs have obvious traits and delicately communicate aesthetic senses of oriental cultures. The scale is seen as one of cultural traits of a product' (Pei-Ling & Ming-Chyuan, undated, pp. 1).

These specifically Japanese skills were transferred from craft to mainstream industrial production in the 20th century, and gave Japan a tremendous advantage in the modern electronic industry.

And this leads us to the question: what are the particular characteristics of Indian craft that are valuable in today's world? Perhaps it is the frugal use of resources. This frugality, I suggest, is a part of the ethos of the Indian civilization. It was evident in India's spectacular Mangalyaan mission, it is there in every Indian household's careful housekeeping and it is the defining feature of Indian craft, now being adopted by the corporate world as *'jugaad innovation'*. Frugality is evident in the Agaria's methods of iron smelting – their furnace is a simple construction of 'earth mixed with a little rice husk' (Sahasrabudhey, undated). The artisan is naturally frugal; it is part of artisanal respect for and relation to nature. Nature provides India with an abundance of plant life, and crafts-persons in the past used it prudently, husbanding nature while using its gifts as resource. The Agaria used wood fallen from trees for their charcoal, rather than cutting the trees. Ravindra Sharma of Kala Ashram in Adilabad says people used to say they were going into the forest to *pick* firewood, rather than to *cut* it. Colonial administrations of course did not see this distinction, they banned iron-smelting by the Agaria 'to preserve the forests'.

This was ironic, as the State's hegemony over India's forests has sounded their death knell. In contrast to artisans' frugal use of forest resources, sustained over centuries, the State's management has consisted of rapid destruction of the forest in collusion with corporate industry. While artisan industry conserves nature, high-energy industrialization is at war with it. Big industry can swallow up whole forests, whole ways of life, to feed its greed for raw materials. A classic case is the current battle between the Dongria Kondh people and the Vedanta Corporation, to preserve or destroy Niyamgiri, the ancient hill sacred to the Kondh. Extracting its bauxite from their sacred hill would destroy the local environment and the life of the Dongria Kondh, guaranteed by the Constitution of India. The Government of Odisha offered to sell Vedanta the rights to mine Niyamgiri, which would give Anil Agarwal, the chief shareholder of Vedanta, huge profits. That's not the end of the story: bauxite is the raw material for aluminium smelting, perhaps one of the most damaging of all high-energy industries, closely connected to the arms industry.

The great craft traditions of India are not only part of our past; they are the clues to future industrial production. It is only the myth of a universal modernity that relegates handicraft to an inconsequential niche, and the history of crafts in India to a story of inevitable decline, of a natural transition from tradition to modernity. In this myth mass-production was said to be the modern replacement of handicraft, as part of a natural transition from tradition to modernity. The fallacy of this assumption becomes plain now when mass production itself faces obsolescence. A new paradigm is emerging, an end of the 'carbon era', in which craft production gains new value. Craft production employs low-energy technologies, for which the whole world is now anxiously searching. In the coming post-industrial age the features of craft production that were reckoned as weaknesses – particularly its dispersed, small-scale nature – will be seen in a new light, as socially and environmentally sound practices. It is dispersed and small-scale production supported by small-scale local energy generation that can avoid social ghettoization and concentrations of pollution.

In the heyday of mass production viability was measured only by the productivity of one unit, in which craft was bound to score low. Today energy and environmental costs are beginning to be factored into the economic argument. Today it is clear that the era of fossil-fuel based industries is in decline. Oil is running out and highly industrialized countries are counting the costs of dependence on fossil fuels:

'Coal plants are the nation's top source of carbon dioxide (CO_2) emissions, the primary cause of global warming', says the US Union of Concerned Scientists. For how long will industries dependent on 'dirty energy' score high on the viability scale? As they slide down that scale, the future of craft practice looks ever brighter. The climate crisis threatens life on earth, and India's living craft industries give the country a huge advantage in planning its industrial future.

One of the ways to strengthen the crafts sector would be a law to protect artisans' rights to collect raw material from forests. Sixty years after India became independent, the State continues its colonial relation to forests, with official Forest Departments in control. Many natural mixed forests have been turned into plantations of hardwood trees, which local people are not allowed to touch, and from which the wood is sold to traders on maturity. Meanwhile bamboo, which is easily regenerated and which could support the livelihoods of millions of bamboo artisans all over the country is neglected, and local artisans severely restricted in their access to their primary raw material. Bamboo, that wonder material of natural forests with higher tensile strength than many steel alloys, has been since colonial times given almost free, by the truckload, to paper mills, to be pulped for paper, resulting in the decimation of once plentiful bamboo.

Artisanal activity is tuned into the cycle of life; they do not shrink from using materials that others may regard as untouchable. For example the famous clay water pots made by the *kumhars* of Adilabad and known as 'Adilabad ranjan' owe their cooling properties to the addition of a little horse dung to the clay. Fermentation of indigo for dyeing used to be started with a little urine. Guruppa Chetty the Kalamkari artist from Kalahasti recalls how in his childhood the local indigo dyers used to pay boys under ten years of age a 'damri' to urinate into their pots. Parts of dead animals are critical to artisan activity, the string of the carding bow used to card cotton is made of animal gut, which perhaps explains why cotton carding all over the country was often done by Muslims; since among Hindus handling any part of dead animals, the most important of course being the skin, would automatically put the user into the lowest caste. Leather tanning is an ancient skill of India – leather work is mentioned in the earliest Indian manuscripts. It used to be done using the magical properties of *Terminalia chebula*, the extraordinary myrobalan tree that is one of the stalwarts of Indian medicine, tanning and natural dyeing. There were still leather artisans working in Adilabad district when I first visited Chinnur in 1990, using water from the local *cheruvu* to fill sheep hides with a solution of *karakkaiya*, the local name for myrobalan. Sadly, because of the low social status of the occupation these skilled artisans gave it up some years after we met them. Indian society must take up vigorous campaigns to change feudal attitudes towards skilled work involving 'dirty' materials or processes.

The continued existence of the indigenous cotton textile industry of India in the twenty-first century demonstrates beyond doubt the vitality of contemporary craft practice. Long after the decline and fall of its would-be nemesis, the cotton textile industry of Britain, artisanal cloth making in India continues to produce millions of metres of cloth each year. As it has always done, the craft practice of cotton textile production adapts itself to changing circumstances, accessing new communications technologies, new uses of its products and new marketing channels. It reflects the evolutionary nature of living organisms and the inherent advantages of flexible production. It thereby offsets deliberate neglect by the State and sly cannibalizing of its markets by power-looms.

Cotton weavers and cotton farmers still number in millions and continue to live side-by-side in Indian villages. Together they can make a truly 'green' end-to-end cotton textile production chain, made up of numbers of small scattered units, adding up to a massive whole which would out-compete the high-energy industrial cotton textile industry as fossils fuels deplete and the energy equation changes. For this to happen, the intermediate yarn-making stage between the growing and weaving of cotton must be accessible to both weavers and farmers. The State must take up the research and development of small-scale, low-energy, local cotton spinning as part of its thrust towards a vibrant rural hinterland. Here is a chance for India to look at its pre-industrial cotton cloth technology in a fresh light, as a trailblazer towards future craft-led production, taking its own path to a different industrialization, a different economic system, one that acknowledges the primacy of nature and the goal of a just society. The Kala Cotton initiative to make cloth from a traditional cotton variety (Desor, 2014), and the Malkha fabric made from cotton yarn in small-scale village spinning mills are first steps in this direction.[4]

It is unfortunate that craft production in spite of its large presence in India is not ready to fulfil its potential leadership role in the country's economy. This is because of the anachronistic social matrix in which it is embedded. Artisans are entangled in hierarchic dependence on market intermediaries who control access to credit, market and raw material. This must change, India's craft sector must be brought into the democratic era, and in this the State must play a role. Just as the State takes responsibility to legislate relationships between corporate employers and employees, so it must legally ensure the democratic rights of crafts producers to credit, raw material and market access. Just as the State protects the right to their brand identities for the corporate world, so it must guarantee recognition of the artisan sector's unique products. The State must take up the battle against cheap machine made copies of Indian craft products, whether those copies are made in India or in other countries. Within a legally constituted environment low-energy craft technology will flourish. The numbers of stable rural livelihoods will grow. The climate crisis will be addressed – a prospect that is well within our capabilities to achieve.

The legendary mobility and flexibility of the Indian artisan, able to change the product to suit new markets, able to learn new skills and techniques, able to migrate from village to town and back again, is a historic feature of Indian society. Indian craft products have remained part of contemporary Indian city and village life, declining but holding on at subsistence village levels, thriving where they find new patronage in towns and cities. Village based artisans have discovered the cell phone and the internet to reach new markets. As the cost of small-scale locally generated green energy goes down craft production will become more profitable. Yes, things are looking up for the Indian crafts sector in the post-industrial era; perhaps the Indian state will wake up soon to this fact and give the craft sector its due recognition in the form of credit institutions and guaranteed access to raw material. Perhaps then the shape of an alternative modernity will emerge from the Indian craft-world, changing the village from a backwater to a haven for peaceful productive lives, supporting craft production integrated with nature, a step towards equality in society.[5]

As much as the living traditions of Indian food and Indian music, craft is a strand in the fabric of Indian culture. Craft production in India has resonances of syncretic folk philosophy, embodied in the figure of Sant Kabir Das, the medieval Hindu-Muslim weaver poet. Kabir often invokes craft imagery in his verse and his metaphors of earthen pots and woven threads resonate across the subcontinent, where people still cool drinking water in earthenware vessels and cloth is still woven on the handloom. An object made by a craftsperson contains value other than its monetary cost; it is a repository of the artisan's being. The buyer of a craft object values that intangible content and is prepared to pay for it. An exchange between an artisan and a buyer, even if it is not a face-to-face encounter, is something more than a dry transaction confined to sale and purchase.

As the tide of the times changes in favour of low-energy technologies the living craft industries of India will come into their own, bringing with them hope of redistribution of wealth in society, of regeneration of nature, of freedom from market domination. Craft skills will proliferate, crafts-persons and their abilities will gain respect. Lost or forgotten artisan skills, like blue-glazing of earthenware, or herbal tanning of leather might be rediscovered. Society needs the craftsperson's practical intelligence, gained from constant hands-on interaction with materials. This will be the greatest contribution to society of a resurgent Indian craft industry.

Endnotes

1. See Timeline of the economy of the Indian subcontinent, https://en.wikipedia.org/wiki/Timeline_of_the_economy_of_the_Indian_subcontinent (Last accessed 16 July 2016).

2. www.worldhistorysite.com (Last accessed 16 July 2016).

3. Some years later another French Jesuit again did a brilliant bit of industrial espionage: 'Ironically it was a man of the cloth, Jesuit Father Coeurdoux, who betrayed these fiercely guarded secrets' (Yafa, 2006).

4. See Malkha: The Freedom Fabric, http://www.sustainablecottons.com/638/ (Last accessed 1 May 2016).

5. 'Jharcraft' a state enterprise in Jharkhand state seems to have partially reversed urban migration, by supporting several traditional crafts from raw materials to marketing, credit, and capacity enhancement, though it has weakened more recently (Kothari, 2012; Mayaram, 2015).

References

Bean, S., 1989, 'The Fabric of Indian Independence', in Cloth and Human Experience, A. B. Weiner & J. Schneider, (eds), Washington DC: Smithsonian Institution Press.

Beauchamp, Joan, 1935, British Imperialism in India, London: Martin Lawrence.

Chomsky, N., 1993, 501: The Conquest Continues, London: Verso.

Desor, Shiba, 2014, Strengthening Local Livelihoods with Ecological Considerations in Kutch, Gujarat, Pune: Kalpavriksh. Available at http://www.vikalpsangam.org/static/media/uploads/Resources/kachchh_alternatives_report_titled.pdf (Last accessed July 2017).

Forbes India Magazine, September 25 2014, 'India's 100 Richest Billionaires', http://www.forbes.com/sites/naazneenkarmali/2014/09/24/indias-100-richest-of-2014-are-all-billionaires-for-the-first-time/#3c91fde9758b (Last accessed 15 July 2016).

Hobsbawm, E., 2010, *Age of Revolution: 1789-1848*, UK: Hachette.

Illich, I.,1973, *Tools for Conviviality*, New York: Harper and Row.

Irwin, J., 1962, 'Indian Textiles in Historical Perspective', *Marg*, Vol. XV.

Kothari, A., 2013, 'Being the change', *The Hindu*, 22 April. http://www.vikalpsangam.org/static/media/uploads/Stories_PDFs/harcraft_article_as_pub_the_hindu_21.4.2013.pdf (Last accessed in July 2017).

Marx, K., 1965, *Capital: A Critique of Political Economy*, Moscow: Progress Publishers.

Mayaram, B., 2016, 'Jharkhand mein hatkargha kranti' (in Hindi), http://www.vikalpsangam.org/article/झारखंड में हथकरघा क्रांति-in-hindi/#.WW0kKbFh1E4 (Last accessed in July 2017).

McLellan, D., 2000, *Karl Marx: Selected Writings*, USA: Oxford University Press.

Pei-Ling, Lee and Ming-Chyuan, Ho, Undated, *A Study on the Miniaturization of a Product*, http://www.idemployee.id.tue.nl/g.w.m.rauterberg/conferences/CD_doNotOpen/ADC/final_paper/232.pdf (Last accessed March 23, 2017).

Sahasrabudhey, S., Undated, Agaria-vidya: A Link in the Philosophy of Emancipation Undated, https://www.yumpu.com/en/document/view/36640066/agaria-vidya-a-link-in-the-philosophy-of-emancipation-vidya-ashram (Last accessed 16 July 2016).

Satya, L. D., 1997, *Cotton and Famine in Berar – 1850-1900*, New Delhi: Manohar Publishers.

Srinivasan, S., 2015, 'The Luddites might have been right', *The Hindu*, 14 March, *http://www.thehindu.com/opinion/op-ed/the-luddites-might-have-been-right/article6991180.ece* (Last accessed 15 July 2016).

Srinivasan, S. and Ranganathan, S., 1997, *Wootz Steel: An advanced material of the ancient world*, http://materials.iisc.ernet.in/~wootz/heritage/WOOTZ.htm (Last accessed 14 July, 2016).

Yafa, S., 2006, *Cotton: The Biography of a Revolutionary Fiber*, USA: Penguin Books.

Appendix A

Reprinted from Young India 21-5-1931

IN 1828
The Representation of a Spinner

To the Editor, The *Samachar,*

I am a spinner. After having suffered a great deal, I am writing this letter. Please publish this in your paper. I have heard that, if it is published, it will reach those who may lighten my distress and fulfil my desire. Please do not slight this letter from a poor sufferer.

I am very unfortunate. It would be a long story if I were to write all about my sufferings. So I must write in brief.

When my age was five and a half *gandas (22)* I became a widow with three daughters. My husband left nothing at the time of his death wherewith to maintain my old father-and-mother-in-law and three daughters. He had several businesses. I sold my jewellery for his *shraddha* ceremony. At last as we were on the verge of starvation God showed me a way by which we could save ourselves. I began to spin on takli and charkha. In the morning I used to do the usual work of cleaning the household and then sit at the charkha till noon, and after cooking and feeding the old parents and daughters I would have my fill and sit spinning fine yarn on the takli. Thus I used to spin about a tola. The weavers used to visit our houses and buy the charkha yarn at three tolas per rupee. Whatever amount I wanted as advance from the weavers, I could get for the asking. This saved us from cares about food and cloth. In a few years' time I got together seven *ganda* rupees (Rs 28). With this I married one daughter.

And in the same way all three daughters. There was no departure from the caste customs. Nobody looked down upon these daughters because I gave all concerned, the *ghatakas* and caste people, what was due to them. When my father-in-law died I spent eleven *ganda* rupees (Rs. 44) on his *shraddha*. This money was lent me by the weavers which I repaid in a year and a half. And all this through the grace of the charkha. Now for 3 years we two women, mother-in-law and I, are in want of food. The weavers do not call at the house for buying yarn. Not only this, if the yarn is sent to the market, it is not sold even at one-fourth the old prices. I do not know how it happened. I asked many about it. They say that *bilati* yarn is being largely imported. The weavers buy that yarn and weave. I had a sense of pride that *bilati* yarn could not be equal to my yarn, but when I got *bilati* yarn I saw that it was better than my yarn. I heard that its price is Rs. 3 or Rs 4. per *seer*. I beat my brow and said, 'Oh God, there are sisters more distressed even than I. I had thought that all men of *Bilat* were rich, but now I see that there are women there who are poorer I.' I fully realized the poverty which induced those poor women to spin. They have sent the product of so much toil out here because they could not sell it there. It would have been something if they were sold here at good prices. But it has brought our ruin only. Men cannot use the cloth out of this yarn even for two months; it rots away. I therefore entreat the spinners over there that, if they will consider this representation, they will be able to judge whether it is fair to send yarn here or not.

Shantipur   A representation from a suffering spinner

SAMACHAR DARPAN
(*Economics of Khadi*, pp. 362)

Appendix B

*Testimony of Francis Carnac Brown, Proceedings of the Madras
Board of Revenue no. 407 dated April 9, 1862*

The story of cotton in India is not half told, how it was systematically depressed from the earliest date that American cotton came into competition with it about the year 1786, how for 40 or 50 years after, one half of the crop was taken in kind as revenue, the other half by the sovereign merchant at a price much below the market price of the day which was habitually kept down for the purpose, how the cotton farmer's plough and bullocks were taxed, the *Churkha* taxed, the bow taxed and the loom taxed; how inland custom houses were posted in and around every village on passing which cotton on its way to the Coast was stopped and like every other produce taxed afresh; how it paid export duty both in a raw state and in every shape of yarn, of thread, cloth or handkerchief, in which it was possible to manufacture it; how the dyer was taxed and the dyed cloth taxed, plain in the loom, taxed a second time in the dye vats, how Indian piece goods were loaded in England with a prohibitory duty and English piece goods were imported into India at an *ad valorem* duty of 2 ½ per cent. It is my firm conviction that the same treatment would long since have converted any of the finest countries in Europe into wilderness. But the Sun has continued to give forth to India its vast vivifying rays, the Heavens to pour down upon the vast surface its tropical rains. These perennial gifts of the Universal Father it has not been possible to tax.

Industry, Workers and Nation: Dreaming the Good Dream

Dunu Roy

Summary

This essay sketches the brief history of industrialization in the world and the parallel patterns in Indian industry. Indian industry and its workers are broadly divided into three sectors. One is the formal sector wherein labour laws are somewhat functional primarily because of the organised strength of the workforce (although present trends of mechanization have led to rampant unemployment in this sector). The second is the informal sector, which is enlarged by the displacement of labour from the formal sector. The workers in this sector are self-employed, there is the absence of an employer to negotiate with, lack of access to credit, transportation, markets, skills, and space to carry on livelihoods. The third is the illegal sector, in which working people don't have even the minimum protection of the law as they are deemed illegal.

This essay gives numerous examples that suggest that workers in all these sectors have creatively been registering their opposition to disinvestment and restructuring, privatization and foreign investment, denial of organizing rights and fair wages, contractual labour and labour law reforms, demolitions and evictions, and this has fuelled resistance to the strategy of division and consolidation led by the government and corporations. However, the future of industrial work lies in a radical change of two crucial determinants of capitalist society, that is, competition and profit. The essay provides a few examples of movements that have been trying to challenge these determinants, but the real problem lies in the absence of a politics and theorization that can go beyond these attempts by workers, and challenge and change all structures of exploitation, inequality, and injustice.

Looking Back in Time

A brief history of modern industrialisation should begin with Frederick Taylor's time-and-motion studies that led to the 'Assembly Line' technique integrating the standardisation of parts with inter-changeability and movement of materials. This not only hugely intensified work, but also eliminated the skilled workman as the assembly line promoted a series of repetitive movements designed to speed up the production process and increase profits. But the alienation and boredom of work led to higher rates of absenteeism, turnover of workers, shop-floor disputes, and tardiness. A new technique to counter these problems was the 'Human Relations' discipline of management that tried to publicly recognise the contribution of the worker, and attempted to improve the work environment. But even this approach could not provide relief from the enormous physical and mental stresses of producing more and more, faster and faster. The researchers' next answer to this was 'Automation' which replaced workers in the production process with machines, semiconductors, and the micro-chips. This centralisation of information also led to decentralising production through outsourcing and contractual arrangements, with lower machinery and labour costs, low-skill processes, faster communication, and the ability of capital to move rapidly across borders to locate production where labour is unprotected and wages are low (Kranzberg and Hannan, 2010).

In India there are parallel patterns with significant diversification in industry after the 1950s', leading to an increase in the industrial work force. The new industries in the chemicals, petroleum and electronic sectors had a faster growth rate but were also more hazardous, with increasing risks to workers. The majority of the labour force migrated from the impoverished peasantry, while middle and upper castes grabbed the white collar jobs. Women and children had a lower status at work, and gender, caste, and regional identities were used to divide the workers. The 1990s' witnessed an impressive growth of the plastics industry, higher than anywhere else in the world, replacing traditional materials and creating new markets. This was followed by a quantum jump in the information technology industry, marking the change from manufacturing to services and the idea of cities as 'engines of growth'. This also promoted self-employment and work on contract and piece-rated wages (Qadeer et al., 1989). Currently, the attempt is to amend various laws to make the globalised Indian economy more 'investor-friendly'. The proposed changes in labour laws such as the 1948 Factories Act, the 1961 Apprentices Act, the 1986 Child Labour Act, the 1988 Labour Laws Act, and umbrella legislation for small factories and retrenchment of workers indicate the dominant corporate influence on government (Roychowdhury, 2015).

Working Sectors

Formality

The Indian economy at present may be characterised as developing within three sectors. The first is the 'Formal Sector', wherein labour laws are somewhat functional primarily because of the organised strength of the workforce that can enforce the law. Although these existing laws protect only the 9 per cent labour in this sector, there is an increasing demand by corporations for the 'reform' of even these laws to permit greater 'freedom' to capital. However, it is important to remember, for the *freedom of labour*, that these laws also normatively offer protection to other sections of the workforce, provided they become organised within their own sector. As present trends of mechanisation and automation are allowed to grow unchecked, they are leading to rampant under-and-un-employment and the strength of the working class unions is diminishing. Thus, earlier steel mills used to have a muscular 'sinew' of a 30-40,000 strong workforce; modern steel plants now employ only about 1,000 workers as operators of advanced information technology devices. The displacement of labour from the work process is also related to the privatisation of public enterprises, as well as closures and retrenchments (Alessandrini, 2009; Bhattacharya *et al.*, 2003; CPI (M), 2004).

For instance, the public sector Bharat Gold Mines Limited at Kolar, with a peak employment of 36,000 workers, was declared 'sick' in 1992 and the Board of Industrial Financing and Restructuring considered it for possible revival or closure. A detailed study on behalf of the unions indicated that the mines were still viable but had been deliberately allowed to deteriorate through ill-advised diversification, inadequate asset utilisation, and no investment in research and development since 1962. However, all proposals for revival were rejected and the mines sold to a private company with the labour force reduced to 3,800 workers (Menon, 2002). Similarly, the private sector Kamani Engineering Corporation in Mumbai became sick due to financial mismanagement in the mid-1970s'. The Public Financial Institutions took over control in 1975, through the intervention of the Kamani Employees Union, and there was a dramatic turnaround in the fortunes of the company. But in 1992 the management was subverted by the R.P. Goenka Group, which raised its stakes, and then began to divest the company of its revenues and capital assets through amalgamation with another loss-making Goenka company. The Public Financial Institutions abdicated their responsibilities with the survival of 20,000 workers and a Rs.1 billion company at stake (Radhkrishnan, 1999; Wikipedia, undated).

Informality

The second is the 'Informal Sector', greatly enlarged by the displacement of labour from the formal sector. For instance, in the city of Delhi 60,000 out of 100,000-odd industrial units have a labour force of less than five workers per unit. These units are sweat shops that can fold up at any time and relocate elsewhere, where laws are openly flouted for economic gain, and the workers are not organised enough to force employers to meet their basic demands of wages, shelter, health, education, unemployment benefits, and social security. When workers in this sector are self-employed, there is both the absence of an employer to negotiate with, as also lack of access to credit, transportation, markets, skills, and space to carry on livelihoods (Anonymous, 1997). Plus, when the government was pressurised by multilateral funding institutions to adopt a policy of 'no fresh recruitment' in all government services in 1979 (GoI, 1979), the problem of contractual labour employed at low wages with no benefits became so severe that, in 2013, the Labour Ministry had to instruct all government departments to ensure that the same wages and conditions of work were applicable to contract labour as to directly employed workmen for the same kind of work (GoI, 2013).[1]

It was for regulating this sector that the UPA government set up a National Commission for Enterprises in the Unorganised Sector in 2006, since it was:

'... firmly committed to ensure the welfare and well-being of all workers, particularly those in the unorganised sector who constitute 93% of our workforce. Social security, health insurance and other schemes for such workers like weavers, handloom workers, fishermen and fisherwomen, toddy tappers, leather workers, plantation labour, *beedi*[2] workers, etc., will be expanded' (NCEUS, 2006, pp. 1).

The NCEUS held that,

'Formal workers in India who constitute around 9 per cent of the total workforce have some recourse to social security measures. Informal workers in the Indian economy are estimated by the Commission to be more than 91 per cent of the workforce. They consist of informal workers in the informal sector (85 per cent of total workforce) and informal workers in the formal sector (6 per cent of total workforce). These workers have limited or no formal social security cover which increases their vulnerability during times of illness, old age, unemployment and untimely death. The absence of social security mechanisms is a critical factor in downturns in the condition of these households, many of whom are already very poor.'

(ibid., pp. 123)

Illegality

Finally, there is the 'Illegal Sector', in which working people do not get even the minimum protection from the law because the work in which they are engaged in is regarded as being unauthorised and, therefore, the workers are illegal. For example, during the conflict in Assam in 2003 the 'natives' were mobilised against the immigrant Muslims, mostly working in this sector (Fernandes, 2005). Similarly, the Delhi High Court issued an injunction to Delhi Police in 2000 to form a Special Task Force to arrest and deport the one *lakh*[3] or more 'illegal' Bangladeshis alleged to be residing in the city – mostly migrants from Cooch Behar working as waste-pickers (CCPD, 2005). In most cities, groups such as handcart and rickshaw pullers, sex workers, street entertainers, beggars, etc., are routinely criminalised by the police. The presence of zoning laws and restrictive regulations make it impossible for these workers to enter and work in specific areas on grounds of 'environment', 'security', or 'congestion'. The associated issue of 'illegality' has much to do with elitist notions of 'encroachment', 'migration', and 'morality'. In this sector, women and children are particularly vulnerable to sexual harassment and exploitation with little or no access to legal redress.

The assault on this illegal sector unfolded earlier, sometime in the 1960s', when large-scale evictions of working class settlements, known euphemistically as 'slums', took place as the first urban plans came into being. The climax was reached during the late 1970s' when the declaration of a National Emergency suspended all human rights and the administration had a free hand to demolish and recast as they pleased. It is also important to note that the era of 'public interest' litigation followed the Emergency, as the Court genuflected towards mass discontent and restored many of the civil liberties, particularly of the poor. But the wheel has come full circle. There are currently at least a dozen judicial orders which characterise those who live in slums as 'pick-pockets' and 'hoodlums', holding them responsible for all social evils, and ordaining that they have limited rights to what is being called 'free' shelter. So they should be cramped into 'model' multi-storied tenements to be built by private 'enterprise'. Such an approach purposefully neglects to examine the consistent failure of State agencies over the decades in providing 'legal' shelter as per the urban plans themselves. Since the 1990s' the focus has increasingly shifted from 'illegal' shelter to 'illegal' work (Ramanathan, 2006; Dupont, 2008).

Global Transitions

The emergence of these three sectors in the economy is implicit in the drive by governments to shift from manufacturing to services, and be part of the global economy. The attack on work in general began in the 1990s' when India fell into the trap of structural adjustment laid by the global multi-lateral funding institutions. Another watershed had emerged in 1985 when an environmental group filed a 'public interest' petition in the Supreme Court against mining in the Mussoorie hills, thereby depriving the miners of jobs (RLEK, 1985). In the last thirty years, vested interest groups have used the same line of 'environmental' reasoning to urge the courts to demolish the livelihoods of many millions of ordinary working people, though not all environmental groups would support this. Since 1995, when the first 'green' judgements were handed down, the judges have led the charge against the working class and have undermined the 'dignity' of labour that was present in earlier social discourse (Bhushan, undated; Ghertner, 2008; Desai, 2014). In addition, governments have also used 'democracy' to marginalise the working population. What is seen as new ways of 'participation' in governance, through self-help groups, non-government organisations, corporations, and citizens' associations also marks the attempt of the State to shun its social welfare responsibilities and remove the vulnerable from the mainstream.

There are those who hold that the communities who face the dilemma of having demanded state accountability for decades, and not received anything, are entitled to provide for themselves (assisted by civil society organisations) in areas such as decentralised water harvesting and energy, and it is a tad unfair to call this 'marginalisation'[4]. This is perhaps a view that emerges from experiences with rural communities or middle-class colonies. For working class communities (essentially slums) in cities such infrastructural initiatives are necessarily limited because of lack of access to basic resources such as land and finance. However, they are invited to participate in 'governance' by setting up women's self-help groups to maintain community toilets in slums; or permitting cooperatives of waste-pickers to take up door-to-door waste collection and segregation – both being substitutes for municipal authorities, who are mandated to do these tasks, but where they are expected to earn revenues through user fees, as against much-touted private-public partnerships where the commercial entity invited to provide a similar service is paid by the urban local body (Pallavi, 2014).

Workers' Responses

Formal Workers

Workers in all three sectors have obviously responded to the challenges in their sectors but one can also discern a pattern of moving away from older issues of wages and conditions of work towards structural and cross-sectoral themes. Within the Formal Sector, there has been a marked decline of earlier forms of trade union activity but what remains is significant in its departure from earlier modes. Even a snap-shot of news about workers' protests in the last one year reveals that such protests remain vibrant and are responding to contemporary challenges. The five day national coal strike by unions representing 3 lakh (three hundred thousand) coal miners, in January 2015, for instance, was called to protest the disinvestment and restructuring of state-run Coal India Limited by the BJP government (Dutta *et al.*, 2015). In January too, State policy to attract foreign investments in the railway industry sparked protests by Indian Railway workers who claimed that such a policy would not provide jobs to local labour (*The Hindu*, 2015a). And, in the next month, NVH India auto workers in Chennai were arrested because they were trying to challenge the management's refusal to allow a union to be formed, and to hire contract workers to boost production (*Business Standard*, 2015).

In March 2015 India's port workers launched an indefinite strike protesting privatisation in the country's 200-odd ports (*DNA*, 2015). In April the Road Transport workers' unions called for a nation-wide *bandh*[5] to protest against the Road Transport and Safety Bill 2014 that they felt would reduce their employment (*Economic Times*, 2015). Later in May, the police used water cannons and batons to disperse hundreds of Jammu and Kashmir contractual government employees demanding regularisation of their services (Greater Kashmir, 2015). In June the sanitation workers of Delhi protested over non-payment of salaries (*Firstpost*, 2015). A two-day Indian Labour Conference, addressed by the Prime Minister, failed to prevent a spurt of labour activity, from Maruti's Manesar plant in Gurgaon, where workers, agitating for the last three years, demanded a labour protection policy (*The Tribune*, 2015a), to the contract employees of the Karnataka Power Transmission Corporation and Electricity Supply Companies in Mysore demanding their regularisation (*The Hindu*, 2015b). Union leaders at the Neyveli Lignite Corporation struck work to stop the contract labour system, defying a Madras High Court order of restraint (*The Times of India*, 2015). Mineworkers at Thriveni Earthmovers in Odisha (Industrial Global Action, 2015), the Port Contract Workers' Union at Visakhapatnam (*Express TV*, 2015) and the workers at the General Motors plant at Halol in Gujarat (*Deccan Herald*, 2015) were all active in opposing 'anti-labour' policies of the management and the NDA government.

Even the new information technology-based industries were beginning to face worker protests. Thus, white-collar workers of the Life Insurance Corporation of India and four public sector general insurance companies observed a nationwide strike, protesting against the proposal to increase foreign equity limit from 26 to 49 per cent (*The Tribune*, 2015b). The services of online shopping portals Flipkart and Myntra in Mumbai were severely hit by an agitation in early August of logistics staff demanding better pay and working conditions (*The Indian Express,* 2015). Over 400 delivery boys and shipment sorters working with eKart went on strike asking that e-commerce retailers follow labour laws (*Mumbai Mirror,* 2015). DHL India workers staged a protest at the Mumbai Marathon to highlight victimisation of trade union activists and the violation of OECD guidelines for global multinational companies (ITWF, 2015). Women workers were also at the forefront of organising in this period demanding more attention to gender issues. The women employed with Lok Sabha TV highlighted the lack of security for women employees returning home late from work (*The Hindu,* 2015c). *Anganwadi*[6] workers demonstrated in Uttarkashi seeking government employee status with salaries of Rs 15,000 (*The Tribune,* 2015c), while the women tea garden workers in Munnar struck work for higher wages but also protested against the male domination of the unions (Jacob, 2015).

Informal Workers

Turning now to the Informal Sector, one of the landmarks in its trajectory was the formation of a construction workers' union that drafted a comprehensive model Bill for its protection in 1986. Countering stiff opposition from the builders' lobby, the workers lobbied with the Left and Socialist Parties and finally, The Building and Other Construction Workers (Regulation and Conditions of Service) Act was enacted in 1996.[7] Another milestone was passed when 'Operation Sunshine' was launched in Kolkata in 1996 to clear the streets of vendors, and they organised and fought back (Bandopadhyaya, 2009). Hawkers also came together to stop an illegal commercial complex which the Municipal Corporation of Greater Mumbai planned to build at a hawking site in 1997 (Deshpande, 2002). Street vendors' organisations were founded in Patna[8] and Delhi (Verma, undated), and during Delhi's sealing drives in 2006, trader groups mobilised against allowing 51per cent Foreign Direct Investment in single brand retailing.[9] The National Association of Street Vendors of India was founded in 1998 with the objective of bringing together street vendor organisations for collective action.[10] Cumulatively, all these initiatives eventually paved the way for Parliament to pass the Street Vendors (Protection of Livelihood and Regulation of Street Vending) Act in 2014.

As a consequence of these national campaigns, several alliances came together to cover the entire informal sector. Thus, in 2003, a national meeting was convened in Delhi at which there was representation of construction, forest, fisheries, domestic, home-based, sanitation, rice mill, migrant, and agricultural workers, as well as street vendors, rickshaw pullers, tribal labourers, and weavers. This meeting considered the sad plight of the informal sector workers as an aftermath of globalisation-liberalisation-privatisation and the participants

273

unanimously decided to constitute a national campaign committee for informal sector workers. The campaign then called for comprehensive legal protection for these workers through sectoral tripartite boards that would be empowered to provide employment guarantee, non-employment allowance, insurance, provident fund, pension, child care, accident relief, education scholarship, etc., without gender discrimination (LRS, 2005). Subsequently the Ministry of Labour and Employment floated a draft Social Security Bill for Unorganised Sector workers in 2004, while the National Commission for Enterprises in the Unorganised Sector and the National Advisory Council submitted two other drafts in 2005. However, when Parliament finally passed the Act in 2008, it ignored most of the recommendations of the earlier drafts, and the Act remained confined to providing a few welfare provisions only (Sankaran, 2009).

Illegal Workers

The Illegal Sector poses many more challenges than the others, primarily because of its presumed 'illegality' and, therefore, the absence of legal protection (Shankar, 2015). For instance, in Delhi, the Supreme Court ordered 2,245 polluting industries to be closed in 1996, and three years later expanded this to cover 40,000 industries that were in 'non-conforming' areas. Owners and workers allied together, blocking roads and burning buses for four days, before they fell before police batons and bullets (*The Tribune*, 2000). Waste pickers won a little more leverage in the 1990s' when they asserted their place in the economy and ecology of the city, advocating for planning norms. When the Delhi Master Plan came up for renewal by 2001 they lobbied for the adoption of their norms in the Plan (Sajha Manch, 2003). A measure of their success is that while the Waste Management Acts of 1996 and 2001 do not acknowledge them as an entity, the Municipal Solid Wastes (Management and Handling) Rules notified in 2015 do provide for several enabling rules to be made for their involvement in the process of collection, segregation, and recycling. Lately some waste picker organisations have also been asserting their rights from the perspective of their mitigating role in climate change mitigation (Chintan, 2009).

In Mumbai, for decades, the security of shelter for the working poor has been an issue of great contention, with brutal evictions of slums in the 1980s' to reclaim prime land in the central parts of the city. But various slum dweller organisations have come together to resist. Recently in 2015, they have also attempted to reoccupy the land at Mandala, from which they were evicted several years ago (SACW, 2015). In Jaipur too, many of the active slum groups came together in 2007 to form an alliance that conducted a regular campaign in the slums, as part of the resistance to demolition. Indore has marked some success when, in 1996, the State Government began widening the roads and 5,000 slum dwellers came together to stop the demolition of their hutments. The network also leveraged a 1984 law promising land titles to slum-dwellers, and a Master Plan provision for 15 per cent of housing stock for the poor. In Patna an anti-poor drive, which began in earnest in 1997, was contested by the vendors' union which first extracted verbal assurances that they could occupy space on the footpath, and then surrounded the State Minister for Urban Development and the Housing Corporation to obtain two-roomed flats in four-storied structures (Hazards Centre, 2010).

Hyderabad is one of the fastest growing cities, a hub for the Information Technology industry. This modernisation has seen changes in the land use as older settlements have been removed and driven thousands of the urban poor into homelessness and destitution. In 1997, the government proposed to develop the Musi riverfront for commercial purposes while uprooting the slums on the banks, the slum-dwellers resisted the idea, and used the floods of 2000, that created havoc in the city, to build up public pressure to protect the river. In Visakhapatnam slum dwellers also resisted eviction from their huts and were eventually able to negotiate with the municipality for provision of low-rise (up to two storeys) housing on the same site under the *Rajiv Awas Yojana*.[11] Slum evictions have been happening in almost every part of the old historic city of Lucknow, particularly after the launch of the National Urban Renewal Mission in 2005. Various resistance groups mobilised 12,000 people to protest against the eviction process and the roads were jammed three times. While they were supported by local vendors, councillors, and legislators, yet they could not save two slums that were demolished and resettled in an area 30 km away from the present site.[12]

The above selected cases demonstrate that many workers have creatively been registering their opposition to disinvestment and restructuring, privatisation and foreign investment, labour law 'reforms' and contractual labour, denial of organising rights and fair wages, demolitions and evictions. The strategy of division and consolidation adopted by government and corporations has led to fragmentation, but the expectation of workers that development should eventually benefit them has also fuelled resistance to the strategy. It would be pertinent to mention that there are three kinds of struggles in India that are particularly significant. One is the struggle of the primary producers. Some people limit this to tribal communities, forest dwellers, and fisher-folk. But, clearly, it is a struggle of *all* primary producers, because all of them are losing control over the very resources on which their livelihood is dependent. Then there is the struggle of women, on the issue of gender exploitation and patriarchy, which is also fundamental to capitalism in many respects. There is also the related issue of women belonging to the working class who are facing the double brunt of class and patriarchal exploitation. The third struggle is that of the increasing army of the unemployed and underemployed belonging to different strata of society.

Looking Forward

What is the vision for the future? As illustrated above, there is a conflict between owners and workers in industry and new techniques will constantly be evolved by owners and their managers to increase production on one hand and control workers on the other. While corporations have managed to weaken the strength of the organised work force in the Formal Sector, nevertheless new forms of organisation have also emerged to challenge some of the fundamental premises of disinvestment, privatisation, foreign investment, labour law 'reforms', contractual labour, and denial of organising rights and fair wages. As global corporations increasingly stumble through repeated global crises it will offer more opportunities for the organised work force to find new avenues of struggle and articulation that will challenge the fundamental inequalities between owners and workers.

In the Informal Sector the struggle of incipient worker organisations has been to enact new laws through the legislature to protect their interests and then to get the laws and their rules implemented. The draft laws have also explored aspects of gender, investment, environment, and alliance building in novel ways. However, this mode of struggle has its limits in that it functions within the given legal framework. In the years to come, as the experience of the informal workers matures, more opportunities will emerge to move beyond these given limits. The hardest to tackle has been the Illegal Sector where there is an absence of protective law but, nevertheless, the workers and their families have already mobilised around both work and shelter. Some marginal gains have been made at the policy level but the most innovative aspect has been the linking up of several issues to provide a much more comprehensive platform. As these struggles of the illegal workers grow and spread, they are implicitly bound – by the very illegality within which they function – to question how and why this illegality has been imposed. In this they will transcend the issues that the other two sectors face and thus offer the biggest opportunity to face and engage with the global corporations and their manifold connections to political power.

Current Debates

However, the active debates that have accompanied all these struggles of the different sets of workers have exposed a range of issues which have to come together in an integrated whole. Some of the critical, and profoundly ethical, themes are listed below:

1. What is 'good' for the worker? Which kind of industry will provide jobs? Which will ensure that the work is safe and secure; that there will be restful sleep after hard work; that they will not be jailed for demanding their rights? What should be the amount of capital required to create one job? Should jobs be piece-rated or time-rated? What kind of bonus should be offered? How much emphasis should be given to safety and housing? What is the security of tenure, when can the worker be dismissed?

2. What is 'good' for the community, for society? If wages are raised, will they get frittered away on liquor and drugs? Will expenses go up on hospital care and education? Are industries that are manufacturing alcohol and cigarettes and military equipment really serving a social need? Do their products promote creative work, better nourishment, enjoyable learning, less violence? Will there be more justice and more equality when these industries are set up or when they are closed or sold? What is an ethical society?

3. And, finally, what is 'good' for the environment? Will there be animals in the forest and fish in the ponds when these industries manufacture their products? How will our townships be laid out and where will the children play? Will the slag heaps and the stinking drains destroy the very nature from which workers and their families draw sustenance? Will the water and the air and the land remain safe for our grandchildren? Will there be space for the cow and the goat, the snake and the jackal? Will the heron stand in the paddy fields and the tiger call from the high grass?

Social Determinants

These are the questions that any alternative notion of industrialisation must answer. Some believe that the answers, and the 'visions' and the 'strategies' they encompass, are to be given by the wise ones sitting in research institutions and academia. But, if the working woman is to truly benefit, really define what her world will be like, and establish her notion of 'goodness', then she must not only participate in, but lead the search for answers. A lifetime spent with working people may entitle an academic to lay claim to what they think of such issues and where the search is leading, but a lifetime is never enough. So what are the theoretical pegs on which the answers could hang? In fact, there may be only one collective peg – that industry (and curiously enough, the word 'industry' itself means *hard*

277

work) is conceptually 'good' that provides enough work for enough people at all times; work that is satisfying for the worker and her family, and produces artefacts that promote harmony in society; and work that does not damage the ecological base from which it draws its materials and into which it pours out its wastes. Theoretically then, there are two important social determinants for such work – and such industry – to be possible.

The first is whether society is constructed around a paradigm of 'competition'. If it is, then it is unlikely that there will ever be enough secure work, enough satisfied workers, or enough harmonious neighbourhoods. In a context where sectors are competing with each other for customers; industries are competing for higher productivity; units are competing for skilled (and pliable) workers; and workers are competing for jobs: these are a perfect prescription for a society in a state of tension and, therefore, how can industry be 'good' for the worker or for the community? The second determinant is that of 'profit'. When industry attempts to extract more value from its output than is present in its inputs, then economics attempts to evade the physical laws that are the basis for all industrial production. Consequently, what economists cavalierly call 'externalities' are the hidden costs of that evasion, and eventually they become manifest in both social and environmental distress. When affected communities begin raging for compensation; when nature begins to demand restoration (through further externalities impacting on the social condition): it is then that these externalities are converted into the costs that society has to pay for individual profits.

Practical Answers

The key question we are left with is – have challenges to these two social determinants taken place in the history of workers' struggles? The answer may be an ambivalent 'yes'. The cooperative at Kannur was set up by *beedi* workers in 1969 that banned child labour, paid handsome salaries and benefits, and then diversified into food and fruit processing (Pulikunnel, 1997). The employees of Sonali tea plantation in Jalpaiguri established their cooperative in 1974 and privileged preservation of the bushes over profits from premature plucking (Bhowmik, 2007). In 1989, the workers of Hindustan Lever's factory in Bombay, locked out by the management, began producing and marketing an affordable detergent 'Lock Out' (Vasuki, 1989). Transport workers, dismissed in 1991 by a private company in Chikkamagalur, set up their own unit with two buses, an effort that has now expanded to 60 buses running a network on the basis of social trust (Mavya, 2004). The sex workers of Sonagachi set up a cooperative financial institution in the 1990s' that has enabled sex workers to escape from the clutches of pimps, educate and marry off their children, and even buy property (Singh 2015). The mobilisation of mine workers, many of them women, in Rajasthan around occupational disease and compensation began in 2005, and has subsequently taken up issues of ethical and sustainable mining, and participation in government decision-making (Basu, 2011).

This short list, by no means exhaustive, represents the tip of grass-roots initiatives that seem to have occurred in every decade but that remain largely undocumented. But the problem is not one of story-telling; it is of politics and of theorisation. No political party, except for the undivided Communist Party of India in its early years (and, much to the disgust and chagrin of workers everywhere, that Party too has abandoned its founding principles), has provided unstinted support to these initiatives, either considering them to be economically insignificant, or politically redundant. There has been little intellectual effort either (except for some of the painstaking research referred to in this paper) to theorise how these initiatives can go beyond attempts of workers to survive dismissals and closures, and to be part of a politics of challenging and changing the structures of exploitation, inequality, and injustice that are deeply rooted in contemporary capitalist society. What the past teaches us, though, is that as long as such structures exist and human beings are brutalised by them, people will always rise in revolt. This half-century, given the nature of the debates that are presently taking place, and the scope of information on offer, offers a brilliant chance for the workers' revolts to begin grappling with the twin paradigms of competition and profit.

Endnotes

1. While the Government officially does not confirm that any such ban exists, there is much evidence that the ban was first introduced in 1979 as part of austerity measures, and then renewed from time to time in 1991, 1997, and 2001.
2. Smoking stick made of tobacco rolled in a leaf.
3. Unit amounting to a hundred thousand.
4. Ashish Kothari, personal communication, dated 28 January 2016.
5. Denotes a form of protest where a call is given for a shut-down of all transport and commerce.
6. Child care centres.
7. For more details about the National Campaign Committee for Comprehensive Legislation for construction workers see the website of Nirmana Society (http://www.nirmana.org/) which provided the secretariat for the Campaign.
8. See the website of NIDAN, http://nidan.in/nidanwp/.
9. See the website of India FDI Watch, http://indiafdiwatch.org/?page_id=157.

10. See the website of the National Association of Street Vendors of India, http://nasvinet.org/newsite/.
11. A Central government scheme for housing of the poor.
12. For more details, see Hazards Centre, 2010.

References

Alessandrini, Michele, 2009, *Jobless Growth in Indian Manufacturing: A Kaldorian Approach*, Discussion Paper 99, London: Centre for Financial and Management Studies, SOAS, University of London. Available at: http://www.cefims.ac.uk/documents/research-92.pdf (Last accessed July, 2015).

Anonymous, 1997, Order that Felled a City (Commentary), *Economic & Political Weekly*, Vol. 32 (26), 28 June, pp. 1524-527.

Bandyopadhyay, Ritajyoti, 2009, 'Hawkers Movement in Kolkata – 1975-2007', *Economic & Political Weekly*, Vol.44(17), 25 April, pp. 116-119. Available at: http://re.indiaenvironmentportal.org.in/files/Hawkers%20Movement.pdf (Last accessed July, 2015).

Basu, Pekham, April-June 2011, *Mine Workers of Rajasthan – Emerging Leaders in Veils*, Asia Monitor Resource Centre, No.79. Available at: http://www.amrc.org.hk/content/alu-mine-workers-rajasthan-%E2%80%93-emerging-leaders-veils (Last accessed January, 2016).

Bhattacharya, B.B. and S. Sakthivel, 2003, *Economic Reforms and Jobless Growth in India in the 1990s*, Delhi: Institute of Economic Growth. Available at: http://www.iegindia.org/workpap/wp245.pdf (Last accessed July, 2015).

Bhowmik, Sharit K., 2007, 'Cooperatives and the Emancipation of the Marginalized: Case Studies from Two Cities in India', in *Another Production is Possible: Beyond the Capitalist Canon*, Boaventura de Sousa Santos (ed.), pp. 70-94. Available at: http://www.boaventuradesousasantos.pt/media/Chapter%203(2).pdf (Last accessed January, 2016).

Bhushan, Prashant, undated, 'Sacrificing Human Rights and Environmental Rights at the Altar of 'Development', *The Geo. Wash. Int'l L. Rev.*, Vol. 41(2). Available at: http://docs.law.gwu.edu/stdg/gwilr/PDFs/41-2/5-%20BHUSHAN.pdf (Last accessed July, 2015).

Business Standard, 2015, 'Protesting NVH India Auto workers taken into custody', 3 January. Available at: http://www.business-standard.com/article/companies/protesting-nvh-india-auto-workers-taken-into (Last accessed July, 2015).

CCPD, 2005, *Democracy, Citizens, and Migrants: Nationalism in the Era of Globalisation*, New Delhi: Citizen's Campaign for Preserving Democracy, Hazards Centre.

Chintan, 2009, *Cooling Agents: An Examination of the Role of the Informal Recycling Sector in Mitigating Climate Change*, New Delhi: Chintan Environmental Research and Action Group. Available at: http://www.chintan-india.org/documents/research_and_reports/chintan_report_cooling_agents.pdf (Last accessed July, 2015).

CPI (M), 2004, *No Jobs for Millions*, Communist Party of India (Marxist). Available at: http://cpim. org/content/14ls-elec-booklet-uneployment (Last accessed July, 2015).

Deccan Herald, 2015, 'GM to close Halol plant from June', 30 July. Available at: http://www. deccanherald.com/content/492233/gm-close-halol-plant-june.html (Last accessed October, 2015).

Desai, Renu, 2014, *Municipal Politics, Court Sympathy and Housing Rights: A Post-Mortem of Displacement and Resettlement under the Sabarmati Riverfront Project*, Ahmedabad: Centre for Urban Equity, CEPT University. Available at: http://cept.ac.in/UserFiles/File/CUE/Working%20Papers/Revised%20 New/23%20Municipal%20Politics,%20Court%20Sympathy%20and%20Housing%20Rights%20 A%20Post-Mortem%20of.pdf (Last accessed July, 2015).

Deshpande, Swati, 2002, 'BMC does a turn-around on hawkers', *Times of India*, 14 March, Available at: http://timesofindia.indiatimes.com/city/mumbai/BMC-does-a-turn-around-on-hawkers/articleshow /3710033.cms (Last accessed July, 2015).

DNA, 2015, 'Major ports to go on indefinite strike from March 9', 20 February, Available at: http:// www.dnaindia.com/money/report-major-ports-to-go-on-indefinite-strike-from-march-9-2062716 (Last accessed July, 2015).

Dupont, Veronique, 2008, 'Slum Demolitions in Delhi since the 1990s: An Appraisal', *Economic & Political Weekly*, Vol.43 (28), pp. 79-87, 12 July. Available at: http://www.indiaenvironmentportal. org.in/files/4_24.pdf (Last accessed July, 2015).

Dutta, Indrani and AnumehaYadav, 2015, 'Strike hits coal output', *The Hindu*, 6 January. Available at: http://www.thehindu.com/news/national/fiveday-coal-strike-begins/article6759443.ece (Last accessed July, 2015).

Economic Times, 2015, 'Road Transport and Safety Bill: Staff calls for nationwide strike', 28 April. Available at: http://articles.economictimes.indiatimes.com/2015-04-28/news/61615838_1_road-transport-safety-bill-nationwide-strike (Last accessed July, 2015).

Express TV, 2015, 'Operations at Vizag Port, steel plant hit due to unions strike', 2 September, Available at: http://expresstv.in/Eviewpage.aspx?TitleID=19692 (Last accessed October, 2015).

Fernandes, Walter, 2005, 'The IMDT Act and Immigration in North Eastern India', *Economic & Political Weekly*, Vol.40(30), 5 July, pp. 3237-240.

Firstpost, 2015, 'Delhi: Garbage piles up as striking sanitation workers protest ahead of Kejriwal meeting', 8 June. Available at: http://www.firstpost.com/india/delhi-garbage-piles-up-as-striking-sanitation-workers-protest-ahead-of-kejriwal-meeting-2284960.html (Last accessed July, 2015).

Ghertner, D., Asher, 2008, *Analysis of New Legal Discourse behind Delhi's Slum Demolitions, Economic & Political Weekly*,Vol.43 (20), 7 May, pp. 57-66.Available at: http://indiancities.berkeley.edu/speaker_content/docs/ghertner_asher-EPW2008.pdf (Last accessed July, 2015).

GoI, 1979, *Economy in Administrative and Non-Plan Expenditure of Government*, Order No.G.I.M.F., O.M. No.F. 7 (2)-E. (Co-ord.)179, 6 July. Available at: http://www.icar.org.in/files/delegation-of-power-icar/APPENDIX-III.pdf (Last accessed July, 2015).

GoI, 2013, File No, 14(113) Misc. RLC (Coord.)/2012, Ministry of Finance,23 January. Available at: http://www.cbec.gov.in/resources//htdocs-cbec/deptt_offcr/circ-deptl/labourlaw-compliance.pdf;jsessionid=34D5B8D0A3340504B62B2675F4DB1E1C (Last accessed July, 2015).

Greater Kashmir, 2015, 'Contractual employees stage protest, police use force', 7 May. Available at: http://www.greaterkashmir.com/news/kashmir/contractual-employees-stage-protest-police-use-force/185705.html (Last accessed July, 2015).

Hazards Centre, 2010, *Urban Resistance and Alliance Building*, New Delhi.

Kranzberg, Melvin and Michael T. Hannan, 2010, 'History of the organisation of work', *Encyclopaedia Britannica*, 27 May, pp. 1-11. Available at: http://www.britannica.com/topic/history-of-work-organization-648000 (Last accessed in July, 2015).

Industrial Global Action, 2015, 'Support 1,140 Indian mineworkers organizing at bullying Thriveni', 23 July. Available at: http://www.industriall-union.org/support-1140-indian-mineworkers-organizing-at-bullying-thriveni (Last accessed October, 2015).

ITWF, 2015, 'DHL India workers protest at Mumbai Marathon', International Transport Workers' Federation, 23 January. Available at: http://www.itfglobal.org/en/news-events/news/2015/january/dhl-india-workers-protest-at-mumbai-marathon/ (Last accessed July, 2015).

Jacob, Jeemon, 2015, 'On their own: why Kerala women workers' strike isn't just for wages', *Catchnews*, 10 October. Available at: http://www.catchnews.com/india-news/on-their-own-why-kerala-women-workers-strike-isn-t-just-for-wages-1444473618.html (Last accessed January, 2016).

LRS, 2005, 'Successful Rally of National Campaign Committee of Unorganised Sector Workers',10 December, Lok Raj Sangathan. Available at: http://www.lokraj.org.in/articles/news/successful-rally-national-campaign-committee-unorganised-sector-workers (Last accessed July, 2015).

Mayya, Sureshramana, 2004 , 'Empowering Workers through Cooperative Initiative', The International Society for Third Sector Research Sixth International Conference, July 11-14. Available at: http://at.yorku.ca/c/a/m/k/16.htm (Last accessed January, 2016).

Menon, Parvathi, 2002, 'Death of a Mine', *Frontline*, Vol.19(11), May 25-June 07. Available at: http://www.frontline.in/static/html/fl1911/19110340.htm (Last accessed July, 2015).

Mumbai Mirror, 2015, 'We have no loos, basic facilities', 29 July. Available at: http://www.mumbaimirror.com/mumbai/others/We-have-no-loos-basic-facilities/articleshow/48258829.cms (Last accessed October, 2015).

NCEUS, 2006, *Social Security for Unorganised Workers*, New Delhi: National Commission for Enterprises in the Unorganised Sector. Available at: http://sanhati.com/wp-content/uploads/2013/10/Reports-on-Social-Security.pdf (Last accessed July, 2015).

Pallavi, Aparna, 2014, 'Lessons from two cities', *Down to Earth,* 31 March. Available at: http://www.downtoearth.org.in/coverage/lessons-from-two-cities-43741 (Last accessed January, 2016).

Pulikunnel, A. T., 1997, 'Dinesh Beedi Firm at Crossroads', *Business Standard*, 22 August. Available at: http://www.business-standard.com/article/specials/dinesh-beedi-firm-at-crossroads-197082201007_1.html (Last accessed January, 2016).

Qadeer, Imrana and Dunu Roy, 1989, 'Work, Wealth, and Health: Sociology of Workers' Health in India', *Social Scientist,* Vol.17, (5/6), May-June, pp. 45-92.

Radhakrishnan, Justice S., 1999, *Judgement in KEC International Ltd vs Kamani Employees Union and Ors*, Bombay High Court, 5 August. Available at: http://indiankanoon.org/doc/698074/ (Last accessed July, 2015).

Ramanathan, Usha, 2006, 'Illegality and the Urban Poor', *Economic & Political Weekly,* Vol.41 (29), 22 July, pp. 3193-197. Available at: http://ielrc.org/content/a0606.pdf (Last accessed July, 2015).

RLEK, 1985, *Rural Litigation and Entitlement Kendra vs State of U.P. & Ors*, Supreme Court of India, 12 March, Available at: http://indiankanoon.org/doc/1949293/ (Last accessed July, 2015).

Roychowdhury, Anamitra, 2015, 'Recent Changes in Labour Laws and their Implications for the Working Class', *Sanhati*, January 13. Available at: http://sanhati.com/excerpted/12592/ (Last accessed July, 2015).

SACW, 2015, 'India: Thousands in Mandala (Bombay) take back their land / Solidarity Protest in Delhi on 3 June 2014', *South Asia Citizens Web*, June 2. Available at: http://www.sacw.net/article11214.html (Last accessed July, 2015).

Sajha Manch, 2003, *Dilli Kiski Hai*, New Delhi: Hazards Centre.

Sankaran, T. S., 2009, 'A Critique of India's Unorganised Workers' Social Security Act, 2008', *South Asia Citizens Web*, 16 February. Available at: http://www.sacw.net/article658.html (Last accessed July, 2015).

Shankar, Mridula, 2015, 'Decriminalising sex work: Will India lead the way?', International Health Policies, 23 October. Available at: http://www.internationalhealthpolicies.org/why-decriminalisation-of-sex-work-is-the-way-to-go-an-indian-perspective/ (Last accessed January, 2016).

Singh, Shiv Sahay, 2015, 'Sex workers' cooperative wins award', *The Hindu*, 1 February. Available at: http://www.thehindu.com/news/cities/kolkata/sex-workers-cooperative-wins-award/article6843840.ece (Last accessed January, 2016).

The Hindu, 2015a, 'Railway employees join hands against foreign investment', 20 February. Available at: http://www.thehindu.com/news/cities/Thiruvananthapuram/railway-employees-join-hands-against-foreign-investment/article6915728.ece (Last accessed July, 2015).

The Hindu, 2015b, 'Labourers leader demands end to contract labour system in KPTCL', 10 August. Available at: http://www.thehindu.com/news/national/karnataka/labourers-leader-demands-end-to-contract-labour-system-in-kptcl/article7522390.ece (Last accessed October, 2015).

The Hindu, 2015c. 'Women staff raise safety issue', 3 August. Available at: http://www.mumbaimirror.

com/mumbai/others/We-have-no-loos-basic-facilities/articleshow/48258829.cms (Last accessed October, 2015).

The Indian Express, 2015, 'Logistics staff go on strike, Flipkart Myntra in a fix', 2 August. Available at: http://indianexpress.com/article/business/companies/logistics-staff-go-on-strike-flipkart-myntra-in-a-fix/ (Last accessed October, 2015).

The Times of India, 2015, 'NLC unions face contempt action for going on strike', 29 July. Available at: http://timesofindia.indiatimes.com/city/chennai/NLC-unions-face-contempt-action-for-going-on-strike/articleshow/48259108.cms (Last accessed October, 2015).

The Tribune, 2000, 'Sporadic violence during bandh', 28 November. Available at: http://www.tribuneindia.com/2000/20001128/main3.htm (Last accessed July, 2015).

The Tribune, 2015a, 'Set right the wrongs of Congress govt: Factory workers tell Khattar', July 19. Available at: http://www.tribuneindia.com/news/haryana/set-right-the-wrongs-of-congress-govt-factory-workers-tell-khattar/108413.html (Last accessed October, 2015).

The Tribune, 2015b, 'LIC employees oppose Insurance Bill, observe strike', 10 March. Available at: http://www.tribuneindia.com/news/lic-employees-oppose-insurance-bill-observe-strike/51589.html (Last accessed July, 2015).

The Tribune, 2015c, 'Anganwadi workers protest', 4 March. Available at: http://www.tribuneindia.com/news/uttarakhand/community/anganwadi-workers-protest/49385.html (Last accessed July, 2015).

Vasuki, S. N., 1989, 'A soap opera', *India Today*, 15 February. Available at: http://indiatoday.intoday.in/story/hindustan-lever-workers-start-hawking-lock-out-detergent-power-to-raise-funds/1/323076.html (Last accessed January, 2016).

Verma, Gita Dewan, 2001, *Hawking Hawkers, Part II – Subaltern Story of Hawkers Delhi,* New Delhi: MPISG. Available at: http://architexturez.net/doc/az-cf-22753 (Last accessed July, 2015).

Wikipedia, undated, *KEC International.* Available at: https://en.wikipedia.org/wiki/KEC_International (Last accessed July, 2015).

Regionalization and Localisation of Economies: A Preliminary Sketch for an Ecological Imperative

Aseem Shrivastava and Elango Rangasamy

'I sympathize therefore, with those who would minimize rather than those who would maximize economic entanglement between nations. Ideas, knowledge, art, hospitality, travel – these are the things which should of their nature be international. But let goods be homespun whenever it is reasonably and conveniently possible; and, above all, let finance be primarily national.'

(Keynes, 1933, pp. 757)

Summary

The corporate market economy has equated development with economic growth and that has led to a huge ecological damage and destruction of human communities. Globalisation has resulted in the centralisation of power with few nations and companies, who regulate the tightly networked business economy.

This essay argues for localisation and regionalisation of economies that are ecologically stable and renewable. It would mean clusters of 20-30 villages, at times with a town as a hub, which are collectively self-sufficient at least for basic needs. A Panchayat academy could provide the institutional basis for building capacity for this. Such an economy will be a 'Network Growth Economy'. The essay lists out strategies to achieve a new, decentralised, economic architecture, which will challenge the industrial and globalised economy. The essay gives the example of Kuthambakkam village in Thiruvallur district of Tamil Nadu, established by one of the authors, which anchored itself in the vision of Gram Swaraj. The village now enjoys adequate livelihood opportunities including for dalits, good roads, an effective drainage system, safe drinking water, and energy-efficient street lighting, in addition to having dignified housing for all. This village is an example of an attempt at creating a decentralized, ecologically stable and renewable economy.

Introduction

In the midst of the Great Depression Keynes put forth what would be seen by much of the establishment everywhere today as an absurd view, given the intricate interdependence which has come to characterize economic relations between nations in the decades since he wrote. Keynes's concerns stemmed from the financial perils associated with the 'economic entanglement between nations', of which there was already ample proof in the world around him. His apprehensions have proved only too valid, given the financial events since the closing decades of the last century.

Further, Keynes's observation has even greater gravity today when one places, as one must, the ecological crises which besiege us at the centre of our attention. The ecological condition of the earth has deteriorated rapidly since the time that Keynes lived. The last quarter century of globalization, unfettered by any significant institutional or ideological challenges to the corporate market economy (such as communism under the Soviet model, which sustained, howsoever perversely, a global balance of power for three-quarters of a century), has been marked by the heightening of competition between countries, corporations, and individuals. It is now becoming amply clear that such competitive forces have led the world to an ecologically self-destructive race-to-the-bottom. As each country tries to outdo the other, it cuts deeper into the ecological foundations of its organic life. Additionally, imperial nations continue to do even greater damage to the natural environment of poorer parts of the world. The evidence for accelerating climate change accumulates with each passing week, even as reports of disappearing biodiversity and freshwater, rapidly depleting fossil fuel reserves, and destruction of many diverse habitats and ecosystems – from rainforests to coastlines – keep coming daily. In trying to build 'a smarter planet', we may not have one left in the end!

The reigning ideology today is what may be called 'corporate nationalism', whereby virtually every government around the world is not only reductively equating economic growth with development itself, but, far from being the great balancing force in a disturbingly unequal and unjust world, is actually facilitating the goals of globally agile big business by constantly trying to generate a climate ever more suitable for private investment. Ecological damage, the erosion or destruction of human communities, and detrimental consequences for working people are the necessary by-products of this commitment to easing the climate for private investment. The blurring of the all-important public-private distinction, so fundamental to the functioning of a modern democracy, has also followed.

All this is justified on the grounds that 'growth-at-any-cost' is the only way to generate jobs for a rapidly expanding work-force, especially in a populous country like India with a rapidly expanding young population. While the claim is demonstrably false, this paper addresses another ecological concern that stems from the accelerating pace of the globalised economy. It has to do with the ecological consequences that follow predictably from the *centralisation* of the mainstream, globalised economy. It is argued below that what is termed 'globalization' is in fact centralisation, and it has devastating ecological implications, apart from failing to redeem the promise of jobs. If there is to be an ecologically viable future in which secure livelihoods have a place, there is an urgent need to regionalise and localise economies around the world. Centralised, remote-controlled economies just won't do anymore.

A Brief Historical Prelude

We must situation ourselves historically. Industrial modernity has been sweeping across the world for 250 years, the last twenty five—under the commanding force of information and communication technologies—at a particularly accelerated pace. At the heart of the gamut of changes that it has brought upon human life and society is a technological dynamism which has facilitated a degree of *mobility* (of people, goods, services and capital) unimaginable in pre-industrial societies, or even a few generations ago. Taken together with the commercial expansion of the market economy, the revolution in transport has resulted in the uprooting of human cultures and the *dislocation* of communities across the globe, the rapid spread of information and communication technologies having accelerated the pace of this dislocation – as much mental as physical. The economy that has resulted from this all-encompassing process is ecologically alienated from human culture and the natural world.

So far has this accelerating process of expansion of the market economy gone, and so inevitable has become the response of people to the promptings of the money, land and labour markets that it would be no exaggeration to suggest that, globally speaking, we no longer live in a society, but have instead come to live in a tightly networked economy. The phenomenon is best appreciated if one notices how culturally rooted communities are being quickly eclipsed by business *networks* today. This global reality is even truer in the so-called 'developed' nations, where it all began. Not without basis had Mrs. Thatcher won three national elections in Britain in the 1980s, by raising the slogan 'there is no such thing as society'[1] (There are only families and individuals, she had added).

The Indian peculiarity, however, is that the community (*biradiri,* or its vernacular equivalent in other parts of India) survives, howsoever imperfectly (given the myriad injustices of caste, class and gender), especially in the countryside, as the dominant mode of social identity. No Indian politician, unlike in the West, could win even a Panchayat election in this country by proclaiming publicly 'there is no such thing as society.' In other words, this country is at a strange watershed in its history when it is not clear whether the (globalizing) market will in the end triumph over human society to such a degree that a Thatcher-like slogan will ultimately go down well with Indian electorates. The answer will presumably rest on the possible success of the corporate-dominated market economy in providing jobs and an affordable, decent standard of living to the vast majority of the people, a promise that continues to recede into the elusive horizon, given the state of things.

The Predatory Mainstream Economy

The discussion in the previous section points towards the growing role of economic *distance* in the deepening of the global ecological crisis. The globalisation of national economies over the past generation has led to growing concentrations of income, wealth and power. In a world where financial muscle has become rapidly more important, global economic power is now exercised by large, metropolitan world cities, where the world's money and capital markets are located.

Not only this. Production supply-chains now straddle the earth. Any cutting-edge industrial product, such as a smart-phone, now involves inputs from dozens of far-flung sites across the earth (involving mining, shipping, warehousing, processing, manufacture, packaging, stocking, transportation, wholesaling, retailing, consumption, recycling, and waste disposal). Little wonder then, that 'the shadows of consumption' fall right across the earth as well (Dauvergne, 2008).

In this way, the growing centralisation of economic decision has brought about far greater distances between places where ecologically sensitive decisions are made and the point at which they have their impact. At the receiving end of these decisions – whether involving a big dam or a mining project – is not only the ecosystem which stands in the way of the project, but the communities whose lives, livelihoods, and cultures rest on the survival of the ecosystem. These are communities who have hitherto lived in intimacy with the natural world, but are increasingly alienated from their surroundings, and thus more prone to becoming a source of damage to them, especially if they are led to join the ranks of atomized, aspirational consumers. The relentless urbanisation of the mind is no small part of the reason for growing ecological problems around the world. It is readily forgotten that life in the countryside is lived compellingly closer (and more subject) to nature and is thus, in general, more respectful of ecological limits. With a few notable (urban) exceptions, a few individuals, communities or institutions who have resisted the tide – whatever residual ecological wisdom still lives in humanity comes from its rural cultures.

In India in, say, the year 1915, or even 1965 or 1990, economies were a lot more locally and regionally grounded. Ecologically and culturally speaking, they were far more 'embedded'. If so many ecosystems are found in a disturbed condition today, there should be no surprise, given how far from the damage decision-makers (whether in a corporate or a government bureaucracy) live, and how little of the short-range impact of their decisions they have to bear. Nobody, after all, will discuss land acquisition and mining if gold or oil is discovered under Lutyens' Delhi!

The increasingly adverse relations between town and country have been shaped profoundly by this long process of metropolitan economic expansion and resulting economic centralisation in India. The city lives virtually unmindful of the fact that it treats the countryside as a mere hinterland for resources and a dump for its industrial wastes. The vision of the natural world that is taught to school-children is not one which cognitively integrates, as would befit ecological wisdom, life in the city with the conditions in the countryside. It is an exclusively 'modern' one in which development is reducible to urbanisation, and villages are ultimately meant to disappear, their residents migrating to cities in order to 'catch up' with the leaders of 'development'- no matter how impossible such a dream may be. In some strange sense, the pursuit of economic and political power associated with the 'developed' nations has come to be seen as a search for 'equality'!

Under such existential conditions, inflected by a distorted cognition, and a million attendant illusions, is it any surprise that we find ourselves in a state of rapid ecological deterioration?

By no means is it being suggested that localisation comes without its own bag of problems. The challenges of gender, caste and class are present in the Indian countryside too, as they are in the cities. Any transition to localisation and regionalisation of economies recommended here will have to take these factors into account if it is to successfully address these inequities.

Nor is it being suggested that a neat compartmentalisation of the urban and the rural is always possible anymore in a country like India, where hundreds of millions have now adopted strategies of survival which simultaneously engage individuals and families in economic lives in both cities and villages. Even physically, cities and villages sometimes seem to merge into each other.

The point remains, nonetheless, that with the ascent of television and virtual technologies, the urbanisation and metropolitanisation of the public mind is having harmful consequences for habitats. Cognition, belief, and practice – in relation to both nature and culture – are all mutating at rapid speed in directions unfavourable to the protection and regeneration of nature.

India in 2050: a vision of renewability

If the problems facing us today have to be faced with any degree of success, we first need to imagine a desirable world, before we indicate the strategies and processes which can take us there. Let us abstract temporarily from the conditions and momentum of the present world (which would mean, radically, that the events precipitated by climate change do not overtake us in short order over the next 30-40 years) and consider what might be a world worth working towards, in a little over a generation from now, say by 2050.

The self-reliant village, in the sense of a unit entirely economically self-reliant, has perhaps always been a myth. But a self-reliant *region* is certainly possible to conceive. True localisation and regionalisation of economies would mean that there are clusters of, say, 20-40 villages, with a town or large urban centre as a hub, which are, collectively, mostly self-reliant when it comes to meeting their requirements and desires. Importantly, the relationship between the city and the countryside would need to be radically renegotiated to remove age-old inequities, when it comes to the supply of food and raw materials (also resource flows like water) and the disposal of waste, not to forget the uprooting of human communities in the name of development and progress.

In a viable arrangement such a group of villages would trade actively with each other to supply themselves with goods and services they do not produce themselves. They would have reduced trade with the outside world and would certainly not rely on the latter for meeting basic needs like water, food, energy, and materials for housing and clothing. Essential services like health and education would also be provided locally and regionally. The range of consumption that the modern world has got used to, thanks to an indulgently subsidised energy infrastructure, will obviously be far more limited. But the same conservation principle could likely give birth to new forms of cultural creativity the modern world has seen go into dormancy or eclipse.

Importantly, the infrastructure to run such an economic arrangement would focus on the construction of transport and communication systems and the generation of electricity

– using largely locally produced renewable energy – which would prioritise local and regional needs. Gigantic energy projects are therefore ruled out except in a handful of cases where national public needs justify it or if a region is particularly deficient in the resources for energy generation.

Each region would of course be a part of a communication network which links it to the world. But the physical movement of goods, services, and capital, not to forget people themselves (for economic purposes), would be guided and bounded by a sense of limits – unlike the hectic travel and freight that the modern world has got used to. Needless to add, such a state of affairs can come to abide only with a radical cultural and psychological awakening of humanity, reminding it of its place in the scheme of things.

The Road to Localisation and Regionalisation

Now that we have a sense of the sort of world we are looking for, how do we get there? Here are some of the key strategies which can help forge a new, decentralised economic architecture which may be in a position to help us supersede today's destructive globalisation and face the challenge of the transition from the industrial to an ecological age.

Firstly, human needs and ecological stability and survival are the priorities now, not the expansion of trade and economic growth for the sake of profit and power. Growth is cited widely – by economists of widely divergent political persuasions – as the only route to remove poverty from the world. The actual experience of growth around the world has been quite different. Global data of the last 100 years, especially of the last 35, shows rather emphatically that the underlying aim of growth is not about reduction of poverty, as much as the expansion of big business in the name of reducing poverty.[2]

One point merits explicit comment in this context. We live in a time when the luxuries of yesterday – from cars to washing machines to laptop computers – become the necessities of today. This is often described as consumerism, when in fact there are even more powerful impulses working from the side of competitive production and speedy innovation (not forgetting the technologically shaped professional and social expectations) which are driving the socially competitive consumption. Consumer choice under such cultural circumstances (heavily shaped by invasive 24/7 advertising and multiple messaging) is anything but 'autonomous'. If we are serious about facing the ecological challenge, urgently needed is public discussion and education on the theme, so that democratically guided policies can regulate unsustainable production and consumption.

Secondly, if ecological stability and renewability of the economy is the goal, the *scale* and *speed* of globally expansionary economic activity – involving opaque, remote-controlled

291

economies – would have to be brought under democratic public control. This rational regulation is minimally necessary in order to ensure that positive efforts towards renewability and stability are not overwhelmed by the 'default settings' of the mainstream economy, that the hole is not being dug faster than it can be filled. Democratic public control will include the devolution of powers to regional and local polities.

In other words, we are looking for a decentralised economic architecture in which grassroots human communities, still directly linked to the earth for their livelihoods, have an increasingly bigger role in economic decision-making. At an intermediate level, between such communities and the structures of the modern nation-state, organisational and administrative forms have to emerge and evolve. Some of them are already somewhat on the way through civil society and para-statal interventions (one thinks in India, for instance, of legislation like PESA and others) to ensure that the transition to an ecologically embedded economy is not too violent. A smooth transition is now very hard to imagine, but without effective intermediate structures for fair negotiations, the ruptures will be sudden, and often very destructive, apart from changing the destination that is to ultimately be reached. In general, it will have to be understood widely that human ecological survival is impossible without a radically democratic change in the politics of every contemporary society.

As much as grassroots efforts towards livelihoods must gain necessary space, institutional arrangements for the decentralisation and regionalisation of hitherto globalised economies need to be found. Both resources and markets need to be located much closer to the point of actual production than is the norm in a globalised world. In other words, radical reforms are necessary to the present structures of decision-making which involve heavy political centralization, alienate the economy ecologically, and uproot human communities in the process. In India, the Panchayati Raj Institutions (*gram sabhas* as full village assemblies; in indigenous/tribal areas, councils or other institutions considered locally appropriate) are a step in the right direction. However, these are executive bodies. They do not have *legislative* and financial power that could prevail over decisions taken at the provincial or the national level. Imagine the consequences if such bodies could exercise *veto* power in certain cases!

Thirdly, two things ultimately undergird all economic activity: human labour and energy, derived directly or indirectly through our relationship to the natural world. Extraction and distribution of energy to fuel the vast technological edifice of industrial society currently rest on a highly centralised and heavily subsidised global energy infrastructure disproportionately dependent on fossil fuels. India's growth in recent years has come virtually entirely from the import of petroleum and the extraction of coal, for neither of which it has been paying the enormous external ecological costs (in terms of the health costs of pollution, the economic and other costs of climate change and much else). In coming years, this will have to change and policies would have to price dirty energy to include ecological costs (via things like carbon taxes), while simultaneously enabling greater use of renewable energy.[3]

Energy *production* is also heavily centralised in the contemporary, globalised national economy. This means that networks for the distribution of energy (whether between or within countries) are vast. Wouldn't it save huge amounts of energy if the points of production and use of energy were geographically closer to each other? This is possible to imagine only if the scale, spread, and speed of production and use are reduced. It is worth recalling a simple truth here: urban and metropolitan markets offer captive, clustered populations for the mass markets needed by the mass production of transnational business enterprises. Energy production was centralised and accelerated in the first place only to expand the scale of its outreach across space to a much greater population than was accessing it in the past. So, in localising energy production, we will inevitably be limiting and slowing down the production of energy, conforming to the rhythms of renewable energy production and using non-renewables sparingly where they are absolutely necessary. Something along these lines is already happening through the greater use of solar and other forms of renewable energy, typically produced for local use on a small scale. In some places, local or regional grids are also being considered. These are moves in the right direction. However, in a ruthlessly competitive economy, merely improving energy supply and changing the energy-mix in favour of renewables policies won't do. Policies to control overall demand are urgently needed.

Fourth, if energy demands are to be controlled, policies have to be conceived to alter human settlement patterns to bring points of industrial and energy production closer to points of use. This is of course easier said than achieved. Yet, unless city-dwellers (and the policy-elites who come from their ranks) realise the sheer enormity of their ecological dependence on the countryside, arresting what Rabindranath Tagore had described in his prophetic 1924 essay as 'robbery of the soil' (Tagore, 2007), it is very difficult to see how an ecologically stable, renewable economy can come about in the limited time available. A very large proportion of the energy expenditure of globalised economies goes towards the running and maintenance of transport systems, for the movement of goods, waste, and people.

If ecologically just prices were to be paid for the expense on oil and coal, many of the economic activities of the present world may not prove viable. So, measures like stiff carbon taxes – long overdue in India – will have significant consequences for the way we live, what we buy, use and throw, and how (and how much) we travel. They would also fundamentally influence food choices and discourage such habits as eating fruits out of local season or meat from another continent – since food miles would be heavily taxed.

Very importantly, well-designed high carbon taxes (which will raise the cost of travel and freight) would also alter the distribution of the population between villages and cities. In fact, in some cases, it may be appropriate to design fiscal policies which will actively promote living in smaller and more rural or 'rurban', settlements. It would save the cities from some of the likely catastrophes which otherwise lie in wait. There is no option today except to design policies in countries like India which would lead to rapid urban and metropolitan *shrinkage*. This is in the long-term interest both of the city and the countryside, given growing problems of urban unemployment, congestion and pollution.

Fifth, it is important to note that this state of affairs – whereby at present an ecological and cultural chasm straddles the relationship between town and country – corresponds to a pattern of urbanisation which accompanies a very specific, centralised model of energy and resource-intensive industrialization. Neither industries nor cities have to run like this in the future.

It is entirely possible to imagine an ecological society which has cities and villages, both with industry and services, along with agriculture, fisheries, pastoralism and forest-work in the countryside. However, its *technological* basis is very different from the one dominant in industrial society today. It relies on 'ecologically sound technology', as the biologist Barry Commoner once put it. This technology is designed for small-scale production, more for local and regional use and consumption, instead of for sale in distant markets.[4] An example of the sort of technology we are thinking of is the production, using labour-utilising, low-energy carding machines, of *Malkha* fabric by the Decentralised Cotton Yarn Trust in Telangana and Andhra Pradesh.[5]

Importantly, such technology relies preponderantly on renewable energy (in turn in accord with the seasons and cycles of nature) and local and regional energy grids, instead of global ones. It is possible to describe such technology as humanising 'ecofacture', as distinct from the robotised 'machinofacture'[6] that dominates the globalised economy today. It has immensely greater potential for the generation of creative, dignified livelihoods as compared with increasingly automated industry, which has rendered workers as machine-parts. It is crucial to note here – without incurring slurs of being a Luddite – that technologies like nuclear energy (for instance) are inherently authoritarian because of their secretive and centralised nature, while solar technologies are usually democratic because of their open and dispersed character. This is one reason why most of the cutting-edge research in solar technologies has long been controlled by giant corporations keen to make the last buck from fossil fuels. 'Tools of conviviality', as Ivan Illich was famous for saying, change the very character and nature of production, enabling the small to not just be beautiful, but also the only thing truly sustainable, making work both wholesome and dignified. Such an ecological outlook on technology has the potential to liberate humanity from the industrial slavery of wage-labour on the assembly line.

Sixth, if 'tools for conviviality' are to become the norm (in all areas of the economy, but especially in industry) rather than the exception that they are at present, production in the economy has to be fundamentally reorganized.[7] This will involve, among many other things, the sustained recovery and everyday deployment of what some people call *lokvidya* (peoples' knowledge) (Basole, 2015). This is to be distinguished clearly from what is often called 'indigenous knowledge', but in fact isn't, since the latter involves the 'taming of lokvidya' through a powerful global system of intellectual property rights which putatively tries to democratise such knowledge by making it accessible beyond the communities who are normally privy to them. In practice, however, much appropriation of people's knowhow takes place to enable the patenting corporations to reap huge profits. Biopiracy is only the most prominent example of this ongoing process.

Additionally, a new hierarchy of knowledge and knowhow gets set up which privileges the virtual sphere and its simplifying systematisation of people's practical knowledge, leaving out crucial aspects, recognising only those forms of it which can be virtualised. Not only does lokvidya typically involve 'embodied skill, tacit knowledge and experience' impossible to virtualise, it is also 'often characterised by inbuilt wisdom regarding the uncertainty and unpredictability of ecosystems' (Basole, 2015, pp. 379-80). The systematisation of such knowledge into 'virtual libraries' (such as some of digital libraries of the Government of India), unjustly divorces it from the physical sites from which they arise in the first place.

This is perhaps an appropriate moment to note, parenthetically, that a supportive policy framework would go a very long way in terms of helping to reorganise economies for ecological renewability and socio-economic justice. To take just one instance of the sort of change which would be positive, if the many hundreds of crafts listed by the Government of India could be redefined as 'industry', with all the attendant benefits of policy attention and support that industries derive, it would make 'sunset' activities into economically viable propositions. So far, however, far from taking such a perspective, policy has usually stood in the way of the fundamental reorganisation of production needed.

Seventh, the localisation of economies and the recovery and use of lokvidya dramatically alters the prospects for women's work. It has been correctly argued by advocates of lokvidya that 'development' in India and other countries has typically meant the Westernization of knowledge and cultures and the automation of economies. In the process, one after another, different aspects and areas of women's activity have been effectively stolen from them. Women have been deprived over time of a large variety of domestic industries – from textiles and food production and processing to health care. In the bargain, women's specific areas of strength in lokvidya have been undermined as their work and practical wisdom has neither been recognised nor valued fairly, nor have the opportunities for their exercise expanded. This long process of the appropriation of women's work and knowledge will have to be reversed if economic localisation is to become the normative reality. 'The movement for reorganisation of the production and market of textiles and food materials on the basis of women's knowledge can become the mainstay of emancipating women from the vicious web of exploitation and erecting a promising challenge to globalisation' (Sahsrabudhey, 2015 pp. 201).

Eighth, the credit needs of localised economies have to be thought through carefully. These are going to be small per unit of production, but large in aggregate terms, because of the large population. Globalization has been accompanied by such a heating up of competition that large banks have little interest in lending small sums of money. They do not find the administrative and transactions costs of such investment worth their while. Thus, one has to think of other alternatives. The experience with microfinance has been mixed at best and exploitative at worst, thanks to rates of interest only lower than exorbitant ones charged by moneylenders in the informal market. Is there a way to mobilize small household savings through credit cooperatives? The risk is always that once they cross a certain size, they tend to focus on big loans and lose the very rationale for their existence.

Could there be a way to follow the microfinance model without the high rates of interest? This may be a possible area of experimentation. If interest rates are to be kept within bounds, the initiative for it will have to come from the economically active communities themselves. It is pertinent here to think of experiments around the country – such as in Dharani at Timbaktu (Telangana) and URMUL (Rajasthan) – which have achieved this.[8]

Experiments are also being conducted with local economies that run without money to a considerable degree. Here it is vital to keep in view the fact that traditionally, subsistence economies in South Asia – involving agriculture, pastoralism, forest, fisheries and artisanal work – have not depended upon money except at the margins of their needs. However, conditions have changed today with the rapid commodification and monetisation of resources, especially since globalisation was launched in the 1990s'. So money and credit needs have multiplied.

Finally, marketing networks have to be created if local and regional economies have to be effective. While it is true that the production and consumption of things has to cohere around much smaller areas than is the case with today's dominant remote-controlled economies, not even a transitional future can be conceived without some effort towards building a marketing (and sometimes branding) network. There are many examples from across India of production cooperatives in a variety of areas experimenting with niche marketing of organic products, especially in food, herbal medicines, cosmetic products and textiles. Examples that come to mind are organisations like Navdanya, Nirvaah, Aarohi, and Jharcraft in North India and Dastkar Andhra and Desi in South India.[9]

There are also examples of places which have brought business back to villages when the local panchayat has been supportive. The effort is often pushed further by making preferential trade agreements with neighbouring villages or districts. One such instance, which is a model of success, is drawn from the experience of a village in Tamil Nadu. On this experiment rests the idea of a Network Growth Economy.

The Network Growth Economy (NGE): the experience of Kuthambakkam and beyond

The concept of the self-governing village in the Indian context is to be found in Vedic times, as early as in 1200 BC. There is evidence that even Village Sabhas (councils or assemblies) existed at that time which were working as institutional intermediaries with higher authorities on relevant matters (Debroy and Kaushik, 2005, pp. 77).

During the pre-colonial period, panchayats, both at village level as well as that of the *jaati* (caste), existed and actively looked after the affairs of the village/caste, ensuring adherence to law and order as well as working for justice and social solidarity. During the medieval and Mughal periods this system of village panchayats survived, even thrived. Sir Charles Metcalfe, the then provisional Governor-General of India (1835-36), had called these village communities 'little republics'.[10] At the time of the drafting of the Constitution of India, there was initially no provision for panchayats. This led to major debates and finally a provision was included in Part IV of the Constitution (in the Directive Principles of State Policy), which hence, was not mandatory.

Since independence, many good and bad things have happened in India in the context of Panchayati Raj. Rajasthan was the first state to inaugurate Panchayati Raj. Tamil Nadu did not hold Panchayat elections for fifteen years, till after the 73rd Constitutional Amendment in 1992 was passed. It widens the democratic base, enabling horizontal planning and implementation of development programmes.

To an extent, on account of the failure of a top-down approach to rural development, the government has realized that involving local communities is essential. The decision-making processes should essentially involve those for whom the outcome is intended. Therefore, the role of Panchayats has become significant to ensure community participation through Ward Sabhas (meetings) and Gram Sabhas.

The experience of Kuthambakkam village (in Thiruvallur district of Tamilnadu) is valuable. Here, the Trust for Village Self-Governance (TVSG) has been established by one of the authors (ER). A chemical engineer by training, he was the Panchayat president of Kuthambakkam village from 1996 to 2006.

After years of work, the villagers of Kuthambakkam now enjoy good concrete roads, an effective drainage system, safe drinking water, and energy-efficient street lighting, in addition to having *pucca* (houses constructed with bricks/stone/concrete) houses. The various cost-effective and energy-saving technologies that we have promoted in his village have in turn provided employment to many villagers. It is possible to achieve the same results elsewhere as long as adequate infrastructural facilities are provided to rural populations, leading to an 'economy of permanence'.[11]

With legal backing, Kuthambakkam has anchored itself in Gandhi's vision of Gram Swaraj. Gandhians believe in the panchayat's immense potential for democratic decentralization and devolving power to the people. The basic conviction is that the village panchayats could play an important role in social transformation and in implementation of development programmes.

One of the motivations of the Kuthambakkam experiment was the realisation that the typical Indian village produces a few things, and tries to sell them; most of the things sold are "unfinished products", such as harvested crops, unpasteurized milk, nuts for oil. These are sent off to be processed, packaged, and transported back to the village. Typically, there is a 100 per cent mark-up in price in that process. Villagers think of themselves as consumers only of finished goods, but there is no reason why they cannot also be processors who make the finished goods. In the same move, they can eliminate middleman costs, and also find employment through new economic activity. From this there is self-reliance and a sense of pride.

A Panchayat Academy and a Demonstration-cum-Training centre for Village Industries has also been set up under the banner of Trust for Village Self-Governance. The Trust was registered in January 2000 and has been effective in carrying out training for work in village industries. A huge number of local livelihoods have been generated by using panchayat funds to buy machines (for instance, for pressing of oilseeds), bringing back to the village jobs which earlier were only available in the city. Infrastructure has been developed for establishing village industries by doing simple value addition in local produce and raw materials.

The mandate of the Panchayat Academy is to prepare an effective network of Panchayats in the district to work in a collaborative framework. The Academy is already doing extensive work in sensitization of Panchayat representatives from different parts of Thiruvallur district and other parts of Tamil Nadu and other states.

The aim of the Panchayat Academy is to impart awareness, training, exposure and long-term handholding to dynamic and interested Panchayat leaders who are really committed to the development of their villages. The Trust will focus on women (SHG groups) and youth to include their effective participation in the development process and at the same time make better livelihood or career opportunities, adopting local economic activities.

The proposed project is a conscious effort to strengthen the Panchayati Raj system in villages and, through Panchayats, provide technical and financial assistance to the communities and create an 'enabling' environment for promotion of village industries and micro-businesses.

With the NGE model, the real challenge is to motivate local communities to consume products from their own village or nearby villages. The panchayats have to play a pivotal role towards establishing *habitat solidarity* among the villages of the cluster. It is similar to SHG (self-help group) model in villages. Since SHG movement has been a success in some areas, there is a good chance of success of the NGE model because the local leaders, SHGs and youth are the ones who are going to benefit from this. The processes are to be decided, managed and controlled by them.

The overall approach is that in a cluster of 15-20 villages, different items are produced by separate villages based on mutual understanding and such produce is then marketed to each others' villages on a reciprocal basis. This will enliven economic life among the villages rather than allow leakages to urban markets. The surplus of the network will be exported to the nearest towns and the needed products which are not produced in the network will be imported from the nearest town. By doing things this way, the villages will be secured from the exploitation of external markets and traders. A large number of employment opportunities will also be created in rural areas, reducing migration to cities. With such an approach, prosperity and self-sufficiency can be brought about in clusters of villages.

Further, through the Trust's Demonstration cum Training Centre for Village Industries, people from different villages can come and learn manufacturing methods to make a variety of goods and can also learn how those items can be marketed by the village communities. It is also envisaged to provide full technical support, training and, in special cases, organizing financial support to SHG members to undertake manufacturing of various items in their respective villages. Infrastructure development is already in progress and some of the equipment, tool and machinery have been installed. In addition to demonstration and training, these units will also be used to produce some items through SHG members of Kuthambakkam village. The various government schemes will also be dovetailed to boost this effort.

In order to make this NGE model operational, structured training, capacity-building and hand-holding activities have to be undertaken by the Trust. The Panchayat Academy will develop training modules and organize training programmes periodically for 5 years. It will aim to produce a large number of dynamic, development-oriented and committed panchayat leaders. It will impart adequate energy, information and knowledge to enable the participating panchayat leaders to work effectively on the issues pertaining to development of their respective villages. In a democratic country like India if the people (particularly rural) are really empowered to solve their problems by themselves, it will really bring remarkable changes in the Indian economy through rural prosperity.

The Trust feels that the above initiative is in line with the thinking of the central and state governments to strengthen the Panchayati Raj. Once this model is successfully demonstrated in two clusters of Thiruvallur district, the government of India may then decide to replicate this in other parts of the country. This way, the load on the government will also reduce and it can spend its time and effort more on macro policy issues.

The NGE concept is based on a practical field study carried out by one of the Gandhian Panchayat leaders, his team covering about 15,000 families from twenty villages (approximately a population of 60,000).

The study included the consumption of food items and other goods and materials, which are necessary and form a part of routine life of village communities. The survey also included the sources and locations of value addition for such goods. The other elements of the survey included mapping of local resources, which includes agricultural produce, natural raw materials/minerals, and skills available.

The findings of the study reconfirmed certain facts and figures. It was found that all the commodities used by this group of twenty villages came from urban markets. Most of the local produce was sold to the outside market as raw material. The value addition (plus adulteration) to that local produce takes place in urban industries. These products are then sold back to villages through a multi-tier distribution system at very high prices, to cover overheads and huge profit margins for various middlemen in the chain.

Therefore, a concept was developed, in line with the thinking of Mahatma Gandhi, to evolve a system which enables villagers to use their local resources by converting them into consumable products through value addition for their own use. This process allows them to re-learn the basic knowledge of identifying and solving their own problems. The belief is that such processes will not only contribute towards developing the local economy, but will also provide opportunities to rural populations to understand cross-cultural and social aspects.

The NGE Model has two important elements: first, the Panchayat's role as facilitator, and second, promotion of village industries.

Since this model envisages a number of villages working in a collaborative framework, a network among the panchayat leaders of respective villages will need to be established with a fair amount of mutual understanding. The group of villages in a cluster has to live like a big family and the panchayat leaders would be responsible for establishing a degree of harmony and solidarity among the villagers. This mandate will require good leadership, maturity and team-building qualities in the panchayat leaders so that they can handle the group dynamics while dealing with village communities comprising of different castes and religions. Further, the leaders also have to make efforts to deal with various state and central government departments for mobilizing necessary assistance for their villages under different existing schemes. In order to ensure holistic development of their villages, the panchayat leaders will have to give due importance to matters pertaining to community needs, be it education, health, employment, infrastructure, and village-level industries. The SHG members, other villagers and youth have to be motivated and trained to put up value-adding units for converting locally produced items and raw/waste materials into finished goods, in cooperation with the panchayats. The panchayats, as compensation for providing such support, may charge a tax or fee to generate some revenue for developmental activities.

The Wisdom of Localisation

The entirely self-reliant village has perhaps always been rightly seen to be a myth. However, a self-reliant *region*, whose residents take care of the bulk of their material needs from places close is entirely possible. Despite the hostile environment for such experiments generated by globalisation, there are parts of the country which have successfully created this hope by signing agreements with villages in contiguous areas.

Following the sort of principles illustrated by the Kuthambakkam experience, as well as the others which have been discussed in this paper, it is possible to imagine and bring into existence ecologically stable and renewable economies which will also be much more fair and just than the absurdly inequitable and unsustainable economies which mark the era of development under imperial globalisation.

There is rapidly mounting evidence to show that remote-controlled globalised economies come with formidable ecological perils. Localization and regionalisation of economies is the ecological compulsion of our time. A failure to heed this imperative cannot but bring us closer each day to a catastrophe perhaps still possible to avoid for many.

Endnotes

1. See for details, http://www.margaretthatcher.org/document/106689.
2. See, for instance, the data presented here: Growth isn't Working, London: New Economics Foundation, 2006, available at http://www.neweconomics.org/sites/neweconomics.org/files/Growth_Isnt_Working_1.pdf.
3. See essays on Energy, and Environmental Governance, in this volume.
4. See Barry Commoner, 'Ecology and Social Action', The Albright Lecture given at University of California, Berkeley, March 15, 1973, available at https://nature.berkeley.edu/site/lectures/albright/1973.php.
5. For a more detailed description of this pioneering ongoing experiment, see Shrivastava and Kothari, 2012, Chapter 9.
6. Defined in the Merriam-Webster Dictionary as 'the making of articles by machine; mechanization'.
7. The term 'tools for conviviality', is from Illich, 1973.
8. See www.vikalpsangam.org for articles and case studies on these and other such initiatives.
9. For further information, see http://www.navdanya.org/organic-movement/organic-products, http://www.nirvaaha.com, http://www.aarohi.org, http://www.dastkarandhra.org, http://www.deccanherald.com/content/178372/youngistan-goes-desi-organic-clothing.html.
10. Cited in Srinivas and Shah, 1960.
11. The phrase comes from the title of J. C. Kumarappa's book, The Economy of Permanence, Sarva Seva Sangh Prakashan, Rajghat, Varanasi: 1984.

References

Basole, Amit (ed.), 2015, Lokvidya Perspectives: A Philosophy of Political Imagination for the Knowledge Age, New Delhi: Aakaar Books.

Dauvergne, Peter, 2008, The Shadows of Consumption, Cambridge: MIT Press.

Debroy, Bibek and P. D. Kaushik (ed.), 2005, Energising Rural Development through 'Panchayats', New Delhi: Academic Foundation.

Illich, Ivan, 1973, *Tools for Conviviality*, New York: Harper & Row.

Keynes, John Maynard, 1933, 'National Self-sufficiency', *Yale Review*, Vol. 22, no. 4 (June 1933), pp. 755-69.

Sahsrabudhey, Chitra, 2015, 'Lokvidya Approach to the Women's Movement: Women's Knowledge Holds the Key', in *Lokvidya Perspectives: A Philosophy of Political Imagination for the Knowledge Age*, Basole (ed.), pp. 185-207.

Shrivastava, Aseem and Ashish Kothari, 2012, *Churning the Earth: The Making of Global India*, New Delhi: Penguin Viking.

Srinivas, M. N. and A.M. Shah, 1960, 'The Myth of Self-Sufficiency of the Indian Village', *Economic & Political Weekly*, Volume 12 (37), 10 September, 1960, 1375-78, available at http://www.epw.in/system/files/pdf/1960_12/37/the_myth_of_selfsufficiency_of_the_indian_village.pdf (Last accessed in July, 2017).

Tagore, Rabindranath, 2007, 'The Robbery of the Soil', in *Tagore on Books*, New Delhi: Rupa, pp. 29-45.

Biomass-Based Rural Revitalization in Future India

K. J. Joy[1]

Summary

This essay discusses a distinctive approach to rural revitalisation of which biomass is at the core. The biomass based approach can tie together the livelihood and ecosystem needs, thus paving the way for rural revitalisation – both its economy and ecology. As a long term vision for rural India over the next 100 years or so, the essay posits that all the requirements to lead a good healthy life would be met primarily through renewable energy and materials, especially different forms of biomass. The first part of the vision is the primary production sector in which agriculture would be seen as part of a wider biomass production system. It would not only meet all the basic needs like food, fodder and fuel in kind without going through the market, but would also generate recyclable biomass that would go into the soil as throughput and also have three to five tons of surplus biomass per family that would feed into the decentralised agro-industrial production system. The second part of the vision is the decentralised agro-industrial production system in which the surplus biomass, other local materials like stone, clay, sand and renewable energy (wind, solar, small hydro) are brought together in the form of integrated production cum energy generation units (IPEUs). IPEUs would provide goods, income and electricity, thus paving the way for sustainable prosperity for all. The essay discusses an alternative set of biomass-based technologies in the areas of water, roads and buildings. The essay also cautions that this vision cannot be fully realised within the present system; its full potential can be realised only if it becomes part of the agenda for a radical social transformation.

The Context

Rural India is going through a multi-faceted crisis – a crisis characterised by both stagnation and widespread changes. These widespread changes over the last two-three decades are, in a way, contributing to the further deterioration of the lives and livelihoods of the vast majority of the rural people. The increasing number of farmers' suicides in different parts of India is the most telling evidence of this agrarian crisis.

An important indicator of the stagnation is the decreasing agricultural productivity. The euphoria over Green Revolution and its benefits has ended, with questions being asked about the sustainability of such a production system. There is already a talk about the need for a Second Green Revolution to take care of the ills of the first one.[2]

The relative share of agriculture and allied sectors in the overall economy and the Gross Capital Formation in Agriculture and allied sectors (GCFA) in relation to Gross Capital Formation (GCF) has been declining. GCFA in relation to GCF, at constant prices, declined from 24.7 per cent in 1950-51 to 6.7 per cent in 2007–08 (Planning Commission of India, undated).

We are into what is described as jobless growth. From 1994 to 2005, when the economy grew by about 5-6 per cent, the employment growth turned negative (-0.3 per cent). Along with this, there is informalization of the work force, imbalanced growth between sectors and stagnation of real wages (Shrivastava and Kothari, 2012).

There is relatively unchanging levels of rural poverty during the 1990s' (Datt, 1999) and as a result of agricultural stagnation increasing numbers of employable people in the villages are migrating to urban areas (Gupta, 2005).

The increasing frequency and scale of drought is a matter of concern. The 2015-16 droughts affected more than 330 million people in more than 250 thousand villages of 266 districts from 11 states in India (Singh and Pilla, 2016). Despite all the dams built and irrigation systems developed we as a nation have not been able to drought proof the country. The same story goes with floods. These are going to be further exacerbated by climate change.

Amongst the many changes that are taking place in rural India, the following three are especially important from the point of view of this paper. They are:

- The significant changes in the land use, especially the conversion of both cropped and non-cropped lands into non-agricultural uses, since the mid 80s' and early 90s'. During 1991-2011 more than 3 million ha of cultivable land have been lost while the net cultivated area has reduced by 658,000 ha. Large decreases have been reported in the case of permanent pastures and grazing lands, and culturable wastelands during the same period (Directorate of Economic and Statistics DoA & C, MoA, GoI, as cited in Samuel and Joy, 2015). These changes have significant impacts on the livelihood of the rural poor – mainly landless, herders, dalits, and marginal rain-fed famers. It also impacts a 'balanced' land use that is required for environmental sustainability as these lands are not only livelihood spaces for the rural poor but also ecological spaces performing certain ecological functions within the overall landscape (Samuel and Joy, 2015).

• The change in the agrarian relations and occupational patterns, as the population engaged in agriculture as primary livelihood source is receding. While the share of workers engaged in farming (cultivators and agricultural labourers) has come down by 12.6 per cent in 1991-2011, there is a perceptible increase in the number of non agricultural labour, especially casual labour. Another striking aspect is the decline in 'farmers/cultivators' by about 15 per cent for the same period (Government of India, 2016). Less than one third of the rural households earn a livelihood through cultivation while more than half of the households' main source of livelihood is manual, casual labour (*ibid.*, 2016) showing a relatively high level of proletarianization. About 27 per cent of farmers did not like farming because it was not profitable. Nearly 40 per cent felt that, given a choice, they would take up some other career (NSSO, 2003).

• The changing aspirations of the rural population, especially the younger generation, who are not tied to the land and whose aspirations are different from those previously considered as part of rural farming life. The rural development strategy needs to take account of these changing rural aspirations. Unless we acknowledge and engage with this issue, the task of attracting the new generation to agriculture and biomass based livelihood options would remain a serious challenge.

One of the important signs of rural stagnation and an indication of the crisis is the decreasing trend in the primary productivity of the ecosystem, which is the productivity that we get without the use of inputs external to that ecosystem. Secondary productivity is that which we get through the use of exogenous inputs like applied water, chemical fertilisers, pesticides, and so on. The total productivity of an ecosystem is the combination of the two. There are now evidences that the increased productivity that is reported is very often the function of secondary productivity. Even to sustain the same level of productivity the farmers have to use increasing doses of chemical fertilisers. Though going completely organic or managing our agriculture on the basis of local, renewable resources could be our long term vision, as a transitional strategy we could use exogenous resources, provided such inputs are used in a manner that leads to an enhancement of *primary* productivity of an ecosystem. Low External Input Sustainable Agriculture (LEISA)[3] is a good example of such a strategy.

Rural development strategies and programmes often stop at agriculture and have no systemic connections with the industrial scenario they may propose. Being a young nation the number of persons seeking independent livelihoods would increase significantly over the next few decades and only agriculture and other primary sectors may not be able to ensure livelihoods to these new entrants. Thus we need an approach that can combine and integrate primary sectors like agriculture with a dispersed, decentralised industrial system – basically a transition to an agro-industrial society.[4]

We discuss here a distinctive approach to rural revitalisation of which biomass is at the core. There are many distinctive features of this alternative approach and it is difficult to capture them in a single descriptive term, though we often call it a biomass based approach. These distinctive features include: the way it approaches equity issues and access to resources, its approach to agriculture and allied production as biomass production, the way it approaches the problem of the large and the small and of the local and the exogenous resources, the way it approaches the problem of combining judiciously renewable and non-renewable sources of energy and materials, the way it sees the issue of people's participation and empowerment including knowledge and lastly the problem of dispersed industry and non-farm incomes.[5]

The biomass based approach can tie together the livelihood and ecosystem needs, thus paving the way for rural revitalisation – both its economy and ecology.

Biomass as the Main Provider of our Needs

What is biomass?

Biomass refers to the total mass of all living beings/things within an ecosystem. Life is organised as part of a food chain where photosynthetic activity of the primary producers produces the total amount of food in the ecosystem that regulates the number of organisms that can live within the ecosystem. For our purposes, therefore, we use the term biomass to mean the sum total of all vegetative matter – photosynthetic biomass – produced in the ecosystem. All parts of a plant are biomass and not merely the harvestable portion (Figure 1).

Figure 1: Biomass and its various components

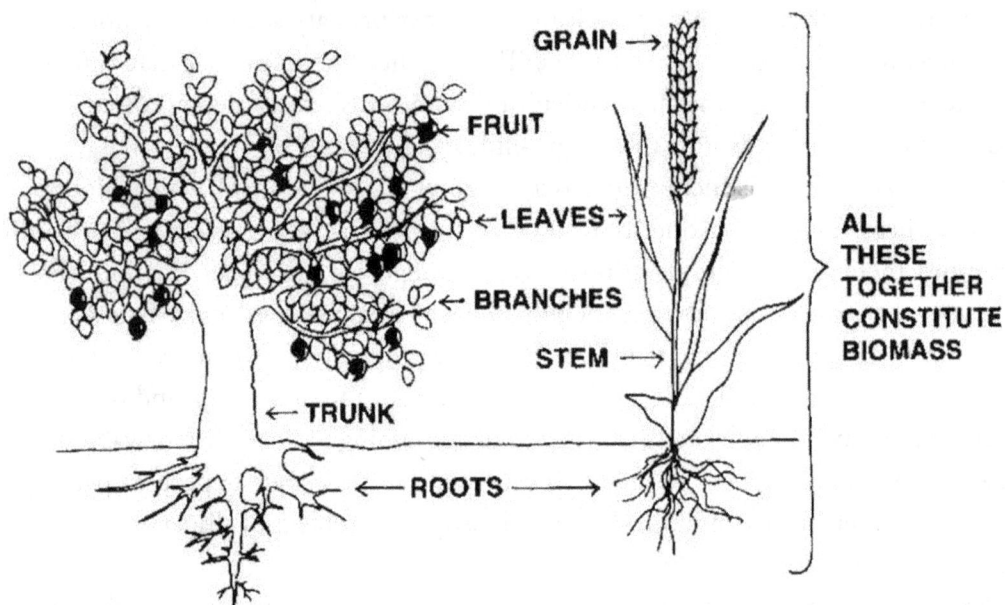

GRAIN →
FRUIT
←LEAVES→
←BRANCHES
STEM →
← TRUNK
←ROOTS→
ALL THESE TOGETHER CONSTITUTE BIOMASS

Source: Paranjape and Joy, 1995, pp. 84

Biomass production and ecosystem productivity in relation to human needs have two distinct but related aspects: potential biomass productivity and its partitioning. Potential biomass productivity represents the total photosynthetic biomass produced within the system while partitioning of this biomass into different products gives us different use values. Potential biomass productivity depends on the sum total of ecosystem relationships and is determined by factors like soil conditions and moisture holding capacity, the total water regime within the ecosystem, and the amount of biomass and nutrients that flow and re-circulate through the ecosystem. The realization of this potential biomass productivity and its partition into different use values is a much more individual matter, depending on species selection, crop and water management, nutrient management, etc (Paranjape and Joy, 1995, Datye *et al.*, 1997, Joy, 1999).

Biomass has been the main provider of human societies: some biomass is consumed directly in the form of food, some used indirectly (as fuel, fodder) and some biomass is sold in the market to meet cash income needs (or also processed for value addition).

Biomass and livelihood needs

In this approach a typical farmer family of five members can meet all its needs – food, fodder, fuel, recyclable biomass for the agriculture system and some surplus biomass for cash income – if it can either produce or get access to about 18 tons (T) of biomass (dry weight[6]) in a year: food and allied needs 2 T, firewood 2 T, fodder 5 T, recyclable biomass 6 T and biomass for cash income 3 T (Figure 2).

Figure 2: Biomass needs of a family of five members

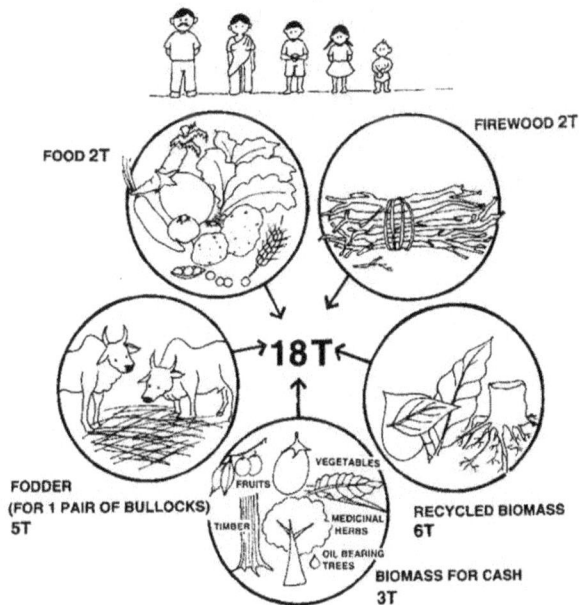

FOOD 2T

FIREWOOD 2T

18T

FODDER
(FOR 1 PAIR OF BULLOCKS)
5T

FRUITS
VEGETABLES
TIMBER
MEDICINAL HERBS
OIL BEARING TREES

RECYCLED BIOMASS
6T

BIOMASS FOR CASH
3T

Source: Paranjape and Joy, 1995, pp. 86

The above estimate is in line with a reasonable upper bound approach (keeping higher values than actually required) with ample scope for optimisation. For example, if the cattle herd is rationalised and two families share one pair of bullocks, about 2.5 T in fodder can be saved[7]. Similarly if the families can shift to fuel efficient devices and methods then part of the biomass earmarked for fuel could be saved; part of it can go back to the soil as throughput and the remaining can be added to the surplus biomass of 3 T. Thus we can safely say that each family can produce a surplus biomass of the order of 3 to 5 T.

This surplus biomass can be handled in a variety of ways. The conventional way is to produce this as perishable commodities like vegetables, fruits or other forms of high value agriculture produce and sell these to meet cash requirements. Efforts are also made to process and turn them into consumer products. However, if this surplus biomass is produced in the form of small dimension timber, bamboo, fibre, oils, medicinal plants, then an additional variety of marketable products become possible. This option has great significance for value addition, thus generating significant non-farm incomes to rural communities.

Biomass Based Future for Rural India

Towards a biomass based rural India

The long term vision for rural India is that over the next 100 years or so, all the requirements to lead a good healthy life would be met primarily through renewable energy and materials, especially different forms of biomass. Here there is a case to learn from the USA, an economy based primarily on fossil energy, reached the threshold around 1970, when its quality of life could not keep pace with economic development (Figure 3). It is in this context the biomass based vision becomes crucial not only for rural India but also urban India, which is consuming materials and energy in volumes from fossil sources at a rapid pace.

Figure 3: Trends in Gross National Product and Sustainable Economic Welfare in the USA, an economy based on fossil energy

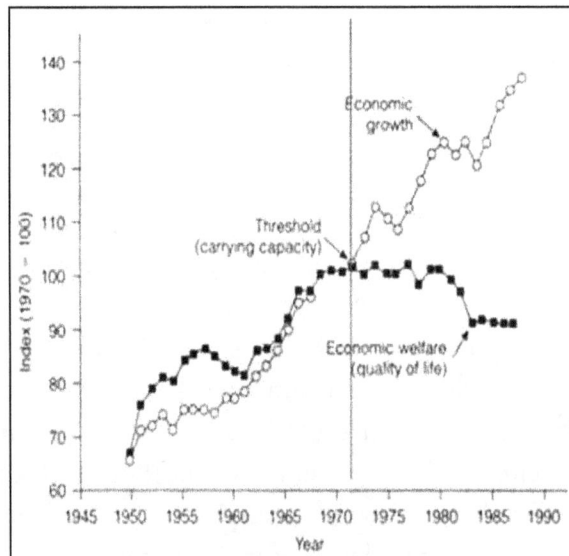

Source: Odum and Barrett, 2005 (The graph is reproduced from Gore, 2014)

The vision has two components. The first is the primary production sector in which agriculture would be seen as part of a wider biomass production system, as described earlier. Here the emphasis is to meet all the basic needs like food, fodder and fuel in kind without going through the market at the scale of a micro-watershed/village or at the most at the level of a cluster of villages. The second part of the vision is the decentralised agro-industrial production system in which the surplus biomass, other local materials like stone, clay, sand and renewable energy (wind, solar, small hydro) are brought together in the form of integrated production cum energy generation units (IPEUs). IPEUs would provide goods, income and electricity.[8]

The land and water sectors would be completely restructured. Every household that depends on land and water for its livelihoods would get sufficient quantities of water to produce the required biomass as part of an equitable water distribution system. All these households would also get access to land with tenurial security and this could take different forms like land re-distribution, collectivization and produce sharing arrangements. Similarly the local communities would have control over the local resources like water bodies, forests, minor minerals like clay, sand, stones, etc. The first take on land, water and other local resources would be to meet basic needs. Land which is not suitable for crop production would be devoted to bulk biomass production (small dimension timber,[9] bamboo, fibres, resins, oils).

There would be two basic organisations. The first one is around biomass production consisting of all households with a support system to take up scientific, socially just and sustainable land and water use planning and use, to take up production of organic inputs and so on. The second one is around the biomass based industrial production system and this would primarily consist of the present resource poor sections such as dalits, agriculture labourers, artisans and women.

IPEUs would be set up at the scale of a cluster of villages. Surplus biomass would be pooled and made available to IPEUs. The local educational and research institutions such as high schools, agricultural colleges, *Krishi Vigyan Kendras* (Agricultural Science Centres) industrial training institutes, engineering colleges and also experienced persons from the community would be drawn into the programme to form resource groups to take up resource literacy campaigns, capability building programmes and also to provide the necessary support systems.

The departure point of the vision presented here is that it does not limit itself to subsistence alone. Sustainable use of land and water is seen in the context of creating a base for a transition to a dispersed agro-industrial society with sustainable resource use and technologies based primarily on biomass, local materials and renewable energy. This vision includes a strategic and judicious use of non-renewable energy and inputs with a possibility of tapering down the use of non-renewables as advances are made in the renewable sectors. It tries to go beyond the polarised discourse of small vs. large, local vs. exogenous, decentralised vs. centralised. It calls for a radically different relationship between these binaries. The emphasis is on the local and decentralised sources and the inputs/resources from the exogenous sources are used to supplement and further strengthen the local resources and not replace them.

Biomass as energy efficient material

The key resource in this transition is the biomass surplus of the order of 3 to 5 T generated per family. Biomass is not simply food and other useful products; it is also energy (encapsulated solar energy). The alternative approach views all materials as energy. For example, let us take the case of cement. Anything between three to five kilograms of coal equivalent energy are required to produce one kilo of cement. Thus use of one kilo of cement is equivalent to the use of about three to five kilograms of coal equivalent energy. Here biomass has a great role in bringing about energy savings. There is a range of technologies that the alternative approach identifies, or has developed, that can bring about significant savings in energy input as materials. The comparison of engineering properties of renewable materials like teak wood, pole wood and bamboo with non-renewables like mild and high tensile steel show that, at current prices and for equivalent performance, pole wood is almost as strong as mild steel and bamboo is superior to high tensile alloy steel (Gore, 2014).

Biomass may be utilised as fuel, as structural material or as a chemical feedstock serving as an alternative route to petroleum based products. Examples are use of dung and residues for biogas, bamboo grids and mats as reinforcement for road bases and surfaces, and cassava used to produce ethanol as additive to petrol, respectively. In each of these uses energy is saved. In terms of coal equivalents, the energy saved when biomass is used as structural material roughly ranges from two to four times its weight, and five or more times its weight when used as substitute for petroleum derived products. If only we treat biomass as energy and actively include it in our energy and local resource use planning, many more options of farm and non-farm incomes become visible. In fact it opens up an alternative pathway to a dispersed industrial society (Paranjape and Joy, 1995; Datye *et al.*, 1997; SOPPECOM, 2007).

As mentioned earlier, the approach does not eschew the use of inputs coming from exogenous and non-renewable sources. However, in the long term, some of the non-renewables like steel and metals could be replaced by carbon fibres and ceramics. In most of the structural applications that are discussed here, biomass is used in combination with other materials like cement and steel – what we could call as composites. In the case of structural applications of biomass, the composites comprise steel, cement (also reinforced soil) and pole wood. Reinforced soil or cement take compressive loads, wood takes tensile loads and steel provides the confinement and connections to bring about composite action. Each of the materials is optimally used for the function it carries out best. The result is a structural or load bearing member or product that matches performance but reduces cement and steel consumption by an order of five or more (SOPPECOM, 2007). Through such replacement and blending, direct energy inputs as well as energy-intensive material input into infrastructure can be drastically reduced as summarised in the table below.

Table 1: Comparison of Conventional Infrastructure Material with Alternate Material

Conventional infrastructure material	Alternate material
Cement	Addition of 15 per cent colloidal silica to cement enhances its strength by a factor of five. Silica could be obtained by controlled burning of rice husk
Steel and metals	Structural components replaced by composites of timber/bamboo, steel wire and cement. Future replacement by carbon fibres, ceramics
Fuels and petrochemicals	Biomass based fuels such as alcohol, biogas, etc., Materials derived from biomass directly
Bricks and concrete	Soil used in conjunction with cement, fly ash, lime, fibres and bamboo for reinforcement. Fuel efficient bricks made from lime and fly ash using solar process can replace concrete

Source: Datye et al., 1997

One of the questions often asked is, where would the biomass come from? Will it not lead to deforestation? Will it impact food security? The biomass that is talked about here is basically in the form of small dimension timber (diameters of the order of 75 to 100 mm), bamboo and fibres of different types. The small dimension timber requires only about five to seven years to reach the usable size and could be produced as part of short rotation forestry under the integrated watershed development, wasteland development and social forestry programmes. It is observed that farmers have a tendency to bring under cultivation even land which is not suitable for shallow rooted, short duration crops as a coping mechanism against drought. With limited but assured water for agriculture the farmers would be able to produce much more from much smaller areas, thus releasing agriculturally non-productive lands (with shallow soils, medium and high slopes), for growing other types of biomass like trees, shrubs, grasses. Fibres like agave, jute, pineapple, can be grown as an under storey (in a multi tiered canopy system) and also can be grown on bunds. Many of the tree species are also amenable to coppicing. Thus a radically different approach to land and water use is the basis of the biomass based rural revitalisation vision presented here.

The defining characteristics of these technologies

Conventional infrastructure technology, by and large, is characterised by:
- Use of highly energy intensive materials and processes
- Very limited use of local materials and resources
- Very small share of local employment and incomes

(Paranjape and Joy, 1995; Datye *et al.*, 1997; Joy, 1999)

The biomass based future presented in this essay relies on a radically different set of technologies which can reverse the above three characteristics. These are characterized by:
- Equal performance or function as compared to the conventional technology
- Equal or reduced cost
- Energy saving and reduction of non-renewable energy consumed typically by a factor of five or more
- Significantly higher use of local labour and materials generating substantial employment and incomes to the local population
- Amenability to modular design, fabrication/ manufacturing in dispersed rural industries and on site assembly
- Opportunities for local skill upgradation and development that have the potential to go beyond the skills imposed by caste traditions

Income generation and energy saving potential

Each kg of biomass material in typical construction applications is expected to earn an income between Rs. 2 and 3 per kg for the biomass producer and add value of up to Rs. 10 per kg, of which Rs. 7 are expected to accrue to the workers. It has thus the potential of opening up wider avenues of livelihood opportunities for the rural poor and the landless if biomass pools are formed and are provided preferential access to them (SOPPECOM, 2007). However, if we take into account the value addition potential of small dimension timber and bamboo in combination with other processable materials like fibre, local clay products, soil blocks, etc., the total income generation can go up to Rs. 12,000/T. If we estimate each ton of wood is equivalent to 700 kWh, then the estimated minimum energy saving of 3,500 kWh/T of biomass processed and used in infrastructure as minimum energy replacement value is about the order of five.

We could treat these as minimum values because the energy saving and income generation involved in other uses of processed biomass like medicinal herbs, natural pesticides, non-edible and edible oils, chemicals like resins and other intermediaries are much higher.

Integrated production cum energy-generation units

The full potential of biomass based processing and value addition would unfold if we combine this with renewable energy sources like solar, wind, small hydro, etc. Energy is required for processing both as heat and as electricity.

An important departure point from the conventional discourse around renewable energy is that the alternative mostly talks of hybrid or cogeneration systems like solar-bio-fuel and wind-hydro systems as they can take care of some of the limitations of single sources, especially the variation in availability (Paranjape and Joy, 1995). The renewable energy sources create dispersed availability of energy and it is important to note that this is a dispersal of productive potential and not merely a dispersal of consumption.[10]

Now the most important issue is: what would be the organisational form that would hold together both these industrial activities – processing of biomass and renewable energy generation – under one roof? The proposition is to set up integrated production-cum-energy generation units (IPEU) for this (Paranjape and Joy, 1995 and Datye et al., 1997). To quote from Paranjape and Joy (1995):

'IPEU is a renewable energy facility that provides energy production and biomass processing in a single workplace-cum-production unit. The advantages of such a system are obvious: on-line waste heat recovery enhances the performance of the energy facility and also provides substantially widened possibilities of income generation through biomass processing. The IPEUs can be sustained if a biomass pool is formed by the people in a local area and it is prioritised for use by the resource poor in the region. In effect, we are suggesting that the renewable resources (biomass) as well as energy facility and the IPEUs be treated as common properties to be utilised in accordance with the idea of the distinction between basic and economic service[11]. In other words, their first use should be stabilisation and expansion of livelihoods and only later or after that should they be used for economic gain' (pp. 150).

The implications of the dispersed energy availability created through IPEUs could be gauged if we compare the potential they create with the international levels of energy consumption and also projections about the energy required for a dignified life. The pre-second World War levels of energy consumption of advanced countries were of the order of 4000 kgoe (kilogram of oil equivalent). More than half of this is accounted by domestic/office heating and transportation. In India, by and large, other than in some regions such as higher Himalaya and Trans-Himalaya, there is no need of such heating, and transportation needs would also be greatly reduced in the type of dispersed agro-industrial society described here. Thus we could safely say that the desirable component of pre-World War standard of living in the advanced countries is more appropriately represented by a per capita consumption level of about 2000 kgoe. The alternative scenario, with vibrant IPEUs all over, creates a production potential of 2400 kgoe per capita. This means that the alternative scenario has the potential of realising more than the desirable component of pre-World War standard of living (Paranjape and Joy, 1995; Datye et al., 1997). There are studies that indicate that an energy availability of 1200 to 1800 kgoe per capita would be required if one has to lead a dignified human life (Prayas, 2015, as quoted by Hande et al., in this volume).

One of the underlying principles of this approach is to treat all ecosystem resources as common property resources and their prioritisation for the livelihood needs of the resource poor. For example it is assumed that the surplus biomass would be pooled and made available to the resource poor families for further processing. This would call for a double movement – one on the part of the state in terms of enabling policies, legislations and resource allocations and the other on the part of the people and peoples' movements to recognise the importance of these ecosystem resources and organise people so that they can manage the ecosystem resources in a sustainable, equitable and democratic manner.

The ecosystem resources could be grouped into: i) land and water, ii) biomass resources which are pooled, iii) other local processable and renewable materials like clay, sand, wastes, etc. and iv) renewable energy facilities and IPEUs. Though there has been considerable experience of institutions around individual resources like water users' associations, joint forest management committees (also community managed forests), watershed committees and farmers producer companies, there has not been much experience or thinking about integrated institutional forms which can manage the four types of ecosystem resources mentioned above. At the moment we can only say that we need not go for a single institutional form – there could be a range of institutional options like cooperatives, thrift groups, registered societies, unions, or even non-profit and joint stock companies so long as they incorporate process of effective regulation by the community to bring about sustainable use, priority allocation to the resource poor and all done in a participatory, democratic manner.

Application of these Technologies

Over the last twenty five to thirty years there have been serious attempts to develop biomass based, energy saving technologies and apply them on the ground. These technologies are based on preservative treated small dimension timber and bamboo, natural fibres and fabrics, and on biomass derived feedstock.

Infrastructure (more specifically construction) and energy are the two sectors chosen for the development of these technologies. Infrastructure is an important precondition as well as concomitant of development. Since these technologies are mostly based on local materials, a major portion of the expenditure accrues as income to the rural people.

Water, buildings and roads are the main sectors where considerable progress has been made. Alternative technologies are now available covering a wide range of applications.[12]

Water

Wood – bamboo technologies in the water sector include reinforced soil/rock fill constructions and gabion structures for dams and water harvesting (both overflow and non-overflow structures) and storage structures. Reinforced soil embankments are used for erosion and landslide control, flood control and lining systems including filters for seepage control of farm ponds, raw water reservoirs and channels. The first timber gabion structure, which could withstand more than three feet overflow on a sustained basis, was built on Ghantia Nala in Dhenkanal, Odisha way back in the 1980s'. The locally available pole wood and stones were used to construct the structure by the local people (Paranjape *et al.*, 1998).

**Figure 4: Timber gabion on Ghantia Nala: under
construction and structure taking overflow**

Source: Vilas Gore

Timber gabions could be an alternative to cement-concrete check dams in the watershed development programmes. In watershed development programmes most of the expenses are made on check dams and if there is a policy direction that promotes the use of local material then it opens up an enormous productive avenue for the rural toilers.

Buildings

Engineered bamboo technologies in this sector include one and two storey residential buildings, community buildings and offices with large spans and building products (beams, trusses, roof slab elements, doors, windows). One of the important innovations is the replacement of steel beams with treated timber and bamboo. The column is a timber-concrete composite one. Saving in concrete is about 75 per cent in the beam design. Steel is replaced by about twice its weight of small dimension timber (Datye *et al.,* 1997). The collaboration between the SOPPECOM/SARMET group[13] and the Inspiration group in Kochi – a team of innovative architects – brought structural stability and aesthetics together. The result has been the beautiful two-storey office building of Inspiration near Kochi.

Figure 5: Two-storey office building of Inspiration near Kochi

Source: Vilas Gore

Roads

Roads are a part of a system which includes flexible pavements, rigid pavements, approach embankments for bridges, and flyovers, and road drainage. In India, the flexible pavements made up of 'stone base with asphalt surface' are virtually getting replaced by the rigid concrete pavements. This is a matter of great concern as the concrete pavements, besides being energy intensive, are low on riding comfort and safety. Asphaltic roads are preferred in the developed nations except for exceptionally heavily loaded pavements on weak soil sub grades. Advances in the technologies the world over have improved the performance of flexible (asphaltic) pavements. The improved asphalt road pavements are virtually free of damages by rutting and pothole damage. The advances include use of high performance synthetic grid reinforcement to strengthen road base, mat reinforcement (example, the glass fibre mat) to strengthen asphalt surfacing as well as synthetic geo-textiles (polypropylene, polyester) for the separation and improved drainage.

There is a great potential for use of biomass based engineered materials in flexible pavements in India. Preservative treated bamboo grids and mats provide a perfect replacement for synthetic plastic grids and glass fibre mats. Composites of natural geo-textiles (jute coir, banana fibres) and synthetic geo-textile would replace synthetic geo-textile for separation and drainage. The efficacy of bamboo grids and natural fabric was well demonstrated for an access road to the truck terminal in a pilot project at CIDCO, Navi Mumbai (*ibid.*). A surfacing of burnt brick/clay tile with a seal coat of asphalt with bamboo strip reinforcement will also be able to withstand the rutting action of bullock cart wheels, a major problem in the rural areas.

Figure 6: Bamboo grid road base reinforcement

Source: Vilas Gore

Contrary to roads in India, where concrete structures have replaced asphalt pavements, fortunately the approach embankments in energy and cost intensive Reinforced Cement Concrete (RCC) have been replaced by reinforced soil embankments. The reinforced soil embankment walls are constructed with synthetic grids and concrete block facia. Here again, there is a great potential of replacing synthetic grids with bamboo grids and pole wood as facings.

Figure 7: Bamboo retaining wall

Source: Vilas Gore

Advances in other areas

In the 1990s' a group of thermal power engineers at Deep Nagar (Bhusaval, Maharashtra) led by the late Ramesh Borole developed an interesting model of solar parabolic collector that could produce industry quality heat. This was a major breakthrough because till then solar energy was primarily used for cooking and heating water. This opened up a different pathway as this energy could be used in many different ways in the dispersed agro-industrial system.

Significant advances have been made over the last couple of decades, globally and in India, around development of dispersed renewable energy sources. There have also been significant developments in the areas of liquid bio-fuels. All these are welcome developments and can aid in the full blossoming of a dispersed agro-industrial system going beyond subsistence, to the path of sustainable prosperity of all.

Limits, Issues and the Way Forward

In this concluding section we discuss some of the critical limitations of the work done so far and also put forward certain suggestions for the realisation of the vision presented here.

1. Though various components, elements and specific technologies have been piloted in different locations, all of them have not been brought together under one umbrella as an IPEU. This work needs to be done and only then we would have a full understanding of all that it takes to function as an integrated system – both technically and socially/organisationally.

2. Though fair amount of work has been done on the technology front, probably the same cannot be said about the organisational components. Of course work has been carried out under different situations and in collaboration with different types of organizations – people's movements, NGOs, educational institutions and commercial ventures. The main issue is how we can bring together the producers of biomass and those who would be putting in their labour to process the biomass. Also there are institutional issues related to pooling of surplus biomass – how to do it, on what terms, how this can be made available to the resource poor, etc. Then there is the issue of mobilising technical and managerial support to the organisation.

3. It calls for a radical restructuring of land and water use. For example equitable access to water to all those who depend on land and water for their livelihoods is a precondition. Similarly access and tenurial security to land in one form or the other is another precondition. A more rational and sustainable land use policy also needs to be in place.

4. There are larger political economy questions that need to be addressed. The present day subsidies very much favour the fossil material and fuel based technologies. This needs to change and more favourable conditions need to be offered to the type of technologies that we have discussed. Climate change offers us a sufficient rationale for such a shift. Also, the government needs to make a conscious policy decision of shifting to such technologies in a phased manner. Employment guarantee schemes could be re-oriented to take care of the labour component of such ventures in the initial phase.

5. Research and development (R&D) and skill development of the rural poor is another area that needs urgent attention. This calls for a re-orientation of the scientific establishment in the country. Similarly, local technical institutions like the Industrial Training Institutes, polytechnics, engineering colleges, could be involved in the skill development of the rural people in a continuing education mode. Similarly there is a

need to create widespread facilities for treating biomass. In the absence of treatment facilities very often people cannot get access to the material required on time and also at an affordable cost. It also involves long distance transport that could negate the energy savings of the alternatives.

6. Changes in technology choices can come about if there is a social demand for such technologies. Here various movements and civil society organisations can play a crucial role. For example, as part of the rehabilitation of project affected persons, the government is supposed to build houses and other infrastructure facilities at the rehabilitation sites. The movements of the project affected persons could take up the demand that these infrastructure facilities be created using the alternative technology options.

Finally there is also the issue of what is possible and what is not, within the constraints of the capitalist system or social relations characterised primarily by class, caste and patriarchy. Though it is true that the present system may allow us to make incremental changes and also to experiment with some of the components of the alternative approach, there should not be any illusions that the integrated alternative which is embedded on the core values of equity, social justice, sustainability and democratisation can be generalized within the present system. It is important that the various social movements working on different issues and with diverse social sections need to engage with the issues detailed in the essay and make them part of the agenda for a radical social transformation.

Endnotes

1. This essay is primarily based on the following sources: Datye, 1997; Paranjape and Joy, 1995; Joy, 1999; Reports and notes of Vilas Gore. The overall approach/vision and specific ideas presented here have evolved over a long period of time and that too, with the efforts of many individuals and organizations. The late K. R. Datye, a visionary, led as well as held together this search. Vilas Gore and Suhas Paranjape contributed significantly to the development as well as grounding of this approach. Society for Promoting Participative Ecosystem Management (SOPPECOM) and Society for Advancement of Research in Materials and Energy Technologies (SARMET) provided the institutional space. I am thankful to Vilas Gore for his inputs.

2. Pl. also see Food and Agriculture Futures essay in this volume.

3. See for details, Reijntes, C., B. Haverkort and A. Water-Bayer, 1992.

4. Pl. also see Localisation and Concluding essays in this volume.

5. For details see Paranjape and Joy, 1995, and Datye *et al.*, 1997.

6. Biomass weight is always given as dry weight as it helps to compare different types of biomass.

7. In fact, with advances in the cattle/goat management techniques such as the Mukta Sanchar Gotha (controlled open grazing) with hydroponics and azola to produce green fodder, even five farmers can come together to set up a unit of 10 animals and 20 poultry birds (*Source*: Notes from Vilas Gore).

8. In this essay we concentrate only on the biomass part of the dispersed agro-industrial production system as the primary sector of agriculture; the aspects related to renewable energy have been dealt with by other essays in this volume – in Mansata *et al.,* and Hande *et al.,* respectively.

9. Small dimension timber is essentially pole wood grown on bunds and lands not suited to food crop production and can be harvested within a relatively short duration of five to seven years.

10. Pl. also see Energy Futures essay in this volume.

11. This distinction between basic service and economic service is much more fully developed – both as a concept as well as in practice – in the case of water and it is closely related to equitable distribution of water. It makes a distinction between two types of water services. The first is the *basic service* that includes water required to meet basic needs like drinking and other domestic water needs (including sanitation and hygiene needs), water for livestock, and water for livelihood activities. The second is the extra, *economic service* over and above the basic service for surplus generation. For details see Paranjape and Joy, 1995.

12. For details about the technologies (designs, materials, cots, etc.) under discussion please see Datye *et al.,* 1997 especially pp. 175 to 189.

13. Primarily Vilas Gore and his team.

References

Datt, Gaurav, 1999, 'Has Poverty Declined since Economic Reforms?' *Economic & Political Weekly*, Volume No. 34 (50) December 11, pp. 3516 – 18.

Datye, K. R. (assisted by Suhas Paranjape and K. J. Joy), 1997, *Banking on Biomass: A New Strategy for Sustainable Prosperity Based on Renewable Energy and Dispersed Industrialisation*, Ahmedabad: Centre for Environment Education.

Gore, Vilas, 2014, Presentation to post graduate architectural students at CEPT, Ahmedabad, 2 March.

Government of India, 2016, *Socio Economic and Caste Census, 2011, Available at* http://secc2011.nic.in/ (Last accessed 29 April, 2017).

Gupta, Dipankar, 2005, 'Wither the Indian Village: Culture and Agriculture in 'Rural' India, *Economic & Political Weekly*, Volume No. 40, (8), 19 February, pp. 751-58.

Hande, Harish, Vivek Shastry, Rachita Misra, 'Energy Futures in India', this volume.

Joy K. J., 1999, 'Biomass-based Production System: An Alternative Approach to Livelihoods' in *Challenges of Agriculture in the 21st Century*, G. M. Pillai (ed.), Dr. Panjabrao Deshmukh Birth Centenary

Memorial Volume, Pune: Maharashtra Council of Agricultural Education and Research (MCAER).

NSSO, 2003, *NSS 59ᵗʰ Round, Situation Analysis of Farmers*, New Delhi: Ministry of Statistics and Programme Implementation, Govt. of India.

Odum, Eugene and Gary W. Barrett, 2005 (5th edition), *Fundamentals of Ecology*, New Delhi: Cengage Learning Publications.

Paranjape, Suhas and K. J. Joy, 1995, *Sustainable Technology: Making the Sardar Sarovar Project Viable – A Comprehensive Proposal to Modify the Project for Greater Equity and Ecological Sustainability*, Ahmedabad: Centre for Environment Education.

Paranjape, Suhas, K. J. Joy, Terry Machado, Ajaykumar Varma, S. Swaminathan, 1998, *Watershed Development: A Source Book*, New Delhi: Bharat Gyan Vigyan Samithi

Planning Commission of India, Undated, 'Data Bank on Agriculture and Allied Sectors', http://planningcommission.gov.in/sectors/agri_html/DataBank.html (last accessed 19 February, 2016).

Reijntes, C., B. Haverkort and A. Water-Bayer, 1992, *Farming for the Future: An Introduction to Low-External-Input and Sustainable Agriculture*, Leusden: Macmillan

Samuel, Abraham and K. J. Joy, 2015, *Changing Land Use, Agrarian Context and Rural Transformation: Implications for Watershed Development*, an extended version of a presentation made during the felicitation conference in honour of Prof. Ramaswamy Iyer in November 2014 at New Delhi [The paper is part of the forthcoming Routledge volume].

Shankar, Vijay, 2016, 'Going Against the Grain', *The Hindu*, 5 February.

Shrivastava, Aseem and Ashish Kothari, 2012, *Churning the Earth: The Making of Global India,* New Delhi: Viking/Penguin Books.

Singh, Ashish and Raghu Pilla, 2016, 'Indian Drought 2015-16: Lessons To Be Learnt', *Counter Currents,* available at: http://www.countercurrents.org/2016/08/27/indian-drought-2015-16-lessons-to-be-learnt/ (last accessed 16 February, 2017).

SOPPECOM, 2007, 'Sarvangin Grameen Abhivruddhisathi Parivarthanachi Paryayi Disha', (article in Marathi), *Samaj Prabodhan Patrika*, Issue 180, October-November, pp. 472-77.

Dare to Dream

M. P. Parameswaran

Summary

This is a vision yet to be realized, but more and more people are thinking on these lines. Pseudo needs or greed manufactured by capitalism, once recognized as such, are to be rejected. Development is increase in the quality of life, including increased longevity with reduced morbidity and increased socially available leisure. Only cooperation can result in this, requiring small self-governing communities. In Kerala a Village Panchayat of 25,000 population and 25-30 sq.km area can become such a community. This essay describes the steps contemplated by one such community to take effective control of its basic natural resources (soil, water and sunlight) and connect them with all local human resources to bring down its ecological footprint by factor of four and still make it fully self sufficient in calories, proteins, vitamins, minerals and fat. The community will equip itself to produce almost all the industrial goods of day to day consumption. They decide, to begin with, to boycott all the goods and services advertised in the media, knowing this will not impair their health. They also know that collective community social security is cheaper and more reliable than individual, commercial insurance. They realise that all of humanity has to become a horizontal network of networks, comprised of self-reliant and increasingly self-sufficient Rurban Republics.

Year 2047

We are celebrating hundred years of independence of my country – India. I am forty years old and live in a 'rurban' area in Kerala, called 'M'. It was a suburban village of a medium city. My grandparents were young when India gained freedom from the British rule a century ago. They used to tell me about the first Independence Day celebration when our first Prime Minister Jawaharlal Nehru made the historic midnight speech about our 'tryst with destiny'. That destiny, subsequently, proved to be an unwholesome one. But Mahatma

Gandhi dreamed about an India which is a large network of self-sufficient, self-reliant village republics. India itself will become a part of horizontally linked Global Network of Self Reliant Local Republics.[1] In his dream humans were not slaves of machines; but the other way round. Production was to be to satisfy needs and not to gratify greed. He dreamed of a political structure with an inverted power pyramid, with the Local Self Government, the Panchayat, as the most powerful element and not the Parliament. He dreamed of an India wherein people are their own masters and not the market.

But others had different dreams, especially Nehru and his colleagues in power. They dreamt of an India, industrialized and modernized, with ever larger enterprises and cities and dams to be worshipped as modern temples. In 1948 Gandhiji was assassinated by a member of an incipient Hindu fascist organization. Gandhiji's dream was rejected even earlier. The rulers in the newly independent India, embarked upon a process of development based on the experience of Capitalist Europe and Socialist Soviet Union. Politically it was to be a federal India, but in actuality the power got concentrated in the Centre, in the hands of fewer and fewer people. Socialism was only a false façade and was discarded soon. Decades of capitalist development brought the country to the brink of an economic, political, social, cultural and philosophical collapse. Fascism was gaining ascendance.

Resistance movements, both political and social, were gathering momentum; people began to realize that the current path of development will lead us to total destruction. They went back to Gandhi and Marx, found in them clear ideas for building a new society based on the experience gained so far. To begin with it was not political parties but peoples' social movements and science movements (PSM) that took the lead. The political movements joined them later. They knew that change cannot be initiated from the top. It has to be the other way round, by local societies, organizations. Self-reliant and self-sufficient communes were gradually formed, like Ralegan Siddhi, Hivare Bazar, and Mendha Lekha.[2] They were still 'dependent' societies' dominated by the State and Central Governments. But, step by step, they began to strengthen their local economy, produce more and more of the necessities of life, reject goods with only vanity values and boycott goods of large scale and corporate enterprises. More and more villages joined them. Their goals became increasingly clearer and sharper. This was conceived as follows: ever increasing happiness to all members of the community. The conditions to be satisfied for this, they realized, are:

(i)   Ever increasing longevity free of morbidity till a balance is reached between birth rate and death rate and population stabilization is achieved;

(ii) Ever increasing freedom from dependence on alienated work;

(iii) Increasing equality, diversity and tolerance;

(iv) Reducing dependence on non-renewable resources and recycling them so that future generations can live a better life than ours.

Some panchayats embarked upon a project to lead their village on to the path of self-reliant local republics. This movement was initiated about three decades ago. I was a ten year old girl at that time. My father was wedded to the concept of 'horizontally connected global network of Self Reliant Village Republics'. The village in his concept was quite different from the traditional Indian villages. It was more akin to what was described in the *Communist Manifesto* – industries dispersed within agriculture, with all the amenities necessary to improve the quality of life – a rural-urban or 'rurban area'. The youth of the village rallied behind him. They transformed the village step by step to what it is today. This is the story of that transformation. This movement was taken up by the youth of many other villages. India is witnessing today a nationwide transformation into a network of self-reliant 'Rurban Republics'.

Preparatory Stage

The first thing that my father and his friends did was to strengthen citizen participation in the governance of the panchayat. The two decade long experience of decentralization and peoples' planning in the state had already prepared the ground for this. Ours was an average panchayat – about 2500 hectares in area with a population of 25000. We had about 6000 households in all. The panchayat was divided into 18 wards each having households ranging from 200-400. Each ward was further divided into neighbourhoods of 40-50 households each. Houses in a neighbourhood are at 'shouting distance' from each other. The adult members in all the households within a neighbourhood formed the Neighbourhood Council (NC). These NCs, became the lively platforms for the above discussion centres for participatory democracy. They understood that various political parties and their ideologies don't make any difference as far as they are concerned. They had read Jayaprakash Narayan's essay, '*Swaraj for the People*' (1962) and decided to put into practice some of the ideas enunciated therein. In the Neighbourhood Councils they discussed about their future representatives or spokespersons – ward members. They fielded the candidates. Gradually they wrested from the political parties the right to choose their representatives who could resign if the citizens ask them to do so. For the first time they could really constitute peoples' panchayat and not 'party panchayat'. Using their united force they could expand the scope of decentralization, wrest more and more powers and resources as well as control over 'state employees'. They set up a Panchayat Development Society and Panchayat Planning Committee. They encouraged the formation of several local study groups – on caste, religion and income divides, on energy, water management, sanitation, health care, social security, education, etc. Each Neighbourhood Council set up sub-committees for all these. Every citizen was persuaded to be a member of one or two sub-committees. This methodology they called 'forcing participation through *commitification*' (persuaded participation by putting people in various committees). Gradually, the citizens began to realize and appreciate their responsibilities as citizens in a democracy. There was nothing anti-constitutional or anti-governmental in this. This can be done in every panchayat if a few people decide to take initiative. The most difficult among these tasks was bridging the divides. A long term plan was conceived for this.

Together with this democratization process they took up another project, in education, which had far deeper impact and implication. Education has two mutually contradictory functions (i) to ensure stability and (ii) to encourage change. We are living in an epoch of change. Unless we change the historic trajectory of progress, we are doomed to total darkness. The present trajectory is one of increased use of non-renewable natural resources, leading to exhaustion of natural resources and accumulation of wastes.

This kind of development is resulting in global warming, climate change and reduction in food production. Industrial production too will come down. Longevity and population will begin to decline sharply, leading to catastrophic situation, as predicted by the authors, Donnella Meadows and others, in *Limits to Growth* (1972, 1992, and 2002).

The development trajectory has to be changed. This requires a generation committed to change and capable of effecting the change. Thus commitment and capability have to be imparted through education. The 'subversive role' of education is more important than its stabilizing role. But no society will destabilize itself. There was an element of critical education in the curriculum developed in Kerala during 1996-97. It was not a fully worked out strategy for change. Widespread opposition came up from vested interests of status quo. It was natural. The experiment failed. But it taught a lesson. Much, much more homework is to be done to initiate a change in education. Having realized this they decided to proceed in a systematic way. They gathered a small group of committed teachers convinced about the necessity of change and began discussing and experimenting – how to use any existing text book and any future text book to impart a new education through classroom activities – imparting values of equity, tolerance, sustainability, democracy, scientific outlook, etc., as well as knowledge and skills necessary for change. They dissected textbooks, discussed situations, arrived at tentative lines of transaction, experimented, discussed results, modified them. Within those years they become confident that using any textbook they can help children to acquire necessary knowledge, skills and values. They began to expand and within five to six years they had a substantial number of teachers committed to change. Its impact began to show up in the ability and attitude of student and youth. I became what I am through the subversive role played by my teacher.

Having established a strong democratic process, having increased citizen participation several fold, having set up study groups and planning councils, they began to rear a new generation with knowledge, skills and attitudes for building a new society. We have much farther to go. But we are confident of reaching there. Already there are hundreds of other panchayats engaged in similar experiments. Sooner or later our number and strength will grow enough to transform the entire society to make a new India.

Action Programme
Children's paradise

The physical, emotional and intellectual health of today's children is the surest guarantee for the health and happiness of future society. The panchayat as a whole, and individual neighbourhood councils severally, took the following decisions:

(i) The entire society will take the responsibility of bringing up its children into physically, emotionally and intellectually strong adults.

(ii) This responsibility will begin from the child-bearing mother. The ICDS should be expanded and deepened to take care of every expectant mother and child. The average birth weight of children will be increased. Safe delivery services will be provided free of cost.

(iii) No child will be allowed to go hungry. 'Kiddies kitchens' will be established in every ward and, if necessary, in every neighbourhood where any child can go to get nutritious food, three times a day. This is to complement and supplement the noon feeding programme.

(iv) The PHC will have a separate paediatric unit. Every child will have periodic health check-up and a health record. All preventive diseases will be prevented.

(v) The school environment will be made congenial to provide a sense of freedom and curiosity for every child. Special care would be taken to develop in them a resistance to various animosities existing in the society outside, or even in one's own homes.

(vi) In schools and in neighbourhood/ward areas, ample facilities for children to play, to be physically and creatively active, will be provided. Regular children's festivals and children's exchange programmes will be held. Every child will be ensured opportunity to be guests of other children in nearby towns or far off.

(vii) Every society will have 'retired' but not tired men and women. Many of them will get themselves involved in social activities. One such activity is to function as surrogate grandmas and grandpas attached to *anganwadis* (integrated child development centres). The presence of a grandmother and grandfather in an anganawadi, besides the teacher, will greatly improve the emotional health of the child.

In short the panchayat will become, on all counts, a 'Paradise on Earth' for children. And today it is so.

Old and Sick

Every society will have a certain number of congenitally or otherwise sick children and old people who require lifetime support. They often become too much a load for any normal family. Often they take recourse to employing a home nurse. The panchayat will take care of them, if necessary. It will set up 'alter homes' for old, terminally sick and born sick children. It will also have, middle aged, destitute women who want society's protection. They will act as daughters to the older people and mothers to the younger people. The presence of aged parents, incurably sick children greatly reduce the quality of life of any family. They can make use of the 'alter homes' facilities to share partially or fully the responsibility of the sick and the old at affordable costs. Having ensured that the children, elders, and sick will be properly taken care of, they turned to the economic life of the society.

Staple food of the people, as everywhere else in Kerala, was rice. The panchayat grew only 20-25 per cent of their rice requirement. Land use details for 2015 are given in Table 1 below:

Table 1: Food Self Sufficiency

Crop	Area (ha)	Production
Rice	256	800 Tonnes
Coconut	600	4.5 Million nuts
Rubber	320	300 Tonnes
Vegetables	120	1000 Tonnes
Tapioca	40	1000 Tonnes
Cashew	60	40 Tonnes
Other crop	200	No consolidated figure

Crop	Area (ha)	Production
Non-agriculture	200	No estimate, widely varying seasonally
Forest	600	

They knew that their panchayat can never become self sufficient in rice. In the long run, humans will have to live with fewer cereals, on a fruit-root-meal diet. Tapioca can be converted into pasta, macaroni, etc, very often preferred by the younger generation. Out of 256 ha of paddy land, they set apart 50 ha for fodder production. Productivity of most of the crops could be doubled and even tripled. Today the land use pattern and production is as below: given in table 2

Table 2: Present Land Use and Production Pattern

Crop	Area (ha)	Production (Tonnes)	Daily per capita Availability (gm)
Rice	200	900	50
Tubers	110	3300	300
Vegetables	160	3200	300
Meat, egg, fish	200	600	30
Milk (fodder)	250	3000	250
Coconut	300	6 million nuts	650

They conceived an integrated production system for milk, meat, fodder and vegetables given in the figure below. They planned about 100 production units, one each for a neighbourhood of 60 houses on an average. The average total area available for those was 10 ha per unit. The annual demand by various items required for 60 households was estimated as follows:

Table 3: Estimated Requirements of the Households

Item	Quantity	Area required
Vegetable	30 Te	1 ha
Tubers	30Te	1 ha

Item	Quantity	Area required
Milk (litres)	20000	2 ha
Meat	4 Te	2 ha
	Total	6 ha³

The integration envisages use of all human and animal excreta in household biogas plants and using the filtered slurry plus cow urine diluted with grey water as fertigant. All the soil nutrients are given back. The necessity of chemical nutrients could be reduced to a minimum. Households are free from LPG. Pests are managed biologically. The products are poison free.

The central unit is a dairy with an annual production capacity of 20,000 litres of milk. It is set up as a producer group with the following divisions:

1. Agriculture
2. Dairy
3. Biogas
4. Finance

The connections amongst these are depicted in Figure 1.

Figure 1: Economic interconnections in a village

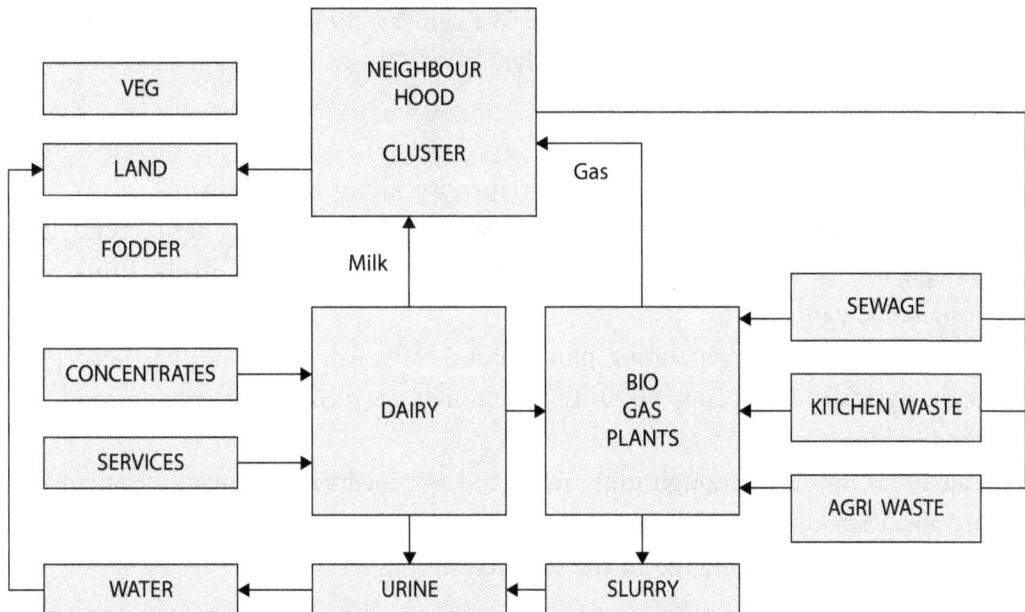

In all there are twenty working members in each company. The households lease out their lands to the producer company to cultivate vegetables, tubers and fodder. They receive rent in kind. They also invest in the company to provide working capital as advance payment to what they purchase – milk, vegetables, etc. It is a consumer supported, worker owned enterprise: Producers and Consumers become one joint family. The entire project was envisaged based on the experience of Joint Liability Group Enterprises under Kudumbasree, the major self-help group (SHG) set up in Kerala in the early 2000s'.

The overall experience of this mode of production has been encouraging. The initial difficulties were the result of the historically developed habits of 'free riding'. But the concept of consumer linked workers' enterprises as the backbone of the local economy caught up and got strengthened. In each panchayat there are more than a couple of hundred such enterprises producing a diversity of products and services. Nothing, including unexpected natural calamities, can make the people go hungry. They have got a revolving stock of food sufficient for six months.

They had set up a dedicated food processing plant, again as a producer company. It is designed to process annually 1500 Te of tapioca – to produce flour, pasta, macaroni, bread, etc., 200 Te of jackfruit, 200 Te of mango and 1000 Te of banana. The plant breaks even at 40 per cent capacity. Some coffee is grown by the panchayat on the hills. About 10,000 jackfruit trees had been planted within forest blanks and 10,000 breadfruit trees as intercrop. We produce some excess food products to exchange for tea, for coffee, for vegetables and fruits that we don't produce. We can say the following things about land and agriculture, of course, a little figuratively:

- Not a bit of land is left as fallow
- Not a drop of water is wasted
- Maximum amount of solar energy is trapped photo-synthetically
- The non-edible portion of the total biomass produced from agricultural land is ploughed back to the soil as compost or biogas slurry. We are on the brink of fully sustainable agriculture
- The forces and walls separating plots, about 1500 Km in length, has been planted with glyricidia producing 6000 Te of biomass to provide for manure and power production
- Panchayat produces enough milk, meat and egg for its own consumption and these are also exchanged for fish and other food
- No force can starve anyone in the panchayat

Industry

As early as the 1920's the panchayat initiated a massive industrialization process; not through mass production, but through production by the masses. It today produces all the soap, washing powder and other toiletries in a medium size plant operated for a cluster of six neighbouring panchayats and a town. It produces all the processed food items for the cluster, in another panchayat. It does not produce any cotton; yarn is brought from outside. It has power looms, with handlooms being used only for very specific design fabrics.

There are many industrial products that cannot be made at panchayat or even at the state level. The examples include computer chips, mobile phones, power equipments, vehicles, etc. But they are all durable goods and their life is extended through a well-knit repair and maintenance network. The annual import cost of all these together will add up to only a small fraction of the GDP of the panchayat.

A whole new industry that has come up is in the field of green technologies – for power, energy, transport, and for construction. The main areas are:

a) *Solar Photo Voltaic*: The panchayat, with its own funds, trained a team of solar engineers and technicians to carry out its massive solar energy project and for quick and efficient maintenance.

b) *Sanitation and Biogas Plant*: It has also got a unit to produce and install toilet linked biogas plants which also receive cow dung from dairies, kitchen waste, market waste and agricultural waste. It is a 'clean panchayat' company. The biogas plants are operated and maintained by the dairy company as mentioned earlier.

c) *Timber Processing*: It has also set up a plant for coconut trunk, bamboo and softwood. It collects all the non-degradable biomass and separates them to timber and fuel. The fuel is used for power production. Timber is used for construction, thus fixing some amount of carbon. The fuel portion is sent to the thermal plant to be burned. Households no longer use firewood, but only biogas supplemented by solar water heaters and induction plates.

Housing

In the 2020s' there were already several unoccupied houses, built as investment. The panchayat decided not to permit to build new houses or flats. It took on lease all unoccupied houses and rented them out to all newly formed families and all existing houseless people. The people declared that a house is not an asset, like gold, to be traded, but a human construct for human habitation. The real estate industry was gradually closed down. This was an essential requirement to make land and labour available for agriculture. Today there is no family in 'M' without a decent liveable house. Building construction being energy intensive, with high embodied carbon footprint, no new homes are built unless absolutely necessary.

Transport

More than 80 per cent of the people work in the panchayat. Children go to neighbouring schools. The health care centres are nearby. Inflow and outflow of commodities have been drastically reduced. Most of the travel is on foot or on cycles. We have built safe paths for pedestrians and cyclists. The roads are good and well maintained. The panchayat has practically no private cars. There is good public transport and a good pool of public taxis available on phone. Every house is connected with phone. It has solved its transport problem. There is a major railway station 15 km away, which is connected by bus. There is an airport 50 kms away, which too is connected by bus.

Water

Every household has potable running water. The panchayat is rich in ground water. They have taken measures to keep it uncontaminated. Local community owned water supply system cater to their needs. Every house now has two water lines – a fresh water line for drinking, cooking, washing and bathing and a grey water line for toilet flushing and gardening.

Energy

One of the earliest programs of the panchayat was to make it energy self-sufficient and reduce carbon footprint of energy. The following elements are taken in:
1. Roof top SPV unit
2. Household biogas unit
3. A pumped storage station for which a site existed
4. Biomass fuelled thermal station

They rescheduled their entire social and economic activity in such a way that high energy consuming activities are done between 10 AM to 4 PM. The evening and morning requirements were brought down by 20 per cent. In the meanwhile, as mentioned earlier, they had trained a group of four engineers and 12 technicians in solar technology. They become part of the Green Energy Company (GEC).

The next thing they did was an intensive solar energy campaign. Every house owner with more than $100m^2$ of built up area has to set up a 5KW SPV unit as his carbon tax for the carbon footprint of the house. Every car owner has to set up a 6-8 KW SPV on his roof, as carbon tax. The excess energy they supply to the grid will be paid for. They were to establish 20 MW of SPV units on the roof top of 6000 households. They achieved this target by 2035.

Education

In the earlier part of this paper we had indicated the early intervention in education. There the importance of subversive role of education was emphasized. Simultaneously it has to play a conservative role too. It has to preserve the present life of the people and also improve it. For these the society has to produce goods and services in agriculture, industry, in the power sector, in textiles, in housekeeping – every sector demands qualified technical persons. The panchayat made a detailed human-power need study and established a number of vocational training schools to train about 3000 technicians, in several hundred trades, after twelve years of general and 'liberal' education of good quality was given to all. After that came vocational education or academic education. Even academic or 'higher' education was planned as preparing for a profession – of production, management, service, research and teaching. At the end of 12th class everybody would acquire a high level of proficiency in the mother tongue, sciences, mathematics, English language and computer usage. Ours is today a cyber society, grounded on our soil. We are a smart society. Every house has a computer. Everybody has access to internet. Everybody can speak fluently in Malayalam and English. We can access the pool of world knowledge. We learn from it. We apply this knowledge to our production. In this way we continuously improve our production – better qualities, lesser input, lesser time, more of products, and of leisure. This situation has been brought about by our generation. Every one of us can play, not badly, one game or another, every one of us can sing a few songs, at least in a chorus, every one of us reads a few books a year, many of us have visited other states and other countries. Education has made us global citizens rooted in our own soil.

Health Care

In the 2020s' we started with the following campaign:
- Complete cleanliness – elimination of flies and mosquitoes – campaign was carried out through extensive peoples' participation, as we did in the literacy campaign of 1989-1991.
- Ensuring clean and safe water for all; the ground water is made safe; based on local water supply.

- Water purification systems were used. Solar water heaters with small modification could become water purifies too.
- Massive citizen education was given to students about unhealthy life style, in eating, in working, in everything.
- Thus vector borne, water borne and lifestyle caused disease load was reduced substantially. Together with this preventive measures, immunization, periodic health check-up too were introduced.
- Curative health care system was strengthened. Once a 'patient' reached the PHC, the ASHA worker would take charge and take the patient, to doctors, to take them around for investigation. There are free ambulance facilities.
- The health of any citizen is the responsibility of the entire society. Our panchayat is freed from alcoholism. It is not total abandoning but tempered consumption. The total alcohol consumption in the panchayat today is less than 10 per cent of what it was in the early decades of the century.

Total Social Security

Today the citizens in our panchayat feel full security. They don't have to worry about employment, food, water, energy, flies and mosquitoes, health care, transport, housing, recreation, children, their education. There is no compunction to amass wealth for future security. This has considerably reduced the corruption rate and crime rate in the panchayat.

Bridging the Divides

The two major divides existing in society are the social divides and the economic divides. Both are legacies of a long history. They knew that these divides will not be bridged through wishful thinking. A multi-front strategy was conceived. It was built on the foundation of the achievements of a century long social reform movements of 19th and 20th centuries. In the schools children were encouraged to learn:

(i)   Origin and development of various religions, their progressive aspects
(ii) Human capabilities and human progress
(iii) Value of diversity
(iv) Value of freedom

There were homes with different castes and religions. Children were often hosted by them. For example even in the days of my grandfather, our home was very cosmopolitan. We had uncles and aunties, coming from all castes – *brahmin, kshatriya, varrior, nambissans, ezhavas, nair,* and different religions like Christian, Hindu and Muslim. The number of such cosmopolitan homes was increasing. It took more than a generation before caste and religion divides were weakened and tolerance and appreciation increased.

Women in Kerala are better educated, but less liberated from traditional taboos. The youth came to the understanding that the false understanding of morality and sex is the main culprit. They argued that a raped woman is not a morally fallen woman but a wounded one as in a car accident. They started an educational campaign to separate sex from morality, to consider it as part of biology just like food and water. Sex, they also argued, is not limited to heterosexuality. It also includes lesbians, gay and transgender, quoting episodes from epics and *Puranas*. There shall not be any discrimination against any sexual attitude. The political clout earned by women – nearly 60% of elected representatives are women – and the economic strength derived from economic activities under Kudumbashri and similar institutions supported by the cultural campaign against false notions on morality are having visible impacts.

We have a long way to go. We understand it. The new generation has taken up the mantle.

The understanding that land is not a commodity, but a production agent gradually brought down land sales. Since everybody had a job, rent from speculative income from land become less important. Unearned income such as rent/interest was seen as unwholesome. Gradually, the share of rent/profit income in the economy became insignificant. The recognition of the category called greed gradually encouraged people to value leisure and freedom and creativity more than accumulation of wealth, which became unnecessary. Vulgar consumption and extravaganza began to be viewed as abnormal. Gradually the pain of social and economic divides began to subside. Practically nobody feels that he or she is socially inferior or superior or economically depressed. Everybody had what they needed.

Yes, we are far better off than our parents and grandparents, thanks to the initiative they took. We can and have to take the initiative forward so that our children and grandchildren will be able to say the same.

Endnotes

1. See also essay on Localisation, and Concluding essay, in this volume.
2. Ralegan Siddhi and Hivare Bazaar are villages in Maharashtra where initiatives have showed pathways towards greater equity based water resource management for participatory village development; while Mendha Lekha is a trailblazer in showing how the gram sabha is the supreme body in getting peoples' rights by accessing the Forest Rights Act in *adivasi* areas. All of these

have shown the value of committed leadership, strong gram sabha and self-governance as keys to self-reliant village development. See also essays on Regionalisation and Localisation of Economies, Biomass-based Rural Revitalisation, and Looking Back into the Future, in this volume.

3. Though a provision of 10 ha area for each unit of 60 households has been made, actually 6 ha would be enough and the remaining 4 ha is kept as risk buffer.

References

Narayan, Jayaprakash, 1962 (reprint 2000), *Swaraj for the People*, Varanasi: Sarva Seva Sangh Prakashan.

Future Bazaar in India

Rajni Bakshi

Summary

The essay briefly traces the history of over 2500 years to map the characteristics of the Indian market culture. However, contemporary notions of growth and technological advancement have changed both modes and relations of production. In a market culture of limitless accumulation, the essay explores the possibility of a culture based on the notion of sufficiency and common good.

The essay visualizes a village level economy, which will be self-sustaining for essentials and capable of expanding space for a non-monetised exchange. Such an economy will have community-based systems of protection and revitalisation of natural resources. The starting point of such a bazaar is to change the aspiration of accumulation into the ethics of commons and public goods.

Introduction

A particularly delicious *kulfi* (ice-cream like desert indigenous to India) is sold from a wooden push-cart parked near Shivaji Park, Mumbai. The *kulfi-wala* (the seller of kulfis) arrives at his chosen spot just as the light is fading over the *maidan* (large open ground) which has given India some of its finest cricketers. Often customers get there earlier, waiting for their favourite kulfi which is sold at a price affordable even for working class people. Some buy a slice of kulfi and eat it on the spot – served on a green leaf with a wooden or plastic ice-cream spoon. Others bring an ice box and carry away big chunks of kulfi to eat at home. Business is so brisk that latecomers are sometimes disappointed – the kulfi-wala has sold all he made for the day and gone home early.

Shivaji Park's coveted kulfi-wala follows a pattern that baffles most business school graduates. If he makes a limited quantity of a much in demand product – why not give it an 'exclusive' branding and charge much more? Or he could mass produce and have outlets all over the city. To those trained in a contemporary market ethos not 'up-scaling' this product is just plain stupid.

Yet that kulfi-wala is one of the countless producers, vendors, entrepreneurs, crafts-persons scattered across India who choose not to expand. They seem to organize their work life around the value of sufficiency – a value that should neither be dismissed as being 'backward' nor romantically valorised.

The quest for a humane and socially embedded market culture in India must grapple with a creative paradox – how to foster systems that are based on sufficiency as a creative value and yet responsive to growth as a necessity. In a country where about 25 per cent of the population has zero assets and hundreds of millions of people don't have adequate nutrition, housing, health care, electricity, water – some expansion of material infrastructure is essential. What forms must this growth take so that it actually serves human and ecological well-being – rather than just being a higher GDP figure? Unravelling or unbundling this paradox is perhaps the most critical challenge that will determine the future not just of India but the equation between markets and societies everywhere.

It is important to appreciate why 'sufficiency' and 'subsistence' are seen as negative within the mainstream discourse. This is primarily because a staggering number of people in India are unemployed or severely under-employed not out of choice but by force of circumstance. Fulfilling more than the basic needs of 600 to 800 million people is both a moral and political imperative. The key question is how this is to be done.

Any visualization of the future of markets and exchange in India must be multi-dimensional. That is, it must be respectful to the entire spectrum of aspirations. From those who are struggling to move beyond elementary survival, to those who see 'sufficiency' as a font of creativity and also those who desire to accumulate surplus assets. A nuanced and intricate understanding of all these dimensions is a pre-requisite for an effective opposition to that stream of economic thinking which assumes that cultivating endless wants is the only reliable basis for ensuring economic dynamism and thus well being.

Here are the suggested parameters of this exercise:

- Map the characteristics of India's market culture which has been thriving un-interrupted for over 2500 years.
- Distinguish this legacy of commerce, of socially anchored bazaars, from the capitalist market ethos within which India is known as an 'emerging market'.
- Explore the spaces for expanding cooperation and co-production.
- Explore the extent to which non-monetary forms of value can carry more weight.

Over 2500 Years of Market Culture

India, like China, has been a land of commerce and markets that have taken diverse forms over at least three millennia. Metal coins as currency appeared simultaneously in Mesopotamia and India in 7th century BC. By the time of the Buddha, about 500 BC, there were multi-layered systems of exchange across India – from village to regional to long distance trade. Unlike Western Europe, where markets more or less collapsed after the fall of Rome to gradually re-emerge from about the 10th Century onwards, this part of the world has seen an uninterrupted evolution of market culture (Thapar, 2002).

In ancient India commerce and trade thrived alongside gift-exchange based on elaborate reciprocal relations. In a pattern seen across the world, gift-exchange in India involved status rather than profit. In her book on ancient India, the historian Romila Thapar described how such exchange persisted in places where clan chiefs were still dominant – with reciprocity being a social norm that served also as an economic function.

Money based exchange co-existed with barter and direct exchange. While the rise of money based exchange intensified commercial trade, other forms of exchange based more on social relations than supply and demand also continued – surviving in some cases right up to the mid-20th century.

Describing the rise of the mercantile community between 300 and 200 BC, Thapar (2002) notes the proliferation of guilds of both manufacturers and merchants – from corn dealers, to gold and silversmiths.

'The picture of this period is that of many people moving in many directions. There were not only *Yavanas'* trading with the subcontinent, but traders from various parts of India finding their way to Central Asia, to West Asia, to the ports of the Red Sea and to South-East Asia. The wide distribution of pottery, artefacts and scripts are also indicators of this movement within the subcontinent and beyond. In many areas there were multiple communities with varying identities that drew upon occupation and caste status, religious sectarian affiliation and the use of a particular language. These were the identities that were to dominate in subsequent centuries.'

(pp. 279)

A multi-tiered system of production and exchange – from the purely village level economy to regional and global – made India a manufacturing hub that was second only to China. The French economic historian Fernand Braudel describes 18th century India as having a natural, strong and successful economy:

'... her agriculture was traditional but productive and high-yielding; her industry was on an ancient pattern, but it was thriving and efficient (until 1810, Indian steel was actually of higher quality than anything produced in England, and inferior only to Swedish steel); the whole country was penetrated by a well-established market economy; there were many efficient trading circuits. Last but not least, India's commercial and industrial strength was based, as one might expect, on a vigorous export trade: she was part of an economic area going well beyond her own shores.'

(Braudel, 1984, pp. 522)

Two factors are commonly attributed for changing India from a vibrant economy to a land of deep and widespread poverty. One factor was the forced de-industrialization driven first by the armies and policies of the East India Company and later the British crown. The other factor was the 18th century revolution in technology that was entirely Euro-centric and introduced both modes of production and profit-making which were severely disruptive of nature's eco-systems and prevailing societal relations.

From Socially Anchored Bazaars to the Capitalist Market Ethos

Re-visiting these well-known elements of Indian history is important primarily because it serves to sift ancient legacies of commerce, and other non-market forms of economic exchange, from the capitalist system that emerged in Europe from the 18th century onwards.

Making this distinction is particularly important because it is not granted much importance in the contemporary discourse about markets.

By the end of the 20th century, particularly after the collapse of communism, the global discourse in corridors of political and commercial power came to revolve around an absolute confidence that 'The Market' is the only way to organize materials and their exchange on this planet. Namely, that production and exchange is most reliably and efficiently driven by the motive of maximizing profits and to do so by responding to cycles of supply and demand – with profit being defined entirely in monetary terms.

This is not to imply that pre-modern forms of economic exchange were perfect or always entirely fair. Traditional 'bazaar' exchanges were marked by multiple power equations and hierarchies that privileged some over others. In India the *jajmani*-system of exchange was based on caste hierarchy and even its in-built reciprocity would not conform to 21st century notions of social justice and dignity for all. Advocates of capitalism have argued that this breaking of old social hierarchies in favour of commodity exchange in 'free' markets was an all-important liberation from injustices of feudal society.

However, this sweeping dismissal of all pre-modern systems of exchange as necessarily unjust has tended to obscure important elements and principles of the equation between pre-modern societies and bazaars. For instance, in his extensive documentation of traditional water systems in North India, Anupam Mishra has highlighted the story of four farmers who accidentally found a stone that could turn base metals into gold. But these farmers chose not to use that stone to amass a large quantity of gold. Instead, they used it sparingly to build four large water bodies which brought prosperity to their area for many generations (Mishra, 2011).

In doing this, those farmers were living out a wisdom that almost all cultures of the world have cherished – that real wealth resides in those materials, processes and natural resources which actually enhance and sustain life, and not just human life. This is the crux of the Greek myth of King Midas – whose very touch turned anything to gold till this power became a curse.

Those who are inclined to treat the story about the four farmers as pure fantasy might consider the tree planting habits of the people of Nimad region along the banks of the Narmada River in Madhya Pradesh. In this region it is common to find three particular trees growing close to each other – the Pipal (*Ficus religiosa*), the Banyan (*Ficus beghalensis*) and the Neem (*Azadirachta indica*). This is due to a cultural tradition, not a nature-generated pattern. People of this region believe that whatever else one might do, life will not be fulfilled unless one has planted and nurtured this combination of trees.

All three trees, significantly, give off no fruit or 'product' that was ever sold in the bazaar. Yet all three are important to the balance of the eco-system and their leaves and bark have multiple medicinal values for both humans and other animals. These three trees – their leaves, bark, etc. – have traditionally remained in the commons and not been commercialized.

For details of a market culture where social, cultural and material relations were inextricably inter-linked we can draw on the work of Ravindra Sharma – artist, story-teller and archivist of the fading cultural practices and modes of exchange in central India. Though Sharma, better known as 'Guruji', was first drawn into the study of local artists and craftsmen in his native Adilabad, this work led him to piece together a picture of how the local economy had functioned even up to the 1960s'. Material life was organized around ensuring that there was enough work for a wide range of producers – potters, iron-smiths, gold-smiths and the multi-layered highly specialized crafts that turned cotton first into thread and then cloth (Bakshi, 1998).

But where do we go from here? Can these legacies inform the present and future? The world that Ravindra Sharma documents is almost entirely swept away by gale force winds of change. Too many of the technological advances and resulting revolutions in infrastructure, modes of production and thus relations of exchange are irreversible. Going back to those modes, in a literal sense, is neither possible nor would it be desirable since contemporary ethical values, notably equal dignity for all, make most of the *jati* based relations of the past unacceptable. Sharma's key insight is that he urges us to look more closely at the core values and principles that informed the traditional systems.

At the risk of over-simplifying a complex reality here is a possible kernel on which markets of the present and future can be visualized.

- Honour the importance of bazaars as a location of conversation, social formation and exchange – as opposed to suspecting market exchange as being necessarily or inevitably exploitative.
- Make a distinction between profit as a means and profit as an end-in-itself. It was from this vantage point that Mahatma Gandhi saw Trusteeship as a futuristic ideal on which practical systems of commercial and social governance could be built.
- Surplus accumulation can play an important role provided it is based on fair, if not equal, access to opportunities and resources. How this can be made possible is the key area of work for researchers, social activists working in tandem with business practitioners at all levels of the economy. At present the village level economy and all those who have bare minimum material resources, or even less, are described as 'the bottom of the pyramid'. If the future is to be not just more equitable but creative, enabling multi-dimensional well-being for humans in balance with ecosystems, it is essential that the pyramid shape itself be dissolved and replaced by what Gandhi described as 'Oceanic Circles' of inter-dependence and mutual creativity (Gandhi, 1946).

Spaces for expanding cooperation and co-production

Building on this frame, what would future markets and production systems look like? Here is an imagined scenario for two vital material needs – food and clothing, in the context of India.

Primacy is given to the 'local' and it is therefore important to clarify, even attempt to define, just what this means. In the economic-social vision outlined by Mahatma Gandhi, 'local' referred to the village economy and by extension a cluster of villages. In the early 21st century some advocates of localization define 'local' as that which lies within a hundred mile radius. This definition is particularly popular within the local food movement that has gathered momentum in the USA and in Europe over the last two decades.

In India Ela Bhatt, founder of the Self Employed Women's Association (SEWA), is perhaps the best known advocate of this principle:

> 'The 100 Mile Principle urges us to meet life's basic needs with goods and services that are produced no more than 100 miles from where we live. This includes food, shelter, clothing, primary education, primary health care, and primary banking.'[2]

For the purposes of this essay the actual measure, of what constitutes 'local', is not as important as the broad idea of anchoring economic activity in the immediate vicinity versus the national and international. The formulation of what constitutes 'local' must be necessarily left open-ended in order to ensure creativity and not make a fetish of it.[3] It is equally important to clarify that celebrating the local should not be equated with an isolationist variety of self-reliance or denigration of national and global linkages. Primacy to local means not a rejection of exogenous exchange but instead ensuring that all exchange – be it immediate – local, regional, national or international – is based on equitable terms of exchange and does not advantage any particular interest group, most of all capital.[4]

Michael Shuman (1998), an American advocate of localism, has conveyed the essential principles thus: 'Going local does not mean walling off the outside world. It means nurturing local businesses which use local resources sustainably, employ local workers at decent wages, and serve primarily local consumers. It means becoming more self-sufficient, and less dependent on imports. Control moves from the boardrooms of distant corporations, and back to the community, where it belongs' (pp. 6).

Food Futures

In considering the future of food it is first vital to note that, according to the Food and Agriculture Organization (FAO), most of the world's food is still produced by more than 500 million family farms spread across the world (FAO, 2014). In 2008 agricultural scientists from across the world released a landmark report known as the International Assessment of Agricultural Science and Technology for Development (IAASTD) which concluded that the business-as-usual model of prevailing industrial agriculture cannot meet the food needs of the 9 billion who are expected to inhabit planet earth within a few decades. Implementing the findings of the IAASTD would mean a significant break from the trend towards farm consolidation and chemical-intensive agriculture. In a nutshell the report said that we cannot go on depleting natural capital, with associated dwindling of genetic variety, and still hope to ensure that everyone on earth has sufficient food.

How then is nutritious and tasty food to be ensured for all? Food production cannot be left entirely to the pure profit motive driven by supply and demand curves of the market. What is needed is a combination of community-action, commercial transactions and a broad framework of government regulations co-created by farmers, consumers and policy makers working in tandem.

That might be possible if:

- Those that are engaged in agriculture voluntarily give first priority to producing crops for local nutritional needs and, on the side, as an extra, plant cash crops for sale in national and international markets.
- Local buyers of these crops can reciprocate and ensure that the farmers are not merely at subsistence level but making a profit. One example of this is the thriving Community Supported Agriculture (CSA) groups in the USA and across the world. In some cases the member-customers of a CSA pre-pay for the crops becoming share-holders of a kind in the farm. The farmer's profit is in cash and consumers' 'profit' lies in the benefit of high-quality, often organic, fresh produce.

While the mainstream discourse of the globalized economy pays little attention to this phenomenon it does have a growing momentum. In November 2015 an international conference on Community Supported Agriculture, was organized in China by Italy based group Urgenci.[5]

In India there are a few examples of direct farmer-consumer links such as the Gorus Organic Farming Association in Pune which serves as a platform linking farmers, consumers and social enterprises, to provide both services and knowledge about growing local exchange. The Hyderabad based Centre for Sustainable Agriculture supports revitalization of local food chains and also aims to influence public policy in favour of both organic and local food.[6]

- Agricultural methods and related technologies would be deployed with a long term perspective to ensure protection or even enhancement of biodiversity, soil health and affordability of the input-costs – namely seeds, pesticides and fertilizers.
- Government policies would focus on supporting and promoting systems of finance and technology which ensure both local food production and purchasing power – instead of defining 'food security' as distribution of food grains from reserves acquired by the government. Protection and regeneration of biodiversity can be linked to a more varied cultivation of food crops, particularly millets. These practices

can also be linked with the Public Distribution System (PDS), thus promoting both better nutrition among the most economically deprived sections and encouraging diversity in agricultural crops (Kalpavriksh & TPCG, 2005).

• Government policies would also ensure a truly level field so that industrial agriculture is not privileged over diverse non-industrial systems of agriculture. One illustration of this is the Dharani initiative of Timbaktu Collective which has enabled farmers, whose soils had become severely depleted due to monoculture and excessive use of chemicals, to shift to organic farming. In addition Dharani has promoted the revival of nutritionally rich millets, which had stopped being cultivated because both government policies and market dynamics pushed for the cultivation of select cash crops, mostly groundnut and rice.[7]

A case study by Kalpavriksh of Timbaktu's work on organic farming and the producers' cooperative concluded that these initiatives have brought about improvements in '... food security and sovereignty through both increased local availability and enhanced incomes, the spread of organic cultivation methods helping in healthier soils and environment, the revival of millets in cultivation and in people's diets, the empowerment of women in the governance of agricultural and other operations, greater economic returns for smallholder farmers showing that economies of scale can work for them also, enhanced livelihoods for the landless, the regeneration of commons, and others' (Kothari, 2014).

Future Cloth

Since Independence Indian handlooms have been treated by governments as a traditional craft that must be protected because it gives livelihood to millions of people. On the contrary, argue social entrepreneurs and activists who have worked in this sphere, handlooms should be seen as a futuristic industry. This claim is bolstered by global awareness about the environmental and social costs of high-energy technologies of the kind that have dominated the world for over 200 years:

'Some say that as energy from steam, oil and electricity ushered in the era of mass production in the 19th century, it will be clean, renewable energy that will take dispersed production industries to the top of the heap in the 21st. As the stock of fossil fuels comes to an end notions of efficiency will change and low-energy manufacturing processes will gain in value. At the same time markets are becoming saturated with the look-alike products of factory production, and there are more and more customers for the individualized products that dispersed production can offer. In this situation household manufacture of cotton textiles in India, particularly if it can use yarn made from cotton fresh from the field, looks as if it will have the last laugh over mass production after all' (Uzramma, 2014).[8]

Realizing this vision is neither easy nor simple, but here are some actions that would help:

- Handloom weavers are ensured a reliable and affordable supply of cotton yarn. At present they depend entirely on yarn produced by spinning mills – with erratic supply often at rates they cannot afford.
- Since the dawn of mill-made cloth in India in the late 19th century, cotton has been taken away – often from the handloom weaver's backyard – to spinning factories. The handloom weaver's economy can change radically if the cotton is locally transformed into yarn. Therefore an NGO based in Andhra Pradesh, the Decentralised Cotton Yarn Trust – has used an innovative machine for cleaning the cotton and making it ready for spinning at the local level – a chain of production that is designed to boost small-scale handloom production. 'Malkha', the fabric created by this process is marketed as a product that empowers the local economy in particular weavers and artisans. Uzramma, one of the promoters of Malkha, writes:

  'the goal of the Malkha initiative is to put all aspects of production, including management, in the hands of the producers, the people who do the actual work – in other words, to achieve true democracy in production. Unlike the corporate model, where almost the entire cadre of top executives is drawn from the elite sectors of society, the Malkha model can be run and managed by people who do not have access to expensive education, or who do not come from a privileged or business background.'[9]

- Laws and policies in support of handlooms make it illegal for mill or power-loom cloth to be sold with false claims that it is handloom cloth. At present, implementation of these laws is extremely inadequate. This leaves handlooms to face unfair competition from falsely labelled mill or power-loom products claiming to be handloom goods. In a fair market place both, the government and trade bodies or chambers of commerce would work to prevent such malpractices.

Farmers and craftsmen's bazaars, including those supported by village or municipal level authorities, are helpful but they are insufficient for addressing the larger problem of fraud in terms of false labelling or overcoming other structural inequities that disadvantage the smaller producers. Since middle-men are often identified as major points of exploitation it is tempting to imagine that removing them would create more equitable equations. This would only be true in a small locality where the producers and consumers are almost neighbours. If emphasis on local economic dynamism is not to be isolationist then regional and long distance exchange must not be discouraged. The challenge lies in ensuring fairness of transaction across all levels of exchange, not in eliminating either middlemen or retailers.

Can Non-monetary Forms of Value Carry More Weight?

Fostering non-monetary measures of value might well be the biggest challenge ahead. Within the realm of mainstream business the concept of triple bottom line – people, planet and profits – has taken hold. This has resulted in the global phenomenon of socially responsible investing which has been boosted by the United Nations Principles of Responsible Investing established in 2006.[10] Socially responsible investing demands that profits be delivered in the form of not just money returns but social benefits and environmental good. However, it is the money profit that remains a non-negotiable, a must.

The rise of micro-finance and social venture capital has given access to credit and capital to people who were otherwise not considered viable clients by conventional banks or investors. However, ironically, the story of micro-finance demonstrates the complex nature of the conundrum. To begin with micro-finance was a way of organizing and circulating local savings. Till the late 1990s', even when extraneous money entered micro-finance it was mostly in the non-profit mode – that is, the micro finance entity was not designed to be a profit generator. This changed with the entry of global investors who promoted for-profit micro-finance on the grounds that the non-profit model could never serve the credit needs of all those at the base of the economy. From 2000 to 2010 this for-profit model dominated the micro-finance field. Freeing millions of people from traditional money lenders who charged up to 100 per cent interest was one of the key achievements of this sector.

However the rapid growth of for-profit micro-finance happened at the cost of the community structures that had served as a vital glue in the self-help groups where non-profit micro-finance had been nurtured. While the for-profit model did reach a much larger number of people it also led to much higher rates of interest and many clients became multiple and serial borrowers – taking loans from one entity to pay off another. As the actual self-help groups disintegrated or were cobbled together only in name, not spirit, local women who were at the centre of the original SHG concept lost control. With the rise of for-profit micro-finance, some borrowers became lenders to others in the village. In some cases the commercially oriented micro-finance entities were charging interest in the range of more than 30 per cent – which was justified as being valid because it was still an improvement on the traditional money lender.

The challenge for a different, an alternative, bazaar culture is neither to valorise the non-profit micro-finance nor demonize for-profit micro-finance, but instead find ways of challenging the dominant pattern of economy which treats rapid circulation of money as an end in itself.[11]

In this context it is important to note the rise of a wide variety of community currencies in different parts of the world. These are community based systems of exchange that aim to partially or entirely free local economic dynamism from dependence on the national currency. This facilitates a wide range of exchanges, usually using some kind of points system, which otherwise would not have happened because the concerned people did not have enough conventional money (Bakshi, 2003).

It is significant to note that community currencies and assorted forms of Local Exchange Trading Systems (LETS) have not sprung up in India – as they have in North and Latin America, Europe, Australia and parts of Asia-Pacific. One reason for this could be that most successful experiments in community currencies have been in post-scarcity societies – where the participants are plugged into the national economy and its currency and join a community currency to supplement income and, often primarily, to foster a sense of belonging to a community. It is important to highlight that even where they are successful community currencies remain relatively marginal to the 'formal' economy and its official national currency (ibid.).

And yet there is one powerful reason why a future vision of bazaar energies must contend with the lessons and experiences of community currencies. Experiments in supplementary currencies highlight two key elements of how to shape bazaars for the greater good. One, such currencies emphasize the role of money as a token of exchange and not as a store of value. Two, they ensure a local multiplier effect – namely that money goes around much more within the local economy as opposed to leaving it to accumulate as surplus at the national and/or international level.

One version of the ideal future bazaar, sometimes posited by social activists, visualizes a scenario where all household and daily needs are met in local markets or *haats*, produced and traded locally, using a combination of local currencies, barter and conventional national currency. Such exchange systems would foster long-term relationships between consumers and producers. The assumption is that as more and more people become both direct producers and consumers this would eliminate inequality in exchange relations since there would be closer knowledge and transparency about the production process and its impacts. It is also assumed that if such local community based systems of exchange became sufficiently powerful they would, as collectives, have greater bargaining power in relation to the regional, national and international levels of exchange.

This vision has to contend with some serious challenges. Firstly, 'community' and socially embedded bazaar mechanisms have to negotiate the complexity of caste and class relations in India. As micro examples across India show, this is possible but it requires concerted effort.

Secondly, if taken literally the scenario outlined above seems ignorant of the massive changes being wrought by technology. There are positive changes of democratizing technologies like cell phones and easy access to the internet. At the same time there are potentially negative implications of the impending economic disruption if, as predicted, robotics and 3-D printers displace hundreds of millions of workers.

This paper does not even attempt to grapple with these complexities. The purpose here is limited to understanding the core aspirations which underlie the vision outlined above. These are:

- Economic and social empowerment at the household level
- Revitalization of the local economy
- Expanded space for non-monetized exchange based on mutuality
- Circles of sharing that make individual or family ownership of many goods and services unnecessary
- Community based systems of inputs to agriculture and joint harvesting of crops, potentially even local manufacture of non-agricultural goods and services
- Community based mechanisms for protection and revitalization of natural resources with robust environmental feedback mechanisms to show when limits are being reached
- An expanded definition of 'value' so that commons and public goods and related phenomenon gain greater importance than accumulation of monetary assets

Many of these aspirations are now acknowledged, some even accepted, within the discourse of multi-lateral agencies, notably the United Nations and World Bank. The difference between that international discourse and the alternatives discourse is that the former treats these aspirations as an add-on, a sweetener, to the existing capital dominated globalized economy. Thus while 'market based solutions' are sought for ensuring social and economic 'inclusion' there is little room for challenging the nature and workings of a market system where monetary profit-motive remains dominant.

The biggest challenge for crafting a meaningful, that is other than fantasy, vision of alternatives is that on the ground, in actual practice, the socially embedded bazaar and the globalized 'market' are often inextricably intertwined. Billions of people are simultaneously living in the many inter-twining spaces of local bazaars and global markets. Thus efforts to transform the 'local' and foster a more socially embedded economy, which do not have a parallel at the national and international level, will only create niche successes.

One way to address this complexity is to lean on the ancient Greek distinction between *Oikonomia* and *Chrematistics* – which was revived in our times by Herman Daly, the father of ecological economics, and John Cobb in their influential book 'For the Common Good: Redirecting the Economy Toward Community'. Oikonomia represents economics for the community and Chrematistics corresponds to private personal preferences. Oikonomia is about costs to and benefits for the whole community. Chrematistics is concerned with individual profit in monetary terms (Bakshi, 2009).

The world we live in at present is a consequence of an exaggerated privileging of Chrematisitcs and an active or implicit belittling of Oikonomia. It is tempting to think that the future can be built by rejecting Chrematistic in favour of Oikonomia. But this may be neither desirable nor possible – if we also want societies based on freedom of choice, expression, action and movement.

Both the 'me' impulse and the 'us' impulse are inherent to human nature. The kulfi-wala who lives by an ethos of 'enough' is as much a part of our social ecosystem as his customer who drives up in an expensive car and lives by the desire to keep accumulating more.

To see greed as good, as essential for economic dynamism, is a constructed belief – not a given of human nature. Similarly, it is a constructed belief that human wants are necessarily unlimited and that's good because consumption led growth is needed to keep the global economy afloat.

The starting point of a future bazaar culture, in India and across the world, is the faith, the confidence, that public policy and mechanisms of finance and exchange can be structured to materially reward and socially honour those who celebrate 'sufficiency' and make a living or profits while serving the common good.

Endnotes

1. The term Yavana is used in Indian texts to refer broadly to people from lands West of the Indus River, notably, Greece, Sindhu (now in Pakistan) and Gandhara (now in Afghanistan).
2. Interview with Ela R. Bhatt, Founder of the Self Employed Women's Association in India, September, 2012, http://www.worldwatch.org/interview-ela-r-bhatt-founder-self-employed-women%E2%80%99s-association-india (Last accessed 2 January, 2016).
3. Pl. see Localisation Future and Dare to Dream essays, and Conclusion in this book.

4. See also Korten, 2010.
5. The Sixth International Community Supported Agriculture Symposium, China, http://urgenci. net/2015/11/ (Last accessed 27 May, 2016).
6. In August 2013, Gorus was registered as a Not-for-Profit Company under section 25 of the Indian Companies Act of 1956, and named Gorus Organic Farming Association. Gorus trains small farmers in Pune district in organic and natural farming practices and provides a market platform with a year-round guarantee of purchase at an assured price. Gorus also provides a weekly basket of organically grown vegetables, fruit, and grocery to more than 200 consumers in Pune city. [http://www.gorus.in/].
7. http://timbaktu-organic.org/ (Last Accessed 4 April, 2016).
8. Uzramma has documented how textile machinery was designed in the 19th century by people who had no clear knowledge of the properties of the cotton fibre and '... sponsored by the merchant class whose only interest was the profitability of the machinery, basically its speed of operation, not its ecological or social cost, nor the quality of the end-product. And there began the long and ultimately tragic history of replacing Indian cotton plant varieties, *G. arboreum* & *herbaceum*, with the American strain, *G. hirsutum*, entirely unsuited to Indian agricultural practices'(Uzramma, 2014). See also Crafts Future essay in this volume.
9. See Malkha: The Freedom Fabric, http://www.sustainablecottons.com/638/ (Last accessed 1 May, 2016) and Deshpande, 2014.
10. http://www.unpri.org (Last accessed 7 January, 2016).
11. Aloysius Fernandez, a veteran of the non-profit micro-finance sector wrote: 'The justification for this neo-NBFC (non-banking financial company) model are primarily these: a) it is sustainable; b) it encourages self help; it is based on the neoliberal principle that the poor should lift themselves up by their bootstraps and by inference government should keep at a distance; c) it has reached the hitherto excluded sector where the official financial institutions have not penetrated and do not show any signs of doing so due to increasing corporate pressures arising from amalgamations, core banking, shortage of staff at the branch level and a focus on a single bottom line namely profit (there are no champions of the SHG-Bank Linkage model at high levels)...' (Fernandez, undated).

References

Bakshi, Rajni, 1998, *Bapu Kuti: Journeys in Rediscovery of Gandhi*, New Delhi: Penguin, pp. 113.

Bakshi, Rajni, 2003, 'Lets Make it Happen: A Backgrounder on Alternative Economics', Mumbai: Centre for Education and Documentation. http://www.doccentre.net/docsweb/Localisation/Lets-make-it-happen.pdf (Last accessed 2 May, 2016).

Bakshi, Rajni, 2009, *Bazaars Conversations and Freedom: for a market culture beyond greed and fear*, New Delhi: Penguin, pp. 69.

Braudel, Fernand, 1984, *The Perspective of the World: Civilization and Capitalism 15th and 18th Century*, Vol. 3, London: Phoenix Press, pp. 522.

Deshpande, Neeta, 2014, *The Key to the Handloom Crisis*, http://www.vikalpsangam.org/article/the-key-to-the-handloom-crisis/ (Last accessed 1 May, 2016).

FAO, 2014, *The State of Food and Agriculture 2014*, Food and Agriculture Organisation, http://www.fao.org/3/a-i4036e.pdf (Last accessed 1 May, 2016).

Fernandez, Aloysius, Undated, *Is Micro Finance leading to a Macro Mess: The AP Ordinance*, http://myrada.org/myrada/rms58 (Last accessed 9 January, 2016).

Gandhi, M.K., 1946, *Harijan* (28 July), https://www.gandhiheritageportal.org/journals-by-gandhiji/harijan (Last accessed on 28 May, 2016).

Kothari, A. 2014, *Very much on the map: Timbaktu Collective*. Pune: Kalpavriksh, http://kalpavriksh.org/images/alternatives/CaseStudies/Timbaktu%20Collective_Case%20study%20report_20Mar2014.pdf (Last accessed 27 May, 2016).

Korten, D., 2010, *10 Common Sense Principles for a New Economy*, http://www.yesmagazine.org/blogs/david-korten/10-common-sense-principles-for-a-new-economy (Last accessed 8 November, 2016).

Mishra, Anupam, 2011, *Aaj Bhi Khare Hain Talaab*, http://www.indiawaterportal.org/articles/aaj-bhi-khare-hain-talaab-book-anupam-mishra (Last accessed on 28 May, 2016).

Shuman, Michael H., 1998, *Going Local: Creating Self-Reliant Communities in a Global Age*, New York: The Free Press, pp. 6.

Thapar, Romila, 2002, *Penguin History of Early India from Origins to AD 1300*, London: Penguin, pp. 279.

Uzramma, 2014, *A cotton textile industry for the future*, http://malkhaindia.blogspot.in/ (Last accessed 15 May, 2016).

Reimagining India's Urban Future

Rakesh Kapoor

Summary

This paper looks at the major challenges that urban India faces in the next three decades and beyond and suggests a vision for an alternative urban future for India 2047. Urban India today faces huge problems of poor infrastructure, highly inadequate water and electricity supply, slums, waste disposal, poor public transport, and so on. Among the underlying causes of this rundown state of Indian cities are poor governance, financial weakness, and lack of innovation and implementation of populist schemes.

Arguing that a better quality of life for Indians – urban and rural – requires fundamental departures from current approaches, mindsets and institutions, the paper suggests a radically different vision for urban *plus* rural India 2047, built around the following components.

- Dispersed urbanization: small towns as development and skilling hubs
- Innovative mechanisms for financing and building small and medium towns
- Public regulatory authorities at multiple levels to regulate the uses of land and water
- Empowering urban local bodies (ULBs) or urban local governments (ULGs)
- Innovation in sustainable resource use and solutions for urban areas to create 'regenerative' and 'smart' cities
- Low carbon cities and resilience to climate change and associated disasters

The suggested future of Indian cities will be based, among other things, on sustainable development through the extensive use of renewable energy sources, minimal waste generation, minimum ecological footprint, provision of decent housing to all citizens and resilience to disasters. Empowered urban local bodies and a decentralized form of governance will be crucial. Ultimately, the challenge for Indians, including our political leaders, is to first of all ***envision*** another future for urban *plus* rural India, and then to take all constituents of our population along to achieve that vision.

Introduction

For decades commentators have stressed the predominance of rural life in India. We take it as a matter of fact that India lives in its villages. By 2047, however, if present trends continue, a major paradigm shift will occur. Half – or perhaps more than half – of India will live in urban areas. And this percentage will thereafter go on increasing significantly during the 21st century. More importantly, the challenges of governance, sustainability, climate change, inclusive growth and innovation – all these will be faced most intensely in the urban half of India. Cities have historically been recognized as important seats of human civilization. This leadership role will be put to test in the 21st century as cities have to deal with the challenges of governance, resource use, global warming and disasters.

This paper is organized in four sections. The first gives an overview of urban population, its distribution and trend of growth in India. In section two, the major challenges that urban India faces in the remaining part of this century and the different facets of the urban challenge lead us, finally, to imagine what urban India 2047 and beyond *can be*. Sections three and four therefore deal with different aspects of the vision for an alternative urban future.

Urban India 2015

Growing urbanization: a snapshot of India and the world

As per the 2011 census India's urban population is 377 million (31.16 per cent) and rural population is 833.1 million (68.84 per cent). In 2001, the urban population was 27.81 per cent and the rural population was 72.19 per cent. For the first time since Independence the absolute increase in urban areas, at 91 million, was more than the absolute increase in rural areas, at 90.4 million, since the last census in 2001. But the projections for the next few decades are significant and indicate the accelerating pace of urbanization. The table below indicates the urban-rural distribution trend over a century and a half.

Table 1: India: Rural-Urban population distribution over the years

Year	Rural (%)	Urban (%)
1901	89.2	10.8
1951	82.7	17.3

Year	Rural (%)	Urban (%)
2001	72.2	27.8
2011	68.8	31.2
Projection for 2050[1]	48.3	51.7

Source: GOI, 2011; UN, 2011 for 2050 projection

It is notable that while it took 110 years for the percentage of urban population to go up from 10.8 to 31.2 per cent (an increase of 20.4 per cent in the extent of urbanization), it will take only another 40 years for another 20.5 per cent increase in the extent of urbanization to 51.7 per cent. India is rapidly becoming an urban nation!

This matches with global trends, only the pace of urbanization in India in the next three to four decades will be among the fastest anywhere in the world. Globally, 54 per cent of the world's population resides in urban areas in 2014. In 1950, 30 per cent of the world's population was urban, and by 2050, 66 per cent of the world's population is projected to be urban. This will be roughly the reverse of the global rural-urban population distribution of the mid-twentieth century (UN, 2014).

Just three countries – India, China and Nigeria – together are expected to account for 37 per cent of the projected growth of the world's urban population between 2014 and 2050. India is projected to add 404 million urban dwellers (with a total urban population of 814 million in 2050), China 292 million and Nigeria 212 million. The fastest growing urban agglomerations that are located in Asia and Africa are medium-sized cities and cities with less than 1 million inhabitants.

Urban settlements

Urban settlements in India can be either Statutory Towns (with a municipality, corporation, cantonment board or notified town area committee) or Census Towns, which are settlements satisfying the following criteria: a minimum population of 5000, at least 75 per cent of male main workers engaged in non-agricultural pursuits and a density of at least 400 per sq km. In 2011 there were a total of 7935 urban settlements: 4041 statutory towns and 3894 census towns. There was an increase of 2532 towns since 2001. The number of metropolitan cities (population above 1 million) in 2011 was 53 (up from 35 in 2001), with 42 per cent of the country's urban population.

According to the McKinsey 2010 report on urbanization, India will have 68 cities of more than 1 million people by 2030 and they will account for almost half of the country's total urban population (Sankhe et al, 2010).

The Challenges before Urban India

Anyone familiar with cities and towns in India is aware of the problems of poor infrastructure, highly inadequate water and electricity supply, slums, waste disposal, poor public transport, etc. The late Ashish Bose, perhaps India's best known demographer, is reported to have said that India's small towns were pictures of hell. The question that inevitably arises is: why have nearly all our cities, with rare exceptions, been such big failures in providing good infrastructure and services and a good quality of living?

The underlying causes for this run-down state of our cities are many, but perhaps have something to do with the fact that in our governance and political culture building good, clean, efficient towns with decent infrastructure and services for all residents and running cities efficiently has simply not been given enough importance. I suspect it has even something to do with India's 'socialistic' ideals that sub-consciously influence our collective psyche and militate against efficiency and excellence in any sphere. Shankar Acharya writes, for instance,

'Five-Year Plan documents paid scant attention to the field until the 1980s'. It was not until 1992 that the 74th amendment to the Constitution empowered urban local bodies in the economic and social governance of the nation. And it was only in 2005 that the Jawaharlal Nehru National Urban Renewal Mission (JNNURM) imparted a serious and long overdue national policy thrust to this area'.

(Acharya, 2014, pp. 36)

The other deep-rooted reason for the woeful state of our cities is the absence of realistic long-term planning. Annapurna Shaw notes that the central government created several important institutions for urban administration and for the training of skilled professionals during the first two Five Year Plans (1951-56, 1956-61).

'These included a Ministry of Urban Affairs, the National Buildings Organization, the School of Planning and Architecture in New Delhi, a Regional and Town Planning Department in the Indian Institute of Technology Kharagpur, and the Town and Country Planning Organization, the technical unit of the Ministry of Urban Affairs... During the 1960s, several states enacted such legislation and created town planning departments which, with the help of central grants, prepared *over 500 master plans for individual cities*. But with the rapid urbanization that followed independence and a threefold increase in urban population from 62 million in 1951 to 159 million in 1981 to 217 million in 1991, these plans were thrown into disarray. *They have remained mostly on paper'* (Emphasis added by author).

(Shaw, 2012, pp. 20)

Thanks to this disjunction between plans and institutions and the real needs of the people, Indian cities and towns have witnessed a host of problems and issues. One of the biggest issues has been the failure to plan for adequate land and housing for city dwellers. Thus by 1991, 21 per cent of India's urban population was residing in slums. In Mumbai this figure was 43 per cent, in Kolkata 36 per cent, and in Delhi 22 per cent (ibid.). In 2001, the slum population, at 52.27 million, was 18.3 per cent of the total urban population and in 2011 it was 65.49 million, 17.37 per cent of the urban population. By some estimates the current slum population in Indian cities is estimated to be 93 million and is expected to cross 100 million by 2017 (Suri *et al.*, 2014; Dash, 2013).

On most other parameters the indicators of urban services and quality of life are poor in India, as the indicators from the McKinsey 2010 report on India's cities and towns given in Figure 1 below show.

Besides these indicators, there are others. For instance, an estimated 18 per cent population in urban areas resorts to open defecation (Mehta *et al.*, 2010). Only 20 out of 85 cities with a population of 0.5 million or more in 2009 had a city bus service (HPEC, 2011).

This situation of urban services is not surprising considering that the running of Indian towns and cities reflects a short-term, misplaced 'welfare' approach, heavily influenced by the peculiar Indian *avatar* of socialism-populism, vide which services are provided and subsidized by the state, but the costs of the same are not recovered from the users, as Table 2 (below) on average cost recovery of selected urban local bodies (ULBs) illustrates. The subsidies – although provided in the name of socialism or public welfare – are more often than not misdirected and cornered by the rich and the middle classes. In the process, the state loses precious revenue that should have been used for infrastructure up-gradation and service provision, which would benefit the really poor or the lower income classes the most. A few simple examples can illustrate this approach.

- Allowing big, private cars of the rich to run on subsidized (and polluting) diesel
- Not charging private vehicle owners adequately for road space and parking space
- The recent example in Delhi of providing free water upto a certain level of monthly consumption.

Figure 1: The current performance of India's cities is poor across key indicators of quality of life

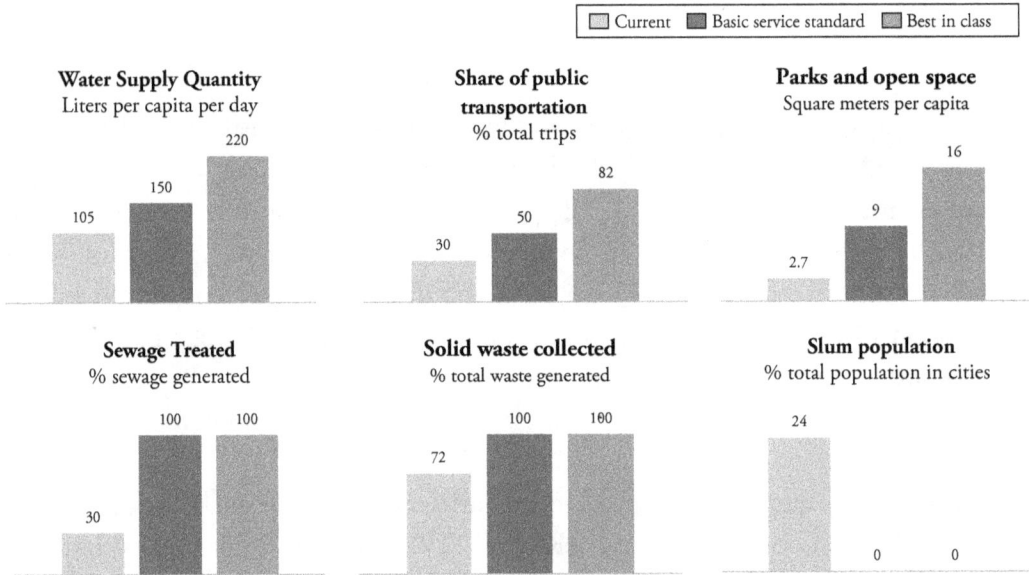

Source: Sankhe et al., 2010

More often than not the benefit of this misdirected subsidy is being cornered by the middle class with small families while the state is losing crucial revenue that could go towards building water supply infrastructure to serve neglected areas with poor residents and extremely poor water supply infrastructure (See Bhalla *et al.*, 2015). The interesting thing is that these misdirected subsidies are provided in the name of socialism or welfare and are widely accepted with little critical scrutiny! Providing cross-subsidies to the poor is perhaps the best option to protect their interests, but sadly, there are few well-designed and properly targeted instances of cross-subsidies one can find in Indian cities.

This situation explains the entrenched financial weakness of Indian cities due to very poor revenue generation through property taxes or through user charges[2]. 'Indian municipalities are among the weakest in the world in terms of access to resources, financial autonomy, and revenue-raising capability' (Mohanty, 2014). According to the High Powered Expert Committee (HPEC) on urban infrastructure and services, 'Urban local governments in India are among the weakest in the world both in terms of capacity to raise resources.....the tax bases of ULBs are narrow and inflexible and lack buoyancy....' (GOI, 2011, pp. XXVII).

Table 2: Average Cost Recovery of Selected ULBs: 2007-08

City	Revenue Expenditure on Urban Services (Rs Lakh)	Revenue Receipts from Urban Services (Rs Lakh)	Average Cost Recovery (per cent)
Metropolitan Cities			
Hyderabad (Andhra Pradesh)	34722	13879	40.0
Bhopal (Madhya Pradesh)	4938	2044	41.4
Jabalpur (Madhya Pradesh)	3240	911	28.1
Lucknow (Uttar Pradesh)	1610	293	18.2
Other Cities			
Amravati (Maharashtra)	2610	204	7.8
Malegaon (Maharashtra)	2000	647	32.3
Palakkad (Kerala)	286	158	55.2
Towns			
Baramati (Maharashtra)	417	143	34.3

Source: GOI, HPEC (2011) based on Budget Documents of ULBs

Discussing the property tax system in India, Rao (2013) mentions that reliable data on revenue collections from property tax by various municipal bodies is not available in India. However, based on an NIPFP study of 2009, he mentions that 'The most optimistic estimate... shows that in 2006-07, on an average, per capita property tax collections was Rs. 486 (about USD10.6) and total collections ranged from 0.16 per cent to 0.24 per cent of GDP.' As may be seen from Table 3 below, this is much below the developing country average of 0.6 per cent, with ridiculously low property taxes as compared to the market value of properties. If one considers all municipal revenues (including property tax), India's municipal revenues-to-GDP ratio was less than 1 per cent of GDP in 2007-08, compared to 6 per cent for South Africa and 7.4 per cent for Brazil (Acharya, 2014).

Kapoor

Table 3: Per Cent of Property Tax Revenue in GDP

	1970s	1980s	1990s	2000s
OECD	1.24 (9.7)	1.31 (9.9)	1.44 (13.65)	2.12 (12.40)
Developing	0.42 (18.7)	0.36 (15.97)	0.42 (13.49)	0.60 (18.37)
Transitional	0.34 (3.67)	0.59 (4.92)	0.54 (7.75)	0.68 (9.43)
ALL	0.77 (14.49)	0.73 (12.89)	0.75 (11.63)	1.04 (3.40)

Note: (Figures in the parentheses show percentage of property tax in total revenues of municipal bodies)
Source: Bahl and Martinez-Vazquez, 2008, quoted in Rao, 2013

This situation not only ensures that India cannot generate enough revenue to invest in the up-gradation of infrastructure and services in its cities, it also ensures that spirit and the functionality of decentralization embodied in the 74th Constitutional Amendment Act (CAA) of 1992 remains elusive.

Mehta *et al.* (2010) observe while reviewing the performance of the JNNURM,

'...pricing of services such as water remains delinked from the cost of service provision, despite this being a requirement under the JNNURM. Thus, despite decentralization and some move towards functional decentralization, urban local governments (ULG) dependence on, and therefore control by, the state and national governments has increased in recent years.'

(pp. 21)

At the same time, it is the state governments, more than the central government that are to blame for this situation and the poor state of ULGs. It is the tardiness, complete lack of imagination and innovation and perhaps old political habits on the part of the leadership in the states that has kept them back from devolving powers to cities and creating effective institutional and support systems to manage them well, while the central government, too, has been responsible in not creating and pushing effective and well-designed policies

364

for urban management. As Mishra (2015) notes, despite allocating funds for 100 'Smart Cities' and now plans for 500 AMRUT (Atal Mission for Rejuvenation and Urban Transformation) cities, '...the Centre cannot build or rejuvenate cities. It can only fund and motivate state governments to do so...' since urban administration is a state subject. Rao (2013) notes that '... placing the local tax powers in the State List has denied them [urban local bodies] the power to determine the base, the rate structure and administrative and enforcement mechanism. Furthermore, it has given the State governments (sic) to abolish the property tax altogether for populist reasons without providing any alternative revenue source, thus denying them an important revenue source and leaving them with large unfunded mandates'. For instance, the Rajasthan State government abolished house tax in 2006 and Haryana abolished it on self-occupied residential properties in 2008, but re-imposed it after the grants for urban development by the Central government was linked to property tax reform.

Thus, besides the disempowerment of Indian cities due to missing revenues (both taxes and user charges), the other factors that contribute to their emaciation are the poor institutional framework to govern cities, and the missing capacities of ULGs to manage and innovate to run cities efficiently (Sankhe *et al.*, 2010; Ahluwalia *et al.*, 2014; Acharya, 2014; Mishra, 2015). **It needs to be emphasized here that running cities 'efficiently' means providing basic services and public infrastructure for all, most of all the poor, and having the human, financial and technological resources to be able to do this.** By no stretch of imagination is an 'efficient' city meant to be a city that excludes or disenfranchises the poor. Instead, it is meant to imply a city that can raise enough resources and charges from its residents (and primarily from the rich residents) and can have the required human and institutional capacities to be able to run the city efficiently for **all** its residents.

Till some of these root causes are addressed, the situation of Indian cities will worsen, not improve, over time. The McKinsey report of 2010 gives a dismal picture of where the quality of urban services is headed if the trends of 2010 continue (Sankhe *et al.*, 2010). Swertsz *et al* (2014) assert that the sustainability of India's urban system in the next few decades poses such a big challenge that it is not just going to be a challenge for India, but a global challenge as well!

Given this dismal picture and deep-rooted causes of disempowerment, where is India's urban future headed?

Alternative Urban Futures, 2047

Reimagining the Indian city of the future

Many scholars and planners have spelt out elements of a vision of sustainable, regenerative cities of the future. The vision laid out, for instance, by Maslin (2009), in the context of his discussion on global warming, is very appealing. I suggest below an outline of a vision for Indian cities of the future. The vision, by definition, is utopian – it is an ideal type. Each element of the vision is desirable but it is clear that in reality all elements will rarely be found in a single instance. The next section, on the other hand, spells out the specific strategies we need to adapt to work towards the vision.

- The city exists in harmony with its hinterland, with an ecological footprint that is not too high, through extensive use of renewable energy sources, appropriate technologies and lifestyles, extremely careful use of resources, demand management and practices such as recycling and reuse of water and careful recharge of groundwater. The city generates the minimum amount of waste possible, segregates its waste at source and is thus able to optimally recycle and treat most of the waste generated.

- The city provides for decent housing for all its residents and thus has no slums, and has mixed use areas so that most people need to travel short distances to work. It has adequate commercial space to provide office/commercial space at low to moderate rates for small businesses.

- The city is very clean with clean drinking water and sanitation for all, a number of green spaces, beautiful public spaces with public art and with adequate facilities for sports for all residents.

- The city has an empowered and responsive local governing body that has the power to levy taxes and raise financial resources and that actively seeks citizen participation in governance of the city. Alternatively, citizen participation could be through direct democracy in neighbourhoods and the elected local governing body of the city coordinates among these neighbourhood units, and handles issues like the overall city budget and building and planning regulations.

- The city is moderately large but not too large so as to permit cycling over shorter or medium distances and also to encourage pedestrians and provide paths for them and cycling tracks. It has very good and adequate systems of public transport so that use of private cars and motorized two-wheeler vehicles is low.

- The city has adopted processes and disaster response strategies based on careful assessment of risk to be resilient to disasters and the impacts of climate change.

- The city is able to develop in harmony with its historical buildings and heritage, and, where possible, is able to preserve its heritage in a way as to attract tourists, while encouraging residents and citizens to be part of this process.
- Considering the distribution of cities in the country, there is a pattern of dispersed urbanization, that is, nearly all regions have moderate-sized vibrant cities and a number of small towns that are hubs for skill development in the area and provide jobs, livelihoods and services to the people of that region so that people do not have to migrate for work over long distances for livelihood and working men or women are not forced to work far away from their families.
- Rivers within or nearby are managed for their landscape, leisure, and nature conservation value. They also form part of urban transport networks, with riverside cycle paths and walkways. Most importantly, the riverbanks and surrounding land absorb rainfall run-off and prevent flooding of built-up areas (this last element has been borrowed from Maslin, 2009).

Strategies towards a desired scenario for urban India

If we want a better quality of life for Indians – urban and rural – and if we want to be prepared for the challenges of the twenty-first century, then radical departures from current approaches, mindsets and institutions are needed. I suggest below a radically different vision for urban India – indeed for urban *plus* rural India – 2047, built around the following components:
- Dispersed urbanization: small towns as development and skilling hubs
- Innovative mechanisms for financing and building small and medium towns
- Public regulatory authorities at multiple levels to regulate the uses of land and water
- Empowering ULBs or ULGs and civic action by urban residents
- Innovation in sustainable resource use and solutions for urban areas to create 'regenerative' and 'smart' cities
- Low carbon cities and resilience to climate change and associated disasters

Small is beautiful: A strategy for dispersed urbanization and prosperity

A number of observers have pointed out the centrality of small and medium towns, or a 'rurbanization' approach, for an inclusive growth strategy for India (Khosla *et al.*, 2006; Indiresan, 2004; Kathpalia *et al.*, 2015; Dahiya, 2012; Sahasranaman, 2012; Singh, 2012). Sahasranaman writes, for instance, that 'sustained development of small and medium cities is possibly the most potent strategy to counter the current trend of lopsided development...

Without urgent and sustained efforts to develop small and medium cities, it will be impossible to develop a meaningful, effective and long term urbanization strategy for India.'[3]

Kathpalia *et al.*, (2015) proposed a dispersed urbanization strategy. They propose the creation of 4000 small towns (the number of blocks in the country is about 7000) either by developing existing small towns or by building new ones, with an average 150,000 population. These towns are to be established 50 to 100 kilometres from existing cities and will cater to the needs of their population and to villages within a 20 km radius (except in remote hilly or desert areas, etc.). These towns will be designed to develop manufacturing, marketing and agricultural processing infrastructure as suitable to local conditions, along with building of power, communication and transport infrastructure, provisions of skills, services and comprehensive network of civic amenities. In particular, these towns will act as hubs to provide skills to young people, which is essential to be able to generate jobs and self-employment for India's multitude of young people.

Dahiya (2012) notes that during 2010–2020 two-thirds of the demographic expansion in the world's cities will take place in Asia, and if cities in Asia are to take advantage of this fact to plan proper infrastructures and alleviate congestion, pollution and slums, 'urban policies must become part and parcel of national development policies, and must include a clear focus on the development of small and medium-sized cities which will accommodate the bulk of urban demographic growth for at least the next two decades' (pp. 59).

Financing small and medium cities

Along with a strategy to create more small towns, a corresponding strategy to finance the building of small and medium cities is essential. The 74th CAA mandated Metropolitan Planning Committees (MPCs) and District Planning Committees (DPCs) to prepare long-term plans. Although the performance of these planning committees has been non-existent or dismal in most states, Sahasranaman (2012) suggests that DPCs would be the ideal vehicles to drive forward the agenda for small and medium cities in India.

The failure to plan for land has been one of the prime reasons for the current state of urban decay in the larger cities. Sahasranaman (2012) suggests a number of innovative ways to achieve this objective. One mechanism that sidesteps the need for land acquisition, while making land available for development is Land Pooling and Readjustment (LPR). In the LPR process,

'a local public authority consolidates numerous small parcels of land owned by different parties, and carries out collective planning of this land. The local authority plans the provision of civic infrastructure amenities such as roads, schools, hospitals and parks, sets aside some portion of land for public sale, and returns the rest to the original landowners. LPR is a self-financing scheme... The provision of infrastructure raises the value of these lands and this increase in value is the compensation to the original landowners who are now returned a proportion of the land that they provided'.

(Sahasranaman, 2012, pp. 62-63)

Although the original owners receive a smaller piece of land than they originally provided, the value of the land they receive is higher. Some portion of the land is set aside for public sale, and proceeds from selling can be used to fund public goods such as schools, hospitals and parks. LPR has been used by some states in India, especially in Gujarat. LPR norms have recently been announced by the central government (TOI, 2015). In Gujarat, Bimal Patel (2015), president of CEPT University, Ahmedabad, shows with a number of examples how private land is regularly appropriated for a variety of public needs. It is appropriated without using the Land Acquisition Act, without 'acquiring' it, without evicting people, without using much force, without costly delays and without burdening the exchequer. Patel mentions that Japan has been using land pooling or reconstitution since at least the 1890s'. He explains the concept of land pooling or reconstitution as follows:

'...imagine that you want to make a path through the middle of a room packed with people. Imagine that two strings parallel to one another and as far apart as the width of the path are stretched across the room. Now, you have two options. You can force all the people between the strings to leave the room and accept compensation for leaving. Or, you can tell everyone in the room to squeeze up to form a path without anyone having to leave the room.'

(Patel, 2015)

Public regulatory authorities to regulate land and water

Due to India's large population and relatively high population density, the issue of land is highly contentious, as has been witnessed in recent debates on land acquisition. However, the matter is dealt with in an ad hoc manner by states, resulting in land mafias and profiteering by speculators at the cost of farmers and other original landowners. At the same time, with a growing economy the demands on land for different purposes (industry, residential, institutional, etc.) are only going to intensify. In this scenario Kathpalia *et al.*, (2015) suggest that the only way to allocate land rationally between different kinds of uses is to have public regulatory authorities at multiple levels (at the *gram sabha* level, the block level, the district and the state). The allocation and regulation of land use is done first at the lowest level of the gram sabha, as per certain norms to be spelt out, and then proceeds upwards to higher levels.

The tasks to be carried out by the public regulatory system will include:

(i) Allocation of land for different purposes, including identifying towns for development as hubs;

(ii) The pricing of land for different uses within a state;

(iii) Framing rules and guidelines for land development and rehabilitation of inhabitants, and for safeguarding land for agriculture, forest purposes and environment protection;

(iv) Monitoring of the actual allocation and implementation of the rules.

Empowering ULBs/ULGs and civic action by urban residents

As discussed in section 2, the strengthening of urban local governments in keeping with the spirit of decentralization embodied in the 74th CAA and the devolution of financial powers and autonomy to them by the state governments is essential to enable our cities and towns to be better managed. The 12th schedule of the Constitution lists 18 economic development and social justice functions that are best devolved to ULBs. These include, among others, urban planning including town planning, regulation of land use and construction of buildings, planning for socio-economic development, water supply for domestic, industrial and commercial purposes, public health, sanitation conservancy and solid waste management, slum improvement and upgradation, urban poverty alleviation, etc.

But the institutional structures of ULBs 'are not uniform across states or even metropolitan (or district) areas, and are plagued with political and administrative problems. These shortcomings make the successful execution of devolved functions a challenging task for the local bodies' (Anand, 2012, pp.1). The experience of nearly all states shows that they have not devolved adequate powers and finances to the ULBs. Moreover, adequate capacities, staff and expertise are also missing in most ULBs. For instance, Vaddiraju (2013) shows that in Karnataka the 74th CAA is not implemented in letter and spirit and governance and planning in the small/medium towns in the state is done through a small, ill-equipped section in the deputy commissioner's/collector's office. Moreover, this task is completely disconnected from the chief planning office in the zilla panchayat (district level local self government body).

Oommen (2015), shows that even the Fourteenth Finance Commission has not treated local governments properly and comprehensively in distribution of finances to them. Avashia *et al.* (2016) note that the JNNURM was the first programme to provide substantial funds for urban local bodies to improve their infrastructure and bring in better governance systems. However, evaluating the urban infrastructure and governance, the authors conclude that the Mission has not been able to substantially improve the functioning and efficiency of ULBs, particularly from performance and personnel management point of view. In this context, they welcome the establishment of a municipal cadre under JNNURM 2.0 as a welcome step towards professionalizing urban governance and creation of a specialized force of officers to manage cities.

Another set of issues vis-à-vis urban local governance relates to going further down to the *mohalla* or neighbourhood level to strengthen democracy by direct involvement and participation of citizens on local issues of relevance. Recent discussions (see, for instance, Teri, 2010; Ramani, 2013; BBMP, 2015) indicate that this is undoubtedly another important way in which local level democracy and citizen participation will be strengthened in future, although at present there is very little progress in this matter.

Direct action and participation by city residents on different aspects of urban governance is going to be an important aspect of urban local governance in future. One can find some examples of this today. For instance, Urban Setu is a civil society initiative in Bhuj town, Gujarat that tries to bridge the gaps of communication and coordination among communities, government and NGOs. The ultimate objective is to institutionalize grassroots urban governance and planning (Desor and Kothari, 2013). Another instance is Participatory Budgeting in Pune. The city has experimented with it since 2006, when it was first introduced formally by the Pune Municipal Corporation (PMC), and citizens' organizations have played an important role in initiating and shaping it (Menon, 2014).

Sustainable, 'regenerative' cities

Globally there is a lot of thinking on the sustainability of cities, on dealing with the challenges posed by climate change and on innovative models for service delivery and urban planning and design. Girardet *et al.* (undated) of the World Future Council conceptualize the regenerative city as a city that:

1. Relies primarily on local and regional supplies
2. Is powered, heated, cooled and driven by renewable energy
3. Reuses resources and restores degraded ecosystems

As against this the resource-wasting city:

1. Uses resources without concern for their origins or destination of their wastes
2. Emits vast amounts of carbon dioxide without ensuring re-absorption
3. Consumes huge amounts of meat produced mainly with imported feed

One of the biggest issues of concern for future cities, and very relevant for India, is the fact that whilst urban areas constitute three to four per cent of the world's land surface, their ecological footprints, which measure the amount of productive land and water needed to produce the goods consumed and to assimilate the resulting wastes, cover most of the productive land surface of the globe.

Giardet *et al.,* document a large number of real examples of sustainable practices from the world's cities. These include solar energy rooftop installations in China; over 100 regions across Germany, encompassing about a quarter of the country's population, that have implemented a 100 per cent renewable energy (RE) target; concentrated solar power (CSP) technology in Spain and USA; urban agriculture program in Cuba, and so on. By 2010 the number of solar water heaters installed in China equalled the thermal equivalent of the electrical capacity of 40 large nuclear power plants.

According to the authors some of the factors limiting the rate of regenerative urban development are:
- Lack of local knowledge about global urban impacts;
- Departmental silos and inadequate financing arrangements;
- Limited efforts to integrate solutions into existing systems;
- Political and financial short-termism;
- Low priority for environmental concerns;
- Exclusion of externalities in product pricing;
- Overlap or conflict in mandates between different government levels.

In addition, one could add a few more factors such as the lack of citizen participation and power in decision-making at the neighbourhood or local levels in cities, and the imbalance of power between urban and rural areas, including the lack of adequate voice amongst rural populations from whom the city draws its resources.

These challenges and factors seem to have a big resonance with the Indian situation.

'Smart Cities' and innovation

The NDA government's proposal to create 100 smart cities has, not surprisingly, led to much discussion. There is much ambiguity about the idea of smart cities, with everyone understanding it differently. The Smart Cities Council, an international, industry-founded advocacy platform, describes it as 'one that knows about itself and makes itself more known to its populace' (Burte, 2014). At the heart of the idea seems to be the use of ICTs embedded into administrative and infrastructural systems (like transport and water supply) for greater efficiency and responsive management. As Burte writes, quoting Hollands (2008),

'...there is no reason why any city, even in the developing world, would not want to be smart. A better information infrastructure, increased operational, economic, energy efficiencies, and a better quality of life for all, are certainly desirable ideals. The question really is whether smart cities can do away with the need to fix our cities in ways that are much more basic?'

'I take an obvious point as already made: that it is necessary to fix the basics before we aim for more techno-managerially advanced systems. If we cannot build and maintain roads without potholes, it is absurd to aim for intelligent pavements.'

(Burte, pp. 24-25)

Similarly, Suri *et al.*, (2014) make the point that,

'Does India really think that the world (and we) can achieve sustainable development without paying attention to cities, or worse, by building 100 (or even 1,000) new, hi-tech, smart cities, while ignoring the imperative of reviving, revitalizing and retrofitting our existing towns?'

(pp. 28)

So, as with a lot of other false oppositions, it is not a question of choosing between smart and non-smart cities. The point is that cities need to be fixed in terms of physical infrastructure, services, preventing the growth of slums or improving conditions in slum areas to decent levels of housing and services, resilience to disasters, managing their finances and institutionalizing good local governance and management capacities. If they can be smart and intelligent through the use of ICTs in addition to all this, that would be a bonus!

Of course there are many ways besides the use of ICTs through which cities can be innovative. Numerous examples from all over the world, including some in India, illustrate this point. Something as simple as painting roofs white to reflect heat and thus reduce the impact of global warming is a good example. But we need good innovative thinking on how to use resources sustainably, how to deal with climate change, how to make cities more humane and participative, and so on. The proposal from Soni *et al.*, to use the water stored in river flood plains aquifers to design and create 'natural cities' belongs to this category. This kind of truly innovative thinking needs to be encouraged, and deserves serious consideration by planners and environmentalists.

Low carbon cities and resilience to climate change and associated disasters

Climate change and associated disasters pose a number of threats to cities. In case of heat stress due to average temperature increases of more than 2 to 4 degrees Celsius above pre-industrial levels in this century a number of cities and regions will face heat deaths and may become uninhabitable (Moriarty *et al.*, 2015).

Cities could well face serious biophysical hazards (urban floods, health problems, geophysical hazards) should greenhouse gas concentrations continue to rise. The cities at greatest risk from biophysical hazards are those that:

- Already face one or more high risks from natural hazards not directly related to climate change
- Face multiple risks from on-going climate change
- Have low financial or administrative resources for adaptation

Many Indian and South Asian cities fall in the category of cities at greatest risk from biophysical hazards. One of the most serious challenges that badly planned and unregulated Indian cities face is that of dealing with earthquakes. The intensity of damage that this can cause in the coming decades, particularly in the Himalayan region, is such that all our skills, knowledge and innovative and managerial capabilities are required to plan for the mitigation of consequences from such a likely event.

Conclusion

The World Urbanization Prospects Report, 2014, of the UN emphasizes that a holistic approach to urban planning and management is needed to improve living standards of urban and rural dwellers alike.

In India, although our challenges are unique and arise primarily from our political-cultural situation, the advantage we have is that we can leapfrog from the current dismal situation to innovative systems of management and designing cities and urban infrastructure and services. The most important thing is that we have to get out of sterile mindsets and either/or thinking that pits one constituency against another, and rural against urban.

Suri *et al.*, make a persuasive case for including the sustainable cities and human settlements goal in the post-2015 sustainable development goals framework.[4] They note, India seems to be vacillating in its support to the Sustainable Cities and Human Settlements (SCHS) goal, as it is called at the moment, aiming to 'build inclusive, safe, sustainable cities and human settlements' with targets that cover urban planning, resilience preparedness, and the integration of housing, transportation and open space.

To my mind, India's support to this goal will reflect, most of all, the recognition that we consider the urban and the rural as two sides of the same human coin, and that we do not want to play divisive and populist politics in playing one against the other.

Ultimately, the challenge is for Indians, including our political leaders, to first of all *envision* another future for urban *plus* rural India, and then to take all constituents of our population along to achieve that vision.

Interestingly, there is enough innovation in the world, and enough models of planning and design that we can draw upon. What we need is an innovating knowledge society, and the willingness to try new approaches. The beginning for this has to come from visionary political leadership. But once we start creating the capacities for innovative thinking in our education systems, and create a trained cadre of urban managers, we could be on the path to the innovative, predominantly urban, knowledge society that could be our best bet for the next hundred years and more. One of the most difficult challenges is to get away from sterile, narrow-minded and puerile political discourse and populism to plan and use innovative best practices for the long term. The challenges India and its citizens will face will be immense, but with political will and imagination we shall be in a much better position to face these. As Vojnovic (2014) says, 'It is politics and not science that hinders the pursuit of urban sustainability' (pp. S43).

Endnotes

1. According to Swertz, *et al.*, 2014, the extent of urbanization in India in 2050 will be 55.9 per cent.
2. Given this analysis, one can understand why the recent moves by the newly elected Aam Aadmi Party (AAP) government in Delhi to slash water and electricity charges are populist, retrograde moves, not to mention the fact that even with full recovery of costs, the environmental costs of providing these services in India are not factored in.
3. At the same time, some influential observers have opposed the thrust or the approach to focus on small towns. According to Sivaramakrishnan *et al.*, 2005, 'there is not much merit in pursuing a program for small and medium towns. While the case for improving urban services is common across the board, a program like the Integrated Development of Small and Medium Towns (IDSMT) has not succeeded in reducing or deflecting large city growth. Whether in comparatively developed states like Maharashtra or Punjab or in other states like Bihar or Rajasthan, it is seen that the growth rates of IDSMT towns continue to be below the average growth rates for the small and medium towns in the state and well below the rate of class I cities' (pp. not available).

4. Since this was originally written, the Sustainable Cities and Communities goal has been adopted by the UN in September 2015 as goal 11 of the 17 Sustainable Development Goals (UNDP, 2016).

References

Acharya, Shankar, 2014, 'Understanding the Urban Challenge', *Economic & Political Weekly*, Vol. XLIX (42), 18 October, pp. 36-38.

Ahluwalia, Isher Judge, Ravi Kambur and P. K. Mohanty (ed.), 2014, *Urbanisation in India: Challenges, Opportunities and the Way Forward*, New Delhi: Sage Publications.

Anand, Vaibhav, 2012, Functions of the Urban Local Bodies, http://financingcities.ifmr.co.in/blog/2012/17/functions-of-the-urban-local-bodies-ulbs/ (accessed 5 May, 2017).

Avashia, V.K. and Amit Garg, 2016, 'Urban Infrastructure and Governance Mission under JNNURM: Have the Reforms Delivered?' *Economic & Political Weekly*, Vol.LI(2), 9 January, pp. 41-57.

Bahl, Roy W., Jorge Martinez-Vazquez and Joan Youngman, 2008, *Making the Property Tax Work*, Cambridge (Mass): Lincoln Institute.

Bruhat Bengaluru Mahanagara Palike (BBMP), 2015, *The Karnataka Municipalities and Certain Other Law (Amendment) Act, 2014*. Available at http://bbmp.gov.in/en/web/guest/act/bye-laws (accessed 16 July, 2016).

Bhalla, Surjit S and Prasanthi Ramakrishnan, 2015, 'No such thing as free water', *The Indian Express*, 18 February, http://indianexpress.com/article/opinion/columns/no-such-thing-as-free-water/ (accessed 9 Jan, 2016).

Burte, Himanshu, 2014, 'The 'Smart City' Card', *Economic & Political Weekly*, Vol. XLIX(46), 15 November, pp. 22 -25.

Dahiya, Bharat, 2012, 'Cities in Asia, 2012: Demographics, economics, poverty, environment and governance', *Cities*, 29 (2012) S44-S61.

Dash, Dipak Kumar, 2013, 'By 2017 India's slum population will rise to 104 million', TNN, Aug 20, http://timesofindia.indiatimes.com/india/By-2017-Indias-slum-population-will-rise-to-104-million/articleshow/21927474.cms (accessed 9 January, 2016).

Desor, Shiba and Ashish Kothari, 2013, 'A bridge not too far', *The Hindu*, 1 December, http://www.thehindu.com/features/magazine/a-bridge-not-too-far/article5407870.ece (accessed 5 May, 2016).

Girardet, Herbert, Stefan Schurig, Anna Leidreiter and Fiona Woo, undated, *Towards the Regenerative City*, Hamburg: World Future Council.

GoI, 2011, Census of India 2011: Rural Urban Distribution of Population, Government of India. Available at: http://censusindia.gov.in/2011-prov-results/paper2/data_files/india/Rural_Urban_2011.pdf (accessed 20 May, 2015).

GoI, HPEC, 2011, *Report on Indian Urban Infrastructure and Services, the High Powered Expert Committee (HPEC) for Estimating the Investment Requirements for Urban Infrastructure Services*, Available at: http://icrier.org/pdf/FinalReport-hpec.pdf (accessed 20 May, 2015).

GoI, 2013, Primary Census Abstract for Slums, Government of India. Available at: www.censusindia. gov.in/2011-Documents/Slum-26-09-13.pdf (accessed 20 May, 2015).

Kathpalia, G. N., and Rakesh Kapoor, 2015, *Management of Land and other Resources for Inclusive Growth: India 2050*, Delhi: Alternative Futures, http://www.alternativefutures.org.in/userfiles/file/ Urbanisation%20paper%20AF%20rev_%20ver5%202015.pdf (accessed 5 May, 2017).

Khosla, Vinod and AtanuDey, 2003, 'RISC – Rural Infrastructure & Services Commons: A Model for Implementing the 'Bicycle Commute Economy', http://www.khoslaventures.com/a-model-for-implementing-the-bicycle-commute-economy (accessed 10 Jan, 2016).

Maslin, Mark, 2009, *Global Warming: A very short introduction,* Oxford, UK: Oxford University Press.

Mehta, Meera, and Dinesh Mehta, 2010, 'A Glass Half Full? Urban Development (1990s to 2010)', *Economic & Political Weekly*, Vol.XLV (28)10 July, pp. 20-23.

Menon, Sanskriti, 2014, Participatory Budgeting in Pune: A critical review, http://www.vikalpsangam. org/article/participatory-budgeting-in-pune-a-critical-review/#.V40krhJCbZQ (accessed 1 July, 2016).

Mishra, Neelkanth, 2015, 'In country-sized states', *Indian Express,* 16 May, Available at: http:// indianexpress.com/article/opinion/columns/in-country-sized-states/ (accessed 20 May, 2015).

Mohanty, P.K., 2014, 'A Municipal Financing Framework', in *Urbanisation in India: Challenges, Opportunities and the Way Forward*, Ahluwalia, Isher Judge, Ravi Kanbur, and P. K. Mohanty (ed.), 2014, New Delhi: Sage Publications.

Moriarty, Patrick, and Damon Honnery, 2015, 'Future cities in a warming world', *Futures,* 66 (2015), pp. 45-53.

Oommen, M. A., 2015, 'Implications for Local Governments', *Economic & Political Weekly*, Vol. l (21), 23 May, pp. 44-46.

Patel, Bimal, 2015, 'Onland, a new way', *The Indian Express*, 6 June, http://indianexpress.com/article/ opinion/columns/on-land-a-new-way-2/3/ (accessed 24 July, 2015).

Ramani, Chitra V, 2013, 'All you wanted to know about Area Sabhas', *The Hindu*, 5 Feb, http://www. thehindu.com/news/cities/bangalore/all-you-wanted-to-know-about-area-sabhas/article4379588.ece (accessed 14 July, 2016).

Rao, M, Govinda, 2013, *Property Tax System in India: Problems and Prospects of Reform*, Working Paper No. 2013-114, New Delhi: National Institute of Public Finance and Policy.

Sahasranaman, Anand, 2012, 'Financing the Development of Small and Medium Cities', *Economic & Political Weekly,* Vol. XLVII, (24), 16 June, pp.59-66.

Sankhe, S., A. Vittal, R. Dobbs, A. Mohan, A. Gulati, J. Ablett, S. Gupta, A. Kim, S. Paul, A. Sanghvi, G. Sethy, 2010, *India's Urban Awakening: Building Inclusive Cities, Sustaining Economic Growth*, McKinsey Global Institute available at "http://www.mckinsey.com/mgi" \t "_blank"www.mckinsey.com/mgi (accessed on 17 September 2017).

Shaw, Annapurna, 2012, *Oxford India Short Introductions: Indian Cities*, New Delhi: Oxford University Press.

Singh, Harsh, 2012, *Structural Innovation for Inclusive Development in Bihar: The Navodaya Shahar Model*, New Delhi: Academic Foundation.

Sivaramakrishnan, K. C., Amitabh Kundu and B. N. Singh, 2005, *Handbook of Urbanization in India*, New Delhi: Oxford University Press.

Soni, Vikram and Arvind Virmani, 2014, 'Natural Cities', *Economic & Political Weekly*, Vol. XLIX, (19), 10 May, pp. 36-40.

Suri, Shipra Narang and Eugenie Birch, 2014, 'India and the Sustainable Cities Goal', *Economic & Political Weekly*, Vol. XLIX (46), 15 November, pp. 26-28.

Swerts, Elfie, Denise Pumain, and Eric Denis, 2014, 'The future of India's Urbanization', *Futures* (special issue on 'India @ 2050'), Vol.56, pp. 43-52.

TERI, 2010, *Enhancing public participation through effective functioning of Area Sabhas*, Project Report No. 2009UD04, prepared for Ministry of Urban Development, Government of India.

The Times of India, 2015, Centre notifies land pooling norms, 27 May, http://timesofindia.indiatimes.com/city/delhi/Centre-notifies-land-poolingnorms/articleshow/47437733.cms (accessed May 27, 2015).

UNDP, 2016, http://www.undp.org/content/undp/en/home/mdgoverview/post-2015-development-agenda/goal-11.html (accessed 13 January, 2016).

United Nations, 2011, *World Urbanization Prospects: The 2011 Revision, Highlights (ST/ESA/SER.A/352)*, Department of Economic and Social Affairs, Population Division.

United Nations, 2014, *World Urbanization Prospects: The 2014 Revision, Highlights (ST/ESA/SER.A/352)*, Department of Economic and Social Affairs, Population Division.

Vaddiraju, A. K., 2013, 'A Tale of Many Cities: Governance and Planning in Karnataka', *Economic & Political Weekly*, Vol. XLVIII (2), 12 January, pp.66-69.

Vojnovic, Igor, 2014, 'Urban Sustainability: Research, politics, policy and practice', *Cities,* 41 (2014) S30-S44.

Alternative Transportation in future India

Sujit Patwardhan

Summary

The expanding Indian cities are facing a huge problem of traffic and transportation. Although most of these cities have extensive urban planning, but despite (or perhaps because of!), flyovers, road widening, and other road infrastructure projects, the problem of traffic is intensifying with each passing year. This essay explores the contemporary scenario of traffic and transport in major Indian cities and details out the vision for the future of transport in India.

Transport planning in India has been predominantly car-centred, and this has resulted in edging out of the bicycle, buses, and other forms of public transport. It has also resulted in high levels of pollution. The essay proposes a people-centric sustainable transport system that can make a city pleasant and safe, where people can walk, cycle and reach destinations without the dependence on automobiles. Central to this is the environment centric city planning that will promote compact forms of residential development, reduced dependence on automobile transport, mixed land use planning, protection of natural assets of the city and effective waste management.

Introduction

In our growing cities, traffic and transportation are cited as one of the most serious problems faced by citizens today.

Although this is most severe in urban areas, it is now being increasingly experienced in peri-urban areas and also spreading to rural areas as demand for mobility outstrips facilities available for people to travel for jobs, education, and other necessities, to urban centres.

Unlike other problems that reduce in intensity with rising incomes and economic prosperity, traffic problems seem to get worse with each passing year, despite all the road-widening, flyovers and other traffic infrastructure that cities build feverishly at great cost (sometimes consuming major portion of their annual municipal budget).

Issues Related to Urban Transport

This is the traffic and transport scenario in a majority of Indian cities today:

Traffic congestion: Without doubt this is the most visible manifestation of the condition of urban transport. Everyone complains of road congestion and the problems it creates for all commuters. Congestion not only causes delays in travel but also adds to the frustration and stress for anyone behind a driving wheel. People stuck in traffic will do everything in their power to avoid congestion, even when it means taking an alternative route that is longer and heavier on fuel consumption, breaking lane discipline, traffic rules and safe driving practices and thus adding to traffic jams and delays. As a graphic image nothing brings out the harrowing quality of urban mobility more forcefully than a photograph of auto vehicles stuck edge to edge in a traffic jam.

Figure 1: Infrastructure does not prevent congestion

Photo Credit: Sujit Patwardhan

Pollution: With headlines in the media screaming about the impact of air pollution on our health and particularly on the health of our children this is another feature of transport that grabs our attention and often evokes a strong emotional response. In recent months Beijing[1] and Paris[2], were forced to ban cars for limited periods to cut air pollution levels never experienced before. Nearer home, Delhi's air pollution has become breaking news not only for the media but also invited strictures from the court. Delhi got the unenviable honour of being ranked as the most polluted city in the world for PM 2.5 (micrograms per cubic meter of particulate matter) compelling Delhi Government[3] to take the most drastic step in tackling air pollution by banning cars with odd and even number plates on odd and even days of the month. While this met with resistance by a section of citizens, it did help to bring down pollution levels.

Accidents: India has one of the worse records for road accidents.[4] Although more accidents take place on inter-city highways, media reports of people killed on the roads rightly makes the news linger in our memory for days. Closely connected with this is the condition of our roads (bad surface, bad speed-breakers, potholes, etc.), that are blamed for many of these accidents. India has the highest number of road accidents in the world. With over 130,000 deaths annually, the country has overtaken China and now has the worst road traffic accident rate worldwide.[5] Indian roads, which account for the highest fatalities in the world, became yet more dangerous in 2015 with the number of deaths rising nearly 5 per cent to 146,000. This translates to 400 deaths a day or one life snuffed out every 3.6 minutes, in what an expert described as a 'daily massacre on our roads'.[6]

Traffic indiscipline and lack of enforcement: In citizens groups and *mohalla* (neighbourhood) committees, this is often vigorously discussed and debated with examples of how different it is in the US or in Europe where drivers as well pedestrians are disciplined and law abiding, on account of which the traffic conditions there are much better than here.

Although these are the most prominent examples mentioned by harassed city dwellers when asked about the condition of their traffic situation, they are actually just symptoms of a much deeper malaise.

Conventional Approach to Tackle Traffic and Transportation Problems

Customary discourse on urban traffic and transport has largely been dominated by road congestion and efforts to overcome it through infrastructure projects aimed at reducing the gap between available road area and the growing number of auto vehicles vying for space on these roads. This is why road widening, building flyovers, elevated roads, adding to parking lots and providing more and more space for auto vehicle movement in public as well as residential areas has been at the core of the existing traffic vision (also called car oriented vision) that has influenced not only urban transport but also land use and city planning for many decades.

However, the urban transportation sector is also responsible for many other negative impacts. For example greenhouse gas emissions from auto vehicles lead to global warming and climate change apart from their impact on human health. With transportation sector accounting for about 60 per cent of total air pollution in major cities, there is a direct relationship between auto emissions and health threatening diseases like respiratory illnesses, common cold, bronchitis, asthma, chronic respiratory diseases, hypertension, heart attacks, cancer, diabetes, and so on.

In many cases such car oriented policies have reduced mobility access and encouraged separation of residential and work areas, forcing residents to spend more money on transportation. For poorer people this can add up to a third of their income, representing a heavy burden on their finances.

With a majority of cities following the outdated approach to traffic and transport planning, it is no surprise that transport and mobility have deteriorated sharply during the last three or four decades – which also represent the decades during which there has been a surge in automobile ownership and use. Just to get an idea of the scale of this problem see the table below showing the number of personal auto vehicles in Pune. The situation in other Indian cities is not very different. As the table shows there has been a massive growth of 197 per cent in the total number of auto vehicles between the years 2000 and 2013. Almost all of these are personal vehicles (cars, scooters, motorcycles).

Table 1: Vehicle Population in Pune

Year	Two Wheelers	Four Wheelers	Total	% increase over previous year
2000	6,09,497	93,507	8,30,609	108.24
2005	9,22,674	1,54,649	12,24,756	106.55
2007	11,25,590	2,12,653	15,07,848	111.44
2010	14,18,585	2,86,763	19,07,794	108.27
2011	15,51,628	3,26,203	20,93,957	109.76

Year	Two Wheelers	Four Wheelers	Total	% increase over previous year
2012	17,05,573	3,74,497	22,67,123	108.27
2013	18,51,785	4,21,644	24,66,417	108.79

Note: For convenience, only figures for two and four wheelers are given, though there are additional vehicles such as trucks, tankers, taxis, ambulances, tractors, etc.

Source: Regional Transport Organisation (RTO), Pune, March 2016

The old approach to meet the challenge posed by exploding growth of auto vehicles has been to build more roads, widen the existing ones (even at the cost of cutting shade giving trees and narrowing the width of footpaths meant for pedestrians). When that is not possible (on account of buildings on either side which can't be demolished without paying a high cost for compensation), flyovers are built to accommodate all these auto vehicles coming on the roads every day. This relentless drive for giving more and more room for automobiles is a common feature of traffic planning in most cities in India – although experience from cities around the globe clearly shows that car oriented planning has failed and there's a need for a totally different approach to tackle this problem.

Cities in industrially advanced countries in US and Europe welcomed the arrival of the motor car, as what was seen as a clean alternative to the horse drawn carriage. It offered a travel mode (form) which was fast, comfortable and personalized – which meant you could travel when you wanted and where you wanted. Post World War II, cities were reconstructed with wide and extensive network of roads and motorways to facilitate easy and fast movement of cars. With rising prosperity and affordable cost of car ownership the motor car became the preferred choice of most families and their numbers grew, edging out not only the animal drawn carriages, but also the bicycle (which was commonly used for short journeys) and public transport vehicles like the tram or the bus, as they lacked the obvious glamour of the motor car. In the US, the car manufacturers actively conspired to decommission streetcars (trams) and used political influence to pour money instead into roads, highways and other infrastructure to promote the motor car. These were the golden years of the automobile and the car industry became a symbol of economic growth in Europe and the US and nothing seemed to threaten its prosperity for as long as one could see into the future.

However as more and more people began to own and use cars, the sheer weight of their numbers began creating problems of road congestion, air pollution, road accidents and destruction of natural and human environment (caused by the need to constantly widen the roads to accommodate more cars) as well as social exclusion and environmental problems. These had not been encountered with such intensity in the past, although critics of car dominated planning had been voicing their concerns for many decades.[7]

By the mid 1970s', these problems, coupled with the steep hike in price of petroleum imports, led to intense debate about the side effects and ultimately a re-questioning of the car dominated way of planning. Several studies and research findings had already come out recommending a change in the way urban traffic was managed. At the Government level also, studies conducted by various ministries (in the UK and other countries in Europe) brought out the need for a drastic change in the existing policy and to move away from the infrastructure based policies relying on increasing number of roads to solve the urban transport problems and, to consider instead, ways to reduce the number of auto vehicles on the city's roads.[8]

New Beginnings

As a consequence of these changes in thinking London introduced the path breaking Congestion Charging for cars entering central London (in 2003).[9] Singapore already had policies in place for controlling the number of cars through a permit system where the permit often cost more than the price of the car being purchased. From 2007, Stockholm, Sweden introduced its own version of congestion charging that varied depending on the level of congestion at the time of the traffic movement each day. Most European cities during this period saw various measures to curb car use in congested and usually older and historical parts of the city. They also took concrete steps to increase the modal share of non-motorised transport (walking and cycling) by building citywide cycle tracks, widening footpaths and in many cases, narrowing the width of roads, for ensuring traffic calming and reducing maximum speeds to under 20 mph[10] (30 km/h) on internal roads.

Although European cities like Amsterdam, Copenhagen, London and Paris were among the first to adopt the new vision for managing their urban transport, this was by no means only restricted to Europe. Curitiba in Brazil, famous for its innovative urban schemes for encouraging recycling and sustainable design long before it was fashionable, and planting trees and creating parks on an enormous scale, was the first city in the world to introduce Bus Rapid Transit (BRT) developed from the late 1960s' to early 1970s'. Recognizing that integrated planning of transportation can assist in planning and growth of the city, Curitiba was one of the first few cities to resist treating transportation as a service that caters to an ever growing demand for vehicles and instead to use it as a tool to improve access and liveability. In 2007 Paris launched Velib – an innovative large scale city bicycle sharing scheme with 20,000 bicycles and 1,800 bike stations located every 300 meters across the whole city that anyone could use, by paying a nominal charge and taking a bike, riding it to any destination within the city and returning it to the nearest bike station at the destination.[11] This has become a great success with people of all incomes for the convenience it offers as well as for its health benefits. One of the positive (unintended) outcomes of many bicycles on the roads was to make car and bus drivers sensitive to the safety needs of NMT (non motorised transport) modes. China, though a late entrant in the sustainable transport world, has in its own dynamic way implemented BRT in many cities and achieved very high ridership levels, and also introduced Velib like city bicycle sharing schemes in many cities that now have ridership levels exceeding that of Paris.

Visioning Urban Transport in 2100

These examples show how there's been a shift away from infrastructure based approach (roads, flyovers, etc.) to one that attempts to address the wider issues of access (to services), equity, environment, and quality of life. As one moves away from car-centric planning, the space taken up for its infrastructure, such as excessively wide roads for fast moving noisy and polluting vehicles, large parking lots and other structures, can be converted to sidewalks (footpaths), bicycle tracks, parks and gardens, etc. The vision of a people-centric sustainable transport can create a city that is pleasant and safe, where children can walk or cycle to school and where shops, offices, places of entertainment, and recreation are within easy distance – accessible without dependence on the automobile.

However it is not enough to merely discard car centric planning because transport is linked to many other urban issues and concerns such as land use, housing, poverty and equity, the informal sector, health, safety and disability, women's issues, children and the elderly, the local government, urban heritage (both natural and built), good governance, economic efficiency, global environment and perhaps many others; and how the city plans its transport impacts all these issues.

Over the past few decades, based on this new vision of people and environment centric planning, a consensus is beginning to emerge about the form and shape of such a sustainable city, which although still a work in progress, can offer many of the following features.

- Compact forms of residential development (not those that lead to sprawl)
- Mixed land use with homes, jobs, schools, shops, and transport stations in close

proximity (not rigid segregation of land use for residential, commercial, educational activities)

- High use of non-motorised transport modes such as walking and cycling, with reduced reliance on automobiles
- Protection of natural assets, built assets and heritage structures (not covering large areas in concrete and channelizing water streams, rivers or allowing heritage to be sacrificed for road widening, flyovers, parking lots, etc.)
- Reduction of waste through separation at source of biodegradable and non biodegradable materials and high percentage of waste recycling (not high levels of landfills and incineration)

Such a city will have a favourable setting for implementing sustainable transport plans – based on non-motorised modes, public transport and minimal dependence on personal auto vehicles. It will also enable creation of car-free zones which become great attractions and boost local commerce.

Today, Indian cities stand at a junction where they can choose to either go along the destructive path followed by Western cities in the first part of the 20th century, dominated by the automobile (major cities like London, New York, Paris, carried out large scale demolitions, road widening and reconstruction for accommodating the motor car with its promise of social and economic boom); or they can understand how this led to a dead end from which cities are still painfully extricating themselves. Indian cities have a real opportunity of leapfrogging over this expensive and crippling phase by choosing the sustainable options.

Fortunately, some enabling policies towards this were introduced in recent years and even though they suffer from some shortcomings they can be a starting point for course correction needed for making transport and transport led urban development more sustainable. The National Urban Transport Policy (2006) is one such document which mandates the need for shifting transport projects away from automobile centric to people centric perspective. The Jawaharlal Nehru National Urban Renewal Mission (JNNURM) announced in 2005 for a period of seven years and extended for a further two year period was aimed at bringing phased improvements in the urban civic service levels. Urban transport projects were a major part of this scheme and were mandated to follow the guidelines of the National Urban Transport Policy for getting Central Government funding. Under the present government the ambitious Smart Cities Mission announced in 2014 also promises central government support for projects promising sustainable transport and city planning. Although policies are often vague and don't always percolate to the city level, these initiatives can become opportunities for bringing desirable changes in the outdated policies under which transport planning has stagnated since independence.

Our cities, as they stand today, have the basic ingredients needed for driving the change towards sustainable urban form. They are still compact, have mixed land use, are not yet highly motorised, posses considerable natural assets, and we as a society are still far from being waste producers at the level of industrially advanced cities. Indeed many Indian cities still possess features that world cities are trying to emulate: compact, 'walkable' areas, mixed land use, those free from automobile domination, possessing many car-free areas, etc. But we are changing fast and presently moving in the wrong direction. We need to preserve many of the features from our traditional cities while adapting to contemporary needs.

There are several examples of good practices in different parts of India. Mall Road in Simla in Himachal Pradesh has, since British times, been completely pedestrian (no auto vehicles allowed).The Simla Road Users and Pedestrians Act, 2007, under which this is protected, covers 14 kilometres of the road which is reserved for pedestrians as the priority and is the world's longest road undertaken for 'pedestrianization', according to Navdeep Asija, the founder of Ecocabs. Fazilka, a border town in Punjab, has the unique distinction of developing Ecocabs[12] – a cycle rickshaw based network that provides door to door service to users who can call up a cycle rickshaw on their phone. This initiative has won the National Award of Excellence in Urban Transport, 2011. In many cities across the country individuals and citizens' groups are actively working towards sustainable transport advocacy and initiatives to change the old traffic vision for the better which will have an impact on the way cities of tomorrow will manage their traffic.

Many cities, for example, Pune, Bhuwaneshwar, Bangalore, are actively pushing the local authorities to invest in preparing citywide cycle networks, adopting 'street design guidelines' (Delhi, Pune) that look at the needs of pedestrians, cyclists and public transport users – not just of automobiles. In several cities like Pune, Chennai and Mumbai, citizens' groups are strongly advocating implementation of higher parking charges as a disincentive against use of personal vehicles and car-free zones. Thought to be an impossible venture for our large cities, these are being seriously considered by cities like Chennai, Pune and Delhi (the last mentioned has announced a car-free Connaught Place sometime soon). [13] Although it is not clear how soon these efforts will take to fully become a reality, the fact that such proposals are being seriously considered is itself a sign of hope and augurs well for sustainable transport vision that is well on its way to go beyond just empty talk.

Indian cities thus have the unique opportunity of choosing sustainable transport as the model for city development which will open doors to not only an inclusive city for all, but in the process, also help to address the broader and diverse issues of health and safety, economic progress, fossil fuel depletion, peak oil and global warming.

Endnotes

1. Details about this are contained in the following links: *Thousands stuck in 50 lane traffic jam in Beijing,* http://www.usatoday.com/story/news/nation-now/2015/10/09/thousands-stuck-traffic-jam-beijing-china-highway/73644000/; *The world's worst traffic jams ever,* http://www.forbes.com/sites/jimgorzelany/2015/10/15/the-worlds-worst-traffic-jams-ever/#2715e4857a0b6b17fc4f6c6c (accessed 2 May, 2017).

2. Schoefield (2014) talks about the drastic measures compelled when pollution reached unacceptable highs and the resistance such a move faced.

3. The Delhi High Court directed the Centre and State governments to come up with comprehensive action plans to put a check on the capital city's 'alarming' pollution rate, saying living in Delhi is like 'living in a gas chamber'. A day after this, the Kejriwal-led government declared the odd-even vehicle rule with the hope it would lower the number of vehicles hitting the road per day, eventually bringing down the city's air pollution rate (Biswas, 2015).

4. 'One serious road accident in the country occurs every minute and 16 die on Indian roads every hour; 377 people die every day, equivalent to a jumbo jet crashing every day; 1214 road crashes occur every day in India' (NDTV, 2013).

5. Krishnan (2010) presents revealing statistics about the frequency and extent of road accidents and the causes for these.

6. In the aftermath of Gopinath Munde's death in a car crash the Times of India published a detailed report about road fatalities across India and the need to bring in a stringent law.

7. Jane Jacobs, a civic activist, made a vitriolic critique of urban planning policy in the United States in the1950s, stating that these destroyed urban communities by creating artificial unnatural urban spaces.

8. The *Road Traffic Reduction Act* empowers the local authorities to draft reports related to the situation of road traffic in order to regulate traffic planning and management, http://www.legislation.gov.uk/ukpga/1997/54/contents (accessed 3 May, 2017).

9. London congestion charging, introduced in 2003, aims to reduce congestion during working hours (Monday – Friday, 7 am – 6 pm). This measure was introduced after extensive public and stakeholder consultation, to discourage excessive use of private motorised transport and encourage other modes, https://tfl.gov.uk/modes/driving/congestion-charge (accessed 3 May, 2017).

10. *Twenty is plenty* – a citizen's campaign across European and American cities was initiated to limit speeds to bring down road accidents and fatalities. It has also been translated into urban

transport policy in some cities, http://www.treehugger.com/urban-design/new-york-city-may-say-twenty-plenty.html (accessed 3 May, 2017).

11. *Velib* – see details at http://en.velib.paris.fr/How-it-works (accessed 4 May, 2017).

12. *Ecocabs* – see details at http://www.ecocabs.org/ (accessed 3 May, 2017).

13. Started on a pilot scale for 3 months, the DMC along with the Traffic Police initiated this to mark pedestrian zones to decrease traffic congestion in this central commercial area in New Delhi.

References

Biswas, Shreya, 2015, 'What is Delhi's new odd-even vehicle rule all about? Where did it come from?' *India Today*, http://indiatoday.intoday.in/story/delhi-odd-even-vehicle-rule-arvind-kejriwal-aap-government-air-pollution/1/541371.html (accessed 30 April, 2017).

Jacobs, Jane, 1961, *Death and Life of Great American Cities*, New York: Random House.

Krishnan, Murali, 2010, *India has the highest number of road accidents in the world*, http://www.dw.com/en/india-has-the-highest-number-of-road-accidents-in-the-world/a-5519345 (accessed 16 March, 2017).

NDTV, 2013, *Road accident statistics in India*, http://sites.ndtv.com/roadsafety/important-feature-to-you-in-your-car/ (accessed 8 May, 2016).

Schoefield, Hugh, 2014, *Paris car ban imposed after pollution hits high*, http://www.bbc.com/news/world-europe-26599010 (accessed 28 March, 2016).

Technological Alternatives for Indian Futures

Dinesh Abrol

Summary

Contemporary technological systems are guided by the dominant neo-liberal knowledge production, which is extremely extractive in nature and generates high inequality in society. Increasingly the research and development institutions are becoming less open to perusal of diversity, centralizing and concentrating on the demand arising from the big business, and have closed their doors to alternate forms of science and technology. For example, the agro-ecosystems and landscapes have drastically degraded due to current models of monoculture and chemical-intensive agriculture. India's growing reliance on the capitalist mode of production and consumption which uses cheap labour and cheap nature is worrisome and needs a response from the protagonists of national democracies, peoples' democracies and socialist democracies.

The essay explores technological alternatives in agriculture and rural industrialization programs, sustainable transportation, energy sector and shelter, housing or habitat development, by ushering in strategies that prioritize changes in the dominant structures and the existing cultural norms of consumption. While the protagonists of democratic visions will be obviously assigning varying weightages when the new and emerging technological options come on their radar, it will have to be the responsibility of protagonists committed to pursuing peoples' democracies and socialist democracies to prioritize the development of new combinations of these technologies as alternatives for the goals of integrated production and habitat planning.

They need to remind themselves that *per se* the industrialization or the support for new and renewal energy technologies cannot bring the unity among the protagonists of democratic visions. The basic needs of peasantry and working class are their priority. The democratic approach demands bringing down the costs of logistics and communication and prioritizing the development of co-location of production through the planning of integrated development of co-products and by-products in services, industry and agriculture. Diversified integrated production of different kinds of use values will have to be the priority. Integrated biomass based solutions for energy and industrial materials that are also compatible with the meeting of the challenge of growing food demand are the need of the hour.

The pathway to technological alternative has to be part of a radical transformation in socio-technical systems, guided by social equity and ecological sustainability. The perusal of technological alternatives therefore also calls for the creation of alternate social carriers of innovation and development.

Introduction

Forecasting of technological alternatives and the assessment of how they will turn out is not easy. Opening and closing of the space for technological alternatives is influenced by the introduction of new and emerging generic technologies. It is difficult to anticipate their potential in advance. It does not get revealed fully in their early stage of development. The history of past efforts is full of false predictions and disappointments. For example, introduction of the technological developments, like the personal computer and the Internet, into the processes of design of socio-technical systems, were not anticipated. Certainly the movements pursuing appropriate technology and environmental concerns did not take these developments into account in India. Historically grown structures support and strengthen certain economic and political interests to the detriment of others, for both the mainstream and radical social movements. Technology users do not make free choices. Knowledge about prevailing and novel options is neither fully objective nor politically neutral. But structural and institutional conditions are subject to change. When contradictions are acute and the protagonists of change become strong, transformative changes happen at an accelerated pace.

Contribution of technological alternatives comes mostly from the perusal of 'unknown knowns' by the social movements. These are doable technologies which the incumbents do not pursue under the influence of arrangements on account of their focus on profit and power. They leave these efforts as 'undone science and technology'. Social movements develop and promote these doable technologies. But evidence also suggests that at a technical level, the success of technological alternatives and products comes at the cost of a process in which the more politically charged design elements and social organizations drop out. Often social movements find their goals being incorporated at a technical level

391

by the mainstream but at a cost of severing the technical goals from the broader political and justice goals.[1]

How technological alternatives can support and strengthen the broader political and justice goals is an important issue for the purpose of strategy formulation for path setting. Investigations show that some movements have been more successful than others in combining the deployment of technological alternatives with the advancement of the broader political and justice goals[2]. In latecomer industrializing countries, much success has come from the industrial restructuring movements. This is undone science as research into the new organizational forms. Industrial access movements have been successful with the perusal of undone science as support for access issues.

How to influence the outcome in favour of accelerating transformative changes is an important question for the movements seeking technological alternatives in India. Assessment of the past efforts that the pro-poor social forces undertook in India with the help of the Khadi and Village Industries Commission, Council of Scientific and Industrial Research (CSIR) and Department of Science and Technology (DST) indicate that social movements have helped generate new research programmes and technologies. Their socio-technical frames have played an important role in the sustainability of social carriers of technological alternatives. As far as the impact of technological alternatives on the broader political and social justice goals is concerned the debate continues on this issue among the protagonists of radical visions till this date (Abrol, 2014a).

Mostly past forecasts have turned out to be too optimistic about the introduction of alternative technologies in the short run and too conservative about the consequences of mainstream technologies in the long run. The role and contribution of technological alternatives in the path formation is connected to the robustness of socio-technical designs and organizational strategies used to embed the social carriers of innovation among the people and the success obtaining in respect of the democratization of national science, technology and innovation (STI) system (Abrol, 2014b). Exercises undertaken for the building of a normative, like a prospective scenario, contain a narrative about how to get there in the longer run. The difference between normative and prospective exercises of technology foresight is that the former does not project technologies to which the society has to adapt but emphasizes how the individuals, institutions and society will have to organize themselves to undertake fundamental changes to realize the desirable futures. For a normative scenario building exercise to be of some consequence a vision must be sketched of desirable futures that are thought to be at least possible, if perhaps not probable.

In this essay we aim to develop the visions of these desirable futures in order to open up the spaces for their own challenge with regard to the creation of technological alternatives. The protagonists of radical visions face the challenge of how to develop suitable social carriers of technological alternatives and organisational forms in the current milieu. The proposed visions are about well-being and good life. These visions are not technologically determined. Although the vision building takes into account the technological possibilities, but their fulfilment does not entirely depend on the realization of technological alternatives. These visions are unlikely to be pursued in their pure form. The country is vast and diverse enough, and the protagonists have sufficient opportunities to experiment with all of these paths. Further the diffusion of new organisational forms and industrial access movements are today influenced by the contra public dynamics emerging due to the challenge from neoliberal ideology. The dynamics of these movements is however not within the scope of this essay.

As things stand a realistic level of progress is only possible with regard to perusal of the goals of national and peoples' democracies. In the longer run the people will have to be mobilized to realize the goals of socialist democracies to attain ecological and social justice for the vast majority of the poor of this world. Since the national and peoples' democracies can help in the organization of social carriers of technological alternatives it is important that their complementary role is acknowledged. Finally, as there are definite limits to any movement being able to plan, control and shape centrally the future of any society in its entirety, the movements must learn to handle the probable futures as frontiers of opportunity as well as states of uncertainty.

Path setting

In thinking about setting the paths and formulating the strategies for the future development of a territory as a 'sustainable region' promoting the diffusion of technological alternatives, it is useful to consider how the visions required to be framed for the realization of a probable sustainable society in India may treat the question of futures of technological alternatives. Three visions that the probable 'sustainable regions' could adopt are ***national democracies, peoples' democracies*** and ***socialist democracies.***

National democracies are envisaged as societies embedded in the capitalist economic system but practicing social harmony, national level economic self-reliance, state regulation of systems of production and consumption and efficiency driven socio-technical systems using productivist 'technological alternatives'.

Peoples' democracies are conceptualized as societies pursuing one of the possible versions of non-capitalist path of economic development which envisages practicing the solidarity and cooperation of petty producers and workers in production, secularism, economic and technological self-reliance planned appropriately at the national or regional level, and developing worker ownership and workplace democracy, socialized investment processes, social control of production and consumption and socially just socio-technical systems of ecologically modernizing 'technological alternatives'.

Socialist democracies are envisioned as societies pursuing another possible version of non-capitalist path of economic development which envisages practicing consciously autonomy of networked systems of production to pursue self-reliance and democracy of the peoples' economies developing at the sub-regional, regional and national level through a joint planning system, democratic control of the processes of design of socio-technical systems and associated societal processes and trade and investment providing for 'socio-ecologically transformational' technological alternatives for production and consumption.

Planning for Sustainable Future Regions

After defining what kinds of futures are desirable the issue becomes one of the way in which protagonists of these visions will need to approach the challenge of making their own respective contributions to the development of technological alternatives in India. Visions for the realization of well-being and good life are guideposts. Particularly as the protagonists are concerned about the implementation of visions for good life they need to understand that the impact of their actions for the perusal of technological alternatives is conditioned by the contemporary trends. These are the weakening of the traditional nation state and the rise of transnational entities, powerful forces of technical change, profound and unequal transformations in health and education outcomes, rising inequalities of wealth and income within countries, contestations between the religious and the secular, post-cold war conflicts and insecurities within and between nations, and so on. They will have to factor in not only that these trends will shape but also will be shaped by the social and group interactions of human beings in the course of political mobilization.

Concepts and tools for a better society are in great demand. Protagonists of change will have to overcome the limitations of their own existing socio-technical framings of technological alternatives. Further there also exist the limitations of disciplinary specializations of the experts associated with the movements. Protagonists will have to pursue their partisan projects keeping in view that the objective knowledge will have to wait for the test of practice to give certitude to their strategies and visions. At the existing level of scientific knowledge, when the practice of reductionism is inevitable and the process of differentiation in sciences is productive, collective endeavour in natural and social sciences (without having to act like natural sciences) should be not to fall in the trap of relativism. They will have to find ways and means to learn from their own past implementation of theory and practice of transformative change.

Very broadly there are four approaches to transition to new forms of development – institutional reforms, planning, social mobilization and engagement with markets. Technological alternatives will have to be envisioned, designed and pursued systematically. This perusal will help them to achieve a greater degree of success against neo-liberal ways which suits big business. Although the current context of neo-liberal, dependent, slavishly imitative mindset is gradually beginning to lose its hegemonic grip across the world, but the protagonists of radical visions need to pursue the immediate challenge of unsettling the neo-liberal hegemons systematically. They will have to learn to cooperate in order to pursue their collective contribution.

Humanity is in the midst of the ongoing struggle worldwide for the realization of 'right to sustainable human development'. The right to protect the 'Basis of Human Development' (*Insani Jeevan Ke Aadharka Adhikar*), 'personal (household) conditions of production', 'natural or external conditions of production', 'general collective conditions of production', which is an inalienable right of the human beings, is the aim of this worldwide struggle. The protagonists need to realize this by uniting with each other in the struggle against neo-liberal globalization. Social progress is equally an important issue. Climate change needs to be addressed with the tools of simultaneously sustaining the struggle for social and ecological justice.

Capitalism requires both, cheap labour as well as cheap nature, to grow. Anthropogenic activity is a problem only because the values of capital are guiding the process of accumulation and development. Known to undermine its capacity to regenerate the *Insani Jeevan ka Aadhar* (basis for human life), increasingly the human means of appropriation of technology and nature are being constrained by social relations of science and production (take finance, IPR, state capacity, etc.). While social progress can be conceptualized by the protagonists for their own respective contexts in distinct ways, but they need to keep in mind that conditions for economic and social reproduction are an outcome of the relations of production and of resources in use. Conditions are required to be changed through the processes of social mobilization – a systemic (structural) change oriented social mobilization.

The protagonists of these visions need to recognize not only the imperative of cooperative perusal of real world experiments but also the imperative of the need to nurture the diversity in knowledge production. The national systems of science, technology and innovation need to be democratized. Knowledge production for social progress can be understood as a process of epistemic modernization of academic disciplines, taking place as a countervailing process to the emerging challenge of neo-liberalization and new public based management for the governance of academic world, and involves recognition of a specific type of ignorance.

Four inter-related challenges face the protagonists of these visions in respect of building of real world experiments and their social carriers on the ground – 1) identification of opportunities for socio-technical system design using relevant heuristics, 2) resource convergence, 3) knowledge production and 4) social mobilization for network development on the ground by building alliances and institutions.

Technological Alternatives and Political Mobilization

The role and relationships emerging from the efforts underway for the perusal of technological alternatives for the establishment of alternate pathways need to be understood as historically evolving contributions of 'Knowledge Production for Social Mobilization' to nation building undertaken by the movements. The protagonists of these three visions need to think about the processes of how mutual interactions and combinations between and among technological developments and their possible reinforcement will occur. It is also clear that the protagonists of these three visions will have to help the nation to selectively delink the system of science, technology and innovation (STI) from the path of imperialist globalization.

There is the need to keep a close watch on the health of the STI system for the impact on directions, diversity and distribution. The multi-class context of knowledge production and utilization requires the building of a political alliance for the creation of technological alternatives for social progress. Protagonists of these three visions will have to mobilize the peasantry, rural labour, middle class professionals and non-big business constituents for their active participation in the real world experiments.

It is necessary to construct the alliance capable of handling the non-antagonistic conflicts and designing the efforts for technological and organizational alternatives building in the region of their respective influence in a sustainable way. Knowledge production has its own politics with which they must engage actively and productively.

Political movements need to invest in the development of real-world experiments to build the social carriers for the development of technological alternatives.

Protagonists face the challenge of how these social carriers can be fostered by them in a sustained way to create a counter-hegemonic process of knowledge production for the realization of their own respective democratic vision. These social carriers should be capable of identifying opportunities, mobilizing resources, undertaking knowledge production and practicing social mobilization required for the purpose of network development on the ground. The protagonists need to realize that the space will have to be opened up by them by engaging with the national STI system using a variety of approaches of collective action.

History tells us that initially, immediately after India gained political independence, the emerging national system of S&T reflected quite a lot of diversity. Consequently there existed opportunities and much more scope for the perusal of diverse innovation trajectories for the implementation of the visions of technological alternatives. In the early years of post-independent India a diverse portfolio of technological implementation programmes was under perusal in the public sector institutions being set up by the country. India was still some time away from the situation of adopting a uniform socio-technical regime in the country as a whole. It was open to providing space to the social movements interested to pursue alternative technologies in most sectors.

Diversity of knowledge generating systems was alive in the system of higher education institutions and R&D institutes being set up by the government. Enterprises of all sizes representing the non-big business sections had access to the emergent science, technology and innovation making efforts of the public sector institutions. For example, there existed across the board quite a lot of space for the national level programmes of solar energy utilization for cooking and water heating, biological reclamation of saline lands, development of vegetable dyes, coal gasification, condensed milk out of buffalo milk, vegetable tanning of leather and many other such technological innovations. After India became independent, because of the nature of political dispensation that had emerged out of the freedom movement, the national S&T efforts reflected quite well, autonomous directions in respect of the programmes of indigenous endeavours with regard to science, technology and innovation and the space for perusal of various types of technological alternatives. All the leaders who had led the freedom movement and who were engaged in the S&T efforts of the Indian nation were still around to exercise influence over the formulation of approaches and strategies for national development.

Closing and Opening of Space for Technological Alternatives

Discussion on how the space got closed gradually for the introduction of alternative technologies and organizational forms in the sectors of agriculture, industry, energy, transport, health and education in the country indicates that contestations undertaken on the basis of knowledge production for technological alternatives became weak in the absence of investment from the protagonists of democratic visions in the conduct of real world experiments. There are a number of possible insights to be gained for the purpose of future political mobilization. Lack of sufficient support for resource mobilization for the perusal of real world experiments was a key weakness of social and political mobilization. In India, the protagonists of democratic visions are known to have quarrelled too often without trying out the real world experiments and the practice to throw up the knowledge for social progress. Knowledge production for undone S&T (technological alternatives) is therefore necessary if we want to win against the big business in the fields of science and technology. The big business could win, and the R&D portfolios of institutions changed. Gradually these interests have acquired power over the national S&T system and other public sector institutions, and the space has been dwindling for the perusal of technological alternatives.

Analysis also shows that when the positive influence of the multi-class character of the freedom movement actually began to fade and the national priorities of science, technology and innovation were turned upside down, the democratic movements actively pursuing counter-hegemony were unable to hold the ground on the front of knowledge production and network development for the diffusion of their own technological alternatives. During the period of the first four decades the Indian state was known not only for supporting research and development (R&D) but also for putting in place the programmes and policies for their systematic diffusion in the area of rural industrialization. The protagonists of democratic visions will have to jointly fight for the democratization of STI system to resurrect this important space. Today the situation is that the state apparatus is hardly willing to discipline the rent seeking activities of the powerful over S&T activities. The control of big business over the STI apparatus is growing. The government is planning to strengthen the institution of private intellectual property rights.

In the way India has implemented import substitution and export promotion strategies it is clear that import dependence has got accentuated rather than being reduced. Today India faces a huge challenge from the situation of growing reliance of the capitalist economic system for the manufacturing sector on imports. The systemic challenge of realization of the visions with regard to the implementation of interconnected technological challenges needs to be dealt with. The path setting exercises will have to take this context into account while formulating their own approaches and strategies. Rather than prioritizing industrialization *per se* the protagonists should be prioritizing autonomous industrialization for sustainable development. The protagonists of democratic visions will have to handle the challenge of capability building of the activists and enrol new actors from the basic classes for the creation of social carriers of technological alternatives.

This challenge will have to be accomplished in the face of reduced diversity and dwindling space within the national system of STI for the practice of technological alternatives. The counter-hegemonic movements lack in the human resources to mobilize the national STI system. It was during the decade of sixties we saw the closure of technological choices taking place in favour of energy and material intensive unsustainable system in a critical sector like agriculture in India. Although this happened because the country needed to deal with the challenge of food grain production, it is also a historical fact that the counter-hegemonic movement was weak. When the new model of agricultural development was being put in place, there was very little done by these movements.

Due to lack of understanding of the systemic (interconnectedness) character of the development of productive forces very little effective contestation was seen in the sphere of knowledge production in the agriculture sector. Environment and health continued to be treated as externalities by the protagonists of autonomous development and democratic visions. We illustrate below this challenge and show how the development of technological alternatives was lost on account of not being able to see the systemic character of development of productive forces. We also finally bring out the possible examples of interconnectedness of productive forces between the agriculture sector and rural industries for the development of a new system of productive forces.

Technological Alternatives: visions and path setting

From the mid-sixties onward, when the mainstream development programme of the government became only one of how to get the Indian peasantry to adopt the system of high external input agriculture, there were still artisanal industries providing inputs to peasantry as well as undertaking processing of outputs arising from the agriculture sector. But once extensive use of chemical inputs and fossil fuel based mechanical energy devices became the mainstream strategy for increasing the production of foodgrains for all the sections of peasantry in the well-endowed agro-ecological regions, the connection of peasantry also became weak.

Compared with the earlier technological system that had crop-livestock interactions at the core and was artisanal labour intensive in respect of the production operations the new technological system was dependent on monocultures. This accelerated the use of external large industry system based inputs of chemical fertilizers and pesticides. Crop rotations that the peasantry in well-endowed regions began to practice ignored legumes and obtained nutrients through external chemical inputs. They began to use chemical pesticides for plant protection. Not only did they deprive the soils of organic matter that used to come from livestock, they also drew a lot of ground water, which has lowered and polluted the water table. They also ended up reducing the use of rural labour and local artisanal industries.

While the full-scale introduction of this new technology system involved a programme of industrialization requiring the replacement of import of inputs needed for its systematic perusal, this path, and the economies of scale and scope, also became gradually responsible for the tilt towards introduction of petroleum based materials and energy inputs into agriculture. Lack of success in the development of technological alternatives affected the use of local materials across the board.

These developments became an important driver of change in the socio-technical system in India and affected the competition faced by the local artisanal industries. An alternate programme of S&T was put forward as a part of the vision that the protagonists of a post-WW II frame of 'national democracy' aimed at – to develop local resource based alternatives for the preparation of raw materials required for the production of nitrogenous fertilizers. However, the efforts were lacking in terms of required support. The success of coal based industrial complexes, including the possibilities of introduction of clean coal technologies and coal as fertilizer was completely stymied. It became very difficult to stem the tide of petroleum based technological alternatives.

Agro-ecological approaches, rural development and national STI system

The model of rural development system, which was proposed in the Higher Education Commission of 1948, known also as the Radhakrishan Commission (RC), received collective support from almost all the major political trends – the Nehruvians, Gandhians and the Left, but came to be marginalized in recent history. The RC model proposed a system of agricultural development with a lot of potential. Focus was on the harnessing of every rain drop and of biodiversity available in every corner. All the agro-ecological regions of the country were to be directed for integrated rural development. This model was abandoned in favour of the model of agricultural development led by capitalist landlords, agribusiness and related new industrial capital.[3]

The RC model of rural university and rural development had the vision of systemic upgrading and development of agro-ecological diverse systems of agriculture and allied sectors, including rural non-farm artisanal knowledge and skills. In this pathway there existed sufficient scope for the rejuvenation of local economies as a system in itself. But under the influence of agribusiness interests we saw the waning of interest of the scientific community in the model of rural development proposed by RC. A model of agricultural education, research and extension, which promoted homogeneity in the selection of cultivars and adopted a strategy of food grain production embedded in the use of high level of external inputs, which did not need local artisanal industry to be upgraded in a systematic way, emerged in the country.

However, the situation went further awry because the model of evaluation of performance of agricultural universities adopted in India was reduced to asking them about how much of agricultural area in the vicinity of colleges and universities had adopted varieties using high external input system of agriculture. In 1966, the National Education Commission endorsed the establishment of this model of evaluation and approved the model of land grant Universities built in United States which was never so centralized and narrow as it was practiced in India under the influence of foreign and local vested interests (Abrol and Pulamte, 2007). The US land grant model was constantly upgraded, and it had a place for basic research. The US is the home of research on decomposition of organic matter, and has major research groups working on soil biology. All these elements have been missing in the Indian case. Today we have a situation that the Indian agricultural research and education system has hardly any receptivity for the alternatives, and the protagonists of these visions will need to pursue an ideological struggle in favour of agro-ecological approaches being used for the development of local economies as a system. Cuba has been witness to such an ideological struggle (Levins, 2008). While this contestation is now well documented, in India the protagonists will have to be ready for such an engagement with the S&T system on agriculture (National Commission on Agriculture, 1976; Abrol and Pulamte, 2007).

Although we are now again witness to the agricultural research system giving some attention to the primacy of organic matter for soil health and agricultural productivity, the need of replenishment of organic matter is also a systemic challenge. The selected systems of monocultures continue to be based on the promotion of high external chemical inputs. While there has always existed the possibility of reduction in the use of external chemical inputs and of undertaking integrated nutrient management, conserving the health of soil, and augmenting the use of rural labour for the production of farm yard manure, composts, azolla, etc., this pathway is, in fact, a good starting point for the intervention of the protagonists of the visions of national democracy and peoples' democracy in India. However, the protagonists of socialist democracies will have to push the system because it is far more compatible with their vision of Indian society. This would allow them to pave the way for the reintegration of crop-livestock sub-systems on the lines of the contemporary version growing in Cuba today. Although the power and attraction of high external input system of agriculture is even today holding away the protagonists of the visions of national and peoples' democracies from dealing with the challenge of changes in the socio-technical system of agricultural development and rural industrialization. But the failure of S&T system in this connection can open up the space for them as well as socialist democracies to intervene far more effectively in respect of social mobilization to deal with agrarian crisis. Agro-ecological approaches do not receive much focus from the larger democratic movement. It is an important area of multiple contestations that need to be carried out with regard the technological alternatives for the future of democratic visions in India.

Broadly the approaches to rural development which are compatible with agro-ecology have been pursued as technological alternatives by movements pursuing peoples' science and ecological agriculture. From India examples can be given of Low External Input System of Agriculture (LEISA) by AME Foundation, Bangalore, Non-Pesticide Management (NPM) by Centre for Sustainable Agriculture (CSA), Hyderabad, Ecosystem level planning for biomass based approach of Society for Promoting Participatory Ecosystem Management (SOPPECOM), Pune, Bio-farm approach of Development Research Communications and Services Centre, Kolkata and Centre for Ecology and Rural Development (CERD), Puducherry, as also Centre for Technology and Development (CTD), Society for Technology and Development (STD), Integrated Rural Technology (IRT).

More opportunities clearly exist at the level of both farm and rural non-farm livelihoods. Knowledge production for the implementation of agro-ecological approach based rural development needs a major push. Today the mainstream system of agricultural education, research and extension is lukewarm to the implementation of agro-ecological approaches. Negative consequences for the state of health of soil and water, incidence of pest and diseases and biodiversity conservation are directly an outcome of this. There is a degradation of agro-ecosystems and landscapes and the meltdown of natural ecosystem service provisions leading to ecological sustainability becoming the bigger barrier to the enhancement of agriculture productivity. The solution for the agrarian crisis lies in changing the production relations and the relations between the resources used in the production. We need to shift from high external input based model to optimal external input model. We need to shift from monocultures to integrated systems.

The protagonists of these visions will have to struggle for affecting changes in the relations between people involved in the production operations, the producer, the labour, the trader, the consumer. They will have to enable the poor peasants, rural labour and artisans and other petty producers to obtain better access to resources, markets and capabilities (Abrol, 2004, 2005). The emerging challenges of food security, livelihood sustainability, public health, right of people to safe food, wider ecological health transformation, regional economic development and social justice can be better dealt with by adopting agro-ecological approaches compared with conventional approaches to agricultural development. The protagonists will have to help the poor and marginalized sections to restore and salvage the existing commons in land, livestock, water, forestry and so on, besides creating new commons in the form of knowledge as a public good.

Technological Alternatives and the Challenge of Sustainable Transportation

In this section we propose to start our discussion with how the development of systems of sustainable rail transportation came to be weakened in India. Although the protagonists of all the three visions need to acknowledge the interconnectedness of transportation and energy sector, it also needs to be recognized that the movement of capital accumulation is shifting away from the primary circuit of capital investment in industrial production towards the secondary circuit of capital investment in urban infrastructure. Urbanization is itself becoming highways, hotels, finance districts, and so on, which are privatized and market driven. This is to allow the capital to maximize the extraction of value from the built environment.

In India the development of the system of public transportation started in the form of railways in the British times. Notwithstanding the major contribution of the freedom movement to the building of India as one country, railways are also considered to be responsible for the integration of India as one market and country. It was possible to develop the rail as a system of public transport. Even while the rail system continues to be built as a state sector institution, the ruling classes have allowed the choice of fuel to go in favour of diesel and petrol. In the case of both of them we are dependent on the imported crude petroleum for their refining and production. We have built an economy which is dependent in rail as well as in road on these products. During the decades of sixties and seventies there was at least some debate on why the rail system based on engines capable of running on electricity is better for this country.

However, the last three decades have seen no such debate. Electrification of rail lines needs to be re-emphasized. Several inappropriate decisions within the realm of urban areas were taken in favour of the system of road transport during the last three decades in India. A road transport system which is using automobiles dependent on petrol and diesel has come to be the dominant system. Road transport has come to be developed to meet far more the needs of upper classes and middle classes. The private sector industry is promoting automobiles rather than promoting bicycles and rickshaws, using all kind of motive forces. Passenger cars have been allowed to grow in number to such a level that it is making the road transportation system untenable in the metros all over the country.

It needs to be emphasized that the infrastructure for road transport is dependent on public provisioning. There is no dearth of new car models which the big business is keen to introduce in the country. It is making acquisitions abroad of even companies which do not make sense from the standpoint of availability of supply of know-how for the fuel systems that we need to learn to reconfigure the transportation and energy system. Road safety in general and safety of vulnerable road users in particular has become a major problem for the people living in the cities of this country. Vehicle emissions need to be given equal importance for ensuring cleaner and more liveable cities.

Unless cities are made safer for pedestrians and bicyclists on one hand, and women, children and the elderly on the other, it would be impossible to obtain optimal use of public transport facilities in the futures. Indian cities should not be allowed to be locked into systems that aim to encourage high speeds and greater use of personal car transport. In this context the protagonists will have to intervene in the policy debates taking place on the alternatives available for the reduction of air pollution and decongestion. Smart cities and bullet trains are becoming the mainstream priority. The protagonists of three visions outlined above should focus on the articulation of demand for the development of rail system as a public system of transportation.

Technological Alternatives for Energy, Shelter, Housing and Habitat Development

Take the case of S&T based innovation activity in the energy system. Immediately after India became independent there was much investment on energy R&D. This interest got subsequently reduced after cheap oil became available. In most sectors directions were set in favour of petroleum based fuels in a short-sighted manner. Dependence on imported petroleum was allowed to grow. Natural gas became the choice after the oil prices rose. Although natural gas is one of the cleanest fossil fuels available at present, it must still be used very judiciously. It needs to be used and conserved for the production of essential chemicals. Kerosene and LPG have ended up displacing the options such as smokeless *chulhas* (hearths) and biogas that made sense for this country. Biogas and smokeless chullhas had received much momentum at one stage. Today nobody talks of them in the mainstream. These days Kerala Shastra Sahitya Parishad (KSSP) is undertaking more efforts on biogas, chulhas, and hot box and electronic chokes for energy conservation.

Today solar and wind energy has the backing of the Indian government. At one time it was an important technological alternative being advocated by the environmental movements. Hydropower has run into problems even while it has had potential to be developed as a technological alternative in India. Today its challenge comes not only due to the inability of the government to minimize displacement and undertake proper rehabilitation of people when displaced, but also from the failure to take precautions on the front of degradation of catchment area and the environmental impacts on account of unregulated development of project areas. As a result, climate change related issues are posing their own challenges for the development of hydropower.

Irrigation has also come to depend on groundwater far more than what is sustainable in the long run. Waterways providing for water transport, the cheapest possible mode of transportation available to us, have remained underdeveloped. Similarly, in the plans for energy and electricity development, the development of clean coal technologies is failing to receive sufficient emphasis from the protagonists of democratic visions these days. An assessment of India's clean energy technology choices indicates that there is no silver bullet in terms of one technology that overcomes all the challenges. In the short and medium run the country will also have to depend on a portfolio of clean coal technologies. Coal technologies emerge competitive with combined cycle gas turbine technologies at even relatively low levels of natural gas prices. Research and development efforts on these technologies will have to aim at simultaneous fulfilment of macroeconomic security, and environmental objectives.

Among the protagonists of democratic visions one can expect different weightages being assigned to the challenges of energy efficiency and use of renewables (solar and wind, hydrogen, and so on). Nevertheless, the development of technological alternatives for integrated habitat planning (combining work and residence, combined heat and power, integrated biomass production capable of providing values of food, fibre, materials, energy, environmental remediation and medicinal plants) will have to be the responsibility of those protagonists who are committed to pursuing peoples' democracies and socialist democracies.

It is obvious that the new and renewal energy technologies will ultimately not unite the protagonists. But the approach to bring down the costs of logistics and communication and the development of co-location of production through the integrated development of co-products and by-products in industry has the potential to unite these three visions behind common technological alternatives where the diversified integrated production of different kind of use values is pursued as a priority. Integrated biomass based solutions for energy and industrial materials that are also compatible with the meeting of the challenge of growing food demand are the need of the hour to deal with the agrarian crisis and make agriculture once more a viable occupation.

Today we face the challenge of habitat development which is not dependent on buildings made out of energy intensive designs and materials that are themselves produced using fossil fuels. Energy intensive materials like cement, steel, glass and plastics are becoming the main materials for the construction of all kinds of buildings, irrespective of viable alternatives being available using alternate materials. Building codes have not been suitably designed to accommodate the practices that would help the country conserve such kind of energy intensive materials. Bamboo is one of the most versatile materials available to the country in abundance in the Northeast. Bamboo is also capable of being grown substantially in other regions.. But it did not receive importance in the R&D programmes of this nation until the last decade. India needed R&D for the development of different types of applications of bamboo based resources.

Cement and steel would be conserved in a big way if attention was given to the development of wood composites as alternate construction materials. Adoption of building designs developed in very different climatic conditions and energy availability is causing havoc. Artisanal industries built around low cost energy conserving material applications and architecture is going out of business. Skills and knowledge of alternate materials and designs continues to languish for the lack of support and have begun to slowly disappear from the scene of habitat development in this country.

Technology Implementation Approaches and Strategies

Technologies are socially constructed. Even when the tool kits are rapidly evolving (for example, life cycle analysis, material flow analysis, industrial ecology tools are available to guide the development of technology) that can measure the degree of sustainability of technological solutions the structures in place prevent the world from envisioning and implementing technological alternatives for sustainable development. The challenge is thus two-fold – one of creating alternative technologies and two of challenging the economic growth paradigm. Societal and technological developments co-evolve and influence each other deeply. The new and emerging technological developments can today support the creation of socio-technical systems that would be possibly more sustainable in terms of the ecological dimension and the social equity and the cultural dimensions. Currently there is much discussion on the impact of new and emerging technologies such as information and communication technologies and biotechnologies on the organisational forms adopted by the working class in the form of trade unions and by petty producers in the form of cooperatives and group enterprises. But evidence suggests that the network forms can be co-evolved by adopting the frame of local economies being upgraded as multi-sectoral network forms of group enterprises led by worker management and active participation of petty producers in enterprise development.

Concluding Remarks

The present socio-technical systems express dominant values, lifestyles and growth drivers of capitalism. Technological alternatives are important. New socio-technical systems will have to emerge from the perusal of paths of radical transformation guided by social equity driven ecological transformation. The perusal of technological alternatives calls for the creation of alternate social carriers of innovation and development (Abrol, 2014a). These social carriers will have to dedicate themselves to the challenge of simultaneous perusal of the quest for social equity and ecological transformation. It is quite important that the processes of radical transformation are explicitly envisioned around the idea of well-being, to be changed through the combined effects of interventions prioritizing alternatives in respect of the development of future forms of social practices, lifestyles, institution building, economy and technology (Abrol, 2014b). Finally the protagonists will have to keep in mind that the process of radical transformation will involve the construction of pathways that aim for not only a change in the power structures but also a cultural change.

Endnotes

1. Technological alternatives are 'Undone S&T' and are embedded in a theory of dynamics of scientific and technological fields and industrial change. The two organizing axes involved in the dynamics of undone S&T are the epistemic conflict dimension and the relationships between social movements and industrial-technological change. Science has become important and more politicized. There is a countervailing trend of epistemic modernization, that is, the opening up of the scientific field to the knowledge needs of the extra field agents in less privileged and dominant positions (See Hess, 2015 on 'Undone Science').

2. The level of conflict with the mainstream efforts on technological pursuits is variable, based again

on the degree of opposition of alternatives to an existing scientific and technological field or to industrial order (ibid.).

3.   See also essay on Food and Agriculture Futures in this volume.

References

Abrol, Dinesh, 2004, 'Lessons from the Design of Innovation Systems for Rural Industrial Clusters in India', Special Issue of *Asialics Journal of Technology Innovation,* Vol. 12(2), September, pp. 67-98.

Abrol, Dinesh, 2005, 'Embedding Technology in Community Based Production Systems through People's Technology Initiatives: Lessons from the Indian Experience', *International Journal of Technology Management and Sustainable Development*, Vol. 4(1), March, pp.1-28.

Abrol, Dinesh (2014a), 'Mobilizing for Democratization of Science in India: Learning from the PSM experience', *Journal of Scientific Temper (JST),* Vol. 2(1&2), Jan.-Apr., pp. 10-32.

Abrol, Dinesh (2014b), 'Pro-poor Innovation-making, Knowledge Production and Technology Implementation for Rural Areas: Lessons from the Indian Experience' in *Innovation in India: Combining Economic Growth with Inclusive Development*, Shyama V. Ramani (ed.), UK: Cambridge University Press, pp. 337-378.

Abrol, Dinesh, and L. Pulamte, 2007, 'The Challenge before Indian Agricultural Universities: Impact and Relevance of the Kothari Commission's Vision and Strategy', in *Perspectives on Education and Development*, Ved Prakash and K Biswal (ed.), New Delhi: National University of Education, Planning & Administration (NUEPA), pp. 337-78.

Hess, David J., 2015, 'Undone Science, Industrial Innovation, and Social Movements', in *The Routledge International Handbook of Ignorance Studies,* Matthias Gross and Linsey McGoey (ed.), London and New York: Routledge, pp.141-54.

Levins, Richard, 2008, *Talking about Trees, Science, Ecology and Agriculture in Cuba*, New Delhi: Leftword Books.

National Commission on Agriculture, 1976, *Report on Research, Education, Extension*, New Delhi: National Commission on Agriculture, Govt. of India.

SOCIO-CULTURAL FUTURES

Between Diversity and Aphasia
The Future of Languages in India

G. N. Devy

Summary

India is a land of 780 diverse living languages. Scholars claim that there are approximately 6000 living languages in the world. Thus, India is home to one out of every eight languages in the world. This essay proposes that languages should be perceived as worldviews rather than just a mode of communication. Delays in recognition and stress on economic viability have resulted in the disappearance of many indigenous languages. The technological revolution in terms of communication has profoundly affected the way the modern world communicates and the languages of several ethnic and cultural groups are facing the threat of elimination.

However, there have been many attempts to document and archive living languages in India. In fact, there have been several research studies funded by the State to document indigenous languages. This essay argues that attention has to be diverted towards supporting languages that are not popular or in the mainstream, or have not reached the cities. This would mean harnessing initiatives to protect languages to a much greater extent, such as by maintaining e-libraries, literary societies and initiating magazines of and for indigenous languages. India will be able to face the challenge of securing its great language diversity only by embracing its multi-linguistic and multicultural identity.

The Declining Language Diversity

It was a remarkable foresight of the makers of the Indian Constitution that they thought of creating a dedicated Schedule of Languages, the 8th Schedule – which initially included fourteen languages – as the languages of administration. The list was subsequently enlarged so as to adjust the intent of the Schedule to the linguistic realities in the country. As of 2015, the Schedule holds a list of twenty two languages. These languages, popularly

411

known as the 'Scheduled Languages' are Assamiya, Bangla, Boro, Dogri, Gujarati, Hindi, Kannada, Kashmiri, Konkani, Maithili, Malayalam, Manipuri, Marathi, Nepali, Oriya, Punjabi, Sanskrit, Santali, Sindhi, Tamil, Telugu and Urdu. The Constitution has empowered individual States by vesting in them the authority to identify any language/s as official languages even if not in the 8th Schedule. Thus, though not in the Schedule, Kokborok (Tripura), Khasi and Garo (Meghalaya) and Mizo (Mizoram) enjoy the status of 'official' languages of administration. Further, a state has the powers to offer primary school education in any language irrespective of its official status. Under this provision, a number of languages of *Adivasi* communities have been introduced in primary schools in Orissa, Chhattisgarh, Andhra Pradesh, Maharashtra and Gujarat where the population speaking those languages is significant. In some states, new link-languages are conceptualized and promoted in order to keep the linguistically diverse states together. Rajasthani (Rajasthan), Pahari (Himachal Pradesh) and Nagamese (Nagaland) are the instances of such state-promoted 'binding' languages.

During the last hundred years, the print media has reached to a number of languages that are not officially recognized or promoted. Though it is not widely known, the number of little magazines, pamphlets and small-circulation books produced in the non-scheduled languages is quite large, a phenomenon that led the National Book Trust (NBT) to making tribal language publications the central theme for the NBT's International Book Fair in 2014. The official radio service –the All India Radio (AIR) – offers slots to nearly 120 languages in its regional programmes. In addition to the languages mentioned so far, there are numerous other major languages in India. Some are native such as Kutchhi (Gujarat), Tulu (Karnataka), Bhojpuri (U.P.-Bihar) and Bagadi (Rajasthan), while others have come from other countries and cultures and were accepted in the course of history as 'our languages'. The 'foreign' languages which are in use in different parts of the country include English (odd to say this is 'still in use' given its increasing spread, unlike the others listed here), French, Portuguese, Bhoti, Iranian, Arabic, Persian/Farsi and Pashto.

Archaeological and historical researches during the last two centuries have made it possible for us to know something about the complex linguistic transitions and migrations that took place over the last five millennia, roughly from the early Harappan times to our time. During this long period, the Indian subcontinent accepted language legacies as distinct as the Avestan of the Zoarastrians, the Austro-Asiatic of the Pacific the Tibeto-Burman of the East and the Northeast Asia. The Indic (or the Indo-Aryan) languages in the northern states together with the Dravidic languages in the south and the Tibeto-Burman languages in the Northeast, each with a great variety of sub-branches – make for the larger bulk of the Indian languages. Throughout the known history of the subcontinent, there has been an active exchange and cultural osmosis between the indigenous languages and the migratory languages, producing in the process great literature in many tongues.

The People's Linguistic Survey of India has estimated that there are nearly 780 living languages in the country at present (Devy, 2014). Scholars claim that there are approximately 6000 living languages in the world. Thus, India is home to one out of every eight languages on earth. The diversity is impressive not only in numerical terms. A language is not just a communication system, it is a unique worldview. Thus, though one can translate a given meaning from one language to another, there are always shades of meaning and nuances in any language that simply cannot be translated into other languages. Hence, the great diversity of languages in India needs be seen as the diversity of worldviews, of the unique ways of perceiving the world.

Despite the vast range of the existing linguistic diversity in India, and the official support that is being given to a relatively large number of languages, the language stock in the country has started showing signs of a rapid decline (Sengupta, 2010). Several historical factors appear to be responsible for the decline. The print technology impacted Indian languages profoundly during the nineteenth century. The languages that were printed acquired importance (Austien, 2009), the ones that remained untouched by it came to be seen more as dialects than as languages, though that was not the case in every instance. Subsequently, the process of state reorganization in the country invoked the principle that a language is a language only if it has printed literature in it. Obviously, languages like Bhojpuri or Gondi, despite having a large number of speakers, were never considered for statehood. The reorganization of Indian states mainly as linguistic states turned the already marginalized and 'non-printed' languages into 'minority' languages. Thus, Bhili, a major language in itself with over 20 million speakers, got divided into four states – Maharashtra, Madhya Pradesh, Gujarat and Rajasthan – and became a minority language in all of them. The Linguistic State Reorganisation Commission was created, in part, in response to the popular language movements in Hyderabad and Punjab. But, in part, it was also in response to the need for defining the federal structure of the newly emergent nation. The popular language movements had a strong emotional tenor and the support of large numbers, primarily from the urban areas. The tribal languages did not have the potential at that point in our history to generate such movements – which several decades later led to the creation of Jharkhand and Chhattisgarh as states. Hence, in the early decades of the post-independence history of India, the languages such as Santali, Mundari, Gondi remained divided uneasily between several states.

The list of 'Mother Tongues' reported by the 1961 Census had 1652 names. Beginning with the 1971 Census, the government decided to include in the list only the languages having more than 10,000 speakers. The list of 1971 had a total of 108 names, with a 109th entry of 'all others' (Nigam, 1972). The policy of using a cut-off figure further eliminated the already marginalized and minor languages. They started becoming increasingly invisible in social practice or political discourse. The relative lack of livelihood possibilities in the areas where the minor and marginalized languages are spoken has led to an exodus to areas where major and mainstream languages are spoken. This too has accelerated the rate at which the Indian language diversity is shrinking. The number of languages that may have disappeared during the last fifty years was estimated to be 250 by the People's Linguistic Survey (carried out in 2010). India seems to have lost nearly a quarter of its 'worldviews' since independence. The grave crisis is confined not to India alone. A similar situation of language loss is being experienced by most countries and in all continents.

There is in our time a worldwide concern about the alarming rise in the incidence of language disappearance. As the global south moves into a new phase of densely urbanized way of life, a somewhat willing concealment of indigenous languages has become a common occurrence. Schools in every country are increasingly engaging in training pupils to use one or the other global language. These global languages or 'mega-languages' have become or are being perceived as threat to the local languages (Lukanovic, 2010; Meierkord, 2012). In a similar way, the idea of nation state, within which is implicit the idea of a language or languages for preserving national unity, has put stress on sub-national languages for a somewhat forced alignment. The sub-national languages, or the 'regional languages' in turn, have learnt to expect the migration of yet smaller language communities within their fold as a natural result of 'development' and 'education', while they themselves feel uneasy in the face of the increasing influence of the 'mega-languages' and the 'national languages'. Thus, quite a hierarchy of fears and anxieties seems to have besieged languages all over the world. The fear and anxiety have taken in their grips even the mega-languages, for distinct continental varieties of these languages are emerging and beginning to become increasingly dissimilar. dissimilar (Barber, *et al.*, 1993; Bragg, 2003). The concern for 'disappearing language' has touched every mind on a scale never before experienced in human history. It is argued that while languages always go through the 'natural cycle' of rise and decline, in our time the incidence of a very rapid decline of natural languages has assumed worrisome proportions (Crystal, 2000; Nettle, 2000;

Florey, 2010). In recent years, as never before in the history of the discipline of language study and linguistics, books on language endangerment and language decline have been appearing in a rapid succession (e.g., Fishman, 2001; Dalby, 2003; Janse & Tol, 2003; Harrison, 2007; Austin, 2008; Aspand and Villiers, 2010).

The discussion on language endangerment and the conservation of threatened languages has received endorsement from UNESCO too (Wurn, 2005; Mosley, 2010).

The Global Language Crisis

Over the last two decades, scientists have come up with mathematical models for predicting the life of languages (Braggs & Freedman, 1993). These predictions have invariably indicated that the human species is moving rapidly close to extinction of a large part of its linguistic heritage. These predictions do not agree on the exact magnitude of the impending disaster; but they all agree on the fact that close to three quarters or more of all existing natural human languages are half in the grave. There are, on the other hand, advocates of linguistic globalization. The processes of globalization have found it necessary to promote homogenized cultures. The idea has found support among the classes that stand to benefit by the globalization of economies. They would prefer the spread of one or only a few languages all over the world so that communication across national boundaries becomes the easiest ever. Obviously, the nations and communities that have learnt to live within only a single language, whose economic well-being is not dependent on knowing languages other than their own, whose knowledge systems are well-secure within their own languages, will not experience the stress of language loss, at least not immediately, though the loss of the world's total language heritage, which will weaken the global stock of human intellect and civilizations, will have numerous indirect enfeebling effects on them too. Since it is language mainly of all things, that makes us human and distinguishes us from other species and animate nature (McMohan and McMohan, 2013), and since the human consciousness can but only function given the ability for linguistic expression, it becomes necessary to recognise language as the most crucial aspect of the cultural capital.

It has taken human beings continuous work of about half a million years to accumulate this valuable capital (Cornballis, 2011). In our time we have come close to the point of losing most of it. Historians of civilisation tell us that probably a comparable, though not exactly similar, situation had arisen in the past some seven or eight thousand years ago (Crystal, 2000). This was when the human beings discovered the magic of nature that seeds are. When the shift from an entirely hunting-gathering or pastoralist economies to early agrarian economies started taking place, we are told, the language diversity of the world got severely affected (Cornballis, 2011; Blench & Spriggs, 2012). It may not be wrong to surmise that the current crisis in human languages too is triggered by the fundamental economic shift that has enveloped the entire world, north or south, west or east. This time though the crisis has an added theme as a lot of the human activity is dominated by human-made intelligence.

The technologies aligned with artificial intelligence have all been depending heavily on modelling the activity of the human mind along the linguistic transactions. The intelligent machines modelled after entirely neurological or psychological systems are still not commonly in use. The language based technologies are now well entrenched partners in the semantic universe(s) that bind human communities together (Gillespie, 2007). Therefore that universe is being re-shaped. Language today is as much a system of meaning in the cyberspace effecting communication between a machine and another machine as much as it has been a system of meaning in the social space achieving communication between a human being and another human being.

Neurologists explain the current shift in man's cognitive processes by pointing to the rapidly changing ways in which the brain stores and analyzes sensory perceptions as well as information. Linguists have raised an alarm about the sinking fortunes of natural languages through which human communication has taken place over the last seven millennia. They have started noticing that the use of human-made memory-chips fed into intelligent machines make heavy dents in the human ability to remember and even the tense patterns of natural languages (Devy, 2014).

Technologists, particularly those astride the leading glory of technology – the ICT – have been talking of network communities as a substitute for civilizations. All in all – there is excitement in the air, and there is alarm in the minds. This is so on all fronts of knowledge, in all aspects of social organizations and all branches of human experience. Collectively, for all nations and all ethnic and cultural groups of humans the vision of a life well beyond our imagination has started appearing on the horizon even if it has not become fully manifest. This makes a mockery of all that the human brain and mind have so far held as being natural and permanent.

In the new experience of the world waiting for all of us, memory as we have so far used it (Rossi, 2006), is expected to be of little use, and imagination as we have so far exercised it is predicted to get entirely transformed. The homo-sapiens, it is believed, moving out of memory, imagination and even language, are poised to enter a post-human phase of the natural evolution (McMohan and McMohan, 2013). Man and the intelligent machine, together, are expected to develop a new image-based system of communication, a new post-human and predominantly externalized memory and a sphere of imagination where multiple frames of existence seamlessly collide.

This image of the things to come – call it a utopia, call it a dystopia – is profoundly unnerving, not because it involves fundamental challenges to the things established; not also because our sense of beauty, ethics and truth will get entirely transformed; but because a lot many communities—ethnic, linguistic, cultural—and innumerable groups on the economic fringes shall have to pay the cost of the transformation by having to face misery, deprivation and extinction.

Probably just as the Industrial Revolution and the associated rise of capitalism in European countries placed the traditional agrarian society at risk, giving rise to the long drawn conflicts between labour and capital, this great transition facing us globally will create strife and, consequently, violence of an unprecedented order. This time too, the post-human societies are likely to get divided between those with access to the digital and those without it.

Already, some linguistic laboratories have started publishing lists of 'digitally dead languages', with over 98 per cent of Indian languages included in the list (Kornai, 2013). Already, the communities not networked are being described as 'non-civil' (and internet based communication is called 'social networking'!). The economies of the world seem to have already resolved that the citizens without unique digital identities can be written off, like characters in Sadat Hassan Manto's stories, as the nowhere people. In our excitement for the utopia of the 'beyond imagination' life and world, it would be tragic if we forgot to look at the struggles and the plight of those who are on the digital fringes. Aphasia,[1] therefore, appears to be spread out for the future of Memory.

Language Erosion and Conservation

The future scenario that I have drawn up in the previous section pertains to a long term future, probably yet several centuries far from us. At present we are not even equipped to grasp the array of effects it will unleash on nations and communities. If one were to think in terms of a relatively shorter time-span, say, of a quarter of a century or so, it may be possible to make somewhat tenable a statement about the changes to come. The short-term future implications for the global language crisis for a country like India are, first and foremost, an increased migration of the economically less privileged classes from one geographical area to another, a marked change in the perception of identity, a more deep-cutting social segregation and, the most regrettably, the alienation of traditional knowledge, ecological as well as sociological. The imbalances created by these projected conditions can well be imagined. And that kind of imagined future is already an important part of the activist rhetoric in vogue. What is, however, not yet imagined is that the massive language-migration may offer India an opportunity to re-imagine the urban habitat? This point calls for some elaboration.

When the state organization was carried out during the two decades after independence and linguistic states were proposed, the assumption was that language would help in keeping the people of a linguistically conceptualized state emotionally bound (Sarangi, 2009; Schwartzberg, 2009). For reasons that had roots in the idea that '*matri-bhumi*'(motherland) and '*matri-bhasha*'(mother tongue) are closely analogous, such a state was seen as a 'homogenous' state. However, owing to the economic and demographic histories of the capital cities of many of the states, a typical mega-city has emerged as being at a fundamental variance from the rest of the state. Thus the linguistic composition of Mumbai is not at all like the linguistic composition of the rest of Maharashtra. The same is the case with Bengalaru, Hyderabad, Kolkata, Chandigarh and Ahmedabad. Yet, the school boards and the text-books boards in the states continue to look at the megapolis and the rest of the state as being one or alike. The language decisions of governments and educational regulatory bodies have ceased to be realistic and appropriate. When in the near future, the larger cities start recognizing their essentially trans-state, even trans-national multilingual character, despite their being capitals of a given linguistic state, a more congenial atmosphere shall emerge for preservation and perpetuation of diverse languages.

Capital cities of most of the states would have to be de-linked from the states in some ways and probably they will have to be given the status of union territories. The de-linking will not be called for merely because of the linguistic composition of the mega-cities, as language remains low in the hierarchy of priorities of any over-populated country. Yet, the economic realities such as the cost-benefit ratio and revenue-efficiency, energy consumption and production abilities, global-market-space and global-skilled-labour available in the key urban centres, all will push the public opinion in the direction of a relatively greater autonomy for such cities.

By 2047, a century from the date of India's independence, cities like Delhi, Mumbai, Hyderabad and Bangalore are likely to have a strong presence of over ten international languages – English (also American?), Korean, Chinese, Arabic, French, Spanish, German, Russian, Italian, Japanese; over thirty scheduled languages (the likely number in 2047); over eight to ten Asian languages and a hundred or more minor and tribal languages. Thus, these cities will be home to nearly 150 or more languages, each of these with their individual 'network communities' – wired and economically productive. Out of sheer economic realism and political pragmatism, the big Indian cities will learn to acknowledge the 'multilingual' nature of their demographic composition and make moves in the direction of establishing multilingual schools, knowledge parks, libraries, book malls, TV channels, radio broadcast, and such. The cities in all probability will play out the 'multicultural phase' of development that European nations studded with migrant labourers have gone through in the recent past (Bianco, 2012). But, given the Indian penchant for 'traditionalism', our lasting love for the past and memory that glorifies the past, and the hardening of the sense of identity bruised by the big cities, the rest of the state(s), made of small towns and deserted villages, tourist resorts and temple towns may return to flashing-points in linguistic chauvinism and cultural jingoism. In this imagined future probably the nation may appear to assuage itself for a while of the mournful awareness that humans have started departing from natural languages a bit too rapidly (Cru, 2010). Yet, in the process, perhaps, India will learn to respect what has always been an essential feature of Indian society for the last five millennia: that a single language as a 'mother tongue' is but a notion in the Indian context. We may wake up to the realization that India has always nurtured and worshiped languages, welcomed languages from foreign lands and tamed even the mightiest of languages (such as Sanskrit and Persian) in the interest of the voice of small communities. It would strike us when natural language itself will be facing a threat to its continuation as never before.

One needs to address a common misgiving that seems to have pervaded the popular sentiment. It relates to the place of the English language. Ever since it was introduced as the main language of knowledge in higher education in India – a slow process (Mayhew, 1926) flagged off by Lord T. B. Macaulay's 'Minutes' (1835) – there have been undercurrents within Indian languages that have looked at English as a challenge to Indian languages. In the years immediately following independence, there have been protest movements in the south against Hindi and an active anti-English campaign in the northern parts of the country. As a result of the epidemic-scale growth in the number of English medium schools in the country in recent years, one notices eruption of '*bhasha-bachao*' (save our language) movements in several states, most particularly in Maharashtra, Gujarat and Punjab. It is easy to understand that the anti-English protests and campaigns shape up as English language has played several key roles in the history of India since the eighteenth century, apart from being just a natural language that came here like many other natural languages. It has been the language of the people who had colonized India. It has been the language through which a lot of what we call 'modernity' is supposed to have reached the Indian shores. It has been the language of the twentieth century Imperialism which the Socialist sentiment in India did not favour so much. Besides, English is today the language of a powerful communication technology and the language associated with the flow of international capital. Being thus so many of the above, and more, it continues to draw anger from a variety of quarters from time to time.

Yet, it is a language that has brought to Indian languages a very huge range of lexical items adding to their power of expression. It is the language which has continued to enrich the literary and dramatic expression in Indian languages by bringing to them literature from all parts of the world. Besides, it is today probably the most effective link language for the Indian republic and a language which brings employment and business more easily than other languages do. Given this extremely complicated and entrenched place of the English language in India, what is in store for us in near future? More specifically, what may be the condition of the Indian languages such as Bangla, Telugu, Marathi, Gujarati and so on? Will English manage to replace all of them completely? Will English one day beat a quiet retreat to the lonely island from where it came to India? It is but natural that these and such other questions should continue to exercise the minds of the nation-loving Indians.

Obviously, there are no easy answers to these questions since human languages are known to have behaved in the most surprising manner in the past. Some very mighty languages are known to have disappeared in the face of some minor challenges; some others have grown taller precisely because they faced threats of extinction. Yet, if one were to try predicting the fortunes of the English language in India, one would have to look at the history of its fortunes in similar situations elsewhere. It is necessary to recall that the English language travelled with the colonial rules to several other continents. It managed to almost entirely replace the indigenous languages in North America, Australia and New Zealand. That did not, however, happen exactly so in African countries like Nigeria, Kenya and South Africa. In India, just as the fortunes of the English language continued to improve, numerous Indian languages too witnessed a remarkable literary and linguistic growth in the same period. Based on this comparative perspective, one can perhaps propose that there had been something in the making of the Indian languages prior to the arrival of English which allowed them to face the encounter in a far more mature way than the languages of the Atlantic and Pacific areas had managed to do. What was this peculiar strength?

If one were to step back in history, one notices that the Indic and the Dravidic languages had previously negotiated the encounter with Arabic and Persian with an equal maturity, themselves surviving in the encounter and linguistically gaining in the process. Given such a history, it is reasonable to assume that the innate multilingualism of Indian culture(s) will see them through in the current encounter with the English language. As a result of the intimacy between the English and the Indian languages, the *bhashas*, they are likely to get suffused with English vocabulary. But so long as the grammars are their own, they need not fear a total annihilation at the hands of English.

The fear of decline should arise from another quarter, namely, the neglect of the minor languages, the dialects, the speech patterns of the indigenous and the coastal communities. These 'other' Indian languages have been like the roots of the main Indian languages. In the past, they have provided the main languages semantic resource and expressive power. Those roots have started drying up as the speakers of the 'other' – the non-scheduled, the oral, the economically less privileged – languages are driven to outward migration in search of livelihood. Already the erosion of the supporting indigenous languages has started showing an adverse impact on the *bhashas*. The situation would be predictably far worse some thirty years from now. So, if the great language diversity of India has to be preserved, promoted and carried forward to the future generations, it would be necessary to turn attention to the indigenous and minor languages.

Language is not only a social system of verbal icons, arbitrarily assembled through ages, it is also a 'means' of carrying forward the cumulative human experience of millennia to the future generations. When language trajectories are snapped, the accumulated wisdom in those languages too gets submerged and continues to survive in severely truncated, irreparable and insensible forms. Essays in this volume on technology and knowledge discuss how, a perceptible shift takes place in our attitude to what knowledge is and, how it is to be transmitted to new generations.[2] They also point to how knowledge in future is to be harnessed for improving sustainability of the planet earth. If we pay heed to those suggestions as much more than a mere wish-statement, the continuation of some of the potentially threatened languages can be ensured. That shall also contribute significantly to the deepening of democracy in a people-friendly and ecology-friendly form. In human history, language was created as a *surplus* of man's cognitive and emotive transactions, a product of the *labour of the mind*. For a very long portion of the human history, language continued to retain its character as a predominantly free system that is sturdily resistant to government controls, market regulations and cultural oppressions.

However, over the last few centuries, particularly since the rise of technologies that apparently function as assistance to language – transport, printing, photography, electronic-language-storage-and-reproduction, digital-encoding-and-decoding of human language – language acquisition, languages transmission and language use have started getting rapidly monetized. Today, as never before, the economically dispossessed classes all over the world are finding it difficult to access language acquisition as per their needs and desires. Thus, throughout the world, we now notice a digit-powered linguistic class and another print and digit-deprived linguistic class. The divide is too deep to bridge by following any conventional or prevailing economic ideologies. A technological reversal in the evolution of languages too is a hugely unrealistic proposition. The only hope for ensuring any future for 'linguistic homo-sapiens' is to envision together and integrate economic development and linguistic federalism. If the rural landscapes and marginalized communities can be safeguarded, the currently threatened languages will find a safe passage to the future; and only if those languages continue to survive shall we have access to the knowledge that helps us to build a sustainable future society. The two are so intimately interlocked.

There have been some noteworthy initiatives in this direction during the last two decades. Several tribal activist groups have started little magazines, in some cases e-books, and literary societies. In 2014, the National Book Trust could find enough printed materials to organize a large exhibition of books and journals in tribal languages. This exhibition was made the centre piece of the World Book Fair in Delhi. Some of the universities have created 'Indigenous Studies' courses. The University Grants Commission (UGC) created new grants during 2013-14 to set up special study centres for indigenous languages in twenty one universities. A few seminars and workshops were held in recent years on the theme of indigenous literature, arts and language by the national Academies. The People's Linguistic Survey of India, a comprehensive study of all living languages, was carried out by Bhasha Research Centre, Baroda. The University Grants Commission has created funds for special research initiatives related to endangered languages. There is now a relatively greater interest in research and documentation of indigenous and endangered languages than any time before. All these impulses and initiatives need to be harnessed fully so that India is able to face the challenge of securing its great language diversity to the extent it is possible, when we celebrate the centenary of our Independence.

Endnotes

1. The Greek term 'Aphasia' is a medical term which describes a patient's inability to speak. It literally means 'the loss of speech'. Aphasia is caused either because the neural instructions do not reach the speech organs, or the speech organs have lost the ability to carry out the brain's command. Here, the term is used to describe not an individual's aphasia but the collective inability to continue one's language.
2. See essays on Technology Futures and Knowledge Futures, in this volume.

References

Asp, Elissa D. and Jessica De Villiers, 2010, *When Language Breaks Down,* New York: Cambridge University Press.

Austin, Peter, 2008, *One Thousand Languages: living, endangered and lost,* Berkley: University of California Press.

Austin, Granville, 2009, 'Language and the Constitution: the half-hearted compromise', in *Language and Politics in India,* Asha Sarangi (ed.), New Delhi: Oxford University Press, pp. 41-92.

Bianco, Joseph Lo, 2012, 'National Language Revival Movements: reflections from India, Israel, Indonesia and Ireland', in *The Cambridge Handbook of Language Policy,* Bernard Spolsky (ed.), Cambridge: Cambridge University Press, pp. 501-522.

Blench, Roger and Mathew Spriggs (eds.), 2012, *Archaeology and Language: theoretical and methodological orientations,* (4 Vols.), Abingdon and New York: Routledge.

Barber, Charles, Joan C. Beal, and Philip Shaw, 1993, *The English Language: a historical introduction,* Cambridge: Cambridge University Press.

Bragg, Melvyn, 2003, *The Adventure of English: the biography of a language.* London: Hodder & Stoughton.

Braggs, I. and H. I. Freedman, 1993, 'Can the Speakers of a Dominated Language Survive as Unilinguals? A Mathematical Model of Bilingualism', *Mathematical and Computer Modeling,* Vol. 18(6), pp. 9-18.

Cornballis, Michael, 2011, *The Recursive Mind: the origins of human language, thought and civilization,* Princeton, NJ: Princeton University Press.

Cru, Josep (ed.), 2010, *The Management of Linguistic Diversity and Peace Processes,* Barcelona: UNESCOCAT.

Crystal, David, 2000, *Language Death,* Cambridge: Cambridge University Press.

Devy, G. N., 2014, *The Being of Bhasha: General Introduction to the People's Linguistic Survey of India,* New Delhi: Orient Blackswan.

Dalby, Andrew, 2003, *Language in Danger,* New York: Columbia University Press.

Fishman, Joshua A. (ed.), 2001, *Can Threatened Languages be Saved?* Clivedon and Sydney: Multilingual Matters.

Florey, Margaret (ed.), 2010, *Endangered Languages of Australia,* New York: Oxford University Press.

Gillespie, Tarleton, 2007, *Wired Shut: copyright and the shape of digital culture,* Cambridge, Massachusetts: The MIT Press.

Harrison, K. David, 2007, *When Languages Die,* New York: Oxford University Press.

Janse, Mark and Sijmen Tol (eds.), 2003, *Language Death and Language Maintenance: theoretical practice and descriptive approaches*, Amsterdam/Philadelphia: John Benjamin Publishing Company.

Kornai, A., 2013, 'Digital Language Death', PLoS ONE8(10): e77056, https://doi.org/10.1371/journal. pone.0077056 (accessed 13 October, 2017).

Lukanovic, Sonja Noval (ed.), 2010, *A Shared Vision: international dialogue – a global paradigm to promote linguistic and cultural diversity*, Ljubljana: Institute for Ethnic Studies.

Mayhew, Arthur, 1926, *The Education of India: a survey of British education policy in India, 1835-1920, and its bearing on national life and problems in India today*, London: Faber and Gwyer.

McMahon, April, and Robert McMahon, 2013, *Evolutionary Linguistics*, Cambridge: Cambridge University Press.

Meierkord, Chritiane, 2012, *Interactions across Englishes: linguistic choices in local and international contact situations*, New York: Cambridge University Press.

Mosley, Christopher, 2010, *The Atlas of the World Languages in Danger*, Paris: UNESCO

Naik, J. P and Nurullah Syed, 1951, *A History of British Education in India during the British Period*, Bombay: Popular.

Nettle, Daniel and Suzanne Romaine, 2000, *Vanishing Voices*, Oxford: Oxford University Press.

Nigam, R. C., 1972, 'Language Handbook on Mother Tongues in Census', *Census of India 1971*, No. 10, New Delhi: Census Centenary Monographs.

Rossi, Paolo, 2006, *Logic and the Art of Memory: the quest for a universal language*, London: Athlone Press.

Sarangi, Asha (ed.), 2009, *Language and Politics in India*, New Delhi: Oxford University Press.

Schreier, Daniel, Peter Trudgill, Edgar W. Schneider, Jeffrey P. Williams (eds.), 2010, *The Lesser Known Varieties of English*, New York: Cambridge University Press.

Schwartzberg, Joseph E., 2009, 'Factors in the Linguistic Reorganization of Indian States' in *Language and Politics in India*, Asha Sarangi (ed.), New Delhi: Oxford University Press, pp. 139-82.

Sengupta, Kamalini (ed.), 2010, *Endangered Languages in India*, New Delhi: INTACH.

Wurn, Stephen, 2005, *Atlas of the World's Languages in Danger*, Paris: UNESCO.

Future of Learning in Indian Schools

Rajesh Khindri and Tultul Biswas

Summary

Education plays a crucial role in the transmission of ideas, life experiences, culture, knowledge, language, etc., from one generation to the other, and the school as an agency of imparting education becomes a vital site of these transmissions. However, school systems are also responsible for reinforcing inequalities and prejudices that are already prevalent in the society.

The dysfunctional government school system in India is populated by students from the most marginalised sections of the society. On the other hand, private schools reflect the highly class stratified Indian society, and do not even engage with the students from the marginalized sections. Such stratification is further amplified with caste, religion, and gender inequalities that are deeply embedded in the Indian society. Inside the classrooms, the academic process is also dismal, be it the government or private schools. Education has been reduced to business and there is no space for the creative and holistic development of a child.

Inspired by the ideas of Avijit Pathak, this essay argues for the vision of future education that can open up opportunities and unleash the potential towards the development of a balanced, just and responsive student and teacher. This essay gives the examples of a few alternate education avenues that have attempted to move away from the conventional school structure and opened new ways of creating an interactive, inclusive, open-ended learning environment.

The Current Situation

Institutionalized learning,[1] or education,[2] has a very short history of only about 500 years as compared to the long, more than 200,000 years of existence of the *homo sapiens*. What purpose does education serve for the human race? And how has it shaped human society? How has human society, in turn, modified the practice of education according to its needs and dynamics? Where are we today? Which aspirations have been met, what are the disillusionments we face and where do we see hope for tomorrow? These are some of the questions that we deal with in this essay.

Let us begin with a critical examination of the state of school education today.[3]

Education plays an important role in the 'transmission' of social experiences – which includes culture, knowledge, language, beliefs, etc. from one generation to the next. 'Schools are, indeed, one important method of the transmission', along with family, community, religion, economy, and politics (Dewey, 2004, pp. 5). However, schools and school systems have also been found to play a significant role in reproducing and legitimizing (or even perpetuating) social and cultural inequalities. Despite stated ideologies of equal opportunity and meritocracy, few educational systems have played a role 'to do anything other than reproduce the legitimate culture as it stands and produce agents capable of manipulating it legitimately' (Bourdieu & Passeron, 1990, pp. 59). What mostly remains unnoticed in society is that the educational achievement of students is also largely influenced by the uneven socio-economic realities that they live in.

The crumbling government school system: The government school system in all parts of the country is witnessing a hitherto unforeseen phenomenon of dysfunction and decimation. This leads to the shift of children coming from powerful and privileged populations towards private schools. This in turn causes further dysfunction of government schools because the vocal populations, that can demand facilities, services and quality of education for their wards, are no longer part of the government school system. The result is a self-perpetuating vicious cycle.

School as an inclusive space: Historically, the Sanskrit *pathshalas* and *gurukuls* of the Indian education system have been spaces for specific caste-borns and the *madarasas* continue to give access to only Muslim children. In contrast to these indigenous structures imparting education, the modern education system put in place by the British was seen more as a space open to all. (It may be wise here to keep in mind that although technically open to all, the modern schools structure forwarded by the British rule in India was still limited in its reach in terms of the class of people who could avail of it). Yet, the very same modern education school system has become fragmented, stratified and largely non-inclusive today. For example, consider the issue of caste in schools. Although blatant forms of caste discrimination like denying entry in school are now rare, subtle ways of denial, exclusion and discouragement on the basis of both caste and class continue to function and become roadblocks to education. Government schools – populated with students from the most marginalized and under-served sections of society – often extend both subtle and

426

overt caste-based discrimination towards these children. Most private schools, on the other hand, do not even engage with these students, as they are high fee-demanding systems, eliminating these groups at the outset. Gender further complicates this scenario, with girls, and especially girls from *Dalit* and backward caste communities being at the lowest rung of the school ladder.

'At the close of the last century it was found that barely 48 percent of Dalit children had completed even primary schooling' (Nambissan, 2009, pp. 9). Un-supportive learning environment, hostile or discouraging attitude of the school structure, teachers and school authorities, lack of basic amenities in schools and lack of home/parental support are some factors that push out these children from schools. 'Even today the vast majority 'drop out' from school well before they complete eight years of education' (ibid.). This is clearly evident from the literacy rate data. Literacy rate of *Adivasi* children was 47.1 per cent against the national average of 64.84 per cent (2001 census).[4] This despite the fact that enrolment rates of Adivasi children have been higher than the national average (86.1% versus 84.8%), showing that many drop out before they finish elementary education.

W(h)ither Right to Education?: While enforcing the Right to Education Act six years ago, the erstwhile Prime Minister of India claimed that all children – irrespective of social or gender category – will have access to free education. April 1, 2013 was then set as the deadline for implementing the key provisions of RTE. More than 3 years beyond the deadline, the ground reality continues to be grim. A striking divide that the RTE has been unable to address is the urban-rural divide. 'More than 47 lakh children out of school belong to rural areas while only 13 lakh come from urban neighbourhoods' (Jain, 2015, pp. 2).

The scenario appears even more alarming when viewed through the caste or religion lens. According to the National Sample Survey estimates, from a report prepared in 2014 by the Social and Rural Research Institute, three out of every four children out of school are Dalit, Muslim or Adivasi. A closer look at the available data reveals that over 32 per cent of those out of schools are Dalits and over 16 per cent belong to the Adivasi communities. According to the same report, 4.43 per cent of Muslim children were found to be out of school, significantly higher than the national average of 2.97 per cent across religions (Jain, 2015).

Thus, although official figures claim that only six million children remain out of school and the drop-out rate in schools has started showing a drop, an analysis of the profile of children still out of school reflects the fact that we are far from achieving the goal of inclusive education.

Inside the classroom: On one hand, discrimination of children on the basis of their socio-cultural backgrounds continues inside the classrooms, on the other, the academic or teaching-learning processes are also on a steady decline – be it government or private schools. As Nambissan (2012) notes, citing several studies that have looked at low-fee private schools, the teaching-learning processes are not that different from government schools, and the school infrastructure and facilities are extremely poor.

In spite of the growing acknowledgement of constructivist approaches to education in the educational discourse at the national level, the content and practice of teaching inside majority of Indian classrooms continues to be teacher-planned and teacher-centric. Very little space exists for the child to learn by exploring and constructing knowledge.

Teacher – the meek dictator: The situation of the teacher in a school classroom today has been aptly described by Krishna Kumar (2006) as 'the meek dictator'. In both government and private school systems, the teacher is the lowest in the hierarchical rungs of the educational structure and hence the least respected. The situation is further demoralized with no space for the teacher to perform as a creative person – contributing to the process of knowledge building of children. Unimaginable levels of micro-planning are the norm of the day in most private schools with very little breathing space for teachers to respond to the different needs of the children they teach or relate their teaching to the diverse environments that they work in. The socio-cultural and natural environment of the students in all classrooms in India, whether rural or urban, varies significantly. In addition, these classrooms encompass students speaking a wide range of tongues as their home language. Taking these diversities into account, in creating teaching materials and planning and executing the teaching processes in a classroom is then but expected from any sensitive and conscientious teacher. However, the present system does not give room to the teacher to take any such initiative or exercise personal agency.

In government schools, the story is that of an overdose of uncoordinated trainings on one hand, and an agonizing non-teaching workload thrust upon teachers, on the other, that ranges from animal census to polio eradication.

The present centralized system of curriculum planning and textbook development has caused further alienation of students from their own language, culture, craft traditions, environment, and even active denigration of these. The situation boils down to the same, whether done by central agencies like the National Council for Education Research and Training (NCERT), the State Councils for Education Research and Training (SCERTs) at the state level, or the private publishers playing in the market driven by profits. The syllabus content largely remains mostly conformist, pro-dominant, with no place for traditional systems of learning including recognizing community elders as 'teachers'. As the written word gets higher priority and status, oral traditions get more and more displaced. The last curriculum and textbook development efforts done by the NCERT in 2005-06 have been a game-changer to some extent. However, even they have failed to give importance to work related knowledge and skills and not just text book learning.

It is in this bleak scenario that we continue to work in the education sector towards a change for the better.

A Vision for Tomorrow

Education, we feel, plays an important role in developing three kinds of sensibilities in human beings. Inspired by the ideas and writings of Avijit Pathak (2009), we see these three areas as:

a) The relationship between a person and other persons – his/her friends or family or his/her community or society at large;

b) The internal dynamics and thought-processes of any person, ranging from the everyday existential frictions of living in a complex world to the deeper inner churnings related to ideas such as truth, trust, democracy and justice;

c) The relationship between humans and nature.

How does learning and education shape these three kinds of human processes/relationships is truly a matter of intrigue. However, let us brave to imagine the unthinkable today! Imagine first of all a living community that is not divided along the lines of caste, class, religion, gender and sexuality or the rural-urban divides. Imagine a collaborative living community where we have people with different skills and abilities, speaking diverse languages, professing different faiths – but all collaborating to make their lives meaningful and working towards a sustainable world.

Now, located in this community, imagine a learning space that is open to learners of all ages – young and old. Imagine people of different ages learning from each other – a child of nine teaching cycling to a man in his thirties, a woman of sixty story-telling to all who are interested. Imagine a space where the learners are active in planning and executing their own learning journeys and are able to seek help and support where needed. Shall we call it a school at all?

In the following sections, we will explore what can be best termed as certain possibilities that can open up opportunities and unleash the potential towards the development of a balanced, just and responsive learner and teacher.

Agency of the Child

On the national level discourse, especially in the context of National Curriculum Framework (NCF) 2005 (GoI, 2005), we have moved away significantly from the paradigm wherein children were presumed to be 'empty vessels' and a teacher's role was that of filling them with knowledge – to a position where it is now acknowledged that the magnitude and intensity of learning that takes place during the first three years of life (before the child reaches school) is enormous. The child is learning continuously while s/he is awake (probably even while s/he is asleep if the role of sleep in memory formation and binding is taken into account), in an extremely supportive environment that provides continuous positive feedback.

However, while this is acknowledged in national documents and discussions, we are yet to see materials and classroom processes that actually imbibe what this means and try to draw upon this rich resource that is available with each and every child in the school. In actual practice, this would mean a shift to classroom transactional processes wherein children are given space to verbalise and share with others most of the time, instead of listening, or repeating, or undertaking a mechanical exercise. Children need to be given space to express themselves orally and bring in all the language and linguistic diversities that they come with and thereby use this multi-lingual resource to enrich the classroom processes.[5] They also must be given the space and scope to articulate in all possible manners like play-acting or trying to create in various other forms. While drawing and painting provide a rich canvas for expression, we need to let them explore many more avenues (like music, abhinaya (*expressive art*), and collaborative games) as well.

Unfortunately, these discussions are usually restricted to pre-primary and early-primary years (not overtly stated, but this is the understanding that is reflected in real practice even in the most alternative schools). Over here, we would like to take up and explore similar dimension for students who are beyond these age groups, for the eight to nine year old children who have started gaining independence to twelve to fourteen year adolescents or young adults.[6] For these children and young adults as much learning takes place out of school as within, because even if one only considers the time factor, compared to 4-6 hours spent in school, they spend about double to three times of their waking active hours in the community or at home. Most children, barring some belonging to the middle class and upper middle class, would be indulging in some activity that provides as much of a learning experience. Probably such opportunities are comparatively less for middle class and upper middle class children who either spend most of the time at home around activities related to school, in the form of home work, projects or assignments or are further burdened with the vagaries of tuitions and coaching.

Providing avenues to youngsters that are meaningful is extremely crucial to make them confident about whatever they are doing, to take them on the path of becoming self-learners, to make them embrace and enjoy the challenges in-built in the process of learning itself. To take this further, creating the space for older children to choose what to learn and when and how to learn, or in other words, explore 'freedom' to learn, will also make learning more meaningful (Coelho & Padmanabhan, 2016). Another area that will require proactive thought and action is to make such avenues and opportunities relevant to all children, including differently-abled children as well as those with learning disabilities.

This requires a change in what we perceive as learning, and what we then convey to children and young adults as the meaning of learning. If even one of these is missing, the 'learning' that takes place is neither valued by others, nor internalised by the individual as something that can lead to confidence building, the kind of confidence that goes hand in hand with the realisation of overcoming challenges and 'learning' something.

We need to examine possibilities of how we can provide avenues to youngsters to bring in the learning from out-of-school interactions to the classroom to enrich the transaction amongst students and between students and teachers. An example is that of the Narmada Jeevanshalas[7] (life schools) run by the Narmada Bachao Andolan. In its early days, the Jeevanshala students living in forest villages or near forests of Jhabua district of M.P. made extensive glossaries of the plant world around them, their names, the uses of their various parts, etc. Similarly, the children of Bodhshala were seen sharing the names of trees whose twigs were being used as '*datoon*' (tooth-brush) while learning about oral hygiene. When the Hoshangabad Science Teaching Programme[8] was active in schools, one has witnessed teachers who gave the entire responsibility of handling kit (the science lab equipment meant for middle schools hands-on experience) to students. These teachers were not burdened by the idea of allowing students to perform experiments in the classes or the fear of the mess that they will need to handle once the class is over. They were also the ones who managed to keep the kit material clean and organized better than others. As a result, children who were given this responsibility became much more adept at a range of skills, including a boost in self-confidence. The idea of *Bal Panchayat*, now spread over many states, whereby children form groups in the community to raise issues related to children's rights and well-being, occasionally bring out a newsletter and take the ownership of taking care of themselves in their own hands also has roots in similar thoughts.

Another critical need is of providing many more meaningful avenues to young students outside the school, because they have the energy, time and the initiative. Such avenues have the capacity of changing the entire learning scenario and environment –

moving from sole dependence on a formal school structure to much more open-ended explorations through peer interactions or interfaces with mentors. One such example that has underlined the possibilities is a network of students' groups set up in Dewas district in early to mid 90s' wherein middle school children organised and ran library-cum-activity centres in their respective villages in community spaces or homes – called *Chakmak* (Flintstone) clubs. At one point there were almost one hundred such informal spaces run by young adults in Dewas district alone. Each *Chakmak* club was anchored by a resource pool of four to six students who organised it as per local requirements, availability of resources, etc., within an overall framework. Over time, many of these turned into spaces of discussion and debate around social issues that provided them a much wider exposure and led to independent perspective building in addition to gaining very important 'soft skills' like confidence, articulation, and leadership. This initiative also later developed into a bedrock for literacy campaign activities in the district with a majority of the *Chakmak* club coordinators taking on roles in the campaign as active change agents.[9]

Another similar effort was taken up around Hoshangabad ten years later. These were called *Bal Samoohs* (Children's Groups). While this was similar in many aspects, it also differed in some ways, especially the focus being on consciously involving children from underserved sections of the society. While Bal Samoohs welcomed everybody, the physical location of these were mostly in settlements that provided easier access to children from underserved communities, essentially to ensure their participation. The forum of Bal Samoohs gave space and recognition to children's and young adults' initiatives through creative expressions like art, theatre, writing, and village-based campaigns on issues of interest and concern to the participating members.

These examples are just to point out and portray the possibilities of engaging with the Agency of the Child, the starting and the end point of the entire enterprise of education. Everybody involved in the enterprise of education at any level should examine whether s/he is using potential of this agency in the processes being suggested and followed.

Education is Defeated in a Non-inclusive Environment

Over the last couple of decades, fragmentation and stratification in the education system has increased to an extent that was unimaginable in the seventies and eighties. Instead of a few limited categories/sets wherein one had a few elite schools like Doon, Scindia, Mayo, Welham and Lovedale at one end, and most other children going to government schools, with a few private schools that were not very different from government schools, one had at the most half a dozen categories. Now there seems to be a continuum starting from the extremely high fee paying private schools affiliated to international boards that charge several thousand rupees per month, down to private schools that charge hundred rupees a month and are meant for populace that can hardly spare that much. Government schools, situated at the lowermost fringe of the continuum, have today become extremely homogenous as they increasingly serve only children from the scheduled castes (SCs), scheduled tribes (STs) and girls, with few children from the other backward castes (OBCs) and those belonging to the general category (Velaskar, 2013). This seems to be the profile in most of the states. While there might be exceptions in certain states and specific areas, this is the predominant profile in the year 2015.

What does this imply? It means that most of the students belonging to a class and a caste-set do not have any exposure to anybody else as far as peer interaction is concerned. Students travelling in AC buses and attending classes in AC classrooms would never get to meet 'middle class' children, let alone have any interaction with children from underserved *bastis* (tenement settlements). Each segment is quite well insulated – there is no question of porosity/mixing. During the first forty years after independence, large public sector undertakings and comparatively inclusive townships[10] provided a space wherein children (and families) from diverse socio-economic and cultural backgrounds lived side by side and this provided an environment rich in diversity, in settlements as well as learning spaces. That has also shrunk drastically and almost evaporated today.

But the next question could be – didn't Right to Education 2009 try to make education more inclusive through the legislation that 25% seats of private schools will be earmarked for children who cannot pay fees? We won't go into the issue of percentages, numbers, etc., in this context, but even within five years it has become apparent that this legislation is in fact being used to weaken the public education system further. In many states, governments are trying to ensure that this quota is utilised to the maximum – which results in shutting/scaling down or merging of government schools due to the decreasing numbers of children enrolling in government schools as a result. In actual fact, it seems to have pushed the government schools towards further homogenising, catering to the segment (of parents) that has no social or political voice to influence the school in any way. And on the other hand, private schools try their best to ward off this intrusion by trying to segregate these students into separate classes or even separate school shifts, by insisting on various kind of additional expenses that the family has to incur in terms of dress, shoes, books, excursion fees... and by use of social exclusion through the medium of instruction.

In such times, one needs to look around for models of inclusive education that would be relevant in today's context, or for voices that propose models that have inclusiveness built into it. For example groups and organisations championing the common schooling system or the concept of neighbourhood schools advocate for schools that serve the children of any neighbourhood irrespective of their religion, caste, class, gender, income levels and family backgrounds. Akhil Bharatiya Shiksha Adhikar Manch (All India Forum for Right to Education) is a network that has brought many of these groups together and given rise to a country-wide debate and discourse on this issue. A small ray of hope is the few groups trying out models of inclusive education at a very small scale, but none-the-less swimming against the tide. Aadharshila School in district Sendhwa, Madhya Pradesh; Centre for Learning, Bangalore; Sholai School, Tamil Nadu; Anand Niketan Democratic School, Bhopal; Students' Educational and Cultural Movement of Ladakh; Marudam Farm School in Thiruvannamalai, Tamil Nadu; Imlee-Mahua School in the Bastar region of Chhattisgarh; Kanavu School, Wynad, Kerala, Vidyavanam, Tamil Nadu are a few examples to quote. Incidentally, even a formal school like St. Mary's in New Delhi admitted a number of children with disabilities in the 90s' at a time when the government was not pushing this kind of inclusion.[11] These need to be nurtured and also studied carefully to figure out possibilities of systems/processes that can make it possible for children of diverse economic and social strata to interact and learn in an atmosphere that enables an exchange of strengths of each other, resulting in a heightened level of humane sensitivity.

Teachers' Agency and the Freedom to Be

While there have been umpteen studies trying to prove or disprove whether teachers are loaded with administrative tasks to such an extent that it impacts teaching time heavily, the fact remains that for a sizeable number of primary schools that have only one or two teachers, even a small amount of this additional load can affect the teaching considerably. However, the issue of import is not about the non-teaching administrative work load, the crucial consideration is the kind of signals a teacher gets from 'higher ups' in the education bureaucracy. Usually, the signal is that the façade of education is to be kept up through filling-up and submitting various kinds of information about status of school, levels of students and so on. And obviously, no school can afford to move downwards. It has to be either stable or has to ensure that it is climbing upwards. So, there is no way a teacher can get out of this mire. Two conversations with government officials in M.P. held in early 2015 indicate how stark and different the reality can be. While the highest bureaucrats in the education department were clear that the state education portal provided exact data regarding number of students in D and E categories (these are the students who have fared worst in the academic transactions in school) at the primary level (showing only a few hundred such students in a particular block), the concerned block official was equally clear that if learning levels were gauged properly, more than half the students in government primary schools in the same block would be found in D and E grades. Probably both echelons are aware of this equally well, but it is a fact that cannot be stated. We are not ready to face a 'proverbial *nangaraja*' or accept that the Emperor has no clothes.

We need to urgently ensure that teachers are conveyed signals that it is fine to be in a difficult spot, fine to take some risks and experiment at her/his level; that some initiatives will deliver and some might not; that s/he will not be taken to task or penalized for these. We need to let the teacher be. And let the teacher be only for interaction with children for the broadest possible educational goals. But how can that be? Why not think out of the box and try. Just a thought – there might be many such possible solutions to be weighed and tried. Just take off all administrative tasks including scholarships, uniforms, books, caste certificates, data collection and uploading ... from the teacher. One way to do that is to appoint a clerk for that (probably a student who has finished schooling or graduation from the respective area). An example to consider is that of Ladakh, where some of the Village Education Committees have been active in providing help to teachers to deal with non-teaching tasks that may have otherwise taken them out of the classroom, and in the process ensuring increase in actual teaching time available. This is just one example... there might be many more possible solutions if we are ready to move out of the box.

On the flip side of this is the question of teacher accountability towards, the children and the community they come from, not just towards the educational bureaucracy. The problem of absentee or present-but-hardly-teaching teachers is also widespread. Nagaland has sorted this out by giving part of the budget for schools, including the salary of the teachers, to the village council to disperse. This has dramatically increased teacher presence in the schools which was otherwise very poor (Pathak, 2014). Another possible way to face this problem squarely is to encourage teachers from within the community itself. This has been tried out by many non-governmental organisations for their varied non-formal or extra-school educational initiatives with positive results. In addition to addressing the problem of teacher absenteeism and/or non-function, this kind of rootedness of the teacher in the students' community and context also enhances the pedagogic process.

Free Access in Local Languages on World Wide Web – possible equaliser

Proliferation of technology and internet are going to further increase rapidly. So anything that is published in print format should also be made available in free access soft version in open source formats in Unicode fonts in all Indian languages, alongside the print version.

Each and every adjective/phrase in the above paragraph is equally important. We have created a mess over the last thirty years by not standardizing Indian language font sets – the government and the private sector have both failed miserably by not pursuing and pushing this agenda. At least now that Unicode fonts have come to the fore, everybody needs to upload content that is as easily searchable in all Indian languages as is possible with English and a hundred other languages. Towards this the government and industry need to develop and populate the Unicode font sets heavily so that there are options available as per niche requirements. Also both propriety and open source softwares should allow Unicode font usage, and equally important, there should be backward linkages with at least a couple of earlier versions of every software as far as Unicode font support is concerned.

Open source formats using open source applications are the need of the hour, so that we don't need to invest heavy financial resources unnecessarily. Over the last few years Firefox and android based applications have proved these. Also initiatives like Wikipedia. Hence a move towards free software movement must be consciously adopted. Wikipedia kind of platforms have to be populated a thousand fold for Indian languages.

In a scenario wherein half the teachers already have smart phones/devices even in rural areas and access to such devices, computers and internet is increasing even for middle and high school students in school and community situations, flooding the web with the best quality educational materials in Indian languages, available under free and open licenses, can provide an opportunity that can be some sort of 'equaliser' across various social and economic strata.

And the Mother of Maladies

The Assessment system – it's been one step forward and two steps backward. Examination system became more and more monolithic and oppressive as the society (or is it the middle class only?) became more and more competitive over the last thirty years or so. From two to three exams over a year, we moved to monthly tests and then weekly tests. Even with the latest schema of CCE (Continuous and Comprehensive Evaluation) most schools/school-systems have introduced unit tests to side-step the actual spirit of formative assessment and abide by the regulations only. If you aren't allowed to conduct exams, just call it by some other name so that the system becomes even more complex, and also futile in the end, as far as learning goes.

Although much has been written and spoken about the futility and ill-effects of year-end or end-of-the-session examinations, yet, the abolishing of board examinations in the elementary school up to and even at class-ten level by the previous UPA regime at the centre was quite unexpected. But within a brief span of three to four years one can hear a massive hue and cry across various geographies and strata to bring back all those exams in the name of quality loss. There is a good chance that the current central Government and most of the states will roll back the no-examination and no-detention policies. And in the meanwhile, various state and central boards have moved to getting test papers prepared at the district, division or the state level even for classes five, eight, nine and eleven.

If one has to identify any one major cause that impacts (and has impacted) learning negatively – it is the machination of the examination system that convolutes focus of everybody involved – teachers, parents, administration and everybody around. It manages to kill all the possibilities of meaningful learning. It takes away too much time and energy to leave room for any creative pursuit.

So, if we have to move forward, the only way is to remove all centralized examinations entirely, including the board exams at class Ten and Twelve. It will allow the teacher maximum possible opportunities to try out different strategies as per the needs of the children s/he teaches and the resources available. In this way, at least those who are keen and interested can deliver their best.

Moreover, what is the point of having duplication by having numerous examinations? Let us leave that to whoever wants to select for admissions or plans to employ. Most of them are in any case doing that. At the most what you can have is some kind of national voluntary test at the end of schooling phase.

And finally, at least some professional board or an autonomous institute needs to take up the cudgels and risk trying out something very different that might seem and sound ridiculous – to provide admissions to a professional course entirely on random selection basis (after ensuring that the applicants are really interested in that particular field), work with (train) this set and show that the entire issue of cut-throat cut-offs is entirely meaningless. And that the randomly selected interested set does as well, compared to a set of top scorers. At least we believe so.

Endnotes

1. 'Learning' as in Webster's dictionary:
    a: the activity or process of gaining knowledge or skill by studying, practicing, being taught, or experiencing something
    b: modification of a behavioural tendency by experience (as exposure to conditioning)

2. The first recorded usage of the word 'education' is in 1531.
    The Webster's dictionary defines it as:
    a: the action or process of educating or of being educated; also: a stage of such a process
    b: the knowledge and development resulting from an educational process

3. The canvas of education is huge in itself, and for a geographically, culturally and linguistically diverse country like India, it is complex, to say the least. For reasons of focus and brevity, the present essay has been limited to the realm of school education and leaves out issues, aspirations and critiques related to higher education. Also note that several other forms of learning, outside of the school system, are not dealt with in detail here.

4. Disaggregated data are not available in the 2011 Census.

5. The need to value and conserve our rich linguistic diversity has been dealt with at length in another essay in this volume (Between Diversity and Aphasia, G. N. Devy).

6. While saying that children start gaining independence, one realises that we are unconsciously restricting thoughts only to middle and upper middle class children, since even 4-5 year old children display this kind of independence in low-income urban settlements and rural hinterland that would constitute not much less than half of Indian population.

7. http://www.narmada.org/ALTERNATIVES/jeevanshalas.html.

8. The Hoshangabad Science Teaching Programme (HSTP) was a field based programme initiated by Kishore Bharati and Friends Rural Centre – two grassroots organisations working in Hoshangabad. Later Eklavya was set up by these two organisations to take up the academic responsibility of the HSTP. The programme gave shape to learning of science in classes 6, 7, and 8 in the government schools of the erstwhile Hoshangabad district of Madhya Pradesh, India, by doing experiments, observing the surroundings and through peer processes.

9. It is as important to provide such avenues within the home as well, but as those cannot be structured, we have limited our discussion to the community based examples above.

10. A word of caution here that the notion of public sector or industrial townships being inclusive is itself a debatable issue as the resources allocated to different strata of people living within these spaces and the unequal ease of access for different categories of people is emerging in recent researches.

11. More information on the schools or learning centres mentioned here can be sought from the following websites:
    http://www.vidyavanam.org/

http://andsbhopal.weebly.com/
http://www.sruti.org.in/?q=sangathan/adharshila-shikshan-kendra
http://www.sholaicloaat.org/
http://www.imleemahuaa.org/
http://cfl.in/
http://www.secmol.org/
http://marudamfarmschool.org/

References

Bourdieu P, and J. Passeron, 1990, *Reproduction in Education, Society and Culture,* SAGE Publications, pp. 59.

Coelho, N., and S. Padmanabhan, 2016, *Imlee Mahuaa: Learning in Freedom the Democratic Way,* Pune: Kalpavriksh.

Dewey, J., 2004, *Democracy and Education: An Introduction to the Philosophy of Education,* New Delhi: Aakar Books.

GoI, 2005, National Curriculum Framework 2005, National Council for Educational Research and Training, New Delhi, Ministry of Human Resource Development, Government of India.

Jain, Mayank, 2015, 'How the right to education is failing the very children it was meant to benefit', *Scroll,* 1 July, http://scroll.in/article/729051/ (accessed on 21 May, 2016).

Kumar, K., 2006 (Revised), *Political Agenda of Education: A study of colonialist and nationalist ideas,* Sage: New Delhi.

Nambissan, G.B, 2009, *Children, Social Exclusion and Development,* Working Paper Series, Volume I, Number 1, Delhi: Indian Institute of Dalit Studies and UNICEF.

Nambissan, G.B., 2012, 'Private Schools for the Poor', *Economic & Political Weekly,* Vol. 47(41), October, 2012 (pp. not available).

Pathak, A., 2009, *Recalling the Forgotten Education and Moral, Quest,* Delhi: Aakar Books.

Pathak, N., 2014, *Communitisation of Public Services in Nagaland: A step towards creating alternative model of delivering public services?,* Pune: Kalpavriksh.

Velaskar, Padma, 2015, 'Educational Stratification, Dominant Ideology and the Reproduction of Disadvantage', in *Education and Society: Themes, Perspectives, Practices,* Meenakshi Thapan (ed.), New Delhi: Oxford University Press.

Further Readings

1. *Access to Elementary Education in India – Country Analytical Review*, R. Govinda and Madhumita Bandopadhyay, NUEPA, Delhi, 2008.

2. Dreze, Jean and G. G. Kingdon, 1999, *School Participation in Rural India*, London: London School of Economics.

3. Govinda, R. (ed.), 2002, India Education Report: A profile of basic education. New Delhi: Oxford University Press.

4. International Institute for Population Sciences, 2000, National Family Health Survey (NFHS-2) 1998-99, Mumbai: IIPS.

5. *Learning Curve*, Issue XXIV, March 2015, ed. Prema Raghunath.

6. Muskaan, 2013, Insights of Education among the Urban Poor – A case study of Bhopal, Bhopal: Muskaan.

7. Nambissan, G.B., 2001, 'Social Diversity and Rural Disparity in Schooling: A study of rural Rajasthan' in Elementary Education in Rural India: A Grassroots View, A. Vidyanathan and P.G. Nair (ed.), New Delhi: SAGE Publications.

8. PROBE, 1999, Public Report on Basic Education in India, New Delhi: Oxford University Press.

9. http://www.ncbi.nlm.nih.gov/pmc/articles/PMC2474466/table/t3-dem-45-0245/

10. http://educationforallinindia.com/Survey-Report-of-%20out-of-school-children-IMRB-MHRD-EDCil-2009.pdf.

11. http://dalitmarch.org/discrimination-education.html.

12. http://www.ibe.unesco.org/National_Reports/ICE_2008/india_NR08.pdf.

13. http://www.india.com/topic/Social-And-Rural-Research-Institute/.

The Future of Arts in India:
Challenges and Opportunities
Towards Revitalization and Sustainability

Sudha Gopalakrishnan

Summary

The essay explores both the inheritance and contemporary representation of art (limited to the performing arts) in India. India has been a land of various traditional art forms, and arts like theatre, dance, and music have also been sites of resistance and ridicule to the dominant establishment. However, market-oriented approach to the performing arts has degraded the legacy of the art forms, and reduced them to mere economic ends.

The essay argues that the future of art has to balance the context-specific significance with relevance to the larger world. A balance of such kind can be struck by creating public spaces, collectives, and organizations that work on exploring and preserving local cultures. Art also has to transgress beyond boundaries to enable the cultural flow and in turn can be systematically archived and preserved. A new possibility of art would entail recognizing its renewable potential or something that creates value.

Context

This paper tries to encapsulate some thoughts on the state of the arts in India, both as inheritance and as contemporary representation, and attempts to look into their future from the perspective of today. For the purpose of this essay, the term 'arts' is limited broadly to the performing arts, in which creativity finds expression through music, dance and drama.

The dance and drama forms of India represent a collective tradition. A study of these forms in their context would throw light on the different processes that undergird its

441

society and culture. Art, in a broad sense, is shaped by life patterns, social order, worldview, as well as cosmological and religious notions of a community. Performing arts have a vital connection to the other areas of human activity including play and daily functions, celebrations and festivals, rites and ceremonies, prayer and worship. Art often shares boundaries with folklore and religion, painting and sculpture. In India, as elsewhere in the world, art was considered not an activity dissociated from life, but a response to it. Art is a way of reflecting, challenging and sometimes transcending the environment from which it emerges. Performing arts like dance and theatre exist in a community that shares and reacts to its meaning. Many art forms and expressions can only be understood with reference to their social, historical and spatial contexts. The arts have the vitality and tenacity to go beyond hierarchies and suggest pathways towards a multicultural society that respects diversities and celebrates intercultural communication. In communities close to nature, music and dance have a primary function, not extraneous to the other activities of life. However, during recent times, these activities, in transitioning into a market-oriented society, have lost their customary and collective significance as participatory activities. They become part of a long process of commoditization, often being reduced to spectacles and objects of consumption.

From early times, people across the world have tried to capture the visual, auditory and kinetic patterns provided by nature, like the wafting breeze, the swaying trees, the rippling streams, the behaviour and movements of birds and other animals in their art. The agriculture-oriented population in the villages of India dependent on a good harvest for survival has devised their own dance and songs consonant with their seasonal activities and daily lives. Animals like the rooster, peacock, horse and the snake, have become the subjects of artistic expression. In many societies, art is intricately connected with occasions when the members of the community gather together, performing for a social occasion, thus reaffirming of social bonds. Perhaps the most important feature of community dances like Theyyam of north Kerala, Ramlila of Rampur and Lai Harouba of Manipur is that they are performed by the participation of all the members of society. Here dance serves to evoke a feeling of camaraderie, generate pleasure, reinforce shared perceptions and values, and strengthen social relations. Many performative events are propitiatory invocations to the forces of nature to maintain peace, prosperity and harmony for the individual and the society. These ritualistic performances integrate penance, incantations, prayers, possession, dance, oracles, spells, feats such as fire-walking, sacrifice and many other elements in their structure. The consecration of time and place by the potency of ritual, sanctification of the atmosphere through incantations and invocations, and the transformation of appearance through ornate and stylized costumes, are all effective devices used in performances to enlarge the field of experience.

Art forms that developed their technique through long years of training and refinement under patrons and mentors have a different course, which is vitally linked to their history, aesthetic concepts and performance technique. With encouragement and support from wealthy patrons including the royalty, these dances gradually become more refined and formal, with the artists honing their skills to cater to an elite audience. Later some of these professional dancers, especially women, began to be attached to temples, and they came to be referred to as *devadasis*, the servants of god. Once formal aesthetic theories began to get crystallized, texts on choreography, dramaturgy and other manuals came to be written. This trend set in across traditions; almost all the 'classical' dances of India have had their origin in entertainments and temple rituals and from their link to the royal courts.

The arts are never static forms of expression, but are in a continuous state of evolution and recreation, conditioned by the needs of their time and context. Theatre, dance and music have also been sites of resistance to established systems of power, displaying an inherent ability of ridiculing, admonishing and challenging the established social order. They have been fostered as much by *darbars* (courtly assemblies), *sabhas* (performance sites, public or private, for musical performances) and temple complexes (for ritualistic and sacred performances like *Kutiyattam, Raslila* and *Krishnattam*), as by open grounds and *maidaans* (public spaces for Therukkuttu, Ramlila). They are what Ramanujan calls 'interactive pan-Indian systems' (1991, pp. 17), having arisen from the large stock of a collective folklore imagination. It is no wonder that many expressions of dance and drama revolved around themes drawn from the Ramayana and the Mahabharata, stories of Radha and Krishna and their local variations.

The continuity of cultural tradition in India proceeds from a cluster of practices perpetuated from generation to generation (*parampara* – tradition). Codified, 'classical' arts in India have evolved and crystallized through sophisticated pedagogical systems. They are imbibed through long years of training and performed according to the skill and imagination of the artist. Many forms of dance that we understand as classical today as well as the different *gharanas* (family lineages) of music were formed over time, integrating concepts from a pan-Indian aesthetic tradition and also assimilating local practices. Knowledge pertaining to different fields was passed down from generation to generation, through schools called *gurukulas* (family of the guru) and transmitted entirely through an unbroken oral tradition. The relationship between master and disciple (*guru-shishya parampara*) is the backbone of the Indian classical tradition; it ensures its continuity and sustenance.

While several art traditions passed on from one generation to the next through *gurukula sampradaya*,[1] it is important to ask questions about social inequalities that were perpetrated through the arts. In many situations, in attempts to valorise specific identities belonging to essentially upper caste ideologies, arts and culture in India have often become sites for segregation, and discrimination among caste, class and gender. Many of these 'elite' arts were not accessible to a major part of Indians belonging to the 'lower' (*shudra* and *atishudra*) communities. However, there have always been challenges and pointed oppositions to such oppressive structures, through contesting narratives (*Jatra, Chakyar Koothu, Tamasha*),[2] and also more strongly in the persona of the comic protagonist in drama. Adopting a subversive perspective on life, he has the freedom to ridicule or criticize anyone in society, and is often an opponent of established authority. His recklessness and libertine boldness in many performance styles become a virtue than a flaw in character, because they bestow on him the license to utter truths that are otherwise concealed.

In the northern part of Kerala, a unique art form called *Poorakkali* exists over generations, which combines ritual, dance and song with discussions on philosophy and the arts engaged in by the subaltern classes. The art tradition combines devotional, visual and intellectual activity and is performed by the socially disadvantaged Asari, Maniyani, and Salia communities[3] among others. The marginalisation of these communities is the reason perhaps why it remains largely unknown. Performed annually as a week-long activity according to the local Malayalam calendar during the months of March-April, it is a spring festival celebrating the spirit of love through fertility cults, a celebratory experience through chanted narratives combined with vigorous dance patterns, and a battle of wits through an oral competition that happens between two groups from the local community. Celebrated as a grand festival held in shrines (*kavus*) dedicated to the local goddess, its participants are villagers who belong to the so-called 'lower' strata of society. This art form integrates rituals associated with the worship of the god of love, dances dedicated to the several deities worshipped in the region and an academic contest on issues ranging from logic, grammar, dramaturgy and philosophy, conducted by locally trained scholars. Many of the participants, not even having the advantage of a systematic curricular study, acquire knowledge of classical textual sources through the oral tradition of learning. An exposure to Poorakkali would help understand the complexity of this unique form of cultural expression and also subvert certain prevailing notions on the 'ownership' of India's scholastic traditions. Arts like Poorakkali reveal that religion, art and learning are not merely matters of individual experience, skill and creative activity, but are processes by which society endorses common values and controls its environment.

The diversity of theatrical traditions in terms of language, region, class and genre becomes a constraint when speaking about a common 'national' theatre. However, regional expressions, largely following a nationalist agenda though confined within a framework borrowed from western theatrical traditions, came up in different parts of India. From the 1940s', direct contact with Western theatre practices reflecting concepts such as nationalism, independence and struggle against social exploitation created a flurry of theatre activity across the country. Resistance theatre movements like the Indian Peoples' Theatre Association (IPTA), and the active involvement of playwrights and actors like Bijan Bhattacharya, Khwaja Ahmed Abbas, Mulk Raj Anand, Sardar Jafri, Rajinder Singh Bedi, Prithviraj Kapoor, Balraj Sahani, as well as dancers like Shanti Bardhan became a strong cultural front to protest against fascism and political violence. In many cases, the adaptation of folk forms like Burra Katha, Tamasha and Jatra on the one hand, and social realism imbibed from Western theatre on the other, led to the democratization and wider appeal of theatre. In Kerala, the Kerala Peoples' Arts Club (KPAC) made a strong impact with landmark plays such as '*Ningalenne Kammyunistakki*' (You Made Me a Communist) and '*Aswamedham*' (The Horse Chariot). Several regions in Bengal, Andhra, and Kerala produced plays based on realism and actively embracing social issues including agriculture labour, famine, gender disparity, health consciousness and educational reforms. During more recent times, mass movements in India such as street theatre have immediacy of impact and dramatic intensity across a wide range of audiences, and several groups in India, including *Jana Natya Manch* (Peoples' Theatre Forum), have engaged in struggles against both immediate and more abiding political and social iniquities in the country.

The Indian theatre movement today is vibrant in all regional languages and with varying engagements with history, politics and tradition, as well as in diverse modes ranging from classical and folk, realist and absurdist, political and historical. Some significant playwrights, directors and artists as well as landmark productions (Bhasa adaptations by Kavalam Narayana Panikkar, '*Charandas Chor*' by Habib Tanvir, '*Ghasiram Kotwal*' by Vijay Tendulkar, '*Andha Yug*' by Satyadev Dubey and Ebrahim Alkazi) are a few examples of the immense range and vitality of theatre practice in India.

Patronage in the Arts

In India, the performing arts have had several systems of sponsorship and sustenance according to the region, community and context. Forms of folk and sacred performances, which were part of village celebrations and calendrical festivals, involved diverse sections of society. Temple-oriented music and dance traditions were protected and fostered by

445

temple administration and royalty, with communities of dancers called *tawaifs*, *devadasis* and different groups of musicians. The patronage of *nautch* girls by courts and the nobility during Mughal rule in north India, as well as the tradition of courtesans in courtly cultures in the south are well known.

Folk traditions faced the challenge of loss of traditional patrons as well as audience with the dwindling of local festivals and social ceremonies that were the main source of sustenance for the rural and traditional artists. The crumbling of feudal patronage affected temple-oriented arts, which were confronted with a democratic, secular audience. Lakshmi Subramanian writes:

> 'The starting point of most of the new works on music has been the formation of the modern classical tradition that was completed around the middle of the twentieth century, when mainly at the initiative of the middle-class Brahman enthusiasts, music and dance had been shifted out of the traditional venues and placed in the modern concert halls and a clearly defined repertoire had been put together to mark the canon and a performing style that produced conceptions of new singing voices as well.'

(Subramanian, 2014, pp. 41-61)

The spirit of nationalism that swept India along with the rise of democracy brought about a shift in text, patronage and performance of the arts. This transformation affected several traditions of theatre, music and dance, from the north to the south. Under the impact of modern education and the search for an 'Indian' identity, traditional arts were recognised as vital links that connect the present with the past. Great changes in patronage, systems of education, training, and new developments in technology brought fresh ideas as well as demands on performing arts across India during this time. From the beginning of the twentieth century, reformers like Rabindranath Tagore, Vishnu Narayan Bhatkhande, Vishnu Digambar Paluskar, Rukmini Devi Arundale and Vallathol Narayana Menon were some of the great pioneers who established institutions dedicated to the arts and scripted changes in format to suit the tastes of a new audience.

After Independence, the government focused on providing impetus and encouragement to art, literature, cultural activities and scientific research. A major initiative of the Government of India, at the national level, to ensure continuity of cultural practice during India's transition to democracy was the establishment of a ministry of culture and national academies for music, dance and drama, for the literary, visual and performing arts of India, as well as the All India Radio and Doordarshan. Some of the activities taken up by the ministry of culture as part of its policy on the protection of culture are establishment of museums and libraries; supporting through fellowships, awards and commemorative events; sponsoring documentation, research and archiving; exchange programmes and festivals abroad. Presently, the three national academies have their counterparts in the states and union territories of the republic. These are similarly constituted and have a similar charter of responsibilities in the regions where they are based. The zonal cultural centres are nodal points, responsible for dissemination of the arts and culture of their respective regions. Broadly, these institutions are engaged in the promotion and preservation of artistic activity in the country. Apart from the government, arts are fostered and kept alive due to the efforts of individuals, groups and locally established institutions across the country.

In spite of the government's avowed policy of encouraging the arts, this support falls short of the need, and there is still much disparity in this patronage. The great diversity of art practices and the dwindling number of practitioners challenge policy-makers and enthusiasts who want to revitalize the space. Urbanization, migration and inroads of electronic media leading to changing lifestyles result in a loss of both skills and audiences, and young people risk losing a legacy they scarcely knew they had. There is gradual disappearance of the art forms as its practitioners are defecting to other professions and the younger generation is not interested.

A Feat of Memory

The past and its lessons are essential to any reckoning with the future. Memory is the reservoir from which a society or individual draws the resources to be able to shape that future. The obliteration of memory by time or historical events is a challenge for any society, especially those that have undergone a forced reshaping of their cultures through processes like colonialism.

Much of India's artistic knowledge, which was an organic part of the lifestyle and often, the livelihood of communities, was interrupted by colonial power. Indigenous knowledge was largely effaced by the colonial agenda since the nineteenth century and the effects of that erasure are evident even now. The postcolonial situation therefore involves an act of willed remembering, and requires a sifting and selection of this past, to bring into the present. This impulse becomes stronger in a context of accelerated globalisation, where it also becomes a struggle to retain and assert cultural identities and local intellectual traditions.

Governments and communities across the world are adopting strategies to safeguard their heritage in the face of a standardising global culture. In India, this perception has an indisputable charge, as global forces overwrite rich oral traditions and a variety of local cultural forms. However, this is not a one-way process. Greater integration with the world also enlarges the cultural space. As scholars of these processes have observed, the periphery also talks back, and cultural traditions mix to create new practices. Cultural change is not only a story of loss and destruction, but also of gain and creativity. India is faced with the same predicament of how to make its own arts and knowledge traditions accessible to the future, even while embracing new ones. These are sources of cultural identity, unique to various communities, and their context-specific significance has to be balanced with their relevance to the larger world.

Imagining a Future of the Arts

What will happen to India's performing arts in the next twenty years – or perhaps in 2050? Envisioning the future of performing arts in a nation spanning several millennia, with diversities in class, caste, region and styles is a challenging task. It throws up questions of ownership and patronage, training and education, perpetration and transaction, providing performance and research opportunities and integration of structures of sustainability. Rather than relying heavily on governmental support, the onus needs to be shifted to the community. Unless the creative energies of the civil society is tapped for assuming a participatory rather than a merely consumerist role, the arts, deemed as classical, folk or modern, have no future on a long term basis. Countless institutional efforts have helped develop different areas of performing arts in the voluntary sector. Initiatives such as SPICMACAY (Society for the Promotion of Indian Classical Music among the Youth) established in 1977, the Chipko Movement (using the power of ritual and poetry for protecting trees), street theatre movements, Dalit theatre movements directed towards specific sectors and social issues have redefined the significance and scope of India's performance space.

Community Participation: The Central Principle in Planning for the Future of Performing Arts

Local cultural organizations can play a key role through providing training and performance opportunities as well as aiding audiovisual documentation and patronage of rural artists in festivals organized by them. Already in different parts of the country, organisations like Virsa Vihar of Amritsar, community institutions like Malerkotla Heritage Society and Changampuzha Park in Edappally, Kochi are presently doing significant work by providing public space and performance opportunities to promote arts from their localized regions.

Such initiatives provide greater opportunities and awakening of interest and lead to a concerted effort to revitalize performing arts and the heritage sector as a whole:

- Creating public spaces for performance of all kinds in other parts of India. Sites such as *maidaan*s, playgrounds, gardens and even fields may be tapped for bringing local performances and festivals back in. For instance, almost every village in north India has a 'Ramlila *maidaan*' traditionally earmarked for recreational activities.
- Creating collectives, organisations and certification of traditional practitioners who currently operate in the non-formal sector and therefore cannot benefit from public sector incentives such as education/training, access to competitive bidding, bank loans, and tax relief.
- Institution of measures such as the recognition of 'Living Masters of Cultural Heritage', with a requirement to take on apprentices in a structured mentorship programme, through stipends for fixed duration.

A Wider Stage

Performance culture has flourished as much in village squares and streets as in courts and elite enclaves. Ramlila maidaans are part of every major town in north India. Today, popular television, cinema and video performances mine this fertile territory, sampling and remixing traditional music and dance. In recent years, there has undeniably been a new abundance of performance opportunities for the arts in India. The Chennai music season is a month-long festival dedicated to classical music and dance, and is gaining popularity year after year. S. Kalidas observes: 'Classical music in democratic India has flowered as never before.... Indian art music now enjoys a global audience and there are highly informed aficionados of Indian music worldwide and some practicing musicians of non-Indian origin too' (Kalidas, 2014, pp. 13-24).

To take a concrete example of these cultural flows, let us examine the case of Punjab. Today, there is national and international interest in Punjabi folk song and dance. The depiction of a certain Punjabi culture, lifestyle, humour and attitudes is a staple in popular cinema. A large Punjabi diaspora around the world, especially in Canada, the UK, the US, Australia and in Southeast Asia enlarges the field of opportunity of an increasing number of artists. '*Bhangra, Giddha, Lokgeet* artists are regularly called by Punjabis and cultural organisations of these countries. Punjabi film industry also has needs for large number of artists. Internet-based radio stations have provided new opportunity to *raagis, dhadhis* and even *bhands* doing comedy performances. Owing to the high demand, a plethora of town-based cultural organisations train young people to cater to this demand'.[4] As there are few to teach these forms, it is important to document performances, especially the traditional ballads and *kissas*. During a field survey in Punjab conducted in 2013, the artists mentioned that they used to perform mainly on wedding and other festive occasions.

While the five zonal cultural centres across India provide performance opportunities to folk artists, they are not equipped to sustain the form or its practitioners. The creation of new opportunities and new audiences and better outreach are vital for sustenance of these age-old practices. For instance, folk media is increasingly recognised as a tool of development communication, particularly in rural areas. Odisha, for one, has organised folk artists under district and block level federations (*Kala Sanskruti Sanghas*) and is training them in development communication and linking them to IEC (Information, Education, Communication) budgets available at the district level. Local NGOs could supplement this effort, to work with communities and help them understand, document and create new expressions with their own traditions. Large-scale rural grassroots art based enterprises can be given recognition and the mandate to document the culture and oral memory-based knowledge of communities around their villages.

I would like to cite the heartening example of a mass-based organisation called Contact Base[5] (a part of another initiative Banglanatak.com, started with objective of creating sustainable livelihood for rural artists and practitioners) headquartered in Kolkata. Starting in 2004, it undertook an initiative called Art for Life (AFL), working with 3200 marginalized communities across six districts in West Bengal, and covering six traditional art/culture forms, with support from the Eastern Zonal Cultural Centre. In 2011, the model was replicated in Bihar (supported by Bihar State Rural Livelihood Project, JEEVIKA) with 1500 people. In less than 18 months time, they had encouraging results:

- Average monthly income of 3200 artists went up from Rs 500 to Rs 3500.
- For 40 per cent people, it is a primary livelihood, for another 40 per cent, it is an important secondary livelihood.
- Around 10 per cent of people are earning more than Rs 12000 per month.
- From 3200 people, it has spread to about 4500 people.
- Sanitation has gone up from less than 10 per cent to above 80 per cent.
- Most of the beneficiary families (mostly illiterate) are sending children to school.
- Fifty artists went to international venues, 500 artists travelled to national festivals, 2500 participated in local ones.
- None of 5000 artists across West Bengal and Bihar have migrated to cities.
- Average age of the folk artist has gone down from 41 to 28 years; youth and women are participating. 174 *Chhau* teams perform on a regular basis, while there were only

twenty one groups in 2004. Chhau groups have again learnt the old steps from their gurus, which have more demand.

- All the village festivals created in 2009-10 are still in place, and are community owned/managed.

State Support

Support and sustenance of the arts, once the preserve of courts, temples and other wealthy individuals are now considered primarily as the state's responsibility. The government, through the Ministry of Culture and its affiliate institutions, serves as the main source of support to performing arts across India. Between them, they offer financial assistance for a plethora of activities – supporting institutions and practitioners, organising festivals and commemorative events, conducting research and documentation, archiving and training, and others. However, given the diversity of artistic expressions in India, there are limits to this top-down approach. A sensitive policy needs to understand the vulnerabilities of the culture sector, revitalize it from a non-productive degrading resource, to a robust, productive asset that involves the participation from all sections of society. This would provide greater opportunities for public participation and involvement in a concerted effort to revitalize the heritage sector.

The dangers of the state influencing and often distorting popular narratives for the use of immediate and long-term political gains cannot be over-stated. When nationalists like Bal Gangadhar Tilak introduced the idea of cultural nationalism in the early twentieth century, which took deep roots in the Indian right wing psyche, he was conscious that the step would arouse the sentiments of Hindu identity to build 'unity' among the people and urge them to come together to fight for a common cause. In India, several political parties, including the 'Hindutva' allies and the more 'liberal secular' forces have exploited the collective strength of religion, culture and popular beliefs in highly charged arenas of the stage, tableaux and oral media. Favourite sites for such contestations have also been the performance of festivals and the demonstration of religious symbolism. These attempts vary from the worship of cow as a sacred animal, to the deification of Pokhran as a venerable site and the celebration of the Ganapati *utsav* as grand public festival(s) in Maharashtra.

Across history down to our times, there have been numerous attempts to curb voices raised for freedom and equality, expressed through artistic manifestations. To take an example, in an aggressive demonstration of the intervention of the state in arts and culture during the last part of the twentieth century, Safdar Hashmi, the activist theatre person and founder of 'Janam' was murdered where he was leading a street play in protest against social evils. In Chhattisgarh, even some of the performances by Gondi women singing songs in their own language for the welfare of their community and promotion of mother tongue are misconstrued as stirring up trouble in the name of political activism.

A more participatory and sensitive approach is needed to craft a comprehensive agenda to resolve each of these situations. Rather than focusing on patronage-based governance, the government should adopt a facilitative role by creating networks of interest and broad parameters of linkage. In an attempt to create and develop innovative models of financial and administrative support that are sustainable over the long term, some of the following processes are suggested, as a future policy intervention:

- Re-examination of the assistance-based approach to effect a change towards a mediatory one.
- Apart from the centrally funded schemes and assistance to institutions and individuals, creation of Heritage and Development Fund – a balanced, well defined funding structure towards state and local level bodies.
- Creation of district level committees with local level participation from multiple sectors such as tourism, education, rural development, PWD in addition to a panel of experts from the local communities. The committee could be in overall charge of planning and implementation of projects.
- Development of innovative models of financial and administrative support that are sustainable over the long term.
- Establishment and maintenance of a web-based clearing house for sharing information on the cultural resources from the local, regional and state levels to the central level. This will be in the form of an inventory, mapping the diverse aspects of cultural heritage in a systematic way. The list of practitioners, agencies, institutions and similar networks in the inventory will aid this process.
- The inventory to have an open-source, internet-based calendar of cultural activities, events, opportunities, for use as a state-wide community platform for promotion of culture.

A Living Archive

To explore how the arts can be sustained, it is important to map existing reserves of knowledge and document them systematically, for easy retrieval and access. Inventory making is critical, not only on the forms and expressions of performing arts across India, recordings of songs and performances and the like, but also information on those who practice and transmit them. Such a database of artists and organisations is critical to extend equitable access to support services, and also to develop creative industries that rely on this base of knowledge.

Many strategies are needed to facilitate the participation of communities, artists and artisans to build the inventory and to identify leaders who can provide ownership of this safeguarding process. It will be important to establish standards for documentation, meta data like authorisation for the sharing of the information gathered. Cultural mapping could be integrated into municipal or local developmental planning. Audiovisual documentation is required, to preserve and make accessible the whole spectrum of the performing arts, ranging from oral and ritual-based traditions, folk expressions, to entertainment-oriented and more codified forms of dance, music and drama. A vast corpus of such material exists in archives across India, but is still not documented, and unless done expeditiously, this knowledge faces the threat of loss.

Digitization of the world's knowledge and its transmission across global networks, no matter how incomplete or incompletely free, have redefined and transformed what we understand as creativity and culture. In India, digitization of archival recordings of legendary performances and performers (e.g., archives of All India Radio, Doordarshan) as well as those of contemporary performers are already underway, but this needs to be coupled with clear strategies of access and dissemination, without impinging on the rights of performers/artists.

Perhaps parallel to the creation of open, physical spaces mentioned above, another area of cultural democratization is the creation of open platforms through web-based and mobile technologies, to make it accessible to a wide population. India records a remarkable internet usage of a 100 million people, and mobile internet use of about 185 million. By end of 2015, it is estimated that more than 200 million had access. Government of India's ICT programme attempts to ensure connectivity to all schools and colleges – rural and urban. Collaborative web platforms and crowd-sourced models of engagement and peer review, and open-source publication are critical. Such web-based platforms reveal an unprecedented opportunity to bring local voices into conversation, and to connect across regions and cultures.

Pad.ma – Public Access Digital Media Archive – is a collaborative platform for content curation in the areas of film and performing arts. It is an online archive of densely text-annotated video material, primarily footage and unfinished films. The entire collection is searchable and viewable online, and is free to download for non-commercial use. The design of the archive makes possible various types of 'viewing' and contextualisation: from an overview of themes and timelines to much closer readings of transcribed dialogue and geographical locations, to layers of 'writing' on top of the image material.

Sahapedia, an open online encyclopaedic resource on Indian arts and culture seeks to provide free access to information, presented in multimedia format, including text articles, photographs, image galleries, audio-video clippings, interactive maps, timelines and lineage trees, PDFs and scans of published articles and books, to animate and deepen the study of these forms.

Seeking Sustainability

To imagine new possibilities for the arts, we need to recognise them not as relics or merely recreational activities, but as renewable resources that can create value. There are worldly aspects to artistic activity, like the need for sponsorship and maintenance.

Parallel to support from the government, corporations and philanthropic foundations need to play a bigger role in arts patronage. The National Culture Fund set up by the Ministry of Culture to facilitate the link with corporate houses has been only partially successful. There are commendable initiatives in the public sector companies and corporate houses like HCL Concert Series and the ITC Sangeet Research Academy, which supports performing arts through creating new venues and new audiences. The National Centre for the Performing Arts in Mumbai was set up as early as 1969 as a multi-purpose cultural institution with an initial grant of four million rupees by the Sir Dorabjee Tata Trust.

In recent years, a significant opportunity in support to the arts came from the amended Companies Act, which mandated a certain portion of the profits as contribution towards corporate social responsibility (CSR). The mandatory nature of CSR has made it possible for corporates and PSUs (Public Sector Undertakings) to give two percentage of the profits towards social causes. This mandate was recently extended to the 'protection of national heritage, arts and culture'.[6] These funds could potentially make a difference to the encouragement of creative expression and the enabling of livelihoods as well as towards restoration, documentation, the establishment of knowledge repositories and the expansion of public access. Though the implementation is at a nascent stage, while channelizing funding towards philanthropic causes, the emphasis of CSR should clearly be on integrity of purpose and transparency in functioning, aimed at a larger cause of social responsibility rather than as an economic benefit. The culture sector needs to recognize that CSR towards the arts is a great opportunity, as well as a challenge in terms of defining and measuring impact.

Skill and Spirit

Performing arts of India are essentially living, skill-based traditions that contain both pan-Indian and local histories, versions of mythologies/narratives/legends, rituals, songs and dances. Even in a rapidly transforming economy, these traditional arts could play a role, by anchoring a society in transition.

Government programmes like the National Rural Employment Guarantee Act or the National Rural Livelihood Mission directed at poverty alleviation and skill enhancement do not recognize the power of arts and culture to transform society, and in fact, lead to the de-skilling of artisans and practitioners by reducing them to manual labour alone to earn their living.

A positive shift in focus would be to rebuild the resource base of traditional knowledge by recognizing the unique cultural legacy of the beneficiaries, and helping to make it economically rewarding. Folk traditions in India are challenged by the loss of traditional patrons as well as audiences. Festivals and social ceremonies are the main source of sustenance for rural and traditional artists. But there are ongoing efforts to link these to a broader market, or to appropriate or repurpose them for different audiences.

A paper by Utpala Desai (2014) traces the efforts of Nishith Mehta, a young musician in his late thirties who studied different traditions of folk music, experimenting and creating his own art:

'The relentless search to identify regional traditions of music led to discovery of many forgotten musicians and singers and... a few who have consciously recreated new traditions from the existing. Armed with information, he ventured to reshape the aesthetic preferences of urban audiences and support livelihood of artists who have, for generations pursued art. His first endeavour in 2007-08 resulted in creation of fusion music of tribal, folk and Algerian singer digitalized as CD. This was followed by Deshaj Sur, a festival of regional folk music in 2013. By 2014 it has matured into a series of experimental music fests called Folk Route/Tribal Route in open air spaces of Amphitheatre. The movement has brought amazing changes in aesthetic preferences of the young audiences and inspired creativity among traditional performers to keep pace with the young.'[7]

There is much discussion about innovation as a valuable strategic resource in planning. Research has established that the contending of ideas from diverse realms sparks innovation. Just as horizontal transference between disciplines creates innovation, the vertical transference between past and present can also stoke creativity. Innovation and tradition are often seen as two poles: incongruent, if not antithetical. But rather than a radical break with the past, could innovation also be seen as continuous improvement, a creativity that draws from the wellsprings of tradition? Similar to the folk and regional forms, theatre is also a site of collaboration and exchange. Many classical genres have served as routes to the discovery of tradition, leading sociologists and theatre scholars to search deep into the processes of 'classicisation' itself.

The future holds much scope in the arts for new interpretations of old themes, mixing genres and blurring lines of artificial divisions of 'classical' and 'folk'. Bollywood, fusion and ballet will interact with the folk/classical and new forms will emerge and redefine existing norms and values. Dance forums like Gati based in Delhi and several others have been probing the creation of a sustainable environment for contemporary dance in India, which will project into the future through experiments and pioneering re-interpretations.

Schooling Matters

Mainstream education in India has by and large denied the opportunity to pursue the arts and art history, music, dance and drama. Schools make no attempt to teach the core principles of aesthetics or the arts to young students. In India, there is a lack of attention to humanistic education in general, and students are not encouraged to pursue these realms, given their seeming lack of use-value or career prospects. The exclusive focus on theoretical knowledge means that the performing arts are even less likely to be studied.

If this is to change, the government must signal the way ahead. The Ministry of Culture and the Ministry of Human Resources Development must work together with a strategic vision for education that draws from cultural traditions. Until 1961, culture was part of the Ministry of Education. After being part of a Ministry of Scientific Research and Cultural Affairs (1961-71), it was linked with Education again until 1999, after which it became an independent ministry. From 2000-2004 and from 2006-2009, it was affiliated to tourism. In the future, the vital connection between culture and education needs to be recognized, with every child having the opportunity to experience the richness of the arts. There is much more that can be accomplished if the Cultural Affairs and the Human Resources Development (HRD) ministries coordinate action to promote arts education.

Instead of going by the generic rules of University Grants Commission, dedicated art education institutions like the Viswa Bharati and the Kerala Kalamandalam need to prescribe their own norms. As things stand, once university status is bestowed on them, UGC norms apply to them, often with a disastrous impact. The gurus, who master the forms they teach through lifelong study and rigorous practice, rather than a one-time degree, get undervalued. They are required to pass examinations in English or the

National Eligibility Test, which have nothing to do with their disciplines or disciples (imagine the indignity of Bismillah Khan or Ravi Shankar or M.S. Subbulakshmi being judged by anything other than the form in which they excelled). This distortion must be resolved, which requires sensitive handling by the ministries of HRD and Culture. The current policy deprives such institutions of the capacity to engage new artist-gurus, and also discriminates against existing ones. Some suggested initiatives to further arts education for ensuring a better future are the following:

- As the first site in educational practice, school curriculum needs to be responsive to education in the arts. More than a text-based study, in-school experiences and lively interactions lead to awakening of interest in young children. Workshops to be organized periodically around themes pertaining to arts, including local artists. Students to be incentivized to participate and creatively contribute to the workshops.
- Establishment of a system of scholarships for promising young culture practitioners to develop the required skills, at the institution of their choice.
- Motivating individual initiatives such as *Aas paas ke khoj* ('exploring the surrounds'), which encourages participation of students in documentation of local heritage.
- Scholarship schemes at school level directed at fostering creativity in culture through involvement of artist-educators.

In India, the emerging field of digital humanities is a 'reinterpretation of the humanities as a generative enterprise: one in which students and faculty are making things as they study and perform research, generating not just texts, but also images, interactions, cross-media corpora, software and platforms' (Burduck, *et al.*, 2012, pp. 10). It also pertains to organising data in multimedia formats through documentation, curation, analysis, editing and hosting, operating on the premise that 'computational tools have the power to transform the content, scope, methodologies, and audience of humanistic inquiry' (ibid., p.123).

The most important lessons for the future of arts through education lie in the gaps that need to be filled in through the reckoning of the needs of a new generation. Arts of the future are inextricably linked to technology and being constantly redefined. From lighting, stage design, settings, digital installations and animations, new avenues of creativity are forever changing traditional concepts and practices in dance and theatre. In the field of music, artificially generated notes through algorithmic coding will produce any sound through re-mixing and customized dissemination.

While forecasting a future, the consequences of this abundant freedom and power vested in cultural production and consumption remain to be seen. Dance, theatre and music will forge links with each other, and also respond to the social, political and other heterogeneous environments across the world. Educational curricula for the future need to make space for fresh ideas in the field of arts for students at different levels of learning to develop their creativity and leave their own impact upon an extensive, rich artistic tradition.

Endnotes

1. Many art forms and craft traditions were passed on through a system of transmission, wherein the student stayed in close proximity to the master and imbibed the skills, imitating and learning the art step by step, and gradually maturing into an experienced artist over time.
2. *Jatra, Chakyar Koothu, Tamasha* are forms of narrative performances popular in Bengal, Kerala and Maharashtra respectively.
3. In the caste structure of Kerala, Asari, Maniyani and Salia communities were considered as backward, and were assigned specific traditional occupations. Asari is a carpenter, Maniyani tended cattle, while Salia is a weaver.
4. I was a lead consultant of an expert group that helped draft the 'Punjab Cultural Policy and Action Plan' during 2013-14. I am indebted to Ananya Bhattacharya of banglanatak.com and her team for their mapping of the intangible heritage assets of Punjab and the drafting of the text on Intangible Cultural Heritage.
5. Information is based on the field work done by Ananya Bhattacharya and her team of Contact Base during the formulation of the Punjab Cultural Policy and Action Plan during 2013-14.
6. Art & Culture: Category: Companies Act, 2013 – Schedule VII (v) protection of national heritage, art and culture including restoration of buildings and sites of historical importance and works of art; setting up public libraries; promotion and development of traditional arts and handicrafts.
7. In the *International Conference on Creativity and Innovation at Grassroots* [ICCIG], IIMA, Jan 19 – 22, 2015, the panel on 'Cultural Diversity and Innovation' looked at the ways to prevent de-skilling of society through large-scale employment programs, which presently build upon manual rather than mental labour ignoring in the process unique cultural and other skills.

References

Burduck, Anne, Johanna Drucker, Peter Lunenfeld, Todd Presner & Jeffrey Schnapp, (eds.), 2012, *Digital Humanities*, Cambridge: Massachusetts Institute of Technology.

Desai, Utpala, 2015, 'Folk Route: Changing Preferences in Urban Spaces', Paper presented for panel on *Cultural Diversity and Innovation*, Indian Institute of Management, Ahmedabad.

Kalidas, S., 2014, *Indradhanush*, New Delhi: Publications Division.

Ramanujan, A.K., 1991, *Folktales from India, Oral Tales from Twenty Indian Languages*, New York: Pantheon Books.

Subramanian, Lakshmi, 2014, 'Music Revivals – Major and Minor: Studying Politics of Performance in Modern South India', in *New Cultural Histories of India: Materiality and Practices*, Partha Chatterjee, Tapati Guha-Thakurta and Bodhisattva Kar (eds.), New Delhi: OUP, pp. 246-274.

Future of Alternative Media in India

Paranjoy Guha Thakurta

Summary

Is alternative media an ideal or a practical possibility? The essay looks at what alternative media should strive for to fetch out in the public sphere, and how it can become more responsive to the segments of the population and issues that are shut out by the profit-driven corporate media. The emergence of oligopoly in the Indian media has resulted in the loss of heterogeneity and plurality. It has become unresponsive and has squeezed its coverage of issues like agriculture, Dalits, marginalized farmers, environmental issues, and so on.

The digitisation of media has resulted in a transformed flow of information in spite of the access divide around the world and gives hope for a democratic future. An ideal scenario would be that aggregation and dissemination of the information in the digital world is not controlled by a powerful few; rather ordinary concerned citizens of the country collect and disseminate information regulated by an independent body, which can deter errant journalists.

Without shying away from the challenges to alternative media, the essay is cautiously optimistic and suggests coming together of people of different backgrounds, yet the same persuasion. Media practitioners should collaborate with whistleblowers, representatives of civil society and political activists to bring out unpleasant truths and deliver greater transparency.

The Context

Across the world and in India traditional forms and practices of journalism and mass communications are undergoing significant changes and being reshaped by the internet and digital technology. What has not changed is the need for factually correct and credible information. Crucial to the sustenance of democracy is the free expression of views, including views that are contrary to those espoused by ruling elites – the spaces for which have been shrinking in India. This does not portend well for the ability of mass media to play the role of the proverbial "fourth estate", the antagonist and adversary to those in positions of power and authority, and by contributing to greater transparency by lowering levels of corruption in society.

The independence of the media, which is meant to ensure checks and balances in the working of other institutions of the state, has been considered indispensable to democracy. If substantial sections of the so-called mainstream media in India and elsewhere have been, and continue to be, remiss in fulfilling its role as the fourth estate, where then is the scope and potential of alternative media? Central to a concept of alternative communication is the notion of a public sphere, which – as conceived by the German Marxist thinker Jurgen Habermas in 1979 – is a network of institutions within civil society (including universities, libraries and the press) which create a space for rational debate enabling the formation of public opinion. Essentially participatory, alternative media is meant to encapsulate the widest possible range of views, especially those of the marginalised and underprivileged sections of society.[1]

Roughly coinciding with the phase of economic liberalization in India in the early 1990s', the government's monopoly over television broadcasting ended and there was a proliferation of TV channels available to Indian viewers, almost all of them privately owned. Unlike other industries purveying products and services, the intensification of competition among TV channels did not result in an improvement in the quality of content. Instead of reinforcing checks and balances to curb misuse and abuse of power and authority and contributing to greater transparency in Indian society, the manner in which information has been disseminated in the public sphere by more media has not led to greater enlightenment as some may have expected (Rajagopal, 2009).

The mainstream media is controlled fully or partly by large corporate houses and treats its audiences as "consumers" rather than as 'citizens', in its efforts to bring buyers or potential buyers closer to sellers of products and services. In the process, what takes a backseat is the media's responsibility in informing the public or even empowering citizens by providing information of use and relevance. The notion of information as a 'public good', vis-a-vis information as a packaged product, often marks the distinction between alternative media and the mainstream media. If the mainstream media largely disseminates information of the kind its target audiences are supposed to want, including news and features that are titillating and trivial – which may be the equivalent of large doses of sex and violence in feature films – the question remains as to what kinds of information

461

the alternative media should strive to highlight which are not adequately covered by the mainstream media.

Such information, analyses and opinions on political, economic, social and ecological issues, which could be considered useful and relevant to much of India's masses and not just its elites, includes information on crop losses, debts of farmers, malnutrition, maternity deaths, infant mortality, waterborne diseases, bonded labour, the status of women, street children or sexual minorities, human rights, workers' unions and the environmental impact of various industrial, infrastructural and mining projects. Such information could also be about newly emerging political demands starting off as underground, illegal protests of the underprivileged, which go on to gain recognition. The growth of the audio-visual media and its wide outreach should have been an active contributor in creating awareness about the issues mentioned, among the illiterate and the marginalized and not just the upper and middle classes. But this process has been slow and halting. The challenge, therefore, is how to make the mass media in India more inclusive and more responsive to the needs and aspirations of the underprivileged.

The Ills of the Mainstream Media

It is not that the mainstream media in India, even if it is largely privately-owned or corporate driven, cannot or do not write on these issues. However these media organisations are businesses that aim at maximizing profits and market shares; revenues from advertising and sponsorships determine the fortunes of these organizations. Certain kinds of information that matter to the public at large can – and often do – get short shrift. As Angela Phillips suggests in her paper 'The Future of Journalism', cost cutting measures in media firms around the world have led to a situation where coverage is not always extensive: the web is now 'too often an excuse for shackling journalists to their desks copying and pasting rather than talking to contacts' (Phillips, 2012).

In the recent past, especially since the Great Recession in the West kicked in from 2008 and the economic slowdown became apparent in countries of the East, including India and China (which present very contrasting 'mediascapes', to use Arjun Appadurai's expression), two simultaneous developments have disrupted the business models of organisations engaged in gathering and disseminating news (Appadurai, 1990).

First, the inevitable and inexorable consequence of an unfavourable economic situation is that corporate entities as well as government bodies tend to cut back, or slow down the increase in expenditures on advertising and marketing services. This, in turn, has had a negative impact on the fortunes of traditional media organizations that have been accustomed to receiving the bulk of their earnings (often more than 90 per cent) from advertisers and sponsors.

The second phenomenon is the exponential rise in the use of the internet as a medium of mass communication as well as personalised communication. The circulation and readership of newspapers, as well as the listenership of radio programmes, had been declining or stagnating in 'developed' countries, even before use of the internet started growing since the mid-1990s', thanks largely to the growth of television. In 'developing' countries like India, however, all media of mass communication – print, radio, television, internet and mobile telephony – have expanded during this period because of relatively narrow audience bases and low literacy levels to start with. For example, the circulation of newspapers and magazines in this country had been growing steadily until recently. Although the census data indicates that the literacy rate (defined as the ability to read and write one's name) grew by an average of over nine per cent between 2001 and 2011, close to one out of four Indians is still officially illiterate. As this proportion decreases, the first documents that those who become literate read after their textbooks are newspapers, which are inexpensive. At the same time, readership of printed publications is bound to decline in the foreseeable future as more people read more on their computer screens and mobile handsets.

As for radio, the number of FM (frequency modulation) radio stations and community radio stations in the country is expected to quadruple over the next few years from around 250 and 150 respectively in early-2015, with the auction of airwaves. India is perhaps the only country in the world that describes itself as a democracy but where news and current affairs programmes on the radio are monopolised by the government-owned broadcaster, All India Radio (AIR) or Akashvani, which is part of the Prasar Bharati Corporation.

Radio broadcasting was thrown open to the private sector in 1999. There have been three rounds of licensing for FM channels so far. In 2011, a minor relaxation was made to allow the broadcast of the FM radio news bulletins of AIR without any addition or modification by private FM radio stations.[2] In 2006, under a new policy, agricultural universities, educational and civil society organizations were allowed to apply for a community broadcasting licence under the FM band 88-108 MHz (MegaHertz), but they could not generate their own news content.[3] Even this policy came eleven years after the landmark 1995 judgment of the Supreme Court in the *Union of India v. Cricket Association of Bengal* case wherein it was held that airwaves were public property to be used to promote public good and express a plurality of views, opinions and ideas. This judgment also strongly critiqued the long-held government monopoly over broadcasting. As per the ruling, freedom of speech and expression guaranteed by Article 19(1)(a) of the

Indian Constitution includes the right to acquire and disseminate information. Further, the right to disseminate includes the right to communicate through any media: print, electronic or audio-visual.[4]

Despite the apparent proliferation of the mass media in India and the existence of numerous publications (nearly 100,000 titles registered with the Registrar of Newspapers for India at the end of 2015), radio stations, television channels (almost 900 have been given up-linking or down-linking permission by the Ministry of Information & Broadcasting) and internet websites, a few players exercise dominance over specific market segments. In other words, India's media markets are often oligopolistic in character. The absence of restrictions on cross-media ownership implies that particular companies or conglomerates dominate markets both vertically as well as horizontally. For instance, *The Times of India* operates vertically across different print media such as radio, television, the internet and print and horizontally by its concentrated presence in particular geographical regions.

One example would illustrate the point: the national capital region of Delhi is the only urban area in the world where sixteen English language daily newspapers are published and distributed but the top two dailies (*The Times of India* and *Hindustan Times*) would account for roughly three-fourths of the total circulation of all English dailies. The question that logically arises is why so many newspapers are then vying with one another for such a small share of the market. The answer lies in the fact that many publications are run not to earn profit for their owners but to enhance their social status, to propagate particular political views, to influence public opinion, and also because the companies that publish these newspapers are sitting on expensive real estate from which substantial rental incomes accrue.

The promoters of media groups have traditionally held other business interests and continue to do so, often using their media interests to further these. There are also instances of promoters who have used the profits from their media operations to diversify into other unrelated businesses. Some of the richest men in India today control and head some of the country's biggest media groups. A notable example would be the Mukesh Ambani-headed Reliance Industries Limited (RIL) which became one of India's biggest, if not the biggest, media groups after acquiring full ownership and managerial control over the Network18 group and a part of the Eenadu group in May 2014.

The growing corporatization of the Indian media is manifest in the manner in which large industrial conglomerates are acquiring direct and indirect interest in media groups. Besides business houses, political parties and persons with political affiliations and religious organisations also own and/or control increasing sections of the media in India.[5] There is also a growing convergence between creators/producers of media content and those who distribute/disseminate the content, thereby restricting competition and fair trade. Across the world and also in India there is (a) vertical convergence wherein the content producer is also the distributor, e.g., the Zee group of television channels and Dishnet, the provider of direct to home (DTH) services, the STAR group and Hathway; (b) horizontal consolidation where the same media group dominates markets for all media in the same geographical area, e.g., the *Times of India* daily newspaper, the Times NOW television channel providing news in English and Radio Mirchi, all controlled by the same media group and the Sun group in Tamil Nadu;[6] and (c) horizontal consolidation on account of the blurring of the dividing line between telecommunications and broadcasting, e.g., Reliance Jio and the Network 18 group plus the Eenadu group and the fact that the head of the Idea Cellular group, Kumaramangalam Birla, is a major shareholder in the India Today media group.

The growing concentration of ownership in oligopolistic markets has led to loss of heterogeneity and plurality. The emergence of cartels and oligarchies could be a sign of an increasingly globalised but homogenized communication landscape, despite the growth of internet technology bringing about a semblance of democratization by allowing for more user-generated content by 'pro-sumers' (producer-consumers). While the growth of the internet has led to a collapse of geo-spatial boundaries and lower levels of gate-keeping in checking information flows, the perceived increase in diversity of opinion has been simultaneously accompanied by a squeeze in the incomes/revenues and profits of a number of traditional media operations in television and print.

The dependence on advertising revenue and the pressures to generate more such revenue has often led to a restriction of coverage to those that would interest the affluent middle-class (the most profitable targets for advertisers); a 'sexing-up' of news content and catering to the 'lowest common denominator'; an uncomfortable closeness between marketing and editorial departments; the diminishing of the role and importance of the independent and professional editor in a media organization; and the transformation of news into a commodity – these are all facets of the 'Murdochization' of substantial sections of the media in India – a reference to the practices often followed by media outlets owned and controlled by the News Corp group headed by Rupert Murdoch, arguably the world's biggest and best-known media mogul. The commercial and corporatized sections of the media in India have been purveying content that is often sensational and emphasizes urban, westernized and consumerist concerns. This chunk of the media emphasises celebrity culture and sex as well as the three 'Cs' that Indians are supposed to be obsessed with, namely, crime, cricket and cinema. Can the alternate or alternative media compete with such mainstream media organisations and, if so, how? There are no easy answers to this question.

There is a growing disconnect between 'mass media and mass reality' in India, argues Palagummi Sainath, former rural affairs editor of the *Hindu* and the 2007 Magsaysay Award winner for journalism, literature and creative communication art.[7] He believes that it is not accidental or incidental that a 'highly engineered disconnect' can be discerned from the priorities of coverage of every major Indian newspaper. He wrote: 'Today for instance there is – in a country with the most number of poor people in the world, (more) than most of Africa combined – not a single full time correspondent on the beat of poverty. No full time correspondent on housing and homelessness, in a country with the most number of homeless people and the second largest housing problem in the world. Show me how many newspapers have a full time labour correspondent or employment correspondent...' (Sainath, 2014).

Developing further his point on skewed coverage by the Indian media, Sainath says that it shows up if one were to look at the number of journalists from India that attend the World Economic Forum in Davos, Switzerland, held every year over ten days. 'At this gathering of billionaires, when it is difficult for the average millionaire to find a hotel room, there are more journalists from India than any other country in the world,' says Sainath (ibid.).

Similar sentiments have been expressed by non-journalists as well. For instance, Nobel Laureate economist and philosopher Amartya Sen and his collaborator Jean Dreze have written that 'perhaps, the biggest barrier to the free operation of the media in democratic India' lay in its overt bias and partiality towards the rich and the influential. This, they argued, is a phenomenon that was rather widespread. 'There are many complex biases that can be detected, but what is remarkably obvious is a serious lack of interest in the lives of the Indian poor, judging from the balance of news selection and political analyses in the Indian media' (Dreze and Sen, 2013).

The media watchdog website, *the hoot.org*, set up by the Media Foundation and edited by Sevanti Ninan, conducted a quantitative and qualitative analysis in April-May 2012 to determine coverage across Indian states among five English news dailies – *The Times of India, The Indian Express, Hindustan Times, The Hindu,* and *The Economic Times.* It was found that politics, crime and sports had been prioritized overwhelmingly and an issue like agriculture had not got its due. The study tracked news coverage across twenty eight states over fifty issues of the Delhi editions of these publications.[8] Urban infrastructure and construction of roadways were two of the most widely covered subjects. Merely three per cent of the total coverage was devoted to the issue of agriculture while development news formed twice the coverage of agriculture with 6.13 per cent of the total coverage.

The *Hindu* was the only newspaper with a special section on agriculture at that time. (The *Indian Express* now has a weekly page on agriculture). For example, the *Hindu* carried stories that dealt with the problem of unavailability of gunny sacks to store wheat in Madhya Pradesh and a groundnut variety that does not need much water to thrive. *The Indian Express* carried special features on organic farming in Assam. The other newspapers in the survey only carried news stories that pertained to yield of crops in states, its impact on the economy, and the drought-like situation in Maharashtra. Environmental and wildlife issues too received poor coverage in the five newspapers, the latter receiving three times as much coverage as the former.

Another quantitative study of the coverage of issues by mainstream Indian newspapers by Inclusive Media for Change (im4change), which is based at the Centre for the Study of Developing Societies in Delhi, came to similar conclusions (Mudgal, 2011). On an average, the country's top circulation papers devoted about two per cent editorial space of their national/flagship editions, with predominantly urban readerships, to the issues and concerns of rural India. Out of between 100 and 200 news items per day, these publications used an average of a little over three items on rural themes.

Even amongst these, many stories were not about farmers/villagers or their concerns related to land, livestock, resources or farming. The biggest portion (thirty six per cent) of this meagre news coverage of rural India went to non-agrarian issues such as crime, general news or, political (Naxalite-related) violence, accidents and disasters. Less than a third of this sparse news coverage (28 per cent) was devoted to agrarian themes such as farm production, yield, irrigation, seeds, crop procurement and related issues. These issues were often brought into the focus of the media by bureaucrats, figures of authority and politicians and in a way, many of these stories were about farm-related business or economic activities and not on farmers *per se*.

The im4change study found that a typical rural story was a brief, single or double column item used in the inside pages and presented in a straight, matter-of-fact manner. Explanations or backgrounders or details about the likely causes of an incident were rare. A considerably large number of stories were displayed in the "briefs" sections which carry just a paragraph or two. Only 3.4 per cent of the news items studied pertained to parliamentary or assembly proceedings. More stories (8.1 per cent) were inspired by farmers' protests and public meetings while a slightly larger number of stories (9.1 per cent) originated from press conferences or press releases.

Many commentators have claimed that the Indian media is 'the most exclusionist institution of Indian democracy' with a long history of alienating the Dalits and tribals, at least one-fourth of the country's population. 'If the community of Dalits, who produced a president of India, could produce the Chief Justice of India, thirty Vice Chancellors in the country, 10-15 governors, chief ministers like Mayawati and a deputy PM, why can't they produce a chief sub-editor in a major newspaper?' asks Sainath (2014).

In his book *India's Newspaper Revolution*, Robin Jefferey, noted scholar on the Indian media, says that the absence of 'Dalit men or women in minor editorial jobs on Indian language dailies meant that aspects of the life of Dalits were neglected'. Over and above, the fact that no sizeable daily in India was owned or edited by Dalits meant that 'stories about them were unlikely to receive the constant, sympathetic coverage of stories about, for example, the urban consuming middle class' (Jeffrey, 2003).

The *Hoot* has published a series of articles by Ajaz Ashraf which highlight the lack of social inclusiveness in newsrooms in India's mainstream media organisations. Ashraf reminds us of veteran journalist B. N. Uniyal's response to a question from a Delhi-based foreign correspondent who wanted to contact a Dalit journalist to whom he could speak on the squabble between the media and the late Bahujan Samaj Party leader Kanshi Ram. In his November 1996 article 'In Search of a Dalit Journalist' in the *Pioneer,* Uniyal wrote that in all the thirty years he had worked as a journalist he had never met a fellow journalist who was a Dalit. None of his friends, editors or columnists knew of a Dalit journalist. Of the 686 accredited journalists listed by the government of India's Press Information Bureau that year, 454 had caste surnames, and none of them suggested that they were Dalit. Of the remaining 232, Uniyal called forty seven at random, but drew a blank.[9]

The Digital Divide

The spread of information and communication technologies (ICT), including the internet and mobile telephony, has been rapid and has irrevocably changed the way information is gathered and disseminated. But access to the internet and mobile telephony has been uneven across the world and in India – a phenomenon often euphemistically described as the 'digital divide'.

Here are some statistics from the Geneva-based International Telecommunications Union (ITU) which is part of the United Nations system. According to the ITU's report, *Measuring the Information Society 2014*, 4.5 billion people (out of more than seven billion people on the planet) were still not online and 90 per cent or over four billion persons who were not using the internet were in the developing world. While more than three out of four people are online in the developed countries, one out of three is online in the developing world. While developed countries have about eighty four active mobile subscriptions per 100 people, in developing countries the comparable figure is about twenty one active mobile subscriptions per 100 people.[10]

According to the population and housing census carried out in India in 2011, 63 per cent of households had a telephone (up from nine per cent ten years earlier). There were significant differences between urban and rural areas, with 82 per cent of Indian urban households having access to a telephone compared with 54 per cent of rural households.[11] According to a report by the Internet and Mobile Association of India (IAMAI) and IMRB International, of the 278 million internet users India had in October 2014, 177 million were in urban India, higher by 29 per cent from the previous year. In rural India, the number of internet users increased by 39 per cent to reach 101 million in October 2014. In the same month internet access through mobile devices stood at 119 million users in urban India and 40 million in rural India.[12] It should also be noted that average internet speeds in India tend to be 40-50 times slower than in the United States.

Developing countries such as India with comparatively low internet penetration among the population (roughly one-fifth at present) will not be able to buck international trends in media consumption for too long. As usage charges fall, these trends will accelerate. Consider, for instance, how popular 'free' over-the-top applications like WhatsApp have become among those in the country with access to the internet. In other words, the writing on the wall seems clear: as more mobile handsets become internet enabled and as more laptops are used in the country, the internet will become increasingly important as an aggregator and disseminator of factual information and opinions considered newsworthy. For users, the web will become their daily newspaper, periodical, library of books, radio station, television channel, post office (and much more).

Ideally, the future will see government officers becoming increasingly wary of indulging in corrupt practices or fooling citizens because the latter would be empowered by their gadgets. Modern technology will also make it easier for citizens to be journalists. Perhaps each family will have a journalist, not necessarily in the traditional occupational sense but a person who is able to bring about greater transparency, less corruption and demand more accountability. The dividing line between privacy and transparency will be clearly drawn. However, there are constraints to be overcome. The first issue is the question of access and bridging the so-called digital divide. The second issue is that the internet is dominated by a few corporations (Google, Facebook, etc.), most of the content is in a few languages (notably English) and a substantial part of the commercial/business activities on the net

469

is of one kind: pornography. All these factors constrain the abilities of the internet to empower ordinary people, especially the poor and the underprivileged.

Right now in India, we have multiple bodies, both statutory (such as the Ministry of Information & Broadcasting (I&B), the Telecom Regulatory Authority of India (TRAI), the Central Board of Film Certification (CBFC), the Computer Emergency Response Team (CERT) in the Department of Electronics and Information Technology (DEITY)) and self-regulatory (the Advertising Standards Council of India (ASCI), the Broadcasting Content Complaints Council (BCCC) in the Indian Broadcasting Foundation (IBF) and the News Broadcasting Standards Authority (NBSA) in the News Broadcasters Association (NBA)), resulting in considerable chaos and anarchy. An omnibus regulatory body, say, the Communications Commission of India, would be empowered to be able to punish errant journalists and dissuade criminals and other rogue elements in the journalist fraternity. Such a body would have to be truly autonomous and independent of both the media and the government, even if it is funded by the latter (like the Election Commission of India or the Supreme Court or the Comptroller and Auditor General of India). The body should ideally be headed by a senior media professional who would operate in a transparent manner. Given the current state of the media however, one needs to be far more circumspect.

Signs of Change

With the growth of the internet as a means of mass communication, one needs to keep in mind the views of the United Nations Special Rapporteur on Freedom of Expression and Opinion, Frank La Rue's report on state surveillance and freedom of expression that acknowledges that technological innovations have 'facilitated increased possibilities for communication and freedom of expression, enabling anonymity, rapid information sharing, and cross-cultural dialogues'.[13]

The future being spoken of is one of different forms of journalistic endeavours. From situations in which a single journalist works for a particular story, more journalists are likely to be called on to play the role of curators of information and as editors of large volumes of content to meet the requirements of specific audiences for reportage of news and analyses of information. At the heart of this is the ubiquitous smart-phone – some three billion of them were in circulation in the world in early-2015. This means that there are three billion people who are potential journalists with stories to tell who can shoot video and put them on live-streams, take photographs, edit, upload and participate in news gathering. The idea: new technologies will enable people from all over the world to tell their own stories where the news organisations will 'act as hubs for independent producers, moving away from producing content and towards harnessing the plurality of voices that exist'.[14]

The future could also be where the line between media and communication becomes fuzzier, where various forms of daily communication including those in the hands of ordinary people become reliable sources of information and analysis, where oral traditions are brought back in (aided by digital media, as in the case of CGNetSwara, referred to later). These will further democratise media, accompanied by the technology-created freedoms and the regulatory mechanisms mentioned above.

While it is true that every citizen cannot become a journalist, a gatherer of credible information or an effective communicator who is able to successfully reach out to large audiences, what cannot be denied is that it is currently easier than ever before for ordinary citizens to gain access to what were earlier cumbersome tools of the trade that media persons had access to, namely, computers, video cameras and recording instruments, and communication devices. This is undoubtedly the way forward for India, one of the few countries in the world where the expansion of cable and satellite television preceded the growth of telephony. It seems almost incredible to recall that till as recently as October 2014, there were more television sets in India with cable and satellite connections than the number of phones (both land-lines and mobile phones). The extremely fast growth in the use of mobile cellular phones in India implies that the hand-set is going to be the favoured means of not just communications but also obtaining and exchanging information in the coming years.

The report by the UN Special Rapporteur La Rue warns that over time the governments of nation-states have expanded their powers to conduct surveillance, lowering the threshold and increasing the justifications for such surveillance, which could lead to unimaginable state surveillance intrusions. The report explains that metadata can be easily accessed, stored and misused. Metadata comprises humongous amounts of transactional data such as personal information on individuals, their location and online activities, logs and related information about emails and messages that they send and receive. The report states that 'communications data are storable, accessible and searchable, and their disclosure to and use by State authorities are largely unregulated. Analysis of this data can be both highly revelatory and invasive, particularly when data is combined and aggregated. As such, States are increasingly drawing on communications data to support law enforcement or national security investigations. States are also compelling the preservation and retention of communication data to enable them to conduct historical surveillance'.[15]

Sainath (2014) writes: 'At the global level, six major companies control the world of media, including the internet. The ownership concentration on the internet is far more dangerous than the monopolies of print or TV media. The extent to which a newspaper has monopoly is limited to a few cities; there is a limit to what it can do. The monopolies on the internet – of Google, Facebook, Apple, and Microsoft – are far more serious. The digital monopolies own your personal data. They follow your transactions. The ads come to your email based on how you have used your card. They sell, trade in, and profit from your data.'

With the rapid spread of the internet will come not just the growth in the distribution of propaganda and pornography but a proliferation of rumour, gossip and unverified information – misinformation (through ignorance or laziness) as well as disinformation (or information that is known to be false but deliberately placed in the public domain). The importance of checkers and gatekeepers of facts, especially information that is fast-flowing and time-bound, will necessarily grow. After all, discerning readers, listeners and viewers will always want information that is factually correct, reliably sourced and authentic, together with views from credible experts (even if these are highly opinionated and/or biased).

In the United States, several non-profit news ventures came up to fill the void left in local news and reporting in the wake of disruption in the news industry in the last decade. The Knight Foundation which has funded many of these organisations – *The Bay Citizen, Chi-Town Daily News, Crosscut, Minn Post, New Haven Independent, St. Louis Beacon, The Texas Tribune and the Voice of San Diego* – has tracked their progress since 2011. While sustainability of these organisations was always a concern, a 2013 report – 'Finding a Foothold: How Non-profit News Ventures Seek Sustainability' – by Knight which examined eighteen non-profit news organisations found that they had begun to generate revenue and building audience. A follow-up report in 2015 – 'Gaining Ground: How Non-profit News Ventures Seek Sustainability' – analyses trends among twenty local, state and regional non-profit news organisations. The key findings indicate stability though reliance on foundation funding remains, and a few appear to be rapidly approaching a sustainable business model.

Signs of Hope

Clearly, this is the way ahead in India as well. There are notables that can be followed. In India, the *Economic and Political Weekly* (EPW), founded in 1966 (to succeed the *Economic Weekly*, launched in 1949 and shepherded by Sachin Chandhuri), is funded and owned by the Sameeksha Trust, a registered charitable trust. It is considered one of the most prestigious journals of its kind.[16]

Of late some media entities have been the beneficiaries of philanthropic funds. A trust called the Independent and Public Spirited Media Foundation, supported by Rohini Nilekani, who sold a portion of her shares in Infosys for 164 crores (1 billion 64 million) rupees, decided to extend grants to individuals and organisations in the areas of governance, legal services, environment and new media.[17] The online media portal, India Spend was one of the beneficiaries. The site registered as a trust also received funds from Vikram Lal of the Eicher Group and the Pirojsha Godrej Foundation. Its co-founder Govindraj Ethiraj looks up to organisations like ProPublica in the United States which defines itself as 'an independent non-profit newsroom that produces investigative journalism in the public interest'. ProPublica invites readers for tips on malpractices and scandals. Engagement of this nature enables it to solicit donations from the public.[18] Another online news portal in India, Scroll.in has raised funds from the philanthropic venture capital fund Omidyar Network founded by eBay founder Pierre Omidyar, whose family office has provided a mix of grants and equity money of around $125 million (roughly 760 crore, or 7.6 billion rupees) in India so far.[19] *The Wire* website, founded in May 2015 by journalists Siddharth Varadarajan, Siddharth Bhatia and M. K. Venu, states that it seeks to 'reimagine' itself as a 'joint venture in the public sphere between journalists, readers and a concerned citizenry' breaking away from the 'traditional models of family-owned, corporate-funded and controlled or advertising-driven newspapers, websites and TV channels'. This is what it states about itself: '...the business model that underpins most Indian news media seldom allows editors the freedom they need. Worse, it has slowly eroded professional standards of reporting and contaminated the media ecosystem with toxic practices like rampant editorializing, paid news and 'private treaties.' Increasingly, media houses are reluctant to spend money on news gathering; and as they develop secondary business interests and 'no go areas' proliferate, their newsrooms suffer further collateral damage – especially as these interests often depend on proximity to politicians and bureaucrats....'[20]

The founding premise of *The Wire* is that in order to promote 'good journalism' and be 'both editorially and financially independent', it would rely 'principally on contributions from readers and concerned citizens who have no interest other than to sustain a space for quality journalism'. Another website attempting to sustain itself through crowd-funding is *Newslaundry* which, like *the hoot.org*, seeks to critique the media. 'We at Newslaundry are from the world of news and want to turn the mirror on ourselves,' states the website set up by Madhu Trehan, Abhinandan Sekhri, Prashant Sareen and Ropak Kapoor, only the last of whom is not a journalist.[21] The Rajasthan Patrika group has promoted *Catch*

News, a digital platform led by senior journalists Shoma Chaudhury and Bharat Bhushan. (Chaudhury was suddenly asked to leave her post by the owners of the group in February 2016).

There are more such organizations coming up and are expected to get established in the years ahead. There already exist organisations that are taking the first steps towards creating more inclusive, sustainable forms of information dissemination in parts of the country that are otherwise ignored by mainstream media, both geographically and in terms of their demographic. CGNetSwara is a Raipur based voice portal for citizens and citizen journalists. Founded by journalist Subhranshu Choudhary, CGNetSwara circumvents the ban on production of news by private radio channels by allowing *adivasis* (tribes) in remote Gondi-speaking areas of Chhattisgarh in central India to record and listen to audio reports in local languages. Adivasis with a story to tell call a number and an IVR (Interactive Voice Response) system responds asking them to push '1' on the keypad to record a piece of news or '2' if they want to hear items on the day's bulletin board. Submitted news items are also vetted by those conversant with the Gondi language as well as by professional journalists and then put up on the server. A digest in English is listed on the website and also emailed to subscribers.

In 2008, the *Khabar Lahariya* (meaning 'news waves') weekly was launched by Pahal, one of the few rural women's media collectives in India. This publication is written, edited, illustrated, produced and marketed by a group of women, most of them from marginalised Dalit, Kol and Muslim communities, in the Chitrakoot and Banda districts of Uttar Pradesh. The eight-page newspaper provides a mix of news, information, and entertainment specifically for its rural readers, most of whom have low levels of literacy. The publication covers current political news, stories on the functioning of *panchayats*, the bureaucracy, schools and hospitals in the region. Its distinctive reportage of atrocities on women and marginalised sections of society critiques the tendency of contemporary media to sensationalise such incidents. Also distinctive is *Khabar Lahariya's* collective process of production which takes place over a two-day writing, editing and illustrating workshop. *Khabar Lahariya* is a unique example of 'transformative education'. It has enabled rural, Dalit, newly-literate women to enter and transform the public arena of media and information creation, a space traditionally dominated by upper-caste men. In a crucial, innovative way, it strengthens grassroots democracy and challenges entrenched gender and caste relations.

Video Volunteers, an international community media organization that has been equipping grassroots stakeholders in underdeveloped areas since 2003 with video journalism skills, is enabling entire communities to expose underreported stories from their communities and take action to right the wrongs of poverty, injustice and inequality. A recent initiative of the group is called India Unheard which is a community news service seeded by a network of 206 'community correspondents' trained in documentation, storytelling and video journalism across twenty four Indian states. Their stories are from and about India's most marginalized sections: poor women, Dalits, adivasis, religious and linguistic and sexual minorities.

While on the one hand these examples of community journalism create an optimistic picture in the fight to enable people to receive and pass on relevant information, they are few in number. One hopes that in the future, community radio will expand and play a far more active role in the articulation of issues that concern people. The current ridiculous situation where news on radio is still monopolised by the government should hopefully end even as the numbers of FM radio stations and community radio stations quadruple by the end of the second decade of this millennium. Meanwhile, NGO and civil society newsletters and what were previously known as 'little magazines' will be increasingly replaced by 'little websites' as the distribution of hard copies of publications on paper will come down considerably. Folk media like street theatre using songs and dances in local languages and dialects to articulate public grievances and anti-establishment messages should hopefully continue to proliferate within specific communities to expand alternative media spaces. Exciting initiatives on these lines include a troupe of Gondi performers in Chhattisgarh connected to the alternative media initiative CGNetSwara mentioned above,[22] the Kabir Kala Manch and Sambhaji Bhagat in Maharashtra, and Makkal Mandram in Tamil Nadu. More support would have to be provided to those who use the Right to Information Act and act as whistleblowers.

Challenges and Strategies

At present, two contrasting (and contradictory) phenomena are visible in the Indian media. One section of the media has become increasingly corrupt. The insertion of 'paid news', or the masquerading of advertising as news, is rampant, especially in the run-up to elections. Particular media companies have cosy shareholding and financial relations ('private treaties') with advertisers and sponsors. Information considered unpalatable to specific individuals and organizations (including political parties and corporate conglomerates) is blacked out and favourable information highlighted.

The Union government and state governments deploy the services of media managers and 'spin doctors' to control flows of information and opinions. On the internet and the social media (such as Facebook and Twitter), anonymous trolls are used to attack, insult and demean critics and dissidents. The Narendra Modi government has been using such strategies against its opponents in the media. The Prime Minister himself has been a beneficiary of considerable praise from the corporate media. He has preferred one-way communication to question-answer sessions and granted interviews mainly to sympathetic journalists. At the same time, the Modi government has sought to exercise greater control over the government-owned media. Public broadcasters (such as AIR, Doordarshan, Lok Sabha TV and Rajya Sabha TV) have to become more autonomous and independent of those in the government if these are to truly become a 'public' organizations and not just a propaganda division of the government with power being wielded by the Ministry of Information and Broadcasting. However, this may not happen in a hurry.

To undertake reporting which exposes corruption in high places, especially corruption in the ranks of leading politicians, government officials and corporate captains, should one expect those belonging to these sections to support independent journalism in general and investigative reporting in particular? The answer is clearly 'no'. The unearthing of facts and airing of views that are considered critical to those in positions of power and authority within ruling elites implies that the media organization has to be aware of the consequences of adopting adversarial and antagonistic positions against well-funded and influential sections of the country's elites.

Whether it is from government-owned or privately-owned media organizations, there will remain an unfulfilled demand for quality reporting of facts and in-depth analyses of information. In particular, there will be a paucity of coverage of the voices of the less privileged sections of society, including those belonging to the scheduled castes and scheduled tribes, farmers and workers. These sections of the population would not be perceived as large consumers of goods and services provided by those who advertise in the mass media. Hence, those in the media that seek to highlight the concerns of these underprivileged sections of Indian society would inevitably have to seek outlets that are not necessarily corporate-controlled and purely profit-driven. This is an extremely challenging task. Nevertheless, this writer is cautiously optimistic that there will be expansion of alternative avenues for dissemination of news and views that are critical and contrarian in nature thanks partly to the use of technology. If this is indeed to take place, media practitioners will necessarily have to interact more with whistleblowers, representatives of civil society and political activists – indeed, make them partners and collaborators in their endeavours.

Since quality reporting requires time and money, owners and controllers of profit-maximising media organisations will find enough reasons to scrimp and scrounge. Thus, funding for in-depth, long-form, investigative journalism will have to come from a variety of different sources, including from philanthropic organizations, civil society groups, international and multilateral bodies, and perhaps even government-supported agencies that share common goals and aspirations. These goals include the intention to expose unpleasant truths, unravel complexities, bring about greater transparency in public life and hold accountable those who abuse or misuse their discretionary powers. The road ahead for the alternative media in India and across the world is certainly not going to be an easy one.

It will be unrealistic to expect journalist-activists to be driven purely by their personal idealism, their desire to redress individual and public grievances and their intention to change what they perceive as what is wrong and inadequate in society. This means that media practitioners will also have to seek and find alternate, non-traditional sources of funding detailed investigations (especially those that require time and travel) and long-form journalism. Within media organisations, profit-making divisions may be called on to 'subsidise' divisions that inherently do not have the potential to yield quick financial returns. In turn, this would require a change in the attitudes and mind-sets of owners and sponsors of the media. They have to believe that there is more to the media than earning profits, that a vibrant media is an inalienable and integral part of democracy and that the weakening of the credibility of the content that is disseminated is not good for their own reputation. It may be unrealistic to expect the owners and sponsors of the media to become liberal in their outlook overnight. Pressure has to be exerted from those who consume the media. There can be no substitute for a more aware, alert and sensitive citizenry.

Endnotes

Note: all the web pages below were accessed in June 2016.

1. http://unesdoc.unesco.org/images/0009/000951/095174eo.pdf; http://www.amic.org.sg/Resources/Research_Materials/Broadcasting/Namma%20Dhwani%20Ideal%20demonstration%20of%20a%20community%20media%20usage.pdf; and http://thehoot.org/web/Defining-alternative-media-in-the-Indian-context/879-1-1-34-true.html.
2. http://thehoot.org/web/home/story.php?storyid=7093 &mod=1&pg=1&sectionId=7&valid=true.
3. http://unesdoc.unesco.org/images/0021/002173/217381e.pdf.
4. http://thehoot.org/web/home/story.php?storyid=7093&mod=1&pg= 1&sectionId=7&valid=true.
5. See for instance the list at http://www.thehoot.org/story_popup/politics-and-media-control-6046.

6. See http://www.epw.in/journal/2015/35/perspectives/business-politics.html.

7. http://www.thehindu.com/2004/05/14/stories/2004051406111000.html.

8. http://www.thehoot.org/web/No-focus-on-development-issues/6159-1-1-9-true.html.

9. http://www.thehoot.org/web/home/story.php?storyid=6956&mod= 1&pg=1&sectionId=19&valid=true.

10. http://www.itu.int/en/ITU-D/Statistics/Documents/publications/mis2014/MIS2014_without_ Annex_4.pdf.

11. http://www.itu.int/en/ITU-D/Statistics/Documents/publications/mis2014/MIS2014_without_ Annex_4.pdf.

12. http://www.thehindu.com/sci-tech/technology/internet/india-set-to-become-secondlargest-internet-market-by-decemberend-report/article6614417.ece.

13. http://www.ohchr.org/Documents/HRBodies/HRCouncil/RegularSession/Session23/A. HRC.23.40_EN.pdf.

14. https://www.journalism.co.uk/news/why-the-future-of-media-and-news-could-be-curation/s2/ a564628/.

15. http://www.ohchr.org/Documents/HRBodies/HRCouncil/RegularSession/Session23/A. HRC.23.40_EN.pdf.

16. Disclaimer: the author was at the time of going to press, the editor of EPW.

17. http://articles.economictimes.indiatimes.com/2013-08-08/news/41202077_1_rohini-nilekani-indian-institute-pratham-books.

18. http://www.fmp.org.in/events/eventDetail/98.

19. http://www.medianama.com/2014/07/223-scroll-in-funding-omidyar/; http://articles.economictimes. indiatimes.com/2013-08-08/news/41202077_1_rohini-nilekani-indian-institute-pratham-books.

20. http://thewire.in/about-us/.

21. http://www.newslaundry.com/newslaundry-privacy-policy/#!.

22. http://www.vikalpsangam.org/article/gondwana-calling/.

References

Appadurai, Arjun, 1990, *Theory, Culture & Society*, London: Newbury Park and New Delhi: SAGE.

Dréze, Jean and Amartya Sen, 2013, *An Uncertain Glory: India and its Contradictions*, London: Penguin Books and US, Canada: Princeton University Press.

Jeffrey, Robin, 2003, *India's Newspaper Revolution: Capitalism, Politics and the Indian-language Press*, New Delhi: Oxford University Press.

Mudgal, Vipul, 2011, 'Rural Coverage in the Hindi and English Dailies', *Economic & Political Weekly*, Vol. 46 (35), http://www.epw.in/journal/2011/35/special-articles/rural-coverage-hindi-and-english-dailies.html.

Phillips, Angela, 2012, 'The Future of Journalism', a talk delivered at Goldsmiths Leverhulme Media Conference, 6 April.

Rajagopal, Arvind (ed.), 2009, *The Indian Public Sphere: Readings in Media History*, Delhi: Oxford University Press.

Sainath, P. 2014, N.N. Sathyavrathan Memorial talk at the Kerala Press Academy, Kochi on February 16, http://mediamagazine.in/content/structural-compulsions-crony-journalism; and http://thehoot.org/web/Inequalities-and-the-media/6940-1-1-19-true.html.

Knowledge Futures:
Democratic Values and Learning Capacities for Sustainability

Rajeswari S. Raina

Summary

This essay presents a vision of knowledge systems in India in 2047. In the institutions and norms that govern knowledge and its contents, its organization and ways of knowing, these knowledge futures will be very different from the prevalent Science & Technology dominated, centralized, undemocratic and unfair systems. The decentralized and integrated knowledge systems in our future, drawing upon the modern sciences, traditional and indigenous knowledge, moral and ethical principles, involve a wide range of organic intellectuals from diverse walks of life and living systems. Knowledge futures inhabited and shaped by these actors and their norms that understand the inter-linkages and seek synergies between diverse natural, social, physical and financial assets and flows, and cherished as knowledge commons, are predictable. Brewing discontent within the state and much of the public in India about the modern sciences in both public and private sector, articulation of social and ecological disruption, inequality and exclusion from knowledge and policy decisions, and increasing evidence of institutional reform in global knowledge systems, and demand for legal and political accountability of knowledge, will lead to rapid learning and change processes. The desired knowledge futures will emerge from these.

Introduction

Knowledge has always been revered in India. Since the mid-twentieth century, the increasing 'scientization' of policy and politics enabled science to claim an overarching supremacy over other forms and cultures of knowledge. The other forms of knowledge in and the practice of traditional medicine, Indian philosophy and mathematical traditions, typologies of agro-ecological sustainability and ecological justice are still revered or respected in some parts of the country. But their policy relevance and the investigative curiosity they invoke, and the personnel and financial resources they attract, have been steadily eroded.

In the twentieth century, the green revolution, super computer, satellite launches, and pharmaceutical industry narratives were about scientists doing India proud – achieving policy goals especially given the rather grim contexts. In the early decades of the twenty first century, the cell phone, new vaccinations, frugal innovation – especially in the automobile industry, surrogacy and cord blood banking, genetically modified crops, and many such techno-sciences bring narratives about the market and the consumers. Though the context – increasing numbers of hungry, malnourished and poor people, growing inequality, and worsening environmental degradation – is grim for the majority, the consumers of the techno-sciences and the state celebrate the rapid economic growth rates enabled by these techno-science markets. The state does articulate the need for inclusive growth, where the poor will also participate in and gain from the pace of growth. But the highly centralized and rigid Science and Technology (S&T) establishment designed to serve its public sector policy masters and support private corporate (domestic and multinational) or commercial demands, finds it difficult to operationalize the modified policy goal in the context of globalization and market liberalization.

In India, as well as globally, human ingenuity is trapped between the techno-scientific markets it has created and the multiple and linked economic, social and ecological processes and consequences born of its applications. This essay foretells how democratic values and age-old systems of sharing, caring and nurturing diversity will prevail and give India its future knowledge system. The essay presents a different knowledge system, in both its contents and ways of knowing; a decentralized and integrated knowledge system that understands the inter-linkages and seeks synergies between diverse natural, social, physical and financial assets and flows. It is built on authentic democratic values and norms of genuine participation to arrive at ethical decisions. It draws upon evidence from several alternative knowledge forms and interactions, and knowledge-policy continuums; and has a lasting commitment to learning and evolving continuously.

'Knowledge futures' brings two distinct images to us. The first, a picture of the possible futures that knowledge will inhabit and shape, and the second where knowledge is traded, exchanged like any other commodity in futures markets. If we continue to accept our present situation, where knowledge or the need for knowledge coexists and is embodied in financialization options, the second scenario is more likely. All our knowledge enterprises today, whether they are into policy making, higher education, scientific research, production of commodities and services – whether from modern science or using traditional and indigenous knowledge, or marketing them, are marked by ownership and exchange in financial terms. During the early twentieth century – marked by the advances in modern science, even in countries like ours – we had to fight our colonial masters for permission to carry out scientific research. Compared to that, the twenty first century seems to have turned the tables of knowledge.

The very reason why we need knowledge today is because it has a price, a financial value. Conversely, any knowledge about or research on pastures, rural production systems, agriculture, ecosystems, local manufacturing and crafts, ancient languages, philosophy, arts and aesthetics, and even literature that are under-financed and also largely non-monetised in value terms, are not considered necessary. This is a logical corollary of the devaluation and displacement of several forms of indigenous knowledge by modern S&T and the increasing privatization of knowledge through IPRs (Intellectual Property Rights). Thereby, any demand for alternatives in knowledge and policy, say the revival and sustainability of grasslands, or indigenous medicine, brings forth well meaning but highly inadequate attempts to ensure the 'participation' of these 'alternatives' in mainstream S&T, within the boundaries, systems relationships and practice terms laid out by modern S&T.

In this essay we present how, in the early decades of the twenty-first century, the realization that 'there is a choice' dawned on many involved in environmental and gender activism, academic research, civil society organizations, bureaucracy, industry and labour, and social protection.[1] All we needed was the means to make that choice, to shape the knowledge futures that can ensure ecological, economic and social well-being and sustainability. Widening inequality, an oppressive state, unprecedented transfer of wealth to the Western economies (which had by the late 1990s' become rentier economies)[2] and worsening impacts of climate change gave us the triggers to articulate these means. This essay captures the essence of what these knowledge futures look like in the mid-21st century, how we got there, and our capacities to democratize and instil learning capacities.

Knowledge futures: 2047

The Independence Day Centenary Celebrations, 2047, is being celebrated today in every District in the country. In Quilon district,[3] the Leader of the 8000 strong Municipal Knowledge Commissioners delivered the Address to the Democracy.[4] She observed that, '*reducing nutritional inequalities, maintaining our freedom from hunger and poverty and ensuring sustainable ecosystems and societies in a world that had witnessed the worst impacts of climate change, is an evolutionary game which demands constant technological and institutional changes.'* She spoke about her own grandmother,

'...who was the only one of three siblings who stayed home when the others migrated to the USA and Kuwait, to join Kerala's biggest revenue stream (remittances). At the turn of century, my grandmother would never have imagined the institutional changes – the new rules, norms, that led to the organization of the Municipal Knowledge Commissions in India; in every Municipality Knowledge and its organizations, even in 2020, were never within the democratic domain of Municipal Corporations. Whether they were formal S&T labs or institutes, universities, or medical, agricultural and industrial research councils, the traditional ayurvedic or unani medical practitioners, or location specific indigenous and tribal knowledge systems, they were owned (with the exception of some indigenous/tribal knowledge systems) and governed by the Union government or, at best, the State governments of the Indian Union. The local population had no say in shaping either the problems researched by these organizations, or the solutions they recommended to solve local problems. Even assessments of the development problems and technological solutions were conducted by experts with credentials in these organized knowledge forms, irrespective of whether they were from modern S&T or traditional knowledge. Today, each Municipality employs thousands of Municipal Knowledge Commissioners, an idea that was carried home from China by Indian scholars working with Chinese scholars on an IDRC (Canada) sponsored research project 'Systems of Innovation for Inclusive Development' (2009-2012) and was received enthusiastically by knowledge reformers working with 'barefoot engineers,' 'women farmer entrepreneurs' and developing 'radical ecological democracies'.[5] The mandate for each Knowledge Commissioner is to ensure decentralized, democratically deliberated, integrated knowledge systems to understand, research, and apply knowledge for development outcomes that enhance equality, justice and harmony. The direct democratic accountability is to the region – the people and the ecosystems. The outputs of the erstwhile knowledge organizations – whether formal scientific or indigenous tribal systems (publications, patents or specific applications) – are no longer relevant or sufficient. Given the new knowledge commons and norms of democratic governance of knowledge, it is the outcomes evident in the Municipality as well-being and prosperity (not growth rates of economic value-added) that count as integrated knowledge outcomes.

Today, in districts that are not governed by elected Municipalities, the Knowledge Consortia are even more dynamic. Not bound by the structural limitation of a Municipality, our Knowledge Consortia (KC) has been able to choose their structures and norms of institutionalization to integrate the bio-physical and socio-cultural knowledge across Blocks or mandals (or agro-ecologically grouped sets of Panchayats) within the District. Each KC has individuals from different walks of life and work. Its mandate is to ensure deliberation and equal participation of all in decisions made within the District. The KC ensures opportunities for all local manufacturing, farmers organizations (whether they were co-operatives in one or market committees in another), women's groups, civil society organizations, traditional healers and forest managers, and scientific associations) to draw upon and replenish the knowledge platform with specific research programmes. Equal participation of traditional healers, biodiversity managers, local metallurgists, and professional scientists therein, make these platforms the embodiment of democratic decentralized knowledge systems.

The design flexibility of the KCs allows some like the Konkan Regional Platforms to promote generic knowledge for the FAN (Food-Agriculture-Nutrition) innovation systems, and some like the CIS³E (Creativity and Infrastructure for Small Scale Sustainable Enterprises) platforms that now generate employment and income streams for thousands of small-scale enterprises and short value networks. That these knowledge platforms can combine thematically relevant problem definitions, analyses and solutions, as in the clever combination of political geography, mechanical and electrical energy, crafts and engineering, philosophy, hydrology, genomics, economics and languages in CIS³E, removed one of the formidable hurdles – the knowledge silos that had tormented India's decision makers in the previous century.

The Regional Knowledge Coalitions (RKC) of inter-district KCs spread across and co-ordinating knowledge and policy among States have become knowledge centres for resilience and low carbon development. They have foreseen problems (like the two disease outbreaks – zoonoses in 2020 and 2023 – when global temperatures peaked, that could have killed millions of humans and cattle) and dealt knowledgeably and with accountability to mitigate and help farmers, rural and urban households adapt to these changes keeping their shared well-being as the main policy goal. We are proud today that the members of these Consortia and RKCs are sought by several agencies counted as the global intelligentsia. The recent multimillion YeRu (that replaced the US $ currency exchange, pegged the international monetary system in the terms set by the low carbon economies of the South) investment in siddha vaidya (traditional herbal medicine) and the ontology of Asian biodiversity programme led by the Central University of Hyderabad, is a good example. The RKC members whether employed in public sector research organizations, civil society organizations, colleges or traditional medicine communes, are happy to conduct their research here in their home ground, open to universal collaborations. Over the past decade (2030's), they have created and endorsed the norms of responsible innovation, drafted new working conditions, linkages with a wide range of collaborators from indigenous communities in the Andes, Sub-Saharan Africa and Mongolia, and disciplines ranging from soil conservation and pasture management to neutrinos and high energy physics.

The RKCs, where individuals and thematic teams also hold University research and teaching positions, are also home to some of the most exciting experiments and theoretical advances made in molecular and developmental biology, computational chemistry, landscape sciences, and institutional economics, bringing accolades and prestigious awards to India's scientific research system. The creation of these institutions (rules and norms) and spaces (organizations, networks) for democratic deliberation of development problems, scientific research projects, and increasing access to open databases have evolved since the 2020s' when they were first enabled.'

She paused briefly, to dwell on the fact that disciplines like developmental biology which were considered dead at the turn of the century when genetic engineering and nano-technology were applied to reductionist economic ends, would not have made such a powerful comeback if it were not for the institutional arrangements and social mobilization that we had enabled for the sciences, for traditional knowledge and a sustainable world.

'When the Indian team of bio-physicists won the Nobel Prize in physics recently, our scientists insisted that the citation include their fellow philosopher who helped them build their computational models of cell membrane behaviour based on the moral principles of caring and nurturing. Not only did the Nobel committee accept this request, but the IUCN and TWAS mobilized support (both design and finance) for the world's first membrane theory based segregator and bio-digester, which we propose to build in Jaitapur. The moral victory of knowledge for prosperity and sustainable bio-economic systems cannot be more explicit!

The flourishing rural industrial cores, manufacturing and service enterprises run entirely on renewable energy, with resource-to-waste tracking, recycling (wherever possible) and waste management systems adapted and perfected to each specific bio-economic regime was indeed unimaginable in the early 21st century. Today, these bio-villages employing millions of women and men, are not just attractive professional venues, but one of the most creative and peaceful job opportunities sought by educated (not just qualified) Indians. Entire classes of people like domestic workers and sewage workers, have moved into services and manufacturing jobs with each Municipality and these rural industrial cores deploying criteria of social and ecological justice and bio-economic labour-capital ratios to ensure decent and dignified work. Our pledge to ensure the well-being of our fellow citizens in our own districts and towns therein, our own bio-villages, did take its toll on many organizations and development interventions. Institutional change was extremely painful for some; while some learned to adapt and enable further reform. These decision making structures and exclusively expert-led decisions that legitimized the political vested interests of the intermediate regime⁶ had caused enough damage to the economy, people's livelihoods and ecosystems, and were ready for institutional reform. We pioneered the evolution and establishment of an ecological deliberative democracy. We have witnessed our idyll of synchronized sustainable and equitable prosperity and our ideology of ecological and social justice win over bureaucratic rigidity, the top-down hierarchy of the mainstream. We have revived and revitalized the sciences, enabled the blossoming of several local and indigenous knowledge systems, and provided the space for co-evolution of several alternatives. This was our biggest success.

Referring to her own role as leader of a Municipal Knowledge Commission, in charge of comprehensive and integrated knowledge support for sustainable development in Quilon district, she concluded her address, recalling the social mobilization and the institutional arrangements we have now.

'What we have today is unparalleled in the world. The institutional arrangements we are committed to, the principles, rules and norms that govern our organizations are:

- *Decentralization: Decentralized knowledge systems with an intellectual class that is essentially organic, and the 'organic intelligentsia' constituted by drawing and building upon the expertise and experience vested with the community; locally relevant democratic processes within communities for deciding and shaping ecological values, as well as the criteria and locally appropriate parameters that inform every economic and social decision;*

- *Authentic democracy: Community led and community based learning capacities based on shared and openly declared values, with shared causal understandings and methods of validation. These are based on the principles of modern and traditional science as well as other forms of knowledge, values and ethics. Explicit in the institutionalization of knowledge commons, with ownership of knowledge outputs (new technologies, practices, rules or norms) and processes vested with diverse communities of practice, and with open public access to all databases and information sourced, collected and analysed by governments – local, provincial/ regional and national;*

- *Integration: Generic knowledge platforms integrating the social and natural sciences, across scales and species, levels of accountability and governance, to design and implement the local geo-political, agro-ecological, production and services, designed with fiscal and financial support from local governments (which now have the capacity) to establish and fund scientific research;*

- *Equality: Exchange of knowledge and goods and services based on principles of reciprocity and redistribution, with democratically determined exchange mechanisms and appropriate targets of well-being for all in a given location (one agro-ecological zone, a mandal or district for example); Minimal public-private dichotomies, ensured by recent modifications in individual and community rights and legal systems, and authentic direct democracy that obliterates the difference between formal and informal spaces;*

— *Justice and harmony*: *Stemming from the principles of critical balance between human well-being, species diversity and population distributions, based on diverse cultures of cooperative and collaborative behaviour that have been our humane inheritance; Establishment of a 'future' ombudsman to check the injustice meted out to future generations of species (including human), to predict plausible questions and guide the design and workings of an ecologically-socially just society.'*

'Let us not forget that the excellence and social-ecological relevance of our research endeavours stem from these norms that govern our RKCs, Consortia and MKCs. They define their roles and collaborations with leading universities, and State Academies enable their proactive public engagements with communities of traditional and indigenous knowledge, local, regional and global educational and scientific research organizations and industry. With global open source systems and user-friendly software, the concerns about futile duplication and repetitive research have disappeared. A century has passed since independence from colonial rule; but our genuine independence from the global scientific and intellectual slavery came when we began our journey of self-reflection and dialogue, and enabled genuine (Mertonian) universalism and communitarianism (open access and sharing of all intellectual property) in the sciences and other forms of knowledge. Today we have institutions or norms to ensure that this journey of democratic values and learning will evolve and continue'.

Social, political and scientific mobilization

What is it that led to these changes? It all started in the mid-2010s'. Shamed the world over, as home to the largest number of malnourished and undernourished people (children in particular), ranking among the highest in farmers' suicides and violence against women and paradoxically, celebrated as the fastest growing economy in the world, India's educated middle class, peoples' movements and concerned political parties demanded a democratic and enlightened understanding of the fundamental problems and possible solutions. With an impending global financial crisis and increasing extremism and fundamentalism, they demanded a better understanding of causal relationships, questioning the core assumptions made by economists, scientists, bankers, industrialists and policy makers in their decisions. They demanded a better appreciation and understanding of political and economic alternatives, and traditional knowledge systems in the country.

The demand for better understanding of the institutions or norms governing our production investments and technological investments were also driven by a frustrated academia. For once, the social and natural sciences, the universities and all the centralized national research councils, that were always parasitic upon the universities (already weakened by policy neglect, poor funding and petty politics), civil society organizations and domestic industry, were united. They demanded a clear explanation, the exact causal relationships that were driving economic growth, without jobs and social security, with increasing inequality, social and ecological disruptions. But reforms within the sciences and within development policies driven by these reforms in public sector academia had yet another trigger.

A deeply disturbed middle class and the toiling working classes with genuine aspirations for quality education were witnessing its deterioration at the school and higher education levels. For the government, this mixture of increasing aspirations and fear of the changing demographic profile adding a young new workforce was an opportunity and a threat; if carefully deliberated institutional reform was not enabled, a new frustrated and energetic generation might enforce drastic and rapid changes. The demand for dialogue on the nature and processes of institutional reform grew. With increasing financialization of education, it was possible to avail loans to study abroad or in the burgeoning private universities in the country. But employment and immigration laws were becoming more rigid and inward looking as the Western nations were facing high rates of unemployment. An influx of refugees (oil displaced millions) from the middle-east, and no manufacturing sector growth and the irreversible stagnation within domestic state run or aided public sector educational establishments, made choices difficult. In the mid-2010s, religious fundamentalism added to the woes of a failing education system. The middle class wanted a solution. Science and scientific temper were considered the answers of the twentieth century. But a coalition of the sciences with other (including traditional) knowledge systems and social-ecological justice was sought in the twenty first century – a strategic shift from the 'sciences speaking truth to power' to 'plural meanings and knowledge systems making sense together.' This effectively replaced the sole reliance on the allegedly neutral and efficient science reinforcing deeply entrenched inequality and injustice.

When the Union Government's Department of Science and Technology (DST) drafted its S&T policy for the country (in 2013), there was concern that this was a policy by DST for DST and had little to do with India's scientific, developmental or environmental problems. When the Position Paper on S&T for SDGs (ICSU-ISSC, 2014) demanded an integrated framework that could address the connections between natural and social processes, India watched the Western Ghats Ecology Expert Panel (WGEEP, 2011) that made explicit the integration of natural and cultural spaces and processes, trashed by the Government of India.[7] India's economists celebrated growth rates in agriculture (a stunning 3.6 per cent over the period 2009-13, they claimed) which was proof of achieving the policy goal of four percent growth rate in the sector, and added that this growth rate was driven by increasing agricultural commodity prices and favourable terms of trade and not by increasing production or productivity growth. This brought serious concerns about policy and the scientific legitimization of policy. No country had a national agricultural policy goal of four percent growth rate. Every country seemed to be fixated on goals like food and nutrition security, increasing competitiveness of the sector, better livelihoods and incomes for the farm sector, and so on. How was it that India's scientific community supported and legitimized this ridiculous policy goal?

In 2014, the series of reports on '30 years of Bhopal' (the industrial disaster that shook the country and the world in 1984) highlighted the indifference of the state, the callousness of industry and overall complacency of the scientific and academic communities in India to the continuing suffering of those affected, and worsening national capacities for addressing any environmental or natural disaster. That neither Fukushima (2012) nor the American gulf oil spill (2013), or the Uttarakhand and Srinagar floods (2013 and 2014) here, changed anything worth the mention for environmental governance and protection of the poor – those that were always the worst affected – emerged as a sore point discussed in many forums. When public policy and administration, industry and S&T joined hands to dilute (sometimes even subvert) the environmental impact assessment (EIA) protocols[8] and dishonour the scientific and political commitments to sustainable development, there was a serious loss of trust and a gaping democratic deficit that rang tunes of India's civil disobedience movement during the colonial period. People questioned the relationship between the scientific community and policy makers in India.

When eleven State Governments drafted their own organic agriculture policy during the early 2000s', it was a political statement that they should be democratically accountable to their people, natural resources and sustainable development; they can and should perform their duties as assigned in the Constitution of the Republic of India. The conceptualization, design and functioning of the Municipal Knowledge Commissioners and Regional Knowledge Coalitions across several districts in a few States, started in the Universities, in small towns, where intellectuals and local civil society organizations established strong linkages between the basic and applied sciences and policy instruments, with an ethos of integration at and by the community. Several books presenting alternatives in development, a different knowledge-policy relationship, were read and discussed. Among people from various walks of life, the game changers were the public mobilization of information and opinions on alternatives in knowledge and practice.[9] While Down to Earth by CSE occupies pride of place, many others were enabled by Vikalp Sangam that provided a platform for consolidating alternatives in social and ecological well-being, Dr. Noshir Antia's community health services, Timbaktu Foundation's agro-ecological principles, and the formal Krishi Vigyan Kendra 'manned' by a group of village women millet cultivators of the Deccan Development Society. Websites like The Alternative run by a group of eco-enthusiasts and journalists and VikalpSangam, created awareness and commitment among the Indian public. Mobilization of the poor and most vulnerable groups gained strength with networks like National Alliance of Peoples' Movements (NAPM) and organizations like SRUTI, increasing the flow of support to local tribal and women leaders who were fighting for land rights, local knowledge systems and education, and against caste discrimination, illegal forest and natural resource encroachments by the powerful. Local businesses (especially the young IT rich like 'Caring Friends') committed to sustainable ecosystems and societies joined hands with these groups to keep the spark alive and encourage investments that local entrepreneurship could gain from and contribute to. Forums for studying and encouraging social entrepreneurship and bio-economic models (drawing from Georgescu-Roegen's work) to develop the criteria and parameters for sustainable production systems, distribution and consumption were worked out in each regional and local economy with the support of these community based systems – quasi public-private community based initiatives. The amazing results of programmatic co-ordination of scientific research, and integration of education and local production systems (rural industrial, agricultural, and local crafts/traditional manufacturing) were achieved after several iterations. But iterative policy making and learning capacities and Block level decentralization and integration of knowledge and policy demanded way back during the first decade of the 21st century, were finally politically acceptable. The knowledge integration was also a trigger that helped address India's long and painful fight against caste and gender inequalities – by the sheer equality of voices within local and municipal knowledge commissions.

The motto of knowledge and policy for maximizing local value added was driven by the State Science Councils. True to the vision of Amulya Reddy and J. C. Kumarappa,[10] this needed environmentally appropriate and sustainable rural and urban industrialization, using local resources and maximizing the substitution of fossil fuels by other energy sources – all of which needed more and better scientific research. In 2016, the State Science Councils were converted to State Knowledge Academies, including and giving equal voice to NGOs working with local communities and state governments. By shaking off the legacy of big NGOs tied to the privileged apron strings of established patrons in the Union

Government, this brought an end to almost all Centrally Sponsored Schemes, individual discipline-based or commodity based national and international research agendas which used NGOs as tail-end technology disseminators.

Most importantly the State level ownership and promotion of knowledge and development policy transformed the sciences, and the co-evolution of several other knowledge systems. Some State Governments soon boasted 4 per cent of State GDP invested in S&T and other forms of knowledge, though given the other metrics of local entrepreneurship and intellectual processes which S&T actors could invest and promote investment in, the State's own expenditure did not matter as a measure anymore. The painful memories of national S&T expenditures below 0.8 percent of GDP at the turn of the century, with hollow promises of increasing it to 2 per cent, were all forgotten when we decided to redefine and measure our intellectual and scientific research capacities.

Some would argue that India's decision to define and measure our scientific research capacities differently, to move out of the standard CORDIS or OECD definition and measures, was perhaps driven by the realization that we could never compete with countries that had 9.3 (Japan), or 6.5 (Denmark) or the stunning 13.1 (Finland) of scientists per 1000 workforce (measured as Full Time Equivalents (FTE) of scientific research effort, in 2000). When these countries had (in 2010-12) thousands of scientists per million people, India stood at a mere 160, though the other emerging economies like South Africa, China and Brazil were closer to the developed country figures. India's scientific community was distressed at the increasing policy indifference to, and disregard for science. India's civil society organizations and academia were disillusioned with the Government's decisions that overruled and in many cases wanted local knowledge networks completely annihilated. This triggered our decision to define measure and build on the wealth of local crafts and manufacturing skills, traditional knowledge, ecological understanding, and progressive gender relationships. It was a transformative move. It simultaneously pushed thousands of skilled workers into acquiring formal scientific, engineering and technical training, and enabled the scientific workforce to engage with, respect and learn from the traditional knowledge, crafts and skills. It facilitated various forms of knowledge to validate and make sense of each other where needed, refine and re-institutionalise them where possible, and establish their redundancy or wastefulness (be it formal scientific research projects or traditional practices) where necessary.

There was a convergence of several triggers that set off the institutional reform in S&T and the new institutional arrangements in the social and economic arena. A combination of demands by civil society and internal debates within the sciences ensured that science could no longer be isolated from and used to govern social problems; it had to be essentially and organically integrated with society.

Democratic Values and Learning Capacities

By the turn of the century the social sciences, more specifically the social studies of science and technology (STS), had several theoretical insights to offer. In many ways the decentralized organization and governance of research and education in all fields, drew up to STS. As the Gulbenkian Commission had noted, the 21st century, driven by biological sciences and social sciences needed the diversity and location specificity of bio-socio-ecological expertise (Gulbenkian Commission, 1996). India's social science engagement came with tangible questions about knowledge for whom, how, where, and had specific social, economic, political targets.[11] India's intellectuals, many from civil society organizations, activists and academia (social scientists and natural scientists) participated in and shaped many global debates about sustainable development (the lead up to and post-1992), peak oil and the energy crisis (1990s' onwards), agricultural and food crises (recurring since the 1990s' in different parts of the world, leading to the IAASTD (the International Assessment of Agricultural Knowledge, Science and Technology for Development, 2004-2008) and global crisis in 2008-09), increasing financialization of nature (since the mid-1990s') and climate variability and change (since 1990s').

Theoretically, they are the organic intellectuals, the constructors, organizers, the permanent persuaders (Gramsci, 1989). They are not just individuals with specialized knowledge but are specialists and directors of change, who have the Gramscian appreciation of every individual as an intellectual (in their pragmatic occupations or daily work) though conscious of the fact that in this era of global crises some have to perform the functions of intellectual labour, persuading dialogue and convergence between the spontaneous (civil society based) and legally enforced (statist) knowledge. These are organic intellectuals who have immense respect for the matter-of-fact universal truths that science brings to us, but understand the social construction of science and technology, are restive about political decisions legitimized (allegedly exclusively) by scientific evidence, and thereby capable of respect, political and cultural contemplation of other forms of knowing the world, the larger values and principles that have, over the ages, guided civilizations and human interactions with the environment (see Veblen, 1906).

The heady ferment of democratic values and intellectual labour is also fuelled by legal activists appalled at the plight of tribal communities and forests in India in the new 21st century, some who have worked with and on similar questions in South Africa (The Truth and Reconciliation Commission) and the USA (The Innocence Project). Democratizing legal and paralegal work goes hand in hand with capacities to question the modern and mindless capital-intensive industrialization, which denigrates people's privacy, community owned resources and local cultures. The debates on the draft Human DNA Bill (2015) and commercialization of GM crops (which had till mid-2014, a moratorium for 10 years even against open trials) reinforce the demand for the techno-sciences to be placed under an ethical democratic lens, outside and beyond the mere cost-benefit analyses they were subject to. There is a growing demand for public sector science to be strengthened with capacities for public engagement and dialogue, to enable ethical decisions within the sciences and between the S&T and policy interface. But this demand faces a repressive public policy denying opportunities for academia and civil society organizations to work on environmental and human rights issues.

The year 2015 has also been witness to global and local experts demanding more research on: (i) 'inter-connections and synergies' and (ii) human behaviour in public and private decision arenas.[12] The latter is torn between randomized control trials as a social science tool to evaluate people's response to development interventions, and, a revival of heterodox and institutional economics to explain habits of thought, norms and behaviour in a world where the youth (mainly) questioned an economics (yes, the discipline itself) that could not relate to the reality of their world. Following 'occupy Wall Street,' with the degrowth movement gaining strength, and the global knowledge networks in high-end physics, climate change, biodiversity, gender, fisheries, rivers and nutrition, the contending approaches to studying and explaining human behaviour are more clear. Yet, it is painfully evident that the global financial organizations, and international programmes, will invest in experimental economics and trials on human population groups who are now mere recipients, markets for goods and services supplied to them by Governments they elect, but have no authentic democratic dialogue with. This makes the ordinary Indian restive. There is a realization that democratic values need to be strengthened to articulate the interconnections and synergies that are crucial to our well-being – in increasingly being articulated – by several alternatives in the civic space and in some cases by the Government.

Way back in the 1980s', debates about decentralized planning and implementation at the Block level had battle lines drawn around questions of organization of the poor, land, integration, and public participation; the demand for a different 'ethos' of participation and development administration (Dantwala, 1980). Today, the same battle lines have been fortified with free trade, international finance that denigrates human dignity, right to work, and the right to safeguard global and local ecosystems. That a genuine deliberative democracy needs contextual information and location specific articulation of development concerns at the decentralized level remains a sore topic till date. India's climate change negotiations and climate action plans are going full steam with an international and largely Western audience, with no effect whatsoever on integration of climate action plans with the development sectors that millions of Indians live in and work with. As the state and climate experts negotiate and wrangle for economic space within an ecologically constrained world, civil society and a select few in India's home grown industry and philanthropic organizations[13] seem to invest in creating and nurturing deliberative capacities at the grassroots. A new set of learning forums are coming up. A re-awakening and revival of a nation-wide Chipko movement, where people bind themselves to not just the fates of their trees and forests, but also their water, air, and energy, is imminent. As they fought to gain the right to do scientific research during the colonial years of the twentieth century, India's scientific community will mobilize themselves again, to do the right kind of research in collaboration with several other knowledge systems in democratic ways, with capacities for deliberation, anticipation and inclusion. As India's carnival for science opens its tumultuous repertoire of institutional reforms, new engagements, contents and directions, a mosaic of intense conversations (Visvanathan, 1997), it will be a harbinger of heady times and an ethical sustainable future for the world.

Endnotes

1. Academics, activists and policy makers who participated in and authored three major assessments of sustainability in the early years of the 21st century were key drivers. These, the MEA (2005), IAASTD (2009) and IPCC (2007), along with the global financial crises, from the late 1990s' till the late 2000s', enabled more informed dialogues among activists, academics, industry and governments.

2. As the western developed countries shifted their economic prowess from manufacturing to services and outsourcing of manufacturing, they became rentier economies, exercising monopoly control over global intellectual and financial resources and appropriating all the profits from this new economic order.

3. A district with over 45 per cent urban population (2011), a sex ratio of 1113: 1000 (when the country was veering on a shameful 940:1000) and among the highest female literacy rates in the country and a progressive Municipal Government for over six decades, was perhaps ripe for the first experiments in operationalising knowledge-based deliberations and development interventions.

4. Henceforth, the text in italics presents excerpts from this Address.

5. The Barefoot College of Rajasthan, the women and men of Deccan Development Society, Kalpavriksh and the Vikalp Sangam process it coordinates, the Centre for Indian Knowledge Systems, the Timbaktu collective involving 20,000 families in arid-semi arid lands, eco-restoration of the commons in the drylands by the Foundation for Ecological Security, the rural manufacturing/ processing initiatives of the Centre for Technology and Development, and the Bodo women weavers in ANT, are but a few of the hundreds of such home grown alternatives that this author has witnessed.

6. Recall Raj's concerns (Raj, 1973), about how the fate of the majority of India's population (predominantly rural and agrarian) was controlled by the intermediate regime (a Kaleckian conceptualization of governments and interest groups including domestic businesses, large peasantry and the public sector work-force).

7. The Union Government constituted and accepted the recommendations of an alternate High Level Working Group (2013) which were 'implementable'. The HLWG used the usual framework of economic, social and environmental pillars, that the ICSU-ISSC pleaded be trashed.

8. Whether it is mining (major or minor minerals), dam construction and hydel power or infrastructure and smart cities, the EIAs conducted by India's premier research institutes have found few projects that are questionable due to their environmental impact.

9. Among them Anil Agarwal, Sunita Narain (public engagement in environmental issues), Vandana Shiva, Bharat Mansata, Debal Deb, Bablu Ganguly, Sunil Kaul, Jennifer Liang, P. V. Satheesh, G. V. Ramanjaneyulu, Kavita Kuruganti, Parthib Basu (sustainable agro-ecosystems, seeds, rural crafts and enterprises); Ramaswamy Iyer, Suhas Paranjape, Himanshu Thakkar, Shripad Dharmadhikary, Sagar Dhara, Mihir Shah, P. S. Vijayshankar, Ashish Kothari and K. J. Joy (water, ecological justice, democratic values), M.P. Parameswaran, D. Raghunandan, Meena Menon (labour, science and science education), are a few (I know) among hundreds of activists-academics-policy makers who addressed environmental challenges.

10. Joseph Chelladurai Kumarappa, the Green Gandhian advocated rural industrialization and a Gandhian economics that would lead to sustainable, equitable and ecological well being for all (see Kumarappa, 1947, 1958). Amulya Kumar Reddy, the eminent Professor and electrochemist at the Indian Institute of Science also advocated decentralized and renewable energy systems for self-sufficiency and rural industrialization.

11. Many criticisms of the report were about lack of any mention of these whom, what, and how questions.

12. This chapter has been notably silent on private and corporate S&T and knowledge. It is not for lack of concern about this appropriation and control over knowledge by few powerful actors, but because of the faith in the public policy and civic space and actors therein to transform the current knowledge system, where some leaders like IBM have already demonstrated their 'private' advantages in open source knowledge systems.

13. While major philanthropic organizations funded by the Tatas or Infosys did make a difference, donor networks like Caring Friends demonstrated, and in many ways held a moral torch to the

CSR and private foundations set up by large corporates – public and private – to advance their own interests in the economy. Their direct interaction with and support and mentoring of NGOs, seems to enable a rhizome syndrome that spreads laterally and produces more similar donor networks in the North eastern states, among artisanal workers, and women in the national workforce.

References

Dantwala, M. L., 1980, 'Block Level Planning Revisited', *Economic & Political Weekly*, Vol.15 (30) pp.1279-81.

Gramsci A.,1989 (reprint), 'Prison Notebooks', *in An Anthology of Western Marxism- from Lukacs and Gramsci to Socialist Feminism*, R.S.Gottlieb (ed.), Oxford: Oxford University Press.

Gulbenkian Commission, 1996, *Open the Social Sciences: Report of the Gulbenkian Commission on the Restructuring of the Social Sciences*, Stanford: Stanford University Press.

ICSU-ISSC, 2014, Major Group Position Paper – *The Scientific and Technological Major Group's Vision and Priorities for the Sustainable Development Goals*, Paris: Sustainable Development 2015 Programme.

Kumarappa, J. C., 1947, 'Village Industries', in *Developing Village India*, Randhawa, M. S. (Ed), Bombay: Orient Longman (Revised Edition, 1951), pp. 225-227.

Kumarappa, 1958 (reprint 1984), *The Economy of Permanence: A Quest for a Social Order Based on Non-Violence*, Varanasi: Sarva Seva Sangh Prakashan.

Raj, K.N., 1973, 'The Politics and Economics of "Intermediate Regimes"', *Economic & Political Weekly*, 8(27), pp. 1189+1191-98.

Veblen, T.W., 1906, 'The Place of Science in Modern Civilization', *The American Journal of Sociology*, Vol 11 (5), pp. 585-609.

Visvanathan, S.A., 1997, *Carnival for Science: Essays on Science, Technology and Development*. Delhi: Oxford University Press.

Health Systems in Future India

Abhay Shukla and Rakhal Gaitonde

Summary

The history of the health system in India is marked by consistent gaps between the rhetoric expressed in policy documents, and the actual resources allocated for the realization of these policies. India has a programme like the National Rural Health Mission (NRHM), based on a model of participatory planning and community-based governance, but the implementation is distorted by the logic of private commodification of the health sector under the neo-liberal framework.

This essay argues for a Health Systems Approach to move towards the democratization of the public health care system and socialization of the private health care system. Central to this approach is a Universal Health Care (UHC) model that will bring in the vast majority of public and private health care providers under a single integrated system which would be publicly managed and funded. It will integrate various health systems including traditional systems found in India. UHC will require radical changes in provisioning, governance and financing (such that it can ensure free access to quality health care for the entire population) along with ensuring a decent and secure income and professional satisfaction for health care professionals.

Introduction

'We thus find ourselves at a crossroads: health care can be considered a commodity to be sold, or it can be considered a basic social right. It cannot comfortably be considered both of these at the same time.

This, I believe, is the great drama of medicine at the start of this century. And this is the choice before all people of faith and good will in these dangerous times.'

(Farmer, 2004, pp. 175)

497

India today stands at a crossroads in terms of the development of its health systems. Over the last two and a half decades, regardless of which political party formed the government, it has maintained a continued commitment to the liberalization, privatization and globalization framework, formally ushered in 1991. Despite the dominance of this ideology, the introduction of these processes has been in fits and starts due to a variety of factors, including political pragmatism. Thus there were some gains on the social front during the period of United Progressive Alliance (UPA) I government (2004-2009), with such programs as the Mahatma Gandhi National Rural Employment Guarantee Act (MGNREGA) and the National Rural Health Mission (NRHM) that committed some additional funds to the development of rural areas and to the social sector. However, subsequent experience in the UPA II regime (2009 – 2014) saw a plateauing of these trends, and the recently elected NDA government has begun to reverse or downscale even these limited social sector programs. Social sector expenditure has declined in real terms, and has been slashed for some sectors, such as nutrition (Centre for Budget Analysis, 2015). This has meant that the limited but significant gains made during the early years of NRHM are now under threat due to systematic constriction of funds (Iyer, 2015). Notwithstanding its major delays in releasing the new health policy document, the current government seems to have a clear intention to usher in an insurance based model of 'health assurance', with the private sector playing a major role not only in provisioning but also in decision making.

Given these conflicting trends in the last decade, what is the likely path of development of the Indian health system over the next three decades? Starting with the premise that the health system (as all systems) is emergent from the balance of various forces in a particular society, we chart out two alternative scenarios. One we suggest will obtain if the present policy trends continue unchallenged, which we term the 'dystopian' scenario. The other we suggest is a possibility if a number of counter-hegemonic forces work together over the next three decades to challenge and replace the present trends. This alternative path we term the 'possible utopian' scenario. We further posit the contestation of two predominant perspectives as the primary driving forces. We call these the 'Profit logic' and 'Social logic'.

'Profit logic' describes broadly the logic of maximizing profit and capital accumulation, which overrides human needs and generally corresponds with the mode of operation of much of the private sector, and is dominating the medical-industrial complex. This 'profit logic', however, adapts to locally evolved institutional structures.

'Precisely because health constitutes a terrain that is politically unique, it is also a sensitive one for which different societies exhibit varying degrees of entitlements and protectiveness with regard to publicly arranged social programs....as a result the health industry manoeuvres very carefully when trying to assure or extend its avenues of accumulation......and the industry seeks to optimize its operating environment, given current and probably future circumstances'.

(Loeppky, 2009, pp. 61)

Globalised capital is today the prime purveyor of 'profit logic', driving increasing commercialization of health care, to ensure that this is a continued and intensified arena of unbridled capital accumulation. The globalised pharmaceutical industry, health insurance industry, medical equipment industry, and private medical education 'industry' are all drivers and active accomplices in this process. **This 'medical-industrial complex' is the 'core alliance' promoting profit logic today.**

The dominant neo-liberal model of citizenship that underlies this profit logic undermines democracy and citizenship by first of all replacing collective consciousness with individualistic understanding and by creating '...an alluring connection between the citizenship and the market. To be a citizen is equated with individual integration in the market, as a consumer and as a producer'.

(Dagnino, 2011, pp. 423)

The '**Social logic**' views health and health care as fundamental and universal human rights, recognizes the social causation of health and illness, as opposed to individualistic models of health. This logic seeks to ensure the highest possible level of health for all, while decommodifying health care and removing it from the sphere of capital accumulation, by ensuring its universal availability as a public good, primarily provided through public systems. This logic is assumed to be the underlying basis for the public health system, and includes a commitment to Comprehensive Primary Health Care, as well as promoting the social determinants of health, and the responsibility of the health care system to lead inter-sectoral action on health. This logic has been experimented with in a number of countries, and represents an important tendency in the health sector in many Latin America countries, most notably in Cuba, and in recent decades, for example, in Venezuela.

Accordingly the social logic would necessitate not only socialization of the resources currently locked in the private sector, but also a massive expansion of democracy related to the public health system and the wider set of public systems.

We see deepening of democracy as a key aspect in the countering of the profit with the social logic. This will alter power relationships between the health system and the people, and also lead to large scale democratization of knowledge, and people's active role in planning and shaping the operation of the health sector at all levels, as they 'reclaim' and transform this system.

We will analyze the future scenarios of the health system across four dimensions. The first is the *overall path of development*. The second dimension is the *dynamics of the health system itself*, and in the case of India the manner in which the mixed public-private health system evolved during the past several decades, and the influence of various forces in determining the relative balance of various forces over time. The third dimension is the *dynamics of the health care professionals, including the medical profession*. This needs to be specifically examined, since there is a critical contribution of the health care professionals in the evolution of the health system. Finally we have looked at the dimension of *health care knowledge and technology*, and the way this influences the development of the health system as a whole.

The next section talks about the dystopian scenario. This is followed by a discussion on the possible utopian scenario where we try and predict what would emerge if the 'social logic' were able to effectively counter, and, over time, largely replace the presently dominant 'profit logic' in the health sector. In each of these sections we give a brief discussion of the four dimensions described above.

In the final section we speculate on how to maximize the possibility of the health system taking a turn away from commercialization, towards an alternative future where health care ceases to be a commodity and becomes a universal social good.

Health Systems in Future India: a dystopian scenario
Wider Developmental Scenario and Social Determination of Health

The situation in India today is marked by increasing inequity, massive poverty and vulnerability as evidenced by the finding that for nearly 75 per cent of our rural population, the per capita income based on the highest earning member is less than Rs. 33 per day (Tewari, 2015). The effect of these macro-economic trends on the social sector including health in India has been well documented (Garg, 1998; Purohit, 2004; Pal & Ghosh, 2007; Selvaraj & Karan, 2009). They note, 'the focus of economic policies during this period shifted away from state intervention for more equitable distribution, towards liberalization, privatization and globalization' (Pal & Ghosh, 2007, pp. 1) The authors have noted how, with these trends, there was a contraction of funds available for the social sector with,

500

'very serious implications on the health system which is almost completely funded by the state governments'(ibid.). The authors also note an increase in rural inequality, rich-poor disparity and increase in both inter and intra-state inequality.

This contraction of investment in the social and rural development sector has meant pushing the agricultural sector into a chronic crisis situation, and has severely affected the basic determinants of health, like food, water and education. This form of development has greatly supported the service sector instead, and has led to the concomitant spread of sedentary lifestyles contributing to the upsurge in diabetes, high blood pressure, heart diseases, etc. The current developmental model is also responsible for growth in pollution, including vehicular pollution, occupational hazards, accidents including vehicular accidents, addictions, while fuelling various forms of violence, including suicides.

Despite the federal structure and the possibility of individual states taking up alternative pathways, the given fiscal scenario with increasing centralization of social sector decision making, or alternatively, pushing increasing burden of spending on the states, needs to be radically challenged. If this is not done it will only further deepen inequalities and lead to a worsening access to the basic determinants of health.

The Health System

The history of the development of the health system in India is marked by persistent gaps between the rhetoric expressed in policy documents, and the actual resources allocated for realization of these policies (which is one indicator of actual political commitment to these goals). This has led to inadequate health budgets and consequently increasing influence on foreign donors who push certain selective techno-managerial vertical programs, rather than comprehensive development of the general health system (Banerji, 2015). The Indian health care system has also remained urban-focussed, doctor and hospital–centric and dominated by bio-medicine, while marginalizing indigenous and alternative systems of healing.

By the 1980s' when the ICSSR/ICMR report was submitted, the health system development was already described as being completely dissociated from the reality of the people's lives. The report called for a radical re-think and for nothing short of a 'people's movement' as the only solution for the ailing health system (ICMR & ICSSR, 1981). Yet, following the report there were no moves to take the recommendations seriously.

The gaps that emerged (especially in curative medicine) were occupied by the private sector, especially from the mid-1980s' onwards. With the increasing dominance of the neo-liberal ideology after 1991 accompanied by macro-economic reforms, the stage was set for persistent and systematic under-funding of the public health system (and other public systems) linked with increasing privatization (Rao, 1999). Despite some respite during the early NRHM years (2004-2009), the second generation reforms, where institutions are modified to suit the market logic, were initiated during the UPA-II regime. These trends were marked by the sharp debate between civil society, the Planning Commission and the Ministry of Health, around Health sector reforms to be pursued during the 12th Five year plan (Jan Swasthya Abhiyan, 2016). The pro-privatisation trends seem to have been intensified during the first two years of the NDA-II regime (2014-16), as witnessed by a rash of privatization initiatives like the proposed privatization of PHCs in Rajasthan (Dhar, 2015).

The health system in India today is characterized by a fractured and stratified system of provisioning, with one of the highest levels of out of pocket expenditures in the world, and among the lowest proportion of GDP spent on health by the government (Baru *et al.*, 2006; Balarajan *et al.*, 2011) and a flowering of various 'insurance' schemes with the diversion of huge chunks of public money to the private sector (Selvaraj, 2011).

This will mean a move towards an approach that privileges the quantifiable over the complex social, defining risk factors at a more and more micro-level, focused on individuals rather than populations, and thus towards a privileging of consumption of specific services rather than a more holistic approach to health (Gaitonde, 2012; Graham, 2016). Similarly sustainable public health approaches to complex challenges like pollution, mental health and malnutrition (both over and under nutrition), are likely to get short shrift by public systems with extremely limited capacity, with a private sector driven by profit logic blocking any intervention that could potentially reduce profit (Tesler & Malone, 2008).

Ongoing discrimination in the health care sector on the grounds of gender, caste, religion, membership in ethnic or tribal communities, etc., is likely to be further accentuated, due to powerful polarizing and marginalizing dynamics in society influencing the health sector. Despite the rhetoric, AYUSH systems will be increasingly seen merely as a commodified alternative to western bio-medicine, rather than as a key approach significantly contributing to alternative integrative health care.

Health Care Professionals

There is widespread recognition of the manner in which the medical profession and other health care professionals are being increasingly incorporated into the logic of capital, ranging from highly underpaid nurses in corporate hospitals, to doctors earning cuts from referring patients for totally unnecessary tests and procedures. One key aspect of this process, which is linked with the growing dominance of private medical colleges (which often provide very limited clinical experience to students), is the fact that doctors are getting deskilled, and are becoming more and more dependent on technology in the name of accuracy and efficiency. The nature of medical practice in the coming period is hence likely to be further distorted by the industry's imperative for maximizing profits, which would trump promotion of the well being of patients and the community as a whole, also leading to an increasing de-personalization of the practice of medicine, and rupturing the remaining bonds of trust that once bound the patient and physician. A recent study among Indian physicians showed that, 'structural changes in society get reflected at the institutional and individual levels, and plays a crucial role in shaping attitudes, beliefs and values over a period of time' (Baru, 2010, pp. 94). With growing commercialisation consolidating monopolies of knowledge, the doctor-dominated model would become further skewed, relegating nurses, paramedics, community health workers and practitioners of indigenous systems of medicine to 'assistants' and 'accessories' to the high-tech dominated medical industry.

Health Care Knowledge and Technology

In the present situation, dominated by 'profit logic' and by an increasing commodification of health and health care, medical education and research also take on a commercialised character. Increasingly the demands of the medical-industrial complex determine the pathways taken by development of medical education, drugs and technology (Zachariah *et al.*, 2010).

Such a focus on a quantifiable, techno-managerial approach will mean that complex determinants like caste, gender and class will be neglected in order to accommodate the development of more marketable and profit making technologies (Graham, 2016). Similarly, AYUSH systems of healing would be further relegated to the margins of the health sector.

In terms of the disease profile in the coming period, we are likely to have continuing persistence of both infectious and chronic diseases. Infectious diseases are likely to become highly resistant to various antibiotics, such as the increasing rise of multi-drug resistant TB, and highly drug resistant hospital acquired infections, which will thus require extremely aggressive control methods. Apart from this, continued disruption of ecosystems and public systems in a globalizing world would presage an increase in the likelihood of re-emergence of infectious disease epidemics of rare, unexpected and virulent microbes.

This is likely to be combined with a major increase in chronic diseases linked with changes in lifestyle – including food habits, and also due to the fact that regular exercise, quality diets and leisure would be feasible only for those who are rich, while the poor and struggling middle classes would push themselves to overwork and unhealthy lifestyles, exposing themselves to risk for a range of chronic conditions. There is also likely to be an increase in the number of unexplained illnesses and cancers due to complex influences of pollution and toxins, about which we know little. Given the direction being taken by industrial development, such exposure to toxic chemicals is only likely to increase.

While the approach to these complex issues needs to be at multiple levels, the overarching dominance of the medico-industrial complex in the context of weak public health systems is likely to result in the pursuit of more technological rather than social solutions, further exaggerating inequities (Gaitonde, 2012; Graham, 2016).

Health Systems in Future India: a possible utopian scenario

Let us discuss how various dimensions related to the health sector may develop in a 'possible utopian' scenario.

Wider developmental scenario and social determination of health

In a future governed by the 'social logic', the health system develops based on equity and sustainability, which would prevent ill health and promote health, thus minimizing the numbers of people needing curative health care. In other words, social determinants of health – the social factors responsible for the health of a population, like water supply, nutrition and food security, housing, environmental and working conditions and sanitation, would be addressed and effectively ensured, and this would significantly reduce the requirement for certain types of health care (e.g., those related to bad nutrition, environmental exposures and lifestyles). At the same time, unhealthy influences like accidents, mental stress, exposure to toxic substances, unhealthy processed foods, addiction to tobacco, alcohol, etc., would be addressed through a range of social measures and programmes.

In this chapter focused on future health systems, we will not go into details of how each of these social determinants needs to be ensured through a wide range of public policies, programmes and social initiatives. Some of these are covered in other essays of this book. However, as far as the health system is concerned, two kinds of measures led by this system would be necessary, in conjunction with various broader changes.

Coordination and participation mechanisms to ensure social determinants of health

Strong convergent governance and accountability mechanisms will need to be operationalized to ensure that various social service departments, (e.g., water supply, food security, education, nutrition, sanitation) coordinate their efforts and address major needs concerning provisioning of services, so that social determinants are addressed in keeping with health needs of each population.

Carrying out core public health functions

The health system would need to develop a dedicated cadre, with the skills and mandate to monitor, mobilise and advocate for addressing specific issues related to the determinants of health in each rural or urban locality. This would include close participatory monitoring of health conditions in each community, linking specific, local conditions with general standards, appropriate promotion of clean drinking water, nutrition, environmental conditions and checking negative factors like toxic exposures or addictions.

Development of the Health System

The core of this approach would be moving towards a system for Universal Health Care, which would have the following features.[1]

- Major reduction in ill-health through integrated action on social factors related to health; this would include addressing social determinants of health through participatory inter-sectoral coordination mechanisms from below (socio-political governance mechanisms) and performing essential public health functions (overseeing implementation and technical facilitation by public health services).
- Bringing the vast majority of existing public and private health care providers under a single publicly managed and funded, integrated 'Universal Health Care' (UHC) system which would provide the whole range of essential health services to the entire population
- Major expansion and pro-people re-orientation of public health services in rural and urban areas to meet comprehensive population, social situation and geography based norms.
- Progressive rationalization and socialisation of existing individual, small and medium sized private health care providers, by in-sourcing them into the publicly organised UHC system.
- Right to free, rational health care for all, without exclusions or targeting.
- Elimination of unnecessary medicines, investigations, procedures – massively reducing wastage of resources and damage to health due to over-medicalisation.

505

- Integrated system for urban and rural areas and continuum of care from primary to tertiary levels.
- Systematic integration of AYUSH (Ayurveda, Yoga, Unani, Siddha and Homeopathy) and modern systems of healing, moving from medical pluralism towards evidence based integrative medicine, which draws upon the best elements from each system, develops mutual complementarity, and gives due weight to diverse healing systems.
- Special measures and programmes for excluded populations and marginalised groups.
- Accountable, participatory governance under people's ownership at all levels, enabling significant decentralised health planning in keeping with each area's requirements, health needs and social conditions.

A transformed health system that provides UHC under the social logic would reflect the following feature fronts of provisioning, governance and financing.

A. Provisioning will include:

- There will be an integration of existing public providers at various levels; effective integration of the wide variety of public health care services and providers (e.g., central, state, municipal, ESI, railways etc.), which are currently compartmentalized and fragmented.
- Expanded and strengthened public provisioning through large scale regular recruitment of additional staff, and in-sourcing of some human resources such as specialist doctors in the short to medium term.
- Involvement of sections of regulated private providers and their progressive socialization, especially individual practitioners, small and medium sized providers, genuine not-for-profit hospitals, etc., by including them in the proposed UHC system, to fill the gaps in public health service provisioning.
- Integrated providers in rural and urban areas and at primary, secondary and tertiary levels, to become part of a seamless, comprehensive system of UHC.
- Comprehensive primary health care approach, with focus on strengthening integrated preventive, promotive and basic curative care close to the community. This would ensure that occurrence of illness is minimized, and the majority of illness episodes are dealt with at the primary level, or are linked with a rational referral network, avoiding current over-medicalisation.
- AYUSH and other traditional and folk systems of healing integrated in the UHC system. This could be initiated through an approach of medical pluralism, where AYUSH/other traditional systems will be available to people as a choice at various

levels, and practitioners will be enabled to practice their system. Research institutions for AYUSH would be started or expanded to undertake generation of evidence, enabling movement towards an integrative system of healing, where different systems could be used in complementary manner, even in case of individual patients.

B. People-centred governance will include:

- ### *Multi-stakeholder bodies for participation and accountability in the health sector, integrated with empowered decentralised governance*

  There will be an expansion of the circle of representation, and activating, and reclaiming existing elected representatives. Involvement of elected representatives including Panchayat members, health care providers, civil society organisations, community groups and active community members would ensure broad based representation of diverse popular voices, to both identify the gaps and formulate/implement draft health plans, as experiences in Brazil and Maharashtra have shown us (Cornwall & Shankland 2008; Shukla *et al.*, 2014).

  There will be **promotion of decentralised governance, with genuine devolution of finances and powers**. The multi-stakeholder committees mentioned above would function as subject specific sub-committees of the decentralised elected bodies, going into details of specific health related issues, enabling community feedback and monitoring, while informing elected bodies with planning proposals. Examples of Kerala and Nagaland can guide these (Isaac and Franke, 2001; Bahl, 2005; Pathak, 2014). Both these types of structures – health specific sub-committees and empowered elected bodies – would be integrated with each other, leading to participatory and decentralised health planning, with active inputs from communities. Community based planning and locally appropriate initiatives based on people's action would be actively encouraged through devolution of resources and powers.

- ### *Internal democratisation of the Public Health System*

  Present bureaucratic and top-down decision making in the health system would be replaced by consultative mechanisms, which would involve frontline health staff and service doctors. Encouraging inputs from staff at various levels for improvement in quality of health services would be complemented by resolution of various constraints experienced by health care providers, as components of wider democratisation.

- ### *Forums for mass participation and accountability*

  Forums for direct democracy, where ordinary people can regularly demand accountability and give proposals in an unmediated manner – *Jan sunwais* (public hearings) *or Jan samvads* (public dialogues) will be organised annually with mass participation at various levels. In addition *Swasthya Gram Sabhas / Mohalla Sabhas* (village health assemblies/neighbourhood assemblies) may be organised regularly with participation of community members, health care providers and elected representatives. Further at district / city and state levels, periodic Health Assemblies may be organised, to guide the overall priorities of the health system through democratic inputs.

- ***Ensuring social accountability of private medical services through participatory regulation; all publicly funded services in the UHC system would be made equally accountable as public provisioning***

  Effective regulation, rationalisation and accountability of private health care providers would be an essential component of the process of health system. This would be through legal, social and professional mechanisms embedded in participatory regulation. Further, all publicly funded services in the UHC system, even if provided by private entities, would be treated identical to public services in terms of their accountability requirements, since the public is paying for these. Right to information, public obligations of health care providers, community based monitoring and grievance redress would be made rigorously applicable to all health services.

- ***Comprehensive rights based legislative framework***

  This includes Right to Healthcare Acts, to delineate entitlements right to healthcare for all, while providing a framework for UHC providers and administrators; Public Health Acts to deal with health determinants and public health functions, enabling effective inter-departmental coordination; Clinical Establishment Acts to standardise quality of care, costs and human resources in all clinical establishments, whether public or private, and whether involved or outside of UHC system.

- ***Inclusion and addressing various special health needs***

  Preferential selection of health service providers from socially excluded groups, thus reversing social hierarchy; sensitising all health care providers regarding gender, sexuality, addressing violence, upholding disability rights and ending discrimination; involving organisations, groups of marginalised people in health system planning and monitoring, so that structural violation of health rights is eliminated.

C. Financing for UHC

The dream of Universal Health Care (UHC) cannot be realized without making a quantum leap in the level of public finances available for the health sector. Based on experiences of other developing countries, it is estimated that public health expenditure at the level of around 4 per cent of the GDP may be adequate to support a UHC system that could provide the complete range of health services required by the entire population. This would require manifold increase in public health expenditure in India, which currently is only around 1.2 per cent of the GDP. Further, major changes in distribution of financing would be required to correct both vertical and horizontal inequities, and the per capita public health allocations for urban and rural areas would be equalized.

- The resources for UHC would come mainly from general tax revenues of the Central and State Governments. Elimination of tax exemptions to the corporate sector and business class, implementing a comprehensive financial transaction tax, and taxation of all inherited property would generate substantial revenues.

- Special measures to raise additional resources for the health sector, such as a health tax may be introduced on the lines of professional tax, so that those who are in regular employment or business can contribute to the health budget; a health cess could be charged from owners of personal four-wheeler vehicles for example, and would be applicable to sale of health degrading products. Hospital beds under Charitable Trust ownership would be brought under Public management, bringing thousands of such hospital beds as a resource for the UHC system.

- Termination of various existing commercial insurance-based health schemes would make available huge quantum of funds, which could be preferentially utilized for strengthening public health services and developing the UHC system. Existing Social health insurance resources like ESIS, CGHS, Railways health funds, etc., could be pooled into the financial pool for UHC, while comprehensive and rational health care would be ensured for all these groups of workers by the UHC system, expanding their health care entitlements.

Evolution of the Health Care Professions

A radical departure would be made from the current doctor-centred, specialist-dominated system to a 'Health team' model, where community health workers, paramedics and nurses, public health professionals, basic doctors, AYUSH/other traditional physicians, family physicians and specialists would work together for people's health in an integrated and non-hierarchical manner. As part of a range of changes, this would also be accompanied by a qualitative change in the method of selection, training, deployment and role of health professionals, and capacity building of community health workers and activists, encouraging community-run health initiatives that would be complementary to the public health system.

In the possible utopian scenario, instead of the distortions of market logic, the actual requirements of the universal health care system would guide the selection and training of various cadres of health care professionals, moving from a doctor-centric to a health team oriented education system.

There would be a Comprehensive Human Resources for Health Policy which includes a spectrum of measures for developing a health workforce that would be both socially committed and technically skilled, and could ensure that the needs of the UHC system are fulfilled.

The process for medical education would be radically changed. Based on experiences of the Cuban system for preparing doctors, and emerging new trends in the Venezuelan medical education system (Brouwer, 2011), the next generation of doctors would be preferentially selected from communities of rural and urban working people, with proposed candidates being forwarded by communities, including hitherto marginalised sections of the population. The process of medical education would involve integration of theory and practice, ensuring that interaction with patients and communities is integrated with conceptual training, from the first day of medical education. Large numbers of 'basic doctors' focused on general practice and family medicine would be trained in centres attached to District and Sub-district hospitals. All these graduates would work entirely in the public health system from Community health units onwards, with provisions for progressive upgradation of skills and knowledge and specialisation by only a section of doctors in keeping with specific requirements of the UHC system.

Health Care Knowledge and Technology

There would be large scale demystification and democratisation of health sector knowledge. To equip them for their role in 'co-production' of health care, ordinary people and patients would not remain 'consumers' (of private health care) or 'beneficiaries' (of traditional top-down and patronizing public health services), but would be actively encouraged to become 'protagonists' and 'partners' in the process of health promotion, prevention and healing, in all possible forms. This would include wide dissemination of rational health information including appropriate use of ICT, promotion of rational self-care and family care for minor and self-limiting illnesses, and providing for informed choice of options for treatment.

Health care technology would undergo a massive transformation, linked with 'patient centred and community centred health research'. The current focus of pharmaceutical companies on producing 'me too' variants of drugs with minor, often minimally significant modifications, to corner market shares targeted at the rich and upper middle class, would be replaced by social priority based research on medicines and treatment modalities. There would be a major shift in the nature of producing and using health care knowledge, due to de-commodification of production of medicines, diagnostics and medical equipment and health care.

At the same time, emerging alternative approaches and appropriate technologies would become the basis for design of generalized health system initiatives. Alternative models of health care delivery like Jan Swasthya Sahayog (Chhattisgarh) (Jan Swasthya Sahayog, undated), Tribal Health Initiative (Tamil Nadu) (Tribal Health Initiative, undated) and Shramajibi Swasthya Udyog (W. Bengal) (Gun, 2012) could guide the development of rational and affordable health care delivery models. Similarly, 'hybrid' spaces like the Community Based Monitoring and Planning (CBMP) and Community Action for Health processes supported by NRHM in certain states would be liberated from the constraints currently imposed by the state, and would become the basis to develop generalized processes for community accountability and co-production of health services.

With the generalised operation of social logic, new approaches would include: focus on health knowledge dissemination in popular vernacular languages; documentation of traditional and local healing traditions, and appropriate screening and assessment of these, to foster positive healing methods prevalent in each region; setting up of community herbal gardens and preserving locally available plants of medicinal value; moving towards integrative modalities of health care, drawing upon the strengths of diverse healing systems and other such measures.

The current Intellectual Property Regime (IPR) related to medicines and medical technologies would be abolished, placing medical knowledge in the public domain, while operationalising alternative mechanisms to encourage medicine and health care related innovations.

Averting Dystopia, Realising Possible Utopia

In the previous pages of this essay, we have briefly sketched two radically different, but plausible trajectories for the future development of the health system in India. While there may be differences over details, few would disagree that the dystopian scenario based on all-compassing commercialisation of the health sector is better avoided, and that some set of systemic changes to ensure 'Health and Health Care for All' based on social logic, as envisaged in the possible utopian scenario, would be desirable.

However, as the nation today stands at the crossroads, which factors will decide the choice that India will make in the coming few decades? We would submit that this will depend primarily not on the outcome of academic discussions, but on how unfolding takes place of the political economy of the country in general, and of the health sector in particular, and which social alliances are formed and prevail over others.

We would now outline certain pre-conditions that would be required to move towards the 'possible utopian' scenario:

- A significant section of Indian society recognises and asserts that the current health system is fundamentally incapable of ensuring rational and quality health care for the population, and hence radical alternatives must be urgently developed. Large masses of people become mobilized for health system change, as part of the broader movement for change in the social-political-economic system, and significant political priority is given to the health sector.

- Large scale democratization processes ensure that masses of ordinary people start becoming active subjects of history, and new forms of bottom-up people's power emerge, while socialisation of resources, which are currently under corporate/capitalist control, leads to de-commodification of various spheres of economic and social life. At the same time, public systems and processes are brought under decentralised, democratic control.

- On the broader social and political stage, neo-liberalism is frontally challenged through a broad based coalition of social movements, progressive political forces and organisations of oppressed and exploited social groups.

- The current developmental model is widely questioned, and an alternative model based on social equity and ecological sustainability, comes centrally onto the agenda. Various people-centred alternatives related to health and health care which are currently implemented on a small scale in specific areas, are provided favourable conditions to flourish and inform broader health policy.

Today the 'medical-industrial complex' is the 'core alliance' promoting profit logic with corporate hospitals and large private multi-specialty hospitals leading this process, with allies in the form of a corporate friendly state, the private medical profession, and a consumerist middle class. The state today actively colludes with the private sector ensuring only nominal regulation, while handing over large scale public resources to the private sector through outsourcing and health insurance schemes. The private medical profession aligns with demands for opposing regulation, while the consumerist middle class, enchanted by the barrage of 'latest' tests and procedures offered by glittering medical technology, unwittingly colludes in the process of commercialisation of health care by providing a ready market.

As the contradictions of profit driven health care inexorably unfold, the potential emerges for formation of an alternative broad based social alliance, which could stand up and frontally challenge the 'insatiable animal' of profit driven health care. Diverse sections of working people are today facing large scale deprivation and exploitation in the sphere of health care – landless labourers; marginal, small and middle cultivators in rural areas; diverse range of workers in the unorganized sector, both 'self-employed' and informally employed; the 'unorganised sector workers in the organized sector', toiling for both public and private sectors; and organized sector workers and 'mental workers', who may be somewhat better off economically, but still face insecurity and lack of health care protection, leading to catastrophic expenditures and poor health outcomes. Many of these sections are today converging around resistance movements on issues like destructive development, environmental concerns, sustainable agriculture, food sovereignty and security, right to employment, water rights, etc. All these constituencies could converge to form a **core 'counter alliance' for social logic, along with sections of the health care professionals**, which would have strong objective interest in aligning with the demand for a system of universal health care, leading to free and adequate health care for all, with progressive de-commodification of the health sector. The counter-hegemonic potential of emerging alternatives would feed into a broader movement for democratic and social justice based development. We thus propose that reaching a future 'possible utopian' situation will depend on larger democratic mobilizations, which will use existing spaces and 'imaginations', and would then multiply such initiatives manifold, based on support from the state and society.

And the current associates of the dominant paradigm – the state, the medical profession and the middle class – remain uncertain allies which have a contradictory relationship with profit-driven health care. As an arm of the state, the public health system now faces a looming crisis with budgetary cuts and further cutting down of already inadequate human-power. Frontline public health staffs – especially contractual workers, ASHAs and Anganwadi workers – are displaying restlessness with their employment conditions, which is manifested in the form of sporadic struggles. Countering incipient moves for overt privatization, resistance is expected at various levels even from within the public health system. Regarding the medical profession, now polarization is underway, with individual doctor-run smaller hospitals and nursing homes facing the heat of competition by well-resourced but unscrupulous corporate and large private hospitals. Even most specialist doctors are losing their autonomy, as they are being reduced to well-paid but subjugated subsidiary players dominated by the juggernaut of corporate hospitals. And among the middle class, there is growing disenchantment with private hospitals due to experiences of excessive and irrational care, rising and unaffordable costs, and frequent instances of negligence and malpractice.

In this scenario of opposing tendencies, which one will prevail in the coming decades, which mode will emerge dominant in the health system, a century after Indian independence: profit logic or social logic? The outcome will depend on the extent to which three related tasks are carried out by the forces which seek to promote and generalise social logic in the health sector. Firstly, consolidation and organisation of the core alliance of working people around the demands for right to health and health care, demanding a publicly funded and organized system of Universal Health Care and equitable access to social determinants of health; Secondly, building a broader united front, detaching sections of the forces that are currently allied with the medical-industrial complex; Thirdly, wherever possible developing and upscaling a range of alternatives on the lines mentioned in the 'Utopian scenario', which would provide a positive agenda and concrete options for change on multiple fronts.

Only such a 'grand alliance' can confront and overpower the powerful medical-industrial complex, and establish the undisputed supremacy of social logic in the health system.

To conclude, the trajectory of the health system in India in the coming decades is not a foregone conclusion, and there are grounds neither for unjustified optimism nor despair. Rather, the future will be the outcome of a prolonged and complex struggle between profit logic and social logic, each championed by a range of social forces which are becoming arrayed against each other. In this context, none of us can afford to be passive spectators or detached experts. The outcome of this epic struggle for health and life will ultimately depend upon how social realignments are configured, and in the coming historic confrontations, on which side each of us decides to take their stand.

Endnotes

1. This section is significantly based on the Policy brief on Universal Health Care in Maharashtra, published for Maharashtra Universal Health Care group by SATHI, Aug. 2014.

References

Bahl, A., 2005, 'Communitisation of grassroot health services, Nagaland', Delhi: Central Bureau of

Health Intelligence. Available at: http://www.hsprodindia.nic.in/listdetails.asp?roid=177 (Accessed 15 March, 2017).

Balarajan, Y., S. Selvaraj, & S.V. Subramanian, 2011, 'Health care and equity in India', *The Lancet*, 377, pp.505–515. Available at: http://dx.doi.org/10.1016/S0140-6736(10)61894-6.

Banerji, D., 2015, *A Vision for an Alternate Public Health Service for India*, New Delhi: Oxford University Press.

Baru, R. Arnab Acharya, Sanghamitra Acharya, A.K. Shivakumar, and K. Nagaraj, 2006, 'Inequities in access to health services in India', *Economic & Political Weekly*, 45(38), pp.49–58.

Baru, R. V., 2010, 'Public Sector doctors in an Era of Commercialisation', in *Health Providers in India: On the Frontlines of Change*, K. Sheikh & A. George, (eds.), New Delhi: Routledge, pp. 81–96.

Brouwer, S., 2011, *Revolutionary Doctors*, New York: Monthly Review Press.

Centre for Budget Analysis, 2015, *Of Bold Strokes and Fine Prints: Analysis of Union Budget 2015-2016*, New Delhi.

Cornwall, A. & A. Shankland, 2008, 'Engaging citizens: Lessons from building Brazil's national health system', *Social Science and Medicine*, 66(10), pp. 2173–84.

Dagnino, E., 2011, 'Citizenship: a perverse confluence', in *The Participation Reader*, A. Cornwall, (ed.), London and New York: Zed Books, pp. 418 – 28.

Dhar, A., 2015, 'Rajasthan is privatising primary health care', *The Wire (07.08.2015)*, Available at: http://thewire.in/7981/rajasthan-is-privatising-primary-health-care/ (Accessed 9 November, 2016).

Farmer, P., 2004, *Pathologies of Power: Health, human rights, and the new war on the poor*, Berkeley: University of California Press.

Gaitonde, R., 2012, 'Registration and monitoring of pregnant women in Tamil Nadu, India: A critique', *Reproductive Health Matters*, 20(39), pp.118–24.

Garg, C.C., 1998, *Equity of Health Sector Financing and Delivery in India*, Working Paper, Harvard School of Public Health (June).

Graham, J., 2016, 'Ambiguous capture: Collaborative capitalism and the Meningitis Vaccine Project', *Medical Anthropology*, 9740 (April), DOI, Available at: http://www.tandfonline.com/doi/full/10.10 80/01459740.2016.1167055 (Accessed 27 April, 2016).

Gun, P., 2012, 'The Journey of Shramajibi Swasthya Udyog (Working Class Health Project)', *Sanhati*. Available at: http://sanhati.com/excerpted/5554/ (Accessed 9 November, 2016).

ICMR & ICSSR, 1981, *Health for All: An Alternative Strategy – Report of a Joint Study*, New Delhi: Indian Council for Medical Research and Indian Council for Social Science Research.

Isaac, Thomas T.M. and Richard W. Franke, 2001, *Local Democracy and Development: the Kerala people's campaign for decentralized planning*, New Delhi: LeftWord.

Iyer, M., 2015, 'Budget 2015: Experts slam government for slashing health budget', *The Times of India*,

28 February. Available at: http://timesofindia.indiatimes.com/budget-2015/union-budget-2015/Budget-2015-Experts-slam-government-for-slashing-health-budget/articleshow/46414052.cms (Accessed 9 November, 2016).

Jan Swasthya Abhiyan, 2016, 'Budget 2016-17'. Available at: http://phmindia.org/wp-content/uploads/2016/03/jsa-budget-Press-Release-1st-March-2016-1.pdf (Accessed 9 November, 2016).

Jan Swasthya Sahayog, 'Jan Swasthya Sahayog', Available at: http://www.jssbilaspur.org/ (Accessed 9 November, 2016).

Loeppky, R., 2009, 'Certain wealth: accumulation in the health industry', in *Morbid Symptoms: Health Under Capitalism*, L. Panitch & C. Leys, (eds.) pp. 59–83. New Delhi: LeftWord.

Pal, P. & J. Ghosh, 2007, *Inequality in India: A survey of recent trends*, DESA Working Paper, New York: Department of Economic and Social Affairs, United Nations.

Pathak, N., 2014, *Communitisation of public services in Nagaland: A step towards creating alternative model of delivering public services?* Pune: Kalpavriksh. Available at http://www.kalpavriksh.org/images/alternatives/CaseStudies/Nagaland.pdf (Accessed 15 March, 2017).

Purohit, B.C., 2004, Inter-state disparities in health care and financial burden on the poor in India. *Journal of Health & Social Policy*, 18(3), pp.37–60. Available at: http://www.ncbi.nlm.nih.gov/pubmed/15201118 (Accessed 13 October, 2015).

Rao, M. (ed.), 1999, *Disinvesting in Health: The World Bank's Prescriptions for Health*, New Delhi: Sage Publications.

Selvaraj, S., 2011, *A Critical Assessment of the Existing Health Insurance Models in India*, Available at: http://planningcommission.nic.in/reports/sereport/ser/ser_heal1305.pdf (Accessed 9 November, 2016).

Selvaraj, S. & A. K. Karan, 2009, 'Health Deepening Insecurity in India: Evidence from National Sample Surveys since 1980s', *Economic& Political Weekly*, 44(40), pp. 55–60.

Shukla, A., R. Khanna, & N. Jadhav, 2014, 'Using community-based evidence for decentralized health planning: insights from Maharashtra, India', *Health Policy and Planning*, pp.1–12, doi:10.1093/heapol/czu099. Available at: http://www.heapol.oxfordjournals.org/cgi/doi/10.1093/heapol/czu099 (Accessed 6 November, 2016).

Tesler, L.E. & R.E. Malone, 2008, 'Corporate philanthropy, lobbying, and public health policy', *American Journal of Public Health*, 98(12), pp. 2123–33.

Tewari, S., 2015, '75 percent of rural India survives on Rs 33 per day', *India Today*, 13 July. Available at: http://indiatoday.intoday.in/story/india-rural-household-650-millions-live-on-rs-33-per-day/1/451076.html (Accessed 9 November, 2016).

Tribal Health Initiative, Available at: http://www.tribalhealth.org/ (Accessed 9 November, 2016).

Zachariah, A., R. Srivatsan, & S. Tharu (eds.), 2010, *Towards a Critical Medical Practice: Reflections on the Dilemmas of Medical Culture Today*, New Delhi: Orient Blackswan.

Imagining Utopia:
The Importance of Love, Dissent and Radical Empathy

Arvind Narrain

Summary

One of the questions philosophy has always wrestled with is: what is it that makes our lives meaningful? The answer provided by late capitalism is that it is in forms of consumption, which satisfy various (created) human needs that pleasure and satisfaction and meaning is to be found. The deeply unsatisfactory nature of this answer is best gestured to by the anti-hero in Brett Easton Ellis's marvellous dystopia, American Psycho, who finds out that an existence where to consume is the very definition of what it is to be human kills the human within you.

This essay is written in the spirit of trying to decipher how one derives meaning in life in the contemporary era. While there are many possible answers, this essay will argue that at least two concepts are deeply meaningful to human existence. The first is the notion of love for one person and the second is the notion of love in a wider sense, which can be characterized as the love of justice or empathy for the suffering other.

These two concepts will be explored biographically by going to three queer lives lived on the margins of the societal consensus, namely, the lives of Swapna and Sucheta as well as Chelsea Manning.

Introduction

Swapna and Sucheta committed joint suicide on Feb 21, 2011in Nandigram, West Bengal, as society made it impossible for them to live their lives together. Though their lives were extinguished by societal intolerance, the brief period of their lives, marked as it was by their mutual bond of love was lived with such luminousness as to signpost possible futures of creative existence.

Chelsea Manning in her life showed what it was to be truthful both to an ideal of justice as well as whom one really was. In her life Chelsea struggled both against the rigid norms which defined Chelsea (a woman) as Bradley (a man) as well as the racist norms which refused to see those outside the dominant culture as human beings worthy of equal respect.

While both Swapna-Sucheta and Chelsea Manning had to pay an extraordinarily high price for choosing to live their life in a manner consistent with an ethical notion of whom they were, yet the creative possibilities embodied in their lives convey a vision for the future.

This paper will seek to trace out the utopian possibilities of queer lives by paying close attention to the creative possibilities embodied in these three different lives.[1] Firstly there is the idea of a defiant and subversive love of two people with an intensity and passion, which marks the experience of what it is to be human. Secondly there is the cultivation of a sensibility which allows one to go beyond the love of the individual self to empathize with the suffering of strangers. To love a person regardless of gender or sexuality and to empathize with seemingly distant causes is to dissent from the status quo. This paper will argue that there is an ethical and political stake in the practice of this form of love and cultivation of this form of radical empathy as both have within them the seeds of a very different world.

Swapna and Sucheta: Unquiet Slumbers for the Sleepers in that Quiet Earth

What insistently reminds us of the multiple stories underlying the suicide of Swapna and Sucheta, is a haunting picture by a police photographer who documented the deaths. In this photo we see Swapna and Sucheta lying on a stack of hay, in an image of peaceful repose calling to mind a deep intimacy. There is a *dupatta* (stole), which joins both of them at the waist. Their faces are turned towards each other and their hands are lightly pressed against each other.[2] The picture in its peacefulness and tranquillity unwittingly calls to mind the powerful conclusion of Emily Bronte's *Wuthering Heights*. Such is the power of stillness, peace, and a sense of eternal repose which the picture communicates that like the narrator in *Wuthering Heights*, we can't imagine unquiet slumbers for these two young lovers.

What accounts for the death of these two young girls who seem so wrapped up in each other even as they seem to lie in tranquil slumber? The work of Sappho for Equality, an organization advocating for the rights of sexual minorities uncovers some part of the story of what lay behind that awful image of great serenity.[3]

Swapna and Sucheta were two cousins who were very close to each other. Sucheta was the older cousin who had been giving tuitions for over one and a half years to Swapna. Sometimes the two girls would stay over in each other's houses after the tuitions. The two families ostensibly got worried by the 'closeness' of the two cousins and jointly decided to do something about it. Doing something about it meant that Sucheta's parents decide to get her married. Sucheta tried to resist the family pressure by saying that she was not interested in getting married as she wanted to study further. The family however forced her into getting married.

According to Sucheta's husband, regardless of the marriage, the bond between the girls was so deep that they would still meet each other regularly. This story of an incredible, all embracing deep friendship, which marriage was not able to destroy continued to trouble the two families. There were hints dropped by Sucheta's father and mother that such levels of closeness between two girls is not good. Similarly Swapna's father also observed that maybe the girls were too close and that not all people took that relationship well. Swapna's father also notes in a telling comment that they tried to isolate the two girls from each other.

On the fateful day, Sucheta had come to her parent's house to go to a fair and after sometime she was not to be found in the house. When her parents went to look for her they found the bodies of both Sucheta and Swapna lying together in that image of peaceful togetherness, which seemed to sum up the aspiration of their lives. In death they seemed to have found the togetherness, which was impossible to achieve in life. What gave an added poignancy to the joint death was the suicide note, which expressed their desire to be cremated together. It is almost as if their wish was to find another more tolerant and accepting world, which would honour their deep desire to be together.

The suicide note left by Swapna gives some more clues as to what lay behind the awful deaths:

'Then I started talking with Sucheta. She was very naughty then. She used to do whatever pleased her. She made me laugh with her strange antics.... We got more into talking and hanging out. Then she loves me very much. I love her very much too. ..If I didn't see her one day, I felt like my world was lost. Her family members misunderstood us... They didn't accept our love.... That's why I have decided to leave this world.... If we die together, please keep us at the same place, however that is possible. And if we live, we will go far away, far, far away, and will never return....'[4]

The tragedy of the death is compounded by the unwillingness of the family to fulfil the wishes of the dead girls. The girls wished to be together in death and strikingly the Inspector of Police, offers help to the two families to cremate the two bodies. However in a painful rejection the families do not even claim the bodies. Unclaimed bodies will be burnt along with other abandoned bodies without the rituals of mourning which accompany the sending off of a loved one. There is a particular poignancy in the fact that not even death is able to reconcile the families with their daughters. The ties of kinship are irrevocably sundered by the acts of love between the two girls and in the eyes of the family the girls have no greater claims on them than those of strangers.

This is a tragedy comprising many elements. It is a story of a deep love, which did not fear to look death in the face. It is also a story of a chosen death, the protagonists of which were unafraid to proclaim boldly and bravely as to why they preferred death to life. It is also a story of a betrayal of deep bonds of kinship that link fathers and daughters, mothers and daughters as well as husbands and wives. When even the body is unclaimed by those who owe sacred duties to one so close in blood to them, how does one account for it?

The Idea of Love: Self Completion, Mania and Philia

To understand the nature of this deep bond between Swapna and Sucheta, we need to go to their own words. The word Swapna uses unambiguously is love. What does love mean for Swapna and Sucheta? There are at least three ideas of love one can trace in Swapna's letter.

Eros as self completion

The most powerful articulation we get from Swapna and Sucheta about the nature of their love is that of the lover completing oneself. As Swapna's suicide note says:

> 'She loves me very much. I love her too. More than my life. But I don't know why. But if I didn't see her or talk to her, I felt very bad. She also felt this way. She herself loves me very much.'[5]

The idea of the lover as a person who completes oneself has deep roots in thinking about the idea of love. We need to go back to the Greeks and Plato's *The Symposium* to understand this idea of love. In *The Symposium*, Aristophanes makes his speech about love in which he invokes a time before time when there were three human genders. The male gender originated from the sun, the female gender from the earth and the combined gender from the moon (Plato, 1999).

What was unique about these three genders was each person had two heads, four legs and four arms and was like a ball, complete in himself/herself. These human beings were fully self sufficient and paid no heed to the Gods. In fact they were so arrogant that they tried to climb up to heaven to attack the Gods. Zeus, wondering what to do about this rebellion, decided that the best course of action would be to split these beings into two. Being split in two by Zeus, the two halves longed to reunite with each other and according to Aristophanes that is how the idea of love was born.[6]

In this ancient Greek idea of love the gender of the lover was irrelevant. The Greeks would not have been surprised by Swapna's passionate declaration that 'if I didn't see her or talk to her, I felt very bad. She also felt this way.' It was natural for women to love women, men to love women as well as men to love men. The only thing which mattered in this rendering of the myth was to account for the passionate feeling. The passion or intensity for the other spoke a deep truth. The reason for the passionate attachment lay in the original split and the human desire for completion. Within the terms of this myth there is no natural and unnatural desire, there is only a simple accounting for why it is human for us to fall in love with another human being.

Eros as mania

In Swapna's suicide note she says,

> 'She loves me very much. I love her too. More than my life. But I don't know why. But if I didn't see her or talk to her, I felt very bad. She also felt this way. She herself loves me very much. Perhaps more than I do. If I didn't see her one day, I felt like my world was lost'.[7]

We need to go to Plato's Phaedrus for an account of what does it mean to be possessed by the mania called Eros (Plato, 2005). Socrates describes the mania of love in the following terms:

> 'it does not willingly give up (the pleasures of love), nor does it value anyone above the one with beauty, but quite forgets mother, brothers, friends, all together, loses wealth through neglect without caring a jot about it, and feeling contempt for all the accepted standards of propriety and good taste in which it previously prided itself, it is ready to act the part of a slave and sleep wherever it is allowed to do so, provided it is as close as possible to the object of its yearning; for in addition to its reverence for the one who possesses the beauty, it has found him to be the sole healer of its greatest labours. This experience, my beautiful boy, the one to whom my speech is addressed, men term love.'

(pp. 33)

If we think of the powerful unbreakable bond between Swapna and Sucheta and relate it to the idea of Eros as described by Plato, we begin to understand something more of that relationship. Clearly the bond can't be described within the contemptuous terms of either carnality or as mere 'friendship'. There was something in the relationship which disturbed both families. The mysterious indefinable 'something' which disturbed both families can best be described as the manic pull of Eros. The mania of Eros overshadowed every other consideration as far as Swapna and Sucheta were concerned. They were not willing to 'value anyone above the one with beauty,' and their love 'but quite forgets mother, brothers, friends, all together'.

It is this utter absorption in each other to the detriment of conventional societal obligations which both families seem to have found difficult to tolerate. Clearly this bond is not of this world, does not have the mundane quality of 'dispensing miserly benefits of a mortal kind' (ibid., pp. 38) but rather partakes of some part of the mania described by Plato.

Being possessed by Eros is about experiencing a heightened state of being. This is not to be scorned at. As Socrates put it, 'the ancients testify to the fact that God sent madness is a finer thing than manmade sanity' (ibid., pp. 24).

The lives of Swapna and Sucheta embody this way of living, in which one is completely alive and the meaning of life and living is never in question. In a contemporary context, where love and living are domesticated by the market, family, community, religion and nation, the example of what being possessed by 'mania' could mean for the very notion of the good life is vital.

Eros as philia: Language and laughter as forming togetherness

A bond cannot be sustained purely on sexual passion alone. The bond needs to be nourished by other ways of human relating. Perhaps the most powerful way of nourishing this bond is through the art of being together, 'sharing in speech and reason.' For that is what it means for human beings to live together, not just to 'pasture in the same place like cattle' (Nussbaum, 2001, pp. 369).

Conversation and laughter are the two gifts which human beings have which are crucial tools in forging togetherness. The suicide note invokes the power of these everyday forms of togetherness as embodied in both conversation and laughter.

'Then I started talking with Sucheta. She was very naughty then. She used to do whatever pleased her. She made me laugh with her strange antics. I scolded her and she used to leave.

She never listened to my words. Then I started liking her. We got more into talking and hanging out....'[8]

This notion of 'talking and hanging out' as well as laughing as an invaluable part of the bond forged by Eros is evoked by literature and biography down the ages. Two moving examples are the bond of Penelope and Odysseus as evoked in Homer's *Odyssey* as well as the love of Karl Marx and Jenny Van Westphalen.

In Odysseus's long journey back home, he ends up staying at an island inhabited by the goddess Calypso as her lover. In Homer's description, though Calypso is beautiful as only Goddesses can be, and the sexual bond is pleasurable, Odysseus longs to go back home to his wife Penelope who he knows is not as beautiful and who will become even less beautiful as time goes by. Calypso promises him immortality and a life free of the pains he is destined to encounter should he go back home to Penelope. Yet, Odysseus requests Calypso to let him go. The reason why Penelope who ages and will become less beautiful is preferable to the deathless goddess, emerges most poignantly in the scene when after a separation of twenty years, Odysseus finally gets back to his home and meets Penelope:

'But the royal couple, once they'd reveled in all
The longed for joys of love, reveled in each other's stories,
The radiant woman telling of all she'd borne at home,
Watching them there, the infernal crowd of suitors
Slaughtering herds of cattle and good fat sheep-
While keen to win her hand-
Draining the broached vats dry of vintage wine.
And great Odysseus told his wife of all the pains
He had dealt out to other men and all the hardships
He'd endured himself-his story first to last-
And she listened on, enchanted...
Sleep never sealed her eyes till all was told.'

(Homer, 1996, pp. 465)

The joys of the bond of Eros as captured in the joy of togetherness and conversation is what Homer so movingly describes. The multiple ways in which human beings relate to each other and the relational richness of Eros is what we get in this powerful description of the bond between Odysseus and Penelope. We don't get a hint about Penelope's jealousy that Odysseus has slept with Calypso, what we get is an affirmation of what makes the bond between Odysseus and Penelope rich, multifaceted and irreplaceable.

In a moving recollection of her father, Karl Marx, Eleanor Marx says that, while Karl Marx was thought by many to be a 'morose, bitter, unbending, unapproachable man' the contrary was true. He was 'the cheeriest, gayest soul that ever breathed' 'brimming over with humour'. Eleanor Marx sees her father's personality as intrinsically linked to her father's love for her mother, Jenny Van Westphalen. According to Eleanor Marx, 'Karl Marx would never have been what he was without Jenny von Westphalen. Never were the lives of two people – both remarkable – so at one, so complementary one of the other' (Marx & Aveling, 2003, pp. 203).

While the bond was at one level a political one, forged by a common commitment to the working class, Eleanor Marx emphasizes the seemingly quotidian bonds which kept them together.

> 'And I sometimes think that almost as strong a bond between them as their devotion to the cause of the workers was their immense sense of humour. Assuredly two people never enjoyed a joke more than these two. Again and again – especially if the occasion were one demanding decorum and sedateness, have I seen them laugh till tears ran down their cheeks, and even those inclined to be shocked at such levity could not choose but laugh with them. And how often have I seen them not daring to look at one another, each knowing that once a glance was exchanged, uncontrollable laughter would result. To see those two with eyes fixed on anything but one another, for all the world like two school children, suffocating with suppressed laughter that at last despite all efforts would well forth, is a memory I would not barter for all the millions I am sometimes credited with having inherited.'

> (ibid. pp. 208)

Clearly the vitality of the relationship of Swapna and Sucheta finds an echo in the loves of Karl and Jenny Marx as well as Penelope and Odysseus. The bond of Swapna and Sucheta formed as it is by both laughter and conversation, evokes an older history of being together. As such, the vitality of the bond gestures to something integral to happiness in human lives. In the contemporary context, marked as it is by grave and continuing injustice, laughter and conversation can make life liveable.

Taking forward the lives of Swapna and Sucheta

Remembering as an act of defiant creation Swapna's suicide note ends with a poignant plea as well as a dream of another world.

'If we die together, please keep us at the same place, however that is possible. And if we live, we will go far away, far, far away, and will never return.'[9]

Of course this dream is not fulfilled, as Swapna and Sucheta did not go far, far away nor were their bodies cremated together. In fact their bodies are not even given the dignity of a send off by their loved ones as their respective families even refused to publicly mourn their deaths. This powerful crisscrossing of the currents of love and hate, recalls the story of Antigone written almost 2400 years ago by the Greek dramatist Sophocles. The tragedy of Antigone, the daughter of Oedipus, is perhaps one of the most influential in western thought, having opened out innumerable creative possibilities in western culture (Steiner, 1986).

In the play, Antigone's two brothers engage in a fratricidal struggle for the throne of Thebes. Polynices attacks Thebes to take the crown from Eteocles. In this conflict the two brothers kill each other and Creon, Antigone's uncle, becomes the king. Creon decrees that Polynices the traitor will be denied the rites of burial and his carcass become the prey of dogs and vultures. Antigone willfully disobeys the King's order and goes on to attempt to bury her brother Polynices. Being discovered by Creon's guards, she is produced before Creon. Creon asks her how she could bury her brother who was a traitor.

In a powerful confrontation with Creon she asserts her right to bury her brother by claiming that Creon's manmade edicts are not strong enough to overrule the unwritten, unalterable law which compels her to give her brother the dignity of a burial (Sophocles, 1984). As a result of this defiance, Antigone is ordered to be buried alive by Creon. This elemental confrontation between manmade law as embodied by Creon and the call of conscience as embodied by Antigone has given voice to numerous struggles around the world.

In a famously subversive rendering, Jean Anouilh performed his version of Antigone in front of the German SS officers when France was under occupation, where Antigone to the watching French, stood for the French resistance against the German occupation (Anouilh, 1946).

In South Africa Athol Fugard wrote a brilliant play called the Island where prisoners on Robben Island perform a two man version of Antigone called the Trial of Antigone and this play was performed before the prison guards as well as all the prisoners. Antigone in a metaphorical sense stood in for blacks in apartheid South Africa and Creon stood in for the apartheid state (Fugard, 1976).

In Argentina, Griselda Gambaro wrote *Antigona Furiosa*, in which the unclaimed body of Polynices stood in for the 50000 people who were 'disappeared' by the Argentine military. Antigone represented the Mothers and the Grandmothers of the Plaza De Mayo who insisted on the right to have their children back. Gambaro's work gave voice to the disappeared, defended those who died, and demanded a proper burial as an act of 'defiance, mourning, and remembrance' (Paulson, 2012).

The story of Swapna and Sucheta, partakes of this global history of 'defiance, mourning and remembrance.' There is something elemental in that story of them being joined in love while to hate is the nature of their society. Like Antigone and her willed suicide, the two Indian Antigones prefer to embrace death, rather than give in to societal prohibitions of their love.

The failure of the parents to claim the bodies of their daughters, tells us about the limits of kinship. Antigone's will to mourn her brother speaks again not in the simple terms of the name of the family against the state but rather about a bond formed at the limits of family.[10] If the family chooses to disown their daughters by not claiming the bodies and publicly mourning them, who then will speak on behalf of Swapna and Sucheta?

The challenge which Swapna and Sucheta are posing to us is to ask the question as to how will we mourn them? The only answer can be that we need to remember the intensity of their lives and the tragedy of their needless deaths in the same way that Jean Anouilh, Griselda Gambaro and Athol Fugard choose to remember the tragedies of their societies. In Gambaro, Fugard and Anouilh the confrontation is between an all powerful Creon and an Antigone who only has the intensity of her moral passion. Our two Indian Antigones really stand in for 'a millennially outraged, patronized, excluded womanhood' (Steiner,1986, pp.150). They stand in for the principled assertion that yes we will lead our lives in accordance with our own inner convictions and that rather than allow these deeply felt convictions to be trampled upon by a barbaric society which does not understand or accept our love we will rather consciously and bravely embrace death.

The importance of mourning is that it is an act of remembrance of those who can no more fight for justice, or those whose voices have been stilled. If they are not to be forgotten, then it is the speech of the living which must remember them. We owe it to these girls and many others like them to multiply their stories as signs of queer existence and challenge the orders of Creon which forbid the mourning of lesbian deaths.[11]

To remember these deaths is to make a commitment that what happened to Swapna and Sucheta should not happen to others like them. The only genuine tribute one can pay to Swapna and Sucheta is to commit to working to ensure that the society of the future will be more accepting of lives such as Swapna's and Sucheta's.

Chelsea Manning: Broadening the circle of empathy

Powerful as the story of Swapna and Sucheta is, one is left wondering whether there are other ways of loving?

The famous Pakistani poet, Faiz Ahmed Faiz , in his poem, 'Don't ask me for that love again', powerfully articulates this question. Faiz begins by describing his beloved in the sublime language of love poetry:

> A glimpse of your face was evidence of springtime.
> The sky, whenever I looked, was nothing but your eyes.
> If you'd fall into my arms fate would be helpless.

This creation of a private utopia composed of the beloved and he, is however insistently challenged by the world outside. As the poet put it:

> As I went into alleys and in open markets
> Saw bodies plastered with ash, bathed in blood.
> I saw them sold and bought, again and again.
> This too deserves attention.

On an almost wistful painful note the poet concludes:

> There are other sorrows in this world,
> Comforts other than love
> Don't ask me, my love, for that love again.
>
> (Faiz in McClatchy, 1996, pp. 395)

The conclusion that Faiz came to is not one favoured in the contemporary world. Clearly one of the 'lacks' in the contemporary world is an unwillingness to open one's eyes and see a world outside the private and personal. The injustices which are perpetrated on a global scale, by forces too large to comprehend let alone fight, create a sense of personal helplessness. In fact one can argue that in the contemporary world, the retreat into the private and personal may be a default position for the large majority too bewildered by the forces which perpetrate injustice on a global scale.

In times such as this, when the desire to retreat inwards is immensely attractive, we need the examples of lives which seek to deepen the bond of empathy. We need empathy to move outward in concentric circles, breaking the shackles of prejudice to embrace suffering humanity. Such is the challenge before us in the contemporary era increasingly divided and subdivided by loyalties of class, caste, region and nation. It is in this context, when people owe their greatest loyalty to their nation and are prepared to kill on behalf of their country, that we need ethical voices to remind us of our common humanity.

In the contemporary world, one such remarkable figure is Chelsea (formerly Bradley) Manning. Private Manning moves from being a loyal soldier of the US army to becoming one of its most courageous dissenters. Private Manning at the end of this journey from loyal soldier to dissenter also transitions from the male gender (Bradley Manning) to the female gender (Chelsea Manning).

Private Manning was an information analyst with the US army who leaked information regarding the war in Iraq and Afghanistan, as well as thousands of diplomatic cables with respect to US foreign policy. As a consequence of this act, Manning was arrested, kept in solitary confinement in a small cell for a period of over nine months for twenty three hours a day. During the pre-trial detention, Manning was tortured using Guantanamo bay techniques including harsh lighting, stress positions and enforced nudity.

After three years of pre-trial confinement, the trial was finally conducted and resulted in Chelsea Manning being sentenced to thirty five years in prison for violations of the Espionage Act. The serious consequences of making public US military documents must surely have been known to Chelsea Manning. What motivated her to place at risk her personal freedom and liberty?

To understand the motivations of Chelsea Manning one can do no better than go to her statement at her trial. Chelsea Manning understands that the significance of the documents that she is releasing to the public domain,

> 'This is possibly one of the more significant documents of our time removing the fog of war and revealing the true nature of twenty-first century asymmetric warfare.....'[12]

When Chelsea Manning refers to asymmetric warfare what she is referring to is the enormous power to kill on a mass scale which is at the disposal of the US military. This power to kill should come with a deep rooted responsibility, and what Chelsea Manning responds to almost viscerally is not only the lack of responsibility but rather the almost inhumane joy in killing which seems to motivate the US troops. One of the videos which Chelsea Manning made public exposed the cold blooded killing of twelve civilians including two Reuters journalists, by a US Apache helicopter crew in Iraq. The killing was initially justified by the US Military as within the rules of engagement even as the US military refused to release the video. Manning chanced upon the video documentation and she was shocked by what she saw:

'The most alarming aspect of the video to me, however, was the seemingly delightful blood-lust the Aerial Weapons Team seemed to have.............

They dehumanized the individuals they were engaging and seemed to not value human life, and referred to them as quote-unquote "dead bastards," and congratulated each other on their ability to kill in large numbers. At one point in the video there is an individual on the ground attempting to crawl to safety. The individual is seriously wounded. Instead of calling for medical attention to the location, one of the aerial weapons team crew members verbally asks for the wounded person to pick up a weapon so that he can have a reason to engage. For me, this seemed similar to a child torturing ants with a magnifying glass.'[13]

Chelsea Manning's shock transforms to a conviction that the American public needs to know what happened:

'I wanted the American public to know that not everyone in Iraq and Afghanistan were targets that needed to be neutralized, but rather people who were struggling to live in the pressure cooker environment of what we call asymmetric warfare.'[14]

There might not be much in common between Chelsea and the Iraqis who were the victims of the US invasion. Yes Chelsea Manning chose to speak out and bear witness to wrongs her country has done. What describes best this sentiment of solidarity and empathy towards those who are so different, is what Christopher Lee calls radical empathy. According to Lee, radical empathy can be 'provisionally defined as a politics of recognition and solidarity with community beyond one's immediate experience' (Lee, 2015, pp. 191).

In Lee's understanding the exemplar of the politics of radical empathy was the anti-colonial writer and activist, Frantz Fanon who is born in St. Martinique, yet in the course of his life became a comrade in the Algerian liberation struggle. Reflecting on what drove Fanon to empathize with the Algerian cause, Fanon's wife Josie Fanon, says 'people have often wondered why he should have taken part in the liberation of a country that was not his originally. Her reply was that only 'narrow minds and hearts' for whom race or religion 'constitutes an unbridgeable gulf' fail to understand, there was no contradiction or dilemma for Fanon, only necessity' (Lee, 2015, pp. 31).

Like Fanon, Chelsea transcends the limits of her origin and is able to establish a human connection with those who are very distant in both geographical and cultural terms. Chelsea Manning embodies a contemporary politics of radical empathy which takes forward the heroic struggle against forms of neo-colonialism by exposing its brutal face. Chelsea Manning is a dissenter in the best sense of the word.[15]

The Importance of Being Chelsea Manning

Interestingly, there is a deep internal dimension to Chelsea's remarkable act of dissent. Chelsea, just when she is sentenced to thirty five years in prison, makes public her gender identity. Chelsea (formerly Bradley) Manning read out a statement:

> 'As I transition into this next phase of my life, I want everyone to know the real me. I am Chelsea Manning. I am a female. Given the way that I feel, and have felt since childhood, I want to begin hormone therapy as soon as possible.'[16]

No less than the public act of speaking out was the act of speaking out about the truth of who she wanted to become. There is not just a public and outer dimension to Chelsea's deep moral convictions but also a private and inner dimension.

The importance of Chelsea Manning's life stems from one fundamental aspect. To Chelsea the self was not a given, something like an inert object. Rather in Chelsea's understanding the human self was always in the process of becoming. In Emerson's terms, Chelsea's voyage of discovery is about working on the realization that the self is 'unattained but attainable' (Emerson, 909). Chelsea's journey is also one with Foucault's journey who famously said that 'The main interest in life and work is to become someone else that you were not in the beginning' (Foucault, 1998, pp. 9).

What is truly remarkable about this journey is that it goes deep within as much as it goes outward. There is a recognition that something is not quite right with the world as it exists, just as there is recognition that there is something not quite right about who I am.

The recognition that there is something wrong with the world is an understanding that to unthinkingly conform to the demands of society is to do serious damage to the self. Conformity produces what Emerson calls living in 'secret melancholy' and Thoreau describes as 'the mass of men living lives of quiet desperation' (Cavell, 2004, pp. 25).

It is precisely this conformity which is responsible not only for individual unhappiness as Thoreau and Emerson put it, but also the infliction of needless suffering through heedless wars whose necessity is never challenged.

It is the lack of an informed and knowledgeable society attuned to the costs of war which allowed for the US government to invade Iraq without serious domestic opposition. Thus Chelsea Manning's impulse to tell the truth about the Iraq war, regardless of the consequences, is at one with the impulse of other heroic dissenters like Thoreau himself in his day as well as Socrates, Martin Luther King and Mahatma Gandhi.

Where Chelsea Manning goes beyond is in articulating the fact that working on the self is not only about broadening the range of ethical concerns but also about being true to who you are in the deepest sense. By questioning the 'truth' that a person born biologically a man should live for his whole life as a man, Chelsea Manning challenges the socially imposed borders of gender and sexuality, thereby giving the notion of freedom another dimension.

The moral compass which is so strongly a part of Chelsea Manning is inseparable from her gender identity. Her being transgender and her willingness to be herself, truthfully and without adornment or artifice is one with her strong moral drive to make her government accountable even at high personal cost. Chelsea Manning exemplifies an ethical life, that is, a life devoted to a practice of freedom.

Imagining utopia

What can one derive as a utopian vision for the future from the lives of Swapna and Sucheta and Chelsea Manning? All three lives are pregnant with utopian possibilities and gesture towards ways of living in the contemporary era which could be deeply meaningful.

The lives of Swapna and Sucheta are an exemplar of how the love between two people can be passionate, playful, meaningful and subversive as well as open out possibilities for future generations. Swapna and Sucheta invoke the little joys of life which should be a part of any utopia. The idea of love encompasses the everyday joys of laughter and togetherness as well as the ability to live with the person of one's choice. These are little joys which become even more significant in a context in which they are denied to human beings. In India the fact that Section 377 criminalizes the intimate lives of LGBT people is a denial of the right to human happiness. Taken from the perspective of the LGBT community, utopia lies in the absence of a criminal law which sanctions LGBT lives and the loosening of social and religious orthodoxies which constrain all efforts of the LGBT community to form intimate attachments.[17]

However utopia cannot just be a personal utopia for the LGBT community. In a world marked by grave and continuing forms of injustice, to achieve some measure of personal happiness (important as it is) can never be enough.

Part of the problem in the world is that even in progressive communities, our empathy is divided up. If you are gay your empathy is only for gay causes and if you are a religious minority your empathy is for religious minority causes only.

In such a situation in which empathy flows only within narrow grooves, there is a case to be made for broadening the grooves so that the heart feels more keenly the suffering of the stranger and the other. Utopia would surely be a state where the human heart is moved by all forms of suffering.

In specific a utopian future vision would be a space where social movements move from being focused on single issues to understanding the connections to other forms of suffering inflicted on human beings.

This utopian aspiration for the future of social movements, is best gestured to by the life of Chelsea Manning who in the remarkable actions of her life, embodied a politics of radical empathy towards strangers in distant lands. Of course this inspirational aspect of Chelsea Manning's life finds echoes in other lives as well.

To take an example from contemporary India: in 2016, India was convulsed with the suicide of a young Dalit scholar, Rohit Vemula, at the Hyderabad Central University. Rohit was persecuted for his political belief and actions by a vindictive university administration and finally unable to cope with this, he decided to take his own life. He left behind a suicide note which movingly recalled a creative life which was so tragically lost. Rohit Vemula in his suicide note said that:

> 'The value of a man was reduced to his immediate identity and nearest possibility. To a vote. To a number. To a thing. Never was a man treated as a mind. As a glorious thing made up of star dust; In every field – in studies, in streets, in politics, and in dying and living.'[18]

The eloquence of the suicide note hinted at the remarkable life that was lost. The life that Rohit Vemula lived was as inspirational as the note he left behind. One aspect of Rohit's remarkable life was his passion for politics not defined as single issue politics but rather politics as a broad tent.

It is precisely this broad tent approach to politics which allowed Rohit to see not only discrimination on caste as an issue of importance but also discrimination against Muslims and issues such as the death penalty.

In fact it was the stance taken by Rohit's organization, the Ambedkar Study Circle, on this broader terrain of politics which got him into trouble. The fact that the Ambedkar Study Circle conducted programmes on multiple human rights issues (including the anti-Muslim pogroms in Muzzafarnagar as well on the death penalty) resulted in vindictive action by the university authorities.[19]

It was the broad platform that the Ambedkar Study Circle espoused which the state found very threatening. Unlike single-issue identity politics, this form of political thinking and action could not be easily managed and controlled, and instead needed to be silenced.

The silencing of Rohit parallels the thirty five year prison sentence for that other heroic dissenter Chelsea Manning.[20] There are echoes of Chelsea's bravery in the actions of the young Rohit Vemula who refuses to see the world within narrow 'identity' frames. They both call out to us to embrace a politics of radical empathy, which broadens the notion of what it is to be human.

What all these lives gesture towards is the possibility of another world. We should not have to suffer death for wanting to live with the one that we love. Similarly we should not be tortured and imprisoned for seeking to speak the truth about the injustices our societies inflict.

In seeking to bring into being a fragile utopia in an insensitive world, these visionaries keep alive the future. The fact that they dared to act against what society expected of them and acted instead in accordance with their internal selves, has introduced an aspect of magical possibility into everyday, quotidian and humdrum lives. To attend to these lives is to demand that their dreams must become our present.

Endnotes

1. The word 'queer' itself inhabits a new political wisdom. For some it is a re-imagination of ideas of love and relationships; and for others a restructuring of the law, politics and society and a challenge to the way we inhabit the world. It represents those who fall out (and/or choose to stand out) of the contours of the hetero-normative social order.

2. The image of Swapna and Sucheta as captured by the photographer can be viewed in a documentary film made by Debalina Mazumdar titled 'The Unclaimed', https://www.youtube.com/watch?v=Ox95MVCXNsY (accessed 10 August, 2015).

3. The narrative documented is from Mazumdar's documentary, mentioned above.

4. Suicide Note on file with Sappho for Equality, 2011.

5. ibid.

6. As Aristophanes puts it, 'that's how, long ago, the innate desire of human beings for each other started. It draws the two halves of our original nature back together and tries to make one out of two and to heal the wound in human nature. Each of us is a matching half of a human being, because we've been cut in half like flatfish' (Plato, 1999, pp. 24).

7. Suicide Note on file with Sappho for Equality.

8. ibid.

9. ibid.

10. Judith Butler in her reading of the myth of Antigone, observes that Antigone's relationship to Polynices is complicated. After all they are both the children of Oedipus who married his own mother. Antigone's story according to Butler posits the emergence of new forms of relationships which are formed outside the traditional kinship ties that bind, for example a brother to a sister.

11. See Mazumdar's documentary film, op. cit.

12. http://www.bradleymanning.org/news/bradley-mannings-statement-taking-responsibility-for-releasing-documents-to-wikileaks.

13. ibid.

14. ibid.

15. Edward Snowden expressed powerfully the value of acts of dissent such as the one by Manning – 'The individuals who make these disclosures feel so strongly about what they have seen that they're willing to risk their lives and their freedom. They know that we, the people, are ultimately the strongest and most reliable check on the power of government. The insiders at the highest levels of government have extraordinary capability, extraordinary resources, tremendous access to influence and a monopoly of violence, but in the final calculus there is one figure that matters: the individual citizen. And there are more of us than there are of them' (Scahill, 2016, pp. xviii).

16. http://www.huffingtonpost.com/2013/08/22/bradley-manning-chelsea-manning_n_3794629.html (accessed 12 September, 2015).

17. Section 377 of the Indian Penal Code criminalizes what it calls 'carnal intercourse against the order of nature'. The law allows for deep intrusions by both state and non state actors into the domain of one's private and intimate life putting in jeopardy the right to dignity, privacy, equality and expression. For a more in depth analysis of the impact of Section 377 on LGBT lives see the essays in Gupta & Narrain (2011).

18. http://indianexpress.com/article/india/india-news-india/dalit-student-suicide-full-text-of-suicide-letter-hyderabad/ (accessed 12 August, 2016).

19. http://indianexpress.com/article/india/india-news-india/behind-dalit-student-suicide-how-his-university-campus-showed-him-the-door/ (accessed 12 August, 2016).

20. At the time of going to press, Chelsea Manning has been released through a Presidential pardon.

References

Anouilh, Jean, 1947, *Antigone*, New York: Random House.

Butler, Judith, 2000, *Antigone's Claim*, New York: Columbia University Press.

Cavell, Stanley, 2004, *Cities of Words*, Cambridge: Harvard University Press.

Emerson, Ralph Waldo, 1909, *History cf. in The Works of Ralph Waldo Emerson*, Vol II, New York: Fireside Edition, http://oll.libertyfund.org/titles/emerson-the-works-of-ralph-waldo-emerson-vol-2-essays-first-series (accessed 5 October, 2017).

Faiz Ahmed Faiz, 1996, 'Don't ask me for that love again', cf. in *The Vintage Book of Contemporary World Poetry*, J. D. McClatchy (ed.), New York: Random House, pp. 395.

Foucault, Michel, 1998, *Ethics*, New York: New Press.

Fugard, Athol (with John Kani & Winston Ntshona), 1976, *Sizwe Bansi is Dead and The Island*, New York: Viking.

Gupta, Alok and Arvind Narrain, 2011, *Law like Love*, New Delhi: Yoda Press.

Homer (Translated by Robert Fagles), 1996, *Odyssey*, New York: Penguin.

Lee, Christopher, 2015, *Frantz Fanon, Towards a Revolutionary Humanism,* Ohio University Press, Athens.

Marx, Eleanor Aveling, 2003, 'Karl Marx: A few stray notes', in *Marx's Concept of Man*, Erich Fromm, New Delhi: Bloomsbury.

Nussbaum, Martha, 2001, *The Fragility of Goodness*, Cambridge: Cambridge University Press.

Paulson, Nancy Kason, 2012, 'In Defense of the Dead: Antigona Furiosa, by Griselda Gambaro', *Romance Quarterly*, Vol. 59(1), pp. 48–54.

Plato, 1999, *The Symposium*, London: Penguin.

Plato, 2005, *Phaedrus*, London: Penguin.

Scahill, Jeremy, 2016, *The Assassination Complex*, London: Serpents Tail.

Sophocles, 1984, 'Antigone', in *Three Theban Tragedies*, Robert Fagles (ed.), New York: Penguin.

Steiner, George, 1986, *Antigones*, Oxford: Clarendon Press.

Envisioning Dalit Futures

Anand Teltumbde

Summary

Dalits have lived in the most inhuman conditions all through history. The colonial rule, that brought various opportunities to Dalits, catalyzed the Dalit movement. The latter, however, could cater only to a very small population and a large section of Dalits in rural areas and urban slums still languishes for want of basic needs.

The essay sketches the current state of Dalits and then takes on to present the vision for the Dalit future in India. The Dalit movement has failed to recognise class consciousness, such that, the policy like reservations, has only benefitted better off sections of the subject caste. The majority of Dalits still don't have access to elementary education, health, employment, democratic rights and modernity, as caste identities continue to dominate the Indian public sphere.

The essay argues for the need of multi-parametric empowerment viz. individual, socio-economic, socio-political and socio-cultural empowerment of the Dalits. Central to this is the abolishment of caste and communal consciousness from the public spaces so that we can march towards a society based on the principles of liberty, equality and fraternity.

Introduction

Dalit is a quasi-class term[1] for the people belonging to the castes considered untouchables in the Hindu social order. While its origin is obscure, it appears to be in vogue in Marathi and certainly used by Mahatma Phule in the modern sense. It evolved through the movement led by Babasaheb Ambedkar. Dalits are formally outside the framework of the caste system mapped by the *Chaturvarna*.[2] They are as such called *a-varna* (non-varna) or outcaste. Though loosely considered to be the lowest stratum of the Hindu society, they mark a break from the caste segment. Being physically excluded for millennia from the caste society, they approximately mirror a similar social structure as of the caste segment, with numerous castes and sub-castes strung in a notional hierarchy. In colonial times, they were known by various names such as Untouchables, Depressed Classes, *Harijan*s – a paternalistic term devised by Mahatma Gandhi – culminating into an administrative term 'Scheduled Castes', being formally included into a schedule prepared in order to implement certain measures won for them by Ambedkar in the Round Table Conferences at London of 1930-32.[3] This official term only includes the Dalits belonging to Hinduism, Sikhism (from 1956) and Buddhism (from 1990) and not to other religions like Christianity and Islam.

Dalits, as Scheduled Castes, account for 16.6 per cent of the Indian population, which in absolute terms is 201 million.[4] If they were a country, they would have been the fifth most populous country just after China, India, United States and Indonesia, and third if all the Dalits were considered.[5] They have lived in most inhuman conditions without property or dignity all through history. Only from the medieval times, with the advent of Islam in India, the escape from this state had become possible for them (Sengupta, 1984). The real change however materialised during the British colonial rule, which brought them huge economic opportunities, modern education, and western liberal institutional framework, marking a kink in their history, and catalysing the birth of the Dalit movement (Teltumbde, 1999). Over a century since then, although a miniscule section of the Dalits appear to have made significant progress marking their presence in every sphere of life, a vast majority of them in rural areas and urban slums still languish in relatively the same as or worse than the state they were in a century before (Teltumbde, 2015a).

The paper seeks to imagine the optimistic future for these hapless people over the coming decades. In order that this exercise is not shorn of reality, it necessarily takes stock of their current state, and the salient historical factors that shaped it in order to sketch out the likely scenario if the present state is simply extrapolated. It is only then that one could think of radical departures to reach the desired state. It lists out salient measures that need to be taken to reach that state. Thus, while they could be seen in the realm of 'do-ability', they cannot be without hurdles. The paper tries to take stock of these hurdles in accomplishing this vision in the concluding section.

Context to the Present

The Dalit movement, born in the early years of the twentieth century, initially with the reforms to uplift some Dalit castes (Jadhav, 1991), was completely metamorphosed under the legendary leadership of Ambedkar, who provided it with the intellectual foundation and contemporary political dimension.[6] Ambedkar, deeply influenced by Pragmatism and Fabianism[7] during his studentship in Columbia University, and following the legacy of his predecessors, had started off with a modest expectation of certain reforms in the Hindu society to alleviate the woes of the Dalits. But realising its futility, he soon turned towards politics and won several concessions for the Dalits from the colonial state, which included political reservations, and reservations in public educational institutes and employment.[8]

Ambedkar played a significant role in the Constituent Assembly, as its member and the Chairman of its most important committee, the Drafting Committee. The Constitution abolished the practice of untouchability and adopted a slew of measures for protecting and promoting the interests of the Dalits[9] – reservations in political representation in parliament and state assemblies; in the admissions to the educational institutions aided by the state and in public employment, have been the most significant of them. As such all these reservations were instituted during the colonial times, right from 1937.[10] These reservations were extended to the tribal people, creating a separate schedule for them.[11] The Constitution also provided for the state to identify the Other Backward Castes (OBC) in future for extending similar support and concessions.[12] With hindsight, it can be clearly seen that all these formulations were done to dilute the exceptional premise of reservations and giving new lease of life to castes (Teltumbde, 2015a) as a divisive weapon (along with religion) to manipulate people for perpetuating the class rule of a single party through the-first-past-the-post election system (Teltumbde, 2010; 2014).

In the euphoria of having accomplished a historic task, Ambedkar exhorted the Dalits to shun agitational methods and adopt constitutional means to resolve their grievances. But he himself was disillusioned within just three years, such that he publicly disowned the Constitution and spoke of burning it down.[13] He was completely disillusioned by the post-colonial governance of the country and resigned from the Nehru cabinet with an alibi of volte face of Nehru on the Hindu Code Bill, which symbolized his ambitious reform in the Hindu society. After ending the uncomfortable bonhomie with the Congress, he contested a Lok Sabha election in 1952 but was defeated by an unknown Congress candidate,[14] which repeated two years later in a by-election (Jadhav, 1991). Despite failing health and mounting frustration, he contemplated floating a non-communist opposition party and had written to prominent progressive leaders of those days. It was a nostalgic reversal to his strategy of Independent Labour Party (ILP) to fight the dual enemy of capitalism and Brahmanism (Jaffrelot, 2009). He soon fulfilled his vow taken two decades earlier[15] by embracing Buddhism along with half a million of his followers. It was in this congregation of the Dalits who came for conversion that he had announced his plan of floating the Republican Party of India for the first time. However, he did not live to see it materialize – he died within two months thereafter on 6 December, 1956. In Ambedkar's liberal schema 'moral code' governing the individual's behaviour occupied an important place, which was taken by Buddhism as the religion that could stand in consonance with modern science. Buddhism also was his antidote to castes in Hinduism, as he fancied the idea that he would make entire India a Buddhist country. A large number of the Dalits became Buddhists following him, but they mostly belonged to the populous constituent caste of the Dalits in every province, which identified with Ambedkar as equivalent of Mahars – his own caste.[16]

Present State of the Dalits

The Constitution outlawed untouchability but not castes. On the contrary, castes were consecrated in the Constitution as the basis for extending the affirmative action policies in favour of the Dalits, the Tribals and the OBCs. With castes surviving, untouchability, which was just an aspect of caste, was not expected to disappear. Naturally, a number of studies/surveys conducted right up to the recent years,[17] have consistently revealed that untouchability is prevalent in both rural and urban India, in both visible and subtle ways. Among the recent surveys, Action Aid's all India survey of 565 villages in twelve states (Punjab, Uttar Pradesh, Bihar, Madhya Pradesh, Chhattisgarh, Rajasthan, Maharashtra, Orissa, Andhra Pradesh, Karnataka, Kerala, and Tamil Nadu) in 2001-2 is important. It revealed inter alia that various forms of untouchability were rampantly practiced in most (60-70 per cent) villages. A recent (2010) study titled 'Understanding Untouchability: A Comprehensive Study of Practices and Conditions in 1,589 villages', was based on a survey conducted in Gujarat from 2007-10 by the Navsarjan Trust, in collaboration with the Robert E. Kennedy Centre for Justice and Human Rights. It brought out the obnoxious practice of untouchability being still intact in Gujarat. The latest NCAER report of the India Human Development Survey (IHDS-2) — the largest pan-Indian non-government household survey — carried out in 2011-12 for economic and social variables across multiple categories, also revealed that 27 per cent people practiced untouchability in some form (NCAER, 2014).

The Constitution basically reflected the Congress thinking, representing the emergent bourgeoisie class. All the upper caste reformers, best represented by Gandhi, vehemently spoke against untouchability but defended castes. Untouchability was too crude a practice to defend and hence it needed to be abolished. Castes could, however, be a potential weapon in their hands to divide people and hence would not be done away with. Untouchability was a mere symptom and hence would not disappear without the disease of caste being eradicated. Indeed, surpassing the colonial stratagem of divide and rule, the new ruling classes skilfully preserved both the potent weapons to divide people – caste and religion. Like abolishing untouchability, the Constitution had a plethora of provisions to claim secular credentials, but avoided including 'secularism' – separating religion from politics. Like castes, religion was preserved with an alibi of bringing in reforms. One can see that it was just an alibi, as the only reform in the post-colonial India was outlawing the practice of *sati* (the practice of a widow immolating herself on her husband's pyre) in 1987, and that too amidst the outrage sparked by an infamous incident of burning a seventeen year old woman Roop Kanwar in Rajasthan (Teltumbde, 2015b). Similar intrigues can be discerned in the provision of much acclaimed reservations. Reservations could be an exceptional policy for exceptional people as they were instituted in the colonial times. In order to continue them there was no need of original castes as they were based on an administrative category – Scheduled Castes, which had superseded them. If the ruling classes willed, castes also could have been outlawed along with untouchability. But they intended otherwise. Next, if they wanted to extend all provisions for the SCs to the tribal people, the latter could have been simply included into the existing schedule, renaming it suitably if required. By doing so the stigma associated with the schedule would have been diluted as the tribal communities did not have castes. They however created a separate schedule substituting caste with tribe. The Constitution included a still vaguer provision for extending similar provisions in favour of the classes (OBCs) to be identified by the state at a future date, which were socially and educationally backward (Art. 340). It was designed to be a can of caste worms the lid of which could be opened at an opportune time. As it happened, this lid was opened by the Prime Minister V.P. Singh in 1990. It not only set caste worms free but also unleashed competitive claims to backwardness to get reservations. In a country like India, caste based reservation cannot be considered as a remedy for backwardness. It could only be sparingly used, over and above the pro-people orientation in policy frameworks, such that all people get empowered on certain basic parameters like health care, education, livelihood security, etc.

The reservations, moreover, tend to benefit the already better off sections and create a narrower band of well off people, thereby aggravating inequality among the subject groups. While reservations in educational institutions and public employment brought varying degree of benefits to a section of the Dalits, political reservation, on the contrary, proved a device for their enslavement. They were meant only for 10 years, but have got renewed automatically without anyone in particular ever asking for it.

More than reservation the associated concessions of economic nature (waiver of fee and scholarship) helped large sections of the Dalits. The reservations in educational institutions proved particularly helpful while entering coveted professional institutions, as they lacked material resources necessitated for competing with others. The reservations in public employment had likewise played a crucial role as they marked not only the fruition of education, but also constituted motivation for the Dalits to get education. The implementation of these reservations has always been lackadaisical. Therefore, the gap between the prescribed and the actual fulfilment got widened as one went up from the lowest (Class D) to the highest (Class A). There is another category called 'sweepers', which until the 1980s' was a virtual monopoly of the Dalits but now no more. From early 1990s', their percentage representation began to decline. The new economy establishments such as airports, malls, hospitals, and office complexes have modern equipments and gadgets handled by liveried 'janitors' provided by service companies, who scarcely belong to the Dalits. While the percentage fulfilment of job reservation improved gradually over the years, from the mid-1990s', with the ascendance of privatization ethos, its base itself has been eroded by over 1.7 million jobs, effectively bringing the reservations to an end.

The reservations have accentuated the divide among the Dalits – both, inter as well as intra castes. While intra caste divide is suppressed under caste identity, the inter caste divide has led to ugly quarrels for the share of reservations, which surfaced first between Malas and Madigas in Andhra Pradesh in 1995 and by now has spread to most states, completely demolishing the idea of the Dalit.

If one takes a dispassionate glance at the situation of the Dalits, one is pained to see that except for the rise of a miniscule middle class – which is just about ten per cent – their relative condition largely remains the same as at the dawn of the Dalit movement. On most development parameters Dalits still significantly lag behind the non-Dalit population.[18] The Dalits are not a homogenous people; there is inequality among them, both social and economic. For instance, a section of them called manual scavengers are almost untouchables even to other Dalits. Despite the laws to eliminate manual scavenging system and the persistent struggle of its victims, there is little improvement. There are about 13 *lakh* (1.3 million) manual scavengers in the country living in abominable conditions.

The Dalits are predominantly a rural people, their urbanization ratio being half of that for the general population. The post-independence policies in rural India, such as land reforms and Green Revolution, were systematically driven, while meeting the needs of the capitalists, to create a class of rich farmers from among the populous shudra castes, as an ally of the central ruling classes. This change entailed many concomitant changes in the social and political sphere. In the political sphere, the newly empowered and enriched shudra castes developed political ambition and floated their own regional parties and with their sheer numbers began threatening the mainstream parties. The castes and communities, particularly the marginalized ones like the Dalits, became important – and thereby vulnerable too – for political manipulations. In the social sphere, on account of spread of capitalist relations in rural areas, the traditional *jajmani* relations of interdependence were decimated, reducing the Dalits to be the rural proletariat utterly dependent on the farm wages from the rich farmers. The erstwhile upper caste landlords were replaced by the shudra caste rich farmers who assumed the baton of Brahmanism. The resultant class contradiction between the Dalits as farm labourer and the rich farmers would spill out through the familiar fault lines of castes, giving rise to a new genre of atrocities. It first erupted in Kilvenmeni in Tamil Nadu, where forty four Dalits, mainly women and children, were burnt alive by the landlords and their henchmen in 1968. These atrocities would soon spread all over and assume menacing proportions. The caste atrocities, which could be taken as proxy for casteism, did not show any definitive trend until the 1980s', but after 1990 it clearly depicts a secular rising trend.[19] The rising agrarian crisis in rural India due to neoliberal policies and growing cultural assertion of Dalits have been the major cause for this rising trend in atrocities.

Sketching the Scenario

To extrapolate the current trend as the Dalit future into the next three to four decades and beyond from the current trend might prove to be a scary exercise. On the one side, the tiny Dalit middle class has become overwhelmingly visible in the towns and cities of India and in the form of a sizable Diaspora, that has taken 'Dalit' and Ambedkar into international arena; or in the form of the Dalit capitalists who have been flaunting their Mercedes and BMWs and claiming that they are 'job givers and not job seekers'; or in the form of certain outfits like BAMCEF (The All India Backward (SC, ST, OBC) and Minority Communities Employees Federation) who hold their five star conferences from *taluka* to international levels; or in the form of politicians who never forget to display their power and riches. On the other hand, the 90 per cent Dalits, sans any support, are being pushed off the margins by the social Darwinist juggernaut of neoliberal policies. In the times of general crisis, the caste divide rather works towards scapegoating the Dalits. Thus, it is difficult to conceive the future scenario of the Dalits in generic terms.

While the urban middle class of the Dalits is economically well off, the umbilical cord of many of its members still links them to their caste. Even otherwise most have to fall back to their caste for their need of social belonging. This linkage stands them automatically in an advantageous position as opinion leaders, although they no more understand the issues of the masses, leave apart possessing their consciousness. What gets projected, as a result, to the outside world, are the class concerns of the urban middle class. This has been an unfortunate feature of the Dalit movement right from the beginning. It is through this process that reservations have overwhelmed all other issues of the Dalits. The lower strata, rather than identifying with others of their ilk, prefer to be led by their own caste-men, obviating the germination of class consciousness. The caste identity naturally leads to fragmentation along the sub-castes, resultantly giving numerous groups among the Dalits divided along the caste and class lines.

The caste ties weaken with each passing generation. The second and third generation of the urban middle class Dalits do not display the same intensity of caste consciousness as their parents. With their next generation, the caste ties perhaps would be too weak to be relevant. Many of them would have married inter-caste and living far away from their locales. Although their number is bound to grow, they would still be insignificant vis-a-vis the majority, for whom caste would still constitute a life-world for a foreseeable future. It is the future of these people that is the focus of this paper. Castes are a complex of social and economic processes and hence need both to mitigate them. What the Dalits need is the multi-parametric empowerment, viz., individual, socio-economic, socio-political and socio-cultural empowerment, proxied by such variables as health and education; land and employment; democracy; and modernity, respectively. Paradoxically, neoliberal policies have created a severe crisis along each of these dimensions.

India never had a proper public health care system, which has further deteriorated under the onslaught of neoliberal policies with the alibi of fiscal discipline. Similar impact is seen on all public services. The education system, which had evolved into a multi-layered system, stands legitimised through the so called Right to Education Act and is fast moving towards privatization. Many schools meant for the lower strata, both in rural and urban areas, are closing down.[20] Education is becoming secularly inaccessible to the Dalits as it was ritually forbidden until colonial times. While, elementary education is accepted as the public good by the government, higher education is declared to be private good to be provided with commercial logic. The social Darwinist ethos of neo-liberalism has eroded democracy. It is reduced to a sterile ritual of periodical elections but without any voice to people. The state wearing all masks of democracy is transformed into a fascist state out to curb any dissent right in the bud. Culturally, there has been an upsurge of fundamentalism and a move towards anti-modern values in response to globalization driven under the new policies. The rise of Hindutva[21] and its aggressive reversal of whatever little was accomplished by way of absorption of modern values is aggravating the crisis of living for the Dalit masses.

Visions for the Future

Although India needs a thorough going revolution to do away the accumulated rot, it may be pure wishful thinking to imagine it happening over a foreseeable future of a few decades. Alternately, if revolution itself is rethought as a series of reforms, the tactical steps towards the strategic goal, the frustration stemming from impossibility of the goal may be overcome and all people could be motivated to contribute to a series of changes that are seen as doable. My vision for a horizon of three to four decades will be to see India moving towards abolishing castes and communal consciousness and tangibly marching towards equality and justice. It is crucially pivoted on a premise that Dalit emancipation is not a sectarian issue but is integral with emancipation of humankind. The following reforms may be initiated to be accomplished over this time horizon. While they fall well within the realm of peoples' imagination and so can be considered feasible, they are not sans hurdles. Rather, many of these innocuous looking reforms could be alarming enough to the ruling classes, that they would pose a formidable resistance. In face of the demand coming from the larger masses of the people, who could hopefully be mobilized for them, the resistance might melt away.

1. *Outlaw castes*

The vision for the Dalit emancipation as Ambedkar had articulated has been the annihilation of castes.[22] Unfortunately, the entire infrastructure of the Dalit movement itself being based on castes, it has become extremely difficult to actualize it. Ambedkar was led to believe that caste system was rooted in Hindu scriptures and hence unless they were destroyed, it would not be possible to annihilate castes. Seeing the latter as an impossible task, he chose an exit path of conversion to Buddhism. The experience of centuries with previous conversions (to Islam, Christianity and Sikhism) as well as of the nearly six decades with conversion to Buddhism itself, clearly invalidates this belief. Instead of emancipating the Dalits, these conversions have infected the new religious societies with castes. The post-colonial ruling classes intrigued not only in preserving castes but also providing them with multi-layered fortification by making a Dalit icon in Ambedkar as its chief architect, and directly associating a plethora of benefits with them. The contemporary castes are thus sourced more from the Constitution than any Hindu religious scriptures. As Marx had prophesied, the spread of capitalist relations indeed loosened the ritualistic hold of castes. If they had been supplemented with proper pubic policies, the castes could have been nearly routed out by now. The current castes are a cultural residue basically enlivened by the constitutional provisions. I am aware, millennia-old social structures may not be erased merely with public policy but it can surely be choked to its eventual demise. If the Constitution abolished castes and all the so-called social justice paraphernalia, and stipulated a framework for people oriented policies, castes could be rendered irrelevant within years. Abolition of castes in the Constitution would mean abolition of caste identities from public spaces. What would remain is the secular inequality which may be dealt with by the peoples' class struggle.

2. *Institute true 'secularism'*

Secularism is separation of religion from politics. Religion would be the private affair of people, which may gradually be weakened by promoting scientific temper in society. But the state should neither assume any role in religious affairs of people nor should it allow people to bring in religion in public spaces. Although, it may not be conventionally identified with the Dalits as they are a miniscule minority community, they are negatively impacted by the religious upsurge in society, particularly that of Hinduism. Moreover, insofar as Hinduism is source ideology of castes, it directly conflicts with their project of annihilation of castes. It also has huge implications in building up class unity of the people. There is no point in claiming that Indian Constitution is already secular in its *sarva dharma sambhava* (equality feelings for all religions) attitude. It has been a vile subterfuge for the ruling classes to use religion as a scalpel to manipulate people.

3. *Revamp reservations*

Reservations may be delinked from castes by creating a separate schedule, with definitive metrics to be phased out within a definite time frame. Insofar as the BCs/OBCs are the major perpetrators of caste atrocities on the Dalits, their intermingling might help dampen their contradictions. The reservations thereafter should be revamped to be family based. The families within the schedule, defined as a unit of married couple with their children, would get preference over those who had already availed of reservation. The schema can be drawn scientifically and implemented easily with the help of technology. It would dampen the public appeal that exists today for reservations and pave the way for their abolition.

4. *Abolish political reservations*

Although the original struggle waged by Ambedkar was for reservations in political institutions such as legislative assemblies, parliament, local government institutions, etc., he became increasingly sceptical about their utility, particularly after the Poona Pact. In the joint electorates, the consent of majority community being necessary for election, the reserved candidates have to be theoretically subservient to the majority. This process empirically produced only 'stooges', to use Kanshiram's famous term. Even Ambedkar himself had realized the impossibility of any Dalit getting elected against the majority candidate through his own contests in 1952 and 1954. He was sceptical about it even while writing the Constitution, but the events had overwhelmed him and he had to agree, albeit with the limitation of 10 years. It is time they are scrapped immediately.

5. *Replace the FPTP with the PR system*

Castes and religion in conjunction with the First-Past-the-Post (FPTP) type of election method has ensured perpetuation of rule of the traditional elites, India's new ruling classes. The FPTP system could be said to be singularly unsuitable for India with its fragmented polity into infinite castes, ethnicities, races, languages, religion, etc. It was a deliberate choice of the ruling classes, treating them as default as coming from British system. It should be replaced by the customized Proportional Representation (PR) system. The FPTP system in theory itself negated democracy as at least forty per cent people would never find their representation in ruling bodies. The PR system overcomes that lacuna. With the possibility of representation, even the smaller castes/communities would be motivated to coagulate and demolish the concept of dominant community. As a system that guarantees representation to every citizen it is certainly better than the FPTP system.

6. *Abolish private property in land*

Land is a crucial asset for rural people of which the Dalits are a part. It signifies not only their economic well-being but also their social and political status. Land distribution is so skewed in India that the top 9.5 per cent households own 56.6 per cent land. Ten per cent households do not own any land and if homestead land is excluded, 41.6 per cent are the landless. Needless to state, the incidence of landlessness is far more pronounced among the Dalits than among the general population. Caste being integral with the village power structure and land being its signifier, it holds almost the key to the caste question. It can be accomplished by abolition of private property in land beyond homesteads. All cultivable lands may be nationalized and parcelled out to village collectives formed by the families desirous of cultivating lands in common on the basis of established local knowledge and relevant modern technologies. The compensation for taking over the lands can be easily designed for attenuating returns over a certain period after which the title would be fully passed to the state. The state should undertake to provide the knowledge, technology, and credit inputs to these collectives. All other land should be in commons, governed by village collectives that are run on democratic and egalitarian basis.[23] It will bring in community management of village assets and ecology on the basis of decentralized participatory democracy which would submerge the existing contradictions that manifest through the familiar fault lines of castes. The state should catalyse and facilitate this structural change. The economic stakes in common enterprise within a village or cluster of villages will further help to negate the residual traces of castes.

7. Universal public health care system

Although not specifically concerned with the Dalits, the incidence of health deficiencies being far larger among them, a universal health care system needs to be instituted.[24]

8. Neighbourhood school system

Education, like health, constitutes the basic instrumentality in peoples' empowerment. The state must provide free, compulsory, and equal quality education to all children up to minimum higher secondary level, that is, 12th standard, through a neighbourhood school system. This should include the education of the children from 0 to 6 ages along with their nutritional care, which constitutes their foundation. The Constitution of India, Part IV, had envisaged such a system of education (although not explicitly stated) up to the age of 14 years, but it was changed to exclude 0 to 6 years vide the 83rd Constitutional amendment. The present multi-layered education system, paradoxically legitimated by the Right to Education Act, with its intrinsic elitist bias, has virtually excluded the Dalits from meaningful education. The proposed system will eliminate the foundational inequality and ensure that the new born children are brought up with the same inputs.[25]

9. Manufacturing and service cooperatives

There may be significant potential in setting up manufacturing and service units as decentralized community cooperatives in rural areas depending upon their location and resources. There is a case of Kutumbakkam village near Chennai which demonstrated possibility of such entrepreneurship in the present circumstances, catalysed just by a single individual without any institutional support.[26] In the context of jobless growth in the organised sector, these community enterprises will not only sustain the rural masses but also will root out caste consciousness. If in future institutional support is made available through the above said reforms, it could have immense possibilities. At the minimum, there is a huge promise of agro-based industries using local resources within sustainability paradigm. The potential for biomass energy through agricultural waste, organic manure for organic farming, agro-based industries, ancillaries, and even for becoming the human-power-intensive supply node for conventional industries hold out infinite possibilities.[27] They could create jobs within the villages and still be part of global supply chains. Likewise, the service sector has rapidly grown and is expected to further grow. Many of the services, which were performed by the poor people, are getting corporatized, benefitting the capitalist. They could be recaptured by local people eliminating rent-seeking intermediaries.

10. *Decentralized development*

Village agro-cooperatives can be the harbinger for decentralized development in rural India. The surplus generated through the village based cooperatives and allied industries could be ploughed back into the developmental project for the local communities. They could build schools, hospitals, training centres, recreation centres, etc., based on their specific needs. The principle of decentralized and sustainable development could be better deployed by the people themselves than the so called experts. The regional, state and central planning bodies may coordinate these development initiatives but they would essentially remain 'bottom up'. Many such experiments have been carried out in certain pockets of the country holding out promise for scaling them up. See for example, the initiative of the Dalit women farmers of Deccan Development Society, at www.ddsindia.com; see also other examples at www.vikalpsangam.org. The state should provide inputs in terms of technology and management for planning for local development on a sustainable basis. Involvement of entire village population across caste and communities into economic activity with common interests will surely help in eradicating caste consciousness. This, and other measures listed above will effectively sensitise people at the grassroots about the importance of environment for their sustainable living.

11. *Make directive principles operative*

Ambedkar's vision for India is relegated to either inert phrases of the Preamble or its Part IV that contains the Directive Principles of State Policy, both of which are unenforceable. Both remain a moral force in the paradigm of increasing amorality. While the ruling classes would overdo one of its articles (Art 48) that bans cow slaughter, the rest are conveniently ignored. This misdirected Article should be scrapped lest it unleashes the biggest disaster on the rural economy. In view of this experience, both the preamble and the Directive Principles should be made enforceable.

12. *Montesquieu's principle for democratic governance*

The sixteenth century French philosopher Montesquieu gave the Doctrine of Separation of Powers between the three wings of the democratic government to have a system of checks and balances. He had warned that placing power in the hands of only one organ or group in a government entails tyranny. The Executive and Legislature in India have theoretically been fused together with only the higher judiciary having the semblance of independence. Even that is sought to be eroded these days and it is a matter of time that it is gone. These checks and balances are particularly important to the lower strata of the society as it assures them the basic rule of law.

13. *Anti-Discrimination Commission*

With the above reforms, most factors responsible for the enduring misery of the Dalits would be done away with. However, such structural remedies cannot completely rectify processes, which would display at the least cultural drag. This residue may be controlled by the institution of an Anti-Discrimination Commission, which would be a watchdog against the practice of discrimination on account of castes and communities. It could be vested with summary powers to punish the violators.

14. Accountability in governance

The state obligations are discharged by the public servants. The entire state apparatus having been adopted in entirety from the colonial regime tends to behave in a highhanded manner with an utter lack of systemic accountability. For instance, the biggest violators of the law are the state functionaries themselves. The law for abolition of manual scavenging is violated by the government departments. The state governments file false affidavits that they do not have any manual scavengers. The people-oriented accountability structure needs to be created with republican ethos, where people of India as sovereign shall be supreme. The above listed reforms will necessarily impinge upon the governance structure towards people-orientation. Nonetheless, conscious efforts in this direction shall be invested, making the entire state oriented to serve the people.

Conclusion

The times are opportune to push these reforms as the crises of democracy have already reached past its zenith, which occasionally manifest into peoples' ire against the ruling classes, be it corruption or VVIP (Very Very Important People) culture. They are suppressed by the increasingly authoritarian state with its might.

The objective condition of the Dalits is expectedly worse. On every conceivable dimension, they are fast losing out. Their politics has long become the adjunct of the ruling classes. Socio-culturally there has been little difference in their condition. Economically, their condition is fast worsening as the job opportunities in the organized sector are drying up and they are being thrown into uncertainty in the exploitative informal sector. The spectre of hopelessness is gripping their youth. As a matter of dejection with the status quo it is reflected in their nostalgic devotion to Dr. Ambedkar; but since it is mediated through their middle classes, they do not realize it. The system appears sans options and that itself has become its shield against change. The above reforms, conceived well within the parliamentary framework and largely unthreatening, may constitute an option for people.

However, there are a plethora of hurdles too in the path. The major one rather, is expected from the Dalit side itself. The tiny Dalit middle class has hegemonic hold over the Dalit masses as it was to be the custodian of their interests. It exhibits array of visions ranging from the cultural renaissance through Buddhism to the empowerment through political opportunism and lately to the economic resurgence through Dalit capitalism. All these of course are singularly divorced from the woes of the Dalit masses, but the latter are still dragged along after them like herds of deer running after a mirage. Dalits had embraced Buddhism following Ambedkar but failed to even create an alternate cultural paradigm away from the Hindu frame. Ambedkar brought the Dalit question into politics and saw it to be the master key to all their problems. Kanshiram and Mayawati creatively exploited this dictum, taking their Bahujan Samaj Party to repeatedly capture political power, but in course of time it became just another ruling class party. The economic sphere remained largely neglected in the emancipation schema of the Dalits, on account of their early contention with communists, identified with economism.[28] Whatever little of economics remained in the Dalit universe was confined to reservations. While reservations are still uncritically relied upon, a section supporting the dominating dictum of global capital has begun flaunting Dalit capitalism, ignoring Ambedkar's caution that Brahmanism and capitalism as the two enemies of the Dalits (Keer, 1990). These diverse, confusing and reactionary overtures of the Dalit middle classes shall be the biggest hurdle in the path of these reforms.

The other hurdles shall be raised by the ruling classes. Even though couched as reforms well within the liberal framework of politics, in the context of the current system, they are too radical to be swallowed. Each one would seriously dent their interests and hence they would not give in without resistance. But any change from the status quo is expected to meet with such resistance from the entrenched classes. Only the determined movement of the masses can overcome it. If the people see this to be a viable and valuable option, to build such a movement may not be a far cry, notwithstanding the continuing neoliberal onslaught to transform them into self-seeking discrete individuals and overtures of the fascist State to curb any dissent in the bud.

Endnotes

1. Dalit, denoting a collective of all the erstwhile untouchable castes that negates ritual differences between them and highlights their occupation in social production, their relation to the means of production, their service role in social organization, the dimensions of the share of social wealth and mode of acquiring it—all elements of Lenin's definition of class (Lenin, 1965 pp. 421).
2. It is the system in which society is stratified into four *varnas*—*Brahman, Kshatriya, Vaishya and Shudra*—determined by birth and held in hierarchy, attributed to *Purushsukta* in *Rig Veda*.
3. The three Round Table Conferences were held in London to decide upon the constitutional reforms in India as per the report of the Simon Commission. Dr. Ambedkar won separate electorates against the fierce opposition of Gandhi (Aktor & Deliege, 2010, pp.111).
4. Primary Census Abstract, Census of India, 2011 (Government of India, 2011).
5. The total estimated population of the Dalits would exceed 320 million, if one adds 20 million of Christian Dalits and 100 million of Muslim Dalits to the official figure.
6. Right in his speech in the Mahad Conference in March 1927, Dr. Ambedkar sought to link the Untouchables' struggle for civil rights to the French Revolution and adopted 'Educate, Organize, Agitate', the Fabian slogan, as the mast of his fortnightly paper, *Bahishkrit Bharat (Ostracized Bharat)*.
7. The influence of John Dewey, the proponent of pragmatism and also an American Fabian, pervaded Ambedkar's life as noted by many scholars (Mukherjee, 2009, pp. 345-70; Mitra, 2013, pp. 301).
8. Political reservations, along with preferment policy for admissions into educational institutions and public employment, came through the Poona Pact between Gandhi and Ambedkar. The present quota system in place of preferment policy was instituted in 1943 at the instance of Ambedkar while he was a member of the Viceroy's Executive Council.
9. They can be clubbed under protective and developmental measures. See Extracts from the Constitution of India, especially relevant to Social Justice & Empowerment. Available at: socialjustice.nic.in/pdf/constprovmsje.pdf (last accessed on April, 2015).
10. Ambedkar won separate electorates for the Dalits in the Round Table Conferences, but succumbing to pressures from Gandhi, who had declared fast unto death against them, he signed the Poona Pact, which was incorporated into the Government of India Act, providing for the political reservations.

11. The Constitution (Scheduled Tribes) Order, 1950. Available at: http://lawmin.nic.in/ld/subord/rule9a.htm. (last accessed on 4 April 2015). See also essay on Adivasi futures in this volume.

12. Article 340 of the Indian Constitution, provided for promotion of the welfare of the OBCs.

13. Extract from Rajya Sabha, 2 September 1953. Rajya Sabha Official Debate. Available at: http://rsdebate.nic.in/handle/123456789/588187 (last accessed 4 April, 2015).

14. He was defeated by a Chambhar candidate, N. S. Kajrolkar (Venkatarangaiya, 1953).

15. On 13 October 1935, in a public meeting at Yewale (near Nashik) he declared his firm resolve, 'though I have been born a Hindu, I will not die a Hindu' (Sangharakshita, 2006, pp. 61).

16. Out of the total Buddhist population of 7,955,207, 73.4 % were in Maharashtra. The other states with significant Buddhist population are: Karnataka 3.9 lakh (390,000) and Uttar Pradesh 3 lakh (300,000); data from the Census of India, 2011, Table 21: Distribution of Population by Religion.

17. Primary surveys include the Wai taluka (block) survey conducted in 17 villages in 1958; Gokhale Institute of Politics and Economics survey conducted in 25 villages in 1962; Harijan Sevak Sangh survey conducted in 192 villages in 1970; Marathwada survey conducted in 95 villages in 1991 (Thorat, 2007).

18. See, Selected Socio-Economic Statistics India, 2011. Available at: mospi.nic.in/mospi_new/.../sel_socio_eco_stats_ind_2001_28oct11.pdf (last accessed 4 April, 2015).

19. The atrocities, as recorded by National Crime Research Bureau (NCRB) have risen from 33,507 in 2001 to 47,064 in 2014. See NCRB, 1994 and 2014. Also see Teltumbde, 2016.

20. Nearly 70,000 rural schools are closed/being closed down under the 'merger and rationalisation' programme, *The Hindu*, 13 October, 2014.

21. Represents the upper caste counter-revolution that believes India is a Hindu nation with its basis in Hindu culture that valorizes hierarchy.

22. One need not accept his prescription as in 'Annihilation of Castes', but his basic diagnosis of the Indian society that it should be completely rid of castes is indisputable.

23. See also essays on Power Futures, Concluding essay, and the essay Dare to Dream, in this volume.

24. See essay on Health Futures in this volume.

25. See essay on Education Futures in this volume.

26. See essay on Localization in this volume.

27. See essay on Biomass based rural revitalization in this volume.

28. The communists, according to the Marxian metaphor of 'base-superstructure' valorised economic struggle and ignored all others, including the caste struggle. The Dalit movement did not agree and in the process took an exactly opposite stand valorising socio-religious struggle and ignoring economic struggle (Omvedt, 2006, pp. 75).

References

Aktor, M. and Robert Deliège, (eds), 2010, *From Stigma to Assertion: Untouchability, Identity and Politics in Early and Modern India*, Copenhagen: Museum Tusculanum Press.

Government of India, 2011, Census of India, Primary Census. Abstract. http://www.censusindia.gov.in/2011census/hlo/pca/pca_data.html. (last accessed 18 January, 2016).

Jadhav, K.N., 1991, *Dr. Ambedkar and the Significance of His Movement*, Mumbai: Popular Prakashan.

Jaffrelot, Christophe, 2009, *Dr. Ambedkar's Strategies Against Untouchability and the Caste System*, Indian Institute of Dalit Studies, Working Paper Series, Volume III (4).

Keer, Dhananjay, 1990, *Dr. Ambedkar: Life and Mission*, Mumbai: Popular Prakashan.

Lenin, V., 1965, 'A Great Beginning', *in V. I. Lenin, Collected Works*, Vol. 29, Moscow: Progress Publications, pp. 421.

Mitra, Keya, 2013, 'Ambedkar and the Constitution of India: A Deweyan Experiment' in *Democratic Experimentalism*, Brian E.Butler (ed), Amsterdam: Rodopi.

Mukherjee, Arun P., 2009, 'B.R. Ambedkar, John Dewey, and the Meaning of Democracy', *New Literary History*, Volume 40(2), Spring. pp. 345-370.

NCAER, 2014, *Biggest caste survey: One in four Indians admit to practising untouchability*, http://www.ncaer.org/news_details.php?nID=91 (last accessed 18 January, 2016).

NCRB, 1993 & 2014, *Crime in India*, New Delhi: National Crime Research Bureau.

Omvedt, Gail, 2006, *Dalit Visions*, Hyderabad: Orient Blackswan.

Sangharakshita, 2006, *Ambedkar and Buddhism*, New Delhi: Motilal Banarsidass.

Sengupta, Subodh Chandra, 1984, *Swami Vivekananda and Indian Nationalism*, Kolkata: Sahitya Sansad.

Teltumbde, Anand, 1999, *Theorising the Dalit Movement: A Viewpoint*, http://www.ambedkar.org/research/THEORISING%20THE%20DALIT%20MOVEMENT.htm. (last accessed 18 January, 2016).

Teltumbde, Anand, 2010, *The Persistence of Castes, The Khairlanji Murders & India's Hidden Apartheid*, London: Zed Books.

Teltumbde, Anand, 2014, 'By the ruling class, for the ruling class', *The Hindu*, 23 April.

Teltumbde, Anand, 2015a, 'On Reservations', *Mainstream Weekly*, Vol. LIV(1), 26 December, pp. 71-80.

Teltumbde, Anand, 2015b, 'Contents and Discontents of Indian Secularism', *in Secularism under Siege: Revisiting the Indian Secular State*, Zahir Ali (ed.), New Delhi: Aaka, pp. 181.

Teltumbde, Anand, 2016, 'Two Years of an Ambedkar *Bhakt* and the Plight of Dalits', *Economic & Political Weekly*, June 4, Vol LI(23), pp. 10-11.

Thorat, Sukhadeo and Prashant Negi, 2007, *Exclusion and Discrimination: civil rights violations and atrocities in Maharashtra,* Working Paper Series, Vol. II(2), 2007, New Delhi: Indian Institute of Dalit Studies.

Venkatarangaiya, M., 1953, *The General Election in the City of Bombay,* Bombay: Vora & Co.

Envisioning India without Gender and Patriarchy?
Why Not?

Manisha Gupte

Summary

The notions of patriarchy that legitimise the control of men over women's production, reproduction, and sexuality dominate the present world. Envisioning India without gender and patriarchy might be difficult, but the essay treads this path and brings out glimpses of India without gender binaries and patriarchy. A society without gender binaries will refute sexual interactions as power-laden transactions; people will have reproductive and sexual rights; women will have open and safe access to private and public spaces and inequalities related to caste, class and religion would be abolished.

The essay argues for an intersectional approach and re-visioning of politics through lived realities of the subordinated, to fight the issues of inequality and injustice. This will force the removal of any kind of hierarchies related to caste, gender, class, ethnicity, and sexuality and also strengthen the values of equality and democratic participation by centre-staging the knowledge and the wisdom of people who witness and experience discrimination.

Introduction[1]

During the past few years, young women from different countries have asked me if it was safe to travel to India, implying whether sexual assault was part of Indian culture. From being the 'dowry death' capital of the world, we had suddenly become its 'rape' capital. My reply would be that, of course rape happens in India all the time[2] and that sexual violence, especially from family members often doesn't even come to light. Having said that, I would ask, if 'date rape' was part of western culture. My intention was not to rebuff allegations, nor to insult another culture, but to emphasise that patriarchal manifestations differ globally. Date rape happens *because* people have the freedom to date a number of people before choosing one's steady partner. Crimes against women in public places at night happen *because* women are outside the home in the dark, and crimes in the name of honour happen *because* young people exercise agency against the diktats of their elders. The constant tension between structures and agency can manifest in the form of increased backlash violence, yet on the other hand, it also offers sites for resistance and change.

Gender and Patriarchy in the Indian Context

Patriarchies all over the world (however distinct they might appear)[3] share certain commonalities, such as the rule of the father/male elder over most women and some men; men's legitimised control over women's production, reproduction and sexuality; gender roles and relations based on power and inequality; gender binaries; and the hegemony of the heterosexual family over all other forms of cohabitation or shared living.

Within Brahminical patriarchy[4] – a structure unique to India – caste, class, gender, sexuality and communalism interact and shape each other through endogamous marriage, wherein notions of purity, pollution and inherent hierarchy prevail. Control over women becomes crucial in maintaining boundaries between castes (Chakravarti, 2003). Historically, inclusion into the Hindu caste system entailed a proscription on women's remarriage, and relinquishing women's economic autonomy and right to choose sexual partners (Gatwood, 1985). In rural Pune district where I have worked since 1987, emulation of 'upper' castes meant not only giving up widow re-marriage or considering a woman's second marriage inferior, but also boycotting households where women had sexually 'transgressed' (Gupte, 2013). Within the double standards of brahminical patriarchy, poor and Dalit women had to be sexually available to powerful men. Thus, control of upper caste women's sexuality through child marriage, *sati* (the practice of a widow immolating herself on her husband's pyre), or enforced ascetic widowhood, and enforced cohabitation for untouchables as a rule could exist side by side.[5]

Control over women's wombs becomes imperative in patriarchy to ensure the purity of the male seed, because only legitimate heirs (sons) can carry forward the family name, property and fame. Accordingly, at no cost should women get pregnant outside marriage, and at no cost should they refuse to have a child within marriage. Families, kinships, markets and the State also manipulate women's wombs, deciding when a uterus is a useful or useless organ.

Manipulation of women's sexuality can take different forms. The Bedias of the states of Madhya Pradesh, Rajasthan and Uttar Pradesh,[6] often raise daughters to do sex-work, but veil and segregate their daughters-in-law (Agrawal, 2008). Strict, yet discrete codes of conduct for different women within the same family ensure the economic survival of the family, while ensuring chaste wives for the sons. The diminution and stigmatisation[7] of *devadasis* (slaves of gods) (Tilley, 2011), who in the past were accomplished artists, earners and valued members of their natal family in Southern India, is another example of how patriarchy and caste subverted what might once have been a matrilocal or matrilineal system.

The moot point is not whether matriarchy, matriliny, matrilocality or any other form of woman-headed communities ever existed in India. Besides, patriarchy would be a faulty template since matriarchies of the past didn't exist as mirror images of current patriarchies. Suffice to say that the gender just society of the future would neither be patriarchal nor matriarchal.

Public and private patriarchies[8] operate hand in hand to disenfranchise women in both spaces, denying equal access to public institutions and experiences (Walby, 1990). Thus deeper structures that perpetuate discrimination or violence, be they patriarchy, caste, class, heteronormativity,[9] racism or majority status in any society need to be constantly addressed. A constantly evolving and dynamic approach to patriarchal controls would be the way forward, with race, ethnicity, caste, gender, class, sexuality, livelihood options, physical and mental ability, nation states and cultural nationalism becoming integral to our understanding of patriarchy. The growing engagement of feminist groups with issues of sex-workers, people living with disabilities, people with diverse gender orientation or same-sex preference signifies such strengthened progressive politics.

Challenges to Dismantling Multiple Patriarchies

The current political scenario is hardly conducive for progressive movements to thrive. Ethnic 'cleansing' outside the home along with control of one's own women within the home, and the impunity with which 'rape-culture' (where brutal sexual violence against women is normalised) is justified, can silence women and minorities at the same time (Baxi, 2005).[10]

Increasing incidents of moral policing during the past decade indicate men's perceived loss of control over women's sexuality. Some of these include enforcement of dress codes; protests against Valentine's Day celebrations; attacks on women going to pubs; Islamophobic[11] terms such as *'love jihad'* (holy war propagated through love and marriage);

Operation Majnu (whereby the police/vigilante groups sniff out courting couples from secluded spots, publicly humiliate them and 'hand over' the girl to her parents); notifying parents when couples elope or start proceedings to marry under the Special Marriage Act, 1954; or, 'retrieving' girls after inter-caste or inter-religious marriages.

The increasing involvement of women in obscurantism and violent politics[12] reiterates the fact that no overarching commonality of experience unites all women, because they are divided along the lines of caste, class and religion (Butalia, 2001). Sisterhood solidarity crumbled when thousands of Hindu women marched to endorse the so-called sati of Roop Kanwar, a young woman in Rajasthan; when Muslim women marched in large numbers in the 1980s' to protest against the Supreme Court's judgement to grant maintenance rights to Shahbano, a seventy five year old Muslim woman; or when women enthusiastically participated in the tearing down of the Babri Masjid in 1992 and in the pogrom against Muslims in Gujarat in 2002. Sadly, communalism, in spite of being a patriarchal ideology that victimises women, has succeeded in drawing them out in great numbers to participate in the agenda of divisive and violent hate politics (Sarkar *et al.*, 1995). We know that women also participate in controlling, monitoring and in punishing deviance or exercise of choice by younger women of the household and are often complicit in crimes in the name of honour. This reminds us once more that patriarchy is not merely about physical male or female bodies, but that our location on other intersections determines whether we take on regressive or emancipatory positions.

The presence and support of a progressive group helps women recognise the connection between the personal and the political, and to address domination within private and public spheres (Gupte, 2012a). However, if external theorisation or activism substitutes 'insider' wisdom, participation and leadership, it cannot document or analyse patriarchy fully (Guru, 2002; Kamble, 2008). Dalit women's standpoint critiqued brahminical patriarchy and showed how the theorisation of intrinsic linkages of caste, patriarchy, sexuality and control over knowledge (evident in the life-mission and writings of Jotirao and Savitribai Phule and Ambedkar) had not received adequate attention, either at the level of theory or strategy of Indian feminism.

Conversely, progressive movements involved in caste or class struggle also urgently need to centre stage gender issues. Except in some instances,[13] a strong women's agenda was missing in many progressive movements in spite of the fact that women participated fully – feminist positions were often regarded as being divisive and irrelevant to the Indian context, or a threat to male hegemony within movements (Sen, 1990; Vindhya, 1990). Restrictive sexual mores and the control of romantic or sexual behaviour have been part of some progressive movements, with political groups taking on the role of the institution of the family; some others have essentialised women's nurturing or peaceful qualities, romanticising women's relationship with nature (ibid.).

What would India without Gendered Binaries and Patriarchy Look Like?

Faiz Ahmed Faiz, our great contemporary South Asian poet has promised us a compelling vision: "*Laazimhainke hum bhi dekhenge, woh din ke jiska waada hain*!![14] The very thought is heady, challenging and full of promises! Here are a few glimpses of a future without gendered binaries and patriarchy.

a) *Gendered roles and binaries*

Children brought up by parents who have transcended gender-binary roles, responsibilities, expectations and behaviour would not consider any task as being 'masculine' or 'feminine'. An androgynous man for example would consider housework to be his work as well, and not just as 'helping' his wife out. Similarly, a woman would not merely be 'supplementing' the household income.

People born intersex (individuals with genitalia that don't strictly conform to male/ female bodies)[15] would have full rights, with parents of newborns having empathetic peer support to deal with immediate issues arising at birth; thus bodies would not be mutilated at birth to be straitjacketed into the male /female binary. Sex assigned at birth would not be thrust upon any individual for life, and the full range of quality health care would be made available for any person who might want to change their body to another gender.

b) *The institution of marriage*

The right whether or not to marry, whom to marry, when to marry, how to marry and for how long to remain married would vest with the persons concerned, and not be dependent on parental authority or caste/religious considerations. Neither would discrimination against same-sex marriages or cohabitation exist. Separation and divorce would be made available on the requirement or demand of individuals, wherein property rights, custody (and rights) of children as well as full dignity of both partners would be protected.

'Marriage' could acquire wholly new forms in a society without patriarchy. No special benefits (legal, social, religious, economic or cultural) would be accorded to anybody just because they were legally married. Conversely, no rights of women (such as their name, identity, inheritance rights, place of residence and so on) would be taken away at marriage.

The patriarchal and hierarchal division between cohabiting married women and widowed[16]/separated/deserted/never married women, whether through obvious symbols of marriage, food or dress restrictions, segregation or discrimination would be challenged, including by women themselves. Further, even terms such as 'pre-marital' would be contested because they presume that marriage is *the* inevitable option in people's lives, and that some people are merely biding or wasting time until they locate the right spouse!

Motherhood would not be linked to marriage either. Hierarchy based on motherhood, be it infertility, childlessness, having no sons or bearing children outside marriage would be challenged. When women's real or perceived dependence on men would cease to exist then love, sexuality and parenthood would be based on intrinsic values such as shared joy and responsibility, rather than on the patriarchal institution of marriage. The institution of marriage and its counterpart, the institution of prostitution would wither away in a gender/caste/class/race equal society because sexual interactions (paid or unpaid) would no longer remain one-way, power-laden transactions, whether in the private or public sphere.

c) *Family and kinship*

Like marriage, the 'family' would metamorphose into a self-chosen and changing unit, based on mutual sharing and caring; moving beyond bloodlines, kinship, marriage or descent. The traditional hierarchy of the patriarch over all women and most men of the household and kinship would be over, and social parenting would be considered at par with biological parenting. Because of enhanced inter-generational understanding, parental control and traditional expectations including decisions related to careers, faith, sex and marriage, which impair children's aspirations, would cease to exist. Children won't be forced to bear names of their fathers or mothers, and certainly not of their caste.[17]

Individual, family, caste, religious or national honour won't be owned by men and embodied by their women. Honour would become an intrinsic value guiding individuals and groups towards enhanced personal ethics. As a result, its expression won't be violent or retributive, but introspective and accountable to basic tenets of human rights (Gupte, 2012a).

d) *Reproduction and sexuality*

Reproductive and sexual rights would exist for everyone, irrespective of marital status, and with respect for diverse forms of sexual expression between mutually consenting adults. They would become an integral part of universally available comprehensive health care for all. The decisions whether or not to have children, or when and how many children would become people-centred; not mandated by the market or State. Adoption, voluntary and safe contraception and abortion, infertility treatment, safe motherhood, parenting skills, health care and non-judgemental counselling would be accessible to anyone and everyone. Undue obsession with proving one's fertility and the quest for biological (or eugenically 'superior') children would not exist.

Sexuality will be discussed openly (even with growing children, in an age appropriate manner) in homes and in schools to make children aware of sexual abuse as well as positive sexuality, and to avoid moral panics or policing of young people. Mutilation or genital cutting of women to control their sexuality would not be acceptable.

Since marriage or motherhood would no longer create a wedge between women in a post-patriarchal society, the hypocritical division between 'good' and 'bad' women based on sexual morality won't exist any longer. The right to say 'No' and the right to say 'Yes' will go hand in hand, as one is meaningless without the other. People would have the right to enter or exit relationships safely, and with dignity and rights.

e) *Public and private patriarchies*

The artificial cleaving of public and private domains would be eliminated, and institutionalised disadvantage for women (for example, considering men to be heads of households, considering domestic violence to be a 'private' affair, or unequal access to property, credit, health care, education or equal wages for similar work) would cease to exist *de jure* (in law) as well as *de facto* (in reality). Women's right to work and choice of livelihood would include equal material and parental benefits, and a safe working environment that is free of harassment, exploitation, discrimination or humiliation.

Women will access public spaces without having to explain why they are there at that time of the day or night. Roads, transport and other public places would be safe and respectful of women's right to mobility. No justification will be accorded to sexual harassment of any kind, nor will victims/survivors of sexual assault or rape be subjected to humiliation or moral scrutiny. Social media that straddle the public and private domain will protect women's rights, without impeding their access to information and recreation.

Since dispossession within the natal family is patriarchy's way of propelling women into marriage, and impelling them to stay there forever, sons and daughters would inherit equally.[18] If and when women want to marry, no dowry or other transactions that denigrate women would exist. If and when couples decide to part, the property accumulated during their stay together would be equally divided between them.

Gender bias in law would be challenged and removed. For example, the gender discrimination in legal age at marriage in India (21 years for boys and 18 for girls) would be corrected because it pre-supposes bridegrooms to be older, more educated and earning partners, but brides to be physically 'mature' enough to bear babies.

f) *Caste*

The process of Sansrikisation (Srinivas, 1962), wherein restrictions are placed on women's sexuality, re-marriage and access to resources in order to move upward in the caste system, would be halted. Further, it would be a matter of shame to say that someone wilfully got their children married within their caste. In the long-term caste (not just 'untouchability') would become illegal since it is an inherently hierarchal and discriminatory structure. As a corollary, caste bodies (and their extra judicial punishments) would become illegal. Annihilation of caste,[19] as proposed by Ambedkar, would be part of the feminist agenda in India, and gender equality would be an integral component of the anti-caste movements.

g) *Violence and discrimination*

In a society where gender inequality has been challenged, gender based violence, and discrimination would never be justified or condoned. Homes especially will become safe for women, because that is where women are most at risk of being beaten, killed or raped. Women's access to justice would not encounter social or cultural obstacles.

Many contemporary issues will become 'non-issues'. For example, sex-determination during pregnancy won't matter, because there would be no discriminatory consequences upon acquiring this information. Similarly we may not require reservations for women once they have equal access to education and political representation, and if all forms of historical discrimination are eliminated. However, as we unearth new areas of discrimination and learn from nascent movements of hitherto unorganised groups, newer special measures (reservations) would have to be introduced in order to make the playing field equal for everyone. These affirmative actions would continue until equality of access opportunity and result is proven.[20]

When differences (natural or artificially created) between people are not used to 'other' someone, or to disadvantage anyone, 'differences' would cease to become discriminatory. These differences would be egalitarian, welcome and necessary because they would enrich society through diversity, be it of clothing, food, music, faiths or genders.

h) *Religion*

Religion would become a personal affair and not linked to governance or functioning of the State in any way. No religious symbols, display or rituals would be observed by State representatives in public spaces and functions. As long as religious holidays remain on the calendar of NGOs, every Indian religion would be represented, so that colleagues can visit people from different religions and participate in diverse celebrations. Patriarchal tenets of religion, such as the son conducting funeral rituals or cohabiting married women being privileged over others would become reprehensible.

In a world where almost every religion is beset with rising intolerance, conservatism and violent identity politics, the fear of cultural nationalism and fascism threaten human co-existence and democracy globally. Therefore special measures would guarantee that minority religions would not be relegated to second class citizenship, having to live in fear of violence, genocide, displacement, exile, stigma and disenfranchisement, nor be constantly expected to prove their 'patriotism' to bigots from the majority religion. Neither would women be at risk of sexual assault in moments of acute or protracted conflict.

Religious leaders would not be considered spokespersons of people following that faith, especially regarding issues concerning women. Human rights, including reproductive and sexual rights would not be compromised in the name of religion. Marriage and related affairs would not be governed by religion, and women would retain the right to their faith (or atheism) in marriage. Secular thought within each religion would be considered equally legitimate in opinion building, including in matters related to faith and religion. Critics of religion would have full freedom and respect; not having to face excommunication, death threats or assassinations.[21] A South Asian (SA) identity could be posited as a secular and inclusive option to narrow down religious identity, thereby including the common experience of western imperialism and colonisation (of most of the eight SA countries), and strategise for peaceful and respectful neighbourly co-existence.

The decision to (or not to) follow a particular belief would not be a 'given' at birth, but a decision made by an informed and consenting adult. Religious identity would be fluid and changeable, ranging from no faith to the practice of single or multiple faiths during any moment in a person's life. People with different religions would easily form a family unit.[22]

i) Intersectional approach to challenging structures of subordination

Since gender itself is an intersectional category that cannot be understood without locating the biological body within socio-political and cultural contexts, an intersectional approach to all our work is imperative. Further, caste and patriarchy will have to be simultaneously eliminated in South Asia because the caste system of Hindus exists in varying degrees, even among non-Hindu religions here. The universal category of class is also inherently linked to women's oppression; thus all progressive struggles would put up a collective resistance to these intersecting systems of domination through a non-hierarchal approach to all human rights of all people. It would avoid the pitfall of perpetual victimhood claims and violent masculinist expression of dissent in emerging identity based campaigns. It would also avoid slipping into the bind of cultural essentialism[23] or cultural relativism.[24] It would be imperative to respect multicultural diversity, and accept the legitimacy of subordinated women's lived realities, without accepting discrimination of any kind 'in the name of culture'. Movements which combine identity and recognition with redistribution (Fraser, 1996) and social justice, have the potential of perpetually remaining dynamic and inclusive. 'One for all, and all for one' would be the only way to move forward for all of us.

j) *Re-visioning our politics through the lived realities of subordinated and marginalised groups*

We need to democratise the feminist movements even further, because hitherto our leadership has largely come from middle-class, urban educated, *Savarna* (privileged 'upper' castes) Hindu activists. Irrespective of how sensitised such a leadership might be, viewing society 'from the top' has its own limitations. Centre-staging the knowledge and wisdom of those who have been marginalised or subordinated through any intersection of domination is imperative, because those at the bottom of the power pyramid, on account of their comprehensive and 'dual view', add significantly new dimensions in understanding power and in dismantling it.

It was through the assertion of autonomous Dalit women's organisations at regional and national levels in the 1990s'[25] (which drew debates and responses both from Left party-based as well as autonomous women's groups) that 'several crucial theoretical and political challenges, besides underlining the brahminism of the feminist movement and the patriarchal practices of dalit politics' were thrown up (Rege, 1998, pp. 42).[26] Unless feminist leadership centre-stages subordinated women, the quest for gender equality will never be fully realised. All we need to do first is to garner courage to unlearn our ways of thinking, being and doing.

Love, Aesthetics and Sense of Humour: Towards a wholesome movement

'Alas, why don't young people join our movements as they did in the 1970s' and 80s', and why do they gravitate instead toward the scarily and steadily growing right-wing?' That is a question we ask of ourselves, and often. Why do women come to our counselling centres when they face domestic violence, yet practice rituals for the long life of their violent husbands? Why do young people find cultural expression in parochial movements, riding noisy motorbikes, flaunting flags of conservative parties?

Along with taking up issues that concern young people of today, aesthetics and a sense of humour will be an integral part of all our movements, and the culturally rich, secular and vibrant new society we want to create. Beauty, celebrations and laughter are required in spite of (and also because of) all the political ugliness that surrounds us. Sadness, injustice and horror will remain all through our lifetimes, but it would be even sadder if all of us just wilted away as sombre, grim and resentful people. Our new movements will teach us the balance of when to take ourselves seriously and when not to.

The feminist movement more easily allows for deep personal friendships that encourage discussion on intimate joys, sorrows and confusions, and wherein laughter, singing, hugging, dancing, shoulder massages, crying, and sharing mundane aspects of caring for children or ageing parents are not considered frivolous, or at variance with one's commitment to social transformation. We need real friendships that support each other even in 'non-movement' moments, so that the traditional family doesn't become the only real support in difficult times such as illness or financial stress. If we truly want to see families that transcend relationships based on bloodlines, marriage, kinship, patriarchy, caste or heteronormativity, now is a good time to begin constructing those.

Possibilities Exist even Today, if only We're Ready to Learn from Them!

- The working class in many ways is able to transcend the strict social mores of those placed 'above' them. I have seen many instances of social parenting among slums/poor households in Mumbai when we[27] worked there in the 1970s' and 80s'. Women breastfed and nurtured each other's children when the mother went out to work. Years later I saw how Zuleikha,[28] born male, but wanting to become a woman all her growing life, was accepted (slowly but surely) by her working class family, even after she ran away as a teenager with a group of *hijras*,[29] wore *sarees* and got herself castrated. The non-judgemental attitude of her family and neighbours helped her return to her studies and complete her doctorate in a reputed academic institution. She is comfortable living 'like a woman' and is proud to have her 'transgender' identity on her passport.
- Sudhir's[30] identity is that of *koti* (transgender) and not hijra. He dresses as a man at home, but as a woman when he does sex-work, or spends time with other kotis. His androgynous and fluid gender identity is not easy, because he really wants to be

a woman all the time. He's married in deference to his mother's wish, and because his wife liked him best from all the proposals that came her way, preferring to marry him than stay with her parents. He loves his wife, but in a non-sexual way. His wife has accepted him along with his transgender identity and his sex-work, but continues to tease and seduce him, knowing well that he dislikes having sex with women. She has negotiated sex with him by drawing out a time-table, to claim her conjugal rights every week. The unusual and playful bond that Sudhir and his wife share in their unconventional marriage caricatures most patriarchal marriages that are based on male-supremacy.

Sudhir is aware of the patriarchal power he possesses within his household. When I asked him how he would feel if his wife did sex-work or got into a same-sex relationship, Sudhir said he would feel unburdened, because then they would understand each other better. He says theirs was a happy marriage because both he and his wife 'were women'. Soft spoken, straightforward and humorous, Sudhir, to my mind is an example of how counter-hegemonic masculinity could be in another, gentler world.

- Even though the closed commune of the hijra community replicates the hierarchy of the private domain of a patriarchal household in some ways (Revathi, 2009) yet, among these fictive kinships the asexual *guru-chela*[31] relationship overrides sexual relationships with men, and lasts for years, sometimes even over a lifetime. Unlike real kinships based on caste and religion, one can change a guru, and thereby abdicate a guru's religious faith each time, after settling financial liabilities.

All relationships within the community are female oriented and matrilineal (labelled as mother, sister, aunt, grand-mother or daughter). New 'relatives' can be obtained when one changes a guru and there is freedom to maintain or disregard ritualistic bonds with earlier fictive relatives. Sexual relationships with men are coveted (with strong sexual jealousies being exhibited too) but they cannot override the internal kinship relationships with other hijras. Many hijras foster or adopt children; sometimes also becoming mothers to men and women from outside the community.[32]

- Kamlabai's[33] home was a deep learning and unlearning exercise for me. A Dalit devadasi engaged in sex-work, she convinced the weeping wife of her Jain *maalak* (favoured client)[34] that she wasn't the cause of marital discord between husband-wife. Kamlabai had learnt the hard way that the only way for women to survive within patriarchy was to work hard and also remain free of men's control over one's sexuality and labour. Her maalak insisted on living with her, with Kamlabai owning her living quarters, maintaining control over her earnings, and even getting him to baby-sit the children of the younger women who worked in her brothel. She encouraged him to visit his wife, children and grandchildren, sending gifts for all of them each time. Within her patriarchal marriage in a conservative household, the wife could neither get her husband to return home, nor could she challenge his exclusively male privilege to have sex outside of marriage. She could only wheedle or cry in front of her husband, sometimes requesting Kamlabai to plead her case. The same man who didn't work at home and was insensitive to his wife's needs, openly did housework in Kamlabai's home, paid off her debts and accepted the fact that she did sex-work alongside their relationship.

- Bhimavva,[35] another Dalit devadasi sex-worker, raised one son in the Muslim faith, because her maalak at the time of his birth was Muslim. This son was not only circumcised, but was also married off to a Muslim girl. Another son was raised Hindu because the maalak at that time was Hindu. Neither of these men were biological fathers of either of the sons. As social fathers, they 'gave their name' to their designated child and were involved in the care of the boys. However, the children remained with the mother when the relationships ended. This kind of fatherhood transcended the patriarchal tenet of having biological sons largely for passage of property from father to son, maintaining a social and emotional bond between father and child beyond bloodlines.

- I found it startling that six major controls of patriarchy (production, reproduction, sexuality, property rights, mobility and decision-making) were challenged in the households of sex-workers, even though autonomy came later in their lives (especially for non-devadasi sex-workers), after they had paid off 'their' debts to the brothel keeper. The 'debts' they were repaying, were amounts for which they had been sold into sex-work, often by family members from the traditional family, or by intimate partners. Having seen the worst face of patriarchy and having no illusions about the institution of the family, sex-workers challenged patriarchal controls knowingly or unknowingly. The presence of SANGRAM and VAMP[36] linked the personal to the political.

- Finally I invite you to visit the household of an activist friend, Sugandhi Francis,[37] in Mumbai whose life holds no contradiction between theory and practice. Her household illustrates how 'family' could be reconstructed transcending bloodline, descent, caste/religion, marriage or kinship. Born in a north Indian Hindu family, Sugandhi married Francis against her parents' wishes and converted to Christianity.

567

Later, Sugandhi stoically dealt with Francis' alcoholism, opium abuse, violence, liver cirrhosis and death, raising their two sons and daughter, and taking care of family expenses. Her major support came in the form of comrades from CITU[38] whose acquaintance Francis had made during one of his jobs. Later Sugandhi remarried a comrade, Dr. Vivek Monteiro,[39] who moved into Sugandhi's household.

Sugandhi's younger son died in a road accident, leaving behind his girlfriend who was living with them, due to her family's opposition to their relationship. When her family came to take her back after his death, the young woman refused to go with them. Sugandhi reasoned that if the accident were to happen after they had got married, 'she would have stayed here'. Eventually this young woman decided to marry a colleague, whose family resisted the match because he was much younger than her. Sugandhi and Vivek actively helped with the wedding, and the new couple is now part of the family too. Recently the boy's family invited the couple to their home in Tamil Nadu, and Sugandhi-Vivek accompanied them as the girl's parents.

As part of supporting survivors of crimes in the name of honour, Sugandhi and AIDWA comrades had rescued Ritu,[40] whose husband and his entire family had been massacred by her brother, leaving her widowed and pregnant at the age of nineteen, because she, a Brahmin had married 'a lower caste Malayali.' Living as Sugandhi's protégé in hiding in her *basti* along with her posthumously born four year old daughter, Ritu later married Sugandhi's older son. The household grew further, to include Ritu as the daughter-in-law (along with the daughter from her previous marriage), and two daughters born later, in her marriage to Sugandhi's son. And finally, Francis' (Sugandhi's ex-husband's) ailing mother in her nineties joined their household a couple of years ago too.

I had the honour to hear the above stories and witness the zest of all the protagonists in spite of challenging life situations. It has renewed my hope, and certainty of witnessing a society without patriarchy. It also reiterates my belief about who the leaders of social movements should be.

Finally, the presence of vibrant movements for democratisation of society, including those that struggle for ecological sustainability, equality and justice in every area of life, is essential to keep the voices of the right-wing subdued and those of the subordinated strong.

Thus, in addition to our individual struggles, we now need to address issues and concerns of those who are as far removed from us as possible. This necessitates giving up hierarchies of class, caste, gender, sexuality or ethnicity related issues within our movements of the 1970s'-80s', and learning from emerging ones, while strengthening the values of equality, redistribution, freedom and democracy in single-identity campaigns. Imbuing freshly emerging perspectives to our struggles is essential, because only the quest for such a compelling and beautiful vision that liberates all, can lend full meaning to our involvement in a struggle for social justice, including gender equality.

Endnotes

1. It is impossible to deal with *all* issues related to patriarchy. Thus, in this paper I have dealt with the ones closest to my heart. This paper substantially reflects my learning (and unlearning) gained through feminist activism and rural community work. It also draws upon my thesis (Gupte, 2012b) which dealt with the ways in which patriarchal honour and power operate in women's lives, and how subordinated women use the most innovative ways to challenge them. Along with academic references, the paper refers to the lived experiences of people's lives, especially women from marginalized, stigmatized and discriminated groups.

2. On an average, three rape cases per hour were registered in India during 2011-2013 (Sasi, 2015).

3. For example the *khap panchayats* of Haryana may seem medieval in the context of urbanized India, or brahminical patriarchy may not be understood in Africa.

4. Chakravarti argues that caste hierarchy and women's subordination are the 'organising principles of the brahminical social order and are closely connected.' In this institution unique to Hindu society, it becomes imperative to control over the sexuality of women from 'upper' castes, not only to maintain patrilineal succession, but also to maintain caste purity.

5. Pauline Kolenda's study quoted in Chakravarti (2003, pp. 83).

6. Many related tribes in parts of South Asia, such as the Badi, Bacchda, Nat, Raj Nat, Nat Purva, Kanjar, Sanshi and so on practice family prostitution. In Maharashtra, a similar practice exists in Jalgaon district.

7. Whereas in the past, wealthy women entered the temple to perform music and dance by dedicating themselves to the goddess (known by different names, such as Yellamma or Renuka) instead of entering into marriage, the current caste composition of *devadasis* is largely Dalit.

8. While patriarchy operates largely in the private sphere it has also 'evolved' in contemporary societies, with men (related and unrelated to them) collectively exerting control and exploiting women in private as well as public spheres (such as in employment).

9. 'Heteronormativity' is the belief that only heterosexual ('opposite' sex) attraction, marriage, romance and sex are 'normal', due to which heterosexual people gain, but those with same-sex attraction lose out in countless ways. Binaried (strictly male-female) and hierarchal genders get promoted through law, religion, culture, media, the medical profession and almost every institution in society. Violence and discrimination against those who don't fall into the heterosexual framework are justified, as are stigma, exclusion and marginalization.

10. See essay on Religious Minority Futures in this volume.

11. 'Islamophobia' refers to an unfounded fear of Islam, and hostility towards anyone or anything Muslim. This belief considers Islam to be backward, inferior, barbaric, violent and incapable of changing. This term, founded in 1991, helps us understand the growing prejudice against Muslims all over the world, through which people, just because of being Muslims, are targeted in the name of addressing terrorism and protecting 'civilization'.

12. Right wing women have existed in India for decades though – the Rashtra Sevika Samiti, an off-shoot of the Hindu supremacist Rashtriya Swayamsevak Sangh (RSS) was founded in 1936.

13. For example, peasant and landless people's movements such as the Bodhgaya struggle in Bihar, the Shahada movement in Maharashtra, Mukti Sangharsh and Stree-Mukti Sangharsh in South Maharashtra, or the movement led by Shankar Guha Niyogi in Madhya Pradesh/Chhattisgarh. Also environmental rights movements such as the sovereignty movement of Dalit women farmers of Deccan Development Society; *mahila mangal dals* of Chipko; all-women's or women-centered forest protection in some villages in Odisha; and anti-violence sangathans like Maati in Munsiari.

14. 'It is imperative that we shall witness the day that has been promised to us.'

15. The Intersex Society of North America estimates that 0.1 per cent to 0.2 per cent (one in 1500 or 2000 births) of all people born, are intersex. Many more with subtler anatomy variations show up later in life; www.isna.org/faq/frequency (accessed on 3 August, 2015).

16. Men's 'widower' identity rarely becomes a marker but women are stigmatized and ostracized lifelong, especially in Savarna Hindu cultures through this labeling.

17. Further, caste will be annihilated in an equal society – see sub-section 'f' in the chapter.

18. This is assuming (or as long as) the right to private property exists, that parents own assets, and wish to pass those on to their children.

19. See essay on Dalit Futures in this volume.

20. Convention on the Elimination of all Forms of Discrimination against Women (CEDAW), http://www.un.org/womenwatch/daw/cedaw (accessed on 20 July, 2015).

21. The killing of rationalists Dr. Narendra Dabholkar in Pune in 2013, and Comrade Govind Pansare and Prof. M.M. Kalburgi in 2015; the hacking of secular bloggers in Bangladesh and the killing of secularists in Pakistan as 'blasphemers' draw our attention to growing violent Hindutva and Islamist ideologies in South Asia.

22. Dalit or adivasi family members belonging to animist, Hindu, Christian or Muslim religions live together in parts of Maharashtra. Examples of Hindu, Sikh (even Muslim) brothers living under the same roof existed in western Punjab (now Pakistan).

23. Cultural essentialism considers certain traits of a culture being unchangeable or immutable. This is dangerous for women's rights, because most human rights of women are violated in the name of culture.

24. The acceptance that 'different' human rights standards can be applied by different cultures defeats the basic attributes of human rights, namely that they are universal, intrinsic, inherent, inalienable and non-hierarchal.

25. For example, the Maharashtra Dalit Mahila Sanghatana, All India Dalit Women's Forum, National Federation of Dalit Women.

26. Rege calls this phenomenon the 'masculinisation of Dalithood and the savarnisation of womanhood', (1998, pp. 42).

27. Zopadpatti Sangharsh Vahini, part of the JP (Jayprakash Narayan) movement.

28. Name changed – one of the narrators in my thesis (Gupte, 2012b). All the other narrators, namely, Kamlabai, Bhimavva, Sudhir and Sugandhi wanted their original names to be used. Informed consent was taken from each of my narrators during my research.

29. Born male, *hijras* renounce their masculinity, often by undergoing ritual castration. They wear women's clothing and live in communes, worshipping Goddess Bahuchara.

30. Sudhir works with two sex-workers' collectives in South Maharahtra and North Karnataka – Sampada Grameen Mahila Sanstha (SANGRAM) and Veshya Anyay Mukti Parishad (VAMP), http://www.sangram.org/. He is a narrator in my thesis.

31. Mentor-novice relationship among hijras.

32. A senior activist of the Mumbai unit of the All India Democratic Women's Association (AIDWA) was raised by her *hijra* uncle and his cohorts. Her husband was also raised in a household of *hijras*. The community got these two foster children married.

33. Kamlabai was the pillar of SANGRAM and VAMP's work in South Maharashtra and North Karnataka. She was not only a friend, but also one of the narrators in my thesis. Her sudden death in 2015 created an irreparable void in the sex-workers' collectives and in the discourse around these issues in India.

34. Even though maalak in traditional rural society in Maharashtra means owner or husband, it has a different meaning in sex-workers' lingo. They 'keep' the *malaak* and get rid of him if he becomes tiresome.

35. Another pillar of SANGRAM-VAMP's work and Kamlabai's best friend, she died within a month of the former's demise. She too was also a narrator in my thesis.

36. SANGRAM and VAMP (www.sangram.org) are the leading voices of sex-workers' rights, working with communities in India's southwest and advocating for dignity, equality and social justice at the national and international levels.

37. Sugandhi was the Secretary of the Mumbai district committee of AIDWA at the time when she was a narrator in my thesis.

38. Confederation of Indian Trade Unions (CITU) – affiliated to the Communist Party of India (Marxist).

39. Maharashtra State Secretary of CITU, and long-term activist in the people's science movement.

40. Name changed.

References

Agrawal, Anuja, 2008, *Chaste Wives and Prostitute Sisters: Patriarchy and Prostitution among the Bedias of India*, New Delhi: Routledge.

Baxi, Upendra, 2005, 'The Gujarat Catastrophe: Notes on Reading Politics as Democidal Rape Culture' in *The Violence of Normal Times: Essays on Women's Lives Realities,* Kalpana Kannabiran (ed.), New Delhi: Women Unlimited, pp 332-383.

Butalia, Urvashi, 2001, 'Women and Communal Conflict: New Challenges for the Women's Movement in India' in Fiona Clark and Caroline Moser (eds) *Victims, Perpetrators or Actors? Gender, Armed Conflict and Political Violence,* New Delhi: Zed Books and Kali for Women, pp. 99-114.

Chakravarti, Uma, 2003, *Gendering Caste: Through a Feminist Lens,* Calcutta: Stree Publications.

Fraser, Nancy, 1996, 'From Redistribution to Recognition? Dilemmas of Justice in a "Post-Socialist" Age' in Nancy Fraser (ed), *Justice Interrruptus: Critical Reflection on the 'Postsocialist' Condition,* New York and London: Routledge, pp 11- 40.

Gatwood, Lynn, 1985, *Devi and the Spouse Goddess: Women, Sexuality, and Marriages in India*, Riverdale, Maryland: The Riverdale Company Inc.

Gupte, Manisha, 2012a, 'Codes of Daily Conduct: Patriarchal and Caste Honour in Rural Maharashtra, India', in Manisha Gupte, Ramesh Awasthi and Shraddha Chickerur, (eds.), *'Honour' and Women's Rights: South Asian Perspectives*, Pune: MASUM-IDRC.

Gupte, Manisha, 2012b, *Walking the Tight-Rope of Honour and Power: Women and the Politics of Patriarchy*, PhD thesis submitted to the University of Pune.

Gupte, Manisha, 2013, 'The Concept of Honour: Caste Ideology and Patriarchy in Rural Maharashtra', *Economic & Political Weekly,* Vol XLVII(18), May, pp. 72-81.

Guru, Gopal, 2002, 'How Egalitarian are the Social Sciences in India?', *Economic & Political Weekly,* Vol. XXXVII (51), December 14, pp. 5003-08.

Kamble, Baby, 2008, (Translated by Maya Pandit), *The Prisons We Broke,* New Delhi: Orient Black Swan.

Revathi, A., 2010, *The Truth About Me: A Hijra Life Story*, Delhi: Penguin India.

Rege, Sharmila, 1998, 'Dalit Women Talk Differently: A Critique of "Difference" and Towards a Dalit Feminist Standpoint Position', *Economic & Political Weekly,* Vol. 33(44), 31 October, WS 39-46.

Sarkar, Tanika, and Urvashi Butalia, (eds.), 1995, *Women and the Hindu Right: A Collection of Essays,* New Delhi: Kali for Women.

Sasi, Priya, 2015, Rape Cases in India – Has anything changed after the Nirbhaya Incident? – Part 1. https://factly.in/rape-cases-in-india-statistics-has-anything-changed-after-the-nirbhaya-incident-part-1/ (accessed 20 July, 2015).

Sen, Ilina, (ed.), 1990, *A Space within the Struggle: Women's Participation in People's Movements*, New Delhi: Kali for Women.

Srinivas, M.N., 1962, *Hinduism and Caste in Modern India and Others: An Essay*, Bombay: Asia Publishing.

Tilley, Rebekah, 2011, 'Saving Women or Policing Sex?' Review article on Lamberg Lucinda's book: *Given to the Goddess: South Indian Devadasis and the Sexuality of Religion*, https://www.as.uky.edu/ saving-women-or-policing-sex-0 (accessed on 20 July, 2015).

Vindhya, U., 1990, 'Women in the Srikakulam Movement', in Ilina Sen (ed.), *A Space within the Struggle: Women's Participation in People's Movements,* New Delhi: Kali for Women, pp 25-49.

Walby, Sylvia, 1990, *Theorizing Patriarchy*, Oxford: Basil Blackwell Ltd.

Future of Religious Minorities in India

Irfan Engineer

Summary

The essay looks at the evolution of religious identities in colonial and postcolonial India and the consequent dilution of community living. Due to the deepening of communal consciousness by cultural entrepreneurs, prejudices and contests have emerged. The Constitution of India has granted privileges to minorities (not defined) without recognizing the differentiated intensity with which they experience discrimination and marginalisation. On the other hand, fundamentalists have used these loopholes to create communal ripples. Taking the example of a Mohalla committee in Bhiwandi, the essay proposes the building of local social networks and groups of diverse communities to tackle communal tensions.

To envisage the future of minorities under the present NDA regime and a society dominated by the capitalist notions of development is difficult. However, alongside the struggle for social justice, inclusion, and livelihoods, the essay envisions of a struggle for democratization of culture. This would mean, an intra-inter struggle of communities and deconstruction of identities by the marginalized, such that the differentiation of the majority and minority becomes irrelevant.

The Context

Religion based identities and consequent majority-minority polarization in South Asia was a consequence of changes that occurred during colonial period. Majority and minority communal identities were an outcome of deliberate policies of the colonial state, popularly called divide and rule policy. Religious identities before British rule were fuzzy (Kaviraj, 1992) and mattered little to the people and the pre-colonial state. Here we would like to distinguish between 'religion' and 'religion based identities'. Subaltern sections were religious, more in the sense of having faith in some supernatural force governing the world to which all beings were subjected to, rather than boundaries drawn to imagine themselves

574

as a community in contradistinction to 'others' separated by the boundary. Therefore, belonging to one religion did not mean being excluded from others. The terms 'Hindus' and 'Muslims' or for that matter 'Christians', 'Jews', etc., were loosely used and did not define an all encompassing, rigidly defined community. For example, Shivaji hailed by Shiv Sena and Hindutva organizations as a 'Hindu Hero', in his letter to Aurangzeb, protesting imposition of *Jaziya* (poll tax), writes, 'Your Majesty, Akbar, the founder of your empire ruled for fifty-two years. He had adopted the excellent policy of treating with peace and equality, Christians, Jews, Muslims, Dadupanthis, Stargazers, Malakas, Atheists, Brahmins, Jains, in fact all the communities' (Pande, 1994).

Notice that Shivaji does not refer to 'Dadupanthis, Stargazers, Malakas, Atheists and Brahmins,' as Hindu community! In the same letter, Shivaji further writes, 'In fact, Islam and Hinduism are both beautiful manifestations of the Divine spirit. The call for Prayers is given in the mosques, the bells ring to the Divine glory in the temples' (Pande, 1994, pp. xxii). Shivaji names the religion as Hinduism, but describes the followers with their diversity rather than defining them as a single community.

In the 1901 Census, the colonial rulers listed 133 social groups as Muslim or partially Muslim. The Muslims too were so diverse, that they hardly constituted a community (Hardy, 1998). The members of the community doing manual scavenging were excluded from the mosque and eateries in many parts of India. Muslims made offerings to local Hindu deities which made them less homogenous (Hardy, 1998). The Muslim converts from untouchable castes such as *halalkhors*, *helas*, etc., were excluded even for matrimonial alliances (Ahmad, 2009). The Turks, Central Asian Muslims, the Pathans, Sayyeds and Shaikhs considered themselves as respectable (*ashrafs*). While the ashrafs themselves constituted into different endogamous groups or *biradaries*, they were small in numbers. More than 90 per cent of Muslims are converts from *shudra* castes (artisans and toilers), economically and educationally 'backward' (this term is used in this essay in a non-pejorative way). The Muslim converts from local communities continued to follow their traditions and customs to various degrees and retain their regional and cultural identities. The varied caste based *biradaries* retained their endogamous matrimonial relations and are referred to as *ajlafs*. Those converted from untouchable castes and involved in manual scavenging are referred to as *arzals*.

The Christians too were largely converted from the indigenous people *(adivasis)*, shudra and *ati-shudra* (untouchable castes).[1] They are referred to as dalit Christians. Those who were converted from the upper castes, e.g., followers of Syrian Orthodox Church in Kerala, continue to exclude the lower caste converts in various degrees. The followers retain their caste based, linguistic and congregational networks. Sikhs too are divided into various *deras*.

575

Those converted from untouchable castes are called *mazhabi* Sikhs and suffer exclusion.

The process of fusing culturally diverse groups of followers of a religion into one community was long drawn out. The cultural entrepreneurs had the onerous task of forging bonds amongst the fellow religionists spread out far and wide with diverse cultural traditions, who were often strangers. In fact, due to limited mobility, people were unaware of existence of fellow religionists outside their familiar small territory. They achieved this feat through numerous ways, but it often included constructing history that projected an ideal golden past; discovering, evolving and constructing sacred symbols with an emotional appeal, mythologies historicised about common sufferings and collective achievements in the past with narratives of heroes and heroic deeds; construction of the 'other' with whom the 'community' was projected to be at constant war; and projection of present common political interests. The cultural entrepreneurs were even encouraged by the colonial masters, as construction of rival and competitive communities helped them project themselves as arbitrators of rival claims and legitimized their hegemony. Simultaneously it undermined and weakened the freedom movement based on inclusion of all and diverse communities on the principle of secularism and democracy. Muslim, Hindu and other communities and communal identities were constructed during the colonial period to facilitate the divide and rule agenda of the colonial government.

Sir Syed Ahmad Khan described India as 'a beautiful bride blessed by two attractive eyes, the Hindus and the Muslims' (Khan, 1887). Sir Syed constructs two communities. He constructs Hindu community alongside the Muslim community even though both communities are necessary for India to constitute attractive eyes of a beautiful bride. Sir Syed strongly advocated for 'his community's' (Muslims) support for the British Government. He advised them to keep away from all political agitations. In all his discourses, Sir Syed continuously refers to the two communities as two different nations. He worked tirelessly to bring awareness among the Muslim community for modern education and negotiated with the British for their share in governance under the colonial structure and seeking larger share by proving the Muslim loyalty to the British.

Mohammed Ali Jinnah started his political career as an ambassador of Hindu-Muslim unity helping bring about a settlement to the vexed problem of share of the Muslim community's political representation. However, he too ended up constructing communal boundaries and notion of a homogenous community with religion as the most significant and defining identity marker. He stated,

'It is extremely difficult to appreciate why our Hindu friends fail to understand the real nature of Islam and Hinduism. They are not religious in the strict sense of the word, but are, in fact, different and distinct social orders; and it is only a dream that the Hindus and Muslims can ever evolve a common nationality... The Hindus and Muslims belong to two different religious philosophies, social customs, and literatures. They neither inter-marry nor inter-dine together and, indeed, they belong to two different civilizations which are based mainly on conflicting ideas and conceptions... It is quite clear that Hindus and Mussalmans derive their inspiration from different sources of history. They have different epics, different heroes, and different episodes. Very often the hero of one is a foe of the other and likewise, their victories and defeats overlap. To yoke together two such nations under a single state, one as a numerical minority and the other as a majority, must lead to growing discontent and final destruction of any fabric that may be so built for the government of such a state.'

(Jinnah, 1940)

The All India Hindu Mahasabha was founded in 1914 under the leadership of Pandit Madan Mohan Malviya and Lala Lajpat Rai. After his release from British jail, V. D. Savarkar provided the ideological leadership to Hindu Mahasabha after writing his treatise on Hindutva. Savarkar through his treatise on Hindutva constructed the political Hindu community on the twin criteria of those who considered the land between river Indus to the Arabian Sea as their holy land and their fatherland. Savarkar included the various castes of Hindus, viz., brahmins, kshatriyas, vaishyas, shudras and 'outcaste' ati-shudras as well as Jains, Buddhists and Sikhs into the fold of political Hindu community, while excluding Muslims, Christians and Jews whose holy land is outside the territory specified by Savarkar.

The cultural entrepreneurs having constructed the boundaries of their respective communities, particularly the Hindu and the Muslim community, proceeded to deepen the communal consciousness by contesting for share in power and terms of sharing political offices and in the process deepening the prejudices against the other. Sir Syed's opposition to the Indian National Congress and his advice to the Muslims to keep away from the party; the partition of Bengal in 1905 which contributed towards encouraging Muslim nationalists; negotiations over the Lucknow Pact in the year 1916; The Nehru report in 1930 and the rejection of the 14 point charter proposed by Jinnah; negotiations for communal demands during the Round Table Conferences and the Cabinet Mission plan were some instances of intense contestations, claims and counter-claims for power sharing between the two communities. These contestations, claims and counter-claims were also punctuated by communal violence which helped deepen the communal prejudices by creating insecurity and fear of the 'other'. Communal violence produced circumstances wherein there was a growing feeling that shared nationalism within one state was difficult, if not impossible. It is out of these contestations that the construction of minority-majority identities consolidated.

Minorities in the Constituent Assembly

Initially the Advisory Committee on Minorities and Fundamental Rights of the Constituent Assembly chaired by Sardar Vallabhbhai Patel recommended joint electorates with reservations for minorities. Minorities were divided into three groups according to their population in the Indian Dominion (omitting the States). Group A were minorities with less than ½ per cent population and included three sub-groups: 1) Anglo-Indians, 2) Parsees and 3) Plains' tribesmen in Assam. Group B consisted of minorities with population not more than 1½ per cent and included Indian Christians and Sikhs. Group C comprised of minorities whose population exceeded 1½ per cent and in this group were Muslims and Scheduled Castes.[2] Provision was made for Anglo-Indians to be nominated by the President and Governors in case they failed to secure adequate representation in legislatures. Parsees were nominally on the list of recognized minorities but they did not want any reservations with provision for future reconsideration on reservations for them if they failed to secure adequate representation. For Indian Christians, there was a recommendation for reservation in proportion to their population in the Central Legislature and in Provincial Legislature of Madras and Bombay. For Muslims and Scheduled Castes, recommendation for provision of reservation on the basis of their population was made. Members of minority communities also had the right to contest from unreserved seats as well. The report also provided that due share of minorities in All India and Provincial services would be kept in view during appointments, along with consideration for efficiency of administration. An officer was to be appointed by the Governors in the Provinces who would report to the Union and Provincial Legislatures the working of the safeguards provided to the minorities (Constituent Assembly Debates, 2003, pp. 243-251). In substance, the provision of the Minority Report scaled down the privileges being enjoyed by the minorities under the British rule, viz. separate electorates and reservations for minorities in Union and Provincial Legislatures larger than their proportion warranted. This was done with the assurance that minorities would not be discriminated if they trusted the majority. The reservations for minorities in the legislatures and in the Cabinet were later withdrawn by a subsequent report of the Advisory Committee on the Minorities, due to the fact that the situation on the ground had changed.

Separate electorates was hotly debated and contested, particularly by some members of the Muslim League. While a member of the Muslim League passionately appealed for separate electorate so that the minorities could select the best candidates to represent them, the rest, particularly the members from majority community, fretted and fumed on such a demand (and on the audacity to put up such a demand in spite of partition and creation of Pakistan).

The Sikhs were contesting only on one issue – that the Schedule Caste converts to Sikhism should also be recognized as Scheduled Castes and this demand of the Sikhs was accepted by the Advisory Committee and the Sardar reported to the Constituent Assembly accordingly.

Amendments suggested by Z.H. Lari tried to find a via media and achieve what the Muslim League wanted, viz., best representatives of minorities without separate electorates. Lari was suggesting through his amendment that elections be held under the system of cumulative votes in multi-member constituencies and the modification that no seats be reserved for the Scheduled Castes. Lari was essentially arguing for proportional representation form of electoral system where minorities would not feel that they are left out. Otherwise, he argued that minorities will suffer as democracy can become tyranny of the majority, that succeeds by force or fraud in conducting elections. Equal electorates afford no representation to minorities. Proportional representation, he argued, was profoundly democratic for it affords cumulative votes and increases the influence of sections who otherwise would be marginalized and have no voice in the governance (CAD, Vol. VIII 16-5-1949 to 16-6-1949, 2003, pp. 283-290).

Indian Constitution

The Constitution of India, without defining minorities, provides two parameters to determine who can be categorized as minorities – religion and language. The only right of minorities which the Constitution recognizes is to preserve their script (Art. 29); right to establish and administer educational institutions of their choice and non-discrimination in matters of grant-in-aid to minority educational institutions. Art. 30 of the Constitution of India states that, 'All minorities, whether based on religion or language, shall have the right to establish and administer educational institutions of their choice.' The Indian Constitution therefore recognizes only religious and linguistic minorities. Justice V. N. Khare in his judgement in the case of (TMA Pai Foundation v. State of Karnataka 2002) explained this Constitutional position further by defining minorities as, 'The person or persons establishing an educational institution who belong to either religious or linguistic groups who are less than fifty per cent of the total population of the state in which the educational institutional is established would be linguistic or religious minorities.' As establishing and administering educational institutions of their choice are an important right of the minorities in India, the reference to educational institution comes whenever minorities are mentioned.

The official stand of the Indian Government in its report to the Human Rights Committee[2] is that there are no ethnic minorities in India. The ethnic minorities are also subsumed as linguistic minorities. The agitation of people of Kashmir, Manipur and Nagaland is therefore not even acknowledged by the Indian state as that of national or ethnic minority for their self-determination. A majority of seven out of eleven judges of Constitutional Bench of the Supreme Court of India, in their recent judgement, have ruled that since the states in India have been carved out on the basis of language of majority persons of that region, minorities – both religious and linguistic – should be determined at the state level (and not whole of India) (ibid.). Justice Quadri, in his separate judgement but concurring with the majority, defined the word minority as 'a non-dominant group' or a numerically inferior group (ibid.).

In the case relating to the Ahmedabad St. Xavier College Society vs. the State of Gujarat, Justice Khanna observed:

'The idea of giving some special rights to the minorities is not to have a kind of a privileged or pampered section of the population but to give to the minorities a sense of security and a feeling of confidence. The great leaders of India since time immemorial had preached the doctrine of tolerance and catholicity of outlook. Those noble ideas were enshrined in the Constitution. Special rights for minorities were designed not to create inequality. Their real effect was to bring about equality by ensuring the preservation of the minority institutions and by guaranteeing to the minorities autonomy in the matter of the administration of these institutions. The differential treatment for the minorities by giving them special rights is intended to bring about an equilibrium, so that the ideal of equality may not be reduced to a mere abstract idea but should become a living reality and result in true, genuine equality, an equality not merely in theory but also in fact...The minorities are as much children of the soil as the majority and the approach has been to ensure that nothing should be done as might deprive the minorities of a sense of belonging, of a feeling of security, of a consciousness of equality and of the awareness that the conservation of their religion, culture, language and script as also the protection of their educational institutions is a fundamental right enshrined in the Constitution. ... The safeguarding of the interest of the minorities amongst sections of population is as important as the protection of the interest amongst individuals of persons who are below the age of majority or are otherwise suffering from some kind of infirmity. The Constitution and the laws made by civilized nations, therefore, generally contain provisions for the protection of those interests. It can, indeed, be said to be an index of the level of civilization and catholicity of a nation as to how far their minorities feel secure and are not subject to any discrimination or suppression.'

(The Ahmedabad St. Xavier College Society & Anr. v.
State of Gujarat, 1974)

The Supreme Court, in *The State of Madras v. Srimathi Champak Dorairajan 1951* held that 'General equality by non-discrimination is not the only need of minorities. Minority rights under majority rule implies more than non- discrimination; indeed, it begins with non-discrimination. Protection of interests and institutions and the advancement of opportunity are just as important. Differential treatment that distinguishes them from the majority is a must to preserve their basic characteristics.'

In TMA Pai Foundation v. State of Karnataka, C.J.I. B.N. Kirpal in his judgement in para 157 stated that, 'Article 30 is a special right conferred on the religious and linguistic minorities because of their numerical handicap and to instil in them a sense of security and confidence, even though the minorities cannot be per se regarded as weaker sections or underprivileged segments of the society.'

The Constitution of India treats all the religious and linguistic minorities on par in matters of rights, whether they are dominant and affluent or stigmatized, discriminated, and whether socially, educationally and economically marginalized or not. However, all minorities do not experience discrimination, exclusion and marginalization with the same intensity. Muslims and Christians have been politically targeted, stigmatized and excluded by Hindutva – the ideology of Hindu nationalists. The Jains, Sikhs and Parsis do not experience the same degree of exclusion and discrimination. The Parsis have a significant section of its community in big industrial and business houses as well as educated and professionals, including lawyers, doctors, etc., that they hardly vie with members of other communities for space in educational institutions – as they have their own community run institutions, affirmative action for livelihoods as there are a lot of philanthropically oriented Parsis and Parsi businessmen and community organizations to take care of their livelihoods. Sikhs are a majority in Punjab. Except the early eighties when Khalistan militants had led to a situation wherein there was rise in prejudices against the Sikhs and which led to anti-Sikh carnage in 1984 in Delhi and other cities in India, there is no grievance of exclusion. The Jain community is also relatively better off economically, educationally and socially and there are no prejudices against them. They are perceived to be believers of non-violence and practitioners of vegetarianism.

While the right not to be discriminated on grounds of religion or language or on any other ground whatsoever should be the fundamental right of every citizen in a democracy irrespective of which community the citizen belongs, parity to all minority communities becomes problematic when special schemes for their welfare are implemented. The welfare schemes for minorities to ensure equality of outcome are justified pointing out the development deficiency in the most backward, discriminated and marginalized minority community – the Muslim community. However the schemes so formulated are implemented for all minority communities and the benefit of the welfare schemes is largely taken by economically better off communities which do not experience discrimination or exclusion in any significant form. For example, the UPA Government appointed a PM's High Level Committee on Social, Economic and Educational Status of the Muslim Community of India headed by Justice Rajindar Sachar (Retd.). The Sachar Committee found that the Muslim community is discriminated and lags behind in educational, social and economical indicators and gave a number of recommendations.[3]

In order to act upon the recommendations of the Sachar Committee, the Government formulated several welfare schemes, including scholarships to encourage education, financial loans to encourage entrepreneurship and business, and schemes for development of minority concentrated districts. However, the schemes targeted all the minorities and members of even Jain, Sikh and Parsi communities qualified for the benefits of the schemes and they benefited more. The study of the Amitabh Kundu Committee points out that after the implementation of the schemes there was no significant change as far as the social, economic and educational status of the Muslim community is concerned (Post Sachar Evaluation Committee, 2014).

In spite of the Constitutional right of citizens not to be discriminated against, amongst other grounds on religion and language, there is no efficacious Constitutional remedy to redress if the rights are, in fact, being violated. The remedy of approaching Constitutional courts is beyond the reach of an overwhelming majority of citizens for three reasons – inordinate delay and prolonged engagement; high costs involved in engaging a good legal team; and the burden of proof to establish discrimination when discrimination is real, subtle, papered over and yet the results are evident.

Security of the Minorities

During scarcity and economic crisis, competition for scarce jobs, livelihood opportunities and state sponsored welfare is intense. Needy individuals, lonely and powerless that they are, depend on the community to which they belong, to access welfare and livelihood. Social capital of the community they belong to becomes crucial for the marginalized to access educational courses, livelihoods and state welfare. Caste, ethnic, linguistic and communal identities acquire importance in such circumstances. Communalization of one community – a process wherein a community of religious followers are transformed into a political community imagining themselves as having common social, economic and political interests – triggers off communalization of 'other' communities as well. Competitive communalism converts religion as faith and spirituality into a tool to define identities and political behaviour. It produces the discourse of majority – minority communities.

Communalization is not a uniform and linear process – it has had its highs and lows and varies from region to region and has its urban-rural dimensions. Communal violence is at once a barometer of communalization and at the same time a contributory factor. Communalization (and therefore, majority-minority consciousness) has been more salient in Northern and Western Indian urban areas (Varshney and Wilkinson, 1995; Engineer, 1995; Rajeshwari, 2004). Communal riots in the 1960s' were localized and urban based, mainly in the North and the West. The Nehruvian idea of culturally diverse and secular India was progressively challenged by Hindutva ideology using communal riots as a tool. They also stalled movements for social justice and inclusion of backward castes.

Frequency and intensity of communal riots increased making minorities feel more and more insecure. In the 1980s' there were major riots practically every year (Engineer, 2004). Insecure minorities too were getting communalized around their demands – no interference in Muslim personal laws; legislation to reverse the Shahbano judgement of the Supreme Court. Alongside the campaign for construction of Ramjanmabhoomi temple in place of Babri Masjid, there were a series of communal riots in North and West India which peaked with riots in several cities simultaneously in 1992-93, after the demolition of Babri Masjid and in several districts of Gujarat in 2002.

The minorities in India have been targets of communal violence. In all 11,855 people have been killed in communal violence between 1950 and 2002 (Engineer, 2004). The major target of the communal violence in India has been Muslims (Ahmedabad in1969, 1984-85, 2002; Surat in 1992-93; Mumbai in 1984 and 1992-93; Bhagalpur in 1989; and other towns like Godhra, Meerut, Aligarh, Moradabad); Sikhs (Delhi in 1984); Christians (in Kandhamal, Orissa in 2007 and 2008). Not only deaths, the businesses, properties and livelihoods of the minorities too are targeted during communal violence leading to forced displacement, further economic marginalization and feeling of alienation. Targeted violence accelerates the process of ghettoization and communal polarization among the communities.

It must also be noted here that though the minorities suffer disproportionately higher casualties than the majority community in communal violence, inevitably there are instances in every riot investigated by this author, wherein members of majority community also save the minority communities from being targeted during communal violence. This is because the saviours are unconvinced by the stereotypes sought to be popularized about the minorities or at least they know the neighbours are not guilty of the stigma sought to be popularized. The security forces can prevent an impending major communal riot if they pay heed to early warnings. However, they normally ignore such early warnings (Engineer, 2013). Security forces in India are also capable of controlling any communal violence within twenty four hours of its outbreak (ibid.). Communal violence however can best be prevented from spreading if there are active social networks of groups from diverse communities engaged in secular pursuits, and, in the process, with each other, and simultaneously linked with administration (Varshney and Wilkinson, 1995). The Mohalla (neighbourhood) Committees in Bhiwandi is one such example that prevented outbreak of communal violence in 1992-93 after the demolition of Babri Mosque, though it is communally sensitive. Active networks of Mohalla Committees composed of citizens from both communities and all socio-economic backgrounds and headed by police officers at beat levels were engaged in addressing the problems of citizens in the late eighties and early nineties. The Committees checked rumours being spread after the demolition of Babri Mosque and countered them effectively. They patrolled their respective areas jointly, with the result that communal riots could be effectively checked.

Future of Minorities

India is undergoing rapid economic transformation and urbanization and being subsumed into the global capitalist structure. The onslaught of global capital is on one hand destroying traditional livelihoods without absorbing most of the displaced people into the industrial economy or providing any alternative livelihoods and thus marginalising them. However, a section of the middle class has burgeoned and augmented its income. The global capital is rewarded with surplus on account of cheap land, natural resources, lower taxation and cheap unorganized labour force. The incomes of the CEOs, MDs and chairpersons too have touched new heights. The net result is growing inequalities which the GDP designed to measure 'growth' manages to conceal.

The displaced, marginalized and excluded from rural as well as urban areas are facing double onslaught under the present NDA regime. NDA's spending on social sectors like health, education, food security, employment guarantee schemes, and housing for the poor has reduced. The Planning Commission, in its Twelfth Five Year Plan document, had suggested the need for financial inclusion of socially backward groups like the minorities, in addition to the SCs, STs and women and to allocate resources for their development. However, the NDA abolished the Planning Commission itself and instead established *Niti Aayog* to focus on appropriate infrastructure planning for industrial development. The excluded would therefore be forced to depend on religious and charitable institutions for survival. The fundamentalists and cultural nationalists are more organized and command resources. They are therefore in a position to establish religio-cultural hegemony over the section of people experiencing marginalisation.

The burgeoning middle class on the other hand faces existential dilemmas with their sudden upward mobility as they adapt to a new social life, seeking new social status and privileges which their newly acquired wealth can purchase. They too flock to the 'Art of Living', Ramdev, Asaram Bapu, Mata Amritanandmayi, etc., and the new religious gurus who re-package religion to appeal to the upwardly mobile middle class through rapidly expanding 24x7 electronic media. They seek new identities, new social status and privileges alongside shopping malls, electronic gadgets, new luxuries and a new way of life that comes along with imported gadgets, goods and culinary tastes. This transforms the individual to a self-centred consumer and grabber at any cost rather than a liberal person with liberal attitudes. Such self centred pleasure indulging the socially alienated consumer needs justification and this is furnished by the 'cultural nationalist' ideologies that target minorities and categorize a section of fellow citizens as 'others' who are potential enemies of the nation (and to the new wealth that has come their way).

However the global capital undergoes cyclical crisis and will plunge into one sooner rather than later as the levels of inequalities cannot be sustained and the society will not remain peaceful. India's Gini coefficient rose to 51 by 2013, from 45 in 1990, signifying rising inequality between urban and rural areas as well as within urban areas (Nair, 2016). According to the data for the year 2016 from Credit Suisse, the richest 1 per cent Indians owned 53 per cent of the country's wealth, up from 36.8 per cent in the year 2000. The richest 5 per cent owned 68.6 per cent in the year 2016, while the top 10 per cent owned 76.3 per cent of the total wealth in 2016, up from, 65.9 per cent. The poorest 50 per cent of the country owned a mere 4.1 per cent of the national wealth (Agrawal, 2016). Eight hundred and thirty six million Indians survive on less than Rs. 20 (less than half-a-dollar) a day and 200 million Indians sleep hungry every night (Bhookh.com, n.d.).

Suicides committed by farmers in India due to agrarian distress increased by over 40 per cent between 2014 and 2015. In 2014 there were 5,650 farmer suicides, while in 2015, the figure crossed 8,000 (Tiwary, 2016).

Inequalities are globally rising at a much faster pace than before. Industrial growth in the world cannot be sustained with rapidly diminishing purchasing power of the bottom 80 per cent to buy their products. The marginalized and excluded people are being mobilized more and more in struggles for justice and better livelihoods and demanding their fair share in the growth. The dalits have been agitating after the Una incident[4] and have expressed their solidarity with the Muslim community. The poorer sections of the politically dominant castes are getting organized to demand livelihoods and their fair share in growth. They want reservations in jobs and education as provided for the Scheduled Castes and backward classes. The Maratha Caste in Maharashtra, Jats in Haryana and Gujjars in Rajasthan have been demanding reservations. Muslims too are demanding reservations in jobs and education. The poorer section of Marathas, Jats and Gujjars mutually support each other. In the times to come, the marginalized sections would question the present model of growth and capitalism itself. As they become more aware and organize to address unsustainable capitalism and wage struggles for justice and their fair share, the religious identities would become less salient in the public arena. On account of depleting purchasing power of the bottom 80 per cent, finance capital too will face crisis, as we witnessed in 2008 in US and the Euro zone debt crisis, triggered off by inability of Greece to service its debts. The rate of growth of economies in the world too has slowed down considerably.

With the BJP led NDA Government in power, soon there will be disillusionment, especially among the landless and farmers in rural areas, workers, dalits, adivasis, other backward classes and women of all castes and communities. Inequality is growing in leaps and bounds. These sections are getting further marginalized even as the richest one per cent is enriching itself and fast entering the billionaire club in the world (Shah, 2015). The state has sufficient resources to ensure the basic needs of all citizens irrespective of their religious, caste, linguistic, ethnic or gender affiliations, including decent housing, basic education, health care and ensuring livelihoods. What we need is the political system and architecture of governance be made more just; accountable to the people; and responsive to the needs of the most marginalized, irrespective of their identities. The succour provided by the elite of a community is at best a small fraction of what is needed. In less than a decade, disillusionment with the identity politics will set in amongst the marginalized. People then will have to resist the neo-liberal policies that allow inequalities to grow and result in marginalized getting further marginalized.

The struggle against the free market ideologies and policies that enable inequalities to grow will mobilize people across all castes and communities. As people of all castes and communities come together in the struggle for justice, equality, accountable governance, and participatory democracy, the interaction among them will demolish prejudices they may have come to acquire against each other.

As people struggle for justice, inclusion and equality, religious identities will become irrelevant for their public life and in day to day interactions with people belonging to other faiths. Faith will be relevant to individuals to answer their philosophical quests like the purpose of life, destiny, etc. Faith may also be a source of moral values and a guide to the notion of a good life. Faith can inspire individuals to be compassionate towards other living beings and nature with which they share their living space. Faith has often inspired individuals to struggle against injustices in the world and to establish a more egalitarian world with social and economic justice. Religion then becomes a source of solidarity and strength, a moral guide to one's social conduct and to attain inner peace through practice of spirituality. Religion in this case helps the individual understand one's own self and subjugate oneself to the larger social cause of welfare of all underprivileged living beings and creation. Religion then does not become a tool for defining a community and construction of community boundaries or a predominant tool of identity.

The struggle for justice and livelihoods includes believers of all faiths and followers of all religions coming together for the shared common cause. Religion was promoted as a tool to define communities and assertion of 'religion based' identities during the colonial rule. Communal identities and differences of majority and minority is neither in the natural order of things nor will it last forever. The future therefore will see communal, ethnic, linguistic, caste, or religio-sectarian identities becoming irrelevant in public spaces. Religion would cease to define one's identity.

How long will it take before the 'majority' and 'minority' discourse becomes irrelevant? This depends on a variety of factors – how strong, networked and organised are the forces struggling for social and economic justice and the vision and the wisdom of their leadership.

Pathway to the Future of Minorities

Hindutva ideology of the ruling NDA Government (elected in May 2014), constructs nationalism on the basis of selective upper-caste traditions. Hindutva seeks to homogenize Hinduism following one supreme leader and use it as a tool to suppress and marginalize all other egalitarian Hindu religious traditions. They problematize the presence of Islam and Christianity on Indian soil. Some ministers and elected representatives within the present dispensation aggressively portray minorities as fit to be thrown out of the nation (Kumar, 2014) or they should live as subjugated lives of second class citizens (Express News Service, 2014) without voting rights (PTI, 2015) and seek to aggressively convert minorities to Hinduism (Qureshi, 2014) and prevent Hindu women marrying Muslim men out of their own choice (Das, 2015). Though the discourse of majority-minority would become irrelevant in future, in fact, presently, the targeting of minorities is communally polarizing a section of people and promoting ghettoization.

Nevertheless, disillusionment with the ruling NDA dispensation is setting in soon. The NDA Government has failed to deliver on its promise of development, checking corruption and giving good governance. The regime may have succeeded in temporarily diverting the attention of the people from the reality on the ground using what it termed as 'surgical strike' on Pakistani territory, after attack on Indian soldiers in Uri by Pakistan based terrorists, heightening conflict with Pakistan and heightening danger of terrorism. Demonetization of nearly 85 per cent of Indian currency and projecting the measure as a tactic to fight corruption, fake currency, black money and terrorism is also a step in that direction, which may have temporarily diverted the attention of some people. But the success may only be temporary. Instilling people with false national or religious pride and misleading people by all sorts of promises that cannot be delivered would not help them win a second term.

The pathway to future wherein majority-minority identities become irrelevant is more likely to pass through tensions, upheavals and strife – both within communities and across the communities. Alongside the struggle for social justice, gender justice, equality, inclusion and livelihoods, wherein people across the communities come together, there will also be struggle for democratization of culture – culture of equality, human dignity of all and scientific temper – a culture that encourages critical questioning and where nothing is so sacred to prevent critical examination. Not only would all the minority communities pass through this internal strife between the liberal-democrats and communal nationalists-fundamentalists, the majority community too would have to pass through it. The seeds of this internal strife are already visible. The Hindu cultural nationalists are being challenged by not only secular minded Hindus but by the religious Hindus as well. The Shanakaracharya of Puri Peetham has opposed the Hindu cultural nationalists a number of times (FP Politics, 2014). The heritage of Kabir, Rohidass, Meera, Tukaram, the varkaris in Maharashtra, Narsi Mehta is invoked daily in popular culture and their compositions appeal to an overwhelming majority of the Hindus. Dalits and the dalit movement will contest the Hindu nationalists strongly.[5]

Within Islam there is a weak reform movement but a rich heritage of rejuvenators of faith using the route of *ijtehad* – re-contextualizing the Quranic message and understanding the word of God in new circumstances. Sir Syed Ahmed, Maulana Mumtaz Ali, Jamaluddin Afghani, Maulana Shibli Nomani, Maulana Abul Kalam Azad, and the *sufi* saints have undertaken the task. Most of them were condemned as heretics and apostates during their times. In recent times, Dr. Asghar Ali Engineer, Maulana Wahiduddin Khan, Syeda Hamid, Sadia Dehalvi and many other Islamic scholars are re-contextualizing/have re-contextualized Islam.

Muslim women are struggling to liberate themselves from the patriarchal interpretation of *Shari'a*.[6] Bhartiya Muslim Mahila Andolan (BMMA), Awaz-e-Niswan and many other Muslim women's organizations are questioning the dominant discourse of *Shari'a* law. The targeted violence experienced by the community pushes the struggles of women back for two reasons – when the entire community's security is at risk, the dominant urge within the community is that of closing ranks to meet the challenge. This urge gives rise to a strong concern for unity, which cannot be achieved if the dominant patriarchal discourse is questioned. The conservative-fundamentalist sections are much better organized within the community using the platform of well knit mosques and *madrasas*. Therefore the voices of gender justice get drowned in this urge to close ranks. During communal violence, women's bodies become the battlefield on which the communal war is played out. Women's security is at an even higher risk. Scores of them face sexual assaults. In such circumstances, patriarchal oppression by their male relatives becomes more acceptable than brutally hostile sexual assaults. Mobility of women reduces greatly and some parents think it prudent to withdraw their daughters from schools, particularly if they have to negotiate a passage through a locality inhabited by 'hostile' community to reach to the schools. After communal violence domestic violence increases but women accessing institutions to redress their grievances reduces.

As the struggle for justice strengthens, it strengthens the voices of gender justice within the community too. Women are an important force in the intra-community strife and voice of social reforms to ensure more a liberal and better regime of gender justice. As the voice of women for gender justice strengthens in one community, it reaches out to women suffering oppression and marginalization in other communities too.

The converts to Islam from backward castes and untouchable sections too are questioning the monolithic-communal 'Muslim' identity. The *ajlafs* are questioning the communal leadership of the *ashrafs* and their construct of the community and the communal issues they focus on. The backward sections are becoming more conscious of both their exploitation and oppression – by the economic system and also the hegemony of Hindu nationalist-*ashraf* combine. The *ajlafs-arzals* are forging alliances with the backward classes from the Hindu community and see their liberation in social justice. They are proud of Islam as well as their social identity and local cultural traditions. Their understanding of Islam is different from that of the *ashraf* led *whahabi-salafi* reading of Islam. Islam for them is declaration of equality and their liberation, for social justice. The deconstruction of the notion of Muslim community by the *ajlaf-arzal* is an important factor in deconstruction of the minority identity. The dalit Christians too feel that their destiny and liberation is closely linked with the other oppressed section, including Hindu dalits and at times question the traditional reading of the Bible.

The future of India is in secular democracy, liberating the people and the country from sectarian perspectives of the feudal, hierarchical, conservative, fundamentalist and hegemonic elite of all the communities taking pride in the 'past achievements' rather than seeing the pathway to the future as greater pursuit of knowledge and knowledge based just and sustainable development.

Endnotes

1. The *shudra* castes in the caste hierarchy were artisan and labouring castes like the weavers, carpenters, potters, land tillers and traditionally had to serve the upper castes. The *ati-shudra* castes on the other hand were compelled to render menial and scavenging services considered polluting. They were therefore treated as untouchables and excluded from the village society, inhabiting outside the village.
2. The minority report was later amended and Scheduled Castes were removed from the list of minorities.
3. Prime Minister's High Level Committee Cabinet Secretariat (Government of India), 'Social, Economic and Educational Status of the Muslim Community of India' (A Report), popularly known as Sachar Committee Report, 2006.
4. Four members of *ati-shudra* castes, also referred as dalits, who were skinning a dead cow were mercilessly flogged in Una town in Gujarat State on the night of 10-11 July 2016, by the upper-caste who accused them of killing a cow. Following the incident, there was a massive protest agitation by dalits demanding land so that they do not have to resort to their traditional occupation of skinning dead cows and can live a life of dignity. Their demand has received a popular response and their agitation is continuing.

5. Several other essays in this volume relate to this theme, including those on the future of Dalits, on Democracy, on Arts, and on Localisation, as also the Concluding essay.

6. See also essay on Gender Futures in this volume.

References

Agrawal, Nisha, 2016, *Inequality in India: what's the real story?* 4 October, https://www.weforum.org/agenda/2016/10/inequality-in-india-oxfam-explainer/ (accessed 23 December, 2016).

Ahmad, Imtiaz, 2009, *Can there be a category called Dalit Muslims?* 31-August, http://www.dalitmuslims.com/2009/08/can-there-be-category-called-dalit.html (accessed 14 July, 2015).

Bhookh.com, *Hunger Facts.* http://www.bhookh.com/hunger_facts.php (accessed 23 December, 2016).

CAD, 2003, *Constituent Assembly Debates,* Vol. V (14-8-1947 to 30-8-1947), New Delhi: Lok Sabha Secretariat.

Das, Madhuparna, 2015, "Love jihad" gets a Bengal reply: Bahu lao, Beti bachao, "purify" Muslim brides', *The Indian Express,* 13-March, http://indianexpress.com/article/india/india-others/love-jihad-gets-a-bengal-reply-bahu-lao-beti-bachao-purify-muslim-brides/ (accessed 28 July, 2015).

Engineer, Asghar Ali, 1995, *Communalism in India – A Historical And Enpirical Study*, New Delhi: Vikas Publishing House Pvt. Ltd.

Engineer, Asghar Ali, 2004, *Communal Riots After Independence – A Comprehensive Account*, Delhi: Shipra.

Engineer, Irfan Asgharali, 2013, *Issues of Communal Violence: Causes and Responses*, Mumbai: Institute for Peace Studies and Conflict Resolution.

Express News Service, 2014, 'Ramzada vs haramzada: Outrage over Union Minister Sadhvi's remark,' *The Indian Express* 2 December, http://indianexpress.com/article/india/india-others/union-minister-spells-out-choice-in-delhi-ramzada-vs-haramzada/ (accessed 28 July, 2015).

FP Politics, 2014, 'Modi's 'Hindu' problem: Too Hindutva for spiritual leaders', *First Post,* 2 May, http://www.firstpost.com/politics/modis-hindu-problem-too-hindutva-for-spiritual-leaders-1506079.html (accessed 28 July, 2015).

Ghose, Sagarika, 2015, 'Wanted: A saffron Amartya Sen – India's right wing has failed to create intellectuals of global stature', *The Times of India,* 22 July, http://blogs.timesofindia.indiatimes.com/bloody-mary/wanted-a-saffron-amartya-sen-indias-right-wing-has-failed-to-create-intellectuals-of-global-stature/ (accessed 28 July, 2015).

Government of India, 2006, *Social, Economic and Educational Status of the Muslim Community of India – A Report,* New Delhi: Prime Minister's High Level Committee for Preparation of Report on Social, Economic and Educational Status of the Muslim Community in India, Government of India.

Hardy, P., 1998, *The Muslims of British India*, First South Asian Edition, New Delhi: Cambridge University Press.

Jinnah, Mohammad Ali, 1940, *Excerpt from the Presidential Address delivered by the Quaid-i-Azam*, 22-March. http://www.columbia.edu/itc/mealac/pritchett/00islamlinks/txt_jinnah_lahore_1940.html (accessed 23 December, 2016).

Kaviraj, Sudipto, 1992, 'The Imaginary Institution of India', in *Subaltern Studies, VII*, Partho Chatterjee and Gyanendra Pandey, New Delhi: OUP.

Khan, Sir Syed Ahmad, 1888, *Speech of Sir Syed Ahmed at Meerut*, http://www.columbia.edu/itc/mealac/pritchett/00islamlinks/txt_sir_sayyid_meerut_1888.html (accessed 26 December, 2016).

— 1887, *Speech of Sir Syed Ahmed at Lucknow*, http://www.columbia.edu/itc/mealac/pritchett/00islamlinks/txt_sir_sayyid_lucknow_1887.html (accessed on 26 December 2016).

Kumar, Manish, 2014, 'Giriraj Singh Wanted to Send PM Critics to Pakistan. Now, He is Minister', *NDTV.com*, 10-November, http://www.ndtv.com/people/giriraj-singh-wanted-to-send-pm-critics-to-pakistan-now-he-is-minister-691021 (accessed 28 July, 2015).

Nair, Remya, 2016, *IMF warns of growing inequality in India and China*, 4 May, http://www.livemint.com/Politics/mTf8d5oOqzMwavzaGy4yMN/IMF-warns-of-growing-inequality-in-India-and-China.html (accessed 23 December, 2016).

National Commission for Religious and Linguistic Minorities, 2007, *Report of the National Commission for Religious and Linguistic Minorities*, New Delhi: Ministry of Minority Affairs, Government of India, 2007.

Pande, B. N., 1994, *Chhatrapati Shivaji*, Delhi: Gandhi Smriti & Darshan Samiti.

Post Sachar Evaluation Committee, 2014, *Post Sachar Evaluation Committee*, (23September), http://iosworld.org/download/Post_Sachar_Evaluation_Committee.pdf (accessed 15 July, 2015).

PTI, 2015, 'Shiv Sena demands withdrawal of voting rights to Muslims', *First Post.com*, 13 April, http://www.firstpost.com/politics/shiv-sena-demands-withdrawal-of-voting-rights-to-muslims-2193715.html (accessed 28 July, 2015).

Qureshi, Siraj, 2014, 'Another Muslim family of 12 becomes Hindu in Agra', *IndiaToday.in*. 27 December, http://indiatoday.intoday.in/story/agra-reconversion-gatheli-ram-rehmat-ali-achhnera-tehsil-ved-nagar-luv-pandit-haji-jamiluddin-agra-rss-mohan-bhagwat/1/409155.html (accessed 28 July, 2015).

Rajeshwari, B., 2004, *Communal Violence in India – A Chronology (1947-2003)*, http://www.nagarikmancha.org/images/1242-Documents-Communal_Riots_in_India.pdf (accessed 27 July, 2015).

Shah, Mihir, 2015, 'Tribal alienation in an unequal India', *The Hindu*. 4 July, http://www.thehindu.com/opinion/lead/mihir-shah-writes-on-tribal-alienation-and-need-for-inclusive-growth/article7383721.ece (accessed 28 July, 2015).

The Ahmedabad St. Xavier College Society & Anr. v. State of Gujarat. 1974 AIR 1389, 1975 SCR (1) 173 (The Supreme Court of India, 1974, 26-April).

*The State of Madras v. Srimathi Champak Dorairajan,*1951, SCR 525 (1951) (The Supreme Court of India).

Tiwary, Deeptiman, 2016, 'Farmer suicides up 40 per cent in a year, Karnataka shows sharpest spike', 19 August, http://indianexpress.com/article/india/india-news-india/farmer-suicide-case-in-india-crop-failure-drought-dry-zones-indian-monsoon-2984125/ (accessed 23 December, 2016).

TMA Pai Foundation v. State of Karnataka, 2002, 8 Supreme Court Cases 481 (The Supreme Court, 31 October).

Varshney, Ashutosh and Steven I Wilkinson, 1995, 'Hindu Muslim Riots in India (1960-63): What We Know', *Towards Secular India – October-December,* Vol. I(4) pp. 34-83.

A Vision for Adivasis

Gladson Dungdung

Summary

Adivasis are the indigenous peoples of India, constitutionally known as the Scheduled Tribes, who have unique identities, traditions, culture, ethos and philosophies of life. The community is known for being casteless, classless, and equitable, with a community-centred economy, co-existence with nature, consent based self-rule, dignity and autonomy. They do not rely on the natural resources merely for livelihood, but their identity, culture, history, autonomy, and existence depend on it. The Indian State denies their existence as the indigenous peoples, but it has made clear provisions in the Indian Constitution and introduced several progressive laws for safeguarding them, including their land, territory, and resources. Despite this, their rights are grossly violated and they are being alienated, displaced, and dispossessed from their land, territory and resources in the name of development, economic growth and national interest. In the above situation and circumstances, the Adivasi community needs to envisage its future. The vision could comprise of five major aspects – social transformation, economic prosperity, political empowerment, cultural revival and community centric development. The vision could be realised by the active participation of the community, the sound use of democratic institutions and constitutional and legal provisions.

Introduction

'Adivasis' literally means aboriginal, original or first settlers, or the original dwellers, or the indigenous people of the land of the land (Dungdung, 2013). The term 'Adivasi' was highly popularised by the Adivasi scholar Jaipal Singh Munda during the Jharkhand statehood movement (Munda and Mullick, 2003). Undoubtedly, Adivasis are the Indigenous Peoples of India (Dungdung, 2013). In the Indian Constitution, they are classified as the Scheduled Tribes (STs), and guaranteed certain special rights and privileges under the Fifth and Sixth schedules, Part XVI and Article 46 of the Constitution.[1] There are 705 individual Adivasi ethnic groups notified as the Scheduled Tribes in 30 States and Union

Territories (Ministry of Tribal Affairs (MoTA), 2013). However, several Adivasi ethnic groups are yet to be notified, in which case the percentage of the Adivasi population would certainly go up. This would have a direct impact on the demography and politics of the country.

Unfortunately, the Indian Government had repeatedly declined to accept the existence of Adivasis as the Indigenous Peoples of India in front of the United Nations' Working Group on Indigenous Populations. Nevertheless, on 13 September 2007 the Indian State became party to the United Nations Declaration on the Rights of Indigenous Peoples, which was, of course, the first official admission of the Adivasis as India's indigenous peoples. Finally, it was legitimized by the Apex Court of India on 5 January 2011, while hearing on an appeal (the special leave petition (Cr) No. 10367 of 2010 Kailas & others Vs State of Maharashtra), the Court said that the tribal people (Scheduled Tribes or Adivasis) are the descendants of the original inhabitants of India and as a group one of the most marginalized and vulnerable communities in India.[2]

According to the 2011 census, the Adivasis are 8.6 per cent[3] of India's total population, which is 104 million. About 85 per cent of them live in Rajasthan, Gujarat, Maharashtra, Madhya Pradesh, Chhattisgarh, Odisha, Jharkhand and West Bengal. About 12 per cent live in Assam, Arunachal Pradesh, Nagaland, Meghalaya, Manipur and Tripura and the rest 3 percent live in other states (MoTA, 2013). The sex ratio for the overall population is 940 females per 1000 males, whereas the sex ratio of Adivasi community is 990 females per thousand males;[4] this manifests the status of gender based equality in the community, which is much better than the Indian society despite having more or less the same kind of patriarchal social order. Overtime, the self-dependent community has been almost compelled to become Government dependent due to various factors rising out of wrong governmental policies. More recently, economic liberalization, globalization and privatization have created terrible impact in the social fabric, economy, politics, culture and idea of community development.

This essay is an attempt to understand and visualize a conclusive and achievable vision for the Adivasi community, based on an analysis of historical facts and the present day context.[5] The vision would comprise of short term and long-term goals, to be achieved by the communities in democratic and participatory ways.

Historical Facts and Present Context

Adivasis have by and large been living in or around the forests with a rhythm akin to nature and thus their life cycle moves round nature. They do not merely depend on the natural resources for their livelihood, but their sole identity, culture, autonomy, conscience, tradition, ethos and existence are based on it (Dungdung, 2016). The 2011 Census data suggests that 89.9 per cent of them still live in the rural areas, and merely 10.1 per cent of them have shifted to urban centres.[6] An Adivasi legendary figure, Dr. Ramdayal Munda describes the true characters of the Adivasi community as 'casteless, classless, based on equality, community based economic system, co-existence with the nature, consent based self-rule, dignity and autonomy' (Munda, 2001, pp.10). Regrettably, these inherent characteristics of the community are rapidly disappearing.

The Adivasi economy could be termed as need based or community centric, with hardly any consideration shown in profit making endeavours (Dungdung, 2016). The rural market was more a place for sharing commodities than selling goods to gain profit. Most of the goods were produced by the community, for instance, oil from seeds, broom, mat, edibles, agricultural equipment, etc. Modernisation, with all its positive impacts on one side, has become detrimental to Adivasi communities by imposing on it the profit based economic system and thus all the ills of market dominant economy. Thus, the Adivasis who produced to exchange goods for goods in the rural markets have been strangled by the profit based rural markets limiting them predominantly as consumers.

In the ancient period, the Adivasis possessed undisputed ownership rights over the natural resources and they judiciously used these resources for their existence (Dungdung, 2013). Consequently, they enjoyed autonomy, peace and prosperity. The situation changed rapidly with the incursion of dominant non-Adivasi communities and turned worse during the British rule. On the one hand, the non-Adivasis destroyed the Adivasi civilization, denied them their indigenous identity and did not accept them as fellow human beings, and the British colonialists, on the other hand, used violence against the Adivasis for grabbing their land, territory and resources and even listed a few of them as criminal tribes.

The British introduced a centrally organized administration, a judiciary and a police system. They also introduced the concept of private property as opposed to the traditional notion of collective usufructuary rights of the community. The communal resources were considered as the 'eminent' domain and taken over. Thus, forests and other individually unclaimed fallow lands were declared as the property of the state (Munda & Mullick, 2003). Gradually, the government enacted various policies which induced the marginalization of the Adivasis. They were deprived from the natural resources merely for the government's revenue yielding measures. The Adivasi economy and identity was destroyed by imposing revenue on land and duties on the forest products.

It is a historically known fact that almost one hundred years before India's first recorded independence struggle of 1857, the Adivasis had revolted against the British colonial rule. This is the community that has a history of struggle for more than three centuries. At the very outset, the community resisted to be ruled over by outsiders. They had been freedom loving people and they valued their freedom to govern and to live as a community. To cite a few examples, the Paharia uprising of 1772, the Kol uprising of 1832, Bhumij Movement of 1832-33, the Santal Hul of 1855 (Horo, 2013), etc., were against the imposition of the idea of State on them. The community could not comprehend the concept of paying taxes for lands and forest products because they were fully aware that everything was from the bounty of nature. Nevertheless, the British government forced levy and taxes on them.

Unfortunately, even after Indian independence the status quo remains the same. The Indian rulers were not different from the colonial rulers when it concerned the monopoly over natural resources. The vested interests, the methods of oppression and the basic ideology remained the same (Anjum & Manthan, 2002). The Adivasis' rights over the natural resources were snatched away through various legislations in the name of national interest, economic growth and development. The data suggests that '…from 1951 to 2004, over 37 million people were displaced in the name of development in India. Twenty six million were forcibly displaced due to dams and canals construction alone. The Government accepts a national figure of over fifty million arising from 'development-related-displacement' (JJDMS, 2004, pp. iii). Perhaps, only twenty five per cent people were rehabilitated in some way and seventy five per cent are still waiting for rehabilitation.

At the same time, there has been huge illegal land alienation in the community despite having special legislation for safeguarding their land. According to the Ministry of Rural Development (Government of India), 60,464 cases regarding 85,777.22 acres of illegal transfer of land were registered till 2001-2002 (MoRD, 2003). Out of these:

- 34,608 cases of 46,797.36 acres of land were considered for hearing and the remaining 25,856 cases related to 38,979.86 acres of land were dismissed;
- After the hearing, merely 21,445 cases of 29,829.7 acres of lands were given possession to the original holders and the rest remain with the non-Adivasis.

Subsequently, 2,608 cases of illegal land transfer were registered in 2003-2004, jumping up to 5382 cases in 2007-2008 (Dungdung, 2013, pp. 123). which indicates that illegal land alienation is increasing rapidly.

However, India's war for natural resources continues even today in the name of cleansing the CPI-Maoist forces. This has resulted in gross violation of civil and political rights of the Adivasis. The cases of brutal killing, molestation, rape, torture and false implications of innocent Adivasi men, women, girls, boys and children are countless (Dungdung, 2015). At a very rough and minimum estimate, from 2001 to 2016, 2,000 innocent villagers have been murdered by security forces – 1,000 in Chhattisgarh, 700 in Jharkhand and 300 in Odisha. Similarly, at least 2,000 Adivasi girls and women have been sexually abused by men wearing government uniforms – 1,500 women in Chhattisgarh, 300 in Jharkhand and 200 in Odisha.[7] According to various reports,[8] Adivasis form the vast majority of 27,000 arrested as 'Maoists' and 'encroachers on government land' in these three States, under various laws, including Unlawful Activities (Prevention) Act, Prevention of Terrorism Act, Arms Act, Explosions Act, Criminal Law Amendment Act and Forest Conservation Act 1980 – 17,000 in Chhattisgarh, 8,000 in Jharkhand and 2,000 in Odisha. Ironically, the Indian State regularly refuses or ignores to take action against the actual perpetrators despite several commission reports having exposed the naked truth.

The Adivasi community seems to be the most vulnerable and politically voiceless, despite political representation with forty seven members in the Indian Parliament and more than 500 members in the Legislative Assemblies of several States, elected from the reserved constituencies to represent the Adivasi community. However, due to compulsions of party dynamics the Adivasi issues are hardly ever raised in the corridors of power. It seems clear that the community suffers from leadership vacuum. Most of the Gram Sabhas and other traditional bodies are also under the clutch of political parties. The community does not possess political power in the real sense due to lack of the politicisation.

The colonial concept of civilisation, and the Indian idea of mainstreaming and inclusion, has resulted in alienation of Adivasis from their land, territory, resources, identity, culture, languages and ethos. The invasion of different communities into Adivasis' territories in different periods, and civilization and mainstreaming processes carried out by the colonial masters, and later, by the Indian government, after portraying the Adivasis as uncivilized, backward, sub-human and so on, resulted in their cultural alienation. For instance, the Mundas started writing their surname as 'Singh' and started wearing the sacred thread similar to the Brahmins, to show their superiority among the Adivasi ethnic groups.

Similarly, the Kherwar and Chero Adivasis used 'Singh' as their surname to associate themselves with the Rajput. However, later, they realized it as a blunder, and made corrections to some extent. But by and large, the cultural alienation has continued. The

Adivasis have alienated themselves from their cultural identity by not writing their surname in public places, changing their food habits, altering their lifestyle, making a shift from community to individual life, and from community based to market economy. Adivasis had once inscribed their name in golden letters in national hockey. Today, their representation is dwindling in games and sports, especially in hockey, which was their strength. To cite an example children tend to imitate cricketers and are seen playing cricket instead of hockey and football inside the forest.

The constitutional provision of reservation, modern education system and mainstreaming processes, created a middle class in the Adivasi community, which took the path of huge cultural alienation. This middle class started adopting most of the cultural practices of the modern Indian society. For instance, individualism is placed above community; discrimination is created on the basis of ethnic groups along the lines of caste, colour, status, race and gender, and so on. The community is also alienated from land, territory and resources. The idea of Adivasi development has taken a backseat. The traditional health system, education system and the idea of rural infrastructure creation through community cooperation are slowly disappearing. The worst is that the modern day health facilities, educational endeavours and rural development programs have failed to enhance the life of Adivasis.

The status of education and health of the Adivasi community is among the worst in the country. According to the 2011 Census, the literacy rate is 59 per cent, with 68.5 per cent male and 56.9 per cent female literacy rate (Bagaicha Research Team, 2016). Quality education is a far dream in the Government run schools. The children of Naxal affected states are trapped in violence, highly knowledgeable about the latest weapons – AK-47s, SLRs, and various other kinds of gun, pistol, bomb and landmine, which the security forces and Naxals use to target each other. But they hardly know anything from their text books. The students of class seven are neither able to read the text books of class five properly, nor can they solve mathematical problems of class three (Dungdung, 2015). The government run schools have become food serving centres and the teachers are busy with various government programs with hardly any time to teach, leading to a high increase in dropout rates from class eight to ten – a staggering seventy per cent. In addition, much of the education in Adivasi areas is run by non-Adivasis, is not in the mother tongue, and does not relate to the cultural, ecological and historical roots of Adivasi lives.

The health status of Adivasi children and women is pathetic, as shown by indicators in Table 1.

Table 1: Health status of adivasi children and women

Mortality rate	National average	Adivasis
Neonatal	39	39.9
Post-neonatal	18	22.3
Infant	57	62.1
Child	18.4	35.8
Under five	74.3	95.7

Source: MoTA, 2013.

Adivasi women and children suffer from high levels of anaemia and malnourishment. For instance, 85 per cent of women and 80 per cent of children of West Singhbhum distict of Jharkhand are anaemic, and 64.3 per cent children aged below five are underweight (Alam, 2014). The availability of the health infrastructure in the Adivasis' regions is another area of serious concern. Across India:

    Health sub-centres required: 31,257
    Operational: 27,958
    Primary Health Centres required: 4674
    Operational: 3957
    Community Health Centres required: 1156
    Operational: 998

Towards a Transformed Future

In the above situation and circumstances, the Adivasis community needs to envisage its future for the next five decades or for a century. The vision could comprise of five major aspects – social transformation, economic prosperity, political empowerment, cultural revival and community centric development. The vision could be realised by the active participation of the community, the sound use of democratic institutions and constitutional and legal provisions.

Social transformation

The majority of the Adivasis, from impoverished to the well-off, live under the stigma of being part of the Adivasi community, resulting in the loss of confidence, mental slavery, dependency, multiple alienation and breakdown of the social fabric. It happened because the Adivasi philosophy was neither scripted nor propagated though it is one of the most progressive philosophies in India. At the same time, the dehumanisation processes continued. The Adivasi community was or, in some areas, still is, in a much better position compared to the Indian society—something never highlighted. Instead, the so-called mainstreaming processes were carried out by the Government(s) as well as non-government organisations, especially the right wing fundamentalist forces, who intend to bury the Adivasi identity.

Social transformation should take place in the Adivasi community on the basis of its philosophy. The doctrine comprises of co-existence and symbiotic relationship with nature, community life, liberty, equality, justice, rights, inclusive development, need-based economic system, consent based democracy and fraternity (caring and sharing). Adivasis live with nature and care for its well-being. The concept of 'exploitation' has no place in Adivasi philosophy; therefore, they do not exploit the natural resources but use it to meet their daily needs. Due to this, Adivasi philosophy also addresses the ecological crisis the world is facing. Liberty is a rich human value and it is one of the pillars of any form of progressive liberalism. Therefore, concepts of development need to be aligned with liberty.

Equality is another pillar of the Adivasi philosophy. There are two parts in equality – general equality and gender based equality. The Indian social structure is largely based on caste, race and gender inequality whereas there is no such concept of inequality in Adivasi philosophy. A poor person and a person from a well-off family can work together in the agriculture field, share a meal, dance holding each other's hands, drink rice beer and attend social functions in each other's families. Conceptually, there is no gender based discrimination in the Adivasi community; therefore, both boys and girls are treated equally (though there may be exclusion of women from political decision-making). The happy consequence is that female foeticide and dowry based torture and killings are unheard of among the Adivasis. However, the processes of mainstreaming have diluted this rich disposition by incorporating the concept of discrimination within tribal ethnic groups, to the detriment of the Adivasi community. Therefore, the lofty concept of equality needs to be brought back into practice through the Gram Sabhas and other traditional institutions.

There is no concept of competition in the Adivasi philosophy which encourages cooperation, caring and sharing, resulting in inclusive growth and development. The community does not care only for the protection of the rights of human beings but the intrinsic rights of animals are also taken care with required diligence. For instance, a hunting dog is given equal share of the prey and the Adivasis do not consume milk to protect the right to food of the calf. Besides, consent based democracy and need based economic system facilitate the Adivasi community to maintain its co-existence with nature. Thus, the Adivasis do not indulge in the evil of manipulation and exploitive practices as they hold cooperation as the mantra of their life.

The justice delivery is part of the Adivasi philosophy. However, it has been suppressed by the introduction of the modern judiciary. The Indian State has officially accepted through the Forest Rights Act 2006 that historical injustice has been inflicted on the Adivasis. Yet the injustice continues at the same pace even today. The modern judiciary system has failed in justice delivery to the Adivasi community precisely because it is under the clutch of the people from dominant classes and the fact that the Adivasis do not have the resources to fight a case. Justice is very costly and unaffordable. Within the given context, the Adivasi community has to be educated to settle all its issues, as far as possible, within the community itself through the traditional judicial system, cultivating a broader perspective drawn from the customary, legal and constitutional framework.

The traditional judicial system of Adivasis, which is known for delivering overnight justice, also faced heavy criticisms and was defamed as the kangaroo court for adopting illegal and unconstitutional punishment to culprits in some stray cases. But the overall picture has been bright as it has done tremendous work in delivering fair justice to the Adivasis within matter of weeks at very nominal cost in cases related to land conflict, family dispute, marriage problems, cattle related dispute, etc. For instance, Parha Raja Simon Oraon of Bero block located in Ranchi district of Jharkhand is one such example, where justice is delivered to the villagers within three weeks. The Adivasis of seven villages under his jurisdiction, do not go to court for any dispute. The traditional system needs to be aligned with the Gram Sabhas under the traditional self-governance system. The enforcement of the traditional judiciary system will also have a positive impact in the Adivasi economy and rebuilding the community solidarity.

The Adivasi community needs to get rid of two major social evils – witch hunting and alcoholism. Both have heavily damaged the community reputation of being gender-sensitive and egalitarian, For instance, approximately 1500 Adivasi women were brutally killed in Jharkhand between the years 2001 to 2016, as witches. Most of the victims were either widows or old women, who were really helpless. The Adivasi community has to resolve to get rid of witch hunting through dialogue and critical awareness.

The excess use of alcohol is another social evil, which has heavily blocked the progress of Adivasis. Many women have been widowed because of excessive of alcohol consumption by married men. Families have been broken and the lives of children have been put at stake. The ill has affected the Adivasi youth too, to the extent of destroying their career. Several kinds of liquor e.g. mahua (*Madhuca longifolia*) – used to brew a local variety of liquor, rice beer, etc., are part of Adivasi culture, which are offered to the deity as well as the ancestors during festivals, religious rituals and social events. However, under the cultural tag, other local and several branded liquors have comfortably entered into Adivasi community resulting in accidental deaths, abuses, killings, wife battering and alienation from land. Therefore, there is an urgent need to curb alcoholism, which could be done by having a series of open dialogues in the Gram Sabhas and other traditional local bodies. Since the Gram Sabha is authorized under the PESA Act 1996 to prohibit the use of alcohol and have control over the local markets, Gram Sabhas need to be strengthened. The Adivasi community should have a vision to rebuild it on the basis of its philosophy. In some parts of India such as some villages in Gadchiroli, Maharashtra, there has indeed been a campaign by Adivasis to stop or seriously regulate liquor.

Economic prosperity

The biggest economic challenge for the Adivasi community is to protect the 'need based economic system' or 'community economy' from the organized attack of the market economy. There has been a constant attempt to submerge everything into the market economy, which has resulted in the centralisation of the economy in the hands of a few people. Therefore, instead of handing over the economic resources to the private business entities under the government's recent 'cashless economy' drive, the community needs to enhance its traditional ways of cooperation, caring and sharing of goods and services by keeping the concept of 'profit' away from the community and market, which will bring sustainability, equity and equal economic prosperity. At the same time, the rural markets need to be maintained as a place of sharing goods and services, which presently have become highly profit making centres. Instead of 'cashless economy' the community could play a big role in promoting 'community economy', which can address everyone's needs and the emerging ecological crisis as well.

The community needs to have control over the village economy through the Gram Sabha precisely because the village economy is fully controlled by the outside business class people, resulting in migration and trafficking of the Adivasi youths. Therefore, the Adivasis need to take up entrepreneurship as a challenge, which will facilitate in gaining back the control on village economy in the long run. At the same time, the community should produce and manufacture necessary goods to meet its needs instead of fully depending on the market for everything, and that is quite possible as the community has a long legacy of production and manufacturing to meet its needs. For instance, the Adivasis of Lathakhamhan village in Simdega district of Jharkhand produce brooms, mats, oil, etc., for their use and sell the surpluses in local market.

Ninety per cent of Adivasi population still depend on agriculture, forestry and animal husbandry. However, due to the lack of irrigation facility, technical support and investment, the economy seems to be more or less stagnant. Therefore, the investment, technical support and availability of irrigation facility can make a huge difference. For instance, in Jharkhand, ninety mega dams, four hundred medium dams and 11,878 smalls dams are available – but the water doesn't reach to the agriculture fields of Adivasis but has been provided to the steel and mining industries. The damage done by these dams is substantial and unjustified. But now that they are there, if the water of these dams is prioritised for village farms through small-scale canal and lift irrigation facilities, there would be higher production of crops. Similarly, the value addition on the forest products would strengthen the Adivasi economy. The community should be given complete ownership on the forest resources, as envisaged (but hardly implemented) under the PESA and Forest Rights Act. The agriculture, fishery, horticulture, animal husbandry and forestry need to be aligned and converted into small scale industries through cooperatives, which will enhance the village economy.

The Tribal Sub-Plan (TSP) could play a big role in stabilising the Adivasi economy. Government of India should ensure the allocation of 8.6 per cent budget under the TSP from the central budget per annum as per the Constitutional provision under the Article 275. This fund needs to be spent on human resource development programmes, village development projects, welfare schemes and economic activities (animal husbandry, traditional poultry, farming, horticulture and micro entrepreneurship). The non-utilisation, diversion and misuse of TSP funds are reasons for halting economic activities. The TSP should have a strong monitoring system with involvement of the community. The most important need is the transformation of the Adivasi population from the State's 'burden' into self-reliant people. This could be done by maximum utilisation of the TSP fund in imparting appropriate higher education, technical knowledge and entrepreneurship skills to Adivasi youths, rather than displacing their own traditional and local skills and knowledge. This will create new opportunities towards appropriate economic prosperity, which, of course, should not be at the expense of the environment and local cultures. It would be a mistake to replicate the model of the mainstream economy.

Mining and industry are other vital areas where the paradigm shift is the need of the hour. The major minerals and other natural resources are located in the Adivasi regions of the country, resulting in heavy mining and industrialisation, with hardly any benefit to the Adivasis. Small-scale quarrying, in keeping with ecological sustainability, controlled by Adivasis, and with benefits coming back to them in entirety, could be tried. However, large-scale mining and industrial activities have to be replaced by more decentralised economic options including rural, small-scale manufacturing, crafts, and agriculture based produce. In many parts of India Adivasi populations have on their own or with help from civil society or government, managed to enhance livelihoods through the use of forest produce (e.g., in Vidarbha region of Maharashtra, using the Forest Rights Act), through crafts and small-scale manufacture (e.g., Jharcraft in Jharkhand), or other means. Such activities will guarantee them livelihood possibilities from generation to generation. There would be a flow of economy into Adivasi villages, which will enhance their standard of living, health, education, nutrition, and so on.

Tourism could be another area of economic activity. Since, the Adivasi regions are full of touristic hotspots with numerous waterfalls, natural landscapes with rising and falling hills, tourists could be easily attracted into the region, which, in turn, will create new economic opportunities. The Central and State Governments should provide the basic infrastructures like approach roads, communication facilities, enhancing the spot, along with availing drinking water and sanitation facilities. The Gram Sabha should be given ownership of these spots and the members trained in the art of tourism. Gram Sabha will collect the entry fee from the tourists and also provide them the basic facility and security. The Gram Sabha can pay ten to fifteen per cent revenue to the State, fifty per cent on staff and rest could go to the Gram Sabha's fund. This will create new job opportunities for the Adivasis and also strengthen the village economy; care will need to be taken that outsiders do not control the tourism economy, and that activities are not destructive to the environment.

Political Empowerment

Politics decides the future of any nation, society and community today. However, the Adivasi community is not able to influence Indian politics for multiple reasons. There permeates the culture of silence in the community and a slavery mindset among the Adivasi political leaders. Therefore, they are not able to use the democratic institutions to the advantage of the Adivasi communities. The politicisation of the Adivasi community has not yet happened in a systematic way. For instance, there have been endless mass resistances against displacement across the Adivasi regions in the country, there were also police firings and brutalities on the public protests, but whenever there is election of local bodies, Legislative Assemblies or Parliament, the Adivasis cast their votes in favour of those political parties whose economic policies alienate them from land, forests and other natural resources. The majority of the Adivasi population becomes the traditional voters of any political party instead of auditing (and if necessary replacing) them on the basis of their performance, policies and programmes. Jaipal Singh Munda had brought the Adivasi politics to the centre stage, but later, he was co-opted by the Congress Party. Thus, the status quo remains. Therefore, the culture of silence needs to be converted into the culture of critical questioning rising out of awareness and education, sharing information and imparting analytical skill. The politicisation of the Adivasi community will bring about the necessary change in the community.

The reestablishment of self-rule through the strengthening of Gram Sabha is another critical area of work. The Gram Sabha is said to be the most powerful body in the democratic system, which has been legitimized through various legislations like PESA, 1996, Forest Rights Act, 2006 and Land Acquisition Rehabilitation and Resettlement Act, 2013. However, in most of the villages, the Gram Sabhas have either become the political party centric institutions or the Government scheme delivery centres. The Gram Sabhas are unable to play a decisive role for the community. The common Adivasis do not really practice their power due to lack of information, legal knowledge and authoritarian attitude. Consequently, the political parties, corporate houses, NGOs, extremist groups and other vested interest groups have gained control over the Gram Sabhas. The people of each village need to be given critical awareness about the role, power and authority of the Gram Sabhas. If the Gram Sabhas are strengthened, the major issues like land alienation, corporate resource grab, trafficking, migration, etc., could easily be curbed. Adivasis can learn from examples like Mendha-Lekha village in Gadchiroli district of Maharashtra, which established self-rule more than two decades ago with the slogan 'Our government in Mumbai and Delhi, but we *are* the government in our village.' Demands can also be made for laws such as the Village Council Act of Nagaland, which empowers village bodies to take most decisions; most states have never extended such powers as per the intent of the constitutional amendment legislated as PESA.

Historically, the Adivasis had their own system of governance, which was free from the police system. The traditional system of governance still exists among several ethnic groups. For instance, there is Manjhi-Pargana system among the Santhals, Manki-Munda system among the Munda Adivasis, Doklo-Sohor system among Kharias and Parha system among the Oraon Adivasis (Pal, 2008). Though majority of them respect their traditional system of governance the imposition of the so-called modern democratic system has played down the importance of this. The voting system has overshadowed 'consent', which was real democracy, where everyone had a say in the decision making process. Presently, the traditional system of governance is restricted to social affairs and its political role has been curtailed. Consequently, the political leaders are riding over the traditional system of governance to secure their vote banks and also having control on the community. This needs to be reversed. The community should have control over politics through the traditional system of governance. It should play a vital role in selecting effective political representatives for the local bodies, Legislative Assemblies and Parliament.

Political leadership building is another core area of intervention. Needless to say that there is a complete lack of the vocal, critical, analytical, inspirational and trustworthy political leaders in the community. It is a big problem that 104 million Adivasis have no credible voice in the Indian Parliament despite having forty seven political representatives. The major problem is that there is lack of perspective, lack of deep knowledge on issues and lack of skills to influence the corridor of power. There is also lack of research team and intellectual support to these representatives. Thus, the Adivasi issues are not raised in the corridor of power. The Adivasi community needs to build credible leadership, create an intellectual support group to the political leadership and create a centre, where political leadership could be trained.

Political unity is another thrust area that needs intervention. Although the Adivasis can play a decisive role in the regional politics in several states, which can have a direct impact in the national politics of India, due to multiple divisions, they have totally failed. There are clear divisions on the basis of ethnicity, religion and region as well. In particular, the division on the ground of religion has damaged the political unity of the community. The right wing Hindutva forces have harvested on the division in different parts of the country. The RSS and its allies have convinced sections of Adivasis that the Christian Adivasis are their main enemy. Consequently, they are engaged in religious conflicts and their votes are largely divided between mainline parties. This division has resulted in land alienation, corporate land grab, police brutalities, race based atrocities and other injustices. There is a crucial need of political unity among the Adivasis, which could be on the basis of the identity of being an Adivasi irrespective of religious beliefs and expressions.

However, the prime long-term political vision of the Adivasi community should be the establishment of autonomy in governance within Adivasi traditions, self-determination and self-rule. The President of India and the Governors of the states were made the custodians of Adivasis through the Constitutional provisions, and the district collectors or deputy commissioners were made watchdog of their land through various legislations but these legal authorities have totally failed in protecting Adivasis' rights. This clearly implies that the State has failed in protecting the rights of Adivasis and also in justice delivery. Therefore, the only way to protect the Adivasis' rights is by acquiring autonomy, self-determination and self-rule in the Adivasis' territories within the constitutional set-up of the Indian union.

Cultural revival

Cultural alienation is one of the major areas that need quick intervention. This could be seen in the deprivation of Adivasis from their community life, identity, languages, religion and sports, etc., the result of a well thought out design of 'mainstreaming'. Whatever the Adivasi community possesses is tagged with negative terms like 'worst', 'impure' and 'wild'. These tags have been thrust in their minds, and convinced them that they need to join the processes of mainstreaming to become a 'civilised' human being. Such cultural alienation could be contained by a cultural revolution, by the propagation of the Adivasi philosophy, to make them understand the actual meaning of being Adivasis. The Adivasi philosophy should be scripted as literature in different ethnic groups and in other regional languages, which will create pride in the Adivasis. This transformation into pride could be done through social events, mass conferences and discussions. Gram Sabhas or tribal councils and assemblies should be the centres for a cultural revolution which can reach to every family.

The first cultural alienation could be seen in the change of lifestyle. Community living is the foundation of the Adivasi community but it has rapidly changed into individualism. Now the community centric activities have been shifted into individual centric, adopted from the so-called mainstream of the Indian society. The community centric activities need to be promoted even in the towns and cities. The community should be made critically aware about the impact of the market economy, which is forcing them to adopt the individual centric life style. The Adivasi co-existence with nature needs to be brought back.

The second major alienation that is taking place is in the area of Adivasi identity. The majority of Adivasis see their Adivasi identity as a stigma. Therefore, they attempt to hide their identity by not writing their surnames. For instance, the majority of Adivasi youth using Facebook do not expose their surname to hide their Adivasi identity. The Adivasi women have started writing their surname like 'Devi' similar to the Hindu women. There are several Adivasi ethnic groups like Kharwar, Gond, Chero, etc., use 'Kumar' for boy and 'Kumari' for girl instead of using their surname. The Adivasis need to be made aware about the importance of their identity and its link with nature.

Third alienation could be seen in the alienation from traditional food. The food habit has also changed very fast. The Adivasi foods like millets, maize, cereals, double boiled rice, food items made of rice are called as food of the backward classes. Therefore, many Adivasis have changed their food habits. For instance, the Chinese food items are served in marriage and other social functions instead of traditional food. The city-dwelling Adivasi children do not want to eat the traditional food for its black colour and prefer to eat the white coloured food items. The racial discrimination has impacted deep alienation in the minds of Adivasi children. The food habits could be restored by propagation of its importance, availability of nutrition in addressing several diseases. For instance, there are several herbs and cereals, which are used as vegetables and other food items, which are medicinal for blood pressure, diabetics etc.

Fourth area of cultural alienation is Adivasi languages, which are disappearing rapidly.[9] Several ethnic groups have lost their mother tongues and adopted Hindi, Bhojpuri, Oriya, Bangla and other languages as their main language. At the same time, the city-dwelling Adivasis, especially youth and children, do not know their languages because their parents did not teach them deliberately to get rid of the stigma of being Adivasis. They encouraged their children to learn English and Hindi, and other regional languages instead. The language could be made alive only by using it. The Adivasi children should adopt three tier languages – mother tongue, Hindi or relevant state language and English as the global language. This could be done through the traditional community learning centres and educational institutions. The mother tongue should be incorporated as primary language in formal schools also, and in later classes to learn state language, or Hindi, and English. Children should also be inspired towards creative writings like poem, stories, articles in their own languages, which could be published in local magazines and journals. Educational centres also need to be transformed to provide most relevant, enjoyable learning that is rooted in Adivasi cultures and ecology along with outside knowledge. Examples of this include Adharshila in Madhya Pradesh, Bhasha Adivasi Academy in Gujarat, Imlee Mahuaa in Chhattisgarh.[10]

The fifth major area is games and sports. Hockey, the national game of India used to be the integral part of the Adivasi community. Jaipal Singh Munda was the first Indian captain, whose team won the Gold in the Olympics. Among nine gold medals India has won in the Olympics, eight medals go to hockey. However, cricket has taken over the fields of hockey, football and other local sports. The youth need to be made aware about the importance of local games and sport, which can also provide them job opportunities. The community should organize annual games and sports festivals at the block, district and state levels.

Additional areas for change are arts and music, of which Adivasis have such an incredible wealth; and health, in which traditional Adivasi knowledge and practices could be added to by modern medicine in an appropriate mix, practiced through community health systems. An example of this is the Tribal Health Initiative in Tamil Nadu.[11]

Community centric development

The idea of inclusive development is part of the Adivasi philosophy. The Adivasi community follows the 'development' model derived from nature, where all the living beings have equal space and opportunity for growth (cultural, intellectual, and social). There is no space for competition, leading to inclusive growth. Therefore, the community centric development is much easier to promote. The focus should be on the development of basic infrastructure like construction of good houses, linking villages with proper roads, availability of well managed health centres and properly administered primary school in every village, availability of electricity, pure drinking water and sanitation facilities in every village. This could be done by the use of TSP fund with community cooperation and its involvement in planning, implementation and monitoring of the rural infrastructure building. However, the community ownership needs to be put in place, which will facilitate in taking care and repairing of the rural infrastructure.

Besides, the rural infrastructure creation, quality services need to be provided in the villages especially in education and health services. Presently, there is lack of quality in the elementary education, the education centres have become food serving centres. Similarly, the health centres are defunct. The teachers, nurses and doctors are paid without providing quality services to the villages. This needs to be changed with community involvement, making available quality teachers and making the medical staff accountable. The Gram Sabha should be given authority for ensuring quality health and education services, building on local and traditional knowledge and adding to it from outside.

Conclusion

Although the Adivasis are the first settlers or indigenous peoples of India, who have a history of more than three centuries of resistance against the imposition of the idea of the State, alienation from lands, territories and resources, and imposition of western concept of development, have forced them to struggle for survival. The invasion of different communities into their territories pushed them to the margins and led to their alienation. Therefore, the Adivasi community needs to envisage its future by designing both short and long term goals. The democratic institutions, constitutional provisions and laws could be used to realise the short-term vision where the community needs to play a prominent role by activating and involving its traditional institutions.

However, in the long-term vision, there must be social, economic, political, cultural and developmental transformation in the Adivasi community. The community must regain its lost lands, territories and resources, where it should enforce the idea of self-determination, self-reliance and self-rule being the part of the Indian union. The vision of the community must be guided by its philosophy. And through this transformation, they can perhaps also help the rest of Indian society to become more equitable, just, and ecologically sustainable.

Endnotes

1. Constitution of India, published by the Ministry of Law and Justice (Government of India) in 2007.
2. The Supreme Court order on the SLP (Cr) No. 10367 of 2010, Kailas & others V State of Maharashtra.
3. See Census Report, 2011, Government of India.
4. ibid.
5. Based on the experience of the author, this article is primarily related to adivasi or tribal populations of central and eastern India, and does not deal with issues of such populations in other parts of India.
6. This data has been taken from the author's upcoming book (*Endless Cry in the Red Corridor*).
7. For instance, see JHRM (Jharkahand Human Rights Movement), 2012.
8. See also essay on Language Futures in this volume.
9. See www.vikalpsangam.org for details of these.
10. See details at http://www.tribalhealth.org.

References

Alam, Mahtab, 2014, 'BJP has ruled Jharkhand for much of its 14-year existence but has delivered precious little', *Scroll.in*, 19 December.

Anjum, Arvind & Manthan, 2002, *Displacement and Rehabilitation*, Pune: National Centre for Advocacy Studies.

Bagaicha Research Team, 2016, 'Deprived of rights over natural resources, impoverished Adivasis get prison: A study of undertrials in Jharkhand', Ranchi: B. R. Team.

Dungdung, Gladson, 2013, *Whose Country is it Anyway?* Kolkata: Adivaani.

Dungdung, Gladson, 2015, *Mission Saranda: A War for Natural Resources in India,* Ranchi: Deshaj Prakashan.

Dungdung, Gladson, 2016, *Adivasi aur Vanadhikar,* New Delhi: Prithvi Prakashan.

Horo, Albert, 2013, 'Jharkhand Movement', *International Journal of Humanities and Social Science Invention,* Volume 2 (4) 1 April, pp.01-06. Available at www.ijhssi.org (accessed on 15 January, 2017).

JHRM, 2012, *Jharkhand Human Rights Report 2001-2011*, Ranchi: Jharkhand Human Rights Movement.

JJDMS, 2004, 'Editorial', *Jharkhand Journal of Development and Management Studies,* December, Vol. 2, pp. iii.

MoRD, 2003, *Annual Report 2002-03*, Delhi: Ministry of Rural Development, Govt. of India.

MoTA, 2013, *Statistical profile of Scheduled Tribes in India 2013*, Delhi: Ministry of Tribal Affairs, Govt. of India.

Munda, R.D. & S.B. Mullick, 2003, *The Jharkhand Movement,* New Delhi: International Working Group on Indigenous Affairs & Binderai Institute of Research and Action.

Munda, Ramdayal, 2001, *Adivasi Astitva aur Jharkhandi Asmitake Sawal.* New Delhi: Prakashan Sansthan.

Pal, Sudhir, 2008, *Hasiye se Hukumat,* New Delhi: Adhar Prakashan.

CONCLUDING PERSPECTIVES

A Debate on the Future is a Debate on the Present
Notes from the Authors' Dialogue

Shrishtee Bajpai and Sarita Bhagat

Introduction

As part of the making of this book, Kalpavriksh and Society for Promoting Participative Ecosystem Management (SOPPECOM), along with Oxfam, organized a three-day dialogue on India's Future from 23 to 25 February, 2016, at Centre for the Study of Developing Societies, New Delhi. The motive behind the dialogue was to enable a platform for cross-fertilization of the ideas across the thirty odd themes that this book covers. The participants were mostly authors and the editors of this book, along with some others who added relevant content for the discussion. In the opening session, Ashish Kothari and K. J. Joy emphasized that the processes of resistance and reconstruction are inherent in imagining the future. They also laid out two primary objectives of the dialogue, first to understand the perspectives on diverse topics from participants engaged in cross-sectoral learning and second to link these to the five pillars of the alternatives that have emerged out of the Vikalp Sangam process.[1] These five pillars – 1) Ecological resilience and wisdom, 2) Direct and delegated democracy, 3) Social well-being and justice, 4) Economic democracy, and 5) Cultural knowledge and diversity – were used as an analytical structure to the dialogue, without getting into the trap of clubbing them into any neat categorizations. This was followed by presentations delivered by experienced activists and academics from across India. Participants shared the key arguments of their papers, their vision for the future and pathways to reach there.

Before envisioning these futures it is important to understand that in the present scenario of fast depleting natural resources and growing inequalities, this is a daunting task. Authors of the papers have struggled to imagine the future and not be completely bogged-down by the present. However, the process of envisioning is crucial as it may influence the course of events and can help to lose the cynicism of the present to retain the hope for the future. One of the common understandings that emerged from this dialogue was to develop certain boundaries (economy, democracy) to help visualise the future and understand different linkages. Also the need to maintain internal consistency in the dialogue to get a futuristic picture – even if we are dreaming wild, we need to ground it on reality.

Ecological Sustainability[2]

Sharachchandra Lele, in his paper 'Environmental Governance in Future India', laid out the proximate causes such as weak enforcement, light green judiciary and socio-economic forces that have led India to what Ramachandra Guha calls an 'environment basket case'. The future of environmentalism has to be about the protection of nature by ensuring quality of life, livelihood generation and maintaining intergenerational equity. The above can be realised if we start to move towards decentralization of operational authority, but with an overarching regulatory authority, democratic accountability, enhancement of technical capability and with effective conflict resolution support. However, during the discussion around the key aspects of the paper, various participants stressed the need to critique the persistent desire to scale up and the idea of unending growth that conveniently vouches for anthropocentric arguments. The baffling question that remains is how do we deal with the pollution of minds? The need for radical transformation in the value systems (away from aspects like selfishness and individualism, consumerism, elitism and anti-democratic functioning) and the process to reach there was a common concern. To explore the paradox of strict laws and environment crises, we need to start with questioning the current development model that displaces natural capital by financial capital.

Political Democracy[3]

Power is inherent in all relationships in society, characterized by inequality, sustained by manipulation, structural or actual physical violence. However, the question is how can these change, either with a conventional revolutionary theory or by using cracks in the system? According to Pallav Das, the future of power lies in radically changing the current cultural practices, systems, and institutions. Power equations will thrive in and support the society that has direct democracy, institutions of representation downwardly accountable with breaks of tenure, expenditure through a common fund with equal access, cooperative ownership of the means of production and no endless growth. Das does not see the abolishment of power as a possibility, but seeks for abolishment of concentration of power. During the discussions, Aseem Shrivastava made an interesting intervention about the socialisation of consciousness and clear distinction between power and freedom. For example, many *Dalits* will accept to be repressed due to the prevalent social order and will never challenge the repressor because of the internalisation of the repressive practices. This point was further augmented by two critical observations made by Bharat Patankar – the need to think about the role of power within the families and power as a medium of love. Spiritual power and the role of moral power were also suggested to be included in the paper.

Discussion of power cannot escape one of its very crucial loci: 'law', which is both, a medium of exercising power, and one of correcting injustices. Power is re-articulated and negotiated in various forms and makes law a site of struggle. Heavy evidence based law deprives a lot of powerless people from accessing justice. The two relationships that become inevitable to examine are: 1) relationship between law and justice and 2) relationship between law and society. The vision of law, for Arpitha Kodiveri, lies in making the judicial process more accessible and creating pluralistic forms of dispute resolutions. Given the current inaccessibility, especially to marginalised sections, creation of mediation centres to address issues of injustice will be crucial. The discussions that followed the presentation were intriguing as they questioned the extent of the role that law can play in society and about the necessity to formalise all relationships. The vision should also take into account the power of customary law and the societies that are self-regulatory and need minimal formal judicial intervention. Procedure of law-making has to go through an overhaul to be able to encompass the contextual realities and law needs to play a lesser role in self-reliant communities.

Human rights trump both power and law. In spite of the range of institutions pushing for human rights, one of the most active civil societies and relatively free media, India has amongst the worst statistics in the world and witnesses horrific human rights violations. Miloon Kothari probes this contradiction[4] and envisions the need of a more rigorous approach to human rights, not in law but as ethical and moral principles. To guarantee that no human rights is violated, one has to ensure self-determination by allowing local people to have the right over the natural resources first and the greater use of the UN human rights frameworks. Human rights in some sense give a space to exercise agency and create a context for mobilisation. However, critiques were raised about the role of UN as an adequate system to protect human rights. Rajni Bakshi felt that human rights have to cut across class/caste and not be handicapped by them and this in turn will require thinking about the nature of human rights institutions. Aseem Shrivastava, made a comment about imagining a future in which human rights norms and law are exceptions and not having to be used all the time. This point was further amplified by K. J. Joy's observation on proliferation of rights and the tendency to transform basic needs (that the state fails to provide) into rights, which results in overshadowing the state's coercive punitive action.

However, can the present parliamentary democracy ensure the protection of human rights or do we need radical changes in the democratic forms? The ideological synthesis by Aditya Nigam reckons for a radical social democracy. His attempt in the paper is to liberate authors like Ambedkar and Gandhi from the historical context and restage these thinkers for the encounters of today. The need for radical social democracy arises from the nature of current parliamentary, representational democracy that does not ensure equality, the fundamental principle of democracy. It, in fact, results in concentration of power and distrust among local and marginalised communities. The discussion around the paper was engaging as it posed a daunting challenge to the way we imagine the future of Indian democracy itself. In addition, what will radical social democracy look like in a post-national world and in fact what will India's future look without a parliamentary democracy? Clearly, these were perplexing questions and Nigam responded to these concerns by stating his limitations so far in the envisioning. He recognises that more thinking is needed on the form of party-less democracy, localization of economic life and ecological principles. The post-national world is not simply 'global', but it is vital to acknowledge that the emancipatory potential of the nation is exhausted and, in fact, the state is now even more repressive and in a relentless fixation on creating new identities.

Can these complexities find their way through multilinear critical theory? This idea stems from the recognition of the complexities and multifaceted realities that human existence abounds. Practice is sometimes ahead of theory, e.g., renewable energy sources, equitable water distribution, other alternatives. Bharat Patankar advocates a multilinear critical theory, which will bring together various movement strands including ecology, marginalized peoples, etc. The hope is of a non-violent struggle, which includes women, Dalits and *Adivasis*. In the course of discussion, participants felt that although the attempt of the paper is optimistic, there would be unrelenting complexity of maintaining internal consistency among multiple strands of theories. For example, there is still distrust between ecology movements and Dalits. Patankar nevertheless affirmed that the emergence of new theory by synthesizing existing ones is pertinent to combat the challenges and contradictions mentioned above. The alternative theories should emerge or should be the expansion of original theories; it is time that we reduce our dependence on original theories of Gandhi and Marx.

Economic Democracy

One of the main steps in making communities self-reliant is to increase local participation in the decision-making process, especially related to the livelihood options. Nine papers presented around the theme 'economic democracy', explored its contours and the discussions that followed each presentation further added to the richness of the ideas. We need plural futures and localization is one form of a plural future, according to the authors, Aseem Shrivastava and Elango R. in their paper, 'Regionalisation and Localisation of Economies'. We are presently in a centralised economy, where globalisation is used as a euphemism. The authors expressed their contention to such a scenario and fore-grounded the immediate need of institutional arrangements that can curb the present trajectory of growth. A new kind of urbanisation and creative thinking about market networks can trigger a movement against the current economic growth model. This includes initiatives from the local people, where appropriately small or regional ecological units become ideal units for economic prosperity. However, during discussions, people expressed apprehensions about the power play of caste, land rights, and human rights, which can complicate the localization process. Questions regarding the role of the state, determination of relations of production and the process of planning in a localized economy were asked. Aseem Shrivastava replied stressing the strong need for the State to recede, as it only tends to aggravate the matter. In addition, ecological problems cannot be tackled with the so-called corporate bureaucracy in place and we need to bring back the discourse of communities participating in the decision-making process.

In tune with the above arguments, K. J. Joy presented a paper on 'Biomass-based Options for "Rural Revitalisation"' and highlighted the need to overhaul the institutional/organizational forms, capacities, pooling of biomass and changes in policy. There is a need for radical restructuring in the social institutions, creating awareness about informed choices and possibility of exploration within and outside the system. The paper illustrates tested models of small-scale biomass production that takes care of all needs of a family and yet produces surplus for agro-industrial production, using energy-saving and locally controlled biomass technologies. However, due to the constraint of resources for research and development in the sector, many interesting trends remain unexplored.

An economic democracy will also have to re-work its ways to deal with labour. Dunu Roy invoked interesting arguments about the emergence of labour relations and a massive conflict between capital and labour. With growing advanced technology, the values of capitalism will always be transferred – for example, self-employment is often capitalism in disguise. The future of industrial labour lies in radical change of two determinants of capitalist society: first, competition (will capitalism be able to revive its internal competition and how will it affect the working class and needed solidarity?) and second, profit (where is the profit coming from without writing off the social and ecological externalities?). These are difficult questions to think about for the future of labour. For Aditya Nigam, the key question was the idea of property. In India, for example, there is preponderance of small ownerships and it is crucial to deliberate, if the future of labour is imagined as the slave of the industry or as a part of industrial cooperatives? There is a massive technological interruption that will unfold in the coming decade and that will result in huge displacements and emergence of large-scale vulnerable unemployment. The formidable question is, are we in a position to deal with a future robotic world? Anant Phadke, emphasized the need to differentiate between demanding labour rights from the State in contrast to seeking welfare from the State.

Definitely, the future that Dunu Roy envisions for labour cannot thrive in the current capitalist markets. Can a different market future be envisioned? Rajni Bakshi posed a pertinent question about the possibility for humanity to redefine the term value. She emphasised the need to look at the evolution of the contemporary meaning of words like profit and value and map the measures and initiatives like Timbaktu Collective that promote non-monetised exchange. Spaces like Vikalp Sangam[5] can be effective platforms to push for solidarity economy. We live in an economy that is not even social let alone a community, an economy that attempts to rationalise, monetise, measure everything and treat 'value' as a superset to society and community. In such a scenario, we need to distinguish between personal and private property, to be able to solve the disjuncture that it tends to create within the communities. The current political discourse and market system is infiltrating the society and dividing it. Extremely crucial to this entire discussion was the concern around the creation of a self-sufficient society. The creation of culture and practices that promote the idea of sufficiency is the most challenging task for the practitioners, intellectuals and others concerned about the alternative world. Adopting a 'degrowth discourse' can be one step towards a solidarity economy.

Currently, rapid urbanisation and the capitalist mode of production have disoriented the way we produce and consume. After the green revolution, India has lost its abundant fertile land and different varieties of cropping patterns. Bharat Mansata and Vijay Jardhari stressed on the need of having a decentralized mode of water allocation, where communities decide the amount of water required by their crops. They envision the future based on integrated watershed management, forest regeneration and agro-ecological models, with participatory decision-making as the crucial element for achieving 'Anna Swaraj' or Food

Sovereignty. However, participants expressed scepticism about the social and financial viability of organic farming and its capability to challenge the emerging mechanistic mode of farming. Participants raised their discomfort regarding the focus on production instead of distribution, and this was brought forth after Aditya Nigam's remark regarding 'capital cannibalism', that has captured all forms of production and distribution and has brutally hindered the claim to access. Rajeshwari Raina suggested bringing the discourse on 'Agriculture in the Environment', where growing crops works in tandem with the principles of nature and not 'Agriculture versus Environment'. Mansata and Jardhari acknowledged these challenges but maintained that ecologically sustainable farming is the only viable future we have.

Vivek Shastry, in his paper, stressed the need to challenge the discourse of infinite growth, which thereby creates infinite energy demand. The focus should be on using clean technologies to distribute energy, with least cost and minimum ecological footprint. The basic precondition for sustainable energy is decentralisation for better access to energy and use innovative technologies which modify with the needs of the local people. To promote green energy and suggest informed choices of alternatives, it is also important to look at the relative efficiency of the fossilized and non-fossilized energy. The need of the hour is to think about questions like why energy, who needs it, and how and how much? Taking into account the consumption patterns of different sections of the population is vital for sustainable and equitable energy future, as industrial modernity results in class based, convenient mode of seeking solutions.

The change in the consumption patterns and living styles will also require a change in the way our cities are designed. Currently, cities are marred with poor infrastructure, inadequate water supply, improper waste segregation and disposal, poor public transport, and so on. Keeping in mind that urbanisation is going to increase in future with large number of people living in slums, Rakesh Kapoor argued for radical departures from the current approaches, mindsets, and institutions, and listed the elements of future cities. These cities will have good risk assessment and disaster planning preparedness, dispersed urbanisation, and management of river and water bodies for conservation, transport, and flood control. However, during the discussions participants felt that the future of cities need to be looked at from the perspective of the poor as well. Without including food, health, education into the vision and democratic science/knowledge generation for sustainable urbanisation, one cannot radically change the future of cities. The beautification plans are usually corporate sponsored and these band-aid solutions cause destruction at the periphery of the cities, often inhabited by poor migrants and the displaced. One has to intently look at the high level of externalities that urbanization creates and go back to the key question of do we need aggregation at the urban centres in the first place?

The paper by Sujit Patwardhan explored another crucial dimension of urban areas – transportation. He briefly navigated through the distorted scenario of transportation in India built in the capitalist mode of production, before moving onto his vision. The vision of transportation in India will have free space for pedestrians to walk and with cycle tracks. In addition, there will be mixed land use to reduce the need for mobility (with work place and residence close to each other as far as possible), use of sustainable energy and parks rather than parking lots. Sujit also highlighted issues like urban agriculture, waste recycling, and creation of recreational spaces to be considered while planning for transportation. However, aspirations and personal desire of accumulation (such as an aspiration for a personal vehicle) came out as a hard challenge that requires cultural interventions. There was a suggestion by a few participants to start thinking about the ways of creating aspiration for public transport. Changing attitudes is always a tough task, but with creative efforts, such changes can steadily be envisaged.

Social Well Being and Justice[6]

A world of ethical and communal harmony would be possible only if the dignity of communities of different ethnicities, faiths, and cultures is respected and within these, of different genders, ages and abilities. Recognition of multiple identities and elimination of minority as a uniform identity is important to create greater state accountability for violence against minorities. Irfan Engineer, after contextualising at length about the contemporary condition of minorities in the country, emphasised the need to develop minority consciousness rather than religious consciousness, which would mean breaking away from any kind of religious identities.

As we speak on the rights, equality and justice of the minorities, Anand Teltumbde emphasised on the institutionalisation of secularism as an essential step to ensure social justice for Dalits. After briefly sketching current social injustice perpetrated on Dalits and the failure of reservations to change the situation for the majority of them, Teltumbde gave a detailed account of the future that he envisions for them in India. The future is in outlawing caste (including through constitutional change), but by itself that will not be enough, and there is a need to create a firewall between religion and state, through secularism. However, for participants, the idea of elimination of reservations was a difficult proposition; even if there have been very few who have actually benefitted from it. Anant Phadke raised concern about the challenge in the process of altering the caste consciousness that pervades society because the annihilation of caste would mean the annihilation of prejudices.

Another very important community that rarely finds its presence in the mainstream social sciences and is subsumed under farmers are the pastoralists. Pastoralists are widespread in India and their contribution to Indian economy is huge (India is the world's largest producer and exporter of milk). In addition, the pastoralist system thrives on a low carbon economy, depending on nature or traditional farming methods for the products, creating positive impact on the biodiversity of pastures and maintaining a balance between the available natural resources and livestock. However, they are usually excluded from the mainstream policy forums and drastically depleting natural resources have further added to their plight. According to Ilse Köhler-Rollefson, considering the above facts, the future of the pastoralist community lies in creating sustainable livestock production and an alternative model of pastoral heritage, and this can be initiated by formally recognising the rights of this community. Rajeshwari Raina felt that the vision should also look into some conflicting exchanges between pastoralists and poor farmers. Miloon Kothari proposed to move towards the global declaration of rights of the pastoralists in tune with recognition of violations within the pastoralist communities, for example, the issue of violence against women.

Cultural Diversity and Knowledge Democracy[7]

The organised and centralized form of science has undermined the traditional knowledge systems and has created unfair, undemocratic science and technology. Rajeshwari Raina proposed decentralized and integrated knowledge systems that produce organic intellectuals from all walks of life. Her vision for the future includes knowledge not bound by structure but inclusion of institutional norms (including traditional and local knowledge) chosen through democracy. This will initiate reciprocity and equality between diverse natural, social, physical, and financial assets, making knowledge as commons. The author proposed to build wider knowledge consortia bringing on board various forms and practitioners of knowledge and linking with international producers of knowledge.

In earlier times, there was a space in mainstream science and technology institutions to deliberate on social-ecological issues; however, that space has considerably eroded. Probably very few people in the country are working on technology alternatives. Dinesh Abrol has been trying to re-envision the connection of technology and rural industrialisation in the hope that technological revolutions will find a space in social revolutions or movements. He argued for technological alternatives that can play a significant role in the realization of sustainable development goals. The pathway to technological alternatives has to be part of a radical transformation in socio-technical systems, guided by social equity and ecological sustainability, requiring alternate social carriers of innovation and development.

The discussion around the two papers raised a very crucial point of disconnection between the traditional knowledge systems, technology and social movements. There is a dire need to link knowledge systems to the ground level political struggles to attack the political and corporate fascism of contemporary times. In connection to democratising knowledge systems and envisioning their space in social mobilisation, Nagmani Rao, argued for ways to explore the connection between public imagination and indigenous knowledge systems. Many knowledge systems are orally transmitted across generations, but, there is absolutely no recognition and according to Ashish Kothari, oral knowledge should find space in the knowledge systems that we recognise.

An art, for example, is an important form of the knowledge system. Art can either be associated with people's way of living or to express resistance in a social movement. However, due to the mainstreaming of particular forms of arts, a few become privileged over the others. Sudha Gopalkrishnan gave an insightful perspective into the current state of performing arts in India, including its codified forms and elite patronage. Creating public spaces is one way to revitalise old performing arts. The future of the arts has to be participatory and decentralized, although state's patronage is important, but it should find means to be even and equal by playing a facilitative role. For example creating district level committees to promote art and associating it with tourism or other sectors. However, various sociological concerns were raised about the envisioning the art's future. Rajeshwari Raina posed an important concern regarding the role of the arts in creating and changing identities and hence the necessity to explore caste dimension of the arts. The egalitarian future of the arts has to recognise the embedded discriminations that traditional art forms have practiced for long and have to broaden the space to become democratic.

Craft is also an important form of traditional knowledge that needs to be rescued from the capitalist mode of production. Uzramma's vision for the future of crafts is a society in which producers own the means of production, capital and marketing. The dominant capitalist mode of production undermines the crafts and other related modes of production and hence it has become imperative to revive the traditional craft industries that require small capital investment, low-energy production and have potential to usher in democratic control. Significant interventions were made by participants regarding the role of intermediaries and crafts as networks to gain identity in the market, rather than monopoly of individual producers. Anant Phadke, raised an important concern regarding the tendency of petty production linked to local markets to move towards the capitalist forms, unless there are cooperatives, collective and state supported systems. Ashish Kothari gave an example of Jharcraft to highlight the need to differentiate between state support and state dependence.

Among all these, media is a distinctive arena that cuts across various themes of culture, politics, power, and social justice. The role of media in cultural diversity and democracy is extremely vital. However, due to intensifying corporate control the fourth estate has been denigrated to becoming like commercial real estate. Paronjoy Guha Thakurta proposed a future of media in India that is not controlled by the few powerful elites and corporations and does not treat people as mere consumers. The alternative media has to challenge power, ensure accountability, and gain independence by generating funds from various other sources and not only through advertisements. Rajni Bakshi made an interesting intervention about the social media being a double-edged sword as it enhances but also undermines democracy, especially when there are very little filters to separate fact from fiction. Vijay Jardhari questioned the sociality of the social media. There is a need to deliberate more on the kind of regulatory institutions that will be required to create socially responsible media.

Conclusion

Ashish Kothari, in his remarks to bind together the discussions, observed that the presentations and the subsequent discussions cut across various themes and had diverse perspectives but it was evident that most of the participants veered towards decentralization and democratization (a more people centred way of living) while addressing the issues of inequality and discrimination. The themes also envisaged to establish a relationship with a larger world order and to dream ecologically and culturally diverse political democracies. The locus for all the discussions was to focus on collectives of the people to make democracies more accountable. Communities were defined in various ways, but the underpinning of all these conceptualizations was the ecological foundations and social justice.

The pressing concern is what are the basic ethical and cultural principles that drive us towards an alternative future? Articulating a framework against the dominating framework in the society is a daunting and challenging task in itself. Henceforth it becomes vital to relentlessly strive towards a basic ethic and framework. An integrated theory for practitioners and theoreticians is vital to go beyond the binaries and explore the relationship between local and exogenous. The dialogue was fruitful as it contributed to the visions, setting boundary conditions and pathways to get to the future.

While making concluding remarks Ashis Nandy brought in perspectives about the virtual world, which is hostile and subjects humans to an 'attractive' economic model that looks spectacular from outside but is excessively authoritarian and repressive. In a world that is increasingly losing touch with the people and democratic power is in the hands of a few so called 'experts', we need to create diverse options for the future. Importantly, an ethical space to build larger coalitions and not remain secluded in separate struggles is imperative. One has to look at a future which people find not only admirable but touchable too.

Endnotes

1. See http://www.kalpavriksh.org/images/alternatives/Alternativesframework4thdraftMarch2016.pdf.
2. Papers on Future of Conservation and Future of Water in India could not be presented but are in the volume.
3. Papers on Democracy Futures and India's Global Role, and the paper 'Dare to Dream', could not be presented but are in the volume.
4. Paper not received in time for inclusion in this volume.
5. See http://kalpavriksh.org/index.php/alternatives/alternatives-knowledge-center/352-s.
6. Papers on Adivasi Futures, Education Futures, Future of Gender, Health Futures and Future of Sexuality could not be presented but are in the volume.
7. Paper on Future of Language Diversity in India could not be presented but is part of the volume.

Looking Back into the Future:
India, South Asia, and the World in 2100

As reported by Ashish Kothari and K. J. Joy

Address by Meera Gond-Vankar to the Vikalp Mahasangam 10, held simultaneously in 30 locations across South Asia, winter of 2100[1]

Welcome to the Vikalp Mahasangam 10,[2] the first time we are organizing a confluence at 30 different locations in South Asia, where thousands of you working on the most exciting initiatives to sustain justice have gathered. Firstly, my compliments and thanks to the incredible team of communicators which has made this possible through the plurinet, the decentralized system that replaced the centrally controlled internet of the first half of the century that just passed. I feel blessed that even as I speak in my language, it is being transmitted in over 300 languages with the help of volunteers from the pluriversities that I will speak about a bit later. I am also deeply honoured that I was chosen to put together this brief account of the transformations that have taken place in the last few decades, based on inputs that came in from countless amongst you who have lived through them. I have tried to be faithful to what I got from you, but inevitably there will be interpretations and mistakes which are mine. There will be many more narratives of this journey out there, and may they all flourish!

I also apologise that when I refer to years or decades in this narrative, I am using the Gregorian calendar. Though fortunately the diversity of calendars and time maps, and indeed of the concept of time, has been increasingly accepted across the world, many of us have grown up using this one as our reference point (even though in my own case, my ancestors used different ones). I hope that you will find easy ways to convert the time periods I use into calendars and time maps of your own liking and convenience.

Those of you who are old enough to have gone through the upheavals in the mid-21st century will remember that we walked through fire. Various kinds of inequities and injustices, ecological collapse, and much else that some of us would like to forget, had peaked

627

by the 2030s' to 50s'. It was a slow climb out of that quagmire created by the combination of capitalism, statism, fascism, patriarchy, casteism, human-centrism and other structural forces. But climb we did, clinging onto the many but scattered and small initiatives that went against the tide, building on those through networks and solidarity, collectively envisioning better futures. It is the last few decades that have seen us move resolutely, though not without hiccups, towards equity, justice, ecological wisdom, sustainability, and peace, and all that is associated with these great transformations. It is the specifics of this remarkable journey that I would like to elaborate upon today. I confess I received so many great inputs from so many of you, I did not have time to make a coherent narrative, so what follows may seem somewhat disjointed, and is not in any order of priority or importance. It is for each of you to decide what in this story is most important for you, which part of this story you'd like to highlight to your own young ones ... or if you are amongst the young ones right now, which ones you'd like to carry with you as inspiration for the rest of your life.

And by the way, I am going to mention several places, movements, and initiatives in my presentation; some of you are from these areas, indeed responsible for the transformations there. But if there are any you don't know about and want more detail, you know where to look: www.vikalpsangam.org!

I start with one of the most remarkable transformations: the dissolution of what used to be a sharp divide between the rural and the urban. Over the last few decades, settlements have become part of larger socio-economic and ecological units of rural, rurban and urban settlements (a continuum with no clear break) that would be able to meet most or all basic needs internally; *sustainable exchange zones* or *swaraj* economies have flourished; governance institutions at these larger cultural and ecological landscapes have been established, accountable to the *gram sabhas* and *mohalla sabhas* they are comprised of (these have been retained in their 'rural' and 'urban' form for the sake of continuity). Typical forms of such eco-regional or bio-regional governance are those covering river valleys (or parts of these where the river is big, such as sub-basins and micro-watersheds), or those on/around a mountain range. Early initiatives on this such as the Aravari Sansad or the river basin authorities in the first two to three decades of the 21st century provided crucial lessons, though often they were only partial successes or sometimes, outright failures, and even though with their own faults such as continuation of caste and gender inequities. Ideas emanating from the work of people like Elango R., Ganesh Devy, Ela Bhatt and others were also useful in conceptualizing these regional economies and governance units. Eco-regional governance also began to reconfigure political boundaries within India, and, as you know by now, the conventional units of districts and states have mostly dissolved or merged into those based on ecological and cultural contiguities.

Linked to the above, and contrary to expectations, at the start of the 21st century, rural-urban migration slowed down to a trickle, and thousands of villages began welcoming back residents who had earlier gone away, including young people who were not even born there. This was because rural areas became economically vibrant, their societies progressively less socially divisive and hierarchical, their *gram sabhas* the locus of enlightened democratic governance that they call *gram swaraj*. Many of them also become a new home for urban youth from elsewhere, who had given up their deadening corporate jobs and taken to rural living, integrating themselves with the local community in mutually beneficial ways, learning farming and crafts and bringing with them new skills and information of use to the village. Even by the early 21st century we were beginning to see examples of this, in villages like Hivare Bazaar (Maharashtra) and Kuthambakkam (Tamil Nadu), or those where the livelihoods programme Jharcraft (Jharkhand) and Kudumbashree (Kerala) were successful. These processes increased as villages were transformed into rurban settlements.

Simultaneously, most cities appear to be well on their way to becoming sustainable: the mega-city syndrome that lasted a century, has been giving way to smaller, manageable ones. These are considerably reducing their parasitic dependence on the countryside, instead having equal exchanges, meeting much of their water, energy, food, and material needs from within or immediate surroundings; dedicating at least seventy five per cent of their roads to public transport and cycling/walking, every colony dominated by public spaces where children can play freely; most colonies declaring themselves zero-waste; and a large majority of the citizens involved in *mohalla sabha* level democracy including local budgeting and planning of public conveniences and spaces that began to be called *nagar swaraj*. Initiatives in Pune, Bengaluru and other cities in the early 21st century had provided some innovations that other urban areas could learn from and take up similar programmes (as startling counter-trends to the dominant megapolis-related problems of unsustainability and non-liveability). Fittingly a national campaign on this was dedicated to Tagore, one of the earliest to write about city-village inequality.

The earlier concentration of industries and institutions in cities slowly gave way to decentralization of production facilities, services, and so on (including health and learning or education). The burgeoning slums of the late 20th and early 21st century underwent dramatic transformations through *in situ* programmes of dignified housing, open spaces, self-reliance in water and energy, vibrant cultural opportunities, a combination of self-governance and accountable city administrations, and predominantly localized livelihoods.

An early example of this was the Homes in the City programme in Bhuj, Kachchh; these and other examples were used around the 2020s' to get a Constitutional amendment building on the 74ᵗʰ Amendment, to provide all the elements of urban decentralization.

Infrastructure has also been increasingly decentralized where technically feasible, and it is more and more renewable and local material based. Fossil-based materials have been phased out and even if they are used, they are restricted or limited and used in such a way as to strengthen the local and renewable material and not to replace them. Some form of 're-wilding' has also been attempted, with green spaces and wetlands, road-side green corridors, innovative nesting and roosting spaces incorporated into the architecture of buildings (some from traditional designs hundreds of years old), all contributing to the revival of wildlife and biodiversity in cities.

Talking about wildlife, and recalling in particular our age-old belief that we are part of nature, and all of life is worthy of respect, I am happy to report that community-based conservation has spread across most of South Asia, with communities on their own or with help from the government, researchers and civil society, managing and conserving natural ecosystems. Latest surveys show that ecosystems (across the rural-urban continuum) with some special attention to wildlife, now cover a third of the country, having been regenerated and interconnected, providing cover for a dramatic recovery of most wildlife populations. Given the increasing focus on sustainability across much of the rest of the landscape and seascape too, biodiversity would be recovering even outside the thirty three per cent of special attention areas. Conventional exclusionary policies of separating people and wildlife, epitomized by tiger conservation in the late 20ᵗʰ and early 21ˢᵗ century, have given way to the recognition that co-existence of various kinds is possible, with adequate attention to the needs of different species, including undisturbed spaces identified collaboratively by experts from both host communities and outside. A major boost towards inclusionary conservation was legislations like the Forest Rights Act that was enacted in early 21ˢᵗ century, and its successors, related to marine areas and freshwater wetlands, combining tenurial security for communities with responsibilities and capacities for conservation. But equally important was the increased recognition of non-legal, customary or community paradigms of living with nature, not straitjacketed by formal western models. Significant documentation work in the first couple of decades of the 21ˢᵗ century had already shown the reality and potential of community conserved areas (CCAs), and of ecological revival even in cities (e.g., lakes in Bengaluru and Salem), and these examples were learnt from and built upon over the next few decades. Most important, we seem to be well on the way to thinking of ourselves as part of nature, and of throwing out the notion of separate areas for humans and the rest of nature; we have most of all our *adivasi*, pastoral, peasant, and fisher populations to thank, for showing us the way towards this mind shift. Within the government, the old Forest Department has been replaced by an Ecosystems Extension Service, tasked primarily to facilitate community-based conservation.

The welcome concern for biodiversity and wildlife has gone hand in hand with some amazing transformations in socio-economic conditions of people. Absolute poverty (including deprivations of any kind of basic needs) has been eliminated … thank you for the applause… it's all due to your efforts! …with everyone having secure access to all basic needs including nutritious and adequate food, clean water and air, sanitation, shelter, energy, conditions of good health and opportunities for learning. While in the early 21st century a series of rights-based legislations helped in this journey, it was realized that it was not adequate to demand the state's accountability towards welfare for the deprived. Indeed such 'welfarism' at times created a new form of deprivation – that of taking away *agency* from people, the ability to self-provision, and when (as often happened in the early decades) the state withdrew or was unable to deliver on welfare schemes, it created a situation of complete collapse, with people not even having their own resources to fall back on. The rights-based policies were gradually converted into policies and social processes of sovereignty and self-reliance, in which communities were able to gain the rights, capacities, and forums for ensuring basic needs, by themselves or in regional relationships of localized production and consumption … and indeed the emergence of a 'prosumer' ((producer – consumer) society. This relates also to the nature of 'work', to which I will return a little later.

Agriculture, pastoralism, fisheries, and forestry have become dedicated to, first and foremost, meeting food and other basic needs locally, through organic or ecologically sensitive methods. Conversion of agriculture from mainly use-value production (use-value production to satisfy various needs and enrich human life) to mono-cultural, high external input based, cash crop production that took place in the middle of the 20th century, has been reversed. Communities are now able to meet most of their primary needs without going through large-scale commodity market systems. These livelihood systems are seen as part of a larger biomass production system to meet food, fodder and fuel needs, to supply necessary nutrients to the soil, and also to provide inputs into the agro-based, decentralized value addition opportunities. Agrochemicals and undemocratic technologies like genetic modification have been phased out; most such livelihoods are based on local seeds and breeds, and local inputs for fertilization and protection. The movements around seeds, sustainable pastoralism, various forms of sustainable agricultural practices and the campaigns against GM crops and hybrid breeds of the late 20th and early 21st century provided the basis for this shift.

Social inequalities and inequities of various kinds are on their way to being considerably reduced, which has been possibly the hardest struggle to achieve. The most obstinate inequities have been those of caste and gender. For those earlier called dalits, and other socially marginalized sections, while the post-Independence policies of reservations played their role in providing some opportunities for access to education and jobs, by the 2030s' these were replaced by a series of measures towards economic and social empowerment and integration, including access to land, mixed housing, incentives for social relations across castes. This enabled such sections to flourish while beginning to eradicate caste identities altogether, moving towards an Ambedkarite vision of a casteless society. Formerly caste and gender based occupations were transformed in such a way that they became caste and gender neutral, and anybody is now able to take up any occupation, having equal access to learning the necessary skills. In the case of gender and sexuality, the first few decades of the 21st century saw increasing mobilization for equal rights to women on a range of fronts (including titles of custodianship to land and equal wages), the recognition of multiple genders and sexualities (the Supreme Court finally relaxed its views on homosexuality, and an increasing presence of young members of parliament reduced the resistance of the conservative lobby), and the legalization and public recognition of same-sex partnerships. Unlike in many other issues of radical change, in these matters a part of the mainstream media also played a positive role of sensitizing the public in the early decades of the 21st century.

Families, as they exist today, are considerably transformed from the past. While they retain their essential feature of being a space for nurturing and care, families as spaces of oppression and exploitation have become considerably uncommon, mainly due to feminist and children's movements in the mid-21st century. There is now equitable sharing of domestic functions and activities, including child rearing, cooking, caring for the elderly, and so on, across genders (without homogenising them); what has also helped considerably is that these responsibilities are also socialized through neighbourhood groups. Caste and religion is no longer a basis for marriages, partnerships or relationships. Families themselves now exist in a bewildering variety of forms, based on partnerships amongst a diversity of genders, for various reasons including (apart from love!) taking care of children and the elderly.

Possibly one of the most moving transformations has been how society now treats those we used to call 'disabled'. We all are abled or disabled in various ways, and the anachronism of treating those with some particular physical or mental impairment issues as being disabled, and of marginalizing those who are in some such ways challenged, has thankfully been discarded. All human settlements have been undergoing transformations to make them accessible and inclusive, especially sensitive to those who have special needs. Focused programmes in learning and education spaces, and in various forms of media, have changed mindsets that used to think of such people as inferior in some way, towards simply seeing them as part of human diversity.

One major source of inequality (economic, social, political), and of unsustainability, the private and state ownership of land, is on the way out. In the early decades of the 21ˢᵗ century, some communities like Mendha-Lekha in central India took the revolutionary step of placing all agricultural land into the village commons, while reclaiming their collective rights to forests, water, and grazing land from state ownership. I still remember the story of this event recounted to me by my maternal grandparents, who were from this region. The positive impact this had on their economic and social lives, spurred others to take similar steps. Quickest were *adivasi* and indigenous areas, which in any case traditionally had more collective ownership or custodianship patterns; non-adivasi agricultural communities took longer to change; and urban areas were the ones with maximum struggle, and where the transformation is still not complete. Family ownership of homes has remained stubbornly resistant to change, but along with other sources of wealth, there is increasing discussion on the need to do away with their inheritance along family lines. In any case, with a far greater degree of equity in other spheres of life, including economic democratization that I will describe below, and with values of sharing and equality being on the ascendance, wealth inequalities with personal inheritance as a major bulwark are now far easier to question.

In a revolutionary transformation from what it was a century ago, and in sync with the re-commoning of land (and other natural resources), the economy has become considerably democratized. Movements resisting the power of private corporations and the nation-state over economic activities, especially of workers in various sectors, led the way. There was a long period in which workers' unions, especially those linked to political parties, were not the transformative force they could have been, and much of the unorganized or informal sector workforce was left out. However, new kinds of worker organisations including unions of waste-pickers, forest workers, fish-workers, and those from industries and mines who revived the approach of people like Shankar Guha Niyogi of the Chhattisgarh Mines Shramik Sangh, supported by civil society organisations, gradually brought in a focus on producer control, working conditions, environmental responsibility, gender equality, and remuneration parity. Starting with the waste-pickers and forest workers unions, that displaced corporations and state agencies, the movement to take over production and service facilities took root. This was a long and hard struggle, for owners of capital, big landlords, and agencies controlling other natural resources were not likely to give in so easily, and had the might of the state behind them. What helped was the combination of resistance and take-over movements with those who were showing alternative forms of production, such as the dozens of producer companies and producer-run cooperatives that sprung up in the first two to three decades of the 21st century, careful not to repeat the mistakes of government-established cooperatives of the previous century. Also helpful was an increasingly vocal consumer movement that realized its interests were in aligning with producers, both moving towards ecologically sensitive and socially just processes, and towards a merger in a transformation of the meaning of 'work' as described below.

Economic transformation is also manifested in the way this Mahasangam has been organized. We have not spent a single rupee on the local arrangements across these thirty sites; all inputs have come in the form of barter or time-sharing. Democratizing the economy has also meant that the earlier financial hegemony – hege*money* if you allow me a small pun! – of monetary institutions has been replaced by a diversity of local, socially-controlled currencies or non-monetised means of exchange. The rupee still exists, as you know, but is mainly for exchanges amongst regions, and is without its former anonymous power. The great economic depressions of the early 21st century had already put into place serious questions about the role of centralized financial institutions like banks or finance ministries, and at one stage people finally refused to allow governments to bail them out. Instead, movements demanded the decentralization of financial powers and arrangements, including through drastic fiscal reforms, and the creation of localized currencies, and so on. Civil society and communities have also revived or brought in new forms of time sharing to exchange skills and expertise on a non-monetary basis. On that note, let us loudly acknowledge the language volunteers, who are today providing us all the translations to make this address understandable!

Connected to this, are the dramatic changes that have taken place in the domain of livelihoods and 'work'. After a period of sharp decline in the late 20th and early 21st centuries, primary sector livelihoods or ways of life (forestry, agriculture, pastoralism, fisheries, and so on), and others directly based on nature such as many crafts, began to see a revival. This was partly due to mobilization by adivasis, small peasants, artisanal fisherfolks, herders, crafts-persons and others, asserting the legitimacy of their livelihoods and their rights to land and other resources, creating several national forums for greater impact. It was also a result of the work of community organisations and civil society groups that innovated to find livelihood options for the youth amongst these peoples, integrating the best of traditional and new knowledge, creating alternative spaces for learning (such as a series of *shalas* in Kachchh, which I am proud to say, my paternal grandparents were part of), asserting the crucial place of women in keeping society alive through such livelihoods (such as in the work of the dalit women of Deccan Development Society, or the rural women of Maati Sanghatan and urban women of SWaCH), and linking them to processes of economic democracy that were taking place in various sectors. Interestingly, there was also a trend of 'professionals' in other sectors, such as Information Technology, wanting to move into primary sector occupations; while initially this tended to be disconnected from those traditionally engaged in such occupations, over time it became a process of mutually synergistic learning and support. Manufacturing and services were significantly decentralized over time, linking with the increasing localization of the economy and political governance, with large-scale centralized production facilities becoming redundant in most sectors. Workers in modern facilities rebelled against the deadening, assembly line kind of labour they were putting in, with most profits cornered by capitalist owners. They demanded both, greater democratic control over working conditions and revenues, as also kinds and patterns of work that were more 'whole' and meaningful. A seamless rural-urban continuum was built on, and reinforced, the possibilities of families being engaged in all sectors of the economy, no longer categorized as simply 'primary', 'secondary', and so on, nor rigidly bound by caste, gender or other such identities.

The changes in 'work' would also encompass bringing back relations of affect, caring and sharing to centre-stage in the economy. In the several decades of the 20th and 21st centuries in which capitalism and modernity were ascendant, these relations (between people and nature, between people within communities, between communities, and so on) had been ignored, or sidelined, or replaced by commercial and exploitative relations, or commodified by giving them a monetary value, such as happened with the market-based measures for combating the climate crisis. This was pushed back by feminists and others who highlighted the basic *human* nature of such relations and their enormous contribution to the sustenance of society as a whole (including economy); and therefore the need to recognize and bring them back where they had been lost or displaced, where necessary in modified forms, to shed them of any inequities that may be embedded in them.

As a consequence of the above, we no longer have the 9-to-5, Monday-to-Friday routine; rather 'work' happens as part of community life, integrated with enjoyment and leisure in a seamless whole and every individual can be many different kinds of things, taking to new levels Marx's vision of being a hunter and pastoralist and critic, all at once. Also back-breaking, monotonous work has gone; remaining mechanical tasks that are essential for society to function are shared by all those who can perform them. Since there is no space for private accumulation which required labour in assembly line like situations, there is much more time for creative activities like reading, writing, music, dancing, painting and so on, often built into the 'work' itself. All of the above was made much more possible by changes in learning and education (more on this in a minute!), re-instating respect to working with the hands and feet, changing the mindset that divided work and enjoyment, producer and consumer, owner and labourer ...and increasing social realization that 'deadlihoods' (destruction of age-old ways of life and their replacement by deadening 'jobs') needed to be replaced again by livelihoods in various forms. We are moving towards operationalising Marx's vision of 'from each according to capacity and to each according to need'.

Consumerism was amongst the hardest of scourges to tackle, ingrained as it had been over generations of advertising-led brainwashing. But greater awareness of the consequences of over-consumption, a mix of incentives and disincentives to curb consumerism, and resistance and protests by victims of destructive development who linked their situation with the consumption patterns of the rich, led to gradual changes. An 'above sane consumption limit' having been established in the 2020s', all those who were over-consuming resources have changed their lifestyles to greater sustainability. In stark contrast to the early 21st century, we are now mildly envious of neighbours who are happy with less, the value of *aparigraha*, which we can loosely translate as being satisfied with what one has, or 'enoughness', having been firmly established in society's ethical framework. I recall when I was young, my grandparents would frequently repeat Gandhi's famous 'greed' versus 'need' philosophy, and I would silently mock them; now most of us realize its enormous importance.

There has also been a remarkable demographic transformation. Firstly, our population has been stabilized at about 1.5 billion, as birth rates dropped dramatically in the 2020s' and 30s' consequent to women's empowerment, improvement in economic security of the poor, and declining hold of religious beliefs privileging male children or prohibiting abortion and birth control. States like Kerala led the way in this phase. Secondly, many of our people have migrated to other parts of the world, welcomed by the people there as a form of multiculturalism and also in recognition of the fact that the Indian subcontinent was feeling stressed due to high human densities.

I may not be exaggerating if I say that an absolutely fundamental part of these amazing transformations has been the change in learning and education. Educational institutions have been transformed into open spaces of learning and welfare amongst the communities as a whole, their facilitators (they used to be called 'teachers'!) coming from both formal and informal, modern and traditional backgrounds, and learners taking part in setting curricula. Learning has moved more towards a combination of Gandhi's *nai taleem* (new learning/ education) principle of integrating head, hands (and feet!) and heart, towards inculcating oneness with the rest of nature, and building mutually respectful relations with the rest of humanity. In many cases communities across the rural-urban continuum have reclaimed learning for children as a collective practice, rather than one that has to happen within the walls of an institution. Imagine, the pluriversities where young adults are now able to learn a diversity of skills, values, perspectives, and knowledge systems, and to interact with people from diverse cultures, used to once be 'universities' where students were moulded to fit into straitjacketed positions within corporations and government agencies!

One striking result of the changes in learning, education, and skilling is that the dependence on 'professionals' has considerably reduced; each of us has the chance to learn the basics of living. For the better part we now are our own doctors, or teachers, or electricians, or cooks, and the like. Of course we still have specialisations, for none of us can be good at everything, but we are out of that phase that lasted several decades into the 21st century, when for every little ailment we ran to a doctor, for every household task we called in a service professional, for every repair we went to a shop. Most of you would not be old enough to recall a time when, if you had a cough or cold, you would line up to see a doctor!

In the first few decades of the 21st century, electronic means of communication spread considerably; many of you may recall or have heard of Facebook, Twitter and so on. Indeed we went through a horrific phase in which many people opted for a chip implanted in their skin, with the aid of which they could transmit all kinds of information about themselves and learn about others, without the need for any face-to-face or physical contact. But serious misuse of this by corporations and governments, the latter in the name of public security, gave rise to mass movements against such intrusive technologies. People increasingly realized the hollowness of exclusively virtual relationships, and there was a resurgence of face-to-face interactions, the re-commoning of village and town squares as places for conviviality and mutual learning, the revival of oral traditions. The term 'social networking' was rescued from its digital capture, to actually mean such interactions! Of course electronic communication remains, and indeed I'm using it right now for the transmission of this address, but with the increasingly democratic control of media as a whole, it does not displace normal communications.

Linked to this was the movement to remove the rigid distinction or dichotomy between abstract thinking and experiential knowledge. For a long period in human history, such separations were based on caste, class or gender hierarchies, and over the last few centuries on the domination of 'western', 'modern' knowledge and epistemologies. These factors were identified and fought against, and all aspects of knowledge were completely democratized. Various forms of knowledge got more integrated and hybridized, even while retaining some distinctiveness, a sort of eclectic unity in diversity. Information in general became freely available, with the Right to Information Act in the early 21st century having played a major role, but now mostly having to be used only in exceptional circumstances, as society has increasingly accepted the principle of knowledge as a commons. Various movements towards open access systems in software and hardware, publishing, medicine, and other fields, that saw their birth a century ago, flourished from the 2020s onwards, and any attempts at privatizing knowledge were stoutly defeated by people defiantly making such knowledge public. This did not mean that individual innovations were no longer considered important; on the contrary, they were given widespread social recognition. Individuals themselves accepted that their ideas and innovations were their gifts to the collective that was sustaining them (a trait that, incidentally, a substantial part of traditional knowledge had, before notions of intellectual property rights came in towards the late 20th and early 21st centuries).

The general trends in democratizing knowledge and acknowledging its diverse nature also affected technology. In the last few decades, technological development and innovations were increasingly subjected to democratic and social regulation to ensure that technologies of destruction and domination are discouraged and nipped in the bud. In the early part of the 21st century there began a move towards recognizing many traditional technologies that had continuing relevance (e.g., mud architecture), bringing them back in some form including through new innovations (for instance, compressed mud blocks with a mix of materials, including biomass, for added strength). There was also, around the same time, increasing technological innovation that was explicitly kept in the public arena, such as open source digital and mapping techniques. The capacity of civil society organisations to also expose or sabotage dangerous technologies (such as genetic engineering) and their purveyors, or produce alternative technologies that worked as well, or better, also steadily increased. For quite some time state and corporate agencies hit back with law suits and worse, but the force of technological democratization (coupled with the movement towards more open knowledge and information, and the undermining of economic concentrations of power through localization) could not be contained. Technologies became more gender sensitive, and there was a shift from single point/criterion assessment of technologies and choices to multi-criteria assessments based on indicators drawn from concerns of sustainability, equity and democratization.

It followed from the principles of knowledge and information democracy, that the media has also been democratized and diversified. The great concentration of media power that characterized the early 2000s, reaching its pinnacle in the empire of one of the Presidents of the then United States, was gradually broken down by a combination of ethical hackers, a series of Wikileak like events, rising popularity of alternative media that asserted the knowledge commons, technologies enabling much wider public access to information and news, and public discontent with the nexus amongst political, economic and knowledge power centres. A bewildering diversity of media has evolved since then, from community radio and street theatre and public video to newspapers and magazines and others, in an equally bewildering diversity of languages. The internet too has been democratized, with multiple people-controlled nodes for its smooth functioning.

None of the above would have been possible were it not for the strong move towards a radical transformation in politics. Early on in the 21st century, peoples' movements realized that democracy (demos+cratis=power of the people), was not about elections! Rather, it was about ordinary people everywhere having the power to be part of decision-making. Democracy was slowly transformed into an embedded form of political *swaraj,* from a top-down, election-based system into one with the locus of power in *gram sabhas, mohalla sabhas,* tribal village and pastoral community assemblies, and larger representative institutions formed of delegates or representatives of these assemblies. A slogan started by a tiny village in the heart of India, Mendha-Lekha in Gadchiroli – 'our government in Delhi and Mumbai, in our village we *are* the government' – resonated across India, and saw various appropriate modifications depending on context ('we govern our village, and our delegates are in the river valley committee', or 'our municipality in Mumbai, but in our neighbourhood our decisions count'). Representative democracy came to be based on this direct or radical democracy. The politics of representation was greatly transformed, emanating from power at the grassroots, subject to strong norms of accountability, transparency, and the right of recall; the nature of political parties got to be less about gaining power (since in any case centralized power was no longer acceptable) and more about genuine representation of cultural and social (including sexual and gender) diversity, organic leadership, and the motivation to serve. Some unease in the relationship between direct or radical democracy at the ground and representation at higher levels remains, but does not seem to have resulted in serious disruptions, since you as an empowered public have not allowed representatives a free rein of power.

(Pause..... as a loud cheer breaks out amongst the Mahasangam participants...)

One complex and contentious question that was debated through this transformation was regarding the continuation and role of the state. As you know, in its widest definition of a governance mechanism at various levels, the state has remained, but considerably transformed from the centralized, nation-state, top-heavy one that existed earlier, to a series of institutions with functions of coordination and facilitation, and no special powers that are not subject to the units of direct democracy. This was clearly one of the arenas of maximum resistance and contestation in the first half of the 21st century, as seen for instance, in the obstacles put by much of the then Forest Department to the democratization of forest governance under the Forest Rights Act enacted in the first decade of the century, and the attempts by right-wing governments to clamp down on civil society dissent. The maturing of peoples' and civil society movements in this phase, enabling them to work with each other much more than earlier, created a substantial political mass that supported direct democracy and reigned in such attempts by the state. Simultaneously the movement towards eco-regional governance, and to review and relax nation-state boundaries in South Asia (and more globally), which I will describe in a minute, helped redefine the form of the state. The character of the state underwent a radical transformation – from a capitalist, upper caste and patriarchal state as it existed for most part of the 20th and early part of the 21st century; instead, the state and its institutions came to represent the interests of all sections of people. Its role underwent a change from a coercive force to one of a facilitator, helping to integrate different interests, conflicts, and so on, that could be resolved at the level of the communities. Remarkably, we are even seeing the dismantling of the police force, and South Asian peoples as a whole are discussing the possible dismantling of the army; if we all agree to this, it will be one of the most amazing transformations of human history.

This also brings me to the issue of crimes – 'crimes' in inverted commas. For a long period of human history, we considered any deviation from what was considered as 'normal', as a crime. Fortunately, enlightened leadership through the mid-2100s' questioned this, and eventually such a view faded away with the gradual realisation that there is nothing like a 'normal' behaviour against which certain behaviours can be stamped as 'deviant' and thus criminal. Pluralism is not only tolerated, but actively encouraged. And at another level the material conditions that existed which forces people to carry out activities that hurt others or affect relations with other fellow beings in the form of violence, robbery, bribe, trafficking, and so on, do not exist any longer. In other words nobody is compelled to enter into these activities to meet one's needs. This does not mean that presently there are no activities that we may still consider as crimes. We have to acknowledge that human nature is not necessarily always benign and generous, even if these characteristics have been significantly enhanced over the last few decades. We do have reason at times to feel angry and hurt and hostile and even vengeful. So 'crimes' still exist, in the form of people doing things that hurt the interests of others, but with decades of encouragement to our positive and generous side, and the decrease in competition to 'acquire' resources, these occur to a much lesser degree. Also, the way such activities and instances are dealt with has qualitatively changed. People who enter into such activities are no longer considered as criminals and put behind bars. Instead they are seen as people who need help and community counselling centres and rehabilitation processes help them realize the hurt their actions cause to others, and how to overcome the impulses or attitudes that cause them. Instead of stigmatizing such people, the emphasis is on empathy and behavioural change. Around 2030 capital punishment was abolished and, increasingly, corporal punishment too has been substantially phased out.

I have mentioned 'culture' several times above, but it will not suffice to talk about it in passing only. A strong fulcrum of all these transformations has been India's incredible cultural diversity and depth. These have become a cause for celebration and strength, rather than the source of divisiveness and conflict that it had become, under the influence of right-wing political and cultural bigots, in the early part of the 21st century. Several prominent individuals and groups had begun movements against the intolerance marking this phase, aiming to reclaim different cultures and identities as the bases for meaningful sharing and learning, indeed as the source of excitement and joy (how boring if we were all the same!). Diverse languages, cuisines, belief and knowledge systems, ways of living and loving, all these and other aspects of culture were once again given pride of place to counter their rapid erosion under the onslaught of capitalism and modernity or right-wing proselytization. Amongst the most important moves was that of changing education systems to integrate local languages, include oral traditions, and to celebrate both local and other cuisines, ethnicities, and other aspects of culture. Already in the early 21st century organisations like Bhasha in Gujarat and SECMOL in Ladakh were showing the way.

In the spirit of diversity, multiple ideologies that promote equity and social justice, sustainability, democratization, dignity, peace, non-violence, and such other positive values, have flourished. From 2010s' onwards we saw a process of grassroots-up visioning, dialogues of practices, concepts, values, worldviews across India and with peoples in other parts of the world. These were combined with lessons from relevant existing spiritual and secular world views and the great thinkers and doers of the past, into an evolving synthesis of values and principles, leaving room for various ideological branches to flourish and co-exist. The Vikalp Sangams (Alternative Confluences) and the Sangam of Sangams and the Convergence of Movements processes initiated in the late 2010s, of which this Mahasangam is a continuation, were a small part of this. Through this the basic values of diversity and pluralism, solidarity, caring and sharing, equity, justice, oneness of life, interconnectedness and reciprocity, peace, creativity, respect for labour, simplicity, and so on, were revived or reinforced. We now have a huge diversity of peoples' charters across the subcontinent, but most of these are based on a common understanding and acceptance of these and other values, which provide a thread linking us all.

Based on the above, religious centralization and inter-religious conflicts have also been on their way out, as each individual and community realized the power of its spiritual and ethical self; enlightened spiritual leadership would remain but attempts to convert this into dogmatic, blind-faith dominated, undemocratic institutions such as the religions that dominated the early 2000s, would be constantly challenged by movements arguing for pluralism and diversity. For a while, there was tension between science-based movements that were seen to be arguing against spiritualism and religion *per se* (though their focus was more on removal of 'blind faith' and superstitions), and movements seeking to reinforce basic spiritual values and ethics. But enlightened leadership on both sides realized that co-existence was not only possible but essential, especially to undermine the power of the scientific and religious orthodoxy. A number of powerful statements on climate crisis and environment by those from within mainstream religions, going against the tide (such as those by the Pope, the Dalai Lama, and several leaders from Islam and Judaism in the decade of the 2010s'), helped build such bridges; the resurgence of indigenous peoples and their nature-based faiths provided additional momentum. The hold of organized, institutionalized religion on the lives of the people, which was on the rise in the 20th and early 21st century, has reduced considerably by the end of the century; instead people have become more 'spiritual' and as Mahatma Phule said, 'seekers of truth/s' (*satyashodhaks*).

But what is life without aesthetics and fun? An incredible diversity of arts and crafts has flourished, reversing the decline seen in many traditional forms in the late 20th and early 21st centuries. This was linked also to the transformation of livelihoods and work and the revival of cultural diversity, as described above, and the realization by 'ordinary' people of their intrinsic abilities to be creative and of the possibility of integrating art in daily life. One of the most interesting processes was the break-down of the division between 'classical' and 'folk' arts, as music, dance, and other art forms began to be delinked from caste and gender connections, and alternative learning centres encouraged learning by anyone interested. This did not of course mean that excellence and brilliance were not recognized; indeed they are, through social means of acknowledgement and reward, and public sponsorship and patronage. We do it in the opening ceremonies of these Sangams and Mahasangams too! New forms of the mentorship or teacher-learner tradition that have discarded anachronistic links with caste, gender or other such problematic identities have come up. Indeed, we are increasingly seeing the integration of arts and values, the view of nature as art and of art as truth: a sort of 'aesth-ethics'.

As in the case of arts and crafts, the arena of sports has also witnessed an explosion of talent. In the 1920s' and 30s' there was increasing abhorrence against elitism and vulgar commercialization in sports, protest against the 'pedestalization' of cricket, and a demand for democratic, widespread access to facilities and training centres. While a competitive spirit remained, acknowledging that it is part of being human, much greater emphasis started being put on cooperative sports and the cooperative spirit balancing out the ills of aggressive competitiveness. Public patronage played an important role in reducing dependence on the state, and eliminating corporate sponsorships. Elite sports like golf declined in response to the general trend towards equality and democratic decision-making of the commons. We now have a situation where almost everyone is a sportsperson of some kind, where excellence is still celebrated but not given superhero status, and where people from India do very well in global events, not only as individual competitors but as ambassadors of cooperation. I am happy to say that through sensitive attention to those with special needs, and the spirit of cooperation taking over, the old distinctions between 'abled' and 'disabled' have begun to dissolve in sports too.

Everything I've described above has been remarkable. But perhaps the most noteworthy has been the change in our relations in South Asia. While India, Pakistan, Bangladesh, Nepal, Bhutan, Sri Lanka, and China still retain their 'national' identities, boundaries have become porous, needing no visas to cross. By the middle of the 21st century various oppressed nationalities of the 20th and early 21st century in the region could chose their own political future. Local communities have taken over most of the governance in these boundary areas, having declared *shanti abhyaranyas* (peace reserves) in previous conflict zones like Siachen, the Kachchh and Thar deserts, and the Sundarbans (the last had become a serious arena of water and land conflict due partly to the climate crisis, during the 2030s' and 40s'). The same applies to the Palk Strait, with fishing communities from both India and Sri Lanka empowered to ensure sustainable, peaceful use of marine areas. A Greater Tibet has become a reality, self-governed, with both India and China relinquishing their political and economic domination over it and rather extending a helping hand where necessary. In the Greater Thar, communities of livestock herders in both India and Pakistan have been similarly empowered for self-governance. In all these initiatives, narrow nationalism is being replaced by civilizational identities, pride, and exchange, a kind of *swasabhyata* (own ethnicity) that encourages respect of and mutual learning between different civilisations and cultures. Both nomadic communities and wildlife are now able to move freely back and forth, as they used to before these areas became zones of conflict and were dissected by fences. In short the trans-boundary elements of nature and resources in the region – like water, forests, migratory species – are being increasingly brought under a regional public good framework of governance.

Indeed, the people of India and the rest of South Asia have been significant movers of an increasingly borderless world, in the sense of the gradual dissolution of rigid nation-state boundaries. South Asia learnt from the mistakes of blocks like the European Union, with its strange mix of centralization and decentralization and continued reliance on the nation state, and worked out its own recipe for respecting diversity within a unity of purpose. This is heavily based, as mentioned above, on community-based governance in areas of what were formerly nation-state boundaries. Peoples' movements across South Asia were key actors towards devising the democratic Global Peoples' Assembly that, sometime in the mid-2100s', began to replace the United Nations. This Assembly has a series of governance mechanisms that do not give permanent or long-term power to any people or individual, are accountable to direct democracy and eco-regional units on the ground, and are meant exclusively for absolutely essential functions such as governance of the global commons (the seas, the atmosphere, and so on), and facilitation of equitable and sustainable cultural and economic relations.

Indeed, let us acknowledge that the transformations in South Asia are not entirely its own doing. We used to pride ourselves for being an ancient civilization (or several, in fact!), for having the world's largest knowledge base, and so on. That pride took quite a beating when we realized, many decades back, that these things meant little if we continued to let our environment be destroyed, tolerated half of our people living in deprivation, and allowed ourselves to become a colonizing country by exploiting countries weaker than us. It was only when we realized that we could learn enormously from peoples' initiatives across the world, just as they could learn from us that transformations could be made more effectively and widely. Still, I guess we could take some pride in having been instrumental in starting (with others) the Global Alternatives Sangam, which ran for some decades till it was incorporated into the Global Peoples' Assembly.

Which leads me to a final point – for the sake of tradition, we have been calling this unbroken series of gatherings Vikalp Sangams or Alternatives Confluences. When they started and for the better part of their history, they were indeed promoting alternatives to the dominant economic, political and social systems of the day. Now that the processes of justice, equity, and ecological wisdom are firmly rooted and flowering, I propose that we make a change. From next confluence onwards, shall we call them 'Vividh Kalpana Sangams' – Confluences of Diverse Imaginations?

Endnotes

1. 2100 as per the Gregorian calendar; for the equivalent in other calendars of the region, listeners and readers may please look up Vikalp Mahasangam on the plurinet.
2. Alternatives Mega-confluence; a process called Vikalp Sangam was initiated in the early part of the twenty first century, which morphed or joined into various kinds of gatherings and confluences including a widespread Sangam of Sangams ('confluence of confluences') and the Convergence of Movements across the subcontinent, aimed at sharing initiatives of and collectively envisioning more just, equitable, and sustainable societies. While mostly localized and small in size, once in 4-5 years much larger gatherings have been organized as Mahasangams.

Profiles of Authors

Dinesh Abrol

Dinesh Abrol holds the full-time position of Professor at the Institute for Studies in Industrial Development (ISID), where he is coordinating the collaborative research programme on Intellectual Property, Innovation and Industrial Development. He has served as Chief Scientist from National Institute of Science, Technology and Development Studies, and is associated with the Centre for Studies in Science Policy (CSSP) in Jawahar Lal Nehru University (JNU). He is responsible for the coordination of joint sustainability studies programme of JNU and University of Sussex. He carries behind him forty years of experience in Innovation System, Science, Technology and Society & S&T policy. He has helped build the Delhi Science Forum, All India Peoples' Science Network and National Working Group on Patent Laws working for open source movement in seeds and pharmaceuticals and against strong intellectual property system and free trade in India.

Tultul Biswas

Tultul has formal training in Chemistry and Sociology and early exposure of teaching Science to elementary school children. Long involvement with the publishing initiative of Eklavya, with a thrust to develop and publish books that portray independent, thoughtful children with an agency of their own. Presently engaged with the Teacher Education and Outreach programme. Mother of a 10-year old daughter, part of the feminist movement, and has a keen interest in folk and classical music.

Rajni Bakshi

Rajni Bakshi is a Mumbai-based author. She is the author of *Bazaars, Conversations and Freedom*, which won two Vodafone-Crossword Awards. Her earlier book, *Bapu Kuti: Journeys in Rediscovery of Gandhi,* inspired the Hindi film Swades. Her other books include *Long Haul: the Bombay Textile Workers Strike 1982-83, A Warning and an Opportunity: the*

Dispute over Swami Vivekananda's Legacy, Lets Make it Happen: a backgrounder on New Economics, and *An Economics for Well-Being.* Rajni serves on the Boards of Child Rights and You (CRY) and Citizens for Peace. She is also a member of the Executive Committee of the Gandhi Smriti and Darshan Samiti, an autonomous body under the Ministry of Culture and a long term associate of Centre of Education and Documentation. Rajni has a BA from George Washington University and an MA from the University of Rajasthan.

Shrishtee Bajpai

Shrishtee is working with the Alternatives programme of Kalpavriksh- Environment Action Group. She holds a Masters degree in Development Studies from Azim Premji University, Bengaluru.

Sarita Bhagat

Sarita is working as a research associate at Society for Promoting Participative Ecosystem Management (SOPPECOM) and is associated with the Forum (Forum for Policy Dialogue on Water Conflicts in India) since four years. She is doing research on various water and sanitation related issues, especially in the Mahanadi basin. Sarita holds a Masters degree in Environmental Studies and Sustainability Sciences from Lund University, Sweden. Her research interest includes water governance and policy, behavior studies and environmental sustainability.

Pallav Das

Pallav Das has pursued a twin-track career in environmental conservation and creative communications. He has designed and launched innovative campaigns, and founded and led private and non-profit organizations, including Kalpavriksh. Pallav has documented some of India's most pressing development challenges through his film work, including films on violence against women and the threat of HIV/AIDS among street children.

Shripad Dharmadhikary

Shripad is an activist, researcher, and coordinator of the Manthan Adhyayan Kendra that studies water and energy policies with a focus on equity, sustainability and justice. His interests include water policy and projects, dams, rivers, environmental flows, water privatisation and coal-water nexus. A graduate engineer from IIT Bombay, he was earlier an activist for 12 years with the Narmada Bachao Andolan. He writes extensively on water issues.

Ganesh Devy

Formerly Professor of English at the Maharaja Sayajirao University of Baroda and Dhirubhai Ambani Institute of Information Technology, Devy is founder of the Bhasha Research Centre, Baroda, and Adivasi Academy, Tejgadh. He has worked extensively with Adivasis and nomadic communities. He led the People's Linguistic Survey of India, a comprehensive documentation of living Indian languages, forming a fifty-volume book series. He has received several awards, including the Padma Shri, Prince Claus Award and Linguapax Award. His books include *After Amnesia*, *Of Many Heroes*, *Painted Words*, *Nomad Called Thief* , *Vanaprastha* (in Marathi), and *Adivasi Jaane Chhe* (in Gujarati). He has co-edited six volumes on indigenous cultures and knowledge. As an activist, he played a leading role in the movement for the rights of Denotified and Nomadic Tribes, and initiated the Dakshinayan Movement of writers and artists.

Muchkund Dubey

Muchkund Dubey is currently President of the Council for Social Development, New Delhi. He is former Foreign Secretary, Government of India, and Professor at the Jawaharlal Nehru University. He was India's High Commissioner to Bangladesh and Permanent Representative to U.N. Organizations in Geneva. He also served at U.N. and U.N.D.P Headquarters. His areas of specialization have been international economic relations, India's social and economic development, international security and disarmament, international development cooperation and world order issues. He has authored two books, *Unequal Treaty: World Trading Order after GATT* and *India's Foreign Policy: Coping with the Changing World,* edited three books and co-edited six books.

Nikhil Dey

Nikhil Dey, is a Founder Member of the Mazdoor Kisan Shakti Sangathan (MKSS), School for Democracy and a co-convener of the National Campaign on People's Right to Information (NCPRI). He has been parts of several campaigns for rights based laws and establishing entitlements for marginalised communities (information, employment, and food security); unorganised sector pensions, people centric accountability mechanisms like social audit, and mechanisms for citizens to fight corruption and arbitrary use of power; and as a part of the Suchna Rozgaar Adhikar Abhiyan, for the right to good quality public education, Shikhsha ka Sawaal. He was a member of the Central Employment Guarantee Council, and the Steering Committee of the Open Government Partnership in

2011–2015, for whom he is currently an 'envoy'. He received the K.L. Bordia award and shared many awards including the Rule of Law Award in 2011 with the MKSS.

Gladson Dungdung

Gladson Dungdung is an activist, author and researcher. He comes from the Kharia Adivasi community in Jharkhand. He is the author of several books including *Endless Cry in the Red Corridor, Mission Saranda: A War for Natural Resources in India* and *Whose country is it Anyway? – Untold Stories from India's Indigenous Peoples*. He served as an honorary member in the Assessment and Monitoring Authority under the Planning Commission of India (Govt. of India) during 2011-13, and was awarded the Samata Ratan Award, 2014, for his extraordinary work for the Adivasi communities of India.

Irfan Engineer

Irfan Engineer is Director of Centre for Study of Society and Secularism. He is Editor, *Indian Journal of Secularism*. He works for communal harmony.

Vasant Futane

Actively practicing organic farming for the last 30 years, Futane engages in conserving and promoting seed diversity, and has been part of the movement against genetically modified seeds. He has developed an orchard of non-grafted indigenous mango varieties. Of late he has been practicing, promoting, and training farmers on contour bunding and sowing, to enable retention of soil fertility. Of special interest to Futane are village self-rule (swaraj), village women's and youth empowerment.

Sudha Gopalakrishnan

Sudha took her doctoral degree in comparative drama, focusing on the theories and practices of comedy in classical Indian and western drama. She has published books and papers relating to aspects of Indian cultures and heritage, including *Kutiyattam: The Heritage Theatre of India,* translations of *Nalacaritam* (Malayalam to English) and *Krishnagiti* (Sanskrit to English), as well as edited volumes. She has worked on policy and practice relating to intangible cultural heritage. Previously she was Mission Director, National Mission for Manuscripts, and is currently Executive Director, Sahapedia, an open online library and archive of Indian culture and history.

Rakhal Gaitonde

Dr. Rakhal Gaitonde completed his MBBS from Government Kilpauk Medical College and MD Community Medicine from Christian Medical College, Vellore. He has since worked in field of community based accountability and governance of health systems in rural Maharashtra and Tamilnadu. He is presently pursuing a PhD with the University of Umea, Sweden and is based at the Centre for Technology and Policy, IIT-M, Chennai. He also works on issues of Environment and Occupational Health supporting a number of pollution impacted communities through research and advocacy.

Manisha Gupte

Manisha Gupte has been actively involved with the feminist and health rights movements in India since the 1970s. She co-founded MASUM, a rural women's organisation in 1987. She has been involved with campaigns and networks related to constitutional and human rights of subordinated and marginalised groups. Her PhD thesis was on the concept of patriarchal honour and its intersectionality with caste, sexuality, gender and other complex systems of domination and exclusion. She engages with feminist and pro-people's organisations at the national and global levels as an advisor, board member and trainer.

Harish Hande

Harish Hande co-founded SELCO India, a social venture, to eradicate poverty by promoting sustainable technologies in rural India in 1995. He has also lead the evolution of SELCO into SELCO Foundation (2010) and SELCO Incubation Centre (2012) which play a critical role in building the ecosystem for sustainable energy solutions in India and the world. At the core of his vision, Harish has worked to empower the poor through energy and livelihoods thus improving their quality of life. In 2011, he was awarded with Asia's prestigious Ramon Magsaysay Award, and SELCO was awarded the Ashden Awards twice in 2005 and 2007.

K. J. Joy

K. J. Joy is a Senior Fellow with the Society for Promoting Participative Ecosystem Management (SOPPECOM), Pune. He has been an activist-researcher for more than 30 years and has a special interest in people's institutions for natural resource management, especially water. His other areas of interests include drought and drought proofing, participatory irrigation management, river basin management and multi-stakeholder processes, watershed based development, water and sanitation, biodiversity, water conflicts and social movements. He coordinates the Forum for Policy Dialogue on Water Conflicts in India, a national level network on water conflicts. He has published extensively on water-environment-development issues.

Vijay Jardhari

Vjay Jardhari is a farmer, seed custodian, Gandhian, and an environmental activist. He has authored many books and publications on biodiverse sustainable agriculture, traditional knowledge, and the conservation of forests. These include: *Barahnaja* (on traditional multi-cropping), and *The Culture of Nutritious Foods in Uttarakhand*. Jardhari has played a key role in the historic Chipko Andolan to protect Himalayan forests, and in the agitation against limestone mining in Uttarakhand. He is currently a central pillar of the Beej Bachao Andolan, a movement to conserve the traditional agricultural knowledge and seed biodiversity of the Himalayas.

Rakesh Kapoor

Rakesh Kapoor, based in New Delhi, is founder-director of Alternative Futures (www.aternativefutures.org.in), working on ideas, policies and innovations to help create alternative futures for India and the world. He explores the future and processes of social transformation from the perspective of India and the South. He is Associate Editor of *Futures*: journal of policy, planning and futures studies (https://www.journals.elsevier.com/futures) and has edited several of its special issues, including two issues on Indian Futures. He is Fellow of the World Futures Studies Federation and was its Director from 2008 to 2014.

Rajesh Khindri

After a basic exposure to sciences during formal education, Rajesh had a long engagement with Hoshangabad Science Teaching Programme (HSTP) from 1986 to 2002 (till the programme lasted) in Eklavya. Currently, he is the editor of Sandarbh, a bimonthly magazine for teachers from 1994. He is interested in dissemination of material and ideas and in issues related to sustainable development.

Ashish Kothari

Founder-member of Indian environmental group Kalpavriksh, Ashish has taught at the Indian Institute of Public Administration, coordinated India's National Biodiversity Strategy and Action Plan process, served on Greenpeace International and India Boards, helped initiate the global ICCA Consortium, chaired an IUCN network dealing with protected areas and communities, and was on the steering committees of the World Commission of Protected Areas and the IUCN Commission on Environmental, Economic and Social Policy. He has (co)authored or (co)edited over 30 books (including *Birds in our Lives,* *Churning the Earth* with Aseem Shrivastava, and childrens' books *Shero to the Rescue* and *Wildlife in a City Pond*). He helps coordinate the Vikalp Sangam process in search of alternative well-being pathways, and a global project Academic-Activist Co-produced Knowledge for Environmental Justice (ACKnowl-EJ).

Kavitha Kuruganti

Kavitha Kuruganti has around 24 years of experience working on development issues, mainly on farm livelihoods, food security and seed sovereignty, democratisation of science & technology, and promotion of ecological farming. She is a Development Communicator by qualification, with a Masters degree in Communication from Central University of Hyderabad. She has worked in a variety of organizations over the years: grassroots, campaign, women's, funding and state-level resource organizations in addition to working along with farmers' movements and forming national networks, from 1993 till date. She is the national convenor of a large informal network called Alliance for Sustainable & Holistic Agriculture (ASHA), which seeks to address the agrarian crisis in India, and promote sustainable farm livelihoods. She is also the Founder member of a recent initiative that focuses on the rights of women farmers called MAKAAM (Mahila Kisan Adhikaar Manch).

Arpitha Kodiveri

Arpitha Kodiveri is an environmental lawyer and legal researcher based in Bangalore. She is currently a senior research associate at the Ashoka Trust for Research in Ecology and the Environment. She has a Masters in Law from UC Berkeley, Boalt Hall School of Law and a Bachelors in Law from ILS Law College, Pune.

Sharachchandra Lele

Sharachchandra (Sharad) Lele is a Senior Fellow in the Centre for Environment and Development at the Ashoka Trust for Research in Ecology and the Environment, Bangalore. Sharad is an interdisciplinary environmental researcher, with a PhD in Energy & Resources from University of California, Berkeley. He attempts to bridge the natural sciences, economics, and political science in understanding the concepts of and pathways to environmentally sustainable and socially just development. He has worked on sustainable forest management and forest governance, forest hydrology and agricultural impacts, long-term impacts of watershed development, and more recently on governance of water resources and water pollution.

Bharat Mansata

Bharat Mansata is a writer and environmental activist, involved in ecological regeneration. He has authored *The Vision of Natural Farming* (on Bhaskar Save, the acclaimed 'Gandhi of natural farming'); and *Organic Revolution* (on the agro-ecological transformation of Cuba since 1990). He has been closely associated with Earthcare Books and Vanvadi since their inception, over two decades ago. Vanvadi is a collective, regenerated forest rich in biodiversity in the foothills of the Sahyadris, between Mumbai and Pune. It conducts various activities, workshops and camps. Bharat is also involved in the movement for conserving and sharing traditional seeds.

Rachita Misra

Rachita Misra works as a Senior Program Manager in SELCO Foundation. With a background in Architecture and Regional Planning, she is particularly interested in understanding the social and political challenges to uneven distribution of resources in varying contexts.

Aditya Nigam

Aditya Nigam is a political theorist based at the Centre for the Study of Developing Societies, Delhi. His recent work has been concerned with the decolonization of social and political theory. In particular, he is interested in theorizing the contemporary experience of politics, populism and democracy in the non-West, alongside larger question of modernity and capitalism outside the Euro-American world. He is the author of *After Utopia: Modernity and Socialism, The Post Colony, Desire Named Development*. He comments regularly on contemporary political issues on the blog, kafila.online.

Arvind Narrain

Arvind Narrain is the co-founder of the Alternative Law Forum, a human rights advocacy and research organisation based in Bangalore. He is also the co-author of *Breathing life into the Constitution: Human Rights Lawyering in India* and co-editor of *Law like Love: Queer Perspectives on Law*.

Meera Anna Oommen

Meera Anna Oommen is Associate Director of Dakshin Foundation, Bangalore. She works on issues related to ecology, conservation science and environmental history. Her recent work focused on incorporating insights from multiple disciplines to understand the dynamics of human-wildlife conflict in forest fringe landscapes. Her interests lie in integrating emerging research in the fields of frugal heuristics and bounded rationality with traditional approaches to develop research methods for conservation research. Meera's current work also focuses on human-animal relationships and the history of hunting in India.

Bharat Patankar

Bharat Patankar is a leading activist of the left wing Shramik Mukti Dal and of the peasant movement in Maharashtra. Bharat Patankar is an activist intellectual who has worked for almost 40 years in movements of workers, farmers, dam evictees, agricultural labourers, the drought eradication movement, alternative cultural movement, women's liberation movement, anti-SEZ and coal-based power plant movement based on alternative energy proposals, rights of farmers on windmills, and radical anti-caste movements. He is one of the architects of equitable water distribution movement in Maharashtra.

M. P. Parameswaran

Born in 1935 in Trissur, Parameswaran has a B. Sc. (Elec. Engg.) from College of Engineering Trivandrum, and a PhD in Nuclear Engineering from Moscow Power Institute. He was a Scientist in BARC 1957-1975, but lost faith in nuclear energy, resigned, and became an activist. He has been with the Kerala Sastra Sahitya Parishad (KSSP) since 1966, headed the Publication unit of CPI(M), and is Founder Secretary of the All India Peoples' Science Network and the Bharat Gyan Vigyan Samiti (BGVS). He has also been active in the Total Literacy Campaign and the People's Plan Campaign of Kerala.

Sujit Patwardhan

A Graphic Designer and Printer by profession, Sujit graduated from the London College of Printing and Graphic Arts, London, UK in 1968. He runs his own printing company, Mudra. Founder Member of Parisar, a citizens' group working in the field of Environmental Awareness, Education and Action in Pune since 1982. He has been involved in urban environmental issues such as the development plan, heritage conservation, and urban traffic. He has also been networking with other NGOs in and outside the city on issues of common interest like sustainable transportation, sustainable agriculture, livelihood security and environmental impacts of mega projects. For over 20 years he has been working in the field of urban traffic and transportation advocacy.

Praavita Kashyap

Praavita has been working with the Mazdoor Kisan Shakti Sangathan (MKSS) since 2013. She holds a degree in Philosophy from St. Stephen's College, Delhi University and a Masters in Human Rights from Sciences Po, Paris. She has been a part of various campaigns over the last three years, including the National Campaign on People's Right to Information (NCPRI) and the Pension Parishad. She has recently finished studying Law at the University of Delhi.

Elango Rangasamy

Elango is a native of Kuthambakkam village near Chennai. A Chemical Engineer by profession, he worked for the Council of Scientific and Industrial Research for 10 years. Resigning from this in 1996, he contested the panchayat election and became the Sarpanch of Kuthambakkam. Using the panchayat as a local self government, his works made Kuthambakkam as a model village for sustainable development. In 2001, he promoted a trust to network panchayats to function as clusters, promoting the local economy in the name of 'Network Growth Economy'. He also started a Panchayat Academy. As of 2017, over 700 village panchayats are in the network.

Aruna Roy

Aruna is Founder-Member, Mazdoor Kisan Shakti Sangathan (MKSS) and National Campaign on People's Right to Information (NCPRI), and the School for Democracy. She was with the IAS from 1968-1975. In 1987, she moved to work with rural poor. She has worked for accessing constitutional rights for the poor, including Right to Information, Employment, Food Security. She was a member of the National Advisory Council from 2004-06, and 2010-13, and a member of the steering committee of the Open Government Partnership (OGP) till 2014. She is President of the National Federation of Indian Women (NFIW). She was the 2016 Professor of Practice at McGill University ISID, Montreal, Canada, and the 2017 George Soros Visiting Practitioner Chair at CEU, Budapest. Awards include the Ramon Magsaysay Award in 2000, the Nani Palkiwala Award and the Lal Bahadur Shastri National Award.

Rajeswari S. Raina

Rajeshwari S. Raina is Professor in the School of Humanities and Social Sciences in Shiv Nadar University. She has a background in the sciences and economics, and is a keen student of the interface between development policy and knowledge. Current research focuses on theoretical and policy challenges, as well as capacities for (a) Sustainable Development Processes to achieve the SDGs, (b) Millet-based nutrition programmes in select States of the Indian Union, (c) Innovation for inclusive development in India and China, and (d) changes in the agriculture-environment knowledge, policy and practice continuum.

Nitin D. Rai

Nitin D. Rai is a Fellow at the Ashoka Trust for Research in Ecology and the Environment. He uses a political ecology approach to understand the implications of state conservation policy and practice for people and landscapes. His recent interests include analysing market-based interventions and corporate investments in biodiversity conservation and local resistance to such initiatives. Nitin is an editor of the journal Conservation and Society.

Hanwant Singh Rathore

Hanwant Singh Rathore is director of Lokhit Pashu-Palak Sansthan, a support organization for pastoralists based in Pali district of Rajasthan. Hanwant has been working with the Raika community for more than 25 years and has been advocating for their rights at national and international level. A major focus of his work has been to save Rajasthan's camels through a community based approach and for this purpose recently he initiated India's first micro-dairy for camel milk, together with Ilse Kohler-Rollefson.

Ilse Kohler-Rollefson

Ilse Kohler-Rollefson is a researcher, activist and writer investigating and promoting ecologically and socially responsible concepts of livestock keeping. Trained as a veterinarian, she is project coordinator of the League for Pastoral Peoples and Endogenous Livestock Development, an international advocacy organisation based in Germany. Ilse has written several books and more than a hundred publications in scientific journals, is a frequent speaker at international conferences and was recently awarded by the President of India.

Dunu (A.K.) Roy

Dunu Roy is a chemical engineer with five decades of experience in rural and urban development, with specific focus on environmental issues. He has worked extensively in the field of environmental planning, research and education. He has been associated with Frea India in Bombay, Shahdol Group in Madhya Pradesh, People's Science Institute in Dehradun, and the World Wide Fund for Nature in Delhi. Currently he is associated with the Hazards Centre in Delhi, a technical support group that provides services to community organizations.

Abhay Shukla

Abhay Shukla is a Public health physician, working on health issues in collaboration with networks of civil society organisations in Maharashtra. He is Senior Programme Coordinator at SATHI, Pune and is a national convenor of Jan Swasthya Abhiyan. He was centrally involved in organising the national Right to Health Care campaign, and contributed to developing the framework of Community Based Monitoring and Planning (CBMP) of health services. Abhay has authored and co-authored several books including *Dissenting Diagnosis*. He is actively involved in campaigns for patient's rights, social regulation of private medical sector, and a system for Universal Health Care.

Aseem Shrivastava

Aseem Shrivastava is a Delhi-based writer and ecological economist. He holds a PhD in Economics from the University of Massachusetts, Amherst. He is the author (with Ashish Kothari) of the book *Churning the Earth: The Making of Global India* (Penguin Viking, New Delhi, 2012), a searing socio-ecological critique of India's development strategy since 1947. He is presently at work on two projects, one on the ecological thought of Rabindranath Tagore, the other an aphoristic, philosophical examination of greed.

Geetanjoy Sahu

Geetanjoy Sahu is a faculty member at the Centre for Science, Technology and Society, School of Habitat Studies, Mumbai. He holds a PhD in Political Science from the Institute for Social and Economic Change (ISEC), Bangalore, and postdoctoral research programme at the Centre for Interdisciplinary Studies in Environment and Development (CISED), Bangalore. His research and teaching interest broadly include environmental policy and governance, environmental jurisprudence and analysis of forest rights implementation and land use pattern in coastal areas. He is the author of *Environmental Jurisprudence and the Supreme Court: Litigation, Interpretation and Implementation* (2013).

Kartik Shanker

Kartik Shanker is Director of Ashoka Trust for Research in Ecology and the Environment, Bangalore. He is on deputation from the Indian Institute of Science, Bangalore where he studies the ecology and evolution of various terrestrial and marine groups. Kartik has worked on the biology and conservation of sea turtles for the last 25 years, and is the author of *From Soup to Superstar*, a historical account of sea turtle conservation in India. He is a founding trustee of Dakshin Foundation and editor of the magazine, *Current Conservation*. He is the author of several children's books, including *Lori's Magical Mystery*.

Vivek Shastry

Vivek Shastry works with the policy and planning group at SELCO Foundation, focusing on energy planning, ecosystem development, and energy-healthcare nexus. Vivek is a J. N. Tata Scholar and Dual Masters graduate from the University of Texas at Austin, with a background in engineering and regional planning.

Anand Teltumbde

Anand Teltumbde is a civil rights activist, political analyst, columnist and author of many books. He has a long association with peoples' struggle spanning over three decades backing his theorizations on various issues. Trained in technology and management from the top institutes in the country, he marshals his insights of the modern techno-managerial world to sharpen strategies of struggles. He teaches Business Analytics in Goa Institute of Management.

Himanshu Thakkar

Himanshu, an engineer from Indian Institute of Technology, Mumbai, is coordinator of SANDRP and editor of the magazine *Dams, Rivers & People*. He has been engaged with issues related to Dams, hydropower projects and rivers for over 25 years. SANDRP is part of the consortium that organizes India Rivers Week since 2014. Himanshu has in the past been associated with the work of Save Narmada Movement, the World Commission on Dams and Centre for Science and Environment.

Paranjoy Guha Thakurta

Paranjoy Guha Thakurta was till the time of going to press, Editor of the *Economic and Political Weekly*. His work experience, spanning four decades, cuts across different media: print, radio, television and documentary cinema. He is a writer, speaker, anchor, interviewer, teacher and commentator in three languages: English, Bangla and Hindi. His main areas of interest are the working of the political economy and the media in India and the world, on which he has authored/co-authored/published books and directed/produced documentary films. He teaches and speaks on these subjects.

Shiv Visvanathan

Shiv Visvanathan is Professor, Jindal Global Law School and Director, Centre for the study of Knowledge Systems, O.P. Jindal University. He is also an Adjunct Professor at Raman Research Institute, Bangalore. Shiv is the author of *Organising for Science*, Oxford University Press (1985) and *A Carnival for Science*, Oxford University Press (1997), *Theatres of Democracy*, Harper Collins (2016) and has co-edited *Foul Play: Chronicles of Corruption*, Banyan Books (1997). He is a regular columnist to many newspapers including *The Hindu, Asian Age, Hindustan Times* and *Financial Chronicle*. He also writes for digital magazines like *Daily O, Scroll.in* and *Quartz*.

Uzramma

Uzramma has been associated with the artisanal making of cotton cloth and in other crafts for twenty-seven years and has founded support agencies for craft production. She has participated in seminars in India and abroad, given lectures and published papers and articles on cotton handloom weaving and natural dyeing. A book, *A Frayed History: The Journey of Cotton in India*, co-authored with Meena Menon, is forthcoming. Uzramma is currently Director of the Decentralised Cotton Yarn Trust and the Malkha Marketing Trust.

Index